"Anyone seeking to find the link between the power of intellectual discourse and policy relevance should read this book. The ASEAN Security Community (ASC), first as a discourse and subsequently as a policy adopted by ASEAN, has to a considerable degree been inspired by the arguments advanced in this book." *Rizal Sukma, Executive Director, Centre for Strategic and International Studies, Jakarta, and an author of the Indonesian proposal for an ASEAN Security Community*

"This groundbreaking study brilliantly illuminates ASEAN's novel approach to issues of national and international security. Theoretically sophisticated and contextually grounded, Amitav Acharya is the rare scholar who succeeds fully in intellectually engaging both security and area specialists." *Peter J. Katzenstein, Cornell University, USA*

"...innovative and stimulating...the theoretical and empirical sophistication that Acharya displays makes this book sure to be a key work on the security and political aspects of ASEAN for academics and policymakers...a vivid and cutting-edge work" *American Political Science Review*

"...a wise book... the author expresses judgments that challenge analysts in Southeast Asia itself to seriously consider what can be done to chart a new course for the region." *Journal of Asian Studies*

"Acharya's book stands as a major contribution to the ongoing Asian security debate and contributes substantially to the quality of that debate's policy analysis." *Survival*

"an invaluable resource for every student of the region." *Pacific Affairs*

"...a fascinating and important book...Regional specialists will find a great deal to mull over in this nuanced and compelling analysis." *Pacific Review*

Constructing a Security Community in Southeast Asia

Third Edition

In this third edition of *Constructing a Security Community in Southeast Asia*, Amitav Acharya offers a comprehensive and critical account of the evolution of the Association of Southeast Asian Nations (ASEAN) norms and the viability of the ASEAN way of conflict management. Building on the framework from the first edition, which inspired the establishment of the ASEAN Political-Security community, this new edition has been extensively updated and revised based on new primary sources that are not publicly available.

Updates for this edition include:

- Expanded and updated coverage of the South China Sea Conflict and how it affects regional order and tests ASEAN unity
- Analysis of new developments in the US role in the region, including ASEAN's place and role in the US pivot/rebalancing strategy and the evolution of the East Asian Community, the newest summit-level multilateral group
- Extensive analysis of the ASEAN Political-Security community
- An examination of US–China relations and China–ASEAN relations
- Coverage of ASEAN's institutional development and the controversy over reform of the ASEAN Secretariat
- An updated outlook on ASEAN's future as a security community and the issue of ASEAN Centrality in the regional security architecture.

The new edition will continue to appeal to students and scholars of Asian security, international relations theory and Southeast Asian studies, as well as policymakers and the media.

Amitav Acharya is Professor of International Relations and the UNESCO Chair in Transnational Challenges and Governance at the School of International Service, American University, Washington, DC. He has been elected to be the 54th President (2014–15) of the International Studies Association (ISA).

Constructing a Security Community in Southeast Asia

ASEAN and the problem
of regional order

Third Edition

Amitav Acharya

Routledge
Taylor & Francis Group

LONDON AND NEW YORK

First published 2001
Second edition published 2009
This edition published 2014
by Routledge
2 Park Square, Milton Park, Abingdon, Oxon, OX14 4RN

and by Routledge
711 Third Avenue, New York, NY 10017

Routledge is an imprint of the Taylor & Francis Group, an informa business

British Library Cataloguing in Publication Data
A catalogue record for this book is available from the British Library

Library of Congress Cataloging in Publication Data
Acharya, Amitav.
   Constructing a security community in Southeast Asia : ASEAN and the
   problem of regional order / Amitav Acharya. — Third edition.
      pages cm. — (Politics in asia)
   Includes bibliographical references and index.
   1. Southeast Asia—Politics and government—1945– 2. National security—
   Southeast Asia. 3. Southeast Asia—Foreign relations. 4. ASEAN. I. Title.
   DS526.7.A26 2014
   355'.0310959—dc23
                                                                    2013038675

ISBN: 978-0-415-74767-7 (hbk)
ISBN: 978-0-415-74768-4 (pbk)
ISBN: 978-1-315-79667-3 (ebk)

Typeset in Times New Roman
by RefineCatch Limited, Bungay, Suffolk

Printed and bound in the United States of America by Publishers Graphics,
LLC on sustainably sourced paper.

Contents

Tables and figures

Tables

Figures

Series editor's preface to the first edition

The Association of Southeast Asian Nations (ASEAN) has enjoyed a mixed institutional experience since its advent in August 1967. The past three decades and more have seen the Association manage intra-mural tensions with some success and also act as a diplomatic community speaking with a single voice during the course of the Cambodian conflict. Since the end of the Cold War, ASEAN has assumed a diplomatic centrality within the ASEAN Regional Forum (ARF) but has also faced evident difficulties in sustaining collective consensus as a result of the impact of regional economic crisis and an enlargement of membership to coincide with geographic Southeast Asia, exempting East Timor. Professor Amitav Acharya has drawn on this mixed institutional experience to address the subject of constructing a security community. At issue in this volume is what kind of model does ASEAN provide for confronting the problem of regional order identified in the subtitle? Professor Acharya has taken as his intellectual point of reference the concept of 'Constructivism', whereby cooperation among states is understood as a social process that can have a positive, and even transforming, effect on their relations through internalising regulatory norms. Indeed, he is a member of the academic school that maintains that norms can have a life of their own and are capable of influencing the behaviour of states so that they come to share a common habit of peaceful conduct.

Professor Acharya is exceptionally well qualified to address this subject and its regional context. He has acquired a wealth of regional field experience and also has established a prodigious record of scholarship combining theoretical perspectives with empirical data. In this volume, he examines and assesses the merits of 'the ASEAN Way' and whether or not the nascent security community is in the ascendant. He sets ASEAN's institutional experience within a structured framework of enquiry, which serves not only as a basis for a deeper understanding of the dynamics of the Association but also as a vehicle for the wider comparative analysis of regional organisations. In the process, he takes the study of ASEAN beyond an account of its historical record. The attendant intellectual appeal extends beyond specialists in Southeast Asian security to the wider community of students of regional and international security.

Michael Leifer

Preface to the second edition

The second edition of *Constructing a Security Community in Southeast Asia* takes into account nearly a decade of further evolution of ASEAN, which marked its fortieth anniversary in August 2007. The major new addition is Chapter 7, tracing and analysing the 'ASEAN Security Community' initiative. This and other chapters update ASEAN's response to both conventional and emerging security challenges since the Asian economic crisis in 1997, including interstate tensions and transnational security issues such as terrorism, the Severe Acute Respiratory Syndrome (SARS), the Indian Ocean Tsunami, environmental degradation, and the challenge of domestic political change. Chapter 6, dealing with ASEAN's role in Asia-Pacific security, has been updated to cover the latest developments relating to the ARF, the emergence of East Asian regionalism (and the East Asian Community idea), and more generally ASEAN's response to the rise of China and its multilateral engagement of China, Japan and India. Modest changes to the conceptual chapter (Chapter 1) have been made to offer some theoretical clarifications.

In terms of source material, I have been able to draw on declassified British records of ASEAN's formative period that were not available when the first edition's draft was completed. These documents, used to revise Chapter 2 on the evolution of ASEAN norms and the emergence of the ASEAN Way, offer interesting new information and insights into differing national perspectives on ASEAN's principles and processes that had to be reconciled to develop and sustain ASEAN. (They do, however, generally confirm my original observations regarding the uniqueness of ASEAN and the strengths and limits of its approach to regional cooperation.) I have also drawn on official documents of the ARF that are not normally available to academics and on both official and non-official sources in Bahasa Indonesia, especially in analysing the ASEAN Security Community idea.

In preparing a new edition, I have been inspired primarily by the response to the first edition from students from around the world who have used this book as a text (to an extent not anticipated by the author) or as a guide and tool for their own research. I am heartened by the scholarly interest and debate the book has generated. It has also turned out to be useful and relevant to policymakers although it was not intended as such, certainly not as a work of policy advocacy. Especially heartening has been the response to the book in China (where a Chinese translation was published in 2004 translated by Professor Wong Zhengyi of Beijing University and published by Shanghai People's Press) and from the wider intellectual community of scholars of international relations theory who are not necessarily interested in Southeast Asian affairs.

The chief intellectual concern of the second edition, like that of the first, is to use and advance the security community concept as an analytic tool, rather than as a descriptive category for ASEAN (the question whether ASEAN has or has not become a true security community). Through this book, I seek to make a contribution to the theoretical study of security communities as well as to the literature on Southeast Asian studies. It reflects my longstanding interest in combining disciplinary and area studies perspectives which, if properly done, can be complementary, rather than mutually exclusionary.

Amitav Acharya
Bristol, UK
August 2008

Preface to the third edition

Asia is the most economically dynamic and strategically significant part of the world today, and the story of ASEAN is an important part of the political and strategic rise and reordering of Asia. Since its first publication in 2001, *Constructing a Security Community in Southeast Asia* has been widely used by scholars and policymakers around the world to study Asia's evolving security architecture amidst momentous changes such as the rise of China and India and the renewed strategic attention given to the region by the United States. It was among the first contributions to renew scholarly interest in the idea of security communities in the post-cold war era. As such it became a key text of the emergent field of comparative regionalism. The book's impact can be seen by the fact that the initial articulation of the ASEAN Political Security Community idea was inspired by its first edition.

International interest in ASEAN, from both the academic and policy-making communities continues to grow, especially with the dramatic expansion of ASEAN's external relations to include all the major powers of the current international system. ASEAN is now an integral part of courses on comparative regionalism taught in universities around the world.

My purpose in bringing out a third edition of the volume is to serve the interest not only of those who have followed the story of ASEAN in the past decades, but also of newcomers to the subject and more generally of those analysing the role of Asia in the twenty-first-century world order.

The third edition expands the book's coverage of key developments that pose new and serious tests for ASEAN's role in regional order, including the escalation of the South China Sea conflict and the US 'pivot' or 'rebalancing' strategy, in which ASEAN figures centrally. Other important developments concern the evolution of the East Asian Community, and ASEAN's institutional development. The conclusion updates the outlook on ASEAN's future as a security community and the core issue of 'ASEAN centrality' in the regional security architecture of Asia.

Amitav Acharya
Washington, DC
3 September 2013

Acknowledgements

I owe a debt of gratitude to many individuals and institutions, including to the Institute of Defence and Strategic Studies, where I was Deputy Director and Head of Research for five and a half years, my various colleagues there, the Department of Politics at the University of Bristol, and the School of International Service at American University, where I have been based since 2009, and my publishers at Routledge. Among individuals, I particularly thank Rodolfo Severino, Surin Pitsuwan, Tommy Koh, Hiro Katsumata, Rizal Sukma, Carl Thayer and the late Barry Wain for sharing their insights and information into the workings of ASEAN. At various stages, Karyn Wang, Morten Hansen, Jack Kwoh, Dan Blank, Shanshan Mei, Goueun Lee provided and Allan Layug invaluable research assistance for the second and third editions, which I gratefully acknowledge. The third edition is dedicated to Louis Goodman, my good friend, neighbour and Dean Emeritus of the School of International Service, American University.

Abbreviations

ACMR	Air Combat Manoeuvring Range
ACWC	ASEAN Commission on the Promotion and Protection of the Rights of Women and Children
ADMM	ASEAN Defence Ministers Meeting
ADMM Plus	ASEAN Defence Ministers Meeting Plus
AEC	ASEAN Economic Community
AFTA	ASEAN Free Trade Area
AICHR	ASEAN Intergovernmental Commission on Human Rights
AIJV	ASEAN Industrial Joint Venture
AMM	ASEAN Ministerial Meeting
APEC	Asia-Pacific Economic Cooperation
APSC	ASEAN Political Security Community
APT	ASEAN Plus Three
ARF	ASEAN Regional Forum
ARF-SOM	ARF Senior Officials Meeting
ASCC	ASEAN Socio-Cultural Community
ASA	Association of Southeast Asia
ASC	ASEAN Security Community
ASCU	ASEAN Surveillance Coordinating Unit
ASEAN	Association of Southeast Asian Nations
ASEAN-ISIS	ASEAN Institutes for Strategic and International Studies
ASEAN-PMC	ASEAN Post-Ministerial Conferences
ASEAN-SOM	ASEAN Senior Officials Meeting
ASEM	Asia Europe Meeting
ASP	ASEAN Surveillance Process
ASTSU	ASEAN Surveillance Technical Support Unit
BIMP-EAGA	Brunei–Indonesia–Malaysia–Philippines East ASEAN Growth Area
CBM	Confidence-building Measures
CENTO	Central Treaty Organization
CGDK	Coalition Government of Democratic Kampuchea
CLMV	Cambodia, Laos, Myanmar and Vietnam
COC	Code of Conduct (in the South China Sea)
CPM	Communist Party of Malaya
CPP	Communist Party of the Philippines
CPR	Committee of Permanent Representatives
CSBMs	Confidence- and Security-Building Measures

CSCA	Conference on Security and Cooperation in Asia
CSCAP	Council for Security Cooperation in Asia Pacific
CSCE	Conference on Security and Cooperation in Europe
CSIS	Centre for Strategic and International Studies
DK	Democratic Kampuchea
DOC	Declaration on Code of Conduct (ASEAN Declaration on the Conduct of Parties in the South China Sea)
EAEC	East Asian Economic Caucus
EAS	East Asia Summit
EASI	East Asia Strategic Initiative
EC	European Community
ECOWAS	Economic Community of West African States
EEZ	Exclusive Economic Zone
EHD	Environment, Human Rights and Democracy
EEPSEA	Economy and Environment Programme for Southeast Asia
EPG	Eminent Persons Group
EU	European Union
FPDA	Five Power Defence Arrangements
FUNCINPEC	Front Uni National pour un Cambodge Independant, Neutre, Pacifique et Cooperatif
GATT	General Agreement on Tariffs and Trade
GCC	Gulf Cooperation Council
GDP	Gross Domestic Product
GNP	Gross National Product
GSP	Generalised System of Preferences
ICJ	International Court of Justice
ICK	International Conference on Kampuchea
ICM	International Control Mechanism
IISS	International Institute for Strategic Studies
IMC	Informal Meeting on Cambodia
IMET	International Military Exchange and Training
IMF	International Monetary Fund
IMT-GT	Indonesia–Malaysia–Thailand Growth Triangle
ISDS	Institute of Strategic and Development Studies
ISG	Inter-sessional Group
JI	Jemaah Islamiyah
JIM	Jakarta Informal Meeting
JLP	Joint Logistics Plan
KPNLF	Khmer People's National Liberation Front
MAPHILINDO	Malaysia–Philippines–Indonesia
MILF	Moro Islamic Liberation Front
MIMA	Maritime Institute of Malaysia
MoU	Memorandum of Understanding
NAFTA	North American Free Trade Area
NATO	North Atlantic Treaty Organization
NETs	Natural Economic Territories
NGO	Non-governmental Organisation

NPCSD	North Pacific Cooperative Security Dialogue
OAS	Organization of American States
OAU	Organization of African Unity
OECD	Organisation for Economic Cooperation and Development
OSCE	Organisation for Security and Cooperation in Europe
PD	Preventive Diplomacy
PECC	Pacific Economic Cooperation Council
PKO	Peacekeeping Operations
PMC	Post-Ministerial Conferences
PRC	People's Republic of China
PRK	People's Republic of Kampuchea
RCEP	Regional Comprehensive Economic Partnership
SEANWFZ	Southeast Asia Nuclear-Weapon-Free Zone
SEATO	Southeast Asia Treaty Organization
SIJORI	Singapore–Johor–Riau
SLD	Shangri-la Dialogue
SLORC	State Law and Order Restoration Council
SIPRI	Stockholm International Peace Research Institute
SNC	Supreme National Council
SOM	Senior Officials Meeting
SAARC	South Asian Association for Regional Cooperation
TAC	Treaty of Amity and Cooperation
TPP	Trans Pacific Partnership
UN	United Nations
UNCLOS	United Nations Convention on the Law of the Sea
UNTAC	United Nations Transitional Authority in Cambodia
USA	United States of America
ZOPFAN	Zone of Peace, Freedom and Neutrality
ZoPFF/C	Zone of Peace, Freedom, Friendship and Cooperation

The evolution of ASEAN-Ten

A chronology

8 August 1967 (Bangkok)	Birth of ASEAN. ASEAN founders from Indonesia, Malaysia, the Philippines, Singapore and Thailand signed the ASEAN Declaration in Bangkok.
27 November 1971 (Kuala Lumpur)	Zone of Peace, Freedom and Neutrality Declaration.
23–24 February 1976 (Bali)	First ASEAN Summit.
24 February 1976 (Bali)	Declaration of ASEAN Concord; Treaty of Amity and Cooperation in Southeast Asia; Agreement on the Establishment of the ASEAN Secretariat.
4–5 August 1977 (Kuala Lumpur)	Second ASEAN Summit.
7 January 1984 (Jakarta)	Admission of Brunei Darussalam.
14–15 December 1987 (Manila)	Third ASEAN Summit.
21–22 July 1992 (Manila)	Applications for Observer status from Laos and Vietnam approved; Instruments of Accession of Laos and Vietnam to the Treaty of Amity and Cooperation in Southeast Asia were accepted.
23–24 July 1993 (Singapore)	Laos and Vietnam at the 26th AMM as Observers; Cambodia at the 26th AMM as a Guest.
22–23 July 1994 (Bangkok)	Laos and Vietnam attended the 27th AMM as Observers; Cambodia and Burma attended as Guests.
17 October 1994	Vietnam applied for membership in ASEAN.
25 October 1994	Cambodia applied for Observer status.
24 January 1995	Cambodia acceded to the Treaty of Amity and Cooperation in Southeast Asia.
12 July 1995	Burma applied for Observer status.
27 July 1995	Burma acceded to the Treaty of Amity and Cooperation in Southeast Asia.
28 July 1995 (Bandar Seri Begawan)	At the 28th AMM, Vietnam was admitted into ASEAN as the seventh member; Cambodia became an Observer; Laos announced its wish to join ASEAN in two years' time; Burma attended as a Guest.
14–15 December 1995 (Bangkok)	The Fifth ASEAN Summit; the first meeting of the seven ASEAN Leaders and their counterparts from Cambodia, Laos, and Burma; Signing of the Treaty on the Southeast Asia Nuclear Weapon-Free Zone by the Leaders of the ten Southeast Asian countries.

15 March 1996	Laos applied for membership.
23 March 1996	Cambodia applied for membership.
12–13 July 1996	Burma became an Observer.
12 August 1996	Burma applied for membership.
30 November 1996 (Jakarta)	The First Informal ASEAN Summit; ASEAN Heads of Government declare commitment to simultaneous admission of CLM (Cambodia, Laos and Burma) countries to ASEAN; informal meeting between the ASEAN Heads of Government and the Heads of Government of the CLM countries.
31 May 1997 (Kuala Lumpur)	Special Meeting of ASEAN Foreign Ministers in Kuala Lumpur reaches unanimous decision to admit the CLM countries in July 1997.
10 July 1997 (Kuala Lumpur)	ASEAN Foreign Ministers 'delay the admission of Cambodia into ASEAN until a later date . . .' following the 'coup' in that country, but agreed that the admission of Laos and Burma 'will proceed as scheduled'.
23 July 1997 (Subang Jaya, Malaysia)	Laos and Burma admitted into ASEAN, one day before the start of the 30th AMM.
15 December 1997 (Kuala Lumpur)	The Second ASEAN Informal Meeting, leaders of the nine ASEAN members agree to 'consultations . . . so as to enable Cambodia to join ASEAN as soon as possible, preferably before the next ASEAN Summit' [in Hanoi in mid-December 1998].
16 December 1998 (Hanoi)	Sixth ASEAN Summit decides to admit the Kingdom of Cambodia.
30 April 1999 (Hanoi)	Cambodia admitted as the tenth ASEAN member.

Source: www.aseansec.org.id (accessed 31 July 2000).

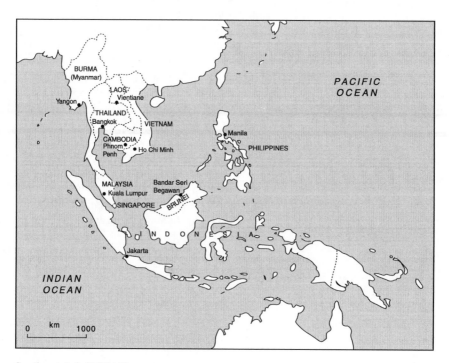

Southeast Asia/ASEAN

Cartography by Gary Haley, PCS Mapping & DTP.

ASEAN 2010: Basic indicators

Country	Total land area (sq km)	Total population (thousand)	Gross Domestic Product at current prices		Product per capita	
			(US$ mn)	(PPP$ mn)	(US$)	(PPP$)
Brunei Darussalam	5,765	415	12,402	19,406	29,915	46,811
Cambodia	181,035	15,269	11,168	28,985	731	1,898
Indonesia	1,860,360	234,181	708,032	1,030,998	3,023	4,403
Lao PDR	236,800	6,230	6,508	16,105	1,045	2,585
Malaysia	330,252	28,909	238,849	415,157	8,262	14,361
Myanmar	676,577	60,163	43,025	76,601	715	1,273
Philippines	300,000	94,013	189,326	351,686	2,014	3,741
Singapore	710	5,077	223,015	291,934	43,929	57,505
Thailand	513,120	67,312	318,709	585,698	4,735	8,701
Viet Nam	331,051	86,930	107,650	291,260	1,238	3,351
ASEAN	4,435,670	598,498	1,858,683	3,107,829	3,106	5,193
CLMV	1,425,463	168,592	168,351	412,951	999	2,449
ASEAN6	3,010,207	429,907	1,690,332	2,694,878	3,932	6,269

Note: PPP stands for purchasing power parity
Source: ASEAN Secretariat

Introduction

Security communities and ASEAN from a theoretical perspective

Identifying the conditions under which states avoid the recurrence of war and establish a durable peace is one of the most difficult challenges for practitioners and theorists of international relations. While there is abundant literature on the causes of war,[1] what leads states to self-consciously abandon war as a means of policy towards other states has been a far more problematic issue and one that has received considerably less attention. Thus, it is hardly surprising that one of the most promising concepts developed to explore 'the conditions and processes of long-range or permanent peace', that of 'security community', developed by Karl Deutsch and his associates in the 1950s, went more or less ignored by a discipline traditionally dominated by the realist paradigm which accepts competition possibly leading to war as an inevitable and permanent condition of international relations.[2]

The concept of security community describes groups of states which have developed a long-term habit of peaceful interaction and ruled out the use of force in settling disputes with other members of the group. In international relations theory, especially for the purpose of this book, the concept has twofold significance. First, it raises the possibility that through interactions and socialisation, states can manage anarchy and even escape the security dilemma, conditions which realist and neo-realist, and neo-liberal, perspectives take as permanent features of international relations. Second, the concept offers a theoretical and analytic framework for studying the impact of international (including regional) institutions in promoting peaceful change in international relations. This framework not only challenges the assumptions of realism and neo-realism, but also goes beyond the intellectual parameters established by the neo-realist–neo-liberal divide, which have formed a major part of the theoretical debate in international relations in the late 1980s and 1990s.

The theory of 'security communities' was among the first major attempts in the period after the Second World War to raise the possibility of non-violent change in international relations. It challenged the dominance of realism with its attendant focus on the security dilemma. The concept of 'security dilemma', proposed by John Hertz in 1950, described how the imperative of self-help guiding the behaviour of states under conditions of anarchy could fuel arms races and conflict.[3] It conceptualised international relations as a 'vicious circle of security and power accumulation' as states are 'driven to acquire more and more power in order to escape the impact of the power of others'.[4] The idea of security community, by contrast, was integral to a perspective that saw international relations as a process of social learning and identity formation, driven by transactions, interactions and socialisation.[5] It recognised the possibility of change being a fundamentally peaceful process with its sources lying in the 'perceptions and identifications' among actors.[6] Such processes could explain why states may develop greater mutual interdependence and responsiveness, develop 'we feelings', and ultimately come to abandon the use of force to settle problems among them.[7] International relations could thus be reconceptualised as a 'world society of political communities, consisting of social groups, a process of political communication, machinery for enforcement, and popular habits of compliance'.[8]

While theoretically challenging, the concept of security community remained on the side-lines of international relations theory. The work of Deutsch and his associates on security community formed an integral part of regional integration theory which dominated the study of regional and international cooperation in the 1960s and 1970s.[9] Along with Ernst Haas's neo-functionalist approach,[10] Deutsch's work (called 'transactionalism') provided conceptual tools for 'investigations into peaceful transnational problemsolving'.[11] But interest in regional integration theory declined sharply with the faltering state of the European Community. The theory was considered 'obsolescent' when EC members failed to respond collectively to the Middle East oil crisis and the American technological challenge in the 1970s.[12] Moreover, as a Euro-centric theory, the liberal-pluralist explanation of regional integration proved to be inapplicable in the Third World context.

The major reason for the lack of interest in security communities, however, had to do with the orthodoxy of a discipline. As Adler and Barnett have put it, international relations scholars have been generally uncomfortable with the language of community – 'the idea that actors can share values, norms, and symbols that provide a social identity, and engage in various interactions in myriad spheres that reflect long-term interests, diffuse reciprocity and trust, strikes fear and incredulity in their hearts'.[13] This was especially evident when integration theory was superseded by theories of complex interdependence and international regimes. The latter proved especially influential in the study of international organisation from the late 1970s.[14] Although it retained some of the insights and concerns of regional integration, especially their 'curiosities about international collaboration via transnational processes within settings of interdependence',[15] the study of international organisations came to be dominated by the rationalistic predispositions of neo-liberal institutionalism. Missing from the picture was the integration theorists' emphasis on the sociological nature of state interactions, especially Deutsch's focus on the development of collective perceptions and identifications, which could lead to a fundamental transformation of the security dilemma. Under Keohane's intellectual leadership, neo-liberal institutionalism[16] accepted the realist premise concerning anarchy as a given of the international system and accepted that cooperation among states, while possible, would arise only in response to states pursuing their short-term self-interest.

The so-called debate between neo-realists and neo-liberals in the 1980s and early 1990s established a relatively narrow parameter for explaining change in international relations. Neo-realism,[17] to a much greater extent than classical realism, is sceptical of the prospects for peaceful change. International institutions, a key agent of peaceful change, are viewed by neo-realists as creatures of Great Power self-interest with only a marginal effect in regulating the behaviour of states. For neo-realists, change occurs as a consequence of shifts, often violent, in the balance or distribution of power. Neo-liberalism accepts that change can occur peacefully through the working of international institutions. Institutions facilitate cooperation by providing information, reducing transaction costs, helping to settle distributional conflicts, and, most importantly, reducing the likelihood of cheating. But while disagreeing with neo-realism that institutions matter only on the margins of international relations, neo-liberal institutionalism would still grant them a limited role. It accepts the basic neo-realist premise that institutions reflect and are conditioned by the distribution of power in the international system.[18] Moreover, institutions are created by self-interested states, and at most constrain state choices and strategies. They do not fundamentally alter state interests and identities (as self-interested egoists). Like neo-realism, neo-liberalism takes state interests as a given. Interests remain exogenous to the process of interstate interactions taking place in a given institutionalised setting. Such interactions do not fundamentally transform the condition of anarchy.[19]

Through the neo-realist–neo-liberal debate, the literature on security communities remained practically stagnant. As Buzan notes, the concept had been 'lying around since the late 1950s', with those who used it doing so 'without looking too far beyond the basic definitions'.[20] It was not until the end of the Cold War that international relations scholars, cognisant that 'states are not as war-prone as believed, and that many security arrangements once assumed to derive from balancing behaviour in fact depart significantly from realist imagery', gave the concept a new lease of life.[21] Not surprisingly therefore, an initial body of work on security communities, done at the regional level, focused on differentiating security communities from other types of security arrangements, such as alliances (defence communities), security regimes and collective security arrangements.[22] Another body of work, at the wider international level, was especially important in identifying and conceptualising different types and stages of security communities and establishing the conditions required for their development.[23] A major impetus for this renewed interest in security communities was the constructivist revolt against neo-realism and neo-liberalism.[24] Constructivism came to be the main theoretical framework for the study of security communities.[25] Its influence in shaping the new discourse on security communities is in three areas.

The first is the social construction of security communities. For constructivists, just as power politics (which is viewed by realists as a given of international politics) is but socially constructed, cooperation among states is also to be understood as a social process that may redefine the interests of the actors in matters of war and peace. The habit of war avoidance found in security communities results from interactions, socialisation, norm setting and identity building, rather than from forces outside these processes (such as the international distribution of power).

Second, constructivist scholarship has injected into the Deutschian literature on security communities a clear focus on the transformative impact of norms on state behaviour. To be sure, all theories of international organisation, including neo-liberal institutionalism, recognise the importance of norms. But constructivism allows for a much deeper impact of norms in shaping international relations. Norms not only 'regulate' state behaviour as in neo-liberal institutionalism, but also redefine state interests and constitute state identities, including the development of collective identities. By focusing on the constitutive effects of norms, constructivism has thus restored some of the original insights of integration theory regarding the impact of socialisation in creating collective interests and identities. As described in the next chapter, norms play a crucial role in the socialisation process leading to peaceful conduct among states, which form the core of security communities.

Third, constructivism allows us to look beyond the impact of material forces in shaping international politics. Neo-realism and most liberal theories take state interests to be shaped by material forces and concerns, such as power and wealth; perceptual, ideational and cultural factors derive from a material base. According to constructivists, while material forces remain important, intersubjective factors, including ideas, culture and identities, play a determining, rather than secondary, role in foreign policy interactions. Thus, constructivism provides important insights into the role of socialisation and identity building (the emergence of 'we feeling') that Deutsch identified as a crucial feature of security communities.

Constructivism remains a somewhat linear perspective, predisposed against the study of crisis points in cooperation which would explain the decline of institutions. In this book, an attempt will be made to examine ASEAN's record in managing regional order by focusing on both its accomplishments and its failures, using a framework that incorporates, but goes beyond, the linear constructivist logic. Overall, however, this book makes a case for adopting a sociological approach to the study of complexities of regionalism, focusing on the role of norms, socialisation and identity as central explanatory tools in the making and unmaking of security communities.

Why ASEAN?

ASEAN provides an important and rich area of investigation into the study of security communities. Since its formation in 1967, ASEAN has lived through a major shift in the regional strategic environment of Southeast Asia. In the 1960s, the outlook for regional security and stability in Southeast Asia was particularly grim. The region was portrayed variously as a 'region of revolt', the 'Balkans of the East', or a 'region of dominoes'. The weak socio-political cohesion of the region's new nation-states, the legitimacy problems of several of the region's postcolonial governments, interstate territorial disputes, intra-regional ideological polarisation and intervention by external powers were marked features of the geopolitical landscape of Southeast Asia. These conflicts posed a threat not only to the survival of some of the region's new states, but also to the prospects for regional order as a whole. Cold War Southeast Asia was polarised as a result of efforts by the revolutionary communist governments in Indochina to export their revolution to the neighbouring states. Vietnam's invasion of Cambodia in 1978 rekindled intra-regional tensions and set the stage for renewed Great Power intervention and rivalry in the region. While the Sabah dispute between the Philippines and Malaysia and the Indonesia–Malaysia–Singapore *Konfrontasi* (meaning confrontation) were the defining features of its regional security environment in the early postcolonial period, Vietnam's invasion of Cambodia and the ASEAN–Indochina polarisation marked the high point of the second Cold War in Southeast Asia.

Against this background, events leading to the establishment of ASEAN in August 1967 did not inspire much hope for the advancement of Southeast Asian regionalism. A year before ASEAN was formed, Kenneth T. Young, US ambassador to Thailand during 1961–63, had written rather pessimistically:

> It is doubtful that political regionalism or area-wide defense will emerge to play a part in encouraging regional equilibrium or regional institutions for political collaboration or collective defense. Centrifugal and divisive tendencies are too strong. Leaders will be more interested in relations with outside countries than among themselves, and more inclined to participate in Pan-Asian or international conferences and organizations than in exclusively Southeast Asian formations. They know that real power and needed resources, which the Southeast Asian countries do not possess, will continue to come from outside the region. Even the common fear of Communist China and the threat of Chinese minorities will not develop any sense of solidarity or serve to coordinate the divergent policies of neutrality and alignment. One political dilemma in Southeast Asia is that these new governments are trying desperately to become viable nation-states in an area where the individual state may, despite internal nationalism and good leadership, be turning obsolescent for the security and development of the area, and where at the same time a sense of regional community and purpose is lacking to complement and reinforce the nation-state.[26]

Indeed, the very survival of ASEAN was placed in doubt as interstate disputes (such as that between Malaysia and the Philippines over Sabah) escalated.[27] Functional cooperation, including trade liberalisation, was also slow to emerge. ASEAN's declaratory blueprint for regional order in the 1970s, such as the Zone of Peace, Freedom and Neutrality (ZOPFAN), was marred by serious contestations.

But ASEAN survived. What is more, by the early 1990s its members could claim their grouping to be one of the most successful experiments in regional cooperation in the developing world. At the heart of this claim was ASEAN's role in moderating intra-regional conflicts and significantly reducing the likelihood of war. The original ASEAN members, Indonesia, Malaysia, Singapore, Thailand and the Philippines, had not fought a war against each other since 1967 when they founded the grouping.[28] In addition, ASEAN could claim an ability to manage regional order by virtue of its leadership role in steering the peace process that culminated in the Paris Peace Agreement on Cambodia in 1991. Buoyed by the international recognition ASEAN received for its role, some of its leaders questioned the utility of Western models of regional cooperation (based on legalistic and formalistic institutions) *vis-à-vis* the ASEAN model, or the 'ASEAN Way', which emphasised informality and organisational minimalism. Such was ASEAN's credibility in the wake of the settlement of the Cambodia conflict that the countries of the Asia Pacific region accepted its nominal leadership and institutional model as the basis for creating a regional multilateral security dialogue, the ASEAN Regional Forum (ARF). ASEAN itself aspired to a role in regulating the behaviour of major powers and in creating a stable post-Cold War regional order in the Asia Pacific.

By the late 1990s, however, ASEAN's image had suffered a major setback. To be sure, ASEAN was never short of critics.[29] But many of them seized on the Asian economic crisis to highlight the shortcomings of the organisation.[30] They pointed to the persistence of intra-ASEAN disputes and ASEAN's failure to develop concrete institutional mechanisms and procedures for conflict resolution. They also cited the continuing differences and disagreements among its members over how to deal with non-members and external powers (such as the differences over ZOPFAN in the 1970s and over Vietnam in the 1980s). ASEAN's tendency to deal with intra-mural conflicts by 'sweeping them under the carpet', rather than resolving them, and its slow pace and modest record in developing economic cooperation, could be cited as further testimony to the limitations of the ASEAN Way. Moreover, in the late 1990s, ASEAN was criticised for not dealing effectively with human rights issues, or transnational problems such as the forest fires in Indonesia that had caused severe air pollution in neighbouring states. In the wake of the Asian economic crisis in 1997, ASEAN's critics also highlighted its inability to provide a united front in dealing with the challenges of globalisation. Intra-ASEAN differences over longstanding norms such as non-interference, evident in the wake of the expansion of its membership to include all ten countries of Southeast Asia, aggravated perceptions of ASEAN's weaknesses. Finally, the ASEAN-led ARF was seen as little more than a talk-shop, much like ASEAN itself. The ASEAN Way of soft institutionalism and dialogue process seemed ineffective in laying the foundations of an Asia-Pacific regional order.

Since then, ASEAN has tried to reform itself. As it crossed 40 years of its existence, ASEAN has undertaken a number of new initiatives, including a vision to build an ASEAN community with three pillars by 2020. An ASEAN security community (partly inspired by the Deutschian academic concept around which this book is written) is one of them. And an ASEAN charter, a constitutional framework for ASEAN that gives the grouping a legal personality, was adopted in 2007. In the wider region, ASEAN has not only continued its effort to bring China (and more recently India) into its normative framework for regional order, it has also helped develop a new process of East Asian regionalism.

The shifting perceptions of, and debates about, ASEAN through its four decades of existence invite several questions. How did ASEAN survive its shaky beginnings? How does one explain ASEAN's role in regional order in Southeast Asia? What explains its decline in the late 1990s compared with the 1980s and early 1990s? Is the 'ASEAN Way', often credited with ASEAN's effectiveness in the past, a myth or a reality? Do the new initiatives of the past few years such as the ASEAN community-building project and the ASEAN Charter mean a rejuvenation of ASEAN? Answering this question causes profound disagreements among scholars and analysts.

This book argues that the concept of security community, originally developed by Deutsch and his associates and recently resurrected and modified by constructivist scholarship, provides the most useful framework for addressing the above questions. This perspective views ASEAN regionalism as a process of interaction and socialisation and focuses on the norms which underpin this process. It also examines identity formation in ASEAN, explored by looking at the claims made by ASEAN elites about regionally specific ways of problem solving and cooperation. The book does not assume, *a priori*, that ASEAN has already become a security community in Deutsch's terms – or perhaps become a fully-fledged security community. Rather, the purpose of this exercise is to use the idea of security community as a framework within which to examine the evolution and nature of ASEAN's political and security role and identify the constraints it faces in developing a viable regional security community.

Such a perspective on ASEAN's role in regional order is scarcely found in the available literature. Despite its abundance, the literature on ASEAN has been and remains overwhelmingly atheoretical, and thus does not lend itself to any neat classification into realist, liberal, constructivist or other categories.[31] But it can safely be concluded that the available literature on ASEAN rarely deals with the question of norms and identity in explaining the evolution and role of ASEAN.

At the risk of oversimplification, one could discern, however, a body of writings on ASEAN that could be described as 'realist', in the sense that it calls into question ASEAN's capacity to shape regional order.[32] For the realist, ASEAN's survival and role have been dependent on, and shaped by, a wider regional balance of power system underpinned by the US military presence. Underlying this view is the quintessential realist assumption that the smaller and weaker states of the international system, whether acting individually or through multilateral institutions, lack the capacity to play a managerial role in ensuring international order and must therefore depend on the resources and leadership of the Great Powers.[33]

Another body of literature on ASEAN may be termed 'institutionalist', in the sense that it takes a generally more optimistic view (although the degree of optimism varies considerably) of ASEAN's capacity for managing intra-mural conflicts and creating the basis for a stable regional order.[34] From a theoretical standpoint, this type of work embraces a broad range of perspectives, including liberal institutionalist (including integrationist) and neo-liberal institutionalist (including regime theory) perspectives. Generally, however, liberal institutionalist perspectives have not been very relevant in explaining ASEAN's successes or failures, especially in the political and security arena. ASEAN was not a major empirical focus of regional integration theory (which had already become 'obsolescent' by the time ASEAN came into the international limelight).[35] Moreover, most liberal theories of cooperation assume background conditions, such as a shared liberal-democratic domestic environment (republican liberalism) and a relatively high degree of mutual economic interdependence (commercial liberalism), for regionalism to succeed. Neither of these conditions, to be discussed in Chapter 1, has been a marked feature of ASEAN.

Neo-liberal perspectives, including regime theory, do not share the belief of integrationist models regarding the sovereignty-eroding potential of institutions. In the case of ASEAN, a small body of literature has investigated its emergence and function as a regional security and economic 'regime' that allows each member to preserve its sovereignty and pursue its own 'national' interest.[36] Thus, Don Emmerson characterised ASEAN as a 'security regime', the latter defined as formal or informal arrangements among states 'to maintain their sovereignty in conditions of peace among themselves and with outside states'.[37] Some of the work on ASEAN economic cooperation also represents this type of approach. Such work views the role of ASEAN as that of a policy-coordinating body, a forum for trade liberalisation, information sharing, and a platform for collective bargaining over such functional issues as access to foreign markets or securing better prices for the primary commodity exports of members. Regional order is enhanced by growing interdependence fostered through trade, investment and other economic linkages.[38] But ASEAN remains primarily a vehicle through which its members pursue their national interests, the content of which remains unchanged (ASEAN as a regime can constrain the aggressive pursuit of national self-interests but not transform them). Regionalism remains largely an exercise in utility maximisation without any sovereignty-eroding or collective identity-shaping impact.

Neither the realist nor the vast majority of institutionalist writings have spent much time in discussing questions central to this book: such as, what are the key norms of ASEAN? To what extent have they been upheld in practice? What effect have they had on the national interests and identities of the ASEAN members? Some available literature on ASEAN displays a constructivist flavour by investigating the elements of the ASEAN Way, and exploring the possibility of identity change.[39] This study is intended to analyse systematically the role of ASEAN's norms in the management of regional order and their effect on the development of collective interests and identities. Proceeding from a constructivist perspective, it examines ASEAN as a security community and, in doing so, hopes to provide a better and more complete understanding of ASEAN than already available.

The conceptual framework of this study goes beyond the neo-realist–neo-liberal divide. It argues that the successes and failures of international and regional institutions are not predetermined for them by forces exogenous to their social practices. This includes the distribution of power emphasised by the realist school. Nor can ASEAN be understood through the neo-liberal prism. While regime theory's view of ASEAN as an informal security arrangement is helpful in understanding ASEAN's role, the accompanying neo-liberal belief that institutions work by 'constraining' state preferences through provision of sanction mechanisms to prevent cheating is not applicable to regional groupings in the Third World. ASEAN, for example, has made no effort to develop such sanctioning mechanisms. Instead, ASEAN has worked by focusing, in a more positive manner, on the task of defining and redefining Southeast Asia's regional identity and developing norms of collective action. As most observers of ASEAN would agree, the organisation's approach to regionalism has been geared to inducing cooperative behaviour from its members through socialisation, rather than 'constraining' uncooperative behaviour through sanctions. A neo-liberal approach predisposes us from examining such constructs as the ASEAN Way and to investigate whether it has led to the emergence of new interests and identities which reflect shared understandings and expectations about regional peace and stability.

In other words, the main reasons for ASEAN's successes and failures can be found by looking at the nature and *quality* of its socialisation process and the norms that underpin it. This perspective is constructivist in orientation. It assumes that state interests and identities derive from their social practices and are not simply exogenous to them.[40] Institutions provide crucial settings within which states develop their social practices and make them understood, accepted and shared by others in the group.[41] ASEAN is not moulded exclusively by material conditions such as the balance of power or material considerations such as expected gains from economic interdependence. Its frameworks of interaction and socialisation have themselves become a crucial factor affecting the interests and identities of its members. The idea of security community, sociologically understood, enables us to analyse ASEAN as a regional institution which both regulates and constitutes the interests and policies of its members on matters of war, peace and cooperation. ASEAN's role in regional order can be studied and evaluated by looking at the extent to which its norms and socialisation processes, and identity-building initiatives, have shaped the attitudes and behaviour of its members about conflict and order in the region, and the extent to which they have led to the development of common understandings, expectations and practices about peaceful conduct.

Notes and references

1   For a comprehensive overview of the literature on the causes of war, see: Jack S. Levy, 'The Causes of War: A Review of Theories and Evidence', in Philip E. Tetlock *et al.* (eds), *Behaviour, Society and Nuclear War*, vol. 1 (New York: Oxford University Press, 1989).

2   Karl Deutsch *et al.*, *Political Community and the North Atlantic Area* (Princeton: Princeton University Press, 1957), p. 3. This book, in the authors' own words, was conceived as a 'contribution to the study of possible ways in which men some day might abolish war'. Ibid. The term security community was coined earlier by Richard van Wagenen, who was a member of Deutsch's team that produced the book.

3   John Hertz, 'Idealist Internationalism and the Security Dilemma', *World Politics*, vol. 2 (January 1950), pp. 157–80.

4   Ibid., p. 157.

5   Donald J. Puchala, 'The Integration Theorists and the Study of International Relations', in Charles W. Kegley and Eugene M. Wittkopf (eds), *The Global Agenda: Issues and Perspectives* (New York: Random House, 1984), p. 189.

6   Ibid.

7   Philip E. Jacob and Henry Teune, 'The Integrative Process: Guidelines for Analysis', in Philip E. Jacob and James V. Toscano (eds), *The Integration of Political Communities* (Philadelphia: Lippincott, 1964), p. 4, cited in Joseph S. Nye, 'Comparative Regional Integration: Concept and Measurement', *International Organization*, vol. 22, no. 4 (Autumn 1968), p. 863.

8   Wolf-Dieter Eberwein, 'The Future of International Warfare: Toward a Global Security Community', *International Political Science Review*, vol. 16, no. 4 (1995), p. 347.

9   Joseph S. Nye, 'Neorealism and Neoliberalism', *World Politics*, vol. xl, no. 2 (January 1988), p. 239. Regional integration theory refers to a body of theoretical writings influential from the 1950s until the mid-1970s covering the origins, functions, and strengths and limitations of regional approaches to peace and cooperation. A selection of writings on regional integration theory includes: Ernst Haas, *Beyond the Nation State* (Stanford, CA: Stanford University Press, 1964); Leon N. Lindberg and Stuart A. Scheingold, *Regional Integration: Theory and Research* (Cambridge, MA: Harvard University Press, 1971); Roger D. Hansen, 'Regional Integration: Reflections on a Decade of Theoretical Efforts', *World Politics*, vol. 21 (January 1969), pp. 242–71; Ernst Haas, 'The Study of Regional Integration: Reflections on the Joys and Anguish of Pretheorising', in Richard A. Falk and Saul H. Mendlovitz (eds), *Regional Politics and World Order* (San Francisco: W.H. Freeman, 1973), pp. 103–31; Donald J. Puchala, 'The Integration Theorists and the Study of International Relations', in Charles W. Kegley and Eugene R. Wittkopf (eds), *The Global Agenda: Issues and Perspectives* (New York: Random House, 1984); Gordon

Mace, 'Regional Integration', *World Encyclopedia of Peace* (Oxford: Pergamon Press, 1986), pp. 323–25; Michael Hodges, 'Integration Theory', in Trevor Taylor (ed.), *Approaches and Theory in International Relations* (London: Longman, 1978); Charles A. Duffy and Werner J. Feld, 'Whither Regional Integration Theory?', in Gavin Boyd and Werner J. Feld (eds), *Comparative Regional Systems* (New York: Pergamon Press, 1980).

10 Transactionalism (Karl Deutsch) examined how increased communications and transactions among societies can redefine their perceptions and relationships and lead to the establishment of security communities in which the use of force becomes illegitimate as a means of problem solving. The other major school of regional integration theory was neo-functionalism (Ernst Haas and Joseph Nye) which held that cooperation in areas of 'low politics' would produce a 'spillover' effect into areas of 'high politics'. Neo-functionalism was a revised version of classical functionalist theory, which, as formulated by David Mittrany, held that the prospects for integration could be enhanced if actors focused their initial efforts on issues of 'low politics', i.e. functional and technical issues, before moving into issues of 'high politics', such as political and military affairs. But classical functionalism was not concerned with the role of institutions in promoting higher and more centralised forms of political authority. This was a gap filled by neo-functionalist theory, developed by Ernst Haas, who also took an expanded view (compared with the functionalist emphasis on technocrats) of the range of actors involved in the integration process, including elements of civil society (e.g. pressure groups).

11 Puchala, 'The Integration Theorists and the Study of International Relations', p. 198.

12 Regional integration theorists were accused by their critics of having overestimated the durability and broader applicability of the conditions that had led to the creation of the EC. Critics argued, for example, that European conditions after the Second World War were somewhat unique; the decline of European nationalism was temporary owing to the scale of devastation caused by the war. Integration theorists had wrongly assumed the end of ideology and the decline of nationalism in postwar Europe. This became further apparent when the EC, despite its evident success in turning age-old rivals France and Germany into members of a permanent security community, failed to come up with a collective response to external challenges, such as the Middle East oil crisis of 1973. That external events could cause states to go their separate ways and opt for national strategies over regional collective action was evident in several cases. For example, when faced with the US technology challenge, Britain, France and Germany ignored the possibility of collective response through the EC, instead adopting national responses. Similarly, Britain joined with the USA in response to the 1973 oil crisis, thereby ignoring and undermining the possibility of a collective response by the EC. All this served to undermine the game plan of the integration theorists, who found the relationship between regional integration and transregional interdependence to be too uncertain and 'turbulent' to justify the view of regional integration as an incremental or linear process.

13 Emanuel Adler and Michael Barnett, 'Security Communities in Theoretical Perspective', in Emanuel Adler and Michael Barnett (eds), *Security Communities* (Cambridge: Cambridge University Press, 1998), p. 3.

14 Robert O. Keohane and Joseph S. Nye, *Power and Interdependence* (Boston: Little, Brown, 1977).

15 Puchala, 'The Integration Theorists and the Study of International Relations', p. 198

16 Robert Keohane, 'International Institutions: Two Approaches', *International Studies Quarterly*, vol. 32, no. 4 (December 1988); Robert Keohane, *International Institutions and State Power: Essays in International Relations Theory* (Boulder, CO: Westview Press, 1989). For a critique, see: Joseph M. Grieco, 'Anarchy and the Limits of Cooperation: A Realist Critique of the Newest Liberal Institutionalism', *International Organization*, vol. 42, no. 3 (Summer 1988).

17 Kenneth Waltz, *Theory of International Politics* (Reading, MA: Addison-Wesley, 1979), pp. 176–93; Robert Gilpin, *War and Change in World Politics* (Cambridge: Cambridge University Press, 1981).

18 'International institutions', write Robert Keohane and Lisa Martin, 'are created in response to state interests . . . their character is structured by the prevailing distribution of capabilities'. Robert Keohane and Lisa Martin, 'The Promise of Institutionalist Theory', *International Security*, vol. 19, no. 1 (Summer 1995), p. 47.

19 A vigorous account of the realist–institutionalist debate can be found in the article by John Mearsheimer in the Winter 1994/95 issue of *International Security* and replies to it in the journal's Summer 1995 issue. John Mearsheimer, 'The False Promise of International Institutions', *International Security*, vol. 19, no. 3 (Winter 1994/95), pp. 5–49. Among the institutionalist

responses, see especially: Robert Keohane and Lisa Martin, 'The Promise of Institutionalist Theory', *International Security*, vol. 20, no. 1 (Summer 1995), pp. 39–51. For an earlier selection of important contributions to this debate, see: David Baldwin (ed.), *Neorealism and Neoliberalism: The Contemporary Debate* (New York: Columbia University Press, 1993).

20 Barry Buzan, Review of *Security Communities, International Affairs*, vol. 76, no. 1 (January 2000), p. 154.

21 Adler and Barnett, 'Security Communities in Theoretical Perspective', p. 4.

22 This was a key aspect of my own early work on security communities, which was done in the early 1990s. Amitav Acharya, 'Association of Southeast Asian Nations: Security Community or Defence Community?', *Pacific Affairs*, vol. 64, no. 2 (Summer 1991), pp. 159–78; Amitav Acharya, 'A Regional Security Community in Southeast Asia?', *Journal of Strategic Studies*, vol. 18, no. 3 (September 1995), pp.175–200. (This article also appears as a book chapter in Desmond Ball, ed., *The Transformation of Security in the Asia/Pacific Region* (London: Frank Cass, 1995). This work was totally unrelated to the parallel work of Adler and Barnett that led to their 1998 volume *Security Communities*, until I was invited by them to contribute a chapter (Chapter 6) to the volume in the final stage of the project.)

23 Adler and Barnett, *Security Communities* (Cambridge: Cambridge University Press, 1998). This volume had been preceded by a number of conceptual and framing papers by the two editors developing a critique of Deutsch and offering a new research agenda. Emanuel Adler and Michael Barnett, 'Pluralistic Security Communities: Past, Present and Future', Working Paper on Regional Security No. 1 (Madison: Global Studies Research Program, University of Wisconsin, 1994); Emanuel Adler and Michael Barnett, 'Governing Anarchy: A Research Agenda for the Study of Security Communities', *Ethics and International Affairs*, vol. 10 (1996), pp. 63–98. See also Emanuel Adler, 'Imagined (Security) Communities: Cognitive Regions in International Relations', *Millennium: Journal of International Studies*, vol. 26, no. 2 (1997), pp. 249–77. My work of 1992 and 1995 focused on Southeast Asia and sought to develop the concept on the basis of the ASEAN experience beyond Deutsch's original formulation, while an essay by Adler published in 1992 focused on the security community in Europe. Emanuel Adler, 'Europe's New Security Order: A Pluralistic Security Community', in Beverly Crawford, (ed.), *The Future of European Security* (Berkeley, CA: University of California Press, 1992), pp. 287–326. For an application of the concept globally, see: Eberwein, 'The Future of International Warfare: Toward a Global Security Community?'

24 Alexander Wendt, 'Anarchy Is What States Make of It: The Social Construction of Power Politics', *International Organization*, vol. 46 (Spring 1992), pp. 391–425; Alexander Wendt, 'Collective Identity and the International State', *American Political Science Review*, vol. 88 (June 1994), pp. 384–96; Alexander Wendt, *Social Theory of International Politics* (Cambridge: Cambridge University Press, 1999); Emanuel Adler, 'Seizing the Middle Ground: Constructivism in World Politics', *European Journal of International Relations*, vol. 3, no. 3 (1997), p. 342. Ted Hopf, 'The Promise of Constructivism in International Relations Theory', *International Security*, vol. 23, no. 1 (Summer 1998), pp. 171–200; Jeffrey T. Checkel, 'The Constructivist Turn in International Relations Theory', *World Politics*, vol. 50 (January 1998), pp. 324–48. Examples of early constructivist case studies can be found in Michael Barnett, 'Sovereignty, Nationalism, and Regional Order in the Arab States System', *International Organization*, vol. 49 (1995), pp. 479–510; Martha Finnemore, *National Interests in International Society* (Ithaca, NY: Cornell University Press, 1996); Audie Klotz, *Norms in International Relations: The Struggle Against Apartheid* (Ithaca, NY: Cornell University Press, 1995); Peter J. Katzenstein (ed.), *The Culture of National Security: Norms and Identity in World Politics* (New York: Columbia University Press, 1996).

25 Emanuel Adler and Michael Barnett, 'Security Communities in Theoretical Perspective', in Emanuel Adler and Michael Barnett (eds), *Security Communities* (Cambridge: Cambridge University Press, 1998), p. 12.

26 Kenneth T. Young, *The Southeast Asia Crisis* (New York: The Association of the Bar of the City of New York, 1966), p. 64.

27 There were exceptions to this pessimism. Some, but not all, British assessments of ASEAN during its early years were cautiously optimistic. 'Despite this caution and the dichotomy between its long-term aspirations and its present limited practical possibilities . . ., ASEAN remains the grouping in the region with the best chance of successfully developing a respectable amount of

meaningful co-operation between its members.' D.F.B. Le Breton from the South West Pacific Department to Mr. Wilford, 'The 4th Ministerial Meeting of ASEAN', 7 May 1971, FW1/1 (London: Public Records Office).

28 Wars in Southeast Asia since 1967 include Vietnam's invasion and occupation of Cambodia between 1978 and 1989, and a border war between Thailand and Laos in 1986. In addition, a near-war situation obtained between Vietnam and Thailand during much of the 1978–89 period. But Vietnam, Cambodia and Laos became ASEAN members in 1995, 1999 and 1997 respectively, and Burma joined in 1997. Thus, it can be said that the ASEAN countries have not fought a war among themselves as ASEAN members.

29 Michael Leifer, *ASEAN and the Security of South East Asia* (London: Routledge,1989).

30 For an overview of the criticism of ASEAN's role in the Asian economic crisis, see: Amitav Acharya, 'Realism, Institutionalism, and the Asian Economic Crisis', *Contemporary Southeast Asia*, vol. 21, no. 1 (April 1999), pp. 1–29.

31 For examples of attempts to view Southeast Asian security from the prism of international relations theory, see: Sheldon Simon, 'Realism and Neoliberalism: International Relations Theory and Southeast Asian Security', *Pacific Review*, vol. 8, no. 1 (1995), pp. 5–24. See also: Shaun Narine, 'Institutional Theory and Southeast Asia: The Case of ASEAN', *World Affairs*, vol. 161, no. 1 (Summer 1998), pp. 33–7; Sorpong Peou, 'Realism and Constructivism in Southeast Asian Security Studies Today', *The Pacific Review*, vol. 15, no. 1 (2002), pp. 1–20; Amitav Acharya and Richard Stubbs, (eds), 'Theorising Southeast Asian Relations', A Special Issue of *Pacific Review*, vol. 19, no. 2 (June 2006).

32 This type of scholarship is best represented by Michael Leifer. Sharing important assumptions of both neo-realism and the English School, Leifer has argued that ASEAN's role in managing regional order has been subject to the prevailing balance (in the sense of distribution) of power, an important determinant of which was the US military presence in the region. See: Michael Leifer, *Conflict and Order in Southeast Asia*, Adelphi Paper no. 162 (London: International Institute for Strategic Studies, 1980); *ASEAN and the Security of Southeast Asia* (London: Routledge, 1989); 'The ASEAN Peace Process: A Category Mistake', *Pacific Review*, vol. 12, no. 1 (1999), pp. 25–38. See also: Tim Huxley, *Indochina as a Security Concern of the ASEAN States*, 1975–81 (Ph. D. dissertation, Australian National University, 1986); 'ASEAN's Prospective Security Role: Moving Beyond the Indochina Fixation', *Contemporary Southeast Asia*, vol. 9, no. 3 (December 1987), pp. 194–207; 'Southeast Asia in the Study of International Relations: The Rise and Decline of a Region', *Pacific Review*, vol. 9, no. 2 (1996). Leifer, however, is not entirely dismissive of ASEAN's role in mitigating intra-regional conflicts. In a 1995 paper, he argued that: 'one can claim quite categorically that ASEAN has become an institutionalised vehicle for intra-mural conflict avoidance and management . . . ASEAN has been able to prevent disputes from escalating and getting out of hand through containing and managing contentious issues'. Leifer, 'ASEAN as a Model of a Security Community?', in M. Hadi Soesastro (ed.), *ASEAN in a Changed Regional and International Political Economy* (Jakarta: Centre for Strategic and International Studies, 1995), p. 132.

33 Such a view is persuasive to some extent, given the fact that many ASEAN leaders themselves have repeatedly acknowledged the impact of the US military presence as a key factor behind regional order and prosperity. Yet, it does not explain the fact that while the US strategic dominance in East Asia remains relatively unchanged in the post-Cold War period, the fortunes of ASEAN have changed over the past decade. It is also at odds with the fact that the most hopeful prospects for regional order in Southeast Asia emerged in the early 1990s, a period when doubts about the US military presence were at their strongest, while today, although US strategic dominance has been reaffirmed, the prospect for regional order and ASEAN's role in managing it is facing its most serious test.

34 A selective listing of such work would include Arnfinn Jorgensen-Dahl, *Regional Organisation and Order in Southeast Asia* (London: Macmillan, 1982); Alison Broinowski (ed.), *Understanding ASEAN* (New York: St Martin's Press, 1982); Alison Broinowski (ed.), *ASEAN into the 1990s* (Basingstoke: Macmillan, 1990); Sheldon W. Simon, *The ASEAN States and Regional Security* (Stanford, CA: Hoover Institution Press, 1982); Muthiah Alagappa, 'Regional Arrangements and International Security in Southeast Asia: Going Beyond ZOPFAN', *Contemporary Southeast Asia*, vol. 12, no. 4 (March 1991), pp. 269–305. While these writings also identify the limitations of ASEAN in managing regional conflict, many works by scholars affiliated with strategic studies

think-tanks in ASEAN, especially members of the ASEAN Institutes of International and Strategic Studies (ASEAN-ISIS), while also falling into this broad category, tend to be, at least until the regional economic crisis, totally uncritical and overly laudatory of ASEAN's achievements. See for example: J. Soedjati Djiwandono, 'The Political and Security Aspects of ASEAN: Its Principal Achievements', *Indonesian Quarterly*, vol. 11, no. 3 (July 1983), pp. 19–26; Jusuf Wanandi, 'Security Issues in the ASEAN Region', in Karl Jakson and M. Hadi Soesastro (eds), *ASEAN Security and Economic Development* (Berkeley, CA: University of California, Institute of East Asian Studies, 1984); Noordin Sopiee, 'ASEAN and Regional Security', in Mohammed Ayoob (ed.), *Regional Security in the Third World* (London: Croom Helm, 1986), pp. 221–31.

35 Attempts to apply regional integration theory to ASEAN can be found in Thakur Phanit, 'Regional Integration Attempts in Southeast Asia: A Study of ASEAN's Problems and Progress' (Ph. D. dissertation, Pennsylvania State University, 1980); Tarnthong Thongswasdi, 'ASEAN After the Vietnam War: Stability and Development Through Regional Cooperation' (Ph. D. dissertation, Claremont Graduate School, 1979).

36 There are few works on ASEAN that utilise the regime perspective. See: Donald Weatherbee, 'ASEAN Regionalism: The Salient Dimension', in Karl Jakson and M. Hadi Soesastro (eds), *ASEAN Security and Economic Development* (Berkeley, CA: University of California, Institute of East Asian Studies, 1984), pp. 259–68. Don Emmerson has also used the term 'regime' to describe ASEAN: see his 'ASEAN as an International Regime', *Journal of International Affairs*, vol. 41, no. 1 (Summer/Fall 1987), pp. 1–16; and 'Indonesia, Malaysia, Singapore: A Regional Security Core', in Richard J. Ellings and Sheldon W. Simon (eds), *Southeast Asian Security in the New Millennium* (Armonk, NY: M.E. Sharpe, 1996), pp. 34–88. Emmerson's emphasis on sovereignty rejects the classical regional integration model, and he does not discuss the impact of ASEAN on regional identity, a major focus for constructivists. See also: N. Ganesan, 'Testing Neoliberalism in Southeast Asia', *International Journal*, vol. 50, no. 4 (Autumn 1995), pp. 779–804.

37 Emmerson, 'Indonesia, Malaysia, Singapore', p. 34.

38 See, for example, some of the essays on economic cooperation in: Hadi Soesastro (ed.), *ASEAN in a Changed Regional and International Political Economy* (Jakarta: Centre for Strategic and International Studies, 1995); Hadi Soesastro and Anthony Bergin (eds), *The Role of Security and Economic Cooperation Structures in the Asia Pacific Region* (Jakarta: Centre for Strategic and International Studies, 1996); M. Hadi Soesastro, 'ASEAN's Participation in the GATT', *Indonesian Quarterly*, vol. 15, no. 1 (January 1987), pp. 107–27; Marjorie L. Suriyamongkol, *Politics of ASEAN Economic Co-operation: The Case of ASEAN Industrial Projects* (Singapore: Oxford University Press, 1988). Soesastro is one of the few scholars of ASEAN who straddles political economy and security studies. Richard Stubbs is another scholar to investigate both the economic and security role of ASEAN. He argues that regional stability in Southeast Asia is a function of rapid economic development in a climate of regional stability. While conceding the contribution of ASEAN, however, Stubbs traces Southeast Asia's prosperity-induced stability to the US strategic involvement in the region, especially as a provider of economic, military and technological aid during the Korean and Vietnam Wars. See: Richard Stubbs, 'War and Export-Oriented Industrialization in East and Southeast Asia', *Comparative Politics*, vol. 31 (April 1999), pp. 337–55.

39 Examples include: Amitav Acharya, 'Association of Southeast Asian Nations: "Security Community" or "Defence Community"?', *Pacific Affairs*, vol. 64, no. 2 (Summer 1991), pp. 159–78; Amitav Acharya, 'A Regional Security Community in Southeast Asia?', *Journal of Strategic Studies*, vol. 18, no. 3 (September 1995), pp. 175–200; Michael Antolik, *ASEAN and the Diplomacy of Accommodation* (Armonk, NY: M.E. Sharpe, 1990). One of the first studies of ASEAN to investigate issues of culture and identity was Estrella D. Solidum, 'Towards a Southeast Asian Community' (Quezon: University of the Philippines Press, 1974). See also: R.P. Anand and Purificacion V. Quisumbing (eds), *ASEAN: Identity, Development and Culture* (Quezon City: University of the Philippines Law Centre and East–West Center Culture Learning Institute, 1981); Michael Haas, *The Asian Way to Peace: A Study of Regional Cooperation* (New York: Praeger, 1989). Moreover, contributions by several key players in the formative stages of ASEAN to the 1975 collection of essays published by the Centre for Strategic and International Studies in Indonesia underscored the identity-building mission of ASEAN. See the essays by: Adam Malik, Mohamad Ghazali Shafie and Rahim Ishak in *Regionalism in Southeast Asia* (Jakarta: Centre for Strategic and International Studies, 1975). For first interpretations of ASEAN from a constructivist standpoint,

see: Amitav Acharya, 'Ideas, Identity and Institution-Building: From the "ASEAN Way" to "Asia Pacific Way"?', *Pacific Review*, vol. 10, no. 3 (1997), pp. 319–46; Amitav Acharya, 'Collective Identity and Conflict Management in Southeast Asia', in Emmanuel Adler and Michael Barnett (eds), *Security Communities* (Cambridge: Cambridge University Press, 1998), pp. 198–227; Alastair Iain Johnston, 'The Myth of the ASEAN Way? Explaining the Evolution of the ASEAN Regional Forum', in Helga Haftendorn, Robert Keohane and Celeste Wallander (eds), *Imperfect Unions: Security Institutions in Time and Space* (London: Oxford University Press, 1999); Nicholas Busse, 'Constructivism and Southeast Asia', *Pacific Review* (1999).

40 Ted Hopf, 'The Promise of Constructivism in International Relations Theory', *International Security*, vol. 23, no. 1 (Summer 1988), p. 176.

41 Ibid., p. 177.

1 Constructing security communities

How do states develop the 'long-term habit' of interacting and managing disputes with others peacefully? The Deutschian framework explained this puzzle by focusing on transaction flows, the spread of transnational values, the development of shared understandings, and the generation of mutual trust.[1] Interactions between states (as well as interaction between social groups) can lead to greater mutual interdependence and responsiveness, including 'discovery of new interests' and recognition of collective identities that would progressively render war illegitimate as a means of problem solving.[2] Constructivist theory offers a range of new insights by further developing and refining the Deutschian framework (which had been criticised for an excessive preoccupation with measuring transactions). The main contribution of constructivism includes its insights into the interplay of institutions, norms and identities that goes into the social construction of security communities.

This chapter provides a framework for understanding the processes and dynamics underlying the making and unmaking of pluralistic security communities. It draws upon the work of Deutsch and his associates, as well as my own previous work (since 1992) on the concept, and the constructivist work on security communities spearheaded by Adler and Barnett around the same time. The chapter proceeds in five parts. The first defines security communities and differentiates them from other forms of international and regional orders. The second section analyses how multilateral (including regional) institutions can play a security community-building role by specifying norms of state behaviour and providing a framework for socialisation that could regulate the behaviour of states and lead to the development of collective interests and identities. The next section looks at the applicability of the concept to the Third World. Like many concepts and theories of international relations, the concept of security community is West European in origin. When Karl Deutsch and his associates first proposed the idea of security community, they were seeking to explain the emergence of cooperation among the developed states of the North Atlantic region. Neither they, nor most of the scholars who have used the concept since, have given consideration to the possibility of security communities in the developing world. Applying Deutsch's model to Third World regions such as Southeast Asia is therefore problematic, because many of the background conditions he and other integration theorists identified as important in the North Atlantic, such as liberal politics and market economics, are often missing from most Third World regions.

The fourth section discusses the emergence and decline of security communities. It identifies the key developments and indicators in the various stages of their evolution. It also discusses the possibility, often ignored in other constructivist studies of international cooperation, that community-building efforts may suffer setbacks or be reversed as a result of increased socialisation and expansion. In other words, this section will outline an evolutionary but non-linear perspective on the construction of security communities. The final section draws the framework of the book, providing brief introductions to chapters and outlining the key questions in terms of which the evolution of ASEAN and the impact of ASEAN's norms will be investigated.

Defining security communities

A security community is distinguished by a 'real assurance that the members of that community will not fight each other physically, but will settle their disputes in some other way'.[3] Such communities could either be 'amalgamated' through the formal political merger of the participating units, or remain 'pluralistic', in which case the members retain their independence and sovereignty.

This book is concerned with pluralistic security communities among sovereign states. A pluralistic security community may be defined as a 'transnational region comprised of sovereign states whose people maintain dependable expectations of peaceful change'.[4] Such a community could be identified in terms of several features, but two are especially important. The first is the absence of war, and the second is the absence of significant organised preparations for war *vis-à-vis* any other members. Regional security communities, as Yalem notes, are groups of states that have 'renounced the use of force as a means of resolving intraregional conflicts'.[5] The absence of war or organised violence need not, however, imply an absence of differences, disputes or conflicts of interest among the actors. Holsti observes that 'some serious differences have arisen among states in security communities', although 'some special characteristics of these relationships have prevented the quarrelling governments from adopting forms of behavior typical in conflicts involving threat or use of force'.[6] Thus it is an ability to manage conflicts within the group peacefully, rather than the absence of conflict *per se*, which distinguishes a security community from other types of security relationships. To quote Deutsch,

> even if some of the prospective partner countries [in a security community] find themselves on the opposite sides in some larger international conflict they conduct themselves so as to keep actual mutual hostilities and damage to a minimum – or else refuse to fight each other altogether.[7]

Security communities are also marked by the absence of a competitive military build-up or arms race involving their members. Within a security community, 'war among the prospective partners comes to be considered as illegitimate', and 'serious preparations for it no longer command popular support'.[8] States within a security community usually abstain from acquiring weapons that are primarily offensive in nature. Neither are they likely to engage in contingency planning and war-oriented resource mobilisation against other actors within the community. To the extent that

> [t]he absence of such advance preparations for large-scale violence between any two territories or groups of people prevents any immediate outbreak of effective war between them ... it serves for this reason as the test for the existence or non-existence of a security community among the groups concerned.[9]

Viewed in this light, the absence of arms racing or contingency planning becomes a key indicator of whether states have developed 'dependable expectations of peaceful change' and thereby overcome the security dilemma. As Deutsch put it, 'the attainment of a security community can thus be tested operationally in terms of the absence or presence of significant organized preparations for war or large-scale violence among its members'.[10]

The task of developing a framework for the study of security communities requires us to differentiate them from other forms of multilateral security cooperation. For the purpose of this book, and drawing on my earlier work on security communities (see Table 1.1 below), I distinguish security communities from three other types of regional security systems. First, a distinction may be made between a *security community* and a *security regime*.[11] In a security regime, as Buzan points out, 'a group of states cooperate to manage their disputes and avoid war by seeking to mute the security dilemma both by their own actions and by their assumptions about the behaviour of others'.[12] This may seem similar to security communities; however, there are important differences. A security regime normally describes a situation in which the interests of the actors 'are neither wholly compatible nor wholly

Table 1.1 Security communities and other frameworks of security cooperation

Security regime:
- Principles, rules and norms that restrain the behaviour of states on a reciprocal basis.
- Competitive arms acquisitions and contingency planning usually continue within the regime, although specific regimes might be created to limit the spread of weapons and military capabilities.
- The absence of war within the community may be due to short-term factors and considerations such as the economic and political weakness of actors otherwise prone to violence or to the existence of a balance of power or mutual deterrence situation. In either case, the interests of the actors in peace are not fundamental, unambiguous or long-term in nature.

Security community:
- Strict and observed norms concerning non-use of force; no competitive arms acquisitions and contingency planning against each other within the grouping.
- Institutions and processes (formal or informal) for the pacific settlement of disputes.
- Long-term prospects for war avoidance.
- Significant functional cooperation and integration.
- A sense of collective identity.

Collective defence:
- Common perception of external threat(s) among or by the members of the community; such a threat might be another state or states within the region or an extra-regional power, but not from a member.
- An exclusionary arrangement of like-minded states.
- Reciprocal obligations of assistance during military contingencies.
- Significant military interoperability and integration.
- The conditions of a security community may or may not exist among the members.

Collective security:
- Prior agreement on the willingness of all parties to participate in the collective punishment of aggression against any member state.
- No prior identification of enemy or threat.
- No expectation of and requirement for economic or other functional cooperation.
- A collective physical capacity to punish aggression.

Source: Amitav Acharya, 'A Regional Security Community in Southeast Asia?,' *Journal of Strategic Studies*, vol. 18, no. 3 (September 1995), pp. 175–200.

competitive'.[13] Indeed, a security regime may develop within an otherwise adversarial relationship in which the use of force is inhibited by the existence of a balance of power or mutual deterrence situation. In this context, the common interest of the USA and the former Soviet Union with regard to nuclear weapons and non-proliferation measures has been cited as an example of a security regime.[14] A security community, on the other hand, must be based on a fundamental, unambiguous and long-term *convergence* of interests among the actors in the avoidance of war. While international regimes do not always or necessarily work to 'constrain' the use of force and produce cooperation, in the case of security communities, the non-use of force is already assumed. Furthermore, security regimes do not necessarily imply that participants are interested in, or already bound by, functional linkages, co-operation, integration or interdependence, while this is an essential feature of security communities. Thus, the Concert of Europe or the Conference on Security and Cooperation in Europe during the Cold War constituted examples of security regimes,[15] while the relationships between the USA and Canada, and among the members of the European Union (EU), are better described as having the attributes of a security community.

Security regimes are more akin to what Deutsch called a 'no-war community'. The latter is a first step towards a fully-fledged security community, but unlike a security community a no-war community is one in which 'the possibility of war is still expected and to some extent preparations are made for it. Sanctions may include continuing defensive preparations for self-help by members.'[16] In a no-war community, prospects for use of force are suppressed by specific circumstances, such as common threat perceptions. War avoidance is based on short-term calculations, rather than on 'dependable' and 'long-term expectations of peaceful change'. Such a community may be relatively easily disrupted by internal or external developments. It is a short step from cooperation and war avoidance to an arms race and military rivalry. Moreover, security regimes are marked by the absence of the 'we feeling'. Institutions for conflict resolution are at best rudimentary or nonexistent.

The idea of a security community is also distinct from that of an *alliance* or a *defence community*. The imperative of war avoidance must be distinguished from that of collective defence. An alliance is usually conceived and directed against a pre-recognised and commonly perceived external threat. Security communities, on the other hand, identify no such threat or may have no function of organising a joint defence against it. A security community implies a relationship of peace and stability among a group of states without any sense of how they might collectively relate to external actors. To be sure, security communities can develop out of common threat perceptions found in an alliance. Moreover, alliances can exist bilaterally or multilaterally within a security community (and such arrangements usually indicate a mature security community with a fairly well-developed collective identity). But this is not to be regarded as an indispensable or even essential characteristic of security communities.

The difference between security community and alliance could be highlighted by applying Lynn Miller's distinction between the 'peace' and 'security' role of regional organisations. The 'peace' role, central to a security community, refers to the 'potential of a regional organization, through its peacekeeping machinery and diplomatic techniques, for controlling the forceful settlement of conflicts among its own members'. The 'security' role, which might be considered integral to a defence community, denotes 'the potential of the organization to present a common military front against an outside actor or actors'.[17]

To be sure, Western security communities usually feature alliance relationships (most EU members are also part of NATO). But, while a defence community may be subsumed within a larger security community (and vice versa), this is not a necessary feature of the latter. The key aim of a security community is to develop the common interests of actors in peace and stability, rather than to deter or balance a common threat. In this sense, a security community is the antithesis of a 'security complex' (in its original formulation) which may be characterised by an 'interdependence of rivalry' among a given group of states as much as an interdependence of shared interests.[18] Conflict avoidance and the peaceful resolution of disputes, which are among the most important shared interests in security communities, are not defining characteristics of security complexes.

Although security communities may be constructed on the basis of shared interests and identities, rather than the perception of a common threat, their identities are usually defined in opposition to the identity of other actors. During the 1980s, ASEAN thrived by consciously emphasising the ideological, economic and political differences between its own members and the Indochinese states. It continues to highlight its own distinctiveness as a regional multilateral institution *vis-à-vis* other multilateral institutions such as those in Europe. Brian Job notes that 'the multilateralism of a security community is intensive among members, membership itself is restricted and, in practice, closely guarded by members'.[19] Security communities usually bring together a group of 'like-minded' actors who often develop common criteria of inclusion and exclusion. But a security community does not need to involve the features of an alliance directed against another state or group of states.

Finally, it is important to distinguish a security community from a *collective security* arrangement. A major difference relates to the means employed to ensure war avoidance. Collective security systems (which tend to be multilateral, while security communities may develop bilaterally) deter war within a group of states by threatening to punish any act of aggression by one member of the grouping against another (although the aggressor is not pre-identified). Security communities, by contrast, inhibit war through the development of reasonably strong and enduring institutions and practices and a sense of 'collective identity'. Second, a collective security system is more concerned with punishing aggression than providing for pacific settlement of disputes. Although collective security institutions such as the UN have developed mechanisms for the pacific settlement of disputes, ultimately, the credibility of collective security depends on the credibility of its punishment mechanism. A security community, on the other hand, seeks to ensure conflict prevention through integrative processes and formal or informal mechanisms for conflict resolution. Third, a security community completely delegitimises the use of force within it. In other words, the use of force has no place in the management of relations among the members of a security community. But war (against an intra-mural aggressor) remains a legitimate instrument in a collective security system.

Unlike a security community, a collective security system is a legalistic device that does not require or anticipate functional cooperation, commercial interdependence or a high degree of transactions. Finally, while viable collective security systems usually require cooperation among the major military powers of the international system, security communities can emerge among any group of states, weak or strong. The idea of collective security is based on a preponderance of physical force, whereas security communities are based on shared norms concerning the non-use of force. Thus, while it will be difficult for regional coalitions of weak states, such as ASEAN, the Gulf Cooperation Council or the Economic Community of West African states, to develop self-reliant collective security systems, collective military weakness need not prevent them from developing into viable security communities. In sum, 'the distinctive character of a security community, in contrast to collective security (or concert) arrangements, is the cognitive transition that has taken place whereby states, in principle, no longer regard or fear force as a mode of conflict resolution *among themselves*'.[20]

Unlike collective security arrangements in the international system, which had been instituted by legal agreement in a quick-fix manner (the League of Nations and the UN) to prevent recurrence of major war, security communities are founded upon norms, attitudes, practices and habits of cooperation which are multidimensional and evolutionary.

Socialisation, norms and identity

Constructing security communities involves developing shared understandings about peaceful conduct, whereby interests previously pursued through war are instead pursued through peaceful means. In the Deutschian formulation, security communities come about as a result of transactions (measured in terms of such indicators as content analysis of mass media, survey data on border crossings and mail flows), a method which led Deutsch to be criticised for an excessive preoccupation with quantitative measurement.[21] Recent constructivist writings on security communities have adopted a qualitative and sociological approach, one which focuses on institutions, norms and the intersubjective process of identity building in the making of security communities.

Institutions

The Deutschian project on security communities was primarily concerned with studying the process of social interactions in its broadest aspect, rather than with the creation and maintenance of specific multilateral institutions or organisations. The development of a security community need not presuppose institutional integration. Security communities may develop on a bilateral basis (e.g. USA–Canada). They can also emerge among actors without the benefit of common membership within a strong and cohesive multilateral organisation such as NATO or the EU, rather than the OECD or the UN. But even though they are not requisites of security communities, formal or informal institutions may provide a framework conducive for their development.[22] The fact that the most important example of a pluralistic security community today, the EU, is also a strong multilateral organisation, reinforces this link. Adler has dubbed such organisations 'security community-building institutions'.[23] Like the EU or the Organisation for Security and Cooperation in Europe, ASEAN may be considered as a security community-building institution.

How do institutions contribute to the making of security communities? Neo-liberal institutionalist theories claim that institutions can mitigate anarchy and facilitate co-operation by providing information, reducing transaction costs, helping to settle distributional conflicts and, most importantly, reducing the likelihood of cheating.[24] This takes a rationalist, utility-maximising and sanction-based view of cooperation. Constructivist theory offers a qualitatively deeper view of how institutions may affect and transform state interests and behaviour. In this view, institutions do not merely 'regulate' state behaviour, they can also 'constitute' state identities and interests. Institutions in this regard act as agents of socialisation, which I define here as regular, formal or informal interaction (dialogue, negotiations, institutionalisation) among a group of actors to manage mutual problems, realise a common purpose, achieve some collective good, and develop and project a shared identity.

To elaborate, neo-liberal institutionalist scholars, like their other rationalist cousins, neo-realists, simply assume state interests without investigating them.[25] Neo-liberal institutionalism accepts that institutions can constrain state action, but it does not concern itself with studying whether institutions may define/create or redefine/recreate the interests of states.[26] The focus is restricted to how existing state interests are pursued by rational state actors through cost–benefit calculations and choice of actions which offer maximum gain (utility maximisation). Constructivists, on the other hand, argue that state interests are not a 'given, but themselves emerge from a process of interaction and socialisation'.[27] This is a sociological rather than rational or 'strategic interaction' view of international cooperation. It helps to illuminate the institutional politics of security communities, covering a deeper and wider terrain. Following Adler, one could argue that investigating regional security community-building institutions

> requires studying the role that international and transnational institutions play in the social construction of security communities. By establishing, articulating and transmitting norms that define what constitutes acceptable and legitimate state behaviour, international organizations may be able to shape state practices. Even more remarkable, however, international organizations may encourage states and societies to imagine themselves as part of a region. This suggests that international organizations can be a site of interest and identity formation. Particularly striking are those cases in which regional organizations have been established for instrumental reasons and later and unexpectedly gained an identity component by becoming a new site for interaction and source of imagination.[28]

Thus, using a sociological lens to study the development of a regional pluralistic security community would mean going beyond the study of how states pursue or hope to realise their national interests through utility-maximising functional measures (such as reduction of tariffs, or creating a dispute-arbitration mechanism) and investigating the extent to which the said regional institution also facilitates:

- the development of trust, especially through norms of conduct;
- the development of a 'regional culture' built around common values such as democracy, developmentalism or human rights;
- the development of regional functional projects that encourage belief in a common destiny (examples include common currency, industrial projects); and
- the development of social learning, involving 'redefinition' and 'reinterpretation' of reality, exchange of self-understandings, perception of realities and normative expectations among the group of states and their diffusion from country to country, generation to generation.[29]

Adopting such a framework does not necessarily lead to a more positive evaluation of institutions. But it certainly provides for a broader canvas. For example, rationalist assessments of ASEAN's record have criticised it for never invoking its formal dispute-settlement mechanism, the 'High Council' provided under the Treaty of Amity and Cooperation. But an adequate evaluation of ASEAN's role in dispute settlement must look into its norms and processes of interaction, which are less tangible but may have a more significant impact in keeping intra-mural peace. By investigating the sociological and intersubjective questions and linkages often ignored by rationalist theories, such an approach looks beyond the formal bureaucratic apparatus and legal-rational mechanisms of institutions. Earlier theories of international organisation and regional cooperation, especially regional integration theory, 'remained closely tied to the study of formal organizations, missing a range of state behaviour that nonetheless appeared regulated and organized in a broader sense'.[30] But as recent institutionalist theories (including neo-liberal theories) acknowledge, the existence of formal institutional structures or legal-rational modes of cooperation does not exhaust the possibility of multilateralism and community building. Multilateralism could involve the 'less formal, less codified habits, practices, ideas, and norms of international society'.[31] These could be developed through consultations, dialogue and socialisation; indeed, the absence of formal legal-rationalistic cooperation may be more desirable (especially in the case of developing countries sensitive to the issue of sovereignty) than the establishment of a formal intergovernmental authority.[32]

Norms

All social communities rely on norms of behaviour. Security communities are no exception. As Holsti puts it, 'mutual acceptance and regular observance of certain rules' is an important indicator of security communities.[33] The definition and functions of norms vary. Kratochwill offers a widely used definition: norms are 'standards of behaviour defined in terms of rights and obligations'.[34] The chief function of norms in this sense is to prescribe and proscribe behaviour. Norms help actors to distinguish between 'normal' and 'abnormal' behaviour and 'to coordinate expectations and decrease uncertainty, to influence decision making, and to legitimate their actions and the actions of others'.[35] Norms contribute to international order by forbidding actions which are subversive of collective goals, by providing a framework for dispute settlement, and by creating the basis for cooperative schemes and action for mutual benefit.[36]

While all theories of international organisation, including neo-liberal institutionalism, recognise the importance of norms, constructivism allows for a much deeper understanding of norms in shaping international relations. Briefly stated, the constructivist definition incorporates both 'regulatory' and 'constitutive' aspects of norms and their effect on state behaviour. Norms not only prescribe and regulate behaviour (the regulatory effect), they also define and constitute identities (the constitutive effect).[37] To put it differently, norms not only establish expectations about how particular actors will behave,[38] they also 'teach' states, which are exposed to norms, new interests and identities.[39]

Moreover, once established, norms have a life of their own. Norms are not epiphenomenal or part of a superstructure shaped by material forces such as balance of military power or wealth. They have an independent effect on state behaviour, redefining state interests and creating collective interests and identities. This is key to understanding the constructivist claim that agents (states) and structures (international norms) are mutually reinforcing and mutually constituted.[40]

Norms help to coordinate values among states and societies. By making similar behavioural claims on different states, norms create parallel patterns of behaviour among states over wide areas. This helps ensure that the principles and practice of peaceful conduct and war avoidance are shared among states and contribute to the development of a sense of community. Moreover, the existence of a security community implies that the norms of the given group of states have already had a constitutive effect, by transforming the identity of states from being that of egoistic and sovereignty-bound actors to members of a social group sharing a common habit of peaceful conduct.

A good way to illustrate the difference between the regulatory and constitutive impact of norms is to look at Deutsch's distinction, discussed earlier, between no-war communities and security communities. No-war communities merely reflect the regulatory impact of norms concerning peaceful conduct among states. In security communities, however, norms have been adopted and adapted to an extent where they constitute the identities of states, reflecting an advanced level of mutual identification producing a 'we feeling'.

Another relevant distinction in assessing the role of norms in security communities is that between legal and social norms made by Katzenstein in his study of the role of norms in shaping national security policy in Japan. A key area of difference between the two is the informality of the latter; legal norms, which are formal and rationalistic principles of law, 'become mostly effective when informal social controls break down'.[41] Social norms are what creates the basis of those informal social controls. This distinction is important in understanding not only the effects of norms, but also their sources. This is because the notion of security community implies an intra-mural relationship that goes well beyond legally binding and enforced commitments. Deutsch stressed that security communities require the emergence of 'some degree of generalized common identity or loyalty',[42] including 'the deliberate promotion of processes and sentiments of mutual identification, loyalties, and "we"-feelings'.[43] In security communities, war avoidance becomes a social habit, rather than a mere legal obligation backed by sanctions.

The core norms of a security community are the avoidance of war or use of force, and the 'avoidance of interference in each other's internal affairs'.[44] But drawing upon Katzenstein's work, I would further differentiate between legal and social norms (which I slightly redesignate as legal-rational and socio-cultural norms) with a view to facilitating a better understanding of the normative basis of security communities and also to understand the sources of norms. Apart from the issue of informality, the two may be differentiated in terms of their primary sources. The most common (if not exclusively so) sources of legal-rational norms in international relations are the universal principles of the Westphalian state system which constitute the basis of modern international law. All international and regional organisations are based on the Westphalian norms of respect for sovereignty, non-interference in internal affairs, non-use of force in interstate relations and the pacific settlement of disputes.[45] Like the UN itself, regional organisations are vested by the UN Charter with a mandate to seek compliance with those norms.[46] Socio-cultural norms, on the other hand, are usually more specific to a group (in the sense that they are more likely to reflect the historical and cultural milieu of the actors), which may explain why they may be effective even as *informal* instruments.

Norms are not static phenomena. As Katzenstein observes, 'Norms are contested and made and remade through politics'.[47] Unlike rationalist theories of international relations, constructivism does not regard norms and identities as a given, or as something that is prior to the process of socialisation.

Constructivism allows for outside or 'universal' norms to be modified or reinterpreted (and sometimes their meaning and scope either expanded or constricted) at the recipient's end through a process of localisation, or to evolve from local discourses and practice.[48] Moreover, some entirely new norms may appear in the local milieu through the early stages of interaction of a social group without necessarily being borrowed and adapted from outside. International (regional) institutions act as agents of diffusion of norms,[49] including the localisation of outside norms and indigenous construction of new norms. Hence the effectiveness of norms cannot be simply measured narrowly by looking at the extent to which a previously articulated norm has affected and shaped the attitude and behaviour of the norm recipient. It also depends on the ability of a social group to modify international norms and create entirely new ones to meet local challenges and suit its local cultural, economic, and political circumstances.

Moreover, the appeal and effects of norms may change and are often context- and issue-dependent.

> The moral importance and functional value of norms . . . change over time. . . . Norms that were initially conceived as moral and functional could become immoral and dysfunctional with the passage of time and with the advent of new challenges. The same stickiness that makes them important can also render them morally unappealing and functionally outdated. Yet, to say that norms arrest progress is not to dismiss their relevance; they are important in shaping both positive and negative outcomes.[50]

Identity

Identity is the third key element in the making of security communities. For realism and most liberal theories, state interests are shaped by material forces and concerns, such as power and wealth; perceptual, ideational and cultural factors derive from a material base. According to constructivists, intersubjective factors, including ideas, culture and identities, play a determining, rather than secondary, role in foreign policy interactions.

Security communities are like other social communities in which members 'have attributes in common, who display mutual responsiveness, confidence, and esteem, and who self-consciously self-identify'.[51] Deutsch viewed the development of security communities as an exercise in identity building, defined as 'some degree of generalized common identity or loyalty'.[52] In the development of security communities, 'the objective compatibility or consonance of major values of the participating populations' must be 'supplemented by indications of common subjective feelings of legitimacy of the integrated community, making loyalty to it also a matter of internalized psychic compulsion'.[53] He also spoke of 'identification' as one of the instruments of integration, with 'identification' being defined as 'the deliberate promotion of processes and sentiments of mutual identification, loyalties, and "we"-feelings'.[54]

Identity is an intersubjective notion. Simply stated, it refers to the 'basic character of states'.[55] Identity formation entails developing a collective sense not only of 'who we are', but also of 'how we differ from others'.[56] It also involves securing outside recognition of the community's own distinctiveness.[57] Ted Hopf defines identities in terms of their

> three necessary functions in a society: they tell you and others who you are and they tell you who others are. In telling you who you are, identities strongly imply a particular set of interests or preferences with respect to choices of action in particular domains, and with respect to particular actors.[58]

The construction of identity is central to the kind of 'we feeling' that Deutsch identified as a key feature of security communities. The notion of identity runs deep into the heart of constructivist approaches because of its central claim that the development of a collective identity can ameliorate the security dilemma among states.[59] Like norms, collective identities can make and redefine state interests and move them beyond the logic of power politics. The collective identity of a social group, like the notion of culture, is not a given that is derived exclusively or even largely from fixed or preordained material sources. Just as norms 'are contested and made and remade through politics',[60] collective identities are made and remade through interactions and socialisation, rather than being exogenous to those processes. For example, until recently, our understanding of the idea of 'region' relied heavily on immutable or preordained features such as geographic proximity, a given physical location, cultural and linguistic similarities among the peoples, and a common historical experience. Today, there is a much greater tendency among scholars to define regions as imagined communities, created by processes of interaction and socialisation which may lead to different conceptions of what constitutes a given region at different points of time.

Benedict Anderson's analysis of nationalism provides an important conceptual basis for a constructivist understanding of the emergence of security communities.[61] Anderson sees the construction of nationalism as one vast exercise in learning, adaptation and collective self-imagination. This process overcomes significant cultural, linguistic, political, and other differences and conflict of material interests between social groups inhabiting different geographic areas and lays the basis of the formation of the nation-state. Like nation-states, security communities can be conceptualised as 'imagined communities'.[62] Imagined security communities involve 'a social construction of generative and self-reinforcing attitudes and behaviours' that may gradually lead to 'the definition and realization of "common identity"'.[63]

Viewed in this light, ASEAN regionalism in general, and the expression 'ASEAN Way' in particular, may be viewed as a continuing process of identity building which relies upon conventional 'modern' principles of interstate relations as well as traditional and culture-specific modes of socialisation and decision making prevalent in the region. The founders of ASEAN had little conception of a regional identity. But they clearly hoped to develop one through regional cooperation. ASEAN came to play a critical role not only in developing a sense of regional identity, but also in laying down the boundaries of Southeast Asia as a region. It drew upon the indigenous social, cultural and political traditions of its members and borrowed, adapted and redefined principles and practices of cooperation from the outside world. Sometimes, supposedly foreign principles and models of regionalism, after having been rejected for lacking 'relevance' in the Southeast Asian context, have been subsequently incorporated into the ASEAN framework after being redefined and adjusted so as to conform to the needs and aspirations of ASEAN's members. Moreover, the supposedly *cultural* underpinnings of ASEAN regionalism have been developed and refined in a self-conscious way through years of interaction since ASEAN's formation. All these remain very much part of an ongoing process. ASEAN regionalism began without a discernible and pre-existing sense of collective identity among the founding members, notwithstanding some important cultural similarities among them. Whether such an identity has developed after more than 30 years of interaction is debatable. But this should not detract from the serious nature of the efforts by ASEAN members to overcome their security dilemma and establish a security community through the development of norms and the construction of an ASEAN identity that would be constitutive of their interests.

Measuring identity formation is one of the most difficult challenges for academic theorists. When can we know that a group of states have achieved a 'we feeling'? The question of collective identity of a social grouping can be examined from several points of reference. One is to look at the overlapping ambit of the national identities of individual member states, and their respective constitutive norms. In the context of ASEAN, for example, this would mean ascertaining the compatibility and overlap between the national identity and preferred norms of one member country, say Thailand, and those of another, say Burma. A second point of reference is the collective identity of a group taken as a whole, for example the notion of the ASEAN Way, which is developed through socialisation and which forms the basis of its collective action. The two points of reference can reinforce each other, but may evolve separately. In other words, a group can develop an identity and approach of its own even if its members' national identities and constitutive norms remain different. The ASEAN Way, in other words, can develop and function despite differing kinds of national identity prevailing among its members.

While there can be several indicators of collective identity, three are especially important. The first is a commitment to multilateralism, including a desire to place on the multilateral agenda an expanding number of issues which have been previously tackled through unilateral or bilateral channels. A second measure of collective identity is the development of security cooperation, including collective defence, collaboration against internal threats, collective security and cooperative security measures. Third, identity formation can be sensed from the boundaries and membership criteria of the group. In the case of regional security communities, the definition of what constitutes a region and commonly held notions about who is included and who is excluded are important indicators of collective identity.

Figure 1.1 illustrates the interplay between norms and socialisation in the making of security communities. The central focus is on the role that norms, both legal-rational (such as non-interference in the internal affairs of members, and non-use of force) and socio-cultural (such as consultations and consensus), could play in the socialisation process which may redefine the interests and identities of the ASEAN members. The role of norms is investigated with respect to their regulatory as well as their constitutive effects, the latter being crucial to the emergence of security communities.

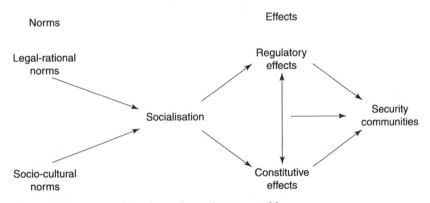

Figure 1.1 Norms, socialisation and security communities.

The framework presented above contests rationalist approaches to the study of international institutions, including ASEAN. The study of ASEAN as 'a security community-building regional organisation' requires us to go beyond a rationalist lens for several reasons. First, ASEAN has made little use of formal and legalistic measures of cooperation. Thus, evaluating it solely or largely by looking at the presence or absence of such mechanisms would yield a limited and misleading picture. Second, a rationalist perspective would limit the scope of investigation to such questions as whether and to what extent ASEAN has enabled its members to realise their predefined national interests. It would be concerned primarily with ASEAN's record in solving disputes and conflict between its members and implementing cooperative projects such as the ASEAN Free Trade Area (AFTA). ASEAN's attempts at regional redefinition and community building (such as the ASEAN Way or 'One Southeast Asia') would be deemed unimportant in the absence of its development of concrete institutionalised mechanisms for cooperation. Little attention would be paid to ASEAN's interest in constructing a new regional identity, including the redefinition of what constitutes Southeast Asia as a region. Moreover, rationalist evaluations, as noted earlier, often have a materialist bias, assuming that norms and regional identity are 'super-structural', their effect conditioned by such material forces as the economic prosperity and the balance of power. This too contributes to a tendency to ignore or dismiss the role of cultural norms and social practices as superficial and having no real impact on the ASEAN states' interest and policy towards each other and in dealing with outside actors.

The point being made here is not that rationalist perspectives and criteria for evaluating ASEAN's record as an evolving security community are irrelevant or unimportant, but that they are unnecessarily limited and unduly restrictive. The perspective adopted here is both broader and deeper and allows us to look at aspects of ASEAN regionalism ignored by most rationalist perspectives. It does not necessarily lead to a more positive evaluation of ASEAN's record, but it provides for a more comprehensive and credible evaluation.

Security communities in the non-Atlantic world?

As noted at the outset, Deutsch's original work on security communities was concerned with the Western world, especially Europe and the North Atlantic.[64] One could identify several examples of amalgamated security communities, including the USA (originally created by the federation of 13 colonies), the UK (created out of the merger of Scotland, Wales, Northern Ireland and England) and Germany (the amalgamation of several hundred principalities, dynastic states, townships and cities).[65] In so far as pluralistic security communities are concerned, Sweden and Norway after 1905, and the USA and Canada after 1815, could be counted as examples of bilateral security communities. Other examples of such communities are the USA and Japan, and Australia and New Zealand. The most prominent example of a multilateral pluralistic security community is the EU, a 'cluster of non-warring peoples in an arena of peaceful conflict-resolution'.[66] In the post-Cold War era, the concept has been further extended. Barry Buzan, for example, speaks of 'a security community among the leading capitalist powers' which draws together Europe, North America, Japan and Australia in a relationship that is of a 'more profound quality than the collective expectation and preparation to use force against someone else that is the essence of alliance relationships'.[67]

In contrast, the label is rarely applied to any segment of the developing world. This is hardly surprising, since the developing world has been, and continues to be, much more prone to conflict and war than the West. As a study by Evan Luard estimated, only two of the 127 'significant wars' during the Cold War (between 1945 and 1986) occurred in Europe, while Latin America accounted for 26, Africa 31, the Middle East 24 and Asia 44. According to this estimate, the developing world was the theatre of more than 98 per cent of all inter-national conflicts.[68] The situation is unlikely to be different in the post-Cold War period. While Western theorists have predicted increased stability in relations among the developed countries, they have been far more pessimistic about the prospects for the developing world. For example, Goldgeier and McFaul argue that the post-Cold War international system will consist of a 'core' sector of stable major powers within which interdependence and shared norms minimise the risk of armed conflict, and a 'periphery' sector (e.g. the develop-ing world) featuring fragile regional security systems marked by a high degree of conflict and disorder.[69] Barry Buzan similarly contrasts the emerging security community among the capitalist Western countries with the continuing anarchy in the developing world.[70] Against this backdrop, finding a suitable case study of a security community, whether bilateral or multilateral, in the Third World has been especially difficult (with the possible exception of

ASEAN and the Southern Cone of Latin America, which has good prospects for developing into a security community).

A second problem in applying the concept of security community to the Third World relates to a widespread assumption among liberal theorists that such communities require a quintessential liberal democratic milieu featuring significant economic interdependence and political pluralism. Although Deutsch's work was not explicitly rooted in assumptions about the pacific effects of liberal democracy and interdependence, the very fact that his main area of investigation was the Euro-Atlantic economic and political milieu has encouraged an implicit correlation between economic and political pluralism and the existence of security communities. This linkage has been made even more explicit in recent writings about the concept. For example, Emanuel Adler argues that

> Members of pluralistic security communities hold dependable expectations of peaceful change not merely because they share just any kind of values, but because they share liberal democratic values and allow their societies to become interdependent and linked by transnational economic and cultural relations. Democratic values, in turn, facilitate the creation of strong civil societies . . . which also promote community bonds and common identity and trust through the process of the free interpenetration of societies.[71]

Both Adler and John Vasquez explicitly invoke the Kantian notion of democratic peace as the philosophical basis of Deutsch's work on security communities.[72] In this view, a true security community is 'a democratic security community', since liberal democracies tend to be more pacific, or, at least, seldom fight each other.

Apart from democratic peace, the idea of security community has been also linked to another well-known liberal dictum popularised by Kant, Adam Smith, Richard Cobden, John Stuart Mill and Thomas Paine, asserting a positive correlation between economic interdependence and peace.[73] The Kantian proposition that 'the spirit of commerce sooner or later takes hold of every people, and it cannot exist side by side with war',[74] is the centrepiece of neo-functionalist and interdependence theories that gained prominence in the 1970s. Although Deutsch's transactionalist approach was concerned with more than just economic interdependence – he used a wide range of indicators to measure integration, including international trade, mail flows, student exchanges and travel – the very idea that an increased volume of interactions may have pacific effects on state behaviour may theoretically apply to all kinds of interactions, including commercial ones. Most theoretical challenges to realist orthodoxy have found it impossible to de-link community from commerce. The post-war surge of theoretical interest in the moderating and transforming impact of trade, interdependence and international regimes on power and anarchy, stimulated by the work of Keohane and Nye, Rosecrance and others, has proven to be a natural complement to Deutsch's transactionalist view of security community.

Economic interdependence may significantly facilitate the development of security communities. Indeed, Yalem contends that security communities require a 'high degree of political and economic integration as a necessary precondition of peaceful relationships'.[75] Theories of regional integration have viewed economic regionalism (including the creation of free trade areas, customs unions and economic unions) as a necessary precondition for improved prospects for regional peace and security. Of particular interest here are insights from the neo-functionalist approach associated with Ernst Haas (which grew out of the classical functionalist theory of David Mittrany), and theories of international interdependence (which incorporated many aspects of neo-functionalist regional integration theory). Both assume the notion of a 'spillover', or a belief that exchanges and cooperation among independent national actors in areas of 'low politics' such as economics and trade could incrementally create common stakes among them in areas of 'high politics'. This serves to make the use of force within such a setting increasingly costly (in terms of its 'uncertain and possibly negative effects on the achievement of economic goals'[76]) and promotes co-operative management of regional peace and security issues.[77] Haas sums up the arguments of the liberal theory in the following terms:

> (1) Increased trade and cross-national investment, especially free trade and capital flows, result in a more highly articulated international division of labour; any disruption in that division of labour causes the belligerents to incur heavy losses of welfare; fearing such losses, countries are less willing to go to war. (2) Increasing popular demands for services on the part of the government limit the amount available for armaments and war; any disruption of welfare services is resented and will cause domestic strife leaders prefer to avoid. (3) Societies committed to welfare-enhancement spin off interest groups dedicated to safeguarding their entitlements; when the nature of the international division of labour creates mutual dependencies among several welfare states, the groups concerned will organize transnationally and thereby outflank their home governments. (4) The more such groups expect of transnational arrangements, the less they expect from their home governments. (5) The more cosmopolitan the knowledge (on which the deepened international division of labour depends) becomes, the less the beneficiaries of that knowledge are willing to disrupt things by war.[78]

But international relations theory is divided on the question of whether interdependence reduces the likelihood of war. No causal connection can be demonstrated between interdependence and war avoidance. As Haas himself has conceded, 'even to assert a simple causal connection between international interdependence and international violence is to skate on theoretical ice which is too slippery for comfort'.[79] Interdependence is 'too patchy and temporary' to permit a causal link with peace.[80]

Furthermore, while interdependence may be strong among Western countries sharing liberal democratic political systems and mature capitalist economies, it tends to be weak among the developing countries. In addition to their illiberal setting, regional subsystems in the Third World tend to be marked by a relatively low level of transactions, especially economic linkages and cooperation.[81] Thus, if the development of security communities is linked to liberal politics and economics, then the possibility of such communities in the Third World would appear to be very remote indeed. Illiberal politics tend to be the hallmark of most Third World states, something recognised by integration theorists as they sought to explain the limits of EU-style regional integration in the Third World:

> Many of the general characteristics of politics in less developed countries are difficult to reconcile with quiet functionalism. Leadership tends to be personalistic; heroes have trouble cooperating. The gap between the literate elite and the illiterate masses, the scarcity of organized interest groups, and the cultural cleavage between city and countryside, which might seem to free the hands of the elites for international integra-tion, have more often resulted in insecurity, isolation, and diversion of attention to internal integration. Scarcity of middle level administrative manpower results in weak governmental and political institutions, which are susceptible to disruption by the

relatively organized institutions such as the army. The adaptability of governments under these conditions tends to be low.[82]

In general, regional economic interdependence and integration in the Third World has been much more elementary than in Europe, 'more obscure in purpose and uncertain in content'.[83] Thus to assume that economic interdependence is a necessary background condition for the development of security communities would make it difficult to use as a framework for analysing and understanding the origins of ASEAN. At the time of its formation and subsequent evolution, ASEAN members neither shared liberal democratic values, nor were bound by a high degree of mutual interdependence. Indeed, a study published in 1978 applying Deutsch's transactions model to the original five members of ASEAN found no evidence of community formation.[84]

But the question may be asked whether a liberal democratic and interdependent setting is a necessary precondition for the emergence of security communities. To restrict the idea of security community to a liberal political-economic setting may needlessly limit the utility of the concept.[85] Whether or not ASEAN can be rightfully regarded as a security community, the conceptual framework is useful for understanding and assessing its evolution and achievements. To explain the emergence of ASEAN, one has to rethink the notion of security community developed by Western scholars. Can a convergence of authoritarian values generate cooperation and war avoidance on a long-term basis? Southeast Asia, and more specifically ASEAN, attests to the fact that community building can proceed despite the absence of a common liberal democratic political culture. Can security communities develop even in an initial absence of economic interdependence?[86] Should interdependence and democracy be viewed as essential preconditions for the development of pluralistic security communities? It may be argued that while common values are necessary for community building, these need not be liberal democratic values. A shared commitment to economic development, regime security and political stability could compensate for a lack of a high degree of economic interdependence. Moreover, if the former conditions are present, they could pave the way for greater economic and functional cooperation. In other words, interdependence could follow, rather than precede, an initial and deliberate attempt at community formation. As the next chapter will show, these factors were central to the evolution of norms and principles of cooperation in the formative years of ASEAN.

Evolution and change in security communities

In an important contribution to the literature on security communities, Adler and Barnett have sketched a social constructivist and path-dependent approach to the origin and evolution of such communities. They identify three stages (*nascent*, *ascendant* and *mature*) in the development of security communities, each of which is marked by a number of characteristics.[87] In the *nascent* phase, a group of states 'coordinate their relations in order to: increase their mutual security; lower the transaction costs associated with their exchanges; and/or encourage further exchanges and interactions'.[88] The initial impulse for such activities may not be specifically geared to creating a security community, but may be 'triggered' by a number of forces drawing states together, such as threat perceptions, expected trade benefits, shared identity and organisational emulation (learning from the experience of other multilateral organisations). Cooperation and coordination at the nascent stage involve both 'bilateral and multilateral exchanges'. Actors may rely on a common institution to promote cooperation, and 'extend and deepen their interactions', and verify compliance.

The *ascendant* phase is marked by tighter military coordination, lessened fears on the part of one actor that others within the grouping represent a threat, and a deepening of mutual trust along with beginnings of a cognitive transition towards intersubjective processes and collective identities 'that begin to encourage dependable expectations of peaceful change'. The main characteristics of the *mature* phase are greater institutionalisation, supranationalism, a high degree of trust, and low or no probability of military conflicts. A mature stage may be 'loosely coupled' or 'tightly coupled' depending on 'their depth of trust, the nature and degree of institutionalization of their governance system, and whether they reside in a formal anarchy or are on the verge of transforming it'.[89] Loosely coupled security communities are minimalist in nature. They are 'a transnational region comprised of sovereign states whose people maintain dependable expectations of peaceful change'. Members of this group expect no military threats from each other and observe self-restraint. Tightly coupled security communities have more stringent standards, including a 'mutual aid society' providing for collective and cooperative efforts to help each other and offer joint solutions to common problems. They should also have some characteristics of supranationalism, or a 'post-sovereign system', which might include common national institutions as well as supranational and transnational institutions, and some form of collective security. Moreover, a tightly coupled community requires 'a system of rules that lies somewhere between a sovereign state and a regional, centralized, government'.[90]

What makes security communities get off the ground? Here, Adler and Barnett have gone beyond Deutsch's emphasis on transactions to suggest a number of possible 'triggering mechanisms'. These consist of both material and normative elements.[91] The material elements include, among other things, common threat (external and/or internal); prospects for capitalising from the existence of the international division of labour or gains from trade; cultural, political, social and ideological homogeneity; and rapid shift in distribution of military power. In addition, security communities can be triggered by 'cataclysmic events' which change the material structures and mindsets and produce new ways of thinking about politics and security. Furthermore, certain domestic, international and transnational factors which create common interest can initiate the push for security communities; these may include a common drive towards democratic polities, or the impact of globalisation. The normative triggers for security communities could include new ideas about cooperation. Important examples of ideational triggers for security communities are the notions of 'common security' and 'cooperative security', ideas which have been particularly important in the development of security institutions in the later stage of the Cold War (in Europe) and the post-Cold War era (in Europe and Asia).

The list of triggers mentioned by Adler and Barnett is not exhaustive. Moreover, the distinction between 'loose' and 'tight' security communities cannot be a sharp one, and there may be some overlap between the nascent, ascendant and mature stages. For example, a *nascent* security community may come into being not just by threat-inspired, utility-driven and institutionally coordinated action aimed at lowering transaction costs. It may also come about by an initial search for a common identity (which is supposed to come later, in the *ascendant* and *mature* phases in the Adler and Barnett schema). The suggested pathway does not exhaust all the possible approaches to security community building, nor does it capture all the features of a particular stage. But it does provide a useful basis for understanding why and when security communities may emerge, and the nature of the interactions that set them apart from other types of security systems.

The idea of security community is often taken as a terminal condition, rather than as a process, because such communities are by definition supposed to have developed 'dependable expectations' of long-term peace. Although Adler and Barnett very briefly consider the possibility that security communities, once established, may unravel, the literature on them does not tell us much about the conditions under which a security community may decay or be disrupted.[92]

I do not see socialisation and institution building as linear processes. Even constructivism is often viewed as a theory of global peace and harmony, but it should, and can, explain both cooperation and conflict. A major theory of international politics should explain failure as well as success, progress as well as setback, of efforts at socialisation and institution building.[93]

A security community, even if it appears to be well established, may unravel in response to a variety of internal and external circumstances. Deutsch himself recognised the possibility of decay in security communities, although he did not specify the conditions that might lead to it. Yet, his assertion that

> [w]hether any specific security community will continue to function in the long run will depend on the ability of its facilities for peaceful adjustment to keep ahead of the strains and burdens which any growth of social transaction may throw upon them[94]

does provide a clue to how security communities may decline. The key point here is the impact of 'strains and burdens' created by increased interactions and socialisation. This provides the basis for a sociological, rather than power-based, explanation of when and how security communities may unravel. An understanding of how security communities may unravel, offered in this book, would thus be a necessary and important complement to explanations of how they come about in the first place.

To elaborate, neo-realist theory would explain major changes in the international system, including the decline of international cooperation, in terms of major shifts in the distribution of power such as that from bipolarity to multipolarity. Such shifts may produce new security threats for states, prompting new external alignments among some of the members that may prove unsettling and divisive for existing groups of states. For example, faced with a rising external power, some states may prefer bandwagoning, while others may prefer balancing.[95] Either could generate new insecurities for states and unravel whatever cooperation might have existed among them. Neo-liberal theories are rather reticent to speak about crisis and decline in institutions. But their assumption that the character of international institutions is 'structured by the prevailing distribution of capabilities'[96] carries an implicit admission that shifts in the balance of power could be the ultimate determinant of the rise and decline of cooperative institutions, including pluralistic security communities.[97]

In contrast, a constructivist explanation of security communities would posit that the sources of decline of security communities are not necessarily external to the socialisation process that constitutes them. Regression in security communities, or the transition of a security community (whether nascent, ascendant or mature) to what might be called a 'decadent security community' (a transitional stage before the community returns to anarchy or an unstable regime or reinvents itself through institutional reform and change), can occur for a number of reasons. Security communities could unravel when they widen or deepen their cooperation. Security communities which have developed new forms of cooperation, or deepened existing ones, may face a situation where resources available to them or the principles governing the conduct of cooperation prove to be inadequate in addressing the new tasks. Similarly, the widening of an existing security community could alter its socialisation dynamic. Since the development of security communities is fundamentally a social process, the induction of previously 'unsocialised' actors could impose new psychological burdens on the community and test its capacity for intra-mural conflict resolution. Moreover, an expanded security community will need to address the specific security problems of the new actors. There may be new material burdens too, especially in cases where the community, having already developed a high degree of economic integration, has to accommodate new entrants which have a lower level of economic development.

Socialisation processes within security communities and those between them and the outside world could be affected by changing norms and ideas about cooperation in the international system. These changes could undermine the ways in which a security community manages intra-mural relationships and deals with external pressures. For example, changing norms concerning sovereignty and the doctrine of non-interference in the internal affairs of states at the global level have affected the way many regional organisations have conducted intra-mural relations as well as relations with extra-regional powers in the past. Security communities, existing or aspiring, which fail to adapt to these changing external conditions could find themselves in crisis.

Two other forces can affect existing security communities in significant ways. One is the effects of globalisation.[98] Karl Deutsch's notion of security communities was articulated before globalisation (or for that matter even interdependence) became a significant concept in international relations theory, although some early trends in interdependence and globalisation were already evident. The benefits of interdependence for interstate peace may be undermined by the effects of globalisation, which is a deeper process (involving transnational production as much as trade) and a more political one (affecting the very authority and legitimacy of the nation-state) than interdependence. Globalisation can unleash new forms of social and political conflict. Although some scholars have examined the linkage between domestic instability and security communities,[99] they have not done so in relation to transnational dangers and security communities. Much of the writing on security communities defines the problem of regional and international order in terms of preventing interstate conflict, without paying comparable attention to domestic or transnational conflict. Yet, such conflicts have become more salient in the past decades, partly due to the effects of globalisation. The classical notion of security communities, in so far as it was geared to examining the possibility and pathways for overcoming the traditional security dilemma and war avoidance among states, has not been examined in relation to transnational or non-traditional dangers. The latter constitute a new type of security challenge, where they can destabilise an entire region or an international order while causing tension and violence among states.

Globalisation generates new forms of conflict,[100] including conflicts over the growth of socio-economic disparities between states, and accelerated movement of people (both legal and illegal). In facilitating the erosion of state sovereignty and authority, the effects of globalisation may benefit some states within security communities more than others, thereby causing interstate jealousy and tensions. Another effect of globalisation is the spread of transnational crime, terrorism, and cross-boundary environmental degradation. The effects of globalisation include dangers that may originate from within the boundaries of a state, but which quickly and suddenly spill over national boundaries. Pandemics and the regional contagion effects of financial crises caused by policy failures in one state are examples of such threats. For example, the Asian financial crisis of 1997 has been called 'globalization's first major crisis'.[101] It was partly the result of the over-dependence of Southeast Asian countries on foreign investment, and partly the handiwork of currency speculators, both intimately linked to financial globalisation. It was also a by-product of the conflict between the demands made by the globalised economy for transparency, accountability and good governance principles and practices on the one hand, and the existing domestic social and political structures in the region with their propensity for corruption, nepotism and lack of transparency on the other. As one study put it, the origin of the crisis had to be seen in the context of 'Southeast Asia's dependence on an impersonal and unpredictable global financial system in which the market's unyielding criticism of economic performance has immediate consequences'.[102] Moreover, the crisis proved to have a contagion effect extending beyond Southeast Asia, thereby further underscoring its links with the global economy. Finally, the crisis prompted a rethink on the benefits of globalisation, although not everyone emulated the Malaysian Prime Minister Mahathir Mohamad's 'war on globalisation' and his currency controls.

Such transnational forces may create pressures for institutional change in security communities. Communities created out of some norms and institutions suited for managing the classic security dilemma may no longer be deemed adequate when the security environment changes and non-traditional threats become more prominent. If communities do not change or adapt, they risk unravelling.

Globalisation has been blamed for approaches to economic development adopted by authoritarian regimes which sustain their domestic and international legitimacy (the so-called 'performance legitimacy'), despite domestic political repression and violence resulting from abuse of human rights. But globalisation, to the extent that it includes a communication revolution and an ideational, as opposed to purely material element, can be a double-edged sword in this respect. The communication revolution associated with globalisation ensures that human rights violations are more easily and widely noticed than ever before, arousing isolation and condemnation of the regime perpetrating such abuses and its regional or international backers. At least, it makes it difficult for a regional group to condone such abuses and remain passive about them. And the globalisation of ideas and values, such as the norms of human rights and democracy, fuels demand for political change in authoritarian states, including those claiming performance legitimacy on the basis of economic growth through foreign investment.

This brings one to a second challenge, often (although not always) linked to the effects of globalisation and its crises: domestic political change in one or several member states, especially in members who play a leadership role. The impact of democratisation on initially illiberal security communities deserves particular attention. Democratisation can affect security communities, especially nascent or ascendant security communities, in both ways. Newly democratic regimes may seek to export their 'revolution', either actively or passively (they may show sympathy for pro-democracy struggles in their neighbourhood), which would make their authoritarian neighbours fearful and hostile. Nationalist sentiments unleashed by democratic transitions may fuel animosity towards neighbours. A more serious threat to regional stability is the possible transboundary spillover effect of domestic strife, including the resurfacing of old ethnic tensions suppressed by the authoritarian regime, that may accompany the democratisation process. Newly democratic rulers, preoccupied with domestic consolidation, may have less time for regional projects, or collective norms and practices for conflict management. Institutions and procedures favoured by an ousted dictator, especially if he happens to be from a leading member state of a regional grouping, may be discredited in the changed political climate. Change in the top leadership of a leading member state can disrupt the socialisation process within regional groups. This may be especially true of regional institutions founded upon close interpersonal ties and informal contacts among leaders and the elite.

Regional institutions established and maintained by authoritarian states could lose legitimacy and support from within the population of their member states that have experienced greater domestic political openness. Democratisation may also call into question the sanctity of existing regional norms and the relevance of mechanisms and practices for pacific settlement of disputes. The spillover effect of democratisation may strain the norms of regional institutions committed to the principle of non-interference in the internal affairs of states. Finally, uneven democratisation within a regional grouping could polarise members over key political issues, including promotion of human rights and democracy through regional means. The non-democratic members are likely to resist strongly any policy proposals for pro-democracy changes coming from the democratic camp.

On the other hand, democratisation may actually improve the conditions for security communities. Democratisation influences foreign policy change in two ways, which can be termed international and domestic legitimation. A newly democratic regime is likely to seek international legitimacy by settling old conflicts and undertaking new foreign policy and security behaviour that contradicts the policies associated with its authoritarian predecessor. Domestic legitimation may entail broadening the foreign policy decision-making system, and securing the participation of other organs of the governments (e.g. parliament) and members of the civil society (NGOs and pressure groups).

Transition to democratic rule brings in its wake availability of greater information about a state's national security and financial policies and assets. This could reduce suspicions among neighbours and expand regional security and economic cooperation. Democratisation may lead to more open and regularised interactions among states, reducing the importance of interpersonal contact and creating pressures for institutionalisation of informal security communities. Last but not least, democratisation may create a deeper basis for regional socialisation by according space to the civil society and accommodating its concerns. Most forms of regionalism in the developing world (indeed anywhere for that matter) have been highly state-centric, which in turn invites opposition to their agenda from domestic and international civic action groups. A grouping of more participatory polities could change that and develop a form of participatory regionalism to increase their ability to offer more effective responses to transnational issues. Socialisation based exclusively on elite-level interactions among authoritarian states does not usually survive the downfall of one or more of the governments. For regionalism to be robust and durable, it must extend to, and incorporate, the civil society.

Framework of the book

This book analyses ASEAN's role in regional order and the obstacles to it. ASEAN regionalism is conceptualised as the process of building a security community in which states develop a reliable pattern of peaceful interaction, pursue shared interests and strive for a common regional identity. Against this backdrop, Chapter 2 provides an historical examination of the development of interstate norms in Southeast Asia. It identifies both legal-rational norms such as the non-use of force, non-interference, regional autonomy and avoidance of military pacts, and socio-cultural norms such as consultations and consensus and a preference for informality over legalistic mechanisms, which are the core elements of the ASEAN Way. The origin and evolution of these norms is examined and how they were institutionalised and expressed within the ASEAN framework is analysed.

Chapter 3 looks at the extent to which ASEAN's norms shaped and were shaped by its handling of the Cambodia conflict. Vietnam's invasion of Cambodia was one of ASEAN's biggest crises and it tested the organisation's collective action agenda. What were the norms at stake, to what extent were they observed, what was the extent of deviation from these norms, and how did they contribute to the political settlement of the conflict? Were ASEAN's policies consistent with its professed norms and corporate culture, and did ASEAN's policy serve to reinforce or undermine the latter?

Chapter 4 discusses how ASEAN's norms and identity have been affected by the expansion of its membership. It assesses whether ASEAN's expansion has been carried out in a manner consistent with its norms. It also addresses whether expansion will affect the future observance of norms and if it might compromise norms such as the principle of non-intervention and the ASEAN Way. This is discussed with particular reference to ASEAN's handling of the entry of Cambodia and Burma, both of which tested ASEAN's norms. Also considered is the extent to which an expanded membership reflects the construction of a new form of regional identity, expressed in concepts such as 'One Southeast Asia'. Will this impose major new burdens on ASEAN, and explain or precipitate its decline?

Chapter 5 examines key developments in intra-ASEAN relations in the post-Cold War period with a view to assessing how they have affected ASEAN's norms and identity as a regional grouping. Five major areas are covered. The first concerns existing and emerging bilateral problems among the ASEAN members, and the prospects for dispute settlement. The second is the military modernisation programmes undertaken by the ASEAN members. Is this development leading to the possibility of an arms race that would subvert ASEAN's claim to be a security community? Third, ASEAN's approach to the Spratly Islands dispute is examined. Although it involves non-member states, this dispute is affecting intra-ASEAN norms and cohesion in a significant way. The fourth area is the development of intra-ASEAN economic cooperation, which could test the impact of economic interdependence on regional peace and provide an indication of the expanding scope of multilateralism, a key indicator of collective identity. Finally, intra-ASEAN defence cooperation, including policy coordination against internal threats, is examined, once again for its implications for multilateralism and collective identity. Overall, this chapter seeks to ascertain whether the handling of these issues by ASEAN members conforms to its norms and processes and whether the grouping has begun to devise new ways of coping with security challenges.

Chapter 6 assesses ASEAN's role in the development and functioning of Asia Pacific multilateralism, i.e. the ASEAN Regional Forum. It examines the extent to which the evolution of the ARF has been based on ASEAN's norms, including the ASEAN Way. As such, it also addresses the question whether ASEAN's norms can provide a credible approach to security cooperation at the wider Asia Pacific regional level. Furthermore, the chapter analyses the burdens imposed on ASEAN by its supposedly 'driver' role in the ARF, which could impede its progress towards a viable security community. The final part of the chapter examines ASEAN's role in the development of East Asian regionalism and the overall place of multilateralism in ASEAN's engagement of Great Powers especially China.

Chapter 7 looks at the crucial issue of institutional reform and change in ASEAN. It highlights the growing challenge posed by non-traditional security threats, which, aside from the effects of the Asian financial crisis discussed in Chapter 5, included terrorism, SARS and the tsunami, as well as the impact of domestic change in Indonesia and Burma. These dangers added to pressure on ASEAN to undertake institutional reform, the most important offshoot being the ASEAN Security Community and the ASEAN Charter.

Together, the aim of these chapters is to ascertain not only whether the norms of ASEAN have had a regulatory impact, but also the extent to which they might have created a sense of regional community (constitutive impact) to foster the long-term habit of war avoidance.

But measuring what is 'regulatory' and what is 'constitutive' is not an easy research task. The theory of norms has provided no standard indicators to measure these effects, although Wendt and Adler and Barnett have made helpful contributions.[103] For the purpose of the book, the framework presented in Table 1.2 is used to assess the effects of ASEAN's norms on regional order. The framework consists of a number of questions grouped under three categories: (1) dispute settlement (management of intra-mural issues); (2) collective action (development of cooperative programmes, including functional cooperation and collective postures *vis-à-vis* outside powers); and (3) collective identity (practices which contribute towards the emergence of a regional identity such as multilateralism, collective defence, etc.). Of these categories, the first helps us measure the regulatory effects of norms; the second straddles both regulatory and constitutive effects; and the third is most directly concerned with assessing the constitutive effects of norms.

Together, these questions constitute a measure of comparability between the chapters and provide an overall framework of discussion for the book, the findings of which will be presented in the conclusion.

It should be noted that the empirical chapters in the book deal with different mixtures of these categories. Chapter 2, analysing the evolution of ASEAN, covers all the three areas, i.e. dispute settlement, collective action and identity formation. Chapter 3, focusing on ASEAN's role in the Cambodia conflict, addresses the questions about collective action listed in the second part of Table 1.2. Chapter 4, dealing with ASEAN's expansion, assesses questions about collective action as well as identity listed in the third part of Table 1.2. Chapter 5, analysing the management of intra-regional relations in the post-Cold War era, deals with questions about all three areas, but in the post-Cold War context. Chapter 6, covering ASEAN's role in Asia Pacific security cooperation, is primarily concerned with

Table 1.2 Constructing security communities: a framework

Questions about norms in dispute settlement

1 In handling intra-regional disputes, has the use of force been resorted to or seriously envisaged?
2 Has there been any indication of competitive arms acquisitions and military planning during the course of the dispute?
3 Does the group provide for institutional mechanisms to settle disputes between members?
4 How often do members resort to such mechanisms?

Questions about norms in collective action

1 Does the group follow its norms in devising functional cooperation, such as economic cooperation?
2 Does the group follow its norms in dealing with outside actors?
3 What is the level of support provided by other members of the group to a member who is involved in a dispute with an outside actor?
4 How does the group handle disunity or breaking of ranks by any member(s) over cooperative and collective action problems?

Questions about collective identity

1 Has there been a growing resort to multilateral approaches to problems compared with the past, including new issues which have been brought under the purview of multilateral cooperation?
2 Has cooperation led to formal or informal collective defence (including policy coordination against internal threats), collective security and cooperative security arrangements?
3 Has it involved and produced new ways of expressing social identity, such as redefining the region?
4 To what extent do countries outside the group recognise its new social identity?

questions about collective action and common identity. And Chapter 7, dealing with trans-national challenges and ASEAN's institutional reform and initiatives, speaks especially to the second and the third sets of questions.

Together, the questions listed in Table 1.2 permit an evaluation of both the regulatory and the constitutive impact of ASEAN's norms. The former is indicated by assessing compliance, while the latter is indicated by the extent to which ASEAN members have adjusted and redefined their national security postures to conform to the collective expectations about behaviour related to matters of regional conflict and order. It is also seen from the identity-building practices of ASEAN, such as its claims about the ASEAN Way and its efforts to develop a 'One Southeast Asia' paradigm of intra-regional relations. The project to construct a pluralistic security community in Southeast Asia can thus be assessed by looking at ASEAN's record in dispute settlement and war avoidance, the progress of collective action, and the development of 'we feelings'.

Notes and references

1 Emanuel Adler and Michael Barnett, 'Security Communities in Theoretical Perspective', in Emanuel Adler and Michael Barnett (eds), *Security Communities* (Cambridge: Cambridge University Press, 1998), p. 4.
2 Philip E. Jacob and Henry Teune, 'The Integrative Process: Guidelines for Analysis', in Philip E. Jacob and James V. Toscano (eds), *The Integration of Political Communities* (Philadelphia: Lippincott, 1964), p. 4, cited in Joseph S. Nye, 'Comparative Regional Integration: Concept and Measurement', *International Organization*, vol. 22, no. 4 (Autumn 1968), p. 863.
3 Karl W. Deutsch et al., *Political Community in the North Atlantic Area: International Organization in the Light of Historical Experience* (Princeton: Princeton University Press, 1957), p. 5. 'A security community is a group of people, which have become "integrated" ', where integration is defined as 'the attainment . . . of a sense of community and of institutions and practices strong enough and widespread enough to assure, for a "long" time, dependable expectations of "peaceful change" among its population'. Ibid. See also Karl W. Deutsch, 'Security Communities', in James Rosenau (ed.), *International Politics and Foreign Policy* (New York: Free Press, 1961), p. 98.
4 Emanuel Adler and Michael Barnett, 'A Framework for the Study of Security Communities', in Emanuel Adler and Michael Barnett (eds), *Security Communities* (Cambridge: Cambridge University Press, 1998), p. 30.
5 Ronald J. Yalem, 'Regional Security Communities', in George W. Keeton and George Scharzenberger (eds), *The Yearbook on International Affairs* (London: Stevens, 1979), pp. 217–23.
6 Kal J. Holsti, *International Politics: A Framework for Analysis*, 5th edition (Englewood Cliffs, NJ: Prentice Hall, 1988), p. 437.
7 Karl Deutsch, *The Analysis of International Relations*, 3rd edition (Englewood Cliffs, NJ: Prentice Hall, 1988), p. 276.
8 Ibid., p. 276.
9 Karl W. Deutsch, 'Security Communities', in James N. Rosenau (ed.), *International Politics and Foreign Policy* (New York: Free Press, 1961), p. 99.
10 Ibid., p. 99.
11 On security regimes see Robert Jervis, 'Security Regimes', *International Organization*, vol. 36, no. 2 (Spring 1982), p. 357.
12 Barry Buzan, *People, States, and Fear: An Agenda for International Security Studies in the Post-Cold War Era* (New York: Harvester Wheatsheaf, 1991), p. 218.
13 Janice Gross Stein, 'Detection and Defection: Security "Regimes" and the Management of International Conflict', *International Journal*, vol. 40 (Autumn 1985), p. 600.
14 Joseph S. Nye, 'Nuclear Learning and US–Soviet Security Regimes', *International Organization*, vol. 41 (Summer 1987), pp. 371–402.
15 Robert Jervis, 'Security Regimes', *International Organization*, vol. 36, no. 2 (Spring 1982), p. 357; Volker Rittberger, Manfred Efinger and Martin Mendler, 'Towards an East–West Security Regime: The Case of Confidence and Security-Building Measures', *Journal of Peace Research*, vol. 27, no. 1 (1990), pp. 55–74.

16 Karl W. Deutsch, 'Security Communities', in James N. Rosenau (ed.), *International Politics and Foreign Policy* (New York: Free Press, 1961), p. 103.

17 Lynn H. Miller, 'The Prospect for Order through Regional Security', in Richard A. Falk and Saul H. Mendlovitz (eds), *Regional Politics and World Order* (San Francisco: W.H. Freeman, 1973), p. 51. See also Amitav Acharya, 'Association of Southeast Asian Nations: Security Community or Defence Community?' *Pacific Affairs*, vol. 64, no. 2 (Summer 1991), pp. 159–78.

18 Barry Buzan, who coined the term 'security complex', defined them as 'local sets of states . . . whose major security perceptions and concerns link together sufficiently closely that their national security perceptions cannot realistically be considered apart from one another'. In its initial formulation, the concept stressed enmity over amity. 'Unlike most other attempts to define regional subsystems, security complexes rest, for the most part, on the interdependence of rivalry rather than on the interdependence of shared interests.' Barry Buzan, 'A Framework for Regional Security Analysis', in Barry Buzan and Gowher Rizvi (eds), *South Asian Insecurity and the Great Powers* (London: Croom Helm, 1986), pp. 3–33. See also: Barry Buzan, 'Regional Security', *Arbejdspapirer*, no. 28 (Copenhagen: Centre for Peace and Conflict Research, 1989). Since then, Buzan has revised this formulation; security complexes may vary from anarchy ('conflict formations') to security communities, where war is unthinkable. Barry Buzan and Ole Wæver, *Regions and Powers: The Structure of International Security* (Cambridge: Cambridge University Press, 2003).

19 Brian L. Job, *Multilateralism: The Relevance of the Concept to Regional Conflict Management* (Working Paper no. 5) (Vancouver: Institute of International Relations, University of British Columbia, 1994), p. 15.

20 Ibid.

21 Puchala, 'The Integration Theorists and the Study of International Relations', p. 187. Deutsch's preoccupation with empirical measurement has been criticised by a number of scholars. Haas argued that Deutsch's transactionalist approach 'does not tell us the content of the messages. . . . It does not explain when and how trust and responsiveness among actors, elites as well as masses, are to occur. . . . Politics, in the sense of demands, negotiations, institutionalization, evolution of tasks, is not really part of the approach since the content of messages is not always treated.' Ernst B. Haas, 'The Study of Regional Integration: Reflections on the Joy and Anguish of Pretheorizing', in Falk and Mendlovitz, *Regional Politics and World Order*, p. 117. Edward Morse questioned 'the adequacy of transaction data to provide sufficient information about the scope and growth of transnational society'. Edward L. Morse, 'Transnational Economic Processes', in Robert O. Keohane and Joseph S. Nye (eds), *Transnational Relations and World Politics* (Cambridge, MA: Harvard University Press, 1972), p. 44. Oran Young found Deutsch's theory to be 'based upon a rather narrow and selective range of indicators of interdependence'. Cited in William C. Olson and A.J.R. Groom, *International Relations: Then and Now: Origins and Trends in Interpretation* (London: HarperCollins, 1991), p. 164. Joseph Nye similarly argues that the 'evidence of increasing transactions is not a good indicator of "integration" because it does not directly measure the growth of community or sense of obligation'. Joseph Nye, 'Comparative Regional Integration: Concept and Measurement', *International Organization*, vol. 22, no. 4 (Autumn 1968), p. 862.

22 Richard W. Van Wagenen, 'Research in the International Organization Field (1952)', cited in Ronald J. Yalem, 'Regional Security Communities', in George W. Keeton and George Scharzenberger (eds), *The Yearbook on International Affairs* (London: Stevens, 1979), pp. 217–23.

23 Emanuel Adler, 'Seeds of Peaceful Change: The OSCE's Security Community Building Model', in Emanuel Adler and Michael Barnett (eds), *Security Communities* (Cambridge: Cambridge University Press, 1998), p. 119.

24 Robert Keohane and Lisa Martin, 'The Promise of Institutionalist Theory', *International Security*, vol. 19, no. 1 (Summer 1995), p. 47.

25 Martha Finnemore, *National Interests in International Society* (Ithaca, NY: Cornell University Press, 1996), p. 9.

26 For an authoritative statement of neo-liberal institutionalism, see: Robert O. Keohane, 'Neoliberal Institutionalism: A Perspective on World Politics', in Robert O. Keohane, *International Institutions and State Power* (Boulder, CO: Westview Press, 1989), pp. 1–20.

27 Jeffrey T. Checkel, 'The Constructivist Turn in International Relations Theory', *World Politics*, vol. 50 (January 1998), p. 326.

28 Emanuel Adler, 'Seizing the Middle Ground: Constructivism in World Politics', *European Journal of International Relations*, vol. 3, no. 3 (1997), p. 345.

29 Emanuel Adler and Michael Barnett, 'A Framework for the Study of Security Communities', in Emanuel Adler and Michael Barnett (eds), *Security Communities* (Cambridge: Cambridge University Press, 1998), pp. 43–4.

30 Stephan Haggard and Beth A. Simmons, 'Theories of International Regimes', *International Organization*, vol. 41, no. 3 (Summer 1987), pp. 491–92.

31 James A. Caporaso, 'International Relations Theory and Multilateralism', in John Gerard Ruggie (ed.), *Multilateralism Matters: The Theory and Praxis of an Institutional Form* (New York: Columbia University Press, 1993), p. 54. Robert Keohane, the leading neo-liberal, accepts that institution building may simply involve the development of 'persistent and connected sets of rules (formal or informal) that prescribe behavioural roles, constrain activity, and shape expectations'. Robert O. Keohane, 'International Institutions: Two Approaches', *International Studies Quarterly*, vol. 32, no. 4 (December 1988), p. 383.

32 Amitav Acharya, 'Preventive Diplomacy: Issues and Institutions in the Asia Pacific Region', Paper presented to the 8th Asia Pacific Roundtable, Kuala Lumpur, 5–8 June 1994.

33 Kal J. Holsti, *International Politics: A Framework for Analysis*, 7th edition (Englewood Cliffs, NJ: Prentice Hall, 1995), p. 372.

34 Friedrich V. Kratochwill, *Rules, Norms and Decisions: On the Conditions of Practical and Legal Reasoning in International Relations and Domestic Affairs* (Cambridge: Cambridge University Press, 1989), p. 59.

35 Neta C. Crawford, 'Changing Norms of Humanitarian Intervention', Paper prepared for the 1994 International Studies Association Conference, Washington, DC, 1 April 1994, pp. 4–5.

36 Kratochwill outlines three ordering functions of norms. First, by 'ruling out' certain methods of individual goal seeking through the stipulation of forbearances, norms define the area within which conflict can be bounded. Second, within the restricted set of permissible goals and strategies, rules that take the actors' goals as given can create schemes or schedules for individual or joint enjoyment of scarce objects. Third, norms enable the parties whose goals and/or strategies conflict to sustain a 'discourse' on their grievances, to negotiate a solution, or to ask a third party for a decision on the basis of commonly accepted rules, norms and principles. Friedrich V. Kratochwill, *Rules, Norms and Decisions: On the Conditions of Practical and Legal Reasoning in International Relations and Domestic Affairs* (Cambridge: Cambridge University Press, 1989), p. 70.

37 Peter J. Katzenstein, 'Introduction: Alternative Perspectives on National Security', in Peter Katzenstein (ed.), *The Culture of National Security: Norms and Identity in World Politics* (New York: Columbia University Press, 1996), p. 5. Martha Finnemore, *National Interests in International Society* (Ithaca, NY: Cornell University Press, 1996), p. 129.

38 Ibid., p. 54.

39 Jeffrey T. Checkel, 'The Constructivist Turn in International Relations Theory', *World Politics*, vol. 50, no. 2 (January 1998), p. 345.

40 Ibid., p. 328.

41 Peter J. Katzenstein, *Cultural Norms and National Security: Police and Military in Post-War Japan* (Ithaca, NY: Cornell University Press, 1996), p. 43.

42 Three other conditions are: (1) mutual relevance of the units to one another; (2) compatibility of values and some joint rewards; and (3) mutual responsiveness. Karl Deutsch, *The Analysis of International Relations*, 3rd edition (Englewood Cliffs, NJ: Prentice Hall, 1988), p. 271.

43 Ibid., pp. 271–72.

44 Holsti, *International Politics: A Framework for Analysis*, 7th edition (Englewood Cliffs, NJ: Prentice Hall, 1995), p. 372.

45 Kal J. Holsti, *International Politics: A Framework for Analysis*, 5th edition (Englewood Cliffs, NJ: Prentice Hall, 1988), p. 436.

46 See: Francis W. Wilcox, 'Regionalism and the United Nations', *International Organization*, vol. 10 (1965), pp. 789–811; Norman J. Padelford, 'Regional Organizations and the United Nations', *International Organization*, vol. 8 (1954), pp. 203–16; Lynn H. Miller, 'The Prospect for Order through Regional Security', in Richard A. Falk and Saul H. Mendlovitz (eds), *Regional Politics and World Order* (San Francisco: W.H. Freeman, 1973).

47 Peter Katzenstein, *Cultural Norms and National Security: Police and Military in Post-War Japan* (Ithaca, NY: Cornell University Press, 1998), p. 38.

48   Amitav Acharya, 'How Ideas Spread: Whose Norms Matter? Norm Localization and Institutional Change in Asian Regionalism', *International Organization*, vol. 58, no. 2 (Spring 2004), pp. 239–75.

49   Andrew Hurrell, 'Norms and Ethics in International Relations', in Walter Carlsnaes, Thomas Risse and Beth A. Simmons, (eds), *Handbook of International Relations* (London: Sage, 2003), p. 147.

50   Amitav Acharya, 'Do Norms and Identity Matter? Community and Power in Southeast Asia's Regional Order', *Pacific Review*, vol. 18, no. 1 (March 2005), pp. 95–118.

51   Donald Puchala, 'The Integration Theorists and the Study of International Relations', in Charles W. Kegley and Eugene R. Wittkopf (eds), *The Global Agenda: Issues and Perspectives* (New York: Random House, 1984), pp. 186–87.

52   Karl Deutsch, *The Analysis of International Relations*, 3rd edition (Englewood Cliffs, NJ: Prentice Hall, 1988), p. 271.

53   Ibid., p. 272.

54   Ibid., p. 272.

55   Ronald L. Jepperson, Alexander Wendt and Peter J. Katzenstein, 'Norms, Culture and Identity in National Security', in Peter J. Katzenstein (ed.), *The Culture of National Security: Norms and Identity in World Politics* (Ithaca, NY: Cornell University Press, 1996), p. 33.

56   The term identity comes from social psychology, where it refers to 'the images of individuality and distinctiveness ("selfhood") held and projected by an actor and formed (and modified over time) through relations with significant "others"'. Ibid., p. 59.

57   This conception of identities is similar to, if somewhat more specific than, that offered by Ted Hopf, 'The Promise of Constructivism in International Relations Theory', *International Security*, vol. 23, no. 1 (Summer 1998), p. 175.

58   Ibid., p. 175.

59   This is implicit in Wendt's assertion that 'through interactions, states might form collective identities and interests'. Alexander Wendt, 'Collective Identity Formation and the International State', *American Political Science Review*, vol. 88, no. 2 (June 1994), p. 384.

60   In using the idea of culture, I share Katzenstein's view that culture is a product neither of deep continuities nor of discontinuities (a product of specific events) of history. Instead of 'invoking history as the autonomous creator of particular aspects of culture, we should be able to point to political processes by which norms are contested and contingent, politically made and unmade in history'. Peter Katzenstein, *Cultural Norms and National Security: Police and Military in Post-War Japan* (Ithaca, NY: Cornell University Press, 1996), pp. 2 and 38.

61   Benedict Anderson, *Imagined Communities* (London and New York: Verso (1983) 1991).

62   Emanuel Adler, 'Imagined (Security) Communities: Cognitive Regions in International Relations', *Millennium*, vol. 26, no. 2 (1997), pp. 249–77.

63   Brian L. Job, *Multilateralism: The Relevance of the Concept to Regional Conflict Management* (Working Paper no. 5) (Vancouver: Institute of International Relations, University of British Columbia, 1994), p. 15.

64   Donald Puchala, 'The Integration Theorists and the Study of International Relations', in Charles W. Kegley and Eugene R. Wittkopf (eds), *The Global Agenda: Issues and Perspectives* (New York: Random House, 1984), p. 118.

65   Kal J. Holsti, *International Politics: A Framework for Analysis*, 5th edition (Englewood Cliffs, NJ: Prentice Hall, 1988), p. 435.

66   Puchala, 'The Integration Theorists and the Study of International Relations', p. 198.

67   Barry Buzan, 'New Patterns of Global Security', *International Affairs*, vol. 67, no. 3 (1991), p. 436.

68   Evan Luard, *War in International Society* (London: Tauris, 1986), Appendix 5.

69   James M. Goldgeier and Michael McFaul, 'Core and Periphery in the Post-Cold War Era', *International Organization*, vol. 46, no. 2 (Spring 1992), pp. 467–92.

70   Barry Buzan, 'New Patterns of Global Security', *International Affairs*, vol. 67, no. 3 (1991).

71   Emanuel Adler, 'Europe's New Security Order: A Pluralistic Security Community', in Beverly Crawford (ed.), *The Future of European Security* (Berkeley, CA: Center for German and European Studies, University of California, 1992), p. 293.

72   Vasquez uses the term 'the democratic security community'. John M. Vasquez (ed.), *Classics of International Relations* (Upper Saddle River, NJ: Prentice Hall, 1986), pp. 288–89. Thomas Risse-Kappen echoes this view; see his *Cooperation among Democracies: The European Influence on US Foreign Policy* (Princeton, NJ: Princeton University Press, 1995), p. 31.

73   For liberal perspectives on the relationship between interdependence and peace, see: Robert O. Keohane and Joseph S. Nye, *Power and Interdependence* (Boston: Little, Brown, 1977), pp. 1–37;

Richard Rosecrance, *The Rise of the Trading State: Commerce and Conquest in the Modern World* (New York: Basic Books, 1986). For a critical review of the liberal argument, see: Ernst B. Haas, 'War, Interdependence and Functionalism', in Raimo Vayrynen (ed.), *The Quest for Peace: Transcending Collective Violence and War among Societies, Cultures and States* (Beverly Hills, CA: Sage, 1987). For realist critiques, see: Kenneth Waltz, 'The Myth of National Interdependence', in Charles Kindleberger (ed.), *The Multinational Corporation* (Cambridge, MA: MIT Press, 1970), pp. 205–23; Barry Buzan, 'Economic Structure and International Security: The Limits of the Liberal Case', *International Organization*, vol. 38, no. 4 (Autumn 1984).

74 Immanuel Kant, 'Perpetual Peace: A Philosophical Sketch', in John A. Vasquez (ed.), *Classics of International Relations* (Englewood Cliffs, NJ: Prentice Hall, 1986), p. 375.

75 Ronald J. Yalem, 'Regional Security Communities', in George W. Keeton and George Scharzenberger (eds), *The Yearbook on International Affairs* (London: Stevens, 1979), pp. 217–23.

76 Robert O. Keohane and Joseph S. Nye, 'Power and Interdependence Revisited', *International Organization*, vol. 41, no. 4 (Autumn 1987), p. 727.

77 On functionalism and neo-functionalism see: David Mittrany, *A Working Peace System* (Chicago: Quadrangle Press, 1966); Ernst B. Haas, *Beyond the Nation State* (Stanford, CA: Stanford University Press, 1964); Ernst B. Haas, *The Uniting of Europe: Political, Economic and Social Forces, 1950–1957*, 2nd edition (Stanford, CA: Stanford University Press, 1968); Joseph S. Nye, 'Comparing Common Markets: A Revised Neo-Functional Model', in Leon N. Lindberg and Stuart A. Scheingold (eds), *Regional Integration: Theory and Research* (Cambridge, MA: Harvard University Press, 1971), pp. 192–231.

78 Haas, 'War, Interdependence and Functionalism', p. 109.

79 Ibid., p. 108.

80 Ibid.

81 For example, the Central American Common Market, once regarded as the very model of the neo-functionalist approach, suffered a long paralysis. The Latin American Free Trade Area was abolished in 1980, as members realised the futility of developing a free trade area and a common market due to different levels of development and conflicts over the distribution of benefits among them. In Africa, similar trends characterised integration efforts with the eclipse of the East African Community. Domenico Mazzeo, 'Conclusion: Problems and Prospects of intra-African Cooperation', in Domenico Mazzeo (ed.), *African Regional Organizations* (Cambridge: Cambridge University Press, 1984), pp. 238–39.

82 Joseph S. Nye, 'Central American Regional Integration', in J. Nye (ed.), *International Regionalism* (Boston: Little Brown, 1968), pp. 381–82.

83 Lincoln Gordon, 'Economic Regionalism Reconsidered', *World Politics*, vol. 13 (1961), p. 245.

84 B. Monte Hill, 'Community Formation Within ASEAN', *International Organization*, vol. 32, no. 2 (Spring 1978), pp. 568–75.

85 Bellamy supports the view that security communities need not begin with a liberal democratic political milieu; see Alexander Bellamy, *Security Communities and Their Neighbours: Regional Fortresses or Global Integrators?* (Basingstoke and New York: Palgrave Macmillan, 2004). Kuhonta calls ASEAN an 'illiberal security community'. Erik Kuhonta, 'Walking a Tightrope: Democracy versus Sovereignty in ASEAN's Illiberal Peace,' *The Pacific Review*, vol. 19, no. 3 (September 2006), pp. 337–58.

86 Deutsch's notion of security community lends itself to interpretations other than those provided by liberal scholars. A careful reading of Deutsch will reveal that he spoke of 'compatibility of major political values' as a condition for the emergence of pluralistic security communities, not necessarily liberal democratic values. Deutsch, *The Analysis of International Relations* (Englewood Cliffs, NJ: Prentice Hall, 1968), p. 196.

87 Emanuel Adler and Michael Barnett, 'A Framework for the Study of Security Communities', in Emanuel Adler and Michael Barnett (eds), *Security Communities* (Cambridge: Cambridge University Press, 1998), pp. 50–7.

88 Ibid., p. 50.

89 Ibid., p. 50.

90 Ibid.

91 Ibid., pp. 50–2.

92 Ibid., pp. 57–8. For a more forceful view that security communities may decline, see: Harald Müller, 'A Theory of Decay of Security Communities with an Application to the Present State of

the Atlantic Alliance', Working Paper (Berkeley, University of California, 4 April 2006). Available http://repositories.cdlib.org/ies/060409 (accessed 9 June 2008).

93   Emanuel Adler, 'Seizing the Middle Ground: Constructivism in World Politics', *European Journal of International Relations*, vol. 3, no. 3 (1997), p. 336; Jeffrey Checkel, 'The Constructivist Turn in International Relations Theory', *World Politics*, vol. 50, no. 2 (January 1998), p. 339.

94   Karl W. Deutsch, 'Security Communities', in James Rosenau (ed.), *International Politics and Foreign Policy* (New York: Free Press, 1961), p. 103.

95   On 'balancing' and 'bandwagoning', see: Stephen M. Walt, *The Origins of Alliances* (Ithaca, NY: Cornell University Press, 1987).

96   Robert Keohane and Lisa Martin, 'The Promise of Institutionalist Theory', *International Security*, vol. 19, no. 1 (Summer 1995), p. 47.

97   In general, the neo-liberal position accepts the conditioning role of anarchy and hence the balance of power, but claims that institutions may mitigate anarchy and lead to cooperation.

98   The definition and meaning of globalisation varies widely. According to Cox, globalisation involves 'growing connectedness and interdependence on a world scale. It is multidimensional: connectedness in politics and the organisation of security, in economics and welfare, in culture, in ecology, in values of all kinds. No area of human activity is isolated; and within each area, no one is untouched by the condition and activities of others.' Robert Cox, 'Economic Globalization and the Limits to Liberal Democracy', in Anthony McGrew, ed., *The Transformation of Democracy*, (London: Polity Press, 1997). A similarly broad view is offered by Giddens, for whom globalisation is 'the intensification of worldwide social relations which link distant realities in such a way that local happenings are shaped by events occurring many miles away or vice versa'. Anthony Giddens, *The Consequences of Modernity* (Cambridge: Polity Press, 1990), p. 64 Other examples of the broad view are Hans-Henrik Holm and Georg Sorensen: globalisation is 'the intensification of economic, political, social, and cultural relations across borders'; Anthony McGrew: globalisation is 'the multiplicity of linkages and interconnections between the states and societies which make up the modern world system'. See: Hans-Henrik Holm and Georg Sorensen, 'Introduction: What Has Changed?' in Hans-Henrik Holm and Georg Sorensen, (eds.), *Whose World Order? Uneven Globalization and the End of the Cold War* (Boulder, CO: Westview Press, 1995); Anthony G. McGrew, 'Conceptualizing Global Priorities', in Anthony G. McGrew et al., *Global Politics: Globalization and the Nation-State* (Cambridge: Polity Press, 1992).

99   For an argument that the absence of large-scale internal conflict is a precondition for security communities, see Laurie Nathan, 'Domestic Instability and Security Communities', *European Journal of International Relations*, vol. 12, no. 2 (2006), pp. 275–99. This argument is supported by earlier writings on security in the Third World, which identified the weaknesses of the post-colonial state structure and lack of regime legitimacy as major sources of internal conflicts in the Third World that tended to spill over into the regional and international arena. Mohammed Ayoob, 'Regional Security and the Third World', in Mohammed Ayoob, (ed.), *Regional Security in the Third World* (London: Croom Helm, 1986), pp. 2–23. I do not see domestic instability as a necessary barrier to the emergence of security communities; in some cases the shared problem of internal conflict management including common concerns for regime survival from domestic threats may unite regimes and create the basis for regional security cooperation, acting as a trigger in much the same way as (or even more than) external threats. Amitav Acharya, 'Regionalism and Regime Security in the Third World: Comparing the Origins of the ASEAN and the GCC', in Brian L. Job, (ed.), *The (In)security Dilemma: National Security of Third World States* (Boulder, CO: Lynne Rienner, 1991), pp. 143–64.

100 See for example, James H. Mittelman, 'The Globalization of Social Conflict', in Volker Bornschier and Peter Lengyel, (eds.), *Conflicts and New Departures in World Society* (New Brunswick, NJ: Transaction Publishers, 1994).

101 Manuel F. Montes, 'Globalization and Capital Market Development in Southeast Asia', Paper Presented to the ISEAS 30th Anniversary Conference on 'Southeast Asia in the 21st century: Challenges of Globalization', Singapore, Institute of Southeast Asian Studies, 30 July–1 August 1998, p. 1.

102 Beyond the Asian Financial Crisis: Challenges and Opportunities for U.S. Leadership (Washington, D.C.: USIP, April 1998), p. 10.

103 Alexander Wendt, 'Collective Identity and the International State', *American Political Science Review*, vol. 88, no. 2 (June 1994).

2 The evolution of ASEAN norms and the emergence of the 'ASEAN Way'

ASEAN was established at Bangkok on 8 August 1967.[1] It brought together five countries – Indonesia, Malaysia, Thailand, Singapore and the Philippines – in one of the most remarkably divergent groups of states. Not only were its members very dissimilar in terms of their physical size, ethnic composition, socio-cultural heritage and identity, and in their colonial experience and postcolonial polities, they also lacked any significant previous experience in multilateral cooperation. Since cultural and political homogeneity could not serve as an adequate basis for regionalism, the latter had to be constructed through interaction. Such interactions could only be purposeful if they were consistent and rule based, employing those rules which would ensure peaceful conduct among the member states. To this end, ASEAN's founders over a period of a decade from its inception adopted a set of norms for intra-regional relations. A Malaysian scholar, Noordin Sopiee, would later describe them as the 'ground rules of inter-state relations within the ASEAN community with regard to conflict and its termination'.[2]

These norms include both the legal-rational and social-cultural variety. The sources of the former were not unique to the region. The principle of non-interference and the principle of non-use of force (and the related principle of pacific settlement of disputes) are common to all international organisations of the modern era, although they took on a special importance in Third World regional bodies because of anti-colonial struggles and the demand for recognition in international affairs.[3] The source of a third principle, that of regional autonomy, may be traced to the 'universalist–regionalist' debate that accompanied the drafting of the UN Charter at the San Francisco Conference.[4] Another important ASEAN norm, avoidance of multilateral military pacts, had its origin in Asian regionalist discourses culminating in the Bandung Asia–Africa Conference of 1955, when a group of Asian regionalists, including India and Indonesia, had framed participation by the newly independent countries in military pacts (such as SEATO and CENTO) led by great powers as constituting a form of intervention in their affairs. Bandung had paved the way for the Non-Aligned Movement to which several ASEAN members would belong (especially Indonesia and Malaysia).[5] This rejection of military pacts morphed into a general unwillingness to participate in multilateral defence cooperation within a regional grouping, especially one which might be perceived to be pro-Western by the Soviet bloc. Hence, ASEAN had to avoid military cooperation in order not to be perceived as a front for the West, or a SEATO through the back door.

ASEAN's adoption of these norms therefore was not so much a matter of conceptual invention, but of their incorporation into a socialisation process to redefine the regional political and security environment. This, however, involved initial contestations and adaptations to define the scope of these norms and render them, including the so-called universal norms, suitable to the local context. Socio-cultural norms played a crucial role in moulding this interaction and compromise involving divergent national positions. While both legal-rational and socio-cultural norms are significant in the construction and expression of collective identities, the latter may be more important in making a particular social group 'distinct' in relation to non-group actors. While the sources of ASEAN's legal-rational norms lay within the structure and dynamics of the international system at large, the notion of the 'ASEAN Way' was founded on elements, especially informality, consultations (*musyawarah*) and consensus (*mufakat*), that were claimed as being unique to Southeast Asia's cultural heritage. And it is these norms that helped ASEAN to overcome initial contestations and reach compromises over the meaning and scope of the legal-rational principles.

The following sections will analyse the evolution of ASEAN's norms and principles by dividing them into four core categories: those dealing with the non-use of force and the pacific settlement of disputes; those concerning regional autonomy and collective self-reliance; the doctrine of non-interference in the internal affairs of states; and, last but not least, the rejection of an ASEAN military pact and the preference for bilateral defence cooperation. This will be followed by a discussion of the 'ASEAN Way'. The final part of the chapter will assess the gap between rhetoric and reality in the development of ASEAN's norms, before examining their impact on ASEAN's political and security role in various issue areas in the subsequent chapters. Particular attention will be given throughout the chapter to analysing the contestations and compromises that marked the emergence, application and adaptation of norms, in keeping with the perspective that normative evolution and change are quintessentially a contested process, and that norms are not static, but are 'made and remade through politics'.

Negotiating Norms: The Bangkok Declaration, 1967

The wording of the preamble of ASEAN's founding Bangkok Declaration of 1967 reflected the contested nature of norm-setting in ASEAN, especially norms of 'regional autonomy' and 'no military pacts'. The most 'controversial paragraphs' of the Bangkok Declaration were the last two (4 and 5) of the preamble:

> **CONSIDERING** that the countries of South East Asia share a primary responsibility for strengthening the economic and social stability of the region and ensuring their peaceful and progressive national development, and that they are determined to ensure their stability and security from external interference in any form or manifestation in order to preserve their national identities in accordance with the ideals and aspirations of their peoples;

> **AFFIRMING** that all foreign bases are temporary and remain only with the expressed concurrence of the countries concerned and are not intended to be used directly or indirectly to subvert the national independence and freedom of States in the area or prejudice the orderly processes of their national development.

An earlier version of the first paragraph, contained in an Indonesian-inspired draft of February 1967, had called on Southeast Asian countries to 'share responsibility' not only for 'the economic and social stability of the region,' but also 'for ensuring the stability and maintaining the security of the region from external interference'. This latter phrase was borrowed from two MAPHILINDO documents signed by Malaysia, the Philippines and Indonesia (the Manila Accord of 31 July 1963 signed by their Foreign Ministers, and the Manila Declaration of 3 August 1963 signed by their leaders). These documents used the expression 'share a primary responsibility for the maintenance of the stability and security of the area from subversion in any form and manifestation'. The Indonesian proposed wording for Bangkok was only slightly different: 'ensuring the stability and maintaining the security' in place of 'stability and security' and 'external interference' in place of 'subversion'.

The original version of the second paragraph, concerning foreign bases, was also contained in the same February 1967 draft. It derived from paragraph 11 of another MAPHILINDO declaration (of 5 August 1963 by the leaders), which read:

> The three Heads of Government further agreed that foreign bases – temporary in nature – should not be allowed to be used directly or indirectly to subvert the national independence of any of the three countries. In accordance with the principle enunciated in the Bandung Declaration, the three countries will abstain from the use of arrangements of collective defence to serve the particular interests of any of the big powers.

Originally, Indonesia had proposed placing these two paragraphs at the very beginning (paragraphs 2 and 3) of the Bangkok Declaration. This, Jakarta had hoped, would differentiate ASEAN sufficiently from ASA (of which it was not a member) and make it appear closer to MAPHILINDO (of which it was a member). More important, the Suharto government wanted to pre-empt domestic critics (from the 'old order' of Sukarno, who had signed MAPHILINDO and conceived it as part of his ideological crusade against the West) who might have accused it of 'having sold out to a western dominated bloc'.

But both Singapore and the Philippines objected to these paragraphs. Manila wished to avoid giving ASEAN the 'political, ideological and racial' flavour of MAPHILINDO, and keep it, like ASA, limited to economic and cultural fields. Singapore 'worked particularly hard first to exclude these references' and later to 'dilute' them by adding to the declaration a list of specific projects (in the end, this list was presented as a separate statement). Thailand went along with Indonesia, and Malaysia 'occupied a middle position'.

In the final signed version of the Bangkok Declaration, as a compromise, the 'shared responsibility' paragraph was split. As a British dispatch interpreted, 'shared responsibility' was limited to 'economic and social stability', hence, 'stability and security from external interference', would be construed 'as the responsibility of each of the individual signatories'. (The author's own interpretation is that even so, reducing the scope for external interference in matters pertaining to security and stability was to become a shared norm, if not a shared responsibility.) The paragraph on foreign military bases was altered from 'should not be allowed to be used' in the MAPHILINDO document to 'are not intended to be used'. The Philippines argued that the change would make the temporary nature of foreign bases appear 'not as a statement of principle, but a statement of fact'. 'It was no more than simple truth that the US bases in the Philippines and the British bases in Singapore were temporary and depended on the consent of the host country and of course there was no question of their being used for the purpose of subversion.'

More importantly, the reference to the Bandung Declaration (of 1955) on the abstention 'from arrangements of collective defence to serve the particular interests of any of the big powers', was entirely dropped. And the two paragraphs were brought from the beginning to the end of the preamble, thereby lessening their importance somewhat. Yet, by placing the foreign military bases issue in the Declaration, Indonesia did manage to meet its domestic concerns and maintain some normative continuity with the MAPHILINDO and Bandung.

Sources: The text of the Bangkok Declaration available at http:// www.aseansec. org/1212.htm (accessed 25 June 2008). The Maphilindo Declaration: 'Joint Statement by the Philippines, the Federation of Malays and Indonesia. Signed at Manila, on 5th August 1963', United Nations Treaty Series 1965. Available at http://untreaty.un.org/unts/1_60000/16/16/00030780.pdf (accessed 25 June 2008). The British reports are: 'ASEAN', British Embassy in Manila to South East Asia Department, Foreign Office, 15 August 1967, FCO 15/23 (London: Public Records Office) and 'Regional Co-operation', British High Commission in Kuala Lumpur to Far East and South Pacific Department, Commonwealth Office, 14 August 1967, FCO 15/23 (London: Public Records Office). The dispatch from Kuala Lumpur was based on a conversation with Zainal Sulong, of the Malaysian Foreign Ministry, who was present in Bangkok, while the Manila dispatch was based on a conversation with Philippine Foreign Secretary Narciso Ramos.

Non-use of force and pacific settlement of disputes

The establishment of ASEAN was the product of a desire by its five original members to create a mechanism for war prevention and conflict management. The need for such a mechanism was made salient by the fact that ASEAN's predecessor had foundered on the reefs of intra-regional mistrust and animosity. An earlier attempt at a regional association in Southeast Asia, the Association of Southeast Asia (ASA), had been made in 1961, but it had collapsed over the Philippines' claim to the former British colony of North Borneo (Sabah), which had opted to join the Malaysian federation. ASA was followed by MAPHILINDO, an acronym for a loose confederation of three independent states of Malaya stock (Indonesia, Malaya and the Philippines) but without displaying an institutional form. Its demise was ensured by Indonesia's challenge to the legitimacy of newly independent Malaysia through a coercive diplomacy known as *Konfrontasi*. The members of the newly formed ASEAN were involved in a number of serious disputes among themselves. War-like tensions obtained between Singapore and Malaysia, and Singapore and Indonesia, reflecting a general distrust of Chinese-dominated Singapore by its Malay-Muslim neighbours.

The idea of ASEAN itself was conceived in the course of intra-regional negotiations leading to the end of confrontation between Indonesia and Malaysia. President Sukarno's *Konfrontasi* had been a prime example of the use of force, however limited, by a postcolonial state in Southeast Asia against a neighbour. In wrecking the prospects for MAPHILINDO, *Konfrontasi* had underscored the importance of regionalism by demonstrating the high costs of the use of force to settle intra-regional conflicts. After fundamental political change, Indonesia's decision to renounce *Konfrontasi* served as a model for its neighbours and raised the possibility of a regional order based on the non-use of force in interstate relations. While interest in regionalism among the five member states of ASEAN was a result of varied geopolitical considerations, all recognised ASEAN's value as a framework through which to prevent a return to a *Konfrontasi*-like situation. As a regional forum under Indonesia's putative leadership, ASEAN would first and foremost constrain Indonesia's possible return to belligerence.

> Indonesia's membership within ASEAN would reduce the possibility of threat to their security posed by their giant neighbour ... Indonesia would appear to be placed in what amounts to a 'hostage' position, albeit in a golden cage. For the new leadership in Jakarta ... it is within ASEAN that Indonesia might be provided with an opportunity to realize its ambitions, if any, to occupy a position of primacy or primus inter pares without recourse to a policy of confrontation.[6]

ASEAN's emergence also served to diminish the prospect of force being used against its smallest constituent, Singapore. Singapore, acutely conscious of its vulnerabilities as 'a Chinese island in a sea of Malays', could use its participation in ASEAN to gain acceptance as part of Southeast Asia and play a bigger role by being able to influence other like-minded countries on issues of mutual interest. Subsequently, another small state, Brunei, would see the usefulness of ASEAN in a similar light. ASEAN membership helped to reduce Brunei's sense of vulnerability against its bigger neighbour, Malaysia. The ASEAN norms of non-interference would lessen the possibility of Kuala Lumpur sponsoring subversion against the monarchy in Brunei which, unlike Sabah and Sarawak, had refused to join the Malaysian federation.

While the experience of *Konfrontasi* lay behind the importance attached to the principle of non-use of force, its first major test was the dispute between Malaysia and the Philippines over Sabah (formerly British ruled North Borneo which had opted to join the Malaysian federation when the latter got its independence from Britain). The origins of the Philippine claim dates back to 1961, but relations between Malaysia and the Philippines suffered a major crisis between April 1968 and December 1969, after the Philippine press reported in March 1968 that a secret army was being trained on the Philippine island of Corregidor to be used for a forceful takeover of Sabah. The Philippines government dismissed the report,[7] but it caused serious concern in Malaysia and the resulting tension put question marks over the survival of ASEAN within a year of its birth.

The rest of the ASEAN members initially maintained public silence over the dispute, lest they be perceived by either side as taking sides and draw ASEAN into its vortex. Privately, however, Indonesia and Thailand urged restraint on both sides and tried to keep the Sabah issue from damaging ASEAN, especially after bilateral talks between Malaysia and the Philippines in Bangkok in June 1968 broke down, and the two countries suspended their diplomatic relations.[8] While maintaining public neutrality in the dispute, both Indonesia and Thailand privately indicated a preference for the Philippines to drop the claim.[9] At a meeting of ASEAN foreign ministers hosted by Indonesia's Adam Malik in August 1968, the 'delegates were able to keep this issue under wraps'.[10] In a sign of the informal approach that would characterise the ASEAN process, Malik persuaded the Foreign Ministers of Malaysia and the Philippines to meet at his residence on the afternoon of 6 August. This meeting produced agreement to a 'cooling-off period', initially for six months, during which any further provocation by either side in word or deed was to be avoided.[11] But Malaysia would insist that any future ASEAN meetings would risk a Malaysian boycott if they went beyond 'various aspects of regional co-operation' and allowed the Philippines to raise the Sabah issue.[12] On 3 December 1968, Malaysian Foreign Minister Tun Razak went further to state that

> Regional cooperation under the banner of ASEAN countries has more or less come to a halt ... this will remain so until the Philippines drops its claim.[13]

Malaysia, however, crucially did not threaten to withdraw from ASEAN. As Razak clarified in January 1969:

> The Philippines claim to Sabah has become a hindrance to the progress of ASEAN but the question of Malaysia's withdrawal from the organisation because of this did not arise at all. Malaysia has pledged its stand on regional cooperation and is determined to see that the Bangkok Declaration of 1967 will be upheld. . . .[14]

But the Sabah dispute had put ASEAN 'on ice'.[15] Malaysia, which was to host the third AMM in August 1969, refused to do anything to convene it. The freeze on ASEAN had to be melted and the job fell on the disputants' ASEAN neighbours: Indonesia and Thailand. In January 1969, the Philippines ambassador in Jakarta announced that Manila would not bring up the question of Sabah in future ASEAN meetings.[16] Both Thailand and Indonesia would send a series of delegations around the region to diffuse the crisis. After one such visit (dubbed a 'non-official visit') to Kuala Lumpur in early March 1969, by Sunarso, the Secretary-General of the Indonesian ASEAN office, when Malaysia was still refusing to sit down with the Philippines, Tunku Abdul Rahman, the Malaysian Prime Minister, remarked, 'If it is our duty to call for a meeting [of ASEAN], then we will have to call one.'[17] This was followed by a major change in Malaysian policy; it agreed that routine technical meetings of ASEAN could recommence then. This had been a major topic between Malaysia and the visiting Indonesian delegation led by Sunarso, thereby suggesting discrete Indonesian good offices.[18] These and other regular ASEAN meetings served as an important channel of communication between Malaysia and the Philippines. At an ASEAN committee meeting in Indonesia in May 1969, the two countries were brought together for the first time in eight months with the exception of an *ad hoc* foreign ministers' meeting in Bangkok in December 1968.

Moreover, it was at an ASEAN foreign ministers' meeting in December 1969 that Malaysia and the Philippines agreed to resume diplomatic relations. The joint communiqué of the meeting credited this positive development to 'the great value Malaysia and the Philippines placed on ASEAN'. The Sabah issue was swept under the carpet. Although the dispute continued to simmer, its muting helped ASEAN to emerge from a cloud of pessimism and uncertainty about its future.

Commenting on the impact of ASEAN in diffusing the Sabah dispute, a British diplomatic memo noted that

> a major influence restraining both Malaysia and the Philippines from open rupture . . . on Sabah seems to have been their reluctance to imperil their standing as ASEAN members . . . While it is, perhaps, too much to expect that a permanent solution can be found in the foreseeable future, we can expect ASEAN to remain an important factor in keeping the temperature down . . . the other members of ASEAN and particularly, perhaps, Indonesia, are best able to take the lead in urging restraint.[19]

Although ASEAN did not have the legal and institutional means to mediate in the Sabah dispute, its members helped to defuse the crisis through their own refusal to take sides, and their efforts at diplomatic persuasion of the two sides to exercise restraint. Not only was the Sabah dispute a milestone in ASEAN's early approach to conflict avoidance, it was also indicative of ASEAN's informal and non-legalistic style of conflict management.

The 1971 Kuala Lumpur Declaration, which mentioned several principles of the UN Charter as the source of ASEAN's norms, listed among them 'abstention from the threat or use of force', and 'peaceful settlement of international disputes'.[20] Chatichai Choonhavan, Thailand's Foreign Minister, stated in 1973, '[t]he immediate task of ASEAN ... is to attempt to create a favourable condition in the region whereby political differences and security problems among Southeast Asian nations can be resolved peacefully'.[21]

The need for the pacific settlement of disputes was held in such importance by ASEAN's founders that they were willing to create formal mechanisms to support this principle within the ASEAN institutional framework despite their known aversion to institutional legalism. Thus, the Treaty of Amity and Cooperation signed in 1976 provided (under Chapter IV, Articles 13 to 17) for an official dispute-settlement mechanism, called a High Council, consisting of ministerial-level representatives from each member state. This Council, as a continuing body, was supposed 'to take cognizance of the existence of disputes and situations likely to disturb regional peace and harmony' and 'in the event no solution is reached through direct negotiations', to 'recommend to the parties in dispute appropriate means of settlement such as good offices, mediation, inquiry or conciliation'. Although this mechanism has never been invoked, this very fact has been cited by ASEAN leaders as indicating an enduring commitment to the non-use of force in intra-regional relations as well as a sign of the grouping's success in intra-mural conflict avoidance and management.

Regional autonomy and 'regional solutions to regional problems'

One of the major points of contention and constraints on regionalism in Southeast Asia since the Second World War had to do with the dependence of the regional countries on extra-regional powers for protection against internal as well as external threats. The strong security links of Thailand and the Philippines with the USA, and those of Malaysia and Singapore with Britain, made security through regional cooperation less urgent. The membership of the Philippines and Thailand in the Southeast Asia Treaty Organisation (SEATO) also created a schism in the strategic perspectives between these two states and Indonesia. The latter was a strong advocate of non-alignment and, even with the advent of a pro-Western regime, opposed any security role for outside powers in the region.

Against this backdrop, the emergence of the principle of regional autonomy was bound to be controversial. Yet, the need for greater self-reliance in managing the region's security problems emerged as a key ASEAN norm. Adam Malik, Foreign Minister of Indonesia, explained this norm most forcefully in 1974:

> Regional problems, i.e. those having a direct bearing upon the region concerned, should be accepted as being of primary concern to that region itself. Mutual consultations and cooperation among the countries of the region in facing these problems may ... lead to the point where the views of the region are accorded the primacy they deserve in the search for solution.[22]

One key measure of this quest for autonomy was ASEAN's careful insistence of keeping the membership of the organisation limited and its leadership firmly in its own hands, rather than accepting the leadership of outside powers, even an Asian power. Under the founding Bangkok Declaration of 1967, membership in the organisation was left open to 'all States in the South-East Asian region subscribing to the ... aims, principles and purposes' of ASEAN. But an important exception to the geographical criteria was made for Ceylon, which was not only allowed, but urged, to join, presumably because its size, influence and resources did not threaten ASEAN's own identity or cohesion (historical and cultural contacts with the Buddhist nation might have been another consideration, but this might also have applied to India, which was not invited).[23] Ceylon did not take up the offer, partly out of concern that ASEAN was too pro-Western and hence might compromise its non-aligned foreign policy. Ironically, its subsequent application in the 1970s to join ASEAN was rejected by the latter on the grounds that it did not belong to Southeast Asia.

ASEAN regionalism was a repudiation of regional associations led by bigger countries, such as India, Japan or Australia. Indonesia rejected not only the SEATO model of a superpower-led military alliance, but also any regional organisation dominated or likely to be dominated by a major Asian or Western power, such as the Asia Pacific Council (proposed by Korea, and including among its members Japan and Australia).[24] Despite Japan's willingness to help ASEAN members, and its launching of the Southeast Asian Ministerial Conference on Development (SEAMCD) to this end, the 'ASEAN group were anxious to stick together and face Japan – "the big economic power of the region".'[25] Recognising such concerns, the Japanese foreign ministry in November 1973 advised Prime Minister Tanaka before his visit to Southeast Asia, to 'express support for the further build-up of ASEAN', rather than 'to launch any new schemes of his own'.[26] Later, the embassy reported that while 'Japan would welcome any sort of group in the area of which she could be a full member, whether it be a reconstituted ASPAC, and ASEAN plus plus, a Development conference given more political content, or some other new post-Vietnam war organisation', Tokyo would 'hope that other countries will take initiatives but she will be hesitant to take the initiative herself'. It also noted that the Southeast Asian response to Tanaka's ideas about a new Asian regional group had been 'discouraging'.[27]

India fared no better. When, after the formation of ASEAN, the Indian government showed interest in involving itself 'in the movement for regional co-operation' in Southeast Asia, especially in an 'association which would be concerned with economic rather than political co-operation',[28] the move was rebuffed by Japan and to a lesser extent Australia, neither of which, ironically were acceptable to ASEAN as members or leaders of regional groups that might subsume ASEAN.[29] Neither was India's participation welcomed by ASEAN members, especially Indonesia.[30]

It may be stressed here that for ASEAN's founding fathers, regional autonomy did not mean autarchy. This would have been absurd given the relative smallness and under-developed status of ASEAN members. Autonomy meant minimizing outside intervention in Southeast Asia, at a time when such intervention was a persistent and worldwide aspect of the Cold War milieu, and when the credibility of outside security guarantees was declining (thereby making them less necessary and perhaps dangerous to rely on). As Leifer noted, 'ASEAN . . . was established by South-east Asian states alone without the intervention or support of a major external power'.[31] While ASEAN's founders sought a 'proprietary role in managing regional order', this role reflected a 'conviction that close cooperation among regional states would have an insulating political effect, thereby overcoming the need for any demeaning policing function being accorded to external powers'.[32] This was in essence ASEAN's quest for regional autonomy.

ASEAN's formation was aided substantially by a common concern among its founding members about the changing role of external powers in the region. Despite their dependence on external security guarantees, all ASEAN members saw dangers in Great Power rivalry in Southeast Asia as its principal manifestation underwent a process of change towards the end of the 1960s, with the Sino-Soviet rift and a new competition for regional influence assuming prominence over traditional Cold War patterns. The prospect of China emerging as the dominant force in the region and, as Prime Minister Lee Kuan Yew of Singapore was to put it later, the related prospect of Southeast Asia becoming 'to her what the Caribbean is to America or Eastern Europe to the USSR'[33] had already constituted one aspect of ASEAN members' collective apprehensions regarding the role of great powers in the region. Sino-Soviet competition, featuring a Soviet quest for regional influence through establishing links in Indochina, its proposal for an Asian Collective Security Arrangement and Chinese warnings concerning Soviet 'hegemonism' made the ASEAN countries appreciate the need for a united response to the new form of Great Power rivalry. At the same time, the relaxation of tensions between the USA and the Soviet Union on the one hand and the USA and China on the other aroused a different kind of concern, that such Great Power compromises would leave the security interests of the ASEAN countries either ignored or undermined. Malaysia's Prime Minister Hussein Onn was to put it succinctly on the eve of the Bali summit when he noted that the big powers

> can create tension in any area . . . especially, when they try to settle their differences and impose their ideologies forcefully in other countries . . . there is a Malay saying that when two elephants fight, the mouse deer wedged in between will suffer.[34]

In this context, the usefulness of regionalism lay in its potential to enhance the bargaining power of small and weak states in their dealings with the Great Powers. Regionalism might not enable the ASEAN states to prevent the Great Powers from interfering in the affairs of the region, but it could, as Lee Kuan Yew pointed out, help them to 'have their interests taken into consideration when the great powers make their compromises'.[35] Adam Malik echoed the sentiment:

> Southeast Asia is one region in which the presence and interests of most major powers converge, politically as well as physically. The frequency and intensity of policy interactions among them, as well as their dominant influence on the countries in the region, cannot but have a direct bearing on political realities. In the face of this, the smaller nations of the region have no hope of ever making any impact on this pattern of dominant influence of the big powers, unless they act collectively and until they develop the capacity to forge among themselves an area of internal cohesion, stability and common purpose. Thus regional cooperation within ASEAN also came to represent the conscious effort by its member countries to try to re-assert their position and contribute their own concepts and goals within the ongoing process of stabilization of a new power equilibrium in the region.[36]

ASEAN's norm of regional autonomy was also influenced by Britain's initial announcement in 1967 of its decision to withdraw its forces from 'east of Suez' by the mid-1970s and that by President Nixon in 1969 of a new US doctrine ruling out future US military involvement in a land war in Asia. He urged US Asian allies to accept the primary responsibility for their own conventional defence with only indirect US assistance. One immediate impact of the Nixon doctrine was to stimulate further Thailand's efforts to steer a more independent course in foreign policy and move towards regionalism. A similar motive lay behind the interest of the Philippines in ASEAN at a time when Manila was keen to shed its image as a client of the USA and to assert its 'Asian' identity. Subsequent US withdrawal from Vietnam was a blow to the credibility of Western security guarantees that had already been undermined by the announcement of Britain's military withdrawal from the region. Reliance on Britain and other Commonwealth partners (Australia and New Zealand) for protection against both internal and external threats suffered when Britain's withdrawal was announced at a time when the development of the region's indigenous defence capabilities was still at a rudimentary stage. Although the impact of that withdrawal was mitigated somewhat by the creation of Five Power Defence Arrangements (FPDA) in 1971 involving Britain, Australia, New Zealand, Singapore and Malaysia, the latter was only a consultative arrangement backed by a small air defence force (centred on Australian combat aircraft) as well as a ground force component (with contributions from Britain, Australia and New Zealand, but Britain and Australia withdrew from this force by the mid-1970s, leaving a New Zealand battalion in Singapore until the end of the 1980s). Against this backdrop, Singapore's Foreign Minister, S. Rajaratnam, observed:

> The British decision to withdraw from the region in the seventies brings . . . to an end nearly two centuries of dominant European influence in the region. The seventies will also see the withdrawal of direct American influence in Southeast Asian affairs. For the first time in centuries, Southeast Asia will be on its own. It must fill what some people call the power vacuum itself or resign itself to the dismal prospect of the vacuum being filled from the outside. . . . We can and should fill it ourselves, not necessarily militarily, but by strengthening our social, economic and political foundations through cooperation and collective effort.[37]

In developing a norm of regional autonomy, the ASEAN members shared two major beliefs concerning the perils of dependence on Great Power security guarantees. The first was that while such guarantees might be useful against a threat of outright aggression, they could not address likely scenarios of revolutionary social challenge. Adam Malik drew attention to this danger when he warned that '[m]ilitary alliances or foreign military presence does not enhance a nation's capacity to cope with the problem of insurgency. The price for such commitments is too high, whereas the negative ramifications for the nation are too great.'[38] Mohamad Ghazali Shafie, a top Malaysian official who later became the country's foreign minister, wrote in 1975 that

> external support for internal insurgencies or for governments combating insurgencies, has the effect of raising the level of violence and complicating both conflict manage-ment and the peaceful resolution of conflicts through political means. Internal stability cannot after all be imposed from the outside.[39]

Second, to seek the help of external powers in situations of domestic instability could undermine the legitimacy of the threatened regime; after all, the most important and painful lesson of the Vietnam War was that relying on external backing in domestic upheavals could 'easily serve to insulate it [the threatened regime] from political and economic realities and render it insensitive to the social forces with which in the long run it must come to terms if it is to survive on its own'.[40]

But negotiating the institutional form that autonomy should take proved to be a conten-tious affair. At a meeting in Kuala Lumpur on 27 November 1971, the ASEAN Foreign Ministers adopted a declaration calling for a Zone of Peace, Freedom and Neutrality (ZOPFAN) in Southeast Asia. This initiative followed and was accompanied by dis-cussions over a Malaysian proposal for the 'neutralisation' of Southeast Asia.[41] Malaysia's idea was inspired by its external and domestic concerns, the latter including the May 1969 race riots, which had exposed the acute tensions between the Chinese and Malay communities. The riots had increased the ruling Malay elite's perception of the threat from China. They feared that Beijing might seek to exploit the pro-China loyalties of Malaysia's Chinese, a fear aggravated by its assumption of China's seat in the UN. In one respect, Malaysia's neutralisation proposal sought to limit China's influence in the region.

A strict neutralisation approach was, however, deemed unfeasible by other ASEAN members for several reasons.[42] Neutralisation as proposed by Malaysia would require formal guarantees from the Great Powers. The Malaysian proposal would create

> a zone in which countries would be neutral and non-aligned. The zone would be free from outside interference, in return the states within it would not take sides in a cold war struggle . . . [Malaysia] envisaged the zone as covering all 10 countries (the ASEAN group, Indochina and Burma). The integrity of the zone would be 'guaranteed' by the major powers.[43]

The issue of guarantees provoked serious uncertainties and reservations about the proposal, from other ASEAN members, especially Indonesia. A guarantee could come in the form of a declaration of recognition and respect for the zone, or it might involve a provision for sanctions (political, military measures) that would have a 'deterrent' value. Even the Malaysians had no simple answer to the question how to secure a guarantee 'which had some real meaning while avoiding giving the major powers any licence to interfere in the affairs of the zone, i.e. without bringing about the very state of affairs they wish to avoid'.

Moreover, while there was 'general agreement on the desirability' of ZOPFAN, there was 'less unanimity on whether neutralisation was the way to achieve it'. Critics of neutralisation in ASEAN wondered whether 'it might be possible to have a zone of "peace" and "freedom" without being "neutral"'.[44] It should be noted that the Kuala Lumpur Declaration on Neutralisation of Southeast Asia did not mention 'neutralisation' in the text, but only in the preamble. The declaration merely stated that the five ASEAN members will 'exert initially necessary steps to secure the recognition of and respect for South East Asia as a zone of peace, freedom and neutrality, free from any form or manner of interference by outside powers'.

Ironically, both Indonesia and Singapore opposed neutralisation, albeit for fundamentally different reasons. For Jakarta, neutralisation under international law meant in effect conceding 'policing rights' to the USA, the Soviet Union and China. Indonesia pushed for a different approach, one that expressed the right of the regional countries to have the exclusive responsibility for managing regional order.[45]

Singapore was worried that neutralisation would undercut the legitimacy of its external security linkages, and viewed the two concepts, neutralisation and ZOPFAN, as separate. Singapore was unenthusiastic about any measure that might restrict its ability to link its security with friendly Western powers, whether physically or normatively.

The Indonesian misgivings about neutralisation had their impact. In March 1972, after visiting President Suharto in Jakarta, Malaysian Deputy Prime Minister Tun Dr Ismail stated that he agreed with Suharto's view that guaranteed neutrality would not mean big power protection. Such protection would mean 'another form of collective colonisation for the whole of South East Asia'. He had explained to the President [Suharto] that 'our concept of a guarantee means acceptance by and respect for neutralisation by the big powers. This does not include protection. We can take care of ourselves.'[46]

At a senior officials meeting to discuss the idea on 6–8 July 1972 held in Kuala Lumpur, Malaysia produced a 'very detailed account of the steps necessary to achieve neutralisation' and a draft treaty, but disagreements over the definition and modalities of the proposal prevented the treaty being given serious consideration.[47] As before, doubts were expressed whether guarantees to support neutralisation could be obtained from foreign powers without giving them a right to interfere in the area.[48] Singapore argued against any rapid withdrawal of major powers as a result of neutralisation. The meeting also reproduced previous disagreements over whether neutralisation was an end in itself or a means to an end. Indonesia and the Philippines saw it as a 'state of being neutral'. Singapore argued that neutralisation was merely a means to an end and that 'other means to achieve the same ends were possible'. It insisted on discussing the 'zone of peace, freedom and neutrality' idea, which was not the same as Malaysia's neutralisation proposal, and argued that there might be other means than neutralisation for achieving ZOPFAN (although it did not mention what the 'other means' were).[49] Indonesia came up with its idea of a Zone of Peace, Freedom and Neutrality though 'national resilience'.[50] The meeting decided to limit itself to discussing the Kuala Lumpur declaration's reference to a zone of peace, freedom and neutrality, rather than neutralisation *per se*. The meeting's main achievement was to produce an agreed definition of ZOPFAN:

> A 'zone of peace, freedom and neutrality' exists where national identity, independence and integrity of the individual states within such a zone can be preserved and maintained, so that they can achieve national development and well-being and promote regional cooperation and solidarity, in accordance with the ideals and aspirations of their peoples and the purposes and principles of the UN Charter, free from any form or manner of interference by outside powers. (original text)[51]

As a result of the disagreement, a proposed ASEAN summit to formally endorse neutralisation was shelved indefinitely.[52] Malaysia backed off from the neutralisation idea and accepted the ZOPFAN concept as conceived by Indonesia, which was also somewhat more acceptable to other members. In sum, the real obstacle to neutralisation was the fact that in order to be credible, it would have to involve strict legalistic prohibitions against foreign military bases and the existing alliance relationships of ASEAN members. Under the neutralisation framework originally envisaged by Malaysia, the regional countries were required to abstain from military alliances with the Great Powers and prevent the establishment of foreign military bases on their soil, while the Great Powers were asked to 'refrain from forging alliances with the neutralised states, stationing armed forces on their territory, and using their presence to subvert or interfere in any other way with other countries'.[53] But while ASEAN countries were keen to espouse the principle of regional autonomy, they were pragmatic enough to realise that complete self-reliance was not feasible under the present circumstances. ASEAN members such as Thailand, the Philippines and Singapore saw their security links with Western powers as a vital ingredient of national security and regional order.

Unlike the original neutralisation proposal, the ZOPFAN did not explicitly deal with foreign military bases or alliances, although these were generally understood to be temporary and only with the expressed agreement of the countries involved, a formulation already laid out in the Bangkok Declaration. Nonetheless, the ZOPFAN ideal contained within it all the principal security considerations and objectives which underpinned the origin and evolution of ASEAN, including the norms of non-interference, non-use of force and regional autonomy. It reflected Malaysia's and Thailand's disenchantment with external security guarantees as well as Indonesia's convictions regarding the dangers of being engulfed by the machinations of the Great Powers. At the same time, it contained enough ambiguity to allow for the continuation of the existing security relationships between the ASEAN members and external powers.

The tension between the ASEAN members' aspirations for regional security autonomy and the continued dependence (however undesirable) of several of them on external security guarantees would remain a stumbling block in the way of realising ZOPFAN. This contradiction reflected disagreements within ASEAN in which Singapore and Thailand stressed the need for external security linkages as opposed to the pro-autonomy views of Malaysia and Indonesia. It was compounded by differing threat perceptions among ASEAN members. The ability of China to pose a long-term security threat to Southeast Asia was a prospect that was viewed more seriously by Indonesia and Malaysia than by other ASEAN partners. Malaysia moved quickly to normalise its ties with the PRC in 1974, partly in order to demonstrate its commitment to ZOPFAN, since the PRC was to be one of the external guarantors under the original neutralisation proposal. Indonesia, however, remained concerned that such a move would encourage Chinese subversion in the region.[54] Thailand and Singapore, for their part, were less optimistic than Indonesia about Vietnam's postwar intentions towards its ASEAN neighbours. Another major area of disagreement was the need for Western security guarantees. Here too the views of Thailand, Singapore and the Philippines regarding the need for a US presence in the region were at variance with the professed principles and objectives of the Bangkok and Kuala Lumpur Declarations, which were strongly espoused by Indonesia and Malaysia. Singapore, reflecting its support for a strong US presence in the region, warned that the ZOPFAN concept made the continuation of US presence all the more necessary since there was no certainty that all the other Great Powers would abide by the restraints on their geopolitical behaviour required by the concept. As Lee Kuan Yew put it, 'in the event of one or more great power not respecting, it may be useful that there would be some [US] naval and air base facilities so that some balance can be maintained'.[55]

These internal obstacles to ZOPFAN came to be obscured by the outbreak of the Cambodia conflict in December 1978 and the accompanying revival of Great Power rivalry (Sino-Soviet) in Southeast Asia. For a long time, ASEAN was able to hold to the convenient position that the realisation of ZOPFAN had to await the resolution of the Cambodia conflict. In this context, ASEAN shifted its attention to a more specific aspect of ZOPFAN, a proposal for establishing a nuclear-weapon-free zone in Southeast Asia. The SEANWFZ idea had been mooted in the ZOPFAN Declaration of 1971, but it was not seriously pursued until the 1980s. Since the realisation of SEANWFZ did not depend upon the settlement of the Cambodia conflict, it was viewed by ASEAN as a step towards ZOPFAN. But some of the problems encountered in the realisation of ZOPFAN, especially intra-ASEAN differences, manifested themselves with regard to the nuclear-weapon-free zone proposal. Moreover, the latter was much more strongly resisted by the USA. The USA argued that a regional nuclear-weapon-free zone covering only the ASEAN states (since Vietnam was unlikely to embrace such an idea) would impose a one-sided restriction on US military deployments in the region, undermining its nuclear deterrence posture without imposing similar constraints on the Soviet Union which would be free to extend its nuclear umbrella to its regional ally, Vietnam. The US objection, in turn, caused greater ambivalence in the attitude of Thailand, the Philippines and Singapore towards the proposal. While the former two states remained tied to the US defence umbrella through bilateral security treaties, Singapore's strong belief in the US role as a regional balancer conflicted with Indonesia and Malaysia's preference for an autonomous and non-aligned regional security framework. In the end, the SEANWFZ proposal remained ill-defined until 1995, with few specifics as to the area to be covered by the proposed zone, the kind of nuclear activities to be prohibited by it, its impact on security arrangements between ASEAN members and external powers, and problems of verification and compliance. Furthermore, differences within ASEAN as well as the adverse US reaction meant that for ASEAN the political costs of SEANWFZ would outweigh its potential benefits for regional security.[56] As a result, the realisation of the nuclear-free-zone concept had to await the end of the Cold War and was not concluded in treaty form until December 1995 (and even then without the approval of the nuclear powers). At the same time, ZOPFAN was further undermined by ASEAN's post-Cold War pursuit of a regional security framework which would 'engage', rather than exclude, the outside powers. This initiative, culminating in the ARF, will be discussed in Chapter 6.

The doctrine of non-interference

Arguably the single most important principle underpinning ASEAN regionalism is the doctrine of non-interference in the internal affairs of member states. As one ASEAN foreign minister put it in 1997, '[n]on-interference in the affairs of another country was . . . the key factor as to why no military conflict had broken out between any two member states since 1967'.[57]

The salience of the doctrine of non-interference in Southeast Asia has long predated ASEAN. As a well-established principle of the modern Westphalian state system, it was firmly enshrined in the charter of the UN as well as the founding documents of numerous regional organisations, such as the OAU, the OAS, and the Arab League. In Southeast Asia, it was a key principle reaffirmed at the Bandung Asian–African Conference in 1955. The doctrine was incorporated in all the major political statements of ASEAN from the outset. The founding Bangkok Declaration of 1967 called upon Southeast Asian states to 'ensure their stability and security from external interference in any form or manifestation'.[58] This injunction was intended to apply not only to interference by extra-regional powers, including the major powers such as the USA, the Soviet Union and China, but also by Southeast Asian countries in the affairs of their own neighbours. The 1971 Kuala Lumpur Declaration on the ZOPFAN, while providing a framework for ASEAN's relations with extra-regional powers, also committed ASEAN's members to 'the worthy aims and objectives of the United Nations', including 'respect for the sovereignty and territorial integrity of all states' and 'non-interference in the affairs of states'. It also recognised the 'right of every state, large or small, to lead its existence free from outside interference in its internal affairs as this interference will adversely affect its freedom, independence, and integrity'. Article 2 of the Treaty of Amity and Cooperation, adopted by ASEAN at its Bali summit in 1976, also contained a statement of the principle of 'non-interference in the internal affairs of one another'. The Declaration of ASEAN Concord, also adopted at Bali, stipulated that 'member states shall vigorously develop . . . a strong ASEAN community . . . in accordance with the principles of self-determination, sovereign equality, and non-interference in the internal affairs of nations'.

With the exception of Thailand, which was never a colony, the ASEAN states were newly independent developing countries. That they should make non-interference the central tenet of intra-regional relations, therefore, was hardly surprising. The sources and exceptional salience of this principle have to be understood, however, in the context of the grouping's search for internal stability and regime security. The norms of non-use of force and regional autonomy reflected ASEAN's concern for security against interstate disputes and extra-regional threats, but the doctrine of non-interference can only be understood in the context of the domestic security concerns of the ASEAN states. As new political entities with 'weak' state structures (e.g. lack of a close congruence between ethnic groups and territorial boundaries) and an equally problematic lack of strong regime legitimacy, the primary sources of threat to the national security of the ASEAN states were not external, but internal. The threat from within outweighed the threat from without. The domestic conflicts of the ASEAN states were aggravated by foreign factors, including interference from close neighbours, but the domestic sources of instability had a 'spillover' effect, causing friction in interstate relations. No framework for regional security cooperation could be meaningful for ASEAN unless it countered the internal enemy and enhanced regime security. Regional order could not be maintained without an agreement on the fundamental importance of regime security anchored in the principle of non-interference.

ASEAN's doctrine of non-interference was, in important part, an expression of a collective commitment to the survival of its non-communist regimes against the threat of communist subversion. This emphasis on internal stability was best illustrated in Indonesia's concepts of 'national resilience' and 'regional resilience', terms that were to become rallying slogans for all ASEAN countries. According to the Indonesian view, domestic stability within the individual ASEAN states was an indispensable prerequisite for regional security and regional collaboration. The concept of national resilience emphasises the non-military, internal dimensions of security. It is

> an inward-looking concept, based on the proposition that national security lies not in military alliances or under the military umbrella of any great power, but in self-reliance deriving from domestic factors such as economic and social development, political stability and a sense of nationalism.[59]

The emphasis on national security and nationalism might seem to go against the spirit of regionalism. The Indonesian view conveys the opposite intent; as Jusuf Wanandi, an Indonesian scholar, has put it: 'if each member nation can accomplish an overall national development and overcome internal threats, regional resilience will automatically result much in the same way as a chain derives its overall strength from the strength of its constituent parts'.[60]

In operational terms, the obligations imposed by ASEAN's doctrine of non-interference on its members had four main aspects: (1) refraining from criticising the actions of a member government towards its own people, including violation of human rights, and from making the domestic political system of states and the political styles of governments a basis for deciding their membership in ASEAN; (2) criticising the actions of states which were deemed to have breached the non-interference principle; (3) denying recognition, sanctuary, or other forms of support to any rebel group seeking to destabilise or overthrow the government of a neighbouring state; (4) providing political support and material assistance to member states in their campaign against subversive and destabilising activities.

Several examples of the first aspect of non-interference in ASEAN may be found during the Cold War period. For example, deference to the principle of non-interference was a reason for ASEAN's refusal to address the genocidal acts of the Pol Pot regime during 1975–78[61] (although it should be remembered that Cambodia was not then a member of ASEAN). Another example was ASEAN's response to the 'People's Power' revolution in the Philippines in 1986. Its initial stance of ignoring the revolt against the Marcos regime was rooted in the doctrine of non-interference. Prior support for Marcos from fellow ASEAN members had included Indonesia's dispatch of military transport aircraft to help the regime fight communist insurgents. ASEAN did not cease its implicit support for Marcos until the dying stage of his regime, and only after strong international condemnation and the withdrawal of US support had stripped it of international legitimacy. It then issued only a mild expression of concern.[62] Subsequent examples of non-interference include ASEAN's non-response to the Thai military's crackdown on pro-democracy demonstrators in May 1992, its decision to admit Vietnam in July 1995 despite its communist political system and, more importantly, its approval of Burma's entry into ASEAN in July 1997 despite international concerns about the legitimacy of the regime (to be discussed in detail in Chapter 4).

The main example of the second aspect of ASEAN's non-interference doctrine can be found in its response to Vietnam's invasion of Cambodia in December 1978. ASEAN criticised the invasion as a serious violation of the doctrine. The invasion was especially galling to ASEAN which had earlier made conciliatory gestures towards Vietnam. It had tried to secure an acceptance of ASEAN's norms, only to be rebuffed by Hanoi. ASEAN foreign ministers, in their first collective response to the invasion, issued on 9 January 1979, urged all countries in the region to 'respect each other's independence, sovereignty, territorial integrity and political system' and to 'refrain . . . from interfering in each other's internal affairs, and from carrying out subversive activities, directly or indirectly, against each other'. What was significant about this statement was its explicit mention of the object to be protected, i.e. the 'political system' of another country, in addition to its national sovereignty and territorial integrity, as well as the identification of the type of activity that it considered as interference, namely 'subversive activities, directly or indirectly'.

The third obligation imposed by ASEAN's non-interference policy on its members was the denial of sanctuary and support to rebels fighting the central authority of a member state. The origin of this policy was rooted in a concern that the transboundary movement of insurgents could become a major source of interstate tension, as reflected in the strained relations between Malaysia and Thailand over the activities of the Communist Party of Malaya (CPM) and Muslim separatists in southern Thailand. (It is worth noting that the hostile attitude of the governments of the Philippines and Malaysia to NGO-sponsored conferences on East Timor in their respective territories provides a post-Cold War example of the continued reluctance of ASEAN states to provide a platform to the dissidents and critics of the governments of fellow members.) While ethnic separatists and rebel groups from Burma, Laos and Cambodia have found sanctuary in Thai territory (with varying degrees of knowledge and connivance of the authorities in Bangkok), Thailand proved to be less tolerant of insurgencies against fellow ASEAN members, such as Malaysia, notwithstanding past Malaysian allegations regarding an allegedly 'soft' attitude by the Thai authorities toward CPM holdouts in southern Thailand. (With the admission of these three countries into ASEAN, the prospects for rebel groups from neighbouring states securing sanctuary inside Thailand are likely to be significantly diminished.)

As noted, the doctrine of non-interference in the context of ASEAN has not meant indifference to each other's domestic needs or strict impartiality in their domestic power struggles. It has meant that ASEAN members have been willing to provide assistance to help each other to counter threats to domestic stability, such as communist insurgency. Thailand, in an apparent willingness to compromise its sovereignty, had even been willing to grant Malaysia the right to engage in cross-border military incursions in 'hot pursuit' of communist guerrillas. As will be discussed in the following section, a series of intra-ASEAN bilateral border security arrangements against cross-border insurgencies, formal and informal extradition agreements, and a strict policy of not providing sanctuary to rebels from neighbouring states, especially between Indonesia, Malaysia and Singapore, attest to this practice of positive action in support of each other's domestic order. While Thailand provided sanctuary to rebels fighting non-ASEAN members such as Burma, Cambodia and Laos before they joined ASEAN, it was less tolerant of insurgencies against ASEAN member Malaysia (although this did not prevent periodic Malaysian complaints about Thai toleration of communist insurgents challenging the Malaysian state).

Moreover, ASEAN's support for regimes threatened from within took political as well as material forms. This was evident from its backing for President Aquino in the Philippines. If ASEAN was slow to recognise the inevitable in Marcos' Philippines out of loyalty to the principle of non-interference (and possibly to a founding member of ASEAN), it was firm in throwing its weight behind Mrs Aquino as she struggled with challenges posed by the communists on the one hand and disgruntled military officers on the other. The decision by all ASEAN leaders to attend the Manila summit in December 1987 despite serious security concerns was celebrated by the media and ASEAN officialdom as a clear endorsement of President Aquino as well as a show of ASEAN solidarity. As Philippine Foreign Secretary Raul Manglapus noted,

> [t]he very holding of the meeting itself . . . is the supreme achievement of the hour . . . they [the ASEAN heads of government] came here in spite of advice from security persons and in spite perhaps, even of their own instincts, in a magnificent show of resolve.[63]

The episode demonstrated ASEAN's support for a member regime *vis-à-vis* its internal enemies.[64]

No military pacts and preference for bilateral defence cooperation

Speculation concerning the question whether ASEAN would include a military arrangement greeted the very birth of the association. At the founding Bangkok meeting, Indonesia's Foreign Minister, Adam Malik had said: 'Indonesia always wanted to see South East Asia develop into a region which could stand on its own feet, strong enough to defend itself against any negative influences from outside the region.' This was seen in diplomatic circles as an indication of Indonesia's desire to add a 'defence element' to ASEAN.[65] But Tun Razak, the Malaysian Foreign Minister, saw no immediate prospect for an ASEAN defence arrangement, although he thought such arrangements were possible 'once we have become good friends with a common interest and destiny'.[66] A few days after the grouping's founding, the Philippines Foreign Minister, Narciso Ramos, rejected any collective security or defence role for ASEAN.

> There is no obligation on the part of any Asian member state to go to the aid of another member state in cases of outside intervention; neither is there any intention or commitment for the Asian states to 'share' in the responsibility of resisting foreign intervention. Each state must look after its own security. (sic)[67]

A visit by President Marcos to Jakarta in January 1968 led to renewed media and diplomatic speculation regarding an ASEAN defence arrangement. More importantly, an interview given by Indonesia's leader Suharto (then as Acting President) to a Japanese newspaper on 3 March 1968 was interpreted as an indication that ASEAN should develop military cooperation. Malaysia's Tun Razak even 'welcomed' this remark, but Indonesian officials promptly disclaimed the report of Jakarta leading any effort to develop ASEAN into a military arrangement.[68]

In truth, Indonesia at this stage was opposed to conventional defence cooperation within the ASEAN framework, although it wanted ASEAN to deal with security issues, broadly defined.[69] Aside from the 'Indonesian dislike of being drawn into any kind of regional defensive grouping' (thanks partly to the lingering effects of Indonesia's earlier opposition to SEATO in the lead-up to the Bandung Conference), this posture recognised the need to prevent the Soviet Union and its allies, especially North Vietnam, from attacking ASEAN as a 'new and more flexible alliance designed to supplement S.E.A.T.O.'[70] The pro-Western outlook of ASEAN members and existing defence ties between individual ASEAN members and the Western powers (such as the US–Thailand and US–Philippines alliances, and the Britain–Australia–New Zealand–Malaysia–Singapore Five Power Defence Arrangements) were conspicuous. In the circumstances, ASEAN members were worried that even if an intra-ASEAN military pact could be formed without directly involving any outside Western power, it would still invite the wrath of the communist powers.

Singapore would go further, unwilling to stress even a political and security role for ASEAN. The city-state wished ASEAN to focus on economic problems, which in its view would exhaust ASEAN's limited resources.[71] Underpinning this position was the republic's faith in the security umbrella of the Great Powers, the UK and USA.

The growing US debacle in Indochina and the approaching Bali summit seemed to provoke a change in the Indonesian attitude towards defence cooperation. In the course of preparations for the first ASEAN summit in Bali in 1976, an Indonesian study paper suggested the formation of a 'joint council' for defence cooperation and the holding of joint military exercises among the ASEAN states.[72] But this idea was discarded by the leaders at the summit. The Prime Minister of Malaysia, Hussein Onn, stated at Bali:

> It is obvious that the ASEAN members do not wish to change the character of ASEAN from a socio-economic organisation into a security alliance as this would only create misunderstanding in the region and undermine the positive achievements of ASEAN in promoting peace and stability through co-operation in the socio-economic and related fields.[73]

While rejecting formal multilateral defence cooperation, the ASEAN leaders did, within the framework of the Declaration of ASEAN Concord signed at the Bali summit, express their approval for the 'continuation of cooperation on a non-ASEAN basis between the member states in security matters in accordance with their mutual needs and interests'. This constituted an endorsement of bilateral border security arrangements and intelligence sharing that had already developed among ASEAN states. For ASEAN members, bilateralism offered several advantages over a formal multilateral alliance system. Mohamad Ghazali Shafie, Foreign Minister of Malaysia, provided the following rationale for bilateralism:

> projects under ASEAN (and other regional bodies) are generally limited in scope and necessarily restricted to the lowest common denominator which is acceptable to all member countries. . . . The limitation of regional cooperation within a formal framework should not prevent countries of the region from trying to forge the closest possible links on a bilateral basis with one another. It may be, for example, that country X would be willing to establish such links on specific subjects and would be prepared to engage in consultations including exchange of information, etc, with country Y which she might

not consider either appropriate or necessary to have with some other third country on a multilateral basis. Such bilateral contacts on any subject and at whatever level which may be mutually acceptable should be pursued as far as possible. In this way, an important criss-crossing network of bilateral links will be established between and among the countries of Southeast Asia. . . . In pursuance of this policy, Malaysia has . . . entered into close bilateral economic/cultural and security/military arrangements with a number of countries in the region. Malaysia's joint border operations with Thailand in the Thai/ Malaysian boundary and with Indonesia on the Sarawak/Kalimantan border of East Malaysia as well as cooperation with Singapore in the context of the Five Power Defence Arrangement, are cases in point in the field of security and defence.[74]

Security cooperation between Malaysia and Thailand to suppress communist insurgency along their common border had been in train since the 1950s. A similar agreement to control border movement was signed between Indonesia and the Philippines in 1964. After the end of hostilities between Indonesia and Malaysia, the two countries entered into active cooperation involving their land, air and naval forces to curb communist insurgency as well as piracy and smuggling along their common border. These bilateral security arrangements expanded in scope following the establishment of ASEAN. A new security agreement between Malaysia and Thailand, signed in 1970, provided for combined operation as well as 'hot pursuit' of insurgents into each other's territory. Similar joint operations against communist insurgents were carried out by Indonesia and Malaysia in 1971. Although ASEAN states deliberated over the need for a multilateral security arrangement against communist subversion (such a move was proposed by President Marcos of the Philippines), bilateral and multilateral intelligence exchanges on the activities of communist and other political opposition groups had become a regular practice by the time of the Bali summit in 1976. The general nervousness felt by ASEAN regimes about their own domestic position in the aftermath of the communist takeover in South Vietnam led to the expansion of such bilateral ties, but not to multilateral defence links.

Moreover, ASEAN's rejection of a military pact was maintained in response to the emergence of a strong Soviet–Vietnamese security partnership and a Soviet naval presence in the region in the early 1980s. Alarmed by the Soviet move, Lee Kuan Yew called for multilateral military exercises among the ASEAN members.[75] Thailand opposed the move.[76] Indonesia also rejected the Lee proposal while reiterating its view that existing bilateral linkages among ASEAN states were sufficient to deal with the emerging security threats and any multilateral exercises, which would be provocative to the 'other side'.[77]

The conscious decision by ASEAN's founders that it should not deal with military issues and that security cooperation should be undertaken only on a bilateral basis had a major impact on ASEAN's ability to manage intra-mural conflict. Many of the intra-ASEAN bilateral security agreements were geared to managing border security problems. As Mohamad Ghazali Shafie put it, the ASEAN countries were wise to create 'mechanisms or apparatus . . . to resolve border problems locally and not at the capitals which would turn a pimple into a boil due to undue publicity'.[78] In this sense, bilateral security cooperation in ASEAN served as a basic building block of multilateralism. Although ASEAN would later organise some forms of defence and security dialogues and cooperation, these are mainly examples of defence diplomacy, rather than operational planning and activities geared to deterring and defeating a common external enemy (one state or more states), which is the hallmark of a military alliance. For example, under the ASEAN Political-Security Community framework, ASEAN instituted a formal meeting of its defence ministers (called

ASEAN Defence Ministers Meeting or ADMM) in 2006, but this or other intra-ASEAN meetings of intelligence, counter-terrorism, police and other security officials are mainly geared to information-sharing and joint measures against non-state (non-traditional or transnational) challenges such as piracy and terrorism and building intra-mural military confidence. They do not constitute a violation of the ASEAN norms of avoiding an intra-mural military pact or alliance in the traditional sense.

ASEAN's social-cultural norms: the 'ASEAN Way' in historical perspective

The 'ASEAN Way' is a term favoured by ASEAN's leaders themselves to describe the process of intra-mural interaction and to distinguish it from other, especially Western, multilateral settings. It is a loosely used concept whose meaning remains vague and contested. Speaking at the height of regional economic crisis three decades after the formation of ASEAN, Singapore's Foreign Minister S. Jayakumar outlined the principles that are considered to be integral to the ASEAN Way. In his words, 'the Asean Way stresses informality, organization minimalism, inclusiveness, intensive consultations leading to consensus and peaceful resolution of disputes'.[79] But other ASEAN leaders and scholars take a broader or narrower view of the term.[80] Moreover, there is considerable room for doubt whether it has been upheld in practice. The ASEAN Way has been criticised as rhetoric and hyperbole that ASEAN officials indulge in defensively to deflect attention from the grouping's shortcomings in ensuring more substantive cooperation. It would be a fair assertion that while the ASEAN Way, especially the elements that refer to informalism and ad hocism, might have been true of intra-mural interactions during ASEAN's formative years, it has been somewhat diluted in later years, especially in the 1990s. Moreover, it has been especially discredited following the outbreak of the regional economic crisis in 1997. With these caveats, however, the concept needs to be examined critically and in its historical context, as it provides an important part of the debates about Southeast Asian regionalism.

The origin of the term is obscure. Some of its early usages implied the close interpersonal ties among the ASEAN leaders. General Ali Moertopo, a senior intelligence official of Indonesia, was one of the first policymakers in ASEAN to have used the term, when, in 1974, he argued that the success of ASEAN was due to 'the system of consultations that has marked much of its work, what I may call the ASEAN Way of dealing with a variety of problems confronting its member nations'.[81] He ascribed the ASEAN Way to 'the fact that most of the leaders representing the ASEAN member countries for the past seven years or more of its existence have mostly been old friends who know one another so well'.[82] Moertopo went on to criticise such an excessively personal approach ('we cannot continue to rely on such a situation that cannot be possibly maintained over a long period of time') and called for 'efforts . . . towards further institutionalisation of regionalism in Southeast Asia'.[83] Ironically, the basis for Moertopo's criticism was subsequently recognised as a major strength of ASEAN.

Some scholars and policymakers viewed the ASEAN Way as a by-product of cultural similarities among the ASEAN societies. Malaysia's former Foreign Minister, Mohamad Ghazali Shafie, argued that 'our common cultural heritage', especially the *kampung* (village) spirit of 'togetherness', not only was a key factor behind secret Malaysia–Indonesia negotiations to end *Konfrontasi*, but also formed the basis of the establishment of ASEAN.[84] Estrella Solidum, a Philippine scholar who is perhaps the first academic seriously to investigate the term, asserted that the ASEAN Way 'consists of cultural elements which are found to be congruent with some values of each of the member states'.[85] In reality, however, the 'cultural' underpinnings of the ASEAN Way of managing disputes and advancing security cooperation could be overstated. Several elements of the ASEAN Way are hardly different from the ordinary qualities of pragmatism and flexibility that are found in national decision-making styles in other cultural settings. Moreover, the so-called cultural underpinnings of the ASEAN Way are not fixed or static, but have been subject to continuous adjustment in response to national, regional and global developments.

The ASEAN Way is usually described as a decision-making process that features a high degree of consultation and consensus. It is a claim about the *process* of regional interactions and cooperation based on discreteness, informality, consensus building and non-confrontational bargaining styles which are often contrasted with the adversarial posturing, majority vote and other legalistic decision-making procedures in Western multilateral negotiations. Aspects of the ASEAN Way can be found in what Peter Boyce, an Australian scholar, once called the 'distinctive and novel' aspects of Southeast Asian styles and techniques of negotiations:

> (1) a disposition to favour summit meetings, especially through the 1960s [this underscores the highly elitist nature of the ASEAN decision-making process], (2) a recourse to *musyawarah* principles and concepts in the conduct of high level conferences, (3) a preference for concealed and often 'unofficial' preliminary transactions by special agents prior to formal ministerial conferences, (4) a preference for *ad hoc* rather than institutionalized practices, (5) an avoidance of judicial or arbitration machinery for the settlement of disputes, (6) readiness to accept mediation or good offices from friendly third parties in the region, and (7) a tendency of at least three ASEAN members [Malaysia, Indonesia and the Philippines] to use the recall of an envoy or down-grading of a mission as a diplomatic practice.[86]

Of the many attributes and elements of the ASEAN Way, two are of particular importance. The first is the preference for informality and a related aversion to institutionalisation of cooperation. The first ever summit of ASEAN leaders did not take place until eight years after the grouping's formation and there were only four summits in the first 25 years of ASEAN's existence. (From 1992, ASEAN began holding a formal summit every three years and from 1996, 'informal' summits were held in between the official summits.) Until the 1990s, the ASEAN Secretariat was kept very small, and its head was called the Secretary-General of the ASEAN Secretariat, rather than the Secretary-General of ASEAN. A former Secretary-General of the ASEAN Secretariat justified this situation by pointing out that it was 'economical not to have any kind of cumbersome and expensive bureaucratic body like the EEC commission'.[87] As ASEAN evolved, the value of close interpersonal contacts among senior government officials came to be increasingly recognised. Carlos Romulo, the Foreign Secretary of the Philippines, was believed to have said: 'I can pick up the telephone now and talk directly to Adam Malik [Indonesia's Foreign Minister] or Rajaratnam [Singapore's Foreign Minister]. We often find that private talks over breakfast prove more important than formal meetings.'[88] As for the latter, it was decided that most of the formal coordinating work in ASEAN would be handled by national ASEAN secretariats located within the foreign ministries of each member country, with the country hosting the annual ministerial meeting assuming the chair of the ASEAN Standing Committee.[89] Managed by the foreign ministers, this vehicle has remained the most active and regularised framework of consultations and decision making in ASEAN.

Explaining the rationale behind the informal setting of ASEAN, Malaysia's Prime Minister, Hussein Onn, observed at the 1976 Bali summit: 'ASEAN has been able to absorb national differences because it is a relatively informal organization without rigid rules of procedure and without elaborate structural machinery.'[90] For Mohamad Ghazalie Shafie of Malaysia, the very fact that the Bangkok Declaration was called a declaration and not a treaty (unlike the Treaty of Rome) was significant, because 'treaty presupposes lack of trust'. Moreover, the word 'association' was meant to differentiate ASEAN from an 'organisation' and thereby convey a sense of looseness and informality.[91] ASEAN's founders believed that such informality was necessary in view of the diversity of views and positions held by the ASEAN members. Agerico Lacanlale, a Philippine scholar, has pointed out that ASEAN's organisational set-up was

> flexible enough to accommodate a diversity of interests without causing the collapse of the organization . . . it is the reluctance to commit themselves to rigid rules of conduct that seems to have strengthened ASEAN. The less the member states feel bound by certain rules, the more willing they are to consult with one another and adopt a common position on common concerns. The fact that the coercive element in their collective conduct is minimized means that joint decisions are arrived at out of free choice and in the spirit of consensus and cooperation.[92]

The looseness and informality that marked ASEAN's formative years became less apparent in the 1980s and 1990s. A proliferation of ministerial and bureaucratic consultations has covered an expanding range of issue areas. There are now numerous ASEAN-related meetings involving ministers, senior officials and parliamentarians coordinating policies in areas ranging from environment, through shipping traffic, to tourism. Indeed, every year, the grouping holds over 200 official meetings under its auspices, a ritual that has become a serious drain on the limited resources of new members like Vietnam and Laos. This has led one analyst to argue: 'ASEAN today is one of the most extensively institutionalised regional associations', with further institutionalisation likely as a result of membership expansion.[93] Since 1995, as noted earlier, ASEAN summitry has become much more frequent. The Singapore summit in 1992 also decided to expand the secretariat, and upgrade the status of the Secretary-General to cabinet rank, with the office redesignated the Secretary-General of ASEAN.[94] Nonetheless, ASEAN has not developed an EU-style bureaucracy with supranational decision-making authority. The ASEAN Secretariat remains subordinate to national secretariats, and its work continues to be limited to economic and technical issues.

ASEAN has remained a loose and informal grouping in many other respects. J.N. Mak, a Malaysian analyst, once noted that the ASEAN dialogue process was 'unstructured, with no clear format for decision-making or implementation' and often lacks a formal agenda; issues are negotiated on an *ad hoc* basis 'as and when they arise'.[95] While this may be overstating the case (it is certainly no longer the case with ASEAN meetings), the proponents of the ASEAN Way continue to acknowledge the virtues of looseness and informality in raising 'the level of comfort' among interlocutors and creating a flexible decision-making environment. This has been especially important to the development of security dialogues and cooperation, not only within ASEAN, but also in the wider multilateral grouping in which ASEAN plays a crucial role, the ARF.

Rear Admiral R.M. Sunardi, a senior official in Indonesia's Defence Ministry under President Suharto, once contrasted the 'Southeast Asian way of enhancing security from that adopted by other sub-regions' of the world. As he saw it, security cooperation in most other cases would be 'framed in a formal structure' because informality would be 'considered improper for the sake of accountability'. He cited the example of confidence-building measures as a primary example of such a formal approach to security cooperation. Referring to the legalistic and mathematical nature of CBM regimes (which must be 'tabulated' and their 'implementation' schedule fixed in advance), Sunardi viewed them as being 'quite a new concept' in Southeast Asia. In his view, for Southeast Asians 'to have confidence in another party does not prescribe any tabulation of what should be done, let alone a fixed schedule for implementation (*sic*).'[96]

ASEAN's tendency to limit institutionalisation was particularly evident in the area of intra-ASEAN dispute settlement. As noted earlier, the very fact that the High Council provided under the Treaty of Amity and Cooperation would never be put to the test (although Indonesia did raise the prospect of its use for settling its dispute with Malaysia over the Sipadan and Ligitan Islands in 1995) has been justified by ASEAN officials not as a failure of regionalism,[97] but as a testimony to the ASEAN members' ability to avoid serious confrontation without resort to formal measures.[98] Indeed, in the mid-1980s, the head of a Malaysian think-tank pointed to 'the intangible but real "spirit" of ASEAN', in 'sublimating and diffusing conflicts as in actually resolving them'.[99] In reality, the High Council framework was at least premature. ASEAN remained, and remains, unwilling to put it to the test for formal internal dispute settlement, even as two intra-ASEAN bilateral disputes between Malaysia and Singapore and Malaysia and Indonesia are now being referred to the International Court of Justice for formal adjudication (as will be discussed in Chapter 5).

Some observers of ASEAN during the early stage of its evolution would note its tendency to emphasise the importance of 'process over the product'. At the fourth ASEAN Foreign Ministers Meeting in 1971, the British embassy in Manila wrote to the Foreign Office in London summarising the remarks of Carlos Romulo, the Foreign Minister of the Philippines, on the ASEAN approach:

> General Romulo summed up the significance of the past 3 or 4 years of work when he said that ASEAN projects had a dual purpose. While they were 'intended to meet some of the pressing problems of the region', they were 'also meant to initiate the process of building confidence in ourselves . . . to solve the region's problems'. Throughout the fourth ASEAN Foreign Ministers' annual meeting the dichotomy between practical possibility and long term aspiration has been apparent in each of the Ministers' statements. There were the usual references to fostering 'the spiritual values of ASEAN' and arriving at a 'moral consensus', thus inevitably inviting the cynical conclusion that ASEAN was inclined to feed on hogwash rather than substantial fare. Time alone will tell whether the cynical view is the more justified, but despite their differences the Ministers appear to have succeeded on this occasion in moving a few steps toward establishing the mutual confidence to which any future progress is inevitably tied.[100]

Next to informality and aversion to formal institutions, the ASEAN Way is characterised by the concept and practice of consensus building. As Singapore's Foreign Minister S. Dhanabalan put it in 1987: 'We have avoided the obvious danger of majority decision-making. . . . We have relied on the principle of consensus, which has stood us in good stead for almost two decades.'[101] Although consensus building is considered to be a common feature of decision making in many Asian societies, in the ASEAN context, the origin of the term is usually traced to a particular style of decision making within Javanese village society. This process has two related components: *musyawarah* (consultations) and *mufakat* (consensus).

As Herb Feith points out, decision making through *musyawarah* and *mufakat* is based on an understanding that

> a leader should not act arbitrarily or impose his will, but rather make gentle suggestions of the path a community should follow, being careful always to consult all other participants fully and to take their views and feelings into consideration before delivering his synthesis conclusions.[102]

Musyawarah may be viewed as a pre-negotiation stage of 'intensive informal and discreet discussions that in the end bring out the general consensus of the community'.[103] During this stage, differences can be aired and the possibility of common ground ascertained before the issues are submitted to more formal official meetings. As Hoang puts it, during the informal prenegotiations stage, 'new positions, proposals or initiatives are floated for extensive consultation . . . so as to make sure that consensus on major issues could be reached at later formal discussions or negotiations'. This practice, Hoang, adds, excludes 'the possibility of the majority imposing views on the minority'.[104]

In a related vein, two Filipino scholars define *musyawarah* as 'consultation on the basis of equality, tolerance and understanding with overtones of kinship and common interests'. In this view, *musyawarah* is a form of 'soft diplomacy as contrasted to sabre-rattling, gunboat diplomacy of the colonial and Big Power variety'.[105] Thus, an important aspect of the consensus-building process is the psychological setting of consultations, which must be non-hostile. Even before the formation of ASEAN, Indonesia's Foreign Minister, Dr Subiandro, had contended that negotiations in the *musyawarah* and *mufakat* would take place 'not as between opponents but as between friends and brothers'.[106] Mak Joon Num notes that in the ASEAN context, consensus means searching for 'an amalgamation of the most acceptable views of each and every member' in a socio-psychological setting in which 'all parties have power over each other'.[107] Sensitive handling of intra-mural differences is a hallmark of consensus building. While parties can debate and disagree on the merit of a particular position behind closed doors, they must refrain from airing these differences in public. Even in situations where ASEAN members find it impossible to arrive at a common position, they must speak and act as though a certain level of unity has been achieved on that particular issue. This means a tendency to play down or give a positive spin to intra-mural differences. A great deal of care must be taken not to isolate or embarrass any individual ASEAN member in international fora. Even when an ASEAN member has advanced a position that is not acceptable to other members, the latter will refrain from acting in ways that may make the member 'lose face' publicly.

The idea of consensus is not an abstract notion, but was conceived as a pragmatic way of advancing regional economic and political cooperation in Southeast Asia. For example, the concept was initially applied to overcome hesitancy and indifference among the ASEAN members towards intra-ASEAN economic cooperation, including ASEAN industrial joint ventures and tariff reductions. As Lee Kuan Yew observed in the context of ASEAN economic cooperation (at a time when ASEAN consisted of only five members: Indonesia, Malaysia, Thailand, the Philippines and Singapore): 'When four agree [to a certain scheme] and one does not, this can still be considered as consensus and the five-minus-one scheme can benefit the participating four without damaging the remaining one.'[108] In this context, consensus building was seen as a way of advancing regional cooperation schemes despite the reluctance of some of the members to participate in them. Lee Kuan Yew described the process in the following terms:

> So long as members who are not yet ready to participate are not damaged by non-participation, nor excluded from future participation, the power of veto need not be exercised . . . when four agree and one does not object, this can still be considered a consensus, and the four should proceed with a new regional scheme.[109]

Consensus as understood in the ASEAN context is not to be confused with unanimity. Rather, it represents a commitment to finding a 'way of moving forward by establishing what seems to have broad support'.[110] In a consensus situation, 'not everyone would always be comfortable', but they tend to 'go along so long as their basic interests were not disregarded'.[111] Although the understanding that consensus need not involve unanimity imparts a great degree of flexibility to decision making at the national and international level, it is also clear that ASEAN-style consensus may be of limited effectiveness in dealing with issues that engage fundamental national interests, including issues of sovereignty and territorial integrity. As a former Secretary-General of the ASEAN Secretariat put it, '[t]he principle of consensus in decision making is a safety device to assure member states that their national interests will not be compromised and nothing can be done against their will'.[112] Moreover, a consensus approach runs the risk of becoming 'a process of determining the realistically achievable objectives given the limits imposed by each member-country's interests'.[113] Bilson Kurus argues that ASEAN's practice of consensus means that 'each and every action taken in the name of ASEAN must either contribute to or be neutral, but not detract from, the perceived national interests of the individual ASEAN member states'.[114] In this sense, the ASEAN Way may be described as a pragmatic and highly deliberate attempt to gloss over national differences that could not be reconciled within a multilateral framework.

In its Javanese conception, the art of forging a consensus requires the strong guiding hand of a village elder. This leads to the question whether, at the regional level, such leadership could be available or desirable.[115] Finally, the ASEAN Way has been criticised for creating a tendency to filter out or exclude contentious issues from the formal multilateral agenda.[116] It is geared more towards conflict avoidance rather than conflict resolution and has led to conflicts being 'swept under the carpet'.[117] This may be helpful in distracting attention from a dispute and buying more time for its final settlement, but critics have found it to be of limited value as conflicts may reappear in the future.

The consensus approach stresses the need for a non-threatening multilateral setting, guided by a shared commitment to moderation and accommodation. This may create enough goodwill among the participants to encourage self-restrained political and military behaviour, based on 'feelings of brotherhood and kinship'.[118] ASEAN's practice of not bringing sensitive issues to the multilateral agenda does not mean that multilateralism has been irrelevant to conflict resolution. It means that multilateralism was viewed by its members not as a legal or formal framework for interactions, but as creating a conducive socio-psychological setting for intra-mural problem solving. Jorgensen-Dahl captures this aspect of ASEAN multilateralism:

> ASEAN served a useful purpose by providing a framework within which the parties could discuss their differences in a 'neutral' atmosphere. . . . The multilateral framework allowed the parties to remain in contact in circumstances which either had caused a collapse of bilateral channels or placed these channels under such stress that they could

no longer function properly. . . . Through the steadily increasing scope and range of its activities . . . it produced among government officials of the five, attitudes which were much more receptive and sensitive to each other's peculiar problems, and which made compromise solutions to conflicting interests a much more likely outcome than before . . . the multilateral setting served to discourage extreme behaviour, modify extravagant demands, and inspire compromise.[119]

The avoidance of sensitive issues on the multilateral agenda by the ASEAN members was also partly due to a recognition that such issues were better dealt with at the bilateral level. Thus, throughout the existence of ASEAN, many issues that are deemed too complicated and sensitive to be placed on the multilateral agenda have been deliberately left to bilateral channels. (As will be discussed in Chapter 5, some ASEAN members opposed a policy of 'flexible engagement', or open discussion of sensitive domestic and bilateral issues at the ASEAN level, on the grounds that this would lead to escalation and internationalisation of tensions.) While Western theories of multilateralism have viewed the two as mutually incompatible, in the case of ASEAN, bilateralism has served as a basic building block of multilateralism.

Norms and identity in ASEAN's evolution

Norms clearly had a major impact on the making of ASEAN regionalism. Speaking in 1985, Musa Hitam, a former Deputy Prime Minister of Malaysia, argued:

> Because of Asean, we have been able to establish the fundamental ground rules for the game of peace and amity between us all. What are these fundamental ground rules? First, the principle of strict non-interference in each other's internal affairs. Second, the principle of pacific settlement of disputes. Third, respect for each other's independence. Fourth, strict respect for the territorial integrity of each of the Asean states. . . . The Asean states have declared these ground rules . . . we have enacted them, we have imbibed them, and most important, we have acted and lived by them.[120]

Norms also played a central role in the development of a nascent regional identity sought by ASEAN. Identity had been a concern of Southeast Asian leaders even before the creation of ASEAN. While some of the leaders of the countries that eventually formed ASEAN did take part in efforts to develop pan-Asian unity undertaken by Prime Minister Nehru of India, or Afro-Asian unity championed by President Sukarno of Indonesia, they also believed that Southeast Asia should have a distinctive place in the Asian regional order and therefore an identity of its own.[121] The idea of a distinctively Southeast Asian grouping had been raised by Aung San of Burma before his assassination in July 1947.[122] The creation of ASEAN reflected a new quest for regional identity building. The Declaration of ASEAN Concord adopted at ASEAN's first ever summit, held in Bali in 1976, urged member states to 'vigorously develop an awareness of regional identity and exert all efforts to create a strong ASEAN community'.[123] Similarly, while the ASEAN Bangkok Declaration of 1967 had assured its members that the grouping would 'preserve their national identities', at the same meeting Foreign Minister S. Rajaratnam of Singapore had urged that

> It is necessary for us, if we are really to be successful in giving life to ASEAN, to marry national thinking with regional thinking [and] we must also accept the fact, if we are really serious about it, that regional existence means painful adjustments.[124]

Rajaratnam's words would indicate an interest on the part of ASEAN's founders to develop an important aspect of community building, what Solidum would later call 'the growth of regional ways of thinking, doing and valuing'.[125]

While identity is sometimes thought of in terms of its traditional cultural roots, it may be argued that the concept of an ASEAN identity was to be derived substantively from its socialisation process. The ASEAN Way itself resulted not so much from preordained cultural sources, Javanese or otherwise, but from incremental socialisation. It emerged not only from the principles of interstate relations agreed to by the founders of ASEAN, but also from a subsequent and long-term process of interaction and adjustment. Thus, in the case of ASEAN, it was not so much that culture created norms, norms also created culture. As Malaysia's Foreign Minister, Abdullah Badawi, would put it later, ASEAN's 'norms have become very much part of the ASEAN culture'.[126] Among these norms were both legal-rational and socio-cultural varieties, the latter including those associated with the ASEAN Way.

Yet, as noted earlier, the norms of ASEAN, including those associated with the ASEAN Way, were not always upheld in practice. As discussed in subsequent chapters, there would be several instances where individual ASEAN members failed to consult their fellow members. Moreover, the practice of consensus seeking would not always produce decisions and agreements acceptable to all members. Although the features of the ASEAN Way might have been crucial in the formative years, where a common fear of domestic insurgency and Vietnamese expansionism helped shape intra-ASEAN unity, they became less important later as the challenges to regional stability have become much more complex and indeterminate. Intra-ASEAN interactions have become progressively more regularised with frequent summits and a large number of regular meetings over a broad range of functional issues. There would be a tendency towards legalism in ASEAN and a willingness to resort to formal procedures, evident in the decision of members to resort to international judicial arbitration to settle their bilateral disputes in the 1990s. With the expansion of its membership, ASEAN would face additional uncertainty as to whether the new members could be socialised into the ASEAN Way.

Many of these difficulties faced by ASEAN in ensuring compliance with its norms and developing common approaches to regional problems would be evident in its handling of Vietnam's invasion and occupation of Cambodia on 25 December 1978. The event not only represented the most serious threat to regional order that AESAN was trying to manage, it also severely tested ASEAN's unity and purpose, as the examination of ASEAN's response to the Cambodia conflict in the next chapter will show.

Notes and references

1 The founding meeting was actually held in two places, the first phase being held in the resort town of Bangsaen, two hours drive from Bangkok, before the ministers moved to Bangkok for issuing the final declaration. Bangsaen was a venue 'with a convenient golf-course, at which emphasis was on ease and informality – "sports-shirt diplomacy"', which would become a hallmark of the ASEAN process. 'Association of South East Asian Nations', Telegram from UK Embassy in Bangkok to Foreign and Commonwealth Office, 11 August 1967 (included in Memorandum for Foreign Office and Whitehall Distribution 15 August 1967), FCO 15/23 (Public Records Office, National Archives).

2 Sopiee mentions four key rules: (1) 'system-wide acceptance of the principle of the pacific settlement of disputes'; (2) 'non-interference and non-intervention in the domestic affairs of member states'; (3) 'respect for each other's territorial integrity and independence'; and (4) 'the principle of not inviting external intervention on one's behalf in the pursuit of disputes'. Noordin

Sopiee, 'ASEAN and Regional Security', in Mohammed Ayoob (ed.), *Regional Security in the Third World* (London: Croom Helm, 1986), p. 229.

3   Jurgen Haacke, *ASEAN's Diplomatic and Security Culture* (London: Routledge, 2002), p. 19.

4   During the drafting of the UN's Charter at the San Francisco conference, the so-called 'universalists', led by the USA, viewed regional arrangements as a potential impediment to the realisation of a universal collective security system. The 'regionalists' (including delegates from Latin America and the Middle East), on the other hand, argued that regional organisations would have a better understanding of threats to peace and stability in their own areas and would be in a better position to intervene in such situations than the distant UN bureaucracy. They also pointed out that investing exclusive authority for settlement of international disputes in the Security Council would amount to 'denying permission to small states in regional groupings the chief responsibility for their own security'. Lynn H. Miller, 'The Prospect for Order through Regional Security', in Richard A. Falk and Saul H. Mendlovitz (eds), *Regional Politics and World Order* (San Francisco: W. H. Freeman, 1973), p. 5. The outcome of this debate was a compromise in which regional organisations were allowed a role in managing peace and security issues, albeit subject to the overall authority and jurisdiction of the UN. Thus the UN Charter listed mediation by regional agencies as one of the techniques of international conflict control (Article 33/1, Chapter VI), while UN members were encouraged to 'make every effort to achieve pacific settlement of local disputes through such regional arrangements' (Article 52/2, Chapter VIII), before taking up the matter with the Security Council. For analyses of the universalist and regionalist positions, see: Minerva Etzioni, *The Majority of One: Towards a Theory of Regional Compatibility* (Beverly Hills, CA: Sage, 1970).

5   For an analysis of the Third World norms concerning military alliances involving the superpowers, see: Amitav Acharya, 'Developing Countries and the Emerging World Order: Security and Institutions', in Louise Fawcett and Yezid Sayigh (eds), *The Third World beyond the Cold War* (Oxford: Oxford University Press, 1999), pp. 78–98.

6   J. Soedjati Djiwandono, 'The Political and Security Aspects of ASEAN: Its Principal Achievements,' *Indonesian Quarterly*, vol. 11 (July 1983), p. 20.

7   Indonesia had intelligence about five other camps, in addition to the one at Corregidor. I.W. Mackey to Mr O'Keeffe, 28 August 1968, FCO 24/341 (London: Public Records Office).

8   After the talks between Malaysia and the Philippines in Bangkok broke down, 'there was considerable apprehension in Djakarta that the dispute would be carried over into the ASEAN Meeting'. 'ASEAN: The Second Ministerial Meeting', Foreign Office and Whitehall Distribution, 19 August 1968, FCO 24/341 (London: Public Records Office).

9   'Although the Indonesian Government continues to maintain a neutral stance in public, in private Malik and other leaders are increasingly impatient of the Filipino attitude.' 'ASEAN: The Second Ministerial Meeting', Foreign Office and Whitehall Distribution, 19 August 1968, FCO 24/341 (London: Public Records Office).

10   I.W. Mackey to Mr O'Keeffe, 28 August 1968, FCO 15/23 (London: Public Records Office).

11   'ASEAN: The Second Ministerial Meeting', Foreign Office and Whitehall Distribution, 19 August 1968, FCO 24/341 (London: Public Records Office).

12   I.W. Mackey to Mr O'Keeffe, 28 August 1968, FCO 15/23 (London: Public Records Office).

13   'Malaysian Statements on ASEAN', Addendum to 'ASEAN as seen from Kuala Lumpur', 14 February 1969, FCO 24/341 (London: Public Records Office).

14   'Malaysian Statements on ASEAN', Addendum to 'ASEAN as seen from Kuala Lumpur', 14 February 1969, FCO 24/341 (London: Public Records Office). This Malaysian position was confirmed by an assessment of the situation in February 1969 by the High Commissioner of New Zealand to Malaysia: 'Malaysia regarded ASEAN as important . . . there was no question of withdrawing from it – and hoped that it would develop and flourish.' The High Commissioner himself expressed 'doubt whether any of its members, including of course Malaysia, would pursue a national interest to the point where there was a real danger that ASEAN would disintegrate'. While 'The Philippines' claim to Sabah has become a hindrance to the progress of ASEAN,' he suggested, 'the question of Malaysia's withdrawal from the organization because of this [Sabah] did not arise at all. Malaysia has pledged its stand on regional cooperation and is determined to see that the Bangkok Declaration of 1967 will be upheld . . .' As a result of the Sabah crisis, he concluded, 'ASEAN is not so much moribund as on ice.' New Zealand's High Commissioner in Kuala Lumpur wrote to the Secretary of External Affairs in Wellington, copy to: London, Washington, Canberra, Jakarta, Bangkok, Tokyo, Hong Kong, Saigon and Singapore, 'ASEAN as seen from Kuala Lumpur', 14 February 1969, FCO 24/341 (London: Public Records Office).

15 'ASEAN as seen from Kuala Lumpur', 14 February 1969, FCO 24/341 (London: Public Records Office).
16 'Malaysian Statements on ASEAN', Addendum to 'ASEAN as seen from Kuala Lumpur', 14 February 1969, FCO 24/341 (London: Public Records Office).
17 'Malaysia, Philippines and ASEAN', British High Commission in Kuala Lumpur to South West Pacific Department, FCO, 14 March 1969, FCO 24/341 (London: Public Records Office).
18 The British felt that 'the Malaysians have now been persuaded' by the Indonesians to take some steps both through ASEAN and bilaterally, and this has caused 'a break with the previously rigid Malaysian position'. 'Malaysia, Philippines and ASEAN', British High Commission in Kuala Lumpur to South West Pacific Department, FCO, 14 March 1969, FCO 24/341 (London: Public Records Office).
19 Mr H.C. Hainworth in Jakarta to the Foreign and Commonwealth Office, London, 30 August 1968, FCO 15/23 (London: Public Records Office).
20 Text of Kuala Lumpur Declaration of 27 November 1971, p. 90.
21 *ASEAN*, 2nd edition (Jakarta: ASEAN Secretariat, 1975), p. 65.
22 Adam Malik, 'Regional Cooperation in International Politics', in *Regionalism in Southeast Asia* (Jakarta: Centre for Strategic and International Studies, 1975), p. 160.
23 A British document of 1969 suggests that for Indonesia, 'Burma, Cambodia and Ceylon would still be very welcome members of the Association.' Vietnam was also 'mentioned in this connection, but not so frequently, and it is not clear which part is referred to'. British Embassy in Jakarta to Foreign and Commonwealth Office, London, 'ASEAN', 8 July 1969, FCO 24/341.
24 In the words of a British assessment of the second ASEAN Ministerial Meeting in Jakarta on 6–7 August, 'Indonesians are likely to continue to be lukewarm in their support for [ASPAC] in which they see the Japanese likely to play the dominating role.' 'ASEAN: The Second Ministerial Meeting', Foreign Office and Whitehall Distribution, 19 August 1968, FCO 24/341.
25 British Embassy in Tokyo to SEAD/FCO, 25 October 1973, FCO 15/1727.
26 British Embassy in Tokyo to SEAD/FCO, 29 November 1973, FCO 15/1727.
27 British Embassy in Tokyo to SWPD, FCO, 26 April 1973, FCO 15/1727.
28 According to a dispatch of the Commonwealth Office, London, based on discussions with the Indian Political First Secretary in London (a Mr Vahali), the Indians 'felt they could make a real contribution'. As a start, India could provide access to its extensive training facilities which were already provided to Southeast Asian countries under the Colombo Plan. India was more interested in a regional association with a 'fairly wide ranging association', stretching from Pakistan to Japan, than a narrower one.
29 The Japanese in particular seemed to have indulged in 'anti-Indian manoeuvres' to deny India a place in the Japanese-led Ministerial Conference for the Economic Development of South East Asia (SEAMCD). The British felt that 'in the long term, India might play a useful role in the development of both economic and political stability in South-East Asia'. 'Even in the shorter run', Indian economic contribution, 'though small, would have an important psychological impact on other developing countries in the region.' Hence in the British view, 'Indian interest in regional co-operation should be encouraged rather than discouraged.' Foreign and Commonwealth Office, London, to British High Commission in New Delhi, 29 April 1968, FCO 15/23 (London: Public Records Office).
30 Commenting on Indonesia's lack of interest in India's membership, the British Embassy in Jakarta noted: 'the unexpressed reason may be that the entry of India into the Association would constitute a challenge to Indonesia's tacitly recognized leadership of it.' British Embassy in Jakarta to Foreign and Commonwealth Office, London, 'ASEAN', 8 July 1969, FCO 24/341.
31 Michael Leifer, *The ASEAN Regional Forum*, Adelphi Paper 302 (London: International Institute for Strategic Studies, 1996), p. 10.
32 Michael Leifer, *ASEAN's Search for Regional Order*, Faculty Lecture 12 (Faculty of Arts and Social Sciences, Singapore: National University of Singapore, 1987), p. 7.
33 Lee Kuan Yew quoted in *Straits Times*, 11 May 1975.
34 *Straits Times*, 7 February 1976.
35 *Sunday Times* (Singapore), 18 March 1978.
36 Adam Malik, 'Regional Cooperation in International Politics', in *Regionalism in Southeast Asia* (Jakarta: CSIS, 1975), pp. 162–63.
37 Statement at the Second ASEAN Ministerial Meeting, Jakarta, 6 August 1968, cited in Thakur Phanit, 'Regional Integration Attempts in Southeast Asia: A Study of ASEAN's Problems and Progress' (Ph.D. dissertation, Pennsylvania State University, 1980), pp. 32–3.

38   Adam Malik, 'Djakarta Conference and Asia's Political Future', *Pacific Community*, vol. 2, no. 1 (October 1970), p. 74.

39   Ghazali Shafie, 'ASEAN's Response to Security Issues in Southeast Asia,' in *Regionalism in Southeast Asia* (Jakarta: CSIS, 1975), p. 23.

40   George McT. Kahin, 'The Role of the United States in Southeast Asia', in Lau Teik Soon (ed.), *New Directions in the International Relations of Southeast Asia* (Singapore: Singapore University Press, 1973), p. 77.

41   Mohamad Ghazali Shafie, 'The Neutralisation of Southeast Asia', *Pacific Community* (October 1971).

42   The British Embassy in Manila summed up the reaction of fellow ASEAN members to Malaysia's neutralisation proposal in the following words:

> Malaysian proposals for the neutralization of ASEAN area, to be guaranteed by the US, the USSR and China, evoked among the other members a reaction rather like that of St. Augustine on chastity: 'Lord, neutralize us, but not yet.' Mr. Thanat, whilst paying lip service to its ultimate desirability, referred to the fate of Belgium: President Marcos said that the concept would take decades rather than years to realize and reaffirmed in another context that the American umbrella was necessary for the security of the smaller Asian powers. The consensus which seems to have emerged was that it was pointless to pursue neutralization until the conflict in Indo-China, which figured prominently in the Ministers' opening speeches as well as in their private discussions, had been resolved. It was meanwhile imperative for members of ASEAN to develop a sense of regional consciousness (Tun Ismail) and 'sound, stable and dynamic national economies' (Rajaratnam). Regional projects were naturally based on 'the lowest common factor' and did little to stir the imagination, but each step forward involved contact and communication at the official level which engendered habits of co-operation and a sense of common purpose.

British Embassy in Manila to The Right Honourable Sir Alec Douglas, 'The Fourth Meeting of the Foreign Ministers of the Association of South East Asian Nations (ASEAN)', 22 March 1971 (London: Public Records Office).

43   'Neutralisation: The Malaysian View', British High Commission in Kuala Lumpur to South West Pacific Department, Foreign and Commonwealth Office, London, 25 July 1972. FCO 24/1269 (London: Public Records Office). This document was based on a confidential meeting between the Malaysian official in charge of neutralisation, Bertie Talalla, and a group of British, Australian and New Zealand diplomatic officials.

44   Ibid.

45   Michael Leifer, *Dictionary of the Modern Politics of South-East Asia* (London: Routledge, 1995), p. 260.

46   'Neutralisation of South East Asia', British High Commission in Kuala Lumpur to South West Pacific Department, FCO, 29 March 1972, FCO 24/1269.

47   The other ASEAN members 'were somewhat taken aback with what they considered a rather premature approach and apparently were not willing to discuss the paper in detail'. 'Neutralisation', British High Commission in Kuala Lumpur to South West Pacific Department, FCO, 18 July 1972 (FCO 24/1269).

48   'Neutralisation', British High Commission in Kuala Lumpur to South West Pacific Department, FCO, 18 July 1972 (FCO 24/1269).

49   Overall, 'the meeting was something of a wrangle and was not repeat not productive'. 'Neutralisation: Officials' Meeting', Telegram from British High Commission in Kuala Lumpur to South West Pacific Department, FCO, 11 July 1972 (FCO 24/1269).

50   Indonesians had gone to the meeting with the position, conveyed to the British diplomat in Jakarta on 4 July 1972, that neutralisation under Great Power guarantee would be 'wholly unacceptable to Indonesia under present world circumstances'. Indonesians understood the Malaysian proposal as being domestically motivated, to improve new Prime Minister Tun Razak's 'internal image'. 'Neutralisation', British Embassy in Jakarta to South West Pacific Department, FCO, undated, filed in the registry on 22 July 1972 (FCO 24/1269).

51   Ibid.

52   Singapore claimed that it was Indonesia, not Singapore, which took the lead in opposing Malaysia's proposal. Singapore merely wanted to keep its options open in view of the changing strategic scene. Singapore regarded the Malaysian proposal as too doctrinaire.

53 Noordin Sopiee, 'The Neutralisation of Southeast Asia', in Hedley Bull (ed.), *Asia and the Western Pacific: Towards a New International Order* (Melbourne and Sydney: Thomas Nelson, 1975), p. 144.

54 Michael Leifer, 'Regional Order in Southeast Asia: An Uncertain Prospect', *Round Table*, vol. 64, no. 255 (1974), p. 311.

55 *Straits Times*, 6 February 1976.

56 Muthiah Alagappa, *Towards a Nuclear-Weapons-Free Zone in Southeast Asia*, ISIS Research Note (Kuala Lumpur: Institute of Strategic and International Studies, 1987).

57 Singapore's Foreign Minister, S. Jayakumar, reported in the *Straits Times*, 25 July 1997, p. 29.

58 For the text of the Bangkok Declaration and all other ASEAN documents mentioned in this book, see: *ASEAN Documents Series, 1967–1988*, 3rd edition (Jakarta: ASEAN Secretariat, 1988).

59 David Irvine, 'Making Haste Slowly: ASEAN from 1975', in Alison Broinowski (ed.), *Understanding ASEAN* (London: Macmillan, 1982), p. 40.

60 Jusuf Wanandi, 'Security Issues in the ASEAN Region', in Karl D. Jackson and M. Hadi Soesastro (eds), *ASEAN Security and Economic Development*, Research Papers and Policy Studies no. 11 (Berkeley, CA: Institute of East Asian Studies, University of California, 1984), p. 305. The idea that regional resilience would *automatically* result from the achievement of national resilience by all ASEAN members may be questioned. A more accurate interpretation of the Indonesian concept is that regional resilience can only come about with the help of cooperation through ASEAN in addition to the realisation of national resilience by all its members.

61 Muthiah Alagappa, 'Confronting the Slorc', *Burma Review*, no. 30 (November–December 1991), p. 13.

62 This stance was broken only in February 1986 with a statement calling upon Philippine leaders to resolve their differences peacefully. The wording of the statement is revealing:

> As member states of ASEAN, Brunei Darussalam, Indonesia, Malaysia, Singapore, and Thailand, have followed with increasing concern the trend of events following the presidential elections in the Philippines.
>
> A critical situation has emerged which portends bloodshed and civil war. The crisis can be resolved without widespread carnage and political turmoil. We call on all parties to restore national unity and solidarity so as to maintain national resilience.
>
> There is still time to act with restraint and bring about peaceful resolution. We hope that all Filippino leaders will join efforts to pave the way for a peaceful solution to the crisis.

'ASEAN Joint Declaration on the Situation in the Philippines', in *ASEAN Documents Series, 1967–1988*, 3rd edition (Jakarta: ASEAN Secretariat, 1988), p. 605. Whether the statement constituted official ASEAN policy may be contested, since its signatories did not include, for obvious reasons, the foreign minister of the Philippines. But it went as far as ASEAN could go in commenting on the domestic affairs of a member state. It is also important to note that the statement not only did not mention any persons or parties by name, but was also decidedly non-committal about the direction in which the Philippine situation might evolve. Although this statement may be viewed as a way of urging (rather than warning) Marcos to refrain from a bloody suppression of the demonstrations, it may also be interpreted as an indication of ASEAN's willingness to accept Marcos if he was able to restore political order and secure his own position as head of the government.

63 *The Other Side of the Summit* (Manila: Department of Foreign Affairs, no date).

64 Hans Indorf, 'A Post-Summit Assessment', in Hans Indorf (ed.), *Association of Southeast Asian Nations after 20 Years* (Washington, DC: Woodrow Wilson International Center for Scholars, 1988), p. 13.

65 According to a British memo: 'Indonesians more perhaps than any of the other signatories, might welcome some defence element in ASEAN'. R.B. Dorman, 'Inaugural Meeting of ASEAN', undated (archived 5 September 1967), FCO 15/23 (London: Public Records Office).

66 'Regional Co-operation', British High Commission in Kuala Lumpur to Far East and Pacific Department, Commonwealth Office, London, 16 August 1967, FCO 15/23 (London: Public Records Office). The same document also quotes a Malaysian Foreign Ministry official present at Bangkok (Zainal Sulong) who believed that Indonesia would at a later stage 'try to give ASEAN an increasingly political and security flavour'.

67 'Philippine Foreign Secretary's Comments on Formation of ASEAN', British Embassy in Manila to South East Asia Department, Foreign Office, 14 August 1967, FO 15/23 (London: Public

Records Office). He refused to comment on Adam Malik's hint of a possible defence role for ASEAN.

68 But the British assessment was that 'There is no likelihood at present of ASEAN developing into a defence association.' From D.F. Murray to Mr Wilkinson, Parliamentary Office, 18 January 1968, FCO 24/341 (London: Public Records Office). They believed, however, that there were 'elements' in the Indonesian military 'who consider that Indonesia's opposition to association with any form of military grouping should be revised'. British Embassy in Jakarta to South East Asia Department, Foreign Office, 21 May 1968, FCO 24/341 (London: Public Records Office). But overall, the British assessed that 'Indonesia will not join any military pact or alliance, but that bilateral military co-operation with other countries in the area is not excluded. The existing arrangements with Malaysia for joint patrols and for the exchange of observers and information in operations against the PGRS [Pasukan Gerilya Rakyat Sarawak, or People's Guerrilla Army Sarawak] on the Kalimantan border are frequently cited as constituting the type of co-operation which is desirable. Some Indonesians have advocated that there should be exchanges of military or security information on a multilateral basis within the A.S.E.A.N. framework. But we have heard no more of this in recent weeks . . . As Adam Malik, the Foreign Minister, has said, the aim should be "security for the stomach".' British Embassy in Jakarta to South East Asia Department, Foreign Office, 21 May 1968, FCO 15/23 (London: Public Records Office). Another British dispatch cited the Indonesian National Secretary to ASEAN, General Rukminto, to the effect that Jakarta continued 'to reject military pacts and efforts to convert ASEAN into a collective military defence organization'. British Embassy in Jakarta to Foreign and Commonwealth Office, London, 'ASEAN', 29 October 1969, FCO 24/341 (London: Public Records Office).

69 In this context, the views of Benny Moerdani, then a counsellor in the Indonesian embassy in Kuala Lumpur who later became a key intelligence official in the Indonesian military, are noteworthy. Moerdani believed that interstate disputes such as the Sabah issue made it 'unrealistic to think of ASEAN developing into a conventional defence pact, although . . . it could do so one day'. 'He did however see it already as some form of security organisation.' Moerdani used the terms 'pertahanan' (defence in Bahasa Indonesia), and 'keamanan' (security in Bahasa Indonesia) in suggesting that ASEAN had a role in the latter, but not in the former. 'ASEAN as Seen from Kuala Lumpur', 14 February 1969, FCO24/341 (London: Public Records Office).

70 'Association of South East Asian Nations', Telegram from UK Embassy in Bangkok to Foreign and Commonwealth Office, 11 August 1967 (included in Memorandum for Foreign Office and Whitehall Distribution 15 August 1967, FCO 15/23 (London: Public Records Office)); British Embassy in Jakarta to South East Asia Department, Foreign Office, 21 May 1968, FCO 24/341 (London: Public Records Office).

71 Singapore Foreign Minister S. Rajaratnam believed that 'A.S.E.A.N. was an association of relatively poor and under-developed countries . . . What the organisation ought not to do was burden itself with responsibility for resolving the ideological, military and security problems of S.E. Asia. Economic problems alone would strain A.S.E.A.N. to the limit for many years to come.' (British wording and the emphasis as in the British document) 'A.S.E.A.N.', British High Commission in Singapore to South West Pacific Department, FCO in London, 31 December 1969, FCO24/341 (London: Public Records Office).

72 Frank Frost, 'The Origins and Evolution of ASEAN', *World Review*, vol. 19, no. 3 (August 1980), p. 10; Tim Huxley, *The ASEAN States' Defence Policies, 1975–81: Military Response to Indochina?*, Working Paper no. 88 (Canberra: Australian National University, Strategic and Defence Studies Centre, 1986), p. 52. See also: *Straits Times*, 10 February 1976. An indication of Indonesia's interest in greater ASEAN military cooperation was the composition of the Indonesian delegation to the pre-summit meeting of ASEAN foreign ministers at Pattaya. The Indonesian delegation included at least four senior military and intelligence officers. Also important was the timing of a strong statement by Indonesian Foreign Minister Adam Malik on the Chinese threat to the region. Just prior to the Pattaya meeting, Malik criticised the complacency that he sensed in the attitude of his ASEAN partners, especially Thailand, towards China. His statement was seen as an attempt to put defence and security at the top of the Bali summit agenda. *Straits Times*, 22 December 1975; 7 February 1976; 10 February 1976; 12 February 1976.

73 *New Straits Times*, 1 April 1976.

74 Mohamad Ghazali Shafie, *Malaysia: International Relations* (Kuala Lumpur: Creative Enterprises, 1982), pp. 161–62.

75 Cited in Michael Richardson, 'ASEAN Extends Its Military Ties', *Pacific Defence Reporter* (November 1982), p. 55.

76 *Bangkok Post*, 11 September 1982.

77 *New Straits Times*, 17 September 1982.

78 Mohamad Ghazali Shafie, 'Reflections on ASEAN: 30 Years and Vision of the Future', Paper presented at the ASEAN Roundtable 1997, 'ASEAN in the New Millennium', jointly organised by the Institute of Southeast Asian Studies and the ASEAN Secretariat, Singapore, 4–5 August 1997, p. 3.

79 Lee Kim Chew, 'Asean Unity Showing Signs of Fraying', *Straits Times*, 23 July 1998, p. 30.

80 For example, while the 'ASEAN Way' usually refers to a particular style of decision making, some scholars have defined it as a combination of norms and style. Noordin Sopiee provides an elaborate list of 13 principles which he claims to be the core principles of the ASEAN Way: (1) rejection of internal and external collective military pacts; (2) rejection of emphasis on peace through military deterrence; (3) the advocacy and practice of 'true peace' measures: the building of confidence, trust, predictability, goodwill and friendship, national resilience, a rich web of productive and warm bilateral relations; (4) the principle of actively seeking and maximising solidarity, common ground, agreement and harmony; (5) the principle of sensitivity; politeness, non-confrontation and agreeability, emphasising 'the ability to agree to disagree without being disagreeable'; (6) the principle of decision making by consensus; (7) the principle of mutual caring; (8) the principle of respect for territorial integrity; (9) the principle of non-intervention in domestic affairs; (10) preference for quiet diplomacy and aversion to excessive public washing of dirty linen and diplomacy through the media and mass mobilisation; (11) the principle of pragmatism; (12) the preference for content rather than form, substance rather than process, non-addiction to Cartesian [approaches] and to legalism; (13) the principle of egalitarianism. While repetitive and in some cases debatable (e.g. many analysts would contest principle 12, which says that ASEAN prefers substance over process; indeed, the ASEAN experience seems to emphasise the 'process over the product'), this is a useful list of the most salient aspects of the ASEAN Way, incorporating both norms and style. Noordin Sopiee, 'ASEAN Towards 2020: Strategic Goals and Critical Pathways', Paper presented to the Second ASEAN Congress, Kuala Lumpur, 20–23 July 1997, p. 9.

81 Ali Moertopo, 'Opening Address', in *Regionalism in Southeast Asia* (Jakarta: CSIS, 1975), p. 15.

82 Ibid., p. 16.

83 Ibid., p. 16.

84 Mohamad Ghazali Shafie, 'Reflections on ASEAN: 30 Years and Vision of the Future', Paper presented at the ASEAN Roundtable 1997, 'ASEAN in the New Millennium', jointly organised by the Institute of Southeast Asian Studies and the ASEAN Secretariat, Singapore, 4–5 August 1997, pp. 1–2.

85 Solidum identifies three sources of the ASEAN Way: (1) the organisational structure and procedures of ASEAN; (2) principles adopted from earlier regional attempts at cooperation; and (3) known cultural similarities. Estrella D. Solidum, 'The Role of Certain Sectors in Shaping and Articulating the ASEAN Way', in R.P. Anand and P. Quisuimbing (eds), *ASEAN: Identity, Development and Culture* (Quezon City: University of the Philippines Law Centre and East–West Center Culture Learning Institute, 1981), pp. 130 and 134–35.

86 Peter Boyce, 'The Machinery of Southeast Asian Regional Diplomacy', in Lau Teik Soon (ed.), *New Directions in the International Relations of Southeast Asia: Global Powers and Southeast Asia* (Singapore: Singapore University Press, 1973), p. 175. The first of these features, a disposition to summitry, may seem to go against what many think to be another key aspect of the ASEAN Way – aversion to institutionalisation. But until the 1990s, ASEAN summits had been an irregular and informal affair. Mere gathering of leaders/officials should not be confused with 'institutionalisation' as the latter involves a degree of bureaucratisation and resort to formal procedures and mechanisms.

87 Phan Wannamethee, 'The Institutional Foundations of ASEAN', in Hans Indorf, *The Association of Southeast Asian Nations after 20 Years* (Washington, DC: Woodrow Wilson International Center for Scholars, 1988), p. 22.

88 Cited in Anh Tuan Hoang, 'ASEAN Dispute Management: Implications for Vietnam and an Expanded ASEAN', *Contemporary Southeast Asia*, vol. 18, no. 1 (June 1996), p. 67.

89 Michael Leifer's study of ASEAN's evolution provides several examples of the ASEAN members' reluctance to create elaborate institutional mechanisms. The rejection of the EC model of a central

permanent bureaucracy was evident from the outset when ASEAN's founding Bangkok Declaration provided for no such body and instead decreed the creation of national secretariats located within the foreign ministries of member states to 'carry out the work of the Association on behalf of that country' and to service various ASEAN ministerial and committee meetings. Even the meeting of the foreign ministers (called ASEAN Ministerial Meeting, or AMM), the top managerial body of ASEAN, was initially supposed 'to be convened as required', although it did become an annual event with the exception of 1970. There was no provision in the Bangkok Declaration for meetings of ASEAN heads of government. The first summit was held in Bali in 1976, where it was decided that further such meetings would be held 'as and when necessary'. While a second summit was held in 1977 in Kuala Lumpur, the third summit could not be held until 1987. This was due to an understanding that the third summit should be held in Manila, but the continuing dispute between Malaysia and the Philippines over Sabah had made Malaysian participation in such a meeting unlikely, thereby delaying the event. In Manila, the ASEAN leaders decided to hold summits every three to five years, but only if 'necessary'. Another important ASEAN institution is the Senior Officials Meeting (ASEAN-SOM), comprising the permanent heads of the member states' foreign ministries. This is where much of the initial consultations and consensus building in ASEAN usually takes place; the annual meeting of the foreign ministers usually endorses the recommendations of the SOM. Despite its importance, the SOM process was not formally recognised in ASEAN's institutional structure. Further indication of ASEAN's aversion to a permanent, supranational bureaucracy can be found in the role of the ASEAN Standing Committee. The Committee consists of the foreign minister of the state due to host the annual ministerial meeting plus the resident ambassadors and high commissioners of the other member states. As such, it has to be reconstituted every year. An ASEAN Secretariat was established in Jakarta in 1976 as a permanent body, but its responsibilities were confined to overseeing economic and technical cooperation, and its Secretary-General was made subordinate to the Standing Committee. The Secretary-General was not given the authority to represent ASEAN in dealings with non-member governments. Moreover, the ASEAN Secretariat had no authority over national ASEAN secretariats. An ASEAN task force set up by the foreign ministers in 1982 recommended several measures to strengthen the ASEAN Secretariat incorporating aspects of the institutional experience of the EC. But these recommendations were rejected by the ministers in 1984, except minor increases in staff strength and budget. Michael Leifer, *ASEAN and the Security of South-East Asia* (London and New York: Routledge, 1989), pp. 24–8. (It should be noted that no major change in the institutional apparatus of ASEAN was made until the fourth ASEAN summit in Singapore in January 1992, and even then the main change was in the area of staff strength and the status of the Secretary-General, rather than the role and authority of the ASEAN bureaucracy.)

90 Cited in Agerico O. Lacanlale, 'Community Formation in ASEAN's External Relations', in R.P. Anand and Purification V. Quisumbing (eds), *ASEAN:Identity, Development and Culture* (Quezon City: University of the Philippines Law Centre and East–West Culture Learning Institute, 1981), p. 399.

91 Mohamad Ghazali Shafie, 'Reflections on ASEAN: 30 Years and Vision of the Future', Paper presented at the ASEAN Roundtable 1997, 'ASEAN in the New Millennium', jointly organised by the Institute of Southeast Asian Studies and the ASEAN Secretariat, Singapore, 4–5 August 1997, pp. 1–2.

92 Lacanlale, 'Community Formation in ASEAN's External Relations', p. 399.

93 Chin Kin Wah, 'ASEAN Institution-Building: The Fourth Wave', Paper presented to the Second ASEAN Congress, Kuala Lumpur, 20–23 July 1997, p. 7.

94 As Chin Kin Wah points out, following the Singapore summit, the ASEAN Secretariat moved to acquire more openly recruited staff, in contrast to the previous practice of being served by nationally seconded staff. The total staff strength more than doubled from the pre-1993 figure of 14 nationally seconded staff. In addition to the Secretary-General, ASEAN has a Deputy Secretary-General, five bureau directors overseeing general affairs, economic cooperation, functional cooperation, ASEAN cooperation and dialogue relations, and the AFTA Unit. The number of assistant directors increased from ten in 1994 to 16 in 1997. Ibid., p. 7.

95 J.N. Mak, 'The ASEAN Process ("Way") of Multilateral Cooperation and Cooperative Security: The Road to a Regional Arms Register?', Paper presented to the MIMA–SIPRI Workshop on 'An ASEAN Arms Register: Developing Transparency', Kuala Lumpur, 2–3 October 1995, p. 5.

96 R.M. Sunardi, 'Maritime Security and Conflict Resolution: Indonesian Perspective', Paper presented to the Symposium on 'The Evolving Security Situation in the Asia Pacific Region: Indonesian and Canadian Perspectives', Jakarta, 26 June 1995, pp. 3–4.

97 Michael Leifer, 'Debating Asian Security: Michael Leifer Responds to Geoffrey Wiseman', *Pacific Review*, vol. 5, no. 2 (1992), p. 169.

98 In reality, what might have contributed to the lack of need to invoke the High Council is the existence of direct bilateral mechanisms and avenues for negotiation, including the previously discussed joint border committees. Moreover, high-level bilateral channels have been used to defuse interstate disputes, such as the Philippine–Malaysia, Indonesia–Malaysia and Thailand–Malaysia territorial disputes, with the Sabah dispute providing a rare example of successful informal third-party mediation (by Indonesia in May 1969).

99 Noordin Sopiee, 'ASEAN and Regional Security', in Mohammed Ayoob (ed.), *Regional Security in the Third World* (London: Croom Helm, 1986), p. 228.

100 British Embassy in Manila to The Right Honourable Sir Alec Douglas, 'The Fourth Meeting of the Foreign Ministers of the Association of South East Asian Nations (ASEAN)', 22 March 1971 (London: Public Records Office).

101 Cited in Phan Wannamethee, 'The Institutional Foundations of ASEAN', in Hans Indorf, *The Association of Southeast Asian Nations after 20 years* (Washington, DC: Woodrow Wilson International Center for Scholars, 1988), p. 22.

102 Herbert Feith, *The Decline of Constitutional Democracy in Indonesia* (Ithaca, NY: Cornell University Press, 1962), p. 40.

103 Kamarulzaman Askandar, 'ASEAN and Conflict Management: The Formative Years of 1967–1976', *Pacifica Review*, vol. 6, no. 2 (1994), pp. 57–69.

104 Anh Tuan Hoang, 'ASEAN Dispute Management: Implications for Vietnam and an Expanded ASEAN', *Contemporary Southeast Asia*, vol. 18, no. 1 (June 1996), p. 67. It should be noted that *musyawarah* and *mufakat* are highly elitist processes. As an Indonesia scholar puts it, such decision making is 'not really a democratic process because decisions are made first, and then people are told about it'. Comments by Dr Almin Siregar at the ASEAN Inter-University Seminar of Social Development, Pekan Baru, Sumatra, Indonesia, 16–19 June 1997.

105 Fred J. Elizalde and Luis D. Beltran, *Of Kingdoms and Brothers: ASEAN Dawn*. Photocopy at the library of the Institute of Southeast Asian Studies, Singapore (no publisher cited, undated), p. 39.

106 Cited in Arnafin Jorgensen-Dahl, *Regional Organisation and Order in Southeast Asia* (London: Macmillan, 1982), p. 166.

107 Mak, 'The ASEAN Process ("Way") of Multilateral Cooperation and Cooperative Security', p. 5.

108 Cited in Roger Irvine, 'The Formative Years of ASEAN: 1967–1975', in Alison Broinowski (ed.), *Understanding ASEAN* (New York: St Martin's Press, 1982), p. 62.

109 Lee Kuan Yew cited in Mary Hogan, 'The Development and Role of ASEAN as a Regional Association' (M. Phil. Dissertation, University of Hong Kong, 1995), p. 88.

110 *Straits Times*, 13 November 1994, p. 17.

111 *Straits Times*, 13 November 1994, p. 17.

112 Phan Wannamethee, 'The Institutional Foundations of ASEAN', in Hans Indorf, *The Association of Southeast Asian Nations after 20 Years* (Washington, DC: Woodrow Wilson International Center for Scholars, 1988), p. 22.

113 Roger Irvine, 'The Formative Years of ASEAN: 1967–1975', in Alison Broinowski (ed.), *Understanding ASEAN* (New York: St Martin's Press, 1982), p. 50.

114 Bilson Kurus, 'The ASEAN Triad: National Interest, Consensus-Seeking, and Economic Cooperation', *Contemporary Southeast Asia*, vol. 16, no. 4 (March 1995), p. 405.

115 Lucian Pye has provided an interesting description of the consensus building in Javanese society:

> in Indonesian villages the process of consensus is wonderful to watch: young hotbloods will expound their views with dramatic passion, the middle-aged will strive to hit the right note so as to suggest wisdom, and then, without the slightest hint that closure might be at hand, an elder will calmly define what the consensus is and deliberations will cease.

Lucian Pye, *Asian Power and Politics: The Cultural Dimensions of Authority* (Cambridge, MA: The Belknap Press of Harvard University Press, 1985), pp. 364–5.

116 Pushpa Thambipillai and Johan Saravanmuttu, *ASEAN Negotiations: Two Insights* (Singapore: Institute of Southeast Asian Studies, 1985).

117 J. Soedjati Djiwandono, 'Confidence-Building Measures and Preventive Diplomacy: A Southeast Asian Perspective', Paper presented to the Symposium on The Evolving Security Situation in the Asia Pacific Region: Indonesian and Canadian Perspectives, Jakarta, 26 June 1995, pp. 6–7.
118 Arnfinn Jorgensen-Dahl, *Regional Organisation and Order in Southeast Asia* (London: Macmillan, 1982).
119 Arnfinn Jorgensen-Dahl, 'The Significance of ASEAN', *World Review*, vol. 19, no. 3 (August 1980), pp. 56–7.
120 Keynote address by Datuk Musa Hitam delivered at the East–West Conference on ASEAN and the Pacific Basin, Honolulu, 29 October 1985, pp. 5–6.
121 Abu Hanifa, one of the Indonesian representatives to the Asian Relations Conference in New Delhi convened by Nehru in 1947, wrote later that the idea of a wholly Southeast Asian grouping was conceived at the conference in response to the belief among the Southeast Asian delegates that the larger states, India and China, could not be expected to support their nationalist cause. At the meeting, delegates from Indonesia, Burma, Thailand, Vietnam, the Philippines and Malay: 'debated, talked, [and] planned a Southeast Asian Association closely cooperating first in cultural and economic matters. Later, there could be perhaps a more closely knit political cooperation. Some of us even dreamt of a Greater Southeast Asia, a federation.' Cited in Christopher E. Goscha, *Thailand and the Southeast Asian Networks of Vietnamese Revolution, 1885–1954* (Surrey: Curzon Press, 1999), p. 255.
122 Amy Vanderbosch and Richard Butwell, *The Changing Face of Southeast Asia* (Lexington, KY: University of Kentucky Press, 1966), pp. 339–40 and 341.
123 *Declaration of ASEAN Concord*, Indonesia, 24 February 1976.
124 A British observer found this statement symbolic of the general premise of ASEAN that would make it a viable organisation. 'It is this apparently genuine wish for closer cooperation coupled with the limited aims and geographical extent of the new organization and the realistic approach of the five Ministers concerned which gives the ASEAN Declaration a healthier sound than some of its predecessors and the organisation itself a better chance of survival.' 'Association of South East Asian Nations', Telegram from UK Embassy in Bangkok to Foreign and Commonwealth Office, 11 August 1967 (included in Memorandum for Foreign Office and Whitehall Distribution 15 August 1967, FCO 15/23 (London: Public Records Office)).
125 Estrella D. Solidum, 'The Role of Certain Sectors in Shaping and Articulating the ASEAN Way', in R.P. Anand and P. Quisumbing (eds), *ASEAN: Identity, Development and Culture* (Quezon City: University of the Philippines Law Centre and East–West Centre Culture Learning Institute, 1981), p. 134.
126 Keynote address by Abdullah Badawi, Foreign Minister of Malaysia, at the Second ASEAN Congress, Kuala Lumpur, 20–23 July 1997.

3 ASEAN and the Cambodia conflict

A regional solution to a regional problem?

The invasion and the decade-long occupation of Cambodia by Vietnamese forces from December 1978 posed the most serious security challenge to ASEAN since its inception. Not only did ASEAN see Vietnam's action as a blatant violation of its norms, but the Cambodia conflict also tested intra-ASEAN relations, thereby threatening its emerging culture of unity and consensus. Differences among ASEAN members as to how to deal with the conflict challenged ASEAN's professed role in the peaceful settlement of regional disputes without interference by outside powers. This chapter reviews ASEAN's role in the Cambodia conflict with the particular purpose of ascertaining the extent to which it contributed to the consolidation of ASEAN's norms and conformed to its professed goal of providing a 'regional solution to the region's problems'.

ASEAN's normative stakes in the Third Indochina War

Norms helped to define ASEAN's stake in the Cambodia conflict. In a strict sense the invasion and the ensuing crisis were outside its framework of seeking a peaceful settlement of regional conflicts: neither Vietnam nor Cambodia were members of ASEAN. For a number of reasons, however, it was of serious and urgent concern to ASEAN.[1] First, ASEAN had for some time considered the possibility of including Vietnam (as well as Laos and Cambodia) within its fold. Its governments had hoped that Vietnam would accept its vision of regional order and adhere to ASEAN's norms of inter-state behaviour even if it did not accept formal membership. Despite past criticisms of ASEAN as a front for Western imperialism, in 1978 Vietnam had raised hopes of a constructive relationship through a brief but visible diplomatic effort to cultivate ASEAN's goodwill. Vietnam's invasion of Cambodia in the same year was a setback to ASEAN's framework for regional order, which had aspired to a partnership with Indochina. The military action taken by Vietnam to overthrow Pol Pot's regime and install a puppet alternative also violated the ASEAN doctrine of non-interference and non-use of force in interstate relations. Furthermore, Vietnam's action was a serious blow to ASEAN's norm of regional autonomy. The conflict over Cambodia precipitated by Vietnam's intervention was, from ASEAN's point of view, not just a local conflict but engaged much broader Sino-Vietnamese, Sino-Soviet and US–Soviet rivalries. Because of strong Soviet backing for Vietnam and militant Chinese opposition to the invasion (including a punitive attack on Vietnam in February–March 1979), ASEAN saw Vietnam's action as dashing its hopes for a reduced Great Power role in Southeast Asia. Instead, it marked the beginning of a period of heightened Great Power rivalry with Sino-Vietnamese confrontation aggravating an existing Sino-Soviet rivalry.

ASEAN's norm of no military pacts within the grouping was also challenged by Vietnam's action. This norm was under pressure as the ASEAN members perceived a direct military threat to one of their number from the instability in Indochina. The removal of Cambodia as a buffer between Vietnam and Thailand and cross-border operations into Thailand by Vietnamese forces against Khmer resistance guerrillas made Thailand the 'frontline' state of ASEAN. The exodus of ethnic-Chinese refugees from Indochina to their shores was also seen by Malaysia and Indonesia as highly destabilising of their delicate social and demographic balances, leading to calls within ASEAN for some form of collective military response to Vietnam.

Norms not only shaped ASEAN's perception of the crisis, but also formed the basis of its response to it. In their first collective response to the crisis issued on 9 January 1979, ASEAN's foreign ministers urged all countries in the region to 'respect each other's independence, sovereignty, territorial integrity and political system'. They also asked all sides to 'refrain . . . from interfering in each other's internal affairs, and from carrying out subversive activities, directly or indirectly, against each other'.[2] ASEAN's response to the crisis was consistent with its key norms and included the following objectives:

- to deny legitimacy to the Vietnamese-installed Phnom Penh government;
- to ensure the international isolation of Vietnam;
- to secure the unconditional withdrawal of Vietnamese forces from Cambodia;
- to prevent Vietnamese encroachment into Thailand;
- to ensure a peaceful, neutral and democratic Cambodia; and
- to ensure ASEAN's leadership in the peace process so that the eventual settlement would protect ASEAN's security interests and would not be completely dictated by outside powers.[3]

While norms influenced ASEAN's objectives, they did not produce a consensus over the means to achieve them. ASEAN's decade-long involvement in Cambodian peacemaking was to be marked by a tension between two approaches. One was a diplomacy of accommodation that sought to address the conflict within an essentially regional framework in which the role of external powers would be kept to a minimum. This approach was favoured by Indonesia and Malaysia and was fully consistent with ASEAN's norm of regional solutions for regional problems, with minimal intervention by outside powers. The other was a strategy of confrontation, the objective of which was to seek Vietnam's isolation from the international community and raise the diplomatic and military costs of its occupation of Cambodia. The latter strategy, identified with Thailand and Singapore, involved organising a resistance coalition front against Vietnam, as well as occasional proposals for intra-ASEAN military cooperation, thereby drawing ASEAN closer to a violation of its norm against military pacts. It also meant seeking close and direct backing from the major external powers, thereby compromising the norm of regional autonomy. Moreover, as these two approaches were often in conflict, they threatened ASEAN's norm of consultations and consensus through the Cambodia conflict.

Regional autonomy versus dependence on outside powers

The formidable challenge facing ASEAN in seeking a political settlement to the Cambodian conflict within a regional framework that would uphold its norms was evident, first and foremost, in the difficulty experienced in getting the various parties directly or indirectly involved to agree to a suitable negotiating forum. The disagreement was shaped by the conflicting interpretations of the causes of the conflict held by the two opposing camps: Vietnam and the regime it installed in Phnom Penh (which had renamed the country the People's Republic of Kampuchea, or PRK) on the one hand, and the combination of ASEAN, China and the Cambodian resistance factions on the other. Vietnam had presented the conflict as a domestic power struggle between rival Cambodian factions, the outcome of which had been the overthrow of the genocidal Pol Pot regime by a Cambodian 'salvation' front. Hanoi's deployment of troops to Cambodia to sustain the Heng Samrin government in power was justified under the terms of a subsequent 1979 security treaty. Hanoi acknowledged the wider geopolitical dimensions of the Cambodia situation, if only to justify its invasion as a defensive move to counter the threat of Chinese expansionism. However, Hanoi rejected the view that it was a direct party to the Cambodia conflict and insisted that the withdrawal of its troops required the prior request of the Heng Samrin regime, the sole legitimate Cambodian government. Further, such withdrawal would only be possible after the Chinese threat had receded.

Such a presentation of the conflict shaped Hanoi's attitude towards peace negotiations. According to Hanoi, the situation in Cambodia, i.e. the rule of the Heng Samrin regime, was 'irreversible' and hence non-negotiable. However, if the regional countries, especially Thailand and other ASEAN states, felt threatened by developments in Cambodia, then this could be addressed by direct talks between Bangkok and Phnom Penh. Vietnam would also be willing to participate in direct talks with the ASEAN states to discuss Thai security concerns within the framework of ASEAN's professed regional security formula, the ZOPFAN. But since Hanoi did not view itself as a direct party to the civil war in Cambodia, it would not submit to the authority of an international forum, including a 1981 UN-sponsored international conference on Cambodia that it had boycotted.

Vietnam's position was clearly articulated in a four-point proposal that emerged at the end of a conference of foreign ministers of the three Indochinese states, held in Vientiane on 17–18 July 1980. The proposal, made in the name of the Cambodian government (PRK), was purportedly addressed to the problem of Thai–Cambodian border tensions. It presented the worsening regional situation as one requiring a mutual understanding between ASEAN and the Indochinese states that would entail acceptance by the two sides of each other's 'legitimate security interests'. It proposed, among other things, the creation of a demilitarised zone along the Thai–Cambodian border to be supervised by a joint commission and discussions between the two countries to resolve other 'relevant' issues of mutual concern, to be confirmed 'by an international conference or by some form of international guarantee'. The proposal was prefaced by a reference to an earlier offer, made in January 1980 by the Indochinese foreign ministers, expressing a willingness to sign non-aggression treaties with Thailand and other ASEAN countries. On 25 September 1980, Vietnam and the PRK confirmed their rejection of the idea of an international conference on Cambodia as put forward by ASEAN that would include all the belligerent parties. Instead, Hanoi tried to persuade Thailand to accept a limited withdrawal of its forces to be decided by Hanoi and Phnom Penh.

Vietnam's presentation of the Cambodia situation conflicted sharply with the view held by the ASEAN states. To the latter, the central issue in the Cambodia conflict was Vietnam's invasion, rather than a domestic power struggle among the Cambodian factions, as Hanoi would have liked the international community to believe. In responding to Vietnam's invasion, therefore, the immediate priority of ASEAN was to deny Vietnam a *fait accompli* in Cambodia. If Vietnam's action went unopposed politically, it could have created a dangerous precedent. ASEAN focused on denying recognition and legitimacy to the Heng Samrin government, to mobilise support for Pol Pot's Democratic Kampuchea (DK), which had been overthrown by Hanoi, and to ensure Hanoi's international isolation both diplomatically and economically.[4] Moreover, ASEAN held that any meaningful negotiation to settle the conflict had to have as its main focus the unconditional withdrawal of Vietnamese forces from Cambodia.

Despite its seemingly hardline stance, ASEAN also had to show that it was serious about its professed norm of the peaceful settlement of disputes. Thus, even as it sought to isolate Hanoi internationally, ASEAN had to come up with a framework for negotiations with Vietnam. In order to facilitate a solution, the ASEAN states were willing to accept a phased, rather than immediate withdrawal. Indonesia and Malaysia were not entirely opposed to a partial withdrawal of Vietnamese troops from Cambodia pending a political settlement over the crucial issue of power sharing among the Cambodian factions. This position carried the implication that if such a settlement were not to be achieved, Vietnamese forces could remain as a guarantor of the Heng Samrin faction. But ASEAN also insisted that any negotiations to settle the Cambodia conflict had to focus on Hanoi's invasion, and that such negotiations could best be conducted within the framework of an international conference. From the outset, ASEAN had focused its diplomatic energies at the UN, mobilising the international censure of Hanoi and securing approval for an international conference on Kampuchea. At the same time, it rejected Hanoi's stated willingness to carry out limited troop withdrawals from the Thai–Cambodian border and its offer of talks between Bangkok and the PRK regime or a dialogue between ASEAN and the Indochina states to discuss mutual security concerns. In ASEAN's view, such a bilateral or regional dialogue would be tantamount to accepting Vietnam's invasion and the legitimisation of the illegal PRK regime. A related factor was the suspicion that Hanoi would use any ASEAN–Indochina conference to divert attention from its military occupation of Cambodia by raising the issue of China's strategic ambitions and role in the region, an issue on which ASEAN remained divided.[5] To this end, ASEAN was willing to rely on an international conference, rather than settle for a diplomatic process consistent with its norm of regional autonomy.

The tension between a regionalist approach and one that sought to internationalise the conflict with a view to isolating and punishing Vietnam with the help of China, the USA and the international community was to plague ASEAN's diplomacy on the Cambodia conflict for a long time. The regionalist approach was favoured most by Malaysia and Indonesia, for reasons described below, and was most clearly represented in the so-called Kuantan Doctrine (also known as the Kuantan Principle), jointly enunciated by the President of Indonesia and the Prime Minister of Malaysia at a meeting in the Malaysian town of Kuantan on 26–28 March 1980. The Kuantan Doctrine contained elements of a possible trade-off between the security interests of Vietnam and those of ASEAN as defined by Kuala Lumpur and Jakarta. Accordingly, Vietnam was to heed the latter's desire to see an end to its dependence on the Soviet Union in exchange for a recognition by ASEAN of Vietnam's security interests in Indochina enshrined into a political settlement of the Cambodia conflict.

As such, the Kuantan Doctrine was clearly consistent with ASEAN's norm of regional autonomy. It reflected the concerns of two key ASEAN members, Indonesia and Malaysia, that the conflict in Cambodia, if unresolved, would become a grave threat to the security of all regional states. In particular, the conflict could aggravate the domestic instability of Thailand, which was already threatened by a massive refugee influx and subjected to repeated threats by Hanoi and the PRK for providing sanctuary for the Cambodian resistance guerrillas. But more importantly, it could pave the way for unwelcome Great

Power meddling, especially Chinese, in Southeast Asian affairs, especially in the wake of the belligerent Chinese response to the crisis in the form of a military offensive against Vietnam in February–March 1979.

The Kuantan Doctrine reflected an intra-ASEAN divide. Malaysia and Indonesia held the view that China posed the real long-term threat to Southeast Asia, and that Vietnam could be a bulwark against Chinese expansionism. This view conflicted with the strategic perspectives of Singapore and Thailand, both identified with the 'hardline' camp within ASEAN, which saw Vietnam backed by the Soviet Union as the main threat to regional peace and security. The Kuantan Doctrine proved unacceptable to Thailand, whose security it was intended to strengthen. In rejecting the formula, Thailand pointed out that in view of Vietnam's refusal to withdraw troops from Cambodia, any concession to Hanoi by ASEAN, such as recognition of its security interests in Indochina, would be ill-timed. Singapore described the Kuantan Principle as a 'bad mistake'. The principle was to suffer an early demise, as indicated by the response of the ASEAN foreign ministers to the border crossing by Vietnamese troops into Thai territory on 23 June 1980 in hot pursuit of Cambodian resistance guerrillas. At a meeting on 26 June 1980, the ASEAN ministers closed ranks and reverted to their original position by calling for the total withdrawal of Vietnamese forces from Cambodia, reaffirming their continued recognition of the DK regime and the idea of 'an independent, neutral and non-aligned Kampuchea, free from foreign interference'. No hint of recognition of Vietnam's security interests in Indochina was offered. Although individual ASEAN countries, especially Indonesia and Malaysia, hinted that a dialogue with Hanoi should resume, the attitude of compromise evident in the Kuantan Principle was no longer apparent.[6] The Kuantan episode confirmed the polarisation of ASEAN into so-called 'hardline' and 'moderate' camps and contributed to the Cambodia stalemate by strengthening Hanoi's belief that ASEAN's internal divisions would favour its strategy of holding out until international opinion changed.

ASEAN and the Cambodia conflict, 1977–82

December 1977–January 1978: Vietnamese Foreign Minister Nguyen Duy Trinh visited all ASEAN states (except Singapore) on a 'peace offensive' while Vietnamese and DK (Khmer Rouge) forces were clashing along their border. He indicated his approval of Southeast Asian initiatives designed to achieve 'peace, independence and neutrality'. He called for enhanced bilateral relations and cooperation between ASEAN and other states in the region.

December 1978: Vietnamese forces invaded Cambodia, overthrew the Khmer Rouge government and installed a government of defectors from the Khmer Rouge led by Heng Samrin.

January 1979: At a meeting in Bangkok, ASEAN foreign ministers issued a statement condemning 'foreign aggression' in Cambodia.

September 1979: ASEAN successfully thwarted a Vietnamese challenge to the credentials of the DK (the ousted Khmer Rouge government) at the UN. The UN General Assembly passed an ASEAN-supported resolution calling for a cease-fire and the convening of an international conference on Cambodia.

March 1980: The President of Indonesia and the Prime Minister of Malaysia enunciated the 'Kuantan Principle' at a meeting in Kuantan, Malaysia.

26–28 March. The Kuantan Principle suggested the possibility of 'trading off' between the security interests of Vietnam and ASEAN, the latter as defined by

Indonesia and Malaysia. It involved Vietnam distancing itself from the Soviet Union in exchange for ASEAN recognition of its legitimate security interests in Indochina.

June 1980: On 26 June, at a meeting of ASEAN foreign ministers, there was a reversion to the original ASEAN position which called for a complete withdrawal of Vietnamese forces from Cambodia.

September 1980: On 25 September, Vietnam and the PRK confirmed their rejection of an offer of an international conference on Cambodia proposed by ASEAN.

January 1981: Following a meeting of Indochinese foreign ministers in Ho Chi Minh City, they issued a proposal on 28 January calling for a regional conference involving the Indochinese and ASEAN states, at which they could discuss their differences. Vietnam further offered to withdraw a portion of its forces from Cambodia or at least from the area near the border with Thailand, conditional upon Thailand relocating Cambodian resistance forces deep into Thailand.

July 1981: The International Conference on Kampuchea (ICK) was held in New York, largely at the instigation of ASEAN. China participated, but Vietnam, the PRK and the Soviet Union boycotted it. At this forum, it was agreed that it was necessary to implement a cease-fire and obtain the withdrawal of Vietnamese forces from Cambodia, which was to be verified by a UN peacekeeping or observer group; the Cambodian factions were to be prevented from employing their forces to interfere in the electoral process; law and order was to be maintained until the coming to power of a government elected in free elections; and free elections were to be held, in which all Cambodians were to be eligible to participate. Plans to disarm the Cambodian factions and to establish an 'interim administration' were dropped, however.

June 1982: On 22 June, the Coalition Government of Democratic Kampuchea (CGDK) was established.

Sources: Amitav Acharya, Pierre Lizée and Sorpong Peou (eds), *Cambodia – The 1989 Paris Peace Conference: Background Analysis and Documents* (Millwood, NY: Kraus, 1991), xxv–xlv; K.K. Nair, *ASEAN–Indochina Relations Since 1975: The Politics of Accommodation* (Canberra: The Strategic and Defence Studies Centre, Australian National University, 1984); Sorpong Peou, 'UN Conflict Resolution in the Cambodian War: An Analysis of the Permanent Five's Role and Its Impact on the Cambodian Peace Process' (Ph.D. Dissertation, Department of Political Science, York University, 1994); Carlyle A. Thayer, 'ASEAN and Indochina: The Dialogue', in Alison Broinowski (ed.), *ASEAN into the 1990s* (Basingstoke: Macmillan, 1990), pp. 138–61.

With the failure of the Kuantan formula, ASEAN moved closer towards its strategy of internationalising the search for a settlement to the conflict with the holding of the first International Conference on Kampuchea (ICK). But the ICK, held in July 1981, did little to advance the search for a political settlement in Cambodia. First, the meeting was boycotted by Vietnam and the Soviet Union. Second, it exposed sharp differences between ASEAN and China over the terms of a settlement.[7] ASEAN's own formula (envisaging total withdrawal of Vietnamese forces from Cambodia, simultaneous disarming of all the four Khmer factions, and the setting up of an interim administration to rule Cambodia pending free elections under UN supervision) did signal a measure of accommodation towards Hanoi by addressing its concern about the return of the Khmer Rouge to power. But China, backed by the USA, rejected the ASEAN proposal on the grounds that it would give the

Vietnamese aggressor and the resistance factions equal status, and insisted that a restored DK government was capable of holding free and fair elections by itself. The ICK exposed the risk that ASEAN's strategy of internationalising the conflict would give external powers such as China a great deal of authority over the terms of the peacemaking.[8] While ASEAN needed China's support in order to 'punish' Hanoi for its use of force in Cambodia, this goal could be realised only at the expense of regional autonomy. Strikingly, Indonesia, despite its considerable empathy with Vietnamese nationalism and its greater suspicion of China's strategic designs in Southeast Asia, went along with this. Jakarta seemed to have little choice, since the alternative would have been to risk the collapse of ASEAN, which it had helped to nurture as a powerful symbol of its post-Sukarno moderation and pragmatism in regional affairs. In return, Indonesia was confirmed as the political leader of ASEAN, by being designated as ASEAN's official interlocutor with Hanoi for all negotiations on Cambodia.

While the regionalist approach based on a formula of accommodation with Vietnam preferred by Indonesia and Malaysia faltered, ASEAN did seek to limit the influence of China on the Cambodia situation (also in the interest of regional autonomy). One key aspect of this move was its backing for a coalition of Cambodian resistance factions, called the Coalition Government of Democratic Kampuchea (CGDK). The CGDK was organised in June 1982 partly as a political move by the Western countries which felt they could not directly support the ousted Khmer Rouge regime in the UN unless it was part of a broader coalition of Cambodian resistance factions. The CGDK, headed by Prince Norodom Sihanouk, included his royalist faction FUNCINPEC as well as a nationalist faction, called the Khmer People's National Liberation Front (KPNLF), led by Son San, a former prime minister. ASEAN's support provided political legitimacy to the coalition. Afraid of growing Chinese influence and aware that the unsavoury reputation of the Khmer Rouge had made unacceptable a political settlement of the conflict that would return it to power, ASEAN's backing for the CGDK was partly inspired by a belief that a Khmer coalition might counter China's confrontational stance centred on the superior military muscle of the Khmer Rouge, to which China was directing most of its military aid. But any hope that the non-communist partners in the coalition would eclipse the Khmer Rouge militarily proved unfounded. The Khmer Rouge remained the dominant military faction, with some 25,000 fighters, compared with 5,000 for the KPNLF, despite ASEAN's efforts to channel some military support to the non-communist members of the coalition. Moreover, lack of unity shown in the demise of the Kuantan formula had undermined ASEAN's collective ability to distance itself significantly from China. This was confirmed by a brief but unsuccessful effort in 1983 by Malaysia to advocate another regionalist approach to conflict management by calling for direct talks between ASEAN, Vietnam and Laos under a 'five-plus-two' formula. Serious Chinese objection put an end to this initiative, and hence to prospects for any immediate breakthrough in peacemaking.[9]

Since ASEAN and Vietnam seemed to share a belief that a military defeat of the other side was a feasible option, the result was a prolonged stalemate on the ground as well as in the diplomatic arena, significantly delaying ASEAN's goal of a peaceful settlement of the crisis. As Carl Thayer observed, 'None of the diplomatic approaches and counter-responses [between ASEAN and Vietnam] in the period prior to 1985 appeared seriously designed to bring a peaceful end to the conflict.'[10]

As previously hinted, another near-casualty of ASEAN's policy towards the Cambodia conflict was its norm against military cooperation within the grouping. The danger to this norm was evident not so much in terms of the prospective emergence of an ASEAN military alliance to deal with the threat perceived from Vietnam. Rather it was in terms of deliberations over possible contingency assistance to Thailand in the event of a spillover of the conflict within Cambodia. Even Indonesia, which had previously denied that it would be obliged to aid Thailand in the event of aggression,[11] came to assert that it would provide aid to any ASEAN nation facing such a prospect. Singapore and Malaysia came up with similar pledges of help to Thailand against Vietnamese attack.

Coming to terms with Thailand's 'frontline' status became the focal point of ASEAN's dilemma concerning security collaboration. Although none of the ASEAN partners gave any specific commitment about the kind of aid envisaged, provision of military aid was assumed to be included. Indonesia's Coordinating Minister for Political and Security Affairs, General Panggabean, stated that Indonesia's assistance could take the form of economic as well as military aid. 'If they [the threatened nation] are short of ammunition, we can give them ammunition.'[12] It was not clear whether this statement reflected the official Indonesian position (a similar comment by the general in late 1970 that Indonesia would provide military assistance to its ASEAN neighbours against attack had been dismissed by Foreign Minister Adam Malik).[13] But it fuelled speculation concerning a major shift in Indonesia's thinking on ASEAN security cooperation. Malaysia was less forthcoming in so far as direct military aid was concerned. Minister Mohamad Ghazali Shafie (then Home Minister) stated that '[o]ur contribution will be in the form of helping the Thais build up their resilience or by sending goods they are short of'.[14] This indicated that Malaysia envisaged provision of logistical support, rather than troop assistance, as the major form of aid to Thailand in the event of a Vietnamese attack. Singapore's position was more or less similar, although the Republic, with its advanced defence production capability, was in a much better position than Malaysia to provide logistical support as well as armaments to its threatened neighbour.[15]

While ASEAN leaders generally hinted that any contingency aid to Thailand could be provided on a bilateral, rather than multilateral, basis,[16] it was evident, as Lee Kuan Yew asserted, that the Vietnamese action had prompted ASEAN policy-making circles to rethink their position on military cooperation.[17] President Marcos appeared to be more receptive to the idea of intra-ASEAN military cooperation, which he thought was necessary as a measure 'to stem the tide of insurgency'.[18] Adam Malik, who had opposed a military role for ASEAN while in office, now proposed that ASEAN should hold a military exercise of 10,000 troops on the Thai–Cambodian border to demonstrate its unity to Vietnam.[19] Thailand, while taking a cautious and ambivalent view towards the need for an ASEAN alliance (because the 'time is not [ripe] yet'), nonetheless supported the idea of joint ASEAN military exercises as a response to the new security situation. In June 1979, Prime Minister Kriangsak Chomanan had observed:

> If the ASEAN governments desire to hold joint manoeuvres, why can't we do it? But we have to wait for the proper time.[20]

At the same time, he expressed readiness to participate in such exercises:

> However, if anyone would like to have joint exercises, we are ready. Manoeuvres can be held in Thailand or if they are held elsewhere, we can send forces there.[21]

Translating the pledges made by Malaysia, Indonesia and Singapore to provide contingency support to Thailand into a framework for ASEAN-wide measures against external threats proved to be difficult. Any temptation to form an ASEAN military arrangement to provide contingency support to Thailand against Vietnam needed to be tempered by the realisation that ASEAN lacked any collective capacity to stand up to an all-out Vietnamese attack. As Lee Kuan Yew warned: 'there is no combination of forces in Southeast Asia that can stop the Vietnamese on the mainland of Asia'.[22] More importantly, the differing perspectives within ASEAN on Sino-Vietnamese rivalry, telescoped by the Cambodia crisis, proved to be a major barrier to greater intra-ASEAN political and security cooperation. This aspect reflected a lack of agreement over the identity of a common external threat that might have served as the basis of multilateral security collaboration. Thailand's policy of seeking China's support against Vietnam served to exacerbate these differences. While the Thai position was based on the calculation that Chinese pressure on the Vietnamese border reduced the threat to Thailand, the Chinese pledge of assistance to Thailand was not conducive to forging an ASEAN security consensus. Malaysia and Indonesia expressed misgivings about the Thai position,[23] eschewing a military role for ASEAN which would have provoked and further alienated Vietnam at a time when both Malaysia and Indonesia continued to harbour hopes of an eventual *rapprochement*. Moreover, the logistical barriers (especially lack of air transport capability) and the operational barriers (lack of practice in joint operations with Thai forces) to such an arrangement were enormous and were recognised in Thai contingency planning. (For the Thais, seeking assistance from the USA (under the auspices of the 1954 Manila Pact and the subsequent Rusk–Thanat agreement) was a much more credible policy against the Vietnamese threat than relying on its ASEAN partners. In fact, it was highly doubtful that the ASEAN states would have ventured to come to Bangkok's aid in the event of a major Vietnamese offensive without some sort of US security guarantee against possible retaliation by Hanoi.)

While the norm against intra-ASEAN military cooperation survived, it paradoxically increased ASEAN's dependence on external powers, thereby eroding the norm of regional autonomy. The US commitment to Thai security against Vietnam was reaffirmed and Washington's military aid to Bangkok as substantially enhanced. Thailand's relations with China acquired the quality of a *de facto* alliance, backed by large-scale arms transfers and an implicit Chinese commitment to provide direct and indirect support to Bangkok in the event of a Vietnamese attack. Indonesia and Malaysia, despite substantial misgivings about China's long-term intentions, acquiesced in the Sino-Thai alliance, while Singapore encouraged it.

ASEAN and the Cambodia endgame

The foregoing analysis shows that the evolution of ASEAN's role in the Cambodia conflict was shaped by two goals: a desire to punish Vietnam for its violation of its norms of regional conduct on the one hand, and a desire to seek a peaceful settlement of the Cambodia conflict without giving too much ground to the external powers on the other. In other words, while seeking to uphold its norm of non-use of force, ASEAN was also trying to maintain its norm of regional settlement of regional conflicts. These goals were not mutually exclusive but they did contribute to an ambivalence in ASEAN's posture, which became even more pronounced as the Cambodian conflict neared its endgame.

As the 1980s drew to a close, ASEAN's policy towards Cambodia was reaping some successes. Vietnam had been isolated internationally, as reflected in increased majorities at the UN General Assembly for ASEAN-sponsored resolutions condemning Hanoi. (For example, the 1989 resolution was approved with 124 in favour, 17 against and 12 abstentions.) Thanks partly to ASEAN's efforts, the cost of the conflict to Vietnam in human, political and economic terms was increasingly steep. Hanoi had been deprived of access to international capital and aid needed for urgent economic development, thus increasing Vietnam's dependence on the Soviet Union which was resented by the highly nationalistic Vietnamese.

ASEAN and the Cambodian peace process, 1987–91

April 1987: Indonesian Foreign Minister Mochtar journeyed to Vietnam for the first time in two years, giving cause for hope for the stalled peace process.

July 1987: Discussions on 27–29 July between Indonesian Foreign Minister Mochtar and Vietnamese Foreign Minister Nguyen Co Thach in Ho Chi Minh City resulted in a joint statement calling for the convening of an informal meeting on Cambodia involving the two sides on an equal basis 'without preconditions or labels'. A first stage of this process would be limited to the Cambodian factions themselves, to be followed by a second stage to which interested regional powers, such as Vietnam, would be invited.

August 1987: At an ASEAN Foreign Ministers Meeting in Bangkok on 16 August the Mochtar–Thach accord was discussed, and it was decided that such a process would only be implemented if Vietnam began to participate immediately after the initial informal discussions of the Cambodian groups.

July 1988: At Bogor on 24–28 July the Jakarta Informal Meeting (JIM I) took place. This involved the four Cambodian factions and focused on 'internal' aspects of the conflict. It did not result in any breakthrough. The PRK abandoned efforts to exclude the Khmer Rouge from the post-conflict political scene and Sihanouk dropped his demand for an international peacekeeping force, downplayed his demand that the PRK administration be dismantled before the holding of elections, and suggested that Cambodia's UN seat could be left vacant. JIM I set a procedural precedent in which the Cambodian groups met in the morning, and were joined in the afternoon by ASEAN, Laos and Vietnam. An informal working group was established to continue discussing the issues.

January 1989: On 6 January, Vietnam offered to withdraw all of its forces from Cambodia by September, dependent on a political solution being reached by then.

January 1989: PRK Prime Minister Hun Sen visited Thailand to enhance dialogue on the Cambodia conflict.

February 1989: JIM II talks were held on 16–21 February, but no progress was achieved due to the wide gulf over the question of power sharing. This appeared to herald the end of regional initiatives to produce a peaceful resolution to the conflict. However, France agreed to explore the idea of another international conference on Cambodia.

July–August 1989: The first Paris Conference on Cambodia was held. It did not produce the desired resolution to the conflict, but did identify a number of fundamental issues: the verification of a Vietnamese troop withdrawal; cessation of military assistance to the four factions; recognition of the importance of refugee problems and other humanitarian issues; the need to reconstruct Cambodia; the prevention of a return to power by the Khmer Rouge; the need to establish an International Control Mechanism (ICM); the question of Vietnamese settlers in Cambodia; and power sharing, establishing an interim government and the holding of general elections.

February 1990: The First Informal Meeting on Cambodia (IMC) was held in Jakarta on 26–28 February between the four Cambodian factions. It released a joint communiqué calling for the following in the interim period: a UN presence at 'appropriate levels'; and the establishment of a 'supreme national body'.

September 1990: The Second IMC was held on 9 September in Jakarta. All four factions participated and made conciliatory speeches. They agreed to establish a Supreme National Council (SNC) as the sovereign representative of Cambodia. The SNC was formally established the next day, with representatives from all four factions.

December 1990: At a meeting in Paris on 21–22 December, the two non-communist resistance factions indicated their willingness to accept a UN role in Cambodia, the total demobilisation of all armed forces, and the holding of elections on the basis of proportionality. The PRK still opposed these things, but the two sides agreed to hold further talks on this.

June 1991: At a meeting in Pattaya, Thailand, on 24–26 June, the Khmer Rouge and PRK appeared to support Sihanouk's plan for the SNC to serve as a 'collegial presidency' led by a relatively weak Secretary-General, and to maintain the status quo, without establishing an interim coalition government, leaving the four factions with autonomous zones. The resistance factions wanted a monitored truce with the demobilisation of forces, a UN peacekeeping force, and a UN role in running the country until elections, but these terms were rejected by the PRK.

August 1991: At a meeting of Cambodian factions in Pattaya on 26–29 August, agreement was reached to disarm 70 per cent of each faction's forces and relocate the remainder to UN-supervised cantonment areas, to a proportional representation electoral system, and to a liberal, multiparty political system with freedom of association and political activity. The UN was also invited to establish a peacekeeping and peacebuilding mission to ensure the implementation of the agreement during the transitional period.

September 1991: A peace agreement ending the conflict in Cambodia was adopted at the reconvened Paris Conference on Cambodia.

Sources: Amitav Acharya, Pierre Lizée and Sorpong Peou (eds), *Cambodia – The 1989 Paris Peace Conference: Background Analysis and Documents* (Millwood, NY: Kraus, 1991), xxv–xlv; K.K. Nair, *ASEAN–Indochina Relations Since 1975: The Politics of Accommodation* (Canberra: The Strategic and Defence Studies Centre, Australian National University, 1984); Sorpong Peou, 'UN Conflict Resolution in the Cambodian War: An Analysis of the Permanent Five's Role and Its Impact on the Cambodian Peace Process' (Ph.D. Dissertation, Department of Political Science, York University, 1994); Carlyle A. Thayer, 'ASEAN and Indochina: The Dialogue', in Alison Broinowski (ed.), *ASEAN into the 1990s* (Basingstoke: Macmillan, 1990), 138–61.

But whether the strategy contributed to the settlement of the conflict itself is more debatable. Until 1986, the situation in Cambodia had been a complete stalemate, on the battlefield as well as at the negotiating table. The stalemate owed much to the fact that both Vietnam and China had remained confident of achieving a military solution to the conflict; China still hoped to oust the regime in Phnom Penh, while Hanoi continued to think of its action in installing a puppet regime in Phnom Penh as 'irreversible'. In this context, ASEAN's persistence in seeking a solution was helpful in breaking the diplomatic stalemate. This occurred in July 1987 when the Foreign Minister of Indonesia, Mochtar Kusumaatmatdja, met with his Vietnamese counterpart, Ngyuen Co Thach, in Ho Chi Minh City and agreed on a two-stage formula dubbed 'cocktail diplomacy', underscoring the informal nature of the contacts towards a settlement of the Cambodia conflict. The first stage of the formula was to include a dialogue among the Cambodian factions themselves, including the PRK regime in Phnom Penh, and the three Cambodian resistance factions. This would be followed by a second stage to include the relevant regional parties, including Vietnam and the ASEAN members.

This seemingly 'regionalist' formula upheld ASEAN's desire to be at centre-stage of the peace process. It could not be easily implemented in the near term owing to divisions among the Cambodian factions themselves, especially the PRK's refusal to sit at the table with the ousted Khmer Rouge leaders, and to the continuing differences and ambivalence among ASEAN members, some of whom were still suspicious of Vietnamese goodwill. To be sure, ASEAN's regionalist approach did pave the way eventually for direct talks between Prince Sihanouk, as the leader of the CGDK, and Hun Sen, Prime Minister of the PRK. It also led to two rounds of regional meetings, called the Jakarta Informal Meetings, in July 1988 and February 1989. These meetings dealt with the complex issue of power sharing among the Cambodian factions, the key to the eventual settlement of the conflict.

But one cannot deny that developments at the international level were significant factors in driving the peace process. While ASEAN was pursuing a regionalist solution to the problem that would limit the role of China and other outside powers, the changing relationship among the USA, the Soviet Union and China created favourable conditions for advancing the peace process. Among the most important developments was Mikhail Gorbachev's assumption of leadership in the Soviet Union and his 'new thinking' on regional conflicts, under which Moscow, keen to improve relations with the USA and seeking to reduce the economic burden of supporting its Third World clients, began to push Vietnam to withdraw from Cambodia. The gradual thawing of the US–Soviet Cold War was subsequently joined by *rapprochement* between Moscow and Beijing. Beijing, which had always viewed Vietnam's occupation of Cambodia as a direct consequence of Soviet support for Hanoi, had made the withdrawal of Vietnamese forces from Cambodia one of the key conditions for normalising relations with Moscow (the other issues being the settlement of the Sino-Soviet border dispute and the end of the Soviet occupation of Afghanistan). As Moscow complied with Beijing's demands by encouraging Vietnam to end its occupation of Cambodia, Beijing began to distance itself from the Khmer Rouge, the key element of its 'bleed Vietnam white' strategy.

While the end of the Cold War was steadily rendering the international context of the Cambodia conflict more conducive to a settlement, ASEAN as a group was becoming somewhat sidelined in the peace process, notwithstanding Indonesia's co-chairmanship of the two Jakarta Informal Meetings, and the two sittings of the Paris Peace Conferences on Cambodia (in 1989 and 1991). This view is reinforced by the instrumental role played in the Paris peace process by the five permanent members of the UN Security Council, as well as the initiatives proposed and undertaken by Australia (which included the comprehensive draft plan for an interim UN administration in Cambodia following the peace settlement, something which would lay the conceptual groundwork for the UN Transitional Authority in Cambodia).[24] And during the last stages of the conflict, ASEAN's own involvement and approach in the peace process was marred by external pressures and intra-mural disunity.[25]

For example, ASEAN's leadership role in the peace process suffered a major setback in July 1990 when the USA announced its decision to withdraw recognition from the CGDK, the Cambodian resistance coalition that included the Khmer Rouge. To the extent that the coalition was the brainchild of ASEAN, and the centrepiece of its diplomatic efforts, US de-recognition was unsettling.[26] The US action also marked the end of its practice of following ASEAN's lead in the Cambodian peace process, a trend that had already been evident with respect to other external players in the Cambodia conflict. To the former Foreign

Minister of Singapore, S. Rajaratnam, the architect of the hardline policy on Cambodia, the US move meant that 'the Cambodia problem has been unceremoniously snatched out of Asean's hands by its Western allies'.[27]

This development was compounded by intra-ASEAN differences starkly evident towards the final stages of the peace process. Indeed, the idea of 'cocktail diplomacy' mooted by Indonesia following the above-mentioned Mochtar–Thach accord of July 1997 had caused a serious rift within ASEAN as Thailand and Singapore indicated their strong disapproval of such a process. This served to undermine ASEAN's influence over the peace process. It is a matter of considerable irony that while ASEAN dithered over the formula envisaged under the Mochtar–Thach accord, this was precisely the course of action over which the interests of the principal external players, the Soviet Union and China, increasingly converged. As the annual general assembly vote on Cambodia approached in 1987, the Soviet Union voiced strong support for the national reconciliation process among the Cambodian factions and criticised ASEAN's backtracking on the Mochtar–Thach accord. China also indicated its approval of the 'cocktail party' concept. Even more significantly, Beijing appeared ready to drop its earlier demand that the restoration of the DK regime must remain an integral part of any Cambodia settlement.

An even more severe test of ASEAN's unity came in the wake of Thai Prime Minister Chatichai Choonhavan's celebrated call for 'turning the Indochinese battlefields into market places'. Thai economic and political initiatives that flowed from Chatichai's policy put ASEAN's political unity and credibility under its most severe stress.[28] Bangkok's move to invite Prime Minister Hun Sen to Bangkok in January 1989 not only brought to the surface deep divisions within the Thai government between the hardline foreign ministry and the prime minister's office, but also caused discomfort and apprehension in other ASEAN capitals, especially Singapore and Jakarta. The former Thai Foreign Minister and a founder of ASEAN, Thanat Khoman, accused the Chatichai government of having 'broken away' from ASEAN.[29] In Singapore, another founding foreign minister of ASEAN, S. Rajaratnam, warned that the Thai initiative could seriously damage ASEAN's credibility as one of the few successful examples of regional political cooperation in the Third World.[30]

Although the Indonesian government did not voice any public criticism of the Thai move, there were indications of considerable disquiet within its military and foreign policy elite over the implications of the Chatichai initiative for ASEAN. A magazine published by the powerful Alumni Association of the National Defence Institute in Jakarta found Thailand's policy 'violating the ASEAN consensus, wherein not a single ASEAN country is justified to make a commitment which is directed to help Vietnam before a comprehensive settlement has been found to the Cambodian problem (*sic*)'.[31] Singapore and Thai hardliners voiced apprehension that the invitation to Hun Sen would legitimise Vietnam's invasion of Cambodia.[32] Later Thai policy was blamed for the hardened position taken by Hanoi and Phnom Penh at the Second Jakarta Informal Meeting (JIM II) negotiations to settle the conflict, thereby perhaps derailing the prospects for a settlement at the first sitting of the Paris Conference on Cambodia in 1989.

Norms, identity and ASEAN in the Cambodia conflict

The Paris Peace Agreement on Cambodia was signed at the end of the second sitting of the Paris conference on 23 October 1991.[33] It was greeted by the ASEAN states with a strong sense of euphoria and self-congratulation. Speaking at the concluding session of the Paris conference, the Chairman of the ASEAN Standing Committee, Foreign Secretary Raul

Manglapus of the Philippines, 'acknowledge[d] with pride and rejoicing the successful contribution of ASEAN to the process that produced this triumphal event'.[34] Malaysia's Foreign Minister reminded the conference delegates that ASEAN had 'always, despite the many obstacles, persisted in its search for a peaceful and comprehensive settlement of the Cambodian conflict' and should therefore be entitled to 'a sense of fulfilment and achievement'.[35] Tommy Koh, Singapore's former Ambassador to the UN, put it differently: 'Without ASEAN there would have been no Cambodia issue. Because if we had not taken up the cause of Cambodia in early 1979, and steadfastly championed it, it would have disappeared.'[36]

The foregoing discussion has referred to the tensions between ASEAN's desire to punish Vietnam so as to defend the sanctity of its norms of non-interference and non-use of force in Southeast Asia's regional order and its desire to seek a peaceful settlement of the conflict so as to uphold its norms of peaceful settlement of disputes and regional solutions to regional problems. The problem for ASEAN, as mentioned earlier, was that it saw itself both as a party to the conflict (given the violation by Vietnam of a key norm of ASEAN) and as a conflict manager committed to a peaceful settlement of the conflict without significant interference by the outside powers. While the two goals were not mutually exclusive, they did create the basis of considerable ambivalence in ASEAN's approach.

It has become increasingly evident in the course of the foregoing analysis that ASEAN's role in the Cambodian peace process had paradoxical effects on its norms and identity. ASEAN was instrumental in raising the profile of the Cambodia issue in the international diplomatic arena. This, in turn, propelled the hitherto obscure grouping into the global limelight. ASEAN could be justly credited with keeping the Cambodia conflict on the international agenda at a time when the international community had little interest in Southeast Asia. The Cambodia conflict had positive effects for ASEAN's pursuit of a regional identity. After having unsuccessfully sought the co-option of Vietnam into a system of regional order founded on its norms, ASEAN presented the Vietnamese invasion as a gross violation of the principle of non-intervention in the internal affairs of states as well as the principle of non-use of force in interstate relations.[37] While organising an international campaign to isolate Vietnam and spearheading a diplomatic settlement of the conflict, ASEAN lost no opportunity to present itself in a more favourable international light *vis-à-vis* Hanoi. Vietnamese 'expansionism' was contrasted with ASEAN's 'good-neighbourliness' and desire for regional political stability (implying a territorial and political status quo in Southeast Asia), Vietnam's alliance with the Soviet Union with ASEAN's professed goal of a ZOPFAN in Southeast Asia, Vietnam's intense nationalism and ideological fervour with ASEAN's pragmatism and developmentalism, and Vietnam's military suppression of the Cambodian rebels with ASEAN's efforts for a political settlement of the conflict. ASEAN's Cambodia posture served not only to enhance its international stature (hence giving it a distinctive identity in international diplomacy), but also, at least initially, to strengthen its intra-mural solidarity. It motivated ASEAN members to overcome conflicting security interests and territorial disputes within the grouping, thereby moving it further on the path towards a security community. The Paris Agreement conformed to terms set by ASEAN from the outset, including the reversal of Vietnam's occupation and the replacement of the regime installed by its invasion through free and fair elections. ASEAN's diplomatic unity, though severely tested by the Cambodia conflict, had not collapsed entirely. As Tommy Koh put it, ASEAN 'always succeeded in evolving a consensus which we could live with'.[38]

But this claim should be kept in perspective. The Cambodia conflict was also a serious threat to ASEAN's unity and cohesion. As the conflict moved towards a political settlement,

Ali Alatas, the Foreign Minister of Indonesia, remarked that it is 'a widespread but histori-cally incorrect assumption that Cambodia is the cement of ASEAN'. As he saw it, the Cambodia issue had been 'divisive'.[39]

Tim Huxley has argued that ASEAN's preoccupation with the Cambodia conflict and its handling of the peace process might have distracted it from its original aims, especially the construction of national and regional 'resilience', entrenched the polarisation of Southeast Asia, and contributed to the militarisation of the region.[40] ASEAN's role in the Cambodia conflict also threatened to compromise its norms. Despite professing a role as a conflict manager, ASEAN was exploiting international concerns about Cambodia in order to isolate and punish Vietnam and pursuing a balancing posture *vis-à-vis* Vietnam and its external backer, the Soviet Union. This strategy relied heavily on securing political and military support from ASEAN's Great Power allies. Whether it achieved ASEAN's objective of securing the removal of Vietnamese troops from Cambodia might be debatable, but it certainly entailed serious compromises to ASEAN's desire for regional autonomy. The prolonged Cambodia stalemate sustained Chinese influence over the security concerns of the grouping; by accepting China's support and role against Vietnam, ASEAN effectively postponed its professed goal of reducing Great Power meddling in the region.[41] ASEAN's strategy of internationalising the Cambodia conflict also increased its political, economic and military dependence on the USA.

For ASEAN, the need for maintaining solidarity against Hanoi at the international level took precedence over diplomatic formulae that might have offered Hanoi the chance of a face-saving exit from Cambodia through regional reconciliation. Instead of providing a neutral political framework for conflict resolution through regional dialogue, ASEAN assumed the role of a subregional political, if not military, alliance against Hanoi in concert with China. The fact that several ASEAN countries stepped up mutual defence cooperation and offered military assistance to Thailand in the event of a Vietnamese attack served to project an alliance posture, thereby undermining ASEAN's role as conflict manager and threatening its norm against defence multilateralism.

In other words, ASEAN's role in the Cambodia conflict came, at least to some extent, at the expense of its norm of providing 'regional solutions to regional problems'. Part of this can be attributed to the nature of the Cambodia conflict, which, despite its roots in historical animosities and cleavages within Cambodian society, was also a product of Great Power rivalry at the global level. While ASEAN was able to play on this rivalry to isolate Vietnam, it remained hostage to developments at the global level before the realisation of its other major objective, a political settlement of the conflict acceptable to ASEAN, could be reached. As one Indonesian scholar predicted in 1988:

> if ASEAN's policy by itself is aimed at finding a final solution to the Kampuchean conflict, then ASEAN has failed or is bound to fail. It is unlikely that separately and on their own any of the countries of the region can possibly solve the problem. The desire that regional problems should be solved regionally without external interference will continue to be what it is – essentially a slogan, at best an aspiration, at least as far as the Kampuchean problem is concerned. In consequence, it is more likely that a solution of the Kampuchean problem will only be reached if the major powers also play their roles.[42]

The Paris settlement opened the door to the broader process of reconciliation between ASEAN and Indochina, especially Vietnam. The objectives of ASEAN's policy towards

Indochina were to change in fundamental ways. Instead of seeking a balance against Vietnam, ASEAN moved towards pursuing a vision of 'One Southeast Asia' which would encompass the Indochinese states (and Burma) in a system of regional order. The next chapter examines the extent to which ASEAN's norms figured in this reconciliation.

Notes and references

1 As Muthiah Alagappa notes:

> ASEAN did not envisage conflict prevention, containment and termination roles in regard to external conflicts. It hoped to eventually include all 10 states in the region, and that – pending inclusion – ASEAN's proposals for peace and security should cover all of Southeast Asia and not just the ASEAN subregion. The Indochinese states and Burma, however, did not subscribe to this view and accede to the 1976 Treaty. Thus, the conflict prevention measures of the Association have not applied to non-ASEAN Southeast Asia.

Muthiah Alagappa, 'Regionalism and the Quest for Security: ASEAN and the Cambodia Conflict', *Journal of International Affairs* (Winter, 1993).

2 For the text of the Bangkok Declaration and all other ASEAN documents mentioned in this chapter, see: *ASEAN Documents Series, 1967–1988*, 3rd edition (Jakarta: ASEAN Secretariat, 1988).

3 For good accounts of ASEAN's interests and role in the Cambodia conflict see: Chan Heng Chee, 'The Interests and Role of ASEAN in the Indochina Conflict', Paper presented to the International Conference on Indochina and Problems of Security and Stability in Southeast Asia held at Chulalongkorn University, Bangkok, 19–21 June 1980, p. 12; Tim Huxley, *ASEAN and Indochina: A Study of Political Responses*, Canberra Studies in World Affairs no. 19 (Canberra: Australian National University, Department of International Relations, 1985); Lau Teik Soon, 'ASEAN and the Cambodia Problem', *Asian Survey*, vol. xxii, no. 6 (June 1982); Michael Leifer, *ASEAN and the Security of Southeast Asia* (London: Routledge, 1989).

4 Chan Heng Chee, 'The Interests and Role of ASEAN in the Indochina Conflict', p. 12.

5 Larry A. Niksch, 'Vietnam and ASEAN: Conflict and Negotiation over Cambodia', Paper prepared for the conference on Southeast Asia: Problems and Prospects sponsored by the Defense Intelligence College and the Georgetown Center for Strategic and International Studies, Washington, DC, 4–5 December 1984, pp. 6–8.

6 Ibid., pp. 516–21.

7 Michael Leifer, *ASEAN and the Security of Southeast Asia* (London: Routledge, 1989), pp. 116–17.

8 China's position was disturbing to ASEAN, as it confirmed suspicions that Beijing's main interest was not in finding a compromise, but to use the Cambodia situation to bog down Hanoi in a protracted engagement in Cambodia that would seriously damage Hanoi's capacity to contest with China for influence in Southeast Asia. Faced with Chinese intransigence, the ICK was rescued only by a last-minute attempt by France to put forward a compromise statement saving it from total failure. The final statement of the conference called for 'appropriate arrangements to ensure that armed Kampuchean factions will not be able to prevent or disrupt the holding of free elections, or intimidate or coerce the populations in the electoral process'. But despite the face-saving gesture, the failure of the ICK was a major blow to the Cambodian peace process, aggravating the stalemate that had already taken root over the refusal of the Indochinese states to accept ASEAN's proposed formula for peace negotiations.

9 Justus van der Kroef, 'Kampuchea: The Road to Finlandization 1983', *Asian Profile*, vol. 13, no. 3 (June 1985).

10 Carlyle A. Thayer, 'ASEAN and Indochina: The Dialogue', in Alison Broinowski (ed.), *ASEAN into the 1990s* (Basingstoke: Macmillan, 1990), p. 154.

11 *Straits Times*, 1 August 1977.

12 David Jenkins, 'Panggabean's False Alarm', *Far Eastern Economic Review*, 8 June 1979, p. 24.

13 Arnfinn Jorgensen-Dahl, *Regional Organization and Order in Southeast Asia* (London: Macmillan, 1982), p. 115. Panggabean's comments assumed significance in view of unsubstantiated press reports circulating in the region that claimed movement of 'secret military air traffic' between Jakarta and Bangkok carrying 'military equipment as well as personnel'. These reports proved to be unfounded. Jenkins, 'Panggabean's False Alarm', p. 24.

14 *New Straits Times*, 21 November 1979.
15 This was confirmed by General Saiyud Kerdphol, the former Supreme Commander of Royal Thai Armed Forces, in a personal interview with the author. According to General Saiyud, both Malaysia and Singapore were informally involved, along with the USA, in a plan to provide contingency assistance to Thailand in the event of a major escalation of the Cambodia conflict spilling over into Thailand. This plan, worked out by General Saiyud himself and dubbed 'Joint Logistics Plan' (JLP), envisaged provision of armaments, including 'common items' such as ammunition and 105 mm and 155 mm guns, by Singapore and Malaysia from the latter's own stocks. According to General Saiyud, steps were taken to 'identify and mark' such items for emergency shipment. The JLP was a 'classified' plan worked out at the 'highest level' of the governments of the countries involved. It was to be activated in the event of a major threat to Thailand, not minor skirmishes on the border, but if Thailand faced the prospect of an open attack by Vietnam backed by the Soviet Union, resulting in the seizure of Thai territory. Personal interview, Bangkok, 26 June 1989 and 28 July 1989.
16 *Straits Times*, 27 June 1979.
17 *Straits Times*, 7 March 1979.
18 *Straits Times*, 4 March 1980.
19 *Star*, 9 May 1984.
20 *Bangkok World*, 9 June 1979.
21 Ibid.
22 Cited in Rodolfo C. Garcia, 'Military Cooperation in ASEAN', *Pointer* (April–June 1987), p. 9.
23 Carolina Hernandez, 'Regional Security in ASEAN: A Philippine Perspective', Paper presented to the Asiatic Research Centre Conference on East Asian Security: Perceptions and Realities, Seoul, Korea University, 25–26 May 1984, p. 12.
24 For an overview of the peace process, see: Amitav Acharya, Pierre Lizee and Sorpong Peou, *Cambodia: The 1989 Paris Peace Conference: Background and Documents* (New York: Kraus, 1991).
25 Michael Vatikiotis, 'Unite and Act', *Far Eastern Economic Review*, 16 January 1992, p. 26.
26 'Decision by US undercuts decade of Asean diplomacy', *Straits Times*, 27 July 1990.
27 'Cambodia: time for Asean to call it a day', *Straits Times*, 3 August 1990.
28 For an excellent discussion of the implications of the Chatichai initiative, see: Donald Weatherbee, 'ASEAN: The Big Loser in Thai Race for Profit in Indochina', *Straits Times*, 5 May 1989.
29 Cited in Surin Pitsuan, 'Thailand Speaks with a New Voice', *International Herald Tribune*, 6 April 1989.
30 S. Rajaratnam, 'Riding the Vietnamese Tiger', *Contemporary Southeast Asia*, vol. 10, no. 4 (March 1989).
31 Cited in *Straits Times*, 2 June 1989.
32 *International Herald Tribune*, 26 January 1989; *International Herald Tribune*, 30 January 1989; *Straits Times*, 14 March 1989.
33 The Final Act of the Paris Conference, signed on 23 October 1991, consisted of three documents: (1) 'An Agreement on a Comprehensive Political Settlement of the Cambodia Conflict'; (2) 'An Agreement Concerning the Sovereignty, Independence, Territorial Integrity and Inviolability, Neutrality and National Unity of Cambodia'; and (3) 'Declaration on the Rehabilitation and Reconstruction of Cambodia'. The first document contained annexes on 'the mandate for UNTAC, military matters, elections, repatriation of Cambodian refugees and displaced persons, and the principles for a new Cambodian constitution'.
34 Statement of HE Raul S. Manglapus, Secretary of Foreign Affairs of the Republic of the Philippines, on the Occasion of the Ministerial Session of the Paris Conference on Cambodia, 23 October 1991, p. 1.
35 Statement by HE Datuk Abdullah Ahmad Badawi, Minister of Foreign Affairs of Malaysia, at the Paris Conference on Cambodia, 23 October 1991, p. 2.
36 Tommy Koh, Singapore's former Permanent Representative to the UN, cited in *Straits Times*, 22 October 1991, p. 6.
37 On ASEAN's response to the Vietnamese invasion of Cambodia see: Chan Heng Chee, 'The Interests and Role of ASEAN in the Indochina Conflict', Paper presented to the International Conference on Indochina and Problems of Security and Stability in Southeast Asia held at

Chulalongkorn University, Bangkok, 19–21 June 1980, p. 12; Muthiah Alagappa, 'Regionalism and the Quest for Security: ASEAN and the Cambodia Conflict', *Journal of International Affairs* (Winter, 1993).

38 *Straits Times*, 22 October 1991, p. 6.
39 'Live and Let Live', interview with Ali Alatas, Foreign Minister of Indonesia, *Far Eastern Economic Review*, 11 July 1991, p. 13.
40 Tim Huxley, 'ASEAN Security Cooperation – Past, Present and Future', in Alison Broinowski (ed.), *ASEAN into the 1990s* (Basingstoke: Macmillan, 1990), p. 90.
41 Tim Huxley, 'ASEAN's Prospective Security Role: Moving Beyond the Indochina Fixation', *Contemporary Southeast Asia*, vol. 9, no. 3 (December 1987), pp. 194–207.
42 J. Soedjati Djiwandono, 'Indonesia, ASEAN and the Pacific Basin: Some Security Issues', in Dora Alves (ed.), *Cooperative Security in the Pacific Basin: The 1988 Pacific Symposium* (Washington, DC: National Defense University Press, 1990), p. 244.

4 Extending ASEAN norms
Benefits and burdens of ASEAN-Ten

If ASEAN had developed the attributes of a 'community' towards the end of the Cold War, then its scope was clearly less than 'regional', with membership limited to only one – ideologically 'like-minded' – segment of Southeast Asia. ASEAN was not identical with Southeast Asia. Its framework for regional order, including a ZOPFAN, was boycotted and vigorously opposed by the Indochinese states notably at the Non-Aligned summit in Sri Lanka in 1976. Moreover, the peaceful relations among the ASEAN members and hence its claim to be a regional security community owed much to common concerns over the domestic threat from communism and to cooperative efforts regionally to balance Vietnamese power. ASEAN functioned more as a subregional alliance than a regional security community. With the settlement of the Cambodia conflict, which removed the principal source of polarisation in Southeast Asia, ASEAN's role in building a Southeast Asian security community required a fresh appraisal. It had developed as an inward-looking subregional entity, but was faced with the challenge of developing a wider regional security community involving Vietnam, Laos, Cambodia and Burma.

ASEAN policymakers were not unaware of this challenge. Not long after the Paris Agreement, Thailand's Prime Minister, Anand Panyarachun, contended that ASEAN would have to seek a new regional order that embraces all nations of Southeast Asia in 'peace, progress and prosperity'.[1] Indonesia's Foreign Minister, Ali Alatas, offered an even loftier challenge, which was consistent with the declaratory security doctrine of ASEAN as enunciated from 1967:

> one quintessential dividend of peace in Cambodia to strive for would be the dawning of a new era in Southeast Asian history – an era in which for the first time Southeast Asia would be truly peaceful and truly free to deal with its problems in terms of its own aspirations rather than in terms of major power rivalry and contention; an era marking the beginning of a new Southeast Asia, capable of addressing itself to the outside world with commensurate authenticity and able to arrange its internal relationships on the basis of genuine independence, equality and peaceful cooperation.[2]

This chapter examines ASEAN's efforts to realise its professed goal of 'One Southeast Asia', a grouping of the ten countries of Southeast Asia during the 1990s, leading to the admission of Burma as the tenth member in 1999. The expansion of ASEAN is important in assessing its prospects of becoming a security community for two main reasons. First, given the different political and ideological characteristics of the new member regimes and their domestic vulnerabilities, the process of expansion itself has provided a major test of the very norms underpinning ASEAN regionalism, such as the doctrine of non-interference. Second, an expanded ASEAN means new political, economic and strategic challenges for the grouping. As discussed in Chapter 1, the theory of security communities holds that an increase in the scope and intensity of interactions may impose new 'burdens' or strains on an emerging security community, and even lead to its unravelling. ASEAN's expansion, aimed at developing a wider regional community of One Southeast Asia, made regional interactions more complex and introduced a greater diversity to the political and security predicament and outlook of the members of the grouping. It generated new sources of intra-mural tensions involving the new members that must be managed, and rendered the task of maintaining a common position *vis-à-vis* external powers more difficult. By increasing the scope of regional interactions, and seeking to socialise the new member into a regional community, ASEAN expansion also put pressure on the ASEAN Way with respect to conflict prevention and consensus building.

The process of regional accommodation: Vietnam

The Paris Peace Agreements on Cambodia in October 1991 dramatically transformed ASEAN's policy towards Vietnam. However, the beginning of the end of ASEAN–Vietnam rivalry can be traced to a thaw in its core element, namely Thai–Vietnamese rivalry, which in turn was helped by domestic changes in both countries. The most important of these occurred in Vietnam. In 1986, the ruling Communist Party adopted sweeping reforms to its domestic economy under a policy of 'renovation' or '*doi moi*'. This signalled, among other factors,[3] Hanoi's acknowledgement that its occupation of Cambodia had entailed severe economic costs that it could no longer afford. Managing the economic crisis at home to ensure regime survival became a more important concern for Hanoi than maintaining its occupation of Cambodia, justified as a response to external threats.[4] The objective of Vietnamese reform, to create a 'market mechanism economy' with the help of foreign investment and export promotion, dictated necessary adjustments to its foreign relations with the objective of ending its international isolation and improving the political climate for economic ties with its ASEAN neighbours.

Initially, the ASEAN states more or less ignored or dismissed the implications of Vietnamese reform for ASEAN–Indochina relations, choosing instead to focus on Hanoi's continued occupation of Cambodia. Although Singapore and Thailand noted that Vietnam's reform priorities would improve the outlook for a settlement of the Cambodia conflict, Thailand's Foreign Minister Siddhi Savetsila cautioned in June 1987 that Hanoi's commitment to reform appeared 'dubious' and did not signal an end to its attempt to impose 'military rule' on Cambodia.[5] But the advent of a new government in Bangkok under the premiership of Chatichai Choonhavan in August 1988 produced a major shift in Thai policy towards Hanoi. Recognising the political and economic opportunities offered by Vietnam's reforms, Chatichai declared that Thai policy would now aim at 'turning the Indochinese battlefields to marketplaces'.[6] Bangkok indicated a willingness to tolerate some Vietnamese influence in Indochina with the hope that the economic liberalisation of Indochina assisted by trade and investment links with Thailand would gradually reduce the scope for Vietnamese domination and enhance Thai influence in Indochina. The new Thai policy also sought to exploit a similar reform process initiated by the Lao People's Revolutionary Party at its Fourth Party Congress in 1986. Called 'New Economic Management', the package of reforms aimed at decentralising the management of public enterprises, encouraging the private sector, and envisaged closer economic cooperation with neighbours, 'in particular, trade relations with Thailand'.[7]

The new Thai policy was ahead of the official ASEAN position, however, and was greeted with suspicion by some of its members. Not only was Bangkok accused of seeking unilateral economic advantage by promoting rapid trade and investment links with Indochina, but Chatichai's political initiatives on the Cambodia conflict undermined ASEAN's consensual diplomacy.[8] In particular, his invitation to Prime Minister Hun Sen to visit Bangkok in January 1989 caused apprehension in other ASEAN capitals, especially in Singapore and Jakarta. Critics saw Thailand's 'battlefields to marketplaces' strategy as being driven by selfish considerations of economic gain, which would damage ASEAN's hitherto steadfast opposition to the Vietnamese-installed regime in Phnom Penh.[9] As noted in Chapter 3, hard-line military officials in Indonesia feared that the Thai initiative represented a breakdown of the ASEAN consensus on one of the most vital issues of security and stability in Southeast Asia.[10]

The critics of the new Thai policy argued that it would legitimise Vietnam's occupation of Cambodia and ease the pressure on Hanoi to make concessions at the negotiating table over Cambodia's political future.[11] Indeed, the failure of the Jakarta Informal Meetings hosted by Indonesia in 1988 to produce an agreement on power sharing among the Cambodian factions was blamed by Chatichai's critics on Vietnamese intransigence, which had suppos-edly resulted from the Thai government's premature offering of an olive branch to Hanoi.

Against this backdrop, Hanoi's declaration on 5 April 1989 that it would unconditionally withdraw its troops from Cambodia by September failed to produce a coherent ASEAN response towards improving the climate for ASEAN–Indochina relations. There was no question that the Vietnamese initiative removed two of ASEAN's most serious concerns about its occupation of Cambodia: first, Vietnam's ability to pose a security threat to Thailand, and second, Vietnam's alleged desire for domination of Indochina as a single strategic unit. Yet, ASEAN waited for clear proof of Hanoi's sincerity before pronouncing an end to the regional rivalry.[12] Moreover, differences surfaced over whether the end of Vietnamese aggression in Cambodia was a sufficient basis for welcoming Vietnam into the ASEAN fold, both as a partner in functional cooperation and as a formal member of ASEAN.[13] On the one hand, both Malaysia and Indonesia hinted that such a development should not await domestic transformation in Vietnam. As Malaysia's Prime Minister, Dr Mahathir Mohamad, put it, 'if Vietnam subscribes to the ideas of ASEAN, the system of government it practises should not be something that stands in the way of becoming a member of ASEAN'.[14] General Try Sutrisno, then the commander of Indonesia's armed forces, argued that by accepting Hanoi into its fold, ASEAN could 'rid the region of antago-nisms and be a force for cooperation, even with . . . [Vietnam's] communist ideology'.[15] On the other hand, Lee Kuan Yew proffered the view that the Indochinese countries should change their economic and political systems before being allowed into ASEAN.[16] Arguing that 'antagonists do not become bosom friends overnight', Singapore's Trade and Industry Minister, Lee Hsien Loong, stressed the need for the Cambodia issue to be fully resolved before the issue of Indochinese membership 'can be put on [ASEAN's] agenda'.[17]

Intra-ASEAN divisions and doubts over improved relations with Indochina persisted through 1990. This was evident at the time of President Suharto's historic visit to Hanoi in November of that year. Suharto, who became the most senior ASEAN leader to visit Hanoi since Vietnam's invasion of Cambodia, held out the possibility of increased economic cooperation between Indonesia and Vietnam. This prospect was not immediately welcomed by some of Jakarta's neighbours, especially Singapore. The Singapore media warned that '[u]ndue haste in helping Vietnam' might offset the economic and political pressures that had already led Hanoi to seek improved relations with ASEAN. In this view,

ASEAN should 'not allow the potential lucrativeness of the Vietnamese market to detract the grouping from the basic objective of rewriting the history of Vietnamese hegemony in Cambodia'.[18] It is ironic that, despite these protests, Singapore had already developed significant 'unofficial' trade relations with Vietnam and Cambodia.

The process of ASEAN–Indochina reconciliation also revealed the competitive aspect of intra-ASEAN relations, especially in the economic sphere. The Thai concept of 'Suwannaphum', or Golden Peninsula, developed by Prime Minister Chatichai, suggested a belief among sections within the Thai elite that Thailand could become the core of a continental segment of Southeast Asia comprising the three Indochinese states and Burma. In this domain, Thailand would aspire to be the principal engine of growth as well as the leading nation in shaping foreign policy and national security priorities. Such a segment of Southeast Asia might compete with a maritime domain comprising Indonesia as the political leader, and Singapore as the financial and communications hub,[19] thereby paving the way for a new polarisation of Southeast Asia.[20] Although subsequent Thai policy towards Indochina was more subtle than Chatichai's, and Thai business ventures failed to dominate the Indochinese economies, the lingering risk that the development of ASEAN's relations with Indochina might prove internally divisive was indicated in a warning issued by Malaysia's Foreign Minister, Datuk Ahmed Abdullah Badawi, who called upon ASEAN members to 'ensure that regional engagement strengthens rather than weakens it [ASEAN], builds upon successes rather than undermines it, and preserves ASEAN cohesion instead of diluting it'.[21]

But these intra-mural differences were not sufficient to block the progressive normalisation of relations between Vietnam and the existing ASEAN members. The key factor was Vietnam's willingness to facilitate a settlement of the Cambodia conflict, which helped to reduce ASEAN's misgivings. Not only did Vietnam announce the withdrawal of its forces from Cambodia, it also made concessions at the negotiating table (for example, agreeing to dismantle the regime it had installed in Cambodia and agreeing to UN-supervised elections of a new government there; this concession was made after the 1989 phase of the Paris conference, which explains why it failed while the 1991 phase produced an agreement). Thus, it is not surprising that a major breakthrough in Vietnam–ASEAN relations came nine days after the signing of the Paris Agreement on Cambodia, when Vo Van Kiet became the first Vietnamese premier to visit an ASEAN capital since 1978. Welcoming him to Singapore, his host, Prime Minister Goh Chok Tong, announced that a 'new relationship between ASEAN and Vietnam is emerging against a very different world backdrop'. This relationship, Goh added, would lead to 'a more relaxed strategic environment in Southeast Asia as Vietnam's economy and policies become more compatible with the ASEAN countries'.[22] Vo's trip was part of an all-ASEAN tour undertaken between October 1991 and March 1992 as a 'fence-mending exercise' intended to create a favourable climate for the fulfilment of Hanoi's desire to sign the Treaty of Amity and Cooperation as a first step towards membership of the grouping.[23]

That this effort was successful was confirmed by the communiqué issued at the end of the January 1992 ASEAN summit in Singapore. The summit declaration envisaged that ASEAN would forge a closer relationship based on friendship and cooperation with the Indochinese countries, following the settlement on Cambodia. As a first step, the Singapore Declaration opened the door to all countries of Southeast Asia to sign the Treaty of Amity and Cooperation, with Vietnam and Laos being the first signatories, to be followed by Cambodia once its internal political structure was settled through elections held under UN auspices (the membership of Burma, a non-Indochinese state, was not highlighted at this meeting).[24] At the summit, Thai Prime Minister Anand Panyarachun stressed the need for

ASEAN members to 'support the economic reconstruction of Cambodia as well as of Laos and Vietnam, especially through the expansion of trade and economic ties'.[25] Vietnam's satisfaction with the summit decision was conveyed by the armed forces newspaper *Quan Doi Nhan Dan*, which called the Singapore summit the 'most important conference since ASEAN was founded in 1967' and praised its new initiatives as 'important factors contributing to establishing a new security order in the region'.[26] ASEAN–Vietnam relations warmed substantially after a flurry of high-level visits by ASEAN leaders to Hanoi. On 15 January 1992, Thailand's Prime Minister Anand Panyarachun arrived in Hanoi for the first visit by a Thai head of government since 1976.[27] He was followed in April 1992 by Mahathir Mohamad, who became the first Malaysian Prime Minister to visit Hanoi since independence in 1957. A joint commission was set up to promote bilateral ties between Kuala Lumpur and Hanoi. In April 1992, Singapore's Senior Minister and former Prime Minister, Lee Kuan Yew, also paid a first visit to Vietnam and was invited by Hanoi to become an adviser to its reform programme.

Vietnam was formally admitted into ASEAN at its annual ministerial meeting in Brunei in July 1995. While the existing members welcomed Vietnam's entry as a significant strengthening of the grouping's influence *vis-à-vis* the larger powers, concerns were also voiced over the implications of an expanded ASEAN. Singapore's Foreign Minister noted that an expanded ASEAN would face difficulties in achieving consensus on key issues.[28] Vietnamese officials, for their part, contended that their decision to join ASEAN was motivated by three factors: to attract foreign investment, to develop and maintain friendly relations with regional states, and to boost Vietnam's domestic reform process.[29] Moreover, as one Vietnamese writer put it, '[p]olitically, due to ASEAN's high international prestige, ASEAN membership would enhance Vietnam's diplomatic standing and integrate Vietnam's security with the security of the whole of Southeast Asia, thus creating an external environment favourable for economic development'.[30] While Vietnamese officials were careful not to highlight their potential strategic gains from ASEAN membership, Hanoi obviously hoped that it would strengthen its position *vis-à-vis* China in the South China Sea dispute.[31] In addition, Hanoi could now make common cause with its ASEAN partners in resisting Western criticism of its human rights record, which had already become a key issue in ASEAN's dealings with the West.

In joining ASEAN, Vietnam acknowledged a shift in its thinking on, and approach to, regional order in Southeast Asia. To the extent that membership required Vietnam to accept and adhere to the obligations and norms of ASEAN, it could theoretically lay the basis for both sides to be bound eventually within a common political and diplomatic culture. There was also a greater convergence of the two sides' attitude towards the management of Great Power relations. In the words of a Vietnamese scholar, Hanoi's prior approach to Great Power relations was based on 'the old conception which advocated that a country should stand with one great power to oppose another one or neighbouring countries'. (This was a reference to Vietnam's alliance with the Soviet Union to oppose China and the USA.) This approach had conflicted with ASEAN's professed objective of a ZOPFAN, which called for regional autonomy. Hanoi's new approach to regional order was cast differently. As stated by Assistant Foreign Minister Tran Huy Chung, '[w]hat is most beneficial to the Southeast Asian countries is to have appropriately balanced relationships with great powers outside the region, with a view to resolving disputes for influence between them over the region'.[32] This desire for an 'appropriately balanced relationship' was indicative of Hanoi's need for a regional balance of power which could offset the perceived threat of Chinese domination. This coincided with ASEAN's move to seek a more 'inclusive' relationship among external powers which would lead to the establishment of the ARF (to be discussed in Chapter 6).

Testing non-interference: 'constructive engagement' with Myanmar (Burma), 1992–97

The admission of Burma proved to be a far more daunting and controversial task for ASEAN than that of Vietnam and Laos. There was, of course, a common basis for ASEAN's approach to Vietnam and Burma: the norm of non-interference. ASEAN had regarded Vietnam's invasion of Cambodia as a blatant violation of this norm. It was used to justify the policy of isolating Hanoi regionally and internationally. However, when Vietnam completed its military withdrawal from Cambodia, ASEAN, after some initial hesitation, saw no reason to oppose Vietnam's membership in the grouping because of its communist political system. The same logic now formed the basis for ASEAN's determination to include Burma despite the widespread international condemnation of the initiative, which was seen as bestowing legitimacy on a repressive regime. In ASEAN's view, political repression in Burma could not be used to justify the exclusion of Burma, since such a move would consti-tute interference in its internal affairs. (ASEAN's position was also dictated by several other geostrategic factors, to be discussed later, including the need to limit Chinese influence.)

Burma provided the first major test of ASEAN's non-interference doctrine in the post-Cold War setting. In September 1988, after a wave of nationwide pro-democracy demonstrations, political power in Burma was reasserted by an incumbent junta consisting of many of the key supporters of the previous regime headed by General Ne Win. The junta set up the State Law and Order Restoration Council (SLORC) and, in May 1990, organised the first parliamentary polls in three decades. The elections were won decisively (392 out of 485 seats) by an opposition coalition, the National League for Democracy, led by Aung San Suu Kyi (the daughter of the late Burmese nationalist leader, Aung San), who had been placed under house arrest since July 1989. The SLORC refused to convene the parlia-ment and transfer power. It also carried out large-scale arrests of opposition politicians and activists.

These domestic developments in Burma occurred at a time when ASEAN's own leadership in the Cambodian peace process was being undermined by intra-mural differences and also overshadowed by the role of the Great Powers and the UN. ASEAN had begun to face questions about its unity and relevance in the post-Cambodia era. While Cambodia was, on balance, a cementing factor in the evolving relationship between ASEAN and the West, the situation in Burma, and the human rights questions it posed, seemed to be a recipe for potential discord between ASEAN and its 'dialogue partners'.

The 1988 incumbency coup led to the suspension of Western and Japanese aid to Burma, although Japan partially resumed its aid in the following year. The ASEAN countries, however, saw the Burmese situation in very different terms. Western condemnation of the SLORC's abuse of human rights and violation of the democratic process was viewed by ASEAN as outside interference in the internal affairs of a country in the region. This was, of course, not the first time that ASEAN had declined to use a country's human rights record and lack of democratic credentials as a basis for deciding whether or not to engage it diplomatically. ASEAN had chosen not to address the genocidal acts of the Pol Pot regime on similar grounds.[33] ASEAN's response to the Burma situation was to put forward the concept of 'constructive engagement' previously employed in a different context in the case of South Africa.

Like ASEAN's earlier policy on Cambodia, 'constructive engagement' was a response to Thailand's security and other interests. In December 1988, three months after the Burmese junta (SLORC) had reasserted its power, Thailand's Army Commander, General Chaovalit Yongchaiyudh, became the first foreign leader to visit Burma since the coup. The visit was followed by a new economic and security relationship between the two countries. Burmese troops were allowed to cross the Thai border to attack Karen and Mon guerrilla positions. At the same time, Thai logging companies, facing a ban within Thailand, were allowed to operate within the Burmese border. Thai fishing companies negotiated major new contracts in Burmese waters in the Andaman Sea. This led some analysts to suggest a possible *quid pro quo* between the Thai military and the Burmese junta, whereby the latter could carry out lucrative logging operations (through companies with strong links to the Thai military) within Burma in exchange for tolerating Burmese troops' operations against its ethnic rebels inside Thai territory.[34] Indeed, some years later, the short-lived government of General Suchinda Kaprayoon, after reviewing Thai policy towards Burma, concluded that it had to continue the old policy of opposing economic sanctions against Burma because the 'two countries [were] close and share[d] many benefits and interests'.[35]

The nature and scope of the policy of 'constructive engagement' remained somewhat obscure. It is useful to look at the year 1992 as a point of origin for this policy, as it was then that much of the debate between ASEAN and the West over how to deal with Burma took place. Moreover, it was in 1992 that an Indonesian foreign ministry official offered the first explicit definition of the policy. He did so in the following terms:

> [w]e are telling them [the Burma regime] very quietly, in a Southeast Asian way, without any fanfare, without any public statements: 'Look, you are in trouble, let us help you. But you have to change, you cannot continue like this.'[36]

The essence of constructive engagement, in the words of the official, was to refrain from taking steps against the Burmese junta 'which embarrass and isolate them'.[37] Moreover, as noted, a key aim of the policy was to reject interference by the outside powers, especially the Western countries, in Burma's internal affairs. Further, constructive engagement was also moulded in the belief that the possibility of regional implications stemming from the crisis in Burma was a Southeast Asian issue to be handled by the region's countries themselves. The Western call to isolate Burma and punish it with sanctions was therefore a challenge to ASEAN's doctrine of both non-interference and regional autonomy.

ASEAN's policy of constructive engagement had its basis also in the concerns of some of its members regarding the growing international criticism of their record in the area of human rights and democracy. The Burmese crisis unfolded at a time when human rights and democracy were emerging as a major issue in the relationship between the ASEAN members and their Western 'dialogue partners', prompted by the shooting by Indonesian security forces of pro-independence demonstrators in the East Timorese capital of Dili in November 1991. In the midst of an outcry in the international media about the shooting, two Western donor countries, the Netherlands and Canada, suspended aid to Indonesia. While Indonesia retaliated by organising a new aid consortium excluding the Netherlands, Jakarta's international image suffered a major blow. Other ASEAN countries, especially Malaysia and Singapore, were criticised by human rights watchdogs for their internal security detention laws and lack of press freedom. Faced with loss of jobs to foreign (especially East Asian) competition, trade unions and human rights groups in the USA were calling for linking trade privileges for countries such as Malaysia to their provision for workers' rights. Violent military suppression of minority groups in Thailand, the Philippines and Indonesia also attracted a great deal of publicity for the human rights implications.

In September 1991, a meeting of foreign ministers of ASEAN and the EU in Luxembourg saw serious disagreement over the EU's insistence that human rights and environmental concerns should be part of any new economic cooperation agreement between ASEAN and the EU.[38] This position was rejected by ASEAN. Soon afterwards, the Vice-President of the EU Commission warned in Kuala Lumpur that failure to respect human rights would have a 'severe impact' on the EU's relations with developing countries, including ASEAN.[39] Following the Dili incident, the EU refused to negotiate a new cooperation agreement with ASEAN. Even Japan, which had taken a much softer position than Western countries on the ASEAN states' human rights record, seemed to disagree with ASEAN on the issue of aid-conditionality. At the Asian regional meeting on human rights in Bangkok in April 1993, Japan took the position that human rights should not be sacrificed to economic growth and that foreign aid would be linked to the human rights performance of the regime in power. This position was at odds with that of the ASEAN members. Against this backdrop, the policy of constructive engagement became a crucial test of will between ASEAN and the Western countries over the place of human rights and democracy in their political, economic and security relationships.

A key argument against constructive engagement, made not only by the Western governments or human rights advocates, but also by several human rights groups within Southeast Asia, was whether it actually involved a serious effort by ASEAN to persuade Burma to undertake political liberalisation. At the Manila PMC in July 1992, Foreign Minister Gareth Evans of Australia contrasted constructive engagement with ASEAN's diplomacy on the Cambodia conflict, lamenting the fact that ASEAN had chosen not to apply the 'kind of energy that it demonstrated for so long in seeking to resolve the Cambodian problem' to address the situation in Burma. US Under-Secretary of State Robert Zoellick challenged ASEAN to give substance to constructive engagement by 'tell[ing] the military regime it must release all political prisoners' and 'engag[ing] them in good-faith dialogue to restore constitutional government at an early date'.[40]

ASEAN's diplomatic engagement of the Burmese regime was limited and half-hearted, at least in the public arena. Only after intense international criticism and direct pressure from its dialogue partners did ASEAN send Raul Manglapus, Foreign Secretary of the Philippines, on an 'unofficial human rights mission' to Burma in December 1991.[41] The mission was largely unsuccessful as the SLORC refused to allow Manglapus to meet with the detained opposition leader Aung San Suu Kyi. Although ASEAN officials claimed subsequently to have applied private pressure on Burma, the extent and effect of this could not be confirmed.[42]

While officials in ASEAN responded to the criticism of constructive engagement by arguing that the policy had delivered results in extracting concessions from the regime, such as the release of some political prisoners,[43] independent analysts argued that the policy actually had little to show for itself. As the Thai newspaper *Nation* asked: 'A pertinent question is whether Asean's "constructive engagement" can make a leopard change its spots.'[44] Critics argued that the real driving force behind the policy was the economic interests of some ASEAN members, such as Thailand and Singapore, in Burma's newly liberalised economy.[45] ASEAN's pursuit of constructive engagement was further plagued by intra-mural differences. 'Constructive engagement', in the words of an official source in ASEAN, 'means that each [ASEAN] country can do what it wants, say what it wants as it sees fit, but not to take a collective six-country position'.[46] Intra-ASEAN differences were starkly evident when the July 1992 ASEAN Foreign Ministers Meeting in Manila debated the issue of whether to invite Burma's Foreign Minister to attend as a guest. The Philippines, as the host nation, and Indonesia supported extending an invitation. Indonesia argued that such an invitation would give a new seriousness to 'constructive engagement' and would be consistent with ASEAN's vision of 'One Southeast Asia', a regional community encompassing all ten states of Southeast Asia. But Malaysia resisted the move, arguing that the ASEAN Foreign Ministers Meeting was not an appropriate venue for engaging the Burmese junta in a dialogue. Privately, Malaysian officials hinted that their position was one of retaliation against Burma's persecution of the Rohingya Muslims, about 150,000 of whom had fled to Bangladesh by March 1992.[47] As a Muslim nation, Malaysia wished to register solidarity with the Rohingyas, whose plight had been the subject of domestic protest.

Growing international pressure and emerging intra-ASEAN differences were major factors behind ASEAN's decision to delay conferring observer status on Burma at the 1993 ASEAN Foreign Ministers Meeting in Singapore. (At the same meeting, Vietnam and Laos acceded to the Treaty of Amity and Cooperation and secured observer status, while Cambodia's political situation was still too uncertain for it to be considered for observer status.)[48] At this meeting, Thailand's Foreign Minister, Prasong Soonsari, acknowledged that the changes brought about by constructive engagement had been 'slow'.[49] Malaysia's official position on Burma reflected a similar sentiment. It urged ASEAN to demand a timetable for political liberalization in Burma so as to 'stimulate' change, rather than to allow change to 'evolve naturally'.[50]

Ironically, however, Malaysia was to emerge as one of the more outspoken advocates of Burma's admission to ASEAN in 1997, not least because it was the host of the ministerial meeting intended to mark the realisation of the 'One Southeast Asia' concept on the occasion of ASEAN's thirtieth anniversary. But divisions over Burma persisted in intra-ASEAN deliberations leading up to 31 May 1997, when it was decided to grant full membership to Burma. As ASEAN discussed the issue of Burmese membership, Singapore and Indonesia came up with justifications for granting membership on the basis of the non-interference doctrine. Singapore's Prime Minister, Goh Chok Tong, argued that the internal affairs of a country were not relevant to membership in ASEAN. As he put it, 'we have always taken the position that the internal situation of a country is that country's concern',[51] and that 'as far as the internal politics within each country, well, we did not begin Asean by examining that and excluding those that had a different system from ours (*sic*)'.[52] Even more forcefully, Ali Alatas of Indonesia argued that '[I]t is impossible for Asean to apply criteria and conditions for Burma's entry which have never been applicable for other members in the past.'[53] Comments by a Vietnamese Foreign Ministry spokesperson on 10 October 1996 reaffirmed the salience of the non-interference doctrine as the primary justification for granting membership to Burma:

A fundamental principle of ASEAN calls for respect for independence and sovereignty and non-interference in each other's internal affairs. Based on this principle, the member countries regard events that have taken place in Myanmar as entirely that country's internal affair. When and what countries are to be admitted is ASEAN's internal business. Stemming from this fundamental policy and in its capacity as an ASEAN member, Vietnam shares this view.[54]

In contrast, the Philippines and Thailand were known to have opposed the move, and there might have been some reluctance on the part of Singapore as well.[55] On the eve of the 31 May 1997 ASEAN Foreign Ministers Meeting, Philippine Foreign Minister Domingo

Siazon admitted that there was no consensus on the timing of Burma's entry. Even more strikingly, Thailand's Foreign Minister Prachaub Chaiyasan stated that Burma's internal politics 'are an important factor to consider'.[56] It was clear that Thailand and the Philippines were less enthusiastic about Burma's admission than Malaysia and Indonesia. The Philippine government, conscious that its own domestic political system and NGO community wanted it to take a hardline stand on Burma, sought to justify its support for ASEAN's decision by expressing the hope, as Foreign Minister Siazon put it, that the integration of Burma would 'have a positive impact over the long-term on the human rights situation'.[57] Another notable development was the opposition to the move to grant membership to Burma by the ASEAN-ISIS group of regional think-tanks, which for the first time broke from the governmental position on a major regional political and security issue by publicly opposing the move, even while it criticised similar opposition by Western academics as 'interference' in ASEAN's internal matters. One factor that appeared to have helped ASEAN to overcome intra-mural differences over Burma was the US decision to impose sanctions against Burma. The US action made it impossible for ASEAN to delay its admission, since that would imply caving in to US pressure and would thereby compromise its goal of regional autonomy. It is clear that the US sanctions were meant to discourage ASEAN from granting membership to Burma. Nicholas Burns, the US State Department spokesman, had said: '[w]e are trying to use our influence to make the point that Burma should be given a stiff message that it is not welcome'.[58] However, as one ASEAN-ISIS scholar, Kusuma Snitwongse, pointed out, the US sanctions served to 'weaken the case against Burma's admission', causing ASEAN to adopt a 'sort of defiant position vis-à-vis the West'.[59]

While ASEAN had consistently invoked its non-interference doctrine in justifying its engagement policy, there were other more political and strategic considerations at work behind the decision to grant membership to Burma. Among these was a concern with the growing Chinese influence in the country, evident in the economic and military links between the two countries. By accepting Burma as a member, ASEAN was trying to prevent that country from sliding into a Chinese sphere of influence.[60]

A basic irony of ASEAN's policy of constructive engagement was that it could not be regarded as strict non-interference. At best, it implied a particular kind of interference in support of the regime. It is hard to believe that the decision to admit Burma would not have strengthened the domestic position of SLORC *vis-à-vis* the internal pro-democratic opposition. A strict policy of non-interference would have meant taking a neutral position towards Burma. The grant of membership gave the regime a greater sense of international legitimacy. Not surprisingly therefore, ASEAN's move was perceived internationally as sanctioning repression. The decision to admit Burma was criticised by several media and human rights advocacy groups in Thailand, where the *Nation* described it as 'a triumph of evil over humanity', adding that '[t]here is a Thai saying that one rotten fish can spoil the whole basket of fish'.[61] The most trenchant criticism came from Sukhumbhand Paribatra, a Thai parliamentarian, who argued:

> Because image is important, Asean's ability to maintain and to enhance its status as an influential diplomatic community will be determined not by the number of members but by the perceived quality of membership, which in turn, is likely to be determined by the quality of new members. . . . Many groups in the West believe Asean to be a 'club of dictators': it is an unjust label, but an early admission of Burma will simply give sustenance to this prejudice. . . . Why should the Asean governments and peoples have to bear the costs of Slorc's folly and intransigence?[62]

The proponents of constructive engagement argued that such a policy would improve Burma's economic position and thereby induce peaceful domestic political change. But this remained to be proven. Even the highly pro-market weekly *The Economist* was sceptical of the argument: 'Constructive engagement may make sense when dealing with a regime – like China's – that will respond with long-term economic policies to improve the common man's lot. It makes no sense if it sustains regimes that practise only repression.'[63] ASEAN's claim that the policy had worked in helping political liberalisation was flatly contradicted by Aung San Suu Kyi when she was finally released from house arrest in 1995. As ASEAN ministers promptly credited the constructive engagement policy for her release, Suu Kyi herself remarked:

> The question is for whom has it been constructive? Was it constructive for the forces of democracy? Was it constructive for the Burmese people in general? Was it constructive for a limited business community? Or was it constructive for SLORC?[64]

The Burmese episode showed that while ASEAN very much cherished the attributes of a security community, it had no desire to turn itself into a 'democratic security community'. Kantian propositions concerning the linkage between democracy and peace have had little resonance for ASEAN as a regional organisation. Upholding the norms of non-interference and regional autonomy occupies a more central place in ASEAN's approach to regional order than acquiring a more positive international image and developing a regional effort to promote human rights and democracy. ASEAN in this respect proved to be more conservative and sovereignty conscious than regional organisations in Europe, Latin America and even Africa, which have, to varying degrees, accepted the need for intervention to promote human rights and democracy.

The admission of Burma had two major implications for ASEAN's norms concerning non-interference. The policy of 'constructive engagement' was consistent with this norm but the events leading to, and subsequent to, ASEAN's admission of Burma exposed the political and diplomatic, if not economic, costs of sustaining this norm. (The loss of international goodwill for ASEAN was the main damage, although the EU's refusal to negotiate a new economic treaty with ASEAN was an economic cost.) Moreover, the intra-ASEAN debate surrounding the admission of Burma showed that ASEAN's prior consensus on the inviolability of this norm was eroding, especially as a result of democratisation within some of its member states. The fact that Thailand and the Philippines, the two most open polities in ASEAN today, were also the least enthusiastic supporters of Burma's admission shows how changes in domestic politics can affect regional norms in ASEAN. Indeed, in late 1997 when a new Thai government (headed by Chuan Leekpai, who took office in the wake of the Asian economic crisis) proposed the idea of 'flexible engagement' (later called 'enhanced interaction'), it was aimed partly at pressuring the regime in Yangon to undertake political liberalisation (apart from addressing future economic downturns, as will be discussed in Chapter 5).

Cambodia 1997–99: limits to non-interference?

In embracing Vietnam, Laos and Burma, ASEAN refused to consider the domestic political system of a country as a criterion for membership.[65] This policy was consistent with its norm of non-interference as the basis for inter-state relations. But in the case of Cambodia, strict adherence to this norm was severely tested, raising serious doubts concerning its continued relevance.

Since the UN-supervised election in 1993, Cambodia had been under the rule of a coalition government between royalist forces led by Prince Ranarridh and the Cambodian People's Party (CPP, which included members of the Vietnamese-installed communist regime) led by Hun Sen.[66] The power-sharing arrangement was extremely tenuous, with the two factions squabbling frequently over a variety of issues, especially that of how to deal with the still-insurgent Khmer Rouge faction. On 5–6 July 1997, after complaining that Ranarridh was sheltering former Khmer Rouge soldiers, who had surrendered to his faction of the Cambodian army, in order to build his military strength *vis-à-vis* the CPP (and thereby gain an advantage in the parliamentary elections scheduled for 1998), Hun Sen ousted the prince and seized control of the Phnom Penh government, thereby creating yet another period of chaos and turmoil in Cambodian history. The episode also dealt a blow to Cambodia's chances of gaining ASEAN membership in 1997 and to ASEAN's hopes for realising its dream of 'One Southeast Asia' at the time of the thirtieth anniversary of the founding of the organisation.

When the conflict between Hun Sen and Ranarridh escalated in early 1997, several ASEAN leaders travelled to Cambodia to urge restraint and reconciliation between the two. (Among them were Indonesia's President Suharto and Thailand's Prime Minister Chaovalit Yongchaiyudh; the latter's visit in June 1997 was of symbolic importance since it brought Ranarridh and Hun Sen to a joint news conference that announced the capture of the Khmer Rouge leader, Pol Pot.) In the event, ASEAN members reacted with equanimity to the internal turmoil in Cambodia. As signs of a major power struggle there became evident, Ali Alatas, speaking on the eve of ASEAN's Foreign Ministers Meeting on 31 May 1997 to consider the admission of new members, stated that the internal turmoil in Cambodia was no barrier to its entry into ASEAN.[67] On 8 July 1997, after the coup, he was equally cautious: '[w]hat's happening now is a struggle between the two premiers, and is entirely Cambodia's own internal affair. Cambodia is a sovereign state, people can't just go in whenever they want.'[68] At the same time, however, Indonesia suggested convening a special ASEAN Foreign Ministers Meeting to discuss the crisis. (This was a critical move; Suharto had been deeply affronted by Hun Sen's action, including his stated readiness to forgo ASEAN membership, if its leaders interfered in Cambodian affairs.) The meeting, which convened on 10 July, produced the following agreement:

> While reaffirming the commitment to the principle of non-interference in the internal affairs of other states, they [the ASEAN Foreign Ministers] decided that, in the light of unfortunate circumstances which have resulted from the use of force, the wisest course of action is to delay the admission of Cambodia into Asean until a later date.[69]

The meeting also decided to send a delegation headed by Ali Alatas to King Sihanouk and the two co-premiers, Hun Sen and Ranarridh.

In the course of responding to the Cambodian crisis, ASEAN enunciated, or at least restated, an important principle concerning its attitude towards the use of force with significant implications for its doctrine of non-interference. In justifying the postponement of Cambodia's membership, Singapore's Foreign Minister, S. Jayakumar, stated that failure to act would 'imply that Asean was condoning ... the recourse to force to change governments'[70]:

> Any unconstitutional change of government is cause for concern. Where force is used for an unconstitutional purpose, it is behaviour that Asean cannot ignore or

condone. . . . As a principled and constructive organisation, Asean's reputation will be diminished if it does not register its dismay and displeasure at certain conduct unacceptable to the international community.[71]

Had this been a case of use of force by one state against another, then ASEAN's action would have been consistent with its norm of non-use of force. But the Hun Sen coup was a case of one domestic faction using force against another. Thus, Jayakumar's view suggested a possible shift in principle; that is, a domestic power struggle leading to the forcible ousting of an existing government would violate an ASEAN norm.[72] It should be noted that ASEAN could and did find a basis for its action in denying Cambodia membership because of its members' status as signatories to the Paris Peace Agreement. In this sense, the coup was not strictly an 'internal' matter to Cambodia. Jayakumar had invoked the Paris Agreement in justifying ASEAN's decision to send a ministerial delegation to Cambodia.[73] Moreover, ASEAN's response was partly an attempt to cover the embarrassment suffered by Hun Sen's blatant defiance of earlier conciliation attempts by leaders such as President Suharto. Had Cambodia already been admitted to ASEAN, it is unlikely that ASEAN would have done anything about it. Furthermore, Jayakumar's position was not strictly an ASEAN one; it had not been formally enunciated in the same manner by ASEAN as a whole (although Jayakumar restated it as an ASEAN norm in 1998, as discussed in the last section of this chapter). But it did introduce an important area of ambiguity about the norms of ASEAN concerning non-interference and non-use of force.

Hun Sen himself saw ASEAN's action in delaying Cambodia's membership as constituting a blatant interference in Cambodia's domestic affairs. He asked ASEAN to 'stay out of our internal business'.[74] Later, he threatened to withdraw Cambodia's application to join ASEAN with these words: 'I am afraid of joining Asean because of Asean interference in internal affairs'.[75] (Hun Sen's statement was the first time that a Southeast Asian country had turned down, or threatened to turn down, membership of ASEAN in the post-Cold War period; Vietnam and Burma had done so during the formative stages of ASEAN.)

The Jayakumar position was far from a blanket endorsement of collective ASEAN action in matters related to the internal politics of its member states. It disapproved of the forcible ousting of an 'established government'. It did not disapprove of instances when a government itself would use force against its own people. (Such disapproval, which would address criticism of ASEAN's anti-human rights orientation, would be a much more serious breach of non-interference.) However, if the principle of opposing an unconstitutional use of force to change established governments were to be regarded as ASEAN policy, then it could, theoretically speaking, apply to *coup d'états*. For example, if a coup against the regime in Indonesia or in Thailand were to take place, would ASEAN oppose the new government? This remains to be seen.

In essence, ASEAN's decision to delay Cambodia's membership re-affirmed ASEAN's concern with regime security, which, as discussed in Chapter 2, was an important source of its norm of non-interference. What was perhaps new was that, for the first time, this concern with regime security and a principle concerning the use of force in domestic politics had been publicly articulated, in this case by a member country (Singapore), rather than being indicated implicitly.

It is important to note that while the decision to delay Cambodia's membership and send a mission to resolve the crisis might be seen as a mild form of interference, ASEAN did not join the USA or Japan in taking more serious punitive action against the Hun Sen regime, such as a suspension of aid. ASEAN insisted that the act of delaying membership and sending a delegation did not constitute a violation of non-interference. Indonesia's Foreign Minister, Ali Alatas, insisted that '[w]e did not pass judgement on who is right, who is wrong, who is legitimate or who is illegitimate or whether there was a coup d'etat'.[76] He also denied that ASEAN's reaction constituted interference: 'We don't want to interfere but we have the right and the duty, as ASEAN foreign ministers, to discuss what are the implications of this.'[77]

But as Hun Sen was blaming ASEAN for too much interference in the affairs of Cambodia, the doctrine of non-interference came under pressure from an unexpected quarter. It came from those who thought that because of its excessive deference to the non-interference doctrine, ASEAN had not done enough to prevent the Paris accords from unravelling. Chief among these critics was the then Malaysian Deputy Prime Minister, Anwar Ibrahim. In a startling commentary, Ibrahim acknowledged that '[o]ur non-involvement in the recon-struction of Cambodia actually contributed to the deterioration and final collapse of national reconciliation'.[78] To prevent similar state collapses in Southeast Asia in the future, he proposed the idea of 'constructive interventions' including the following steps: (1) direct assistance to firm up electoral processes; (2) an increased commitment to legal and adminis-trative reforms; (3) the development of human capital; (4) the general strengthening of civil society and the rule of law.[79] According to this view, a framework of constructive intervention by ASEAN and other members of the international community in keeping Cambodia committed to the path of national reconciliation would be in the interests of ASEAN, since it cannot afford to have a 'failed state' as a member.

Whether the idea of constructive intervention actually amounted to a break from the doctrine of non-interference is questionable. The measures proposed by Ibrahim took the form of proactive and positive assistance to be carried out only with the consent of the recipient state. They did not imply any kind of coercion or pressure which might be construed as an infringement of the latter's sovereignty. The director of a Malaysian think-tank closely allied to Ibrahim conceded that the concept of constructive intervention

> in no way violates ASEAN's principle of non-interference in the domestic affairs of another country. What it advocates is that Asean must pro-actively involve itself in the resolution of problems that occur in its own neighbourhood, usually with the consent of the member concerned.[80]

Nonetheless, the idea of constructive intervention was met with a cool response from sovereignty-minded ASEAN policymakers. Thailand was most supportive of the concept, however. Its Foreign Minister contended that

> [a]s Asean becomes more open, as growing interdependence means events in one country can send shock waves throughout the region, we need to rethink some of our most basic assumptions, ranging from the meaning of development and cooperation to the implications of non-intervention.[81]

Later, as will be discussed in Chapter 5, it was Thailand that proposed the idea of 'flexible engagement' and 'enhanced interaction', which envisaged a more 'intrusive' form of regionalism in ASEAN.[82] (This was not specifically oriented towards Cambodia, but was proposed as a general framework for ASEAN in the wake of the Asian economic crisis.) Indonesia's Foreign Minister was cool towards the idea, maintaining that while ASEAN needed to be more proactive, Ibrahim's comment was 'not an Asean policy'.[83]

Such diverse reactions were a clear indication that a more intrusive political and security role by ASEAN would strain the existing consensus on its norms and approaches to regional order.

It is also noteworthy that Vietnam's position appeared to differ from those of the rest of ASEAN's members on the question of postponing Cambodia's membership. Vietnam's Foreign Ministry suggested in a statement that while it supported the consensus decision by ASEAN to delay Cambodia's membership, it would have preferred to have ASEAN allow Cambodia to join along with Laos and Burma. Moreover, Deputy Foreign Minister Vu Khoan told a newspaper that Hanoi wanted to see stability in Cambodia, which was interpreted as implying support for Hun Sen.[84] In New York, Prince Ranarridh's decision to meet with all ASEAN envoys to the UN, except the Vietnamese, could also be seen as a sign of how Vietnam's position was perceived by him.

Finally, the circumstances leading to ASEAN's decision to delay Cambodia's membership revealed one of the major pitfalls of expansion. As an editorial in the *Jakarta Post* put it:

> The current developments in Cambodia could serve as a lesson for ASEAN, that although the strategic advantages of accomplishing the long-standing ambition of an ASEAN 10 by the inclusion of Burma, Laos and Cambodia, are undebatable, swift action is not always the most expedient.[85]

When ASEAN adopted the doctrine of non-interference as a fundamental basis of regionalism in Southeast Asia, it was giving expression to the fears and insecurities of all newly independent states concerning their sovereignty. The doctrine was meant to protect ASEAN members from external meddling, rather than internal collapse. This was at a time when ASEAN members were acutely concerned with their survival in the face of perceived attempts at subversion, from both within and without the region (particularly by the communist powers, China and Vietnam). After several decades of state building and the experience of living within the state system, ASEAN members, at least some of them, have displayed a greater self-confidence about their sovereign statehood. A more relaxed attitude towards non-interference may not be necessarily incompatible with the requirements for regional order, however. And it is clear that should ASEAN adopt a policy of intervention, it would not take the form of coercive interference in the domestic politics of a member state, but of proactive and supportive assistance to prevent the collapse of an existing regime and to maintain internal stability in the state. This would be consistent with ASEAN's traditional pro-regime bias, which, as seen in Chapter 2, has been a key basis of ASEAN regionalism in general, and of the doctrine of non-interference in particular.

Cambodia was finally admitted to ASEAN on 30 April 1999. The Secretary-General of ASEAN described the event as the fulfilment of the 'vision of our Founding Fathers to unite all nations of Southeast Asia under one ASEAN roof'.[86] This step towards a collective regional identity notwithstanding, the events leading to its admission had been quite controversial. They had raised questions about ASEAN's ability to handle the burdens of an expanded membership.

The impact of expansion on ASEAN's norms and identity

While membership expansion offered several benefits to ASEAN, it also posed a serious test of its norms. Accession by Vietnam, Burma, Laos and Cambodia to the Treaty of Amity and Cooperation[87] committed them to the regional 'code of conduct' on territorial integrity and peaceful resolution of disputes. This commitment could facilitate intra-regional conflict management. For example, Vietnam's differences with the ASEAN six became more manageable than when Vietnam was outside the ASEAN framework.[88] ASEAN expansion also encouraged subregional economic cooperation, such as the 'growth triangle' concept, which served as a further confidence-building mechanism in interstate relations. Expansion would promote transnational contacts between societies and peoples, helping to bridge gaps in perceptions of self-interest and promoting a greater sense of regionalism.

Expansion was especially beneficial to smaller states such as Cambodia and Laos which, like Brunei and Singapore before them, could now expect to be treated as equal partners with their larger and more powerful neighbours. For Vietnam, Burma, Cambodia and Laos, ASEAN membership marked the end of their isolation in international politics. ASEAN membership made it increasingly difficult for Washington to rationalise and continue its policy of non-relations with Hanoi.[89] As ASEAN members, Cambodia, Laos, Vietnam and Burma would be able to take advantage of the coordination and collective bargaining capacity at multilateral institutions and secure greater resources for their reconstruction and development efforts. The new members could engage the major powers of the world through the ASEAN Post-Ministerial Conferences (ASEAN-PMC), which would be difficult for small states such as Cambodia or Laos left to their own devices. Similarly, new members could pursue their security interests within the ARF, which includes all the major players affecting regional security and stability in the Asia Pacific region.

On the other hand, the circumstances surrounding Cambodia's membership process suggested that the doctrine of non-interference could be facing an erosion as a result of membership expansion. (This adds to other challenges to the non-interference doctrine in the wake of the regional economic crisis discussed in Chapter 5.) This development was suggested by the apparently contradictory message in a statement by the Foreign Minister of Singapore, S. Jayakumar, at the ASEAN Foreign Ministers Meeting in July 1998 at which he outlined the norms of ASEAN:

- Sovereign equality and decisions by consultations and consensus;
- Non-interference in each other's internal affairs;
- Avoidance of the use of force to change established governments or an internationally recognised political order;
- Open economies;
- Making ASEAN the cornerstone of our foreign policies.[90]

What is striking about the above list is the possibility of a certain amount of tension between the second and third principles, which was evident in ASEAN's response to the Cambodia crisis of 1997. How could one maintain a policy of non-interference, yet still reject a change of government in a member state brought about by the use of force (meaning a coup carried out by its own armed forces)? If a violation occurred of the third principle as the result of a coup, ASEAN must at least condemn the event as such. But would not condemning a coup in a member state amount to the violation of the second principle, namely non-interference? In a similar vein, expansion posed additional challenges to ASEAN's norm of non-use of force in settling disputes. It imposed new security burdens on ASEAN, including territorial disputes arising from unresolved maritime boundaries and overlapping exclusive economic zones.[91] Intra-ASEAN ties now face additional bilateral problems, such as Thai–Vietnamese, Thai–Laos (the two had fought a brief low-scale war in the 1980s), Vietnamese–Cambodian and Thai–Burmese disputes over territory and resources. At the same time, whether the new members would abide by ASEAN's norms of non-use of force and pacific settlement of disputes remains uncertain. For example, the Thai newspaper, *Nation*, raised doubts as to whether, as an ASEAN member, Burma would live up to 'regional or international norms of conduct and behaviour'.[92] Citing its occupation of a disputed islet in the Moei River, another Thai paper wondered if Burma would respect ASEAN's norm of non-use of force.[93] The fact that Vietnam was involved in border disputes with a number of neighbouring states, including Cambodia, China, Indonesia, Malaysia and Thailand, increased the burden of intra-mural territorial disputes on ASEAN regionalism. Compounding the problem is the possibility that expansion makes it more difficult for ASEAN to maintain the ASEAN Way. Whether the new members, lacking familiarity with the highly informal and inter-personal way in which ASEAN conducts its business, could be 'socialised' into the ASEAN Way is by no means assured.

Expansion also imposed new burdens on ASEAN's external relations which would further test its norm of regional autonomy while maintaining constructive relations with the major external powers. Relations with the EU had been strained by the latter's vehement refusal to include Burma in its cooperation agreements with ASEAN. Moreover, expansion would draw ASEAN into Sino-Vietnamese rivalry and further raise the importance of the South China Sea dispute in ASEAN's security challenges. As one commentary put it, ASEAN's 'diplomatic border' was moved 'right up to the frontier with China'.[94] Hanoi lost no time in publicising the 'common fear of Chinese policy in the South China Sea' that it shared with other ASEAN members such as the Philippines and Malaysia.[95] Vietnamese leaders suggested that ASEAN's decision to see Vietnam as part of the grouping was due to 'economic and defence reasons', and was linked to ASEAN's fears about China's aggressive posture on the Spratly Islands dispute.[96] But Hanoi's bid to develop an anti-Chinese front carried the risk of exacerbating existing divisions among ASEAN states over perceptions of China, as will be discussed in Chapter 5. Joining ASEAN also created the possibility of dragging Cambodia into a future conflict between China and ASEAN states over issues such as the South China Sea dispute. Given its close ties with China, it may not be in Cambodia's interest to endorse a hardline stand by an ASEAN member, or by the grouping as a whole, against Chinese policy in the South China Sea.

Membership expansion carried major implications for regional identity building. One area affected is policy coordination against internal threats. As noted in Chapter 1, security cooperation against such threats contributes to the development of security communities. ASEAN's expansion enhanced regime security in the new members. In the past, political dissident groups challenging central authority in Cambodia, Burma and Laos might have been able to secure sanctuary in neighbouring states. This had been especially true of Cambodia where successive regimes have been undermined by the ability of groups opposing them to secure sanctuary in Thailand and Vietnam. Under the ASEAN framework, neighbours were obliged to refuse access to any rebel group fighting central authority in the new members.

Expansion also added to regional economic interdependence, another source of collective identity. It raised the volume of both intra-regional trade and ASEAN's total trade.[97] The participation of the new members in the AFTA has contributed to ASEAN's collective competitiveness and expanded the appeal of ASEAN's internal market to foreign investors, a critical issue at a time of potential diversion of investment to other areas such as China and India. For ASEAN, the economic liberalisation programmes of the new members provided new economic opportunities at a time when traditional Western markets were turning protectionist. An expanded ASEAN also helped the competitiveness of the original ASEAN six by providing them with a cheaper source of raw materials and production locations, an important benefit as they graduated out of the Generalised System of Preferences (GSP). In particular, the original ASEAN six stood to benefit from the GSP privileges of the new members (except Burma which does not enjoy GSP privileges as a result of Western sanctions) by using them as export platforms to the rest of the world for textiles, garments and the electronic assembly industry. It also enabled them to free their resources for developing more sophisticated industries in keeping with their evolving comparative advantage. The new members were also expected to derive major benefits from expansion (although they will suffer from a loss of customs revenues). It ended their economic isolation (a common feature of all of them, albeit for different reasons). They benefited from investments from the original ASEAN six, especially in their labour-intensive manufacturing sectors as well as in infrastructure. Moreover, the new members could take advantage of ASEAN's collective bargaining system; membership meant that their access to world markets could be negotiated multilaterally, rather than individually.

Despite these potential benefits, membership expansion posed some serious challenges to ASEAN's unity. Of particular importance here were the different levels of economic development between the ASEAN six and the new members. ASEAN had gone through a membership expansion before, when Brunei joined it following independence from Britain in 1984. But the entry of small, rich and stable Brunei had been a remarkably uneventful affair, compared with the circumstances involving the admission of poor and unstable Burma and Cambodia. The addition of the three Indochinese states and Burma created a real danger of the emergence of a two-tier ASEAN of haves and have-nots.[98] Given the concerns of the new members with regime security, their inclusion into ASEAN also introduced a greater diversity of political outlook within the grouping, especially over questions of human rights and democracy. These differences, along with a failure to relate to the ASEAN Way of diplomacy, contributed to possible disillusionment and alienation on the part of the new members and their questioning of the benefits of ASEAN membership. Add their misgivings (especially on the part of Burma and Vietnam) about moves to dilute the non-interference doctrine (see the last section of Chapter 5) and there could be a *de facto* polarisation within ASEAN between the new and the old members. Such a dynamic was seen in Vietnam's convening of a summit of Indochinese countries prior to the ASEAN summit in Manila in November 1999.[99]

In general, expansion both enhanced and eroded ASEAN's progress towards a security community. Several of its key norms, including non-interference, non-use of force and regional autonomy, faced new tests, and the overall burden on regional problem-solving processes and practices increased. These burdens had a potential to unravel the community-building process in ASEAN. ASEAN's sense of collective identity, a crucial aspect of security communities, was strengthened somewhat, but its extent remained uncertain and its overall impact problematic. Early in the expansion process, Ali Alatas of Indonesia had anticipated that expansion might create new problems for ASEAN, but it would also increase ASEAN's 'ability to deal with these problems now that we are together, not divided nations of seven plus three'.[100] But a less sanguine view of ASEAN's expansion was equally plausible – a view articulated by the *Bangkok Post*: 'there is also the distinct possibility that the happy 10 will become something of a dysfunctional family unless the more progressive members grasp the formidable challenges that the three newcomers, and Slorc (*sic*) in particular, present'.[101]

Notes and references

1 Thai Prime Minister Anand Panyarachun, cited in *Straits Times*, 25 June 1991.
2 Statement by HE Mr Ali Alatas, Minister for Foreign Affairs and Co-Chair of the Paris Peace Conference on Cambodia, Paris, 23 October 1991, p. 4 (text obtained by the author).
3 For an overview of the domestic and external factors behind Vietnamese reform, see: Robert G. Sutter, *Vietnam in Transition: Implications for US Policy* (Washington, DC: Library of Congress, Congressional Research Service, 1989).
4 Carlyle A. Thayer, 'The Challenges Facing Vietnamese Communism', *Southeast Asian Affairs* 1992 (Singapore: Institute of Southeast Asian Studies, 1992), p. 352.
5 *International Herald Tribune*, 16 June 1987.
6 For a discussion of Chatichai's initiative, see: Leszek Buszynski, 'New Aspirations and Old Constraints in Thailand's Foreign Policy', *Asian Survey*, vol. 29, no. 11 (November 1989), pp. 1057–72; Katharaya Um, 'Thailand and the Dynamics of Economics and Security Complex in Southeast Asia', *Contemporary Southeast Asia*, vol. 13, no. 3 (1991), pp. 245–70.
7 Dorothea Arndt, 'Foreign Assistance and Economic Policies in Laos', *Contemporary Southeast Asia*, vol. 14, no. 2 (September 1992), p. 200.
8 Donald Weatherbee, 'ASEAN the Big Loser in Thai Race for Profit in Indochina', *Straits Times*, 5 May 1989.
9 S. Rajaratnam, 'Riding the Vietnamese Tiger', *Contemporary Southeast Asia*, vol. 10, no. 4 (March 1989).
10 Cited in *Straits Times*, 2 June 1989.
11 *International Herald Tribune*, 26 January 1989; *International Herald Tribune*, 30 January 1989; Straits Times, 14 March 1989.
12 Paisal Srichratchanya, 'Wait and See', *Far Eastern Economic Review*, 11 May 1989, p. 21.
13 See: Muthiah Alagappa, 'Bringing Indochina into Asean', *Far Eastern Economic Review*, 29 June 1989, pp. 21–2.
14 *Bangkok Post*, 16 December 1988.
15 *Straits Times*, 14 January 1989.
16 *Straits Times*, 17 January 1991.
17 *Straits Times*, 13 December 1990.
18 *Straits Times*, 23 November 1990.
19 See: Donald Weatherbee, 'Thailand in 1989: Democracy Ascendant in the Golden Peninsula', in *Southeast Asian Affairs* 1990 (Singapore: Institute of Southeast Asian Studies, 1990), pp. 349–50.
20 See: Surin Maisrikrod, 'Thailand and the Indochina Conundrum', *Trends*, 23 February 1992, p. 25. A Thai diplomat warned that '[g]ood relations among ASEAN countries can be adversely affected if initiatives on Indochina are undertaken by any ASEAN member without prior consultation with other ASEAN members'. Asda Jayanama, 'One Southeast Asia: The Issues at Stake', *Vietnam Commentary* (November–December 1991), p. 38.
21 Keynote Address by Datuk Abdullah Haji Ahmed Badawi at the fourth Southeast Asia Forum, Kuala Lumpur, 16 January 1992, p. 7.
22 Goh Chok Tong, 'Towards a Positive Relationship With Vietnam', *Speeches* (Singapore Ministry of Information and the Arts), vol. 15, no. 5 (September–October 1991), p. 9.
23 Douglas Pike, 'Vietnam in 1991: The Turning Point', *Asian Survey*, vol. 32, no. 2 (January 1992).
24 *Straits Times*, 17 February 1992.
25 Ibid.
26 FBIS-EAS-92–025, 6 February 1992, pp. 43–4.
27 Surin Maisrikrod, 'Thailand and the Indochinese Conundrum', *Trends*, 23 February 1992, p. 25.
28 Amitav Acharya, 'The ARF Could Well Unravel', in Derek Da Cunha (ed.), *The Evolving Pacific Power Balance* (Singapore: Institute of Southeast Asian Studies, 1996), pp. 63–9.
29 Carlyle A. Thayer, 'Vietnam and ASEAN: A First Anniversary Assessment', *Southeast Asian Affairs* 1997 (Singapore: Institute of Southeast Asian Studies, 1997), p. 208.
30 Hoang Anh Tuan, 'Why Hasn't Vietnam Gained ASEAN Membership?', *Contemporary Southeast Asia*, vol. 15, no. 3 (December 1993), p. 283.
31 A precedent was set when the ASEAN-led ARF discussed the Spratlys issue on a multilateral basis despite China's opposition. *Straits Times*, 26 May 1995, p. 4. See also comments by former Singaporean Prime Minister Lee Kuan Yew, *Straits Times*, 1 April 1995, p. 3.

32   Cited in Thu My, 'Renovation in Vietnam and Its Effects on Peace, Friendship and Cooperation in Southeast Asia', in Nguen Duy Quy (ed.), *Unity in Diversity: Cooperation Between Vietnam and Other Southeast Asian Countries* (Hanoi: Social Science Publishing House, 1992), pp. 141–42.

33   Muthiah Alagappa, 'Confronting the Slorc', *Burma Review*, no. 30 (November–December 1991), p. 13.

34   John Bray, 'Burma: Resisting the International Community', *Pacific Review*, vol. 5, no. 3 (1992), p. 293.

35   *Nation*, 23 April 1992.

36   *Straits Times*, 26 August 1992, p. 27.

37   Ibid.

38   Michael Vatikiotis, 'Dollar Democracy', *Far Eastern Economic Review*, 26 September 1991, p. 35.

39   *New Straits Times*, 31 October 1991.

40   *Nation*, 25 July 1992.

41   *New Straits Times*, 3 December 1991.

42   For example, Singapore claimed that before hosting the ASEAN Foreign Ministers Meeting in July 1993, it had invited a delegation of Burmese cabinet ministers led by SLORC's First Secretary Lt-Gen. Khin Nyunt as part of ASEAN's constructive engagement policy. The visit was used to tell SLORC 'how much the world has changed' and convey international concerns about Burma's political situation: 'Singapore has expressed concern to junta leaders', *Straits Times*, 29 July 1993, p. 20.

43   *Nation*, 15 July 1992.

44   Editorial in *Nation*, FBIS-EAS-92–050, 13 March 1992, p. 50.

45   *Nation*, 18 March 1992, p. A6.

46   *Straits Times*, 26 August 1992, p. 27.

47   Ibid.

48   *Straits Times*, 27 July 1992, p. 15.

49   *Bangkok Post*, 29 July 1993, p. 8; *Nation*, 29 July 1993, p. A1.

50   *Bangkok Post*, 29 July 1993, p. 8.

51   Reuters Dispatch, 10 June 1997.

52   Ibid.

53   'Friends and Fears', *Far Eastern Economic Review*, 8 May 1997, p. 15.

54   Cited in Carlyle Thayer, 'ASEAN's Expanding Membership', Paper presented to the Workshop on 'ASEAN in Transition: Implications for Australia', Brisbane, 9–10 December 1996, p. 12.

55   *Singapore*, EIU Country Report (London: Economist Intelligence Unit, 2nd Quarter 1997), p. 13.

56   *South China Morning Post*, 31 May 1997.

57   *Nation*, 1 June 1997 (from *BurmanetNews*, 2 June 1997).

58   'ASEAN Will Not Drop Support for Burma Entry After US Action: Analyst', from http://www.burmafund.org/News/burmanet_news.htm accessed 27 April 1997.

59   'Friends and Fears', *Far Eastern Economic Review*, 8 May 1997, p. 14.

60   *Nation* (Editorial), 13 June 1997; Reuters, 4 June 1997.

61   *Nation* (Editorial), 1 June 1997.

62   Sukhumbhand Paribatra, 'Asean and the Slorc Conundrum', *Bangkok Post*, 22 May 1997, p. 13.

63   'Burma's Monsters', *The Economist*, 15 March 1992, p. 17.

64   'Aung San Suu Kyi questions ASEAN's stance', Deutsche Presse-Agentur, 31 July 1995.

65   This is in marked contrast to the policies of the EU as well as the Organization of American States which now makes democratic governance a criterion for membership in the organisation.

66   In the May 1993 election, the Cambodian People's Party led by Hun Sen lost to Ranariddh's FUNCINPEC by a margin of 58 to 51. However, the CPP refused to accept the result, making no secret of its reluctance to hand over the reins of power. It demanded new elections in four provinces, accused UNTAC of bias, and threatened mutiny by its powerful army. Ranariddh refused to serve 'side by side' with Hun Sen as Deputy Prime Minister, as initially envisaged under a plan devised by Prince Sihanouk. Although the two finally agreed to form a coalition government with Ranarridh as the First Prime Minister and Hun Sen as the Second Prime Minister, the CPP maintained a strong position within the coalition government. FUNCINPEC ministers complained of an inability to effect their policies due to resistance from the CPP-dominated bureaucracy. As this author pointed out in an article in 1994, 'the eventual breakdown of the coalition and return of hardline CPP elements to power could not be ruled out'. Amitav Acharya, 'Cambodia, the UN and the Problems

of Peace', *Pacific Review*, vol. 7, no. 3 (1994), pp. 297–308. The stalemate in Cambodia resulted from the fact that no side was able to win the two-thirds majority required to have total authority to shape the terms of the new constitution. Though the overall 'winner', FUNCINPEC remained poorly organised and militarily weak. Moreover, without an overall majority in the 120 seat Constituent Assembly, it could not alone dictate Cambodia's political direction. While it agreed to co-habit with the CPP in forming a Government of National Unity, the interests of the two uneasy partners *vis-à-vis* the Khmer Rouge were not congruent. FUNCINPEC saw the continued existence of the Khmer Rouge as a useful counter to the predominant military power of the CPP.

Indeed, it was the Khmer Rouge question which led to the eventual collapse of the power-sharing arrangement in Cambodia. As the Khmer Rouge disintegrated as a political force, Hun Sen accused Ranarridh of accepting the surrender of Khmer Rouge soldiers and rehabilitating them within his own security apparatus so that he could build up his own military strength *vis-à-vis* the CPP in the lead-up to the 1998 parliamentary election. Ranarridh for his part accused Hun Sen of engineering a revolt against his leadership within the FUNCINPEC ranks.

67　*South China Morning Post*, 31 May 1997.
68　*Jakarta Post*, 8 July 1997, p. 1.
69　*Straits Times*, 11 July 1997, p. 1.
70　Ibid.
71　Cited in *Straits Times*, 25 July 1997, p. 29.
72　*Straits Times*, 12 July 1997, p. 46.
73　*Straits Times*, 11 July 1997, p. 26.
74　Ibid., p. 29.
75　*Straits Times*, 15 July 1997, p. 1.
76　*Straits Times*, 11 July 1997, p. 1.
77　*Jakarta Post*, 10 July 1997, p. 1.
78　*Straits Times*, 15 July 1997, p. 19.
79　Ibid.
80　Abdul Rahman Adnan, 'Asean Turns to "Constructive Intervention" ', *Asian Wall Street Journal*, 30 July 1997, p. 10.
81　*Bangkok Post*, 24 July 1997, p. 6.
82　For details of the Thai initiative, see: Amitav Acharya, 'Realism, Institutionalism and the Asian Economic Crisis', *Contemporary Southeast Asia*, vol. 21, no. 1 (April 1999), pp. 1–29.
83　*Straits Times*, 30 July 1997, p. 14.
84　*Straits Times*, 15 July 1997, p. 19.
85　*Jakarta Post*, 9 July 1997, p. 4.
86　'Statement by the Secretary-General of ASEAN Welcoming the Kingdom of Cambodia as the Tenth Member State of ASEAN', 30 April 1999. Available at http://www.aseansec.org/www. aseansec.org/secgen/accam_s.htm (accessed 2 December, 1999).
87　One analyst envisaged Vietnamese membership in ASEAN by the end of 1994: Martin Gainsborough, 'Vietnam II: A Turbulent Normalisation with China', *World Today*, vol. 48, no. 11 (November 1992), p. 207.
88　Ramses Amer, 'Vietnam and Its Neighbours: The Border Dispute Dimension', *Contemporary Southeast Asia*, vol. 17, no. 3 (December 1995), p. 298.
89　Adam Schwarz, 'Joining the Fold', *Far Eastern Economic Review*, 16 March 1995, p. 21. The USA normalised relations with Vietnam in July 1995 on the eve of Vietnam's entry into ASEAN.
90　'Stick to Basics', Opening Statement by Professor S. Jayakumar, Minister for Foreign Affairs, at the 31st ASEAN Ministerial Meeting, 24 July 1999, Manila. Available at http://www.aseansec.org/ amm/amm31oss.htm, p. 1.
91　Donald E. Weatherbee, 'ASEAN and Indochina: The "ASEANization" of Vietnam', in Sheldon W. Simon (ed.), *East Asian Security in the Post-Cold War Era* (Armonk, NY: M.E. Sharpe), pp. 210–11.
92　*Nation* (Editorial), 1 June 1997.
93　*Bangkok Post* (Editorial), 13 June 1997.
94　'Vietnam Joins ASEAN', *Strategic Comments*, no. 5, 8 June 1995, p. 2.
95　Martin Gainsborough, 'Vietnam II: A Turbulent Normalisation with China', *World Today*, vol. 48, no. 11 (November 1992), p. 207.
96　*Straits Times*, 21 July 1992.

97 For an excellent study of the economic implications of an expanded ASEAN, which is the main source for the discussion in this paragraph, see: *The New ASEANs: Vietnam, Burma, Cambodia and Laos* (Canberra: Department of Foreign Affairs and Trade, 1997).

98 This has been a concern in Vietnam, Laos, Cambodia and Burma. See: Barry Wain, 'Asean's Split Personality', *Asian Wall Street Journal*, 24 December 1998.

99 Cambodian officials believe that the Indochina leaders meeting was a Vietnamese response to the Thai effort to dilute the non-interference doctrine, signifying growing Thai–Vietnamese rivalry over influence in Indochina (author's discussion with a former Cambodian minister, Toronto, 15 November 1999).

100 *Nation*, 1 June 1997 (from *Burmanet News*, 2 June 1997).

101 *Bangkok Post* (Editorial), 13 June 1997.

5   Managing intra-ASEAN relations

Security communities emerge when a group of states collectively renounce violence as a means of resolving their differences with an attendant significant muting of disputes among them. ASEAN came to exhibit such characteristics in its diplomatic role during the Cambodia conflict. As discussed in the previous chapter, ASEAN's collective action over Cambodia had a salutary effect on intra-ASEAN relations. Unity against an external challenge helped to divert attention from intra-mural differences. As early as 1982, S. Dhanabalan, the Foreign Minister of Singapore, was claiming that intra-ASEAN conflicts had 'either become irrelevant or been muted considerably'.[1] In 1986, Dr Noordin Sopiee, head of the Institute of Strategic and International Studies of Malaysia, had claimed that the 'sum total' of ASEAN's contribution to regional peace and stability

> has been to bring the ASEAN area to the brink of what Karl Deutsch has called a pluralistic security community. Such a system is one at peace, where no nation continues to accept war or violence as an instrument of policy against another community member and where no actor seriously prepares for war or violence against another. There is no guarantee that such a situation will be sustained in the future. Peace is always a constant struggle. But to come close to being a security community from a starting point so distant within a time span so comparatively short is no mean achievement. Admittedly the ASEAN security community has in part been the result of other factors, not the least of which was the perception of extra-ASEAN threats. But without the existence of ASEAN there would today be no such quasi-security community. And history tells us that common external threats can lead to division as well as unity.[2]

Dr Sopiee's characterisation of ASEAN as a quasi-security community was a qualified one. It was also premature in two important respects.[3] First there was doubt as to whether intra-ASEAN conflicts had been resolved or had been merely 'swept under the carpet'. There were doubts too as to whether the cohesion generated by Vietnam's invasion of Cambodia would translate into long-term and 'dependable' expectations of peaceful conduct in intra-regional relations. Indeed, as the solidarity induced by the Cambodia conflict began to fade, new challenges testing ASEAN's norms concerning peaceful conduct began to appear.

This chapter discusses the evolution of intra-ASEAN relations in the post-Cold War era. It identifies the security challenges confronting ASEAN, including intra- and extra-mural territorial disputes and the prospects for a regional arms race, and assesses the extent to which ASEAN's norms concerning dispute settlement (the first part of the matrix in Table 1.2) and pacific conduct have mattered in addressing these problems. Two other key issues in intra-ASEAN relations are also examined with a view to ascertaining whether

ASEAN members have continued to adhere to their established norms and practices. The first of these is economic cooperation, guided by the norms of the ASEAN Way (including 'soft institutionalism'). The second area is intra-ASEAN defence cooperation, hitherto guided by the norm of bilateralism. Apart from shedding light on norm compliance, these issues are also important to measuring intra-regional interdependence (itself crucial to security community building) and ascertaining identity formation in ASEAN, as they provide indications of whether ASEAN is developing a greater resort to multilateralism. The final section of this chapter will examine the tension between the principle of sovereignty (and its corollary, the non-interference doctrine) and demands by some ASEAN members for a more interventionist approach to regional transnational issues, which emerged especially in the wake of the economic downturn during 1997–99. The ensuing debate on this issue affects not only ASEAN's capacity for collective regional problem solving, but also the sanctity of its norms and its potential to develop a collective identity.

Intra-regional conflicts and conflict management

The Paris Peace Agreement on Cambodia in 1991 was hailed as settling the last major conflict in the region. There remained a number of sources of interstate and regional tensions in Southeast Asia, however. These sources may be divided into three categories. The first was the spillover effect of domestic conflicts, especially ethnic, political and ideological challenges to state structure and regime security. The decline or collapse of the region's transboundary communist movements, such as the Communist Party of Malaya, or the North Kalimantan Communist Party, had reduced the spillover potential of one major type of intra-state conflict, but a number of domestic separatist movements have continued, some with cross-border security implications. Such separatism had been sustained in Indonesia (Aceh – until 2005), Burma, Thailand, the Philippines and Cambodia. During the 1980s and 1990s, the exodus of refugees from Aceh to Malaysia became a highly sensitive issue in Indonesia–Malaysia relations, while Manila's suspicion that elements in Malaysia's state of Sabah were providing support for Moro separatists in Mindanao had led Philippine politicians to take a hard line on completing a formal renunciation of the claim to Sabah. In a similar vein, suspicions continued in Thailand over Malaysia's alleged sympathy for Muslim separatists in the south of the country. Burma's membership in ASEAN has compounded ASEAN's problems concerning the transboundary spillover of internal political conflicts. The pursuit by the Burmese military of Karen refugees fleeing to Thailand (estimated to be about 100,000 in 1996–97) led to military tensions between the member countries.[4]

Southeast Asia was the scene of some of the worst domestic violence of the late twentieth century. The Khmer Rouge regime in Cambodia killed about 1.7 million (a quarter of the Cambodian population) during its brutal rule between 1975 and 1979. Anti-Communist riots in Indonesia which accompanied the transition from President Sukarno to Suharto, claimed about 400,000 lives. Ethnic and separatist movements in East Timor and Aceh claimed 200,000 and more than 2000 lives respectively.[5] While there are no proper collated figures for ethnic separatism in Myanmar – usually low-scale, random casualties and conflicts, 600,000 'internally-displaced persons' from these conflicts have been recorded.[6] According to one estimate, Myanmar, which was embroiled in six different intra-state conflicts, is the world's most conflict-prone country during the 1946–2003 period, having experienced 232 'conflict-years'.[7] Other conflict-prone countries during this period, in terms of having experienced the greatest number of conflict-years, are Philippines (86 conflict-years), Indonesia (40 conflict-years), Cambodia (36 conflict-years), Republic of Vietnam

(36 conflict-years), and Thailand (35 conflict-years). Although Southeast Asia has witnessed a decline in battle-deaths in keeping with the overall trend around the world, and has been free of major conflict since the fighting in Cambodia (1979–91) ended, internal conflicts in Southern Thailand, Southern Philippines, and Myanmar remain a serious challenge to human security. Military rule, which accounted for some of the worst human rights violations in the region, continues in Myanmar, briefly recurred in Thailand in 2006 and cannot be entirely ruled out in the Philippines.

The main sources of internal conflicts in ASEAN include (1) the lack of fit between the territorial boundaries of the modern 'nation-states' and the ethnic composition of their populations (the members of the same ethnic group straddling national boundaries and individual nation-states containing many different ethnic groups); and (2) struggle for regime survival and demands for political change against authoritarian regimes. While one might consider terrorism as a domestic security threat, because it is sometimes rooted in ongoing domestic conflicts, I would include it in the category of transnational threats, given that the major terrorist organisations tend to draw support from and operate across national boundaries, and retain significant external or extra-regional links (e.g. Al-Qaeda and the Jemmah Islamiah network in Southeast Asia).

Domestic conflicts not only challenge the internal stability of ASEAN states, but also regional stability as a whole. Many domestic conflicts tend to spill over national boundaries, especially when militants or refugees flee the conflict zone and seek asylum in neighbouring states (as happened in the past when members of the Communist Party of Malaya moved across the border into Thailand, and may be happening now with the reported movement of Muslim radicals from Thailand's south coming over to Malaysia). Although it seems to happen rarely these days, such spillovers could become a source of friction between ASEAN member states. Because of the possibility of such spillovers, it might be argued that a true security community requires not just peaceful relations between states, but also within them.

The past decade has seen the end of several long-standing separatist movements in ASEAN, particularly Aceh and East Timor, although the ending of these conflicts did come at a significant human and developmental cost. But the separatist movements in the southern Philippines and southern Thailand have no immediate end in sight, and may well continue into the next two decades (It remains to be seen whether the new Thai government's election campaign pledge to give autonomy to the southern provinces will make any difference; as this will be resisted by the armed forces and autonomy has not ended the southern Philippine conflict). Myanmar too is likely to see periodic flare-up of its myriad ethnic rebellions, as happened in 2009 and 2010.

A second source of intra-ASEAN conflict related to disputes over territory. These included the Malaysia–Singapore dispute over the Pulau Batu Puteh/Pedra Branca Island in the Singapore Strait, the Malaysia–Indonesia dispute over the Sipadan and Litigan Islands in the Sulawesi Sea near the Sabah–Kalimantan border (which was settled also by the International Court of Justice (ICJ) in Malaysia's favour), the Thai–Malaysia dispute regarding their common border, the Malaysia–Brunei dispute over Limbang and the lingering Philippines–Malaysia dispute over Sabah. In 2002, the ICJ awarded the Sipadan and Ligitan islands to Malaysia, thereby settling the legal dispute, but some tensions persisted over the issue between the two countries, leading to incidents and near clashes between their navies in the area. The Singapore–Malaysia dispute over Pedra Branca was settled, again through arbitration by the ICJ, in May 2008 in Singapore's favour.[8] Additionally, a number of disputes exist in the maritime arena over issues such as boundary demarcation, exclusive economic zones, fishing rights and resource exploitation. Indeed, the majority of maritime

Table 5.1 Disputed maritime areas in Southeast Asia with petroleum potential

Area	Countries disputing jurisdiction
The northern Andaman Sea	Burma and India
The eastern Gulf of Thailand	Vietnam, Thailand and Cambodia
The southwestern Gulf of Thailand	Malaysia, Thailand and Vietnam
An area north, west and east of China	Vietnam, Indonesia, Malaysia and Natuna Islands
Off-shore Brunei	Brunei, Malaysia, possibly China, possibly Vietnam
The Gulf of Tonkin	China and Vietnam
The Spratly Islands	Brunei, Malaysia, Vietnam, the Philippines, China and Taiwan
The Arafura Sea	Indonesia (after 1999 East Timor) and Australia

Source: Mark Valencia, 'Energy and Insecurity in Asia', Paper presented to the Conference on 'The Economics of East Asian Security', hosted by the International Institute for Strategic Studies, Chinese Council for Advanced Policy Studies, Canadian National Committee of the IISS, Vancouver, British Columbia, 4–5 March 1997, Appendix 2.

boundaries in the South China Sea and the Gulf of Thailand are in dispute (Table 5.1).[9] This situation led to interstate tensions bordering on violence, exemplified by the arrest in April 1988 by the Malaysian Navy of 49 Filipino fishermen, and the clash in early 1994 between Thai and Cambodian naval vessels in the Gulf of Thailand.

There are several outstanding border issues between Vietnam and some of the other ASEAN member states, notably Malaysia and Indonesia, which may test intra-mural peace. Indonesia and Vietnam are in dispute over the continental shelf of the Natuna Islands in the South China Sea that once led Indonesia to consider the 'possibility of facing a sea battle in the South China Sea'.[10] Thailand and Vietnam contest maritime boundaries in the Gulf of Thailand, although in February 1992, Hanoi publicly stated its desire to reach an agreement on the joint development of disputed areas similar to one it had concluded with Malaysia.[11] Little progress has been made in resolving border demarcation disputes between Thailand and Laos, an issue that has led to armed clashes between the two countries in the last decade. Only 58 km of the 2500 km land border between Thailand and Burma have been demarcated.[12]

Third, relations between Southeast Asian countries are also tested by lingering animosities which have ethnic, cultural, religious and nationalist roots. The case of Singapore–Malaysia relations provides perhaps the clearest illustration of some of these types of conflicts. The two countries have managed to live with each other since the bitter separation of Singapore from Malaysia in 1965, but periodic tensions have underscored the fragility of their bilateral relationship. The almost hysterical reaction in Malaysia to the visit by Israel's President Chaim Herzog to Singapore in 1986 is a case in point.[13] Three years later, Singapore's offer of limited military facilities to the USA, in an apparent effort to share the 'burden' of the US bases in the Philippines, prompted Ahmad Badawi, then Malaysia's Defence Minister, to remind Malaysians that Singapore continued to perceive Malaysia 'as a threat to [its] existence', and in this context, 'the [Singapore] offer . . . [might be] directed as a deterrence directed against us'.[14] Another blow to Malaysia–Singapore defence ties was Kuala Lumpur's decision to suspend its bilateral exercises programme with Singapore's armed forces after discovering a Singapore spy-ring in late 1989. Relations hit a new low in March 1997 over comments contained in an affidavit by Singapore's Senior Minister, Lee Kuan Yew, regarding the lack of public safety in Johor Bahru. Lee's comments, for which he later apologised 'unreservedly', drew strong reactions from Malaysian politicians and the public, including calls for a suspension of the water pact which allows Singapore to draw some 1.5 billion litres of water per day from Johor.[15]

The Asian economic crisis from mid-1997 exacerbated Singapore–Malaysia tensions. Malaysia's frustrations in securing financial assistance from Singapore that might have reduced its need for seeking costly and conditional outside help created greater resentment. The Asian crisis also caused new strains between Singapore and Indonesia. The Singapore–Malaysia row, aggravated by a dispute over relocation of their customs and immigration facilities, and the right of Malaysian workers in Singapore to withdraw their Central Provident Fund (CPF) deposits before turning 55 years, spilled over to their defence relationship, with Malaysia pulling out of a joint exercise scheduled in September under the Five Power Defence Arrangements. Bilateral military cooperation suffered a further blow in September 1998 when Malaysia rescinded a long-standing agreement that allowed Singaporean military and rescue planes to fly through its air space without prior authorisation.[16] Dr Mahathir hinted darkly that Malaysia would like to 'take back our territory bit by bit' from Singapore.[17] Although Singapore denied any fear of a military conflict with its neighbours, it took care to increase its defence preparedness.[18]

On 3 May 2002, Malaysian Prime Minister Mahathir Mohamad was reported by a Malaysian newspaper to have said:

> We can skin a cat in many ways. To skin Singapore, there is not just one method.[19]

Mahathir's comments came after the relations between the two countries deteriorated over Malaysia's supply of water to Singapore. The dispute flared up in 2002 when Malaysia asked for a higher price from Singapore for its water, saying the city-state gets a bargain in the price it pays to Malaysia. (See Table 5.2.) Singapore's refusal to pay more led to tension. The issue became linked to another controversy, Malaysia's desire to replace the existing causeway with a bridge. Singapore, after initially refusing to build its own half of the bridge, relented on condition that Malaysia agreed to discuss the water issue as part of a package deal, a suggestion Malaysia has resisted.

Water in Malaysia–Singapore Relations

The water supply arrangement between Singapore and Malaysia is governed by two agreements signed in 1961 and 1962 (expiring in 2061), respectively. The first one provides for up to 55 million gallons a day (about 250,000 cubic metres), while the second provides for up to 100 million gallons a day (about 450,000 cubic metres). In 2002, Singapore depended on Malaysia for up to 52% of its water needs, the remainder coming from its own sources, including reservoirs, with the 1961 agreement accounting for about 18% of its 2002 needs.

The dispute escalated when Malaysia asked Singapore to increase the price it paid for water from 3 Malaysian sen per thousand gallons of raw river water (about S$0.003 per cubic metre) to RM3.00 per 1,000 gallons (about S$0.30 per cubic metre), or an increase of 100%. Malaysia also indicated a desire to renegotiate the second agreement as well and backdate the price to 1987 or 1988, years where a review of the agreements could have been done (but was not). Singapore would only offer to increase the rate to 45 sen per thousand gallons of raw water (about S$0.048 per cubic metre).

Singapore was trying to obtain 15% of its water requirements through reclamation of waste water ('New Water': drinking water recovered through a dual membrane process (micro-filtration and reverse osmosis) with ultra-violet irradiation to kill any remaining pathogens), and another 10% through desalination, by 2010.

In July 2003, the Malaysian newspaper, *New Straits Times*, pointed out that 'Malaysia has never breached any of its legal commitments. Despite fluctuations in bilateral ties, Malaysia has never withheld from Singapore a single drop of water'. In March 2007, Singapore government sources said that New Water could meet a third of the city-state's water needs by 2011. While the dispute continued, Singapore suggested that the dispute over the price of water be settled through arbitration, although Malaysia wanted to hold further discussions before third party referral.

Sources: 'Thorny Water', September 2002, http://www.yawningbread. org/arch_2002/yax-291.htm, accessed 7 June 2008; *New Straits Times*, July 21, 2003. Associated Press, 16 March 2007, *Straits Times*, reprinted from http://www.malaysia- today.net/2008/content/view/8196/84/, accessed 7 June 2008; Ministry of Foreign Affairs, Singapore, 'Remarks by Minister for Foreign Affairs, Prof. S. Jayakumar, in Parliament in reply to questions on Singapore-Malaysia Relations', 6 February 2004, available at //app.info.gov.sg/data/art_Remarks ByMinisterForForeignAffairsProfSJayakumarInParliamentInReply ToQuestionsOnSingapore-malaysiaRelations_060204.html

Some analysts see the water dispute between Singapore and Malaysia as the most serious challenge to the ASEAN security community that could lead to military conflict, but the threat can be exaggerated.[20] Among other things, Singapore has sought to 'desecuritise' the issue by making serious efforts to become self-sufficient in water supply, through measures such as desalination and 'new water' recycled from used water.[21]

The Pedra Branca dispute, though settled through the ICJ, still has a potential for disagree-ments and conflict. The ICJ ruling resolves only the question of sovereignty, leaving out the issue of maritime boundaries, to be decided through bilateral talks. The Court awarded Pedra Branca to Singapore, but the nearby (0.6 nautical miles to the south) two clusters of granite, the Middle Rocks, to Malaysia. The ruling also decided that the South Ledge, only visible during low tide, and which does not generate its territorial waters, belongs to that state whose territorial waters it lies in. Given the overlap in the territorial sea limits of Malaysia, Singapore and Indonesia (Pedra Branca is only 7.6 nautical miles from Indonesia's Bintan island and 7.7 nautical miles from Malaysia's Johor coast), this would complicate determin-ing the status of maritime boundaries and South Ledge. Among other issues, naval patrols and fishing rights around Pedra Branca and Middle Rocks need to be worked out by a Joint Technical Committee.[22]

In 2004, Singapore indicated that it wanted the bilateral issues, including the water dispute, with Malaysia to be settled through arbitration or adjudication. Malaysia, then under a new and more moderate Prime Minister, Abdullah Badawi,[23] responded that it still preferred a settlement first through bilateral negotiations, albeit through 'quiet diplomacy', although it did not rule out third party solutions.[24] The settlement of the land reclamation issue, for example, has been attributed to Badawi's softer approach to relations with Singapore.[25]

Singapore's ties with Indonesia also suffered after the Asian financial crisis and downfall of Suharto. As a country relatively less affected by the crisis, Singapore was perceived by Indonesia as less than sincere in wishing to help them to ride out the crisis. The deterioration of Singapore–Indonesia relations was even more significant since Singapore's offer of aid was not sufficient to overcome Indonesian ill-feelings. Despite an offer of over US $5 billion in assistance, Indonesia's President Habibie openly criticised Singapore as not being 'a friend in need'.[26] (The real reason for Habibie's anger, which found expression in his calling Singapore a 'little red dot', might have had to do with Lee Kuan Yew's earlier criticism of the choice of Habibie as Vice-President by former President Suharto, which Lee implied would be poorly received by the markets and so hinder Indonesia's recovery.) Indonesian President Abdurrahman Wahid (Gus Dur) in November 2000 contributed to the tensions by saying that water supplies could be easily cut off by a 'Malaysian–Indonesian alliance'.[27] Indonesia, which supplies 80 per cent of Singapore's sand needs, imposed a ban on sand exports to Singapore in 2003, citing environmental and maritime boundary concerns, but really in retaliation for Singapore's reluctance to agree to Indonesia's demand for an extradition treaty in order to be able to prosecute bankers and politicians who had allegedly taken US$13.5 billion from the Indonesian Central Bank during the Asian crisis and other possible white collar Indonesian offenders (mainly ethnic Chinese) who live in Singapore.[28] Singapore finally signed an Extradition Treaty and a Defence Cooperation Agreement with Indonesia in April 2007, but legal loopholes make it unlikely that many Indonesian white collar offenders will be repatriated to Indonesia to face trial. Singapore had wanted to keep the defence and extradition agreements separate, but Jakarta had insisted on linking them. But Singapore–Indonesia ties improved considerably under a new government of Susilo Bambang Yudhoyono.

Other intra-ASEAN bilateral relations are occasionally vulnerable to neo-nationalist sentiments (which have been subsumed within more direct causes, such as the treatment of migrant workers). One example is the crisis in Singapore–Philippine relations in March 1995 over the execution in the city-state of a Filipina maid who had been found guilty of murder. After Singapore had carried out the sentence, despite a plea for clemency from President Ramos, the Philippines retaliated by recalling its ambassador to Singapore (drawing a similar response from Singapore), cancelling a visit by its armed forces chief to Singapore, and postponing a joint naval exercise. Intra-ASEAN relations have also been affected by the movement of refugees and rebels across national borders. Malaysia and Thailand have quarreled over alleged Malaysian sheltering (at least by private groups) of Muslim separatists in southern Thailand.

With the expansion of ASEAN, conflicts and tensions involving the new members have also challenged its political unity. Thailand and Burma were engaged in border skirmishes in February and May 2001, when the Burmese army chased Shan ethnic rebels into Thai territory in Mae Sai, killing two Thai civilians, and drawing Thai mortar fire. This incident was seen as a move by the Burmese junta to test the attitude of the new Thai government (under Thaksin Shinawatra) towards it.[29] A similar incident occurred in May 2001 involving a spillover into Thai territory of Shan State Army rebels fleeing a Burmese military assault. The two sides accused each other of supporting rebel groups fighting the Burmese state and involved in the drug trade. On 29 January 2003, a Cambodian mob burned down the Thai embassy in Phnom Penh because a Thai TV star suggested that the Angkor Wat had been stolen from Thailand. This incident led the Thai government to put its troops on alert (although Prime Minister Thaksin was careful to tell his people 'please understand that the country is not at war', and relations returned to normal after the Cambodian government blamed the incident on 'extremists' and offered an apology and compensation to Thailand).[30] And perhaps the most serious threat to ASEAN's intra-mural peace occurred in 2008, when Thai and Cambodian troops went eyeball-to-eyeball over the Preah Vihar temple.[31]

While none of the intra-ASEAN episodes has produced outright military conflict, they have disrupted security relations and provoked a great deal of loose talk of military retaliation. One symbolic example was the evacuation by the Philippines Air Force from Singapore during the 1995 crisis of Filipina maids who had chosen to leave. Invocation of the 'ASEAN spirit' has been a factor in moderating and diffusing these controversies but it has been effective only at the highest political levels. At the grassroots level, concern about 'ASEANness' has mattered little. This disparity attests to the elitist and state-centric nature of ASEAN regionalism, which is yet to be matched by a strong sense of community at the societal level.

Security communities are not marked by the absence of conflict *per se*, but by the ability of societies and governments to manage such conflict peacefully. Despite periodic tensions, ASEAN leaders have discounted the prospect of armed confrontation over territorial disputes. As a Malaysian Deputy Foreign Minister, Abdullah Fadzil Che Wan, once claimed, '[w]e may have problems but they are not that serious enough to develop into war-like confrontation . . . we do not at any time ever envisage that we should act tough and use military means to solve our problems with our neighbours'.[32] This does not mean, however, that such disputes have not featured military deployments, exemplified in the dispatch of naval units by Indonesia and Malaysia near the disputed islands of Sipadan and Ligitan,[33] and the aforementioned military incidents over fishing jurisdiction between Malaysia and the Philippines.

In conflict management, there have been indications that the ASEAN Way, characterised by an avoidance of legal and formal procedures, has been unravelling. This may be adduced from the decision by Singapore and Malaysia in September 1994 to refer their dispute over Pedra Branca to the ICJ.[34] Their initiative was followed by a corresponding one by Malaysia and Indonesia in early 1997 over their dispute over the Sipadan and Litigan Islands.[35] The Malaysia–Indonesia case was significant in that, while Kuala Lumpur had proposed such judicial arbitration three years earlier, Jakarta had wanted to exhaust all diplomatic options before resorting to it. More importantly, Jakarta had indicated that if the dispute was to be subject to any form of third party mediation, then it should be one 'which we ourselves have established', a reference to the High Council provided for under the Treaty of Amity and Cooperation.[36] This was the first time that an ASEAN member country had publicly advocated resort to that mechanism to settle an intra-mural dispute. The agreement to seek redress through international judicial arbitration is consistent with the ASEAN members' commitment to the norm concerning the peaceful settlement of disputes, but it represented a departure from an avoidance of formal mechanisms, characteristic of the ASEAN Way, and a detraction from its norm of seeking regional solutions to regional problems.

Another important development concerning the emergence of legal mechanisms for dispute settlement is the Southeast Asia Nuclear-Weapons-Free Zone Treaty. Under the Treaty, disputes regarding its interpretation are to be settled by peaceful means, including negotiation, mediation, enquiry and conciliation. If no settlement can be reached within one month, then the dispute may be referred to the ICJ. Despite the availability of this legal mechanism, ASEAN officials have stressed the importance of political dialogue as a means of dispute settlement. Legal procedures are to be used only as a last resort. Nonetheless, the Treaty marks a turning point in ASEAN's approach to regional security cooperation, especially its previous reluctance to embrace formal and legalistic mechanisms for arms control, including the provision for such mechanisms in its Treaty of Amity and Cooperation in Southeast Asia (the High Council provision discussed in Chapter 2).

Against this backdrop, ASEAN presented the image of a house divided in the wake of the Asian crisis. Although outright war did not break out among the ASEAN members, the crisis cast a shadow over ASEAN's potential to evolve into a mature security community. Over a decade and a half since the outbreak of the Asian financial crisis, interstate disputes and tensions within ASEAN have not disappeared . Neither has war become 'unthinkable' – the hallmark of a 'mature' security community.[37] In 2011, ASEAN's then Secretary-General Surin Pitswan warned that 'unresolved and overlapping maritime and territorial claims remain ASEAN's biggest challenge.'[38] But the land boundary dispute between Thailand and Cambodia is also important, as it produced military clashes and seriously challenges ASEAN's claim to be a security community, a grouping of states that have developed 'long-term expectations of peaceful change' and ruled out the use of force in settling their disputes. The Thai–Cambodia conflict is a reminder that domestic politics can become a source of intra-ASEAN discord (as with Thailand's Yellow Shirt–Red Shirt rivalry, which led to the hardening of the Thai position on Preah Viehar), and that new ASEAN members may not always play by the established norms of ASEAN (Cambodia's sheltering of fugitive Thai Prime Minister Thaksin Shinwatra, which went against the spirit of non-interference).

The news is not all bad, however. Singapore–Malaysia relations have steadily improved since the end of the Mahathir and Lee Kuan Yew premierships respectively, witness the recent resolution of their 20-year-old railway land dispute. Indonesia and Singapore also enjoy a better political relationship than the days when Indonesian President Habibie disparaged the city-state as a 'little red dot'. But a variety of bilateral issues between Singapore and its neighbours remain to be settled. With Malaysia, they include, among others, Singapore's access to Malaysian water and, more trivially, alleged violations of Malaysian airspace by Singapore's air force planes. Moreover, the bilateral tensions are not strictly inter-governmental, but also inter-societal. Despite Singapore's increasing turn to ASEAN, it is still regarded by some of its neighbours as somewhat self-centred. The historical perception in Malaysia and Indonesia of Singapore as a wealthy Chinese island in a 'sea of Malays', is a latent source of tension, and might resurface in a future economic crisis in which Singapore is perceived to be unwilling to provide unconditional aid to its neighbours (as Malaysia alleged during the 1997 economic crisis). While Singapore and Indonesia have now reached agreement on their western maritime boundary, and talks are well under way to settle the eastern boundary, there have been tensions over extradition (Indonesians feel that its corrupt businessmen find it easy to flee to or via the city-state rather than face justice at home). The pacifying effect of the ICJ mandated settlement of the Sipadan-Ligitan island dispute has been marred by a new dispute between the two countries over the Malaysian claim to the nearby Ambalat. And the Pedra Branca dispute might still surface as a source of Singapore–Malaysia friction, because the ICJ settlement recognised Singapore's sovereignty over Pedra Branca itself, but awarded the adjacent Middle Rocks to Malaysia.[39]

The China factor: the Spratly Islands dispute

Nonetheless, most of these intra-ASEAN tensions are likely to be low-intensity and should not cause severe disruption of economic development or regional stability. For the next 20 years, the South China Sea conflict will probably remain the 'worst-case' threat to peace and security in the ASEAN region, and possibly the most serious challenge to ASEAN's regional conflict management role.

The Spratly Islands group, consisting of over 230 islets, reefs, shoals and sand banks, is located in the southern part of the South China Sea covering a vast area of about 250,000 square kilometres.[40] Their significance is magnified by the presence of natural resources in the area (such as manganese nodules, fish and oil, although the commercially exploitable potential of the last remains to be proven), as well as their strategic location straddling some of the world's most important sea lanes.

The Spratlys dispute was widely viewed by ASEAN governments as the major 'flashpoint of conflict' in post-Cold War Southeast Asia. It also posed a serious test of ASEAN's unity and of its norms concerning the peaceful settlement of disputes. It was Indonesia, and not ASEAN as a group, which took the lead in developing an informal and non-official approach to the conflict in the form of a series of workshops aimed at 'managing potential conflicts in the South China Sea'. Jakarta, with Canadian support, sought to project its South China Sea initiative as an example of ASEAN's role in regional conflict management.[41] China, Taiwan and Vietnam were not invited to the first workshop, which focused on developing a common ASEAN position on the issue.[42] This changed at the second workshop in Bandung in July 1991, where the ASEAN six were joined by China, Taiwan, Vietnam and Laos.

The workshop series deliberately avoided dealing with sensitive territorial issues. Its proponents argued that the holding of the workshop series was in itself an important confidence-building measure, offering the participants a chance to develop a certain level of transparency regarding national positions on the complex dispute. The series instead concentrated on issues of joint development and functional cooperation, producing agreements on specific projects such as combating marine environmental pollution, which might also have a confidence-building effect. The workshops have also undertaken the task of developing a code of conduct for states of the South China Sea region, with a view to reducing the risk of military conflict among them. Proposals for Confidence Building Measures (CBMs), such as non-expansion of military presences in the disputed areas, and exchanges of visits by military commanders there, were discussed, but proved elusive, with China opposing any discussion of military issues in this forum. Ideas about joint development of resources ran into obstacles, including Beijing's objection to any negotiations involving Taiwan, the unlikely prospect that any of the claimants which already had a military presence on the islands would agree to a withdrawal, and problems in deciding the principles for fair allocation of rights and profit.

ASEAN's collective concern with the conflict was initially expressed in a formal declaration stressing the need for a peaceful settlement of the dispute. The Manila Meeting of ASEAN Foreign Ministers in July 1992 produced the 'ASEAN Declaration on the South China Sea'. The declaration stressed the 'necessity to resolve all sovereignty and jurisdictional issues pertaining to the South China Sea by peaceful means, without resort to force', and urged 'all parties concerned to exercise restraint'.[43] But ASEAN has remained unsure of just how seriously Beijing takes the declaration, with its officials pointing to the frequent mismatch between China's declaratory policy and its actual conduct. For example, at the ARF meeting in Brunei in 1995, China's Foreign Minister surprised his audience by accepting UN conventions (including that on the Law of the Sea) as a basis for resolving the South China Sea conflict. This was a departure from the traditional Chinese policy of claiming the islands on the basis of 'historic' rights. At the same meeting, however, a Chinese Foreign Ministry spokesman repeated China's claim to 'indisputable sovereignty over the islands and their adjacent waters', and rejected a role for the ARF in discussions on the issue.[44]

For some time, China had shown restraint in dealing with the claims made by Manila and Kuala Lumpur. During Philippine President Corazon Aquino's visit to Beijing in April 1988, China reportedly pledged not to attack Filipino troops stationed in the Spratlys.[45] Visiting Singapore in 1990, Chinese Premier Li Peng stated China's willingness to shelve the sovereignty issue and cooperate with Southeast Asian countries to develop resources jointly. However, Beijing continued to pursue its territorial claims with the adoption in February 1992 of a territorial sea law which claimed the entire Spratlys and provided for the use of force in its support. This initiative was followed by the award of a three-year exploration contract to an American company in the South China Sea in an area just 160 km from the Vietnam coast. Further, China's occupation of the Mischief Reef (which came to light in early 1995), lying within waters claimed by the Philippines, marked the first encroachment by China into an area claimed by an ASEAN member. Similarly, 'the first violent incident between China and an ASEAN country' occurred in March 1995 when a Chinese fishing boat was fired upon by Malaysian naval vessels in waters claimed by Kuala Lumpur.[46] Such skirmishes continued around the Mischief Reef area involving the Philippine Navy and Chinese fishing boats.

Both Malaysia and the Philippines established a military presence in the Spratlys. President Ramos of the Philippines warned that the dispute was provoking 'a mini-arms race of sorts'[47] in the Asia Pacific region. In the case of Malaysia, for example, the place of the Spratlys in national defence planning was raised from 'secondary to very much top priority' following Sino-Vietnamese naval clashes in March 1988.[48]

Nonetheless, ASEAN could claim some success in dealing with China on the Spratlys issue. A strong objection by China prevented it from placing the issue formally on the agenda of the ARF.[49] But, ASEAN was able to secure an agreement from Beijing to conduct Sino-ASEAN multilateral consultations on security issues, including the South China Sea conflict. This marked a reversal of Beijing's earlier stance. Further, ASEAN could point to China's agreement to seek a solution to the dispute within the framework of the UN Law of the Sea Convention (UNCLOS, and assurances concerning freedom of navigation in waters claimed by it. ASEAN's efforts brought the dispute into the international limelight, suggesting a diplomatic cost for Beijing should it use force.

Attempts to negotiate codes of conduct were painfully slow. A bilateral agreement was concluded between China and Vietnam in October 1993 which committed the two sides to the non-use of force and to refrain from any action which might worsen relations.[50] Another bilateral agreement between China and the Philippines in August 1995 provided for cooperation in safety of navigation, marine research, rescue operations and environmental protection, and for a negotiated settlement of the dispute.[51] Such agreements did not improve matters between Manila and Beijing, however, further underscoring the need for multilateral approaches.[52] In August 1997, ASEAN agreed to consider a Chinese draft proposal for a framework for political and economic cooperation, which included 'norms of conduct' for their relations and guidelines for the peaceful settlement of disputes. (This draft did not refer to negotiations over sovereignty, however.)[53] A draft code of conduct circulated by Manila at the ASEAN Foreign Ministers Meeting in July 1999 was deemed to have been too legalistic; it took the form of a formal treaty, while other members preferred it to take the form of guidelines (more consistent with the ASEAN Way).[54]

At this point, the risk of possible disunity within ASEAN in dealing with China seemed strong. China had continued to push for bilateral negotiations with the claimants and appears to have made headway with respect to Malaysia. Intra-ASEAN tensions over the Spratlys, rare in the past, had escalated over Manila's discovery in April and June 1999 of Malaysia's construction of structures on two reefs claimed by the Philippines.[55] At the ARF meeting in Singapore in July 1999, Malaysia appeared to move closer to China's position of seeking bilateral solutions to the dispute.[56] Manila felt betrayed by Malaysia and frustrated by the lack of support from fellow ASEAN members in dealing with repeated Chinese encroachments.

But negotiations between China and ASEAN (DOC) continued, leading in November 2002 to the signing of a 'declaration' on a code of conduct in the South China Sea at the

ASEAN summit in Cambodia. The most significant words of the declaration concern an undertaking by the parties 'to exercise self-restraint in the conduct of activities that would complicate or escalate disputes and affect peace and stability including, among others, refraining from action of inhabiting on the presently uninhabited islands, reefs, shoals, cays, and other features and to handle their differences in a constructive manner'.

The DOC did not include a specific commitment to cease the erection of new structures in the disputed area, a commitment sought by the Philippines, but refused by China. A demand by Vietnam that the proposed code should apply to the Paracel Islands (claimed by Hanoi but now occupied by China) was resisted by China, although the problem was overcome through the acceptance of a Philippine initiative which suggested dropping any reference to the geographical boundaries of the declaration, thereby allowing Hanoi to claim coverage of the entire South China Sea. Moreover, the declaration is not legally binding. To arrive at such a code remains stated as a long-term goal of the parties. Malaysia intervened to push through this interim measure even though the Philippines had insisted on a more binding framework. But these shortcomings notwithstanding, the declaration does represent a confirmation of China's gradual move towards a posture of dealing with ASEAN multilaterally on a subject that it had previously insisted on resolving on a bilateral basis. The declaration also reflects the fact that China sees a military confrontation over the Spratlys as being detrimental to its interests. China's satisfaction with the agreement may also have to do with the exclusion of Taiwan as a party to the declaration. This could be seen as an endorsement by ASEAN of its 'One China' policy.

Sceptics then argued that China's restraint in the Spratlys is a tactical move at a time when Beijing was preoccupied with the Taiwan issue. The resolution of the question will release China's energy for attention to its territorial claims against Southeast Asian states. Shen Dingli, a well-known Chinese expert on strategic affairs, fuelled such speculation when he warned: 'Once the Taiwan front is closed, we may turn to the South China Sea'.[57] According to a senior PLA official interviewed by the author, three factors influenced China's efforts to reduce tensions in the South China Sea: (1) a desire to maintain good relations with ASEAN; (2) a need to focus on other priorities of the government, such as the Taiwan issue; and (3) a desire to prevent intervention by 'third parties' (read the USA) taking advantage of the conflict.[58] The PLA was unhappy with the decision by the top political leadership to make concessions on the conflict that freezes Chinese territorial expansion.

Thus, in the early 2000s, the South China Sea dispute seemed to have receded to the background amid other, more pressing, challenges to regional order perceived both by China and by the various Southeast Asian claimants. Even the Philippines, which initiated the idea of a regional code of conduct in 1998, and whose intelligence agency had in July 2002 described the Spratlys as an example of 'China's expansionism in Southeast Asia' and as 'the greatest flashpoint for conflict' in the region,[59] was relieved that an agreement could be finally reached. The former Secretary-General of ASEAN, Rodolfo Severino, argued that the DOC would 'convey a sense of stability in the region'.[60]

But the conflict re-emerged with force towards the end of the first decade of the new millennium. With China's growing naval capabilities (including 'area denial' capability) and increasing 'assertiveness', fears grew in ASEAN about Chinese intentions in the South China Sea. At the ARF meeting in Hanoi in July 2010, the Chinese Foreign Minister Yang Jieche was reported to have looked at Singapore's then Foreign Minister George Yeo and said: 'China is a big country and other countries are small countries, and that's just a fact'.[61] This became a dramatic symbol of Beijing's abrupt departure from its charm offensive. While ASEAN did not want the South China issue to be mentioned in the Declaration of the US–ASEAN summit in September 2010, it did recognise the importance of 'maritime security, unimpeded commerce, and freedom of navigation, in accordance with relevant universally agreed principles of international law, including the UNCLOS and other international maritime law, and the peaceful settlement of disputes.'

A number of Chinese actions since 2009 showed an increasing assertiveness by China in the South China Sea dispute. These included presenting: for the first time ever to the UN Commission on the Limits of the Continental Shelf, its 9-dash line U-shaped map, which claims over 80% of the South China Sea[62]; China's occupation, in April 2012, of the Scarborough Shoal, which has been claimed by the Philippines, by deploying paramilitary ships and erecting a barrier to the mouth of the shoal; and the creation of an administrative region of Sansha City covering the Spratly Islands and Macclesfield Bank in June 2012. Further, in May 2013, China deployed ships at the Second Thomas Shoal, which is located near the Mischief Reef, and where the Philippines has troops stationed since 1999.[63]

These developments had provoked alarm in the international community, and challenged ASEAN, because the international community, including major powers such as the US and Japan expect it to take the lead in managing this dispute and reducing the prospects of an outright armed confrontation. ASEAN's main response has been to press China to conclude a legally binding Code of Conduct (COC) as had been envisaged under the 2002 ASEAN–China DOC. Yet ASEAN's responses have been constrained not only by Chinese resistance, but also intra-ASEAN discord.

Intra-ASEAN discord over the conflict was revealed first in the failure of the Philippine proposal for a Zone of Peace, Freedom, Friendship and Cooperation (ZoPFF/C) in the South China Sea, which Manila had proposed in July 2011. The proposal 'stressed the need to segregate the disputed features [of the South China Sea] from the non-disputed waters.' But according to documents obtained by the author and interviews with ASEAN officials, the proposal failed to make headway because of concerns that 'what might be "disputed" by one country may be considered "non-disputed" by another.' Hence, it may be better to focus on the implementation of the DOC and the completion of the COC.[64]

Even more striking was ASEAN's failure to issue its customary joint communiqué at its last ministerial meeting (ASEAN Ministerial Meeting, or the AMM) in Cambodia held during 9–13 July 2012. Much was made of the fact that this was the first time ASEAN had failed to issue a joint communiqué in its 45-year-history. (ASEAN had similar crises before; it ground to a virtual halt in 1968–69 over the Philippines' claim to Sabah.)

The key factor here was Cambodia's refusal to accept language that specifically mentioned the Scarborough Shoal, along with language calling for respect for EEZs and continental shelf, in the communiqué, as had been proposed by the Philippines. Its position, which had the support of other ASEAN members, including Indonesia, was that the Chinese occupation of the Scarborough Shoal and its granting of an oil service contract in the EEZ and continental shelf claimed were gross violations of the DOC, and hence deserved to be mentioned specifically in the communiqué. Cambodia's Foreign Minister, Hor Namhong, argued that it had not been ASEAN's practice to specifically mention specific bilateral disputes by name. He recalled that the ASEAN practice had been to refer to the conflict area as the South China Sea conflict, rather than by the names of Paracels and Spratlys. He proceeded to suggest that if no consensus was found, the entire paragraph on the South China Sea should be deleted from the communiqué, meaning there would be no mention of the South China Sea dispute in the ASEAN communiqué. This would have been a departure from ASEAN's practice hitherto of mentioning the dispute and updating its response.

Subsequent efforts by Indonesia and Singapore to find a solution to the impasse failed. As a Philippine official who attended the meetings in Phnom Penh described it: '[t]he text of the proposed Joint Communiqué's item/subhead on the "South China Sea" was drafted by the ASEAN foreign ministers and several revisions were made to make the text acceptable to all. However, the Cambodian Chair consistently rejected any proposed text that mentions Scarborough Shoal.'[65] In the end not only the text related to the South China Sea issue, but the entire draft communiqué was abandoned, creating a major setback for ASEAN.

Many observers believe that Cambodia's refusal to accommodate the Philippines and Vietnam resulted at least partly from Chinese pressure and financial incentives. The lesson of the Phnom Penh saga is more about the failure of Cambodia's leadership as the ASEAN Chair, rather than the collapse of ASEAN unity. As Thayer observes, not only 'Foreign Minister Hor Namhong was not conciliatory at the AMM Retreat and his subsequent actions in rejecting repeated attempts at compromise appear obstinate,' but also that 'Cambodia's actions indicate that the idea of an ASEAN Community played second fiddle to its relations with China.'[66] On the other hand, what is also important is that the other ASEAN members, including original members Singapore and Malaysia, had supported a more direct reference to the Scarborough Shoal that Cambodia managed to scuttle. The behaviour of the Philippines which 'made major concessions in its discussions with fellow ASEAN members in order to reach consensus on the key principles in the COC,'[67] demonstrated that the senior members of ASEAN still adhere to the principles of consultations and consensus. At the same time, clouds over ASEAN unity were made distinctly visible. It is 'revealing that ASEAN foreign ministers acquiesced to Cambodia's high-handedness in vetoing the draft joint communiqué drawn up by four of their colleagues. No minister directly challenged Hor Namhong's handling of the discussion/debate at the AMM Retreat'. The episode did raise uncomfortable questions about China's willingness and ability to manipulate intra-ASEAN relationships, taking advantage of divergent interests and playing a 'divide-and-rule' game. It also highlighted the willingness and ability of a new ASEAN member to play by the ASEAN rules and the ASEAN Way.[68]

In justifying its decision to block the Communiqué, Cambodia clarified (in a 26 July 2012 note) that 'The AMM is not a court that could rule against or in favor of anybody, in relation to bilateral disputes.'[69] As a matter of fact, it has never been an official ASEAN policy to specifically exclude discussion or not mention bilateral disputes involving non-ASEAN members or between an ASEAN member and an outside party. And China is certainly not an ASEAN member. Moreover, the Joint Communiqué of the 44th AMM hosted by Indonesia did specifically refer to the Thai–Cambodia border dispute (Part IV, Para 103), urging that the two sides 'peacefully resolve their differences through political dialogue and negotiations . . . with appropriate engagement of Indonesia'.[70] Whether the South China Sea dispute is really a purely bilateral dispute can be questioned, but Cambodia's stance was inconsistent with ASEAN's own policy of talking to China multilaterally over this issue.

ASEAN did some damage control when Indonesian Foreign Minister Natelagawa made a tour of Manila, Hanoi, Bangkok, Phnom Penh and Singapore. This proved useful in reversing the setback to ASEAN's image to some extent. Moreover, on July 20, Cambodia as ASEAN Chair issued a statement containing six principles on the South China Sea on behalf of the ASEAN Foreign Ministers, which reaffirmed ASEAN's commitment to: the full implementation of the DOC; Guidelines for the Implementation of the DOC; the early conclusion of a Regional COC in the South China Sea; full respect of the universally recognised principles of international law including the 1982 UNCLOS; continued exercise of self-restraint and non-use of force by all parties; and peaceful resolution of disputes in accordance with the universally recognised principles of international law including the 1982 UNCLOS. [71]

ASEAN has also managed some concessions from China. China was initially opposed to ASEAN's right to hold prior consultations among its members before meeting China on the South China Sea issue. But the ASEAN–China Senior Officials' Meeting held on 20 July 2011, which agreed on the draft Guidelines for the implementation of the DOC, also recognised that 'ASEAN will continue its current practice of having prior consultations in ASEAN before meeting with China on the implementation of the DOC'.[72] In 2012, China dragged its feet on the issue of a binding code of conduct in the South China Sea, insisting that it would sign such a code of conduct only 'when conditions are ripe.' Instead, it wanted to focus on measures such as holding a seminar on navigation freedom in the South China Sea, and creating technical committees on marine scientific research and environmental protection. These measures would not prejudice its territorial claims and would do little to avert military incidents involving the claimant nations. But in July 2013, at the Brunei AMM, China did show more flexibility and agreed to start formal negotiations on the COC in September 2012. This assuaged ASEAN's concerns to some extent and demonstrated the usefulness of its persistence in holding China accountable to the idea of a COC.

ASEAN's draft COC is a short three-page document. Its principles are not newly drafted, but specifically invoke existing norms and agreements, both regional and global. Key among these is: 'Respect and adhere to the UN Charter; the 1982 UNCLOS; the Treaty of Amity and Cooperation in Southeast Asia; the DOC; and the Five Principles of Peaceful Co-existence.' The draft COC seeks to 'Develop modalities and arrangements for the promotion of settlement by peaceful means of disputes and prevent their escalations that would affect peace, stability and security in the area'. A key provision is the creation of a dispute-settlement mechanism for 'the interpretation and application of the Code of Conduct'. This mechanism would either utilise the provisions of ASEAN's Treaty of Amity and Cooperation or the dispute-settlement mechanisms provided under international law, including the UNCLOS. The draft prohibits reservations to the COC, and although it is to remain in force indefinitely, it provides for a review mechanism of the COC at the Ministerial/Leaders level.[73]

But challenges remain before the conclusion of a COC. Indonesia's Natalegawa cautions that a code 'is not a magic wand that will solve the underlying conflict, the territorial disputes. That's for the parties concerned to negotiate.' At the same time, he stressed the critical importance of ASEAN unity over the issue, which could not be taken for granted. 'As long as ASEAN is united then we will be all right. But as soon as we begin to have an à la carte ASEAN outlook, picking and choosing the piece that we like, that's when things will become more problematic.'[74]

In the absence of progress towards a binding code of conduct, the South China Sea issue has been increasingly internationalised and especially become a point of tension between the US and China. China insists that it can manage the dispute by directly engaging ASEAN without the involvement of outside powers. Yang Jieche insisted 'the territorial and jurisdictional disputes should be resolved peacefully by sovereign states directly concerned through friendly consultations and negotiations.'[75] This was not only a clear signal to the US to keep its nose out of this dispute, but also a warning to ASEAN that it cannot expect to deal with Beijing on this matter as a group, since not all ASEAN members are parties to the dispute. The US–China tensions were heightened at the Annual ARF meeting in Hanoi in July 2010. There US Secretary of State Hillary Clinton asserted a 'national interest in the freedom of navigation and unimpeded lawful commerce' in the South China Sea. At the July 2011, ASEAN Regional Forum Meeting in Bali, Clinton implied that China's claim to the South

China Sea, based on nine dotted lines, was 'arbitrary'.[76] She described incidents sparked by China's actions in the South China Sea as a threat to peace and stability in the region. 'These incidents,' she added, 'endanger the safety of life at sea, escalate tensions, undermine freedom of navigation, and pose risks to lawful unimpeded commerce and economic development.'[77]

Against this backdrop, a major challenge facing ASEAN is whether it can replicate its earlier record in conflict management in the Cambodia conflict of the 1980s in the case of the larger South China Sea dispute so as to limit great power competition and intervention (US–China) at its backyard. Like the Cambodia conflict of the 1980s, the South China Sea dispute(s) is not an intra-ASEAN dispute. But the similarity between the two conflicts ends there. Unlike Soviet-dependent Vietnam in the 1980s, China, the main non-ASEAN party to the dispute, is an emerging superpower. While the Cambodia conflict was mainly a political/ ideological matter, the South China Sea conflict revolves around issue of territorial claim and sovereignty, underpinned by the lure of (as yet unproven) natural resources, especially oil and gas that China so critically needs. Another key difference is that not all ASEAN members are claimants in the dispute, a fact that China uses to insist on bilateral approaches to conflict management, rather than engaging ASEAN as a grouping. The Cambodia conflict was a serious and clear violation of the non-intervention principle, hence ASEAN found it rela- tively easy to mobilise international condemnation of Vietnam, aided by the climate of the Cold War. The South China Sea issue is getting hotter at a time of China's growing inter- national clout notwithstanding the fact that the extent of China's claims (its dotted lines over almost the entire South China Sea) is rightly regarded as dubious by almost everyone else in the region. In the 1980s, ASEAN had little difficulty in securing ever-increasing majorities in the UN General Assembly for its resolution condemning the Vietnamese occupation of Cambodia. Would the African or Latin American countries, who receive billions of dollars in Chinese economic aid, now vote against China in the UN to condemn its military action against Vietnam or the Philippines in the South China Sea, no matter how unprovoked?

The South China Sea conflict holds important lessons for ASEAN's future approach to conflict management. With the resolution of the Cambodia conflict in 1991, it was widely seen as the 'next Cambodia' for ASEAN. But it became muted except for a brief escalation over the 'Mischief Reef Incident' in 1995. Now China having already accumulated sub- stantially enhanced economic and military power, has resurfaced the South China Sea issue with renewed vigour. This is an uncomfortable reminder that ASEAN's traditional practice 'sweeping conflicts under the carpet' does not always work. China in particular is too big a player to be swept under the ASEAN carpet. That approach works as long as the political relations among the parties remain good, as was the case in the heyday of China's 'charm offensive' in Southeast Asia in the 2000s. But it is no substitute for more long-term and definitive mechanisms for conflict resolution.

An arms race?

As early as 1977, an Australian analyst, Ron Huisken, characterised the military programmes undertaken by several Southeast Asian countries, including the members of ASEAN, as a 'slow motion arms race'.[78] This trend could be explained with reference to the emerging rivalry between non-communist ASEAN members and the communist Indochinese states. The post-Cold War military acquisitions in Southeast Asia, on the other hand, have been characterised by some as an intra-ASEAN arms race. That race has been driven by what Tim Huxley once described as 'the widely underestimated competition and latent conflict which undoubtedly exists between various of ASEAN's members', although it has also been inspired by the rise of Chinese military power.[79]

In 1992, the Defence Minister of Singapore, Yeo Ning Hong, stated bluntly that despite the end of the Cold War, 'no country in Southeast Asia . . . has declared a peace dividend. No one has reduced its defence expenditure.'[80] The Foreign Minister of Indonesia, Ali Alatas, drew attention to 'rather disturbing reports of increased arms purchases by several countries in the region'.[81]

An analysis of trends in defence spending in ASEAN member countries shows a mixed picture. Between 1984 and 1994, defence spending of ASEAN states grew in absolute terms. But the increase was less pronounced when measured in constant prices, and a decline in spending was evident when measured as a proportion of GNP. The following figures for Indonesia, Thailand, Malaysia and Singapore, are illustrative (in current US dollars; 1994 constant US dollars in brackets). From 1984 to 1990 to 1994, Indonesia's defence spending 'increased' from 1528m (2114m) to 1667m (1856m) to 2318m; Malaysia's from 956m (1323m) to 1208m (1344m) to 2121m; Thailand's from 1684m (2331m) to 2276m (2533m) to 3777m; and Singapore's from 1315m (1820m) to 1959m (2180m) to 3064m. As a percentage of GNP, the changes are: Indonesia's from 2.5 to 1.5 to 1.4 per cent; Malaysia's from 3.8 to 2.7 to 3.2 per cent; Thailand's from 3.9 to 2.5 to 2.7 per cent; and Singapore's from 5.2 to 4.3 to 4.5 per cent.[82]

The immediate aftermath of the 1997 economic crisis saw a noticeable decline in ASEAN states' defence spending, but it picked up after 2001. Malaysia registered one of the highest increases between 2001 and 2003, and a significant jump over 1998 figures (see Table 5.2). Indonesian defence spending doubled between 1998 and 2004. Thailand did not increase defence spending until Prime Minister Thaksin Shinawatra, before he was ousted in a military coup, promised to raise the Thai defence budget to $5 billion from about $2 billion over the next nine years.[83] After seizing power in 2006, the military government of Thailand increased the defence budget by 34 per cent for 2007 and another 24 per cent for 2008.[84]

Trends in arms procurement by ASEAN members in the 1980s and 1990s showed a clear shift towards conventional warfare capabilities in contrast to the counter-insurgent orientation of the past. The emphasis came to be on developing more capable air and naval forces through the acquisition of advanced fighter planes, maritime patrol aircraft, large surface combatants such as corvettes and frigates, missile-equipped patrol craft, and airborne early warning systems. In the pre-Asian crisis period, the combat aircraft acquisitions included US-built F-16s by Indonesia, Singapore and Thailand; British Aerospace Hawks by Brunei, Malaysia and Indonesia; Russian-built MiG-29s by Malaysia; US-built F/A-18s also by Malaysia and Russian-built Su-30s by Indonesia. Several ASEAN states reconfigured their fighter aircraft for maritime strike operations by equipping them with anti-ship missiles (such as the French *Exocet*). ASEAN navies are being reoriented and expanded beyond their hitherto coastal defence missions. Naval force modernisation in ASEAN ranged from the acquisition by Brunei and the Philippines of missile-equipped large patrol craft, to the acquisition of larger platforms such as corvettes and frigates by Malaysia, Thailand and Indonesia. Indonesia and Singapore developed the region's first modern submarine capability.

The armed forces of the ASEAN states also enhanced their strike warfare capabilities by adding to their inventory of advanced precision-guided missiles, including those geared to air combat, aerial ground attack and air defence roles. And several regional armed forces redesigned their ground forces for 'rapid deployment' missions. For example, Malaysia has developed a Rapid Deployment Force equipped with newly purchased transport aircraft, medium-lift helicopters, amphibious assault ships, light tanks and amphibious infantry

Table 5.2 Military expenditure of ASEAN member states in million US dollars and as a percentage of GDP

	1995	1997	1999	2001	2003	2005	2007
	(% of GDP for 2006)						
Brunei	256	334	269	234	260	249	265
	(5.5)	(7.2)	(6.1)	(5.2)	(5.1)	(3.9)	(3.5)
Burma	N/A	N/A	N/A	N/A	N/A	N/A	N/A
	N/A	N/A	N/A	N/A	N/A	N/A	N/A
Cambodia	171	147	131	117	110	110	72.4
	(5.4)	(4.4)	(3.5)	(2.7)	(2.3)	(1.8)	(1.1)
Indonesia	2613	2653	1710	2367	3319	3410	4160
	(1.6)	(1.3)	(0.9)	(1)	(1.3)	(1.2)	(1.3)
Laos	N/A	44	43	46	N/A	N/A	N/A
	N/A	(2.4)	(2.2)	(2.1)	N/A	N/A	N/A
Malaysia	2055	1858	1847	2087	3020	3120	3455
	(2.8)	(2.1)	(2.1)	(2.2)	(2.8)	(2.4)	(2.2)
Philippines	885	828	807	794	920	865	899
	(1.4)	(1.2)	(1.1)	(1)	(1)	(0.9)	(0.9)
Singapore	3378	4153	4791	4745	5051	5468	6148
	(4.4)	(4.7)	(5.4)	(5)	(5.1)	(4.7)	(4.7)
Thailand	3240	3006	2113	2063	2077	2018	2729
	(2.3)	(2.1)	(1.6)	(1.5)	(1.3)	(1.1)	(1.1)
Vietnam	N/A	N/A	N/A	N/A	N/A	N/A	N/A
	N/A	N/A	N/A	N/A	N/A	N/A	N/A

Source: www.sipri.org/contents/milap/milex/mex_database1.html

combat vehicles.[85] Indonesia maintains a rapidly deployable army division and an armoured brigade; this had in the past been used primarily for internal security missions in East Timor and Aceh.[86] With the lessening of the communist threat, the Philippines (which continued to buy counter-insurgency aircraft) undertook personnel and equipment adjustments to create 'a lean, compact, and mobile force' structure.[87]

The 1997 crisis forced cutbacks in weapons purchases by ASEAN members and slowed down their planned modernisation efforts. But weapon acquisitions picked up in the 2000s. Indonesia, with a US$1 billion export credit from Russia, bought 'Su-27 and Su-30 fighters, submarines, attack helicopters, corvettes, and land systems'.[88] Singapore purchased 12 new F-15SG fighter aircraft from the US, Malaysia 18 SU-30MKMs, and Vietnam 36 SU-27SKs.[89] Thailand purchased six (the eventual total could be 40) Swedish-made Gripen fourth-generation fighter jets along with airborne early warning (AEW) aircraft.[90] It is noteworthy that both Indonesia and Malaysia acquired Russian Su-30MK/Flanker fighter aircraft. Russia emerged as a major arms supplier, selling MiG-29S/Falcrum-C to Burma, and Mi-17, Mi-8 to Indonesia and Malaysia. The cash-strapped Philippines acquired C-130 Hercules transport and Bell-205 and M-113 helicopters from the USA as well as the US-made OV-10 Bronco fighter/ground attack aircraft from Thailand. Both Singapore and Malaysia acquired submarines: Malaysia bought the Scorpene Class from France, while Singapore got Västergötland/A-17 submarines from Sweden. Singapore as usual has been a prolific arms buyer, purchasing, among others, Apache strike helicopters, Seahawk anti-submarine warfare helicopters, and F-15 Strike Eagle aircraft, Hellfire anti-tank missiles and AMRAAM air-to-air missiles from the USA. As Richard Bitzinger contends, the weapons acquisitions by ASEAN members has 'gone far beyond the simple modernisation to include the development of . . . new capacities for force projection and stand-off attack, low-observability (stealth), and greatly improved command, control, communications, computing, intelligence, surveillance and reconnaissance (C4ISR) networks'.[91]

According to estimates by the Stockholm Peace Research Institute, defence spending by the ASEAN countries (excluding Myanmar for which reliable data is not available) has roughly doubled in the past decade (2000–10) (see Table 5.3).[92] Moreover, the ASEAN region has also seen a 'dramatic increase' in arms imports. Between 2005 and 2009, Malaysia's arms imports jumped 722 per cent, Singapore's 146 per cent and Indonesia's 84 per cent. Singapore ranks among the top ten arms importers in the world. This has prompted an expert from SIPRI, Siemon Wezeman, to warn that 'The current wave of South East Asian acquisitions could destabilise the region, jeopardising decades of peace'.[93] Some projections suggest that defence spending in East Asia, including Southeast Asia, will continue to grow rapidly into the next two decades. In June 2011, Singapore's defence minister projected a 60–70 per cent increase in defence spending in Southeast Asia and East Asia in the coming decade compared to the past decade.[94]

But is there an arms race in Southeast Asia? Some observers believe so.[95] The International Institute for Strategic Studies warned in 2006 of the possibility of 'a new small-scale arms race' in Southeast Asia that had 'become evident with the revival of defence spending and arms procurement since 2001'.[96] A somewhat different assessment is that ASEAN's military trends 'even if not constituting an arms race *per se*, could still unintentionally have a deleterious impact on regional security'.[97]

The term arms race implies an underlying dynamic of competition or interaction among two or more actors. As Barry Buzan puts it, 'the term arms race suggests self-stimulating military rivalry between states, in which their efforts to defend themselves militarily cause them to enhance the threats they pose to each other'.[98] The classic conception of the arms

Table 5.3 Defence spending by ASEAN member states, 1990–2010 (in constant (2009) US$ m.)

Country/Year	1990	2000	2010
Brunei	368	304	327
Cambodia	77	121	191 (2009)
Indonesia	1,829	2,025 (for 2001)	6,009
Laos	N/A	24.6	18.4 (2009)
Malaysia	1,495	2,020	3,259
Myanmar			
Philippines	1,060	1,215	1,486
Singapore	3,038	5,855	7,651
Thailand	3,304	2,638	4,336
Vietnam	1,565	N/A	2,410

Source: SIPRI Yearbook, various years. Available at: http://milexdata.sipri.org/

Note: For Myanmar, constant dollar figures are not available. Measured in terms of its local currency (Kyat) current figures, Myanmar's defence spending was 5.4 billon Kyat for 1990 and 63.45 billion Kyat for 2000. SIPRI does not provide Myanmar data for 2010.

race is the so-called 'action–reaction' dynamic developed in the 1960s by the then US Defense Secretary Robert McNamara as a general explanation of the US–Soviet nuclear arms race.[99] But the ASEAN states' military build-up has combined both interactive and non-interactive processes. The interactive nature of the military build-up in Southeast Asia was highlighted in a comment by a senior Thai military official who stated that Thailand's naval forces 'should be at least as well-equipped as those of other members of ASEAN in order to have bargaining power'.[100] Similarly, while evaluating the Russian MiG-29 for possible acquisition, Malaysia's Defence Minister Najib Tun Razak justified the need for such aircraft in the following terms: 'Indonesia, Singapore and Thailand have the F-16 while we have none such fighter aircraft. Owning such aircraft will place our air superiority on par with other countries in the region.'[101] Such statements imply that arms purchases in the region have been driven not only by considerations of prestige (since sophisticated modern armaments such as the F-16 aircraft or naval platforms like frigates are a source of status) but also by mutual suspicions and rivalry.

Nonetheless, non-interactive considerations have also been major factors behind ASEAN's military build-up. While internal security threats to ASEAN governments have been generally on the decline, they continue to influence weapons purchase decisions. For example, Indonesia's defence planning is geared more towards dealing with an internal crisis than towards the highly unlikely prospect of war with another state. Both Indonesia and the Philippines have been accorded archipelagic status but must rely on their own air and naval forces to suppress threats to central control and national cohesion. Malaysia's geography dictates a need to secure lines of communication between peninsular Malaysia and Borneo to ensure national security.

The ASEAN states' defence programmes have also been driven by a quest for greater self-reliance since the removal of US bases from the Philippines. It also reflected a move to replace obsolete equipment. While the aircraft purchases by Singapore and Malaysia seem competitive, some of the regional equipment is also complementary, geared to common security tasks. For example, the maritime surveillance aircraft and radars bought by Singapore, Indonesia and Malaysia are used in their coordinated patrol and surveillance of the Straits of Malacca.

The need for self-reliance aside, perceptions of threat from extra-regional powers, particularly China, and the general sense of a 'power vacuum' in the post-Cold War milieu, form an important basis for the military programmes of the ASEAN states. Some analysts see the trend towards greater sophistication in the military capabilities of several ASEAN nations as being 'at least *in part* due to increased uncertainties about the growth of Chinese military power'.[102] If so, this need not imperil intra-mural peace in ASEAN. A common feeling of uncertainty about the changing regional balance of power is perhaps as important a basis for the ASEAN states' defence programmes as interactive threat perceptions and rivalry within the grouping. Moreover, supply-side pressures resulting from competition among arms manufacturers looking for new overseas markets to compensate for declining domestic procurements in Western countries have been a factor behind acquisitions by ASEAN states. The end of the Cold War led to the greater availability of second-hand equipment from the inventories of major supplier nations which could be sold to regional friends and allies at bargain prices.

In the 1980s and before the Asian crisis, improved economic conditions and purchasing power have also contributed to the military build-up by the ASEAN countries. The impact of the Asian crisis in bringing defence spending and arms procurement down and the reversal of this trend following the economy recovery in the 2000s clearly show that the military build-up in ASEAN is most sensitive to economic conditions. Moreover, weapons acquisitions are also influenced by considerations of economic benefit, such as countertrade opportunities and expanding market access for commodities, including, as in the case of Malaysia, Indonesia and Thailand, 'rice, palm oil and even dried fruits'.[103] Finally, although arms purchase decisions are supposed to be based on a calculation of strategic need and economic affordability, in the ASEAN context, the influence of the military over the government apparatus (as evident in the increase in defence spending by Thailand after the military regime took over in 2006), inter-service rivalry and, importantly, corruption also influence the decision-making process, as in the case of Thailand.[104]

Much of the increases in defence spending and arms purchases in Asia are and will be driven by the bigger players, China, India and Japan, rather than Southeast Asia. Historically, defence spending and arms imports in Southeast Asia have been determined by a variety of factors, of which intra-ASEAN disputes and tensions (e.g. Singapore–Malaysia, and Thailand–Myanmar) are only one part. The other factors include domestic insurgencies, concern for the security and safety of sea lanes from disruption from piracy and terrorism (which are common security concerns of ASEAN members), and of course extra-regional security challenges such as uncertainty over China's strategic intentions or fear of retrenchment of the US military presence in the region. The last factor is important, since Southeast Asia is part of the wider East Asian strategic theatre, hence affected by what goes on in the relationship among the major players. This serves as an impetus for defence spending and arms purchases, but it need not destabilise intra-ASEAN relations *per se*. These distinct intra-ASEAN and extra-ASEAN contexts are important to bear in mind when considering the economic and strategic implications of the perceived 'arms race' in East and Southeast Asia. The largest ASEAN member in terms of population and GDP, Indonesia, is only the sixth highest defence spender in ASEAN, while the smallest ASEAN member, Singapore, is the highest spender with the most capable armed forces. This causes a kind of balance that has served intra-ASEAN stability well in the past and should continue to serve it well into the future.[105] Finally, defence spending in ASEAN has historically been highly sensitive to the economic cycle (unlike South Asia, where defence spending is driven mainly by strategic consideration whether the economies perform well or not). This is a hopeful sign for ASEAN that indicates that its members will not put guns before butter.

To sum up, arms procurement decisions by ASEAN states have reflected a mixture of motives, including, but going well beyond, interstate competition and rivalry. To explain the entire phenomenon of force modernisation as a regional arms race is misleading given the fact that no significant conflict has obtained in other bilateral relationships, such as those between Singapore and Thailand, and between the Philippines and Indonesia. A 1999 study concluded that the military build-up in the region 'may not amount to an arms race' as it was driven by both threat perceptions and other factors such as prestige and strategic uncertainty.[106] This assessment concurred with previous studies by Desmond Ball (1993–94) covering the Asia-Pacific region and this author (1994) for Southeast Asia.[107] There is, however, a trend towards increased defence spending and arms acquisitions throughout the Asia-Pacific region, involving China, Korea, Japan, India and Taiwan. US Defense Secretary Robert Gates warned of an Asian arms race.[108] A competitive military build-up featuring the region's major powers may have a potential to draw in ASEAN, rather than an intra-ASEAN arms race. Hence the need for steps to induce greater restraint, transparency and confidence-building in the wider region.

There have been attempts by ASEAN governments to enhance intra-mural military transparency. These include Lee Kuan Yew's proposal in late 1989 that Singapore and Malaysia could open their military installations for mutual inspection (which was rejected by Malaysia)[109] and Malaysia's proposals concerning greater transparency in weapon acquisitions through the creation of a regional arms register.[110] While some of these have been taken up within the ARF, intra-ASEAN arms regulation has not really progressed. The level of transparency in the defence budgets and policies of ASEAN states improved somewhat with some members states, notably Thailand and Malaysia, having started to issue defence white papers. But the advent of the ARF in 1994 and the establishment of the ASEAN Defence Ministers Meeting (ADMM) in 2006 and the ADMM Plus (which includes the ten ASEAN members plus China, Japan, South Korea, US, Australia, New Zealand and India) in 2010 holds promise in inducing greater levels of defence dialogue and transparency both among the ASEAN members and between them and non-ASEAN powers.

Enhancing economic interdependence

ASEAN's founders hoped that ASEAN would facilitate intra-regional conflict resolution and create 'an environment conducive to economic development and the reinforcement of social and political stability'.[111] But regional economic integration in the European sense had never been a professed goal of ASEAN. The ASEAN states were wary of the harmful effects of regional integration on national economic development: maintaining trade and investment links with the outside world was seen as more important to developing ASEAN's economies than measures to promote intra-regional integration. Such measures would discriminate against more efficient non-regional producers and thus undermine the competitiveness of ASEAN economies in world markets.[112]

A major initiative in economic cooperation had been undertaken in 1977 when preferential trading arrangements were signed which provided for measures to liberalise and increase intra-ASEAN trade. These measures included long-term quantity contracts, liberalisation of non-tariff barriers on a preferential basis, exchange of tariff preferences, preferential terms for financing imports, and preference for ASEAN products in procurement by government bodies.[113] Such arrangements had only a marginal impact on raising the level of intra-ASEAN trade as a proportion of total ASEAN trade from 13.5 per cent in 1973 to a peak of 20 per cent in 1983; it subsequently fell to around 16–17 per cent.[114]

In contrast to intra-mural trade liberalisation, ASEAN was more successful in collective bargaining to seek more favourable economic relations with external trading partners. Beginning in the early 1970s, collective external bargaining was used to secure better commodity prices,[115] an example being bargaining with Japan over the price of natural rubber. ASEAN also used collective bargaining to secure better market access for its products, which led to an increase in the number of items exported by ASEAN members which qualify for lower duties under the EC's generalised system of preferences. In addition, ASEAN has tried to maintain a united position at multilateral trade negotiations, both at the Tokyo and the Uruguay Rounds of GATT negotiations.[116]

In considering the impact of economic interdependence on war and peace, Haas has argued that the increasing enmeshment of a group of actors in functionalist ties at the global level is not really important. What matters is if functional ties 'link them to each other' intra-regionally rather than to the outside world.[117] If this is true, then ASEAN's greater commitment to linkages with the global economy in relation to regional economic integration would seem likely to have a smaller impact on prospects for war avoidance.

ASEAN's interest in intra-regional trade cooperation increased in the early 1990s in response to several developments. The changing orientation of ASEAN economies towards manufacturing provided scope for greater intra-ASEAN division of labour. In addition, the establishment of the North American Free Trade Area and the advent of the EU Single Market raised fears within ASEAN of rising protectionism. This fear was compounded by the stalemate in the Uruguay Round of GATT talks towards the late 1980s, a stalemate blamed by Singapore's Prime Minister, Goh Chok Tong, on the two largest economic powers in the world, the USA and the EU, who could 'hold the entire multilateral trading system to ransom' over a 'single issue like agriculture'.[118] ASEAN also feared a declining flow of investment from the West as the collapse of communism led to the opening up of East European economies.

In response to these developments, ASEAN leaders in January 1992 announced plans to form an ASEAN Free Trade Area (AFTA) within 15 years. In addition, a number of initiatives to promote regional economic cooperation were adopted. These included co-operation in securing greater foreign investment through creating an ASEAN Investment Area, liberalisation of the service sector including tourism, maritime transport, air transport, telecommunications, construction, business and financial services, and cooperation in intel-lectual property matters encouraged through creating an ASEAN Patent System and an ASEAN Trademark System. The evolution and scope of AFTA and these other measures suggested the influence of the ASEAN Way, including a preference for informality, non-adversarial bargaining, consensus building and non-legalistic procedures for decision making. As Stubbs has argued, AFTA was to be based 'more on networks of personal contacts and social obligations than on formal institutions and legal commitments'. The negotiations leading to AFTA could be described as a process of developing 'a vaguely worded statement which did not violate any of the participants' basic interests and, therefore, to which all participants could agree'. This allowed AFTA to be moved forward at a 'pace with which all governments felt comfortable'. In a similar vein, disputes were to be settled through informal discussions behind closed doors and without resort to formal dispute-settlement mechanisms as found in the EU or NAFTA. (There is an AFTA Council to deal

Table 5.4 Intra-and extra-ASEAN trade, 2011 (value in US$ million; share in percent)

Country	Intra-ASEAN trade		Extra-ASEAN trade		Total trade
	Value	Share to total trade	Value	Share to total trade	
Brunei Darussalam	2,912.1	19.6	11,910.2	80.4	14,822.3
Cambodia	3,003.8	23.4	9,840.3	76.6	12,844.1
Indonesia	99,353.2	26.1	281,579.1	73.9	380,932.3
Lao PDR	2,530.3	64.0	1,425.5	36.0	3,955.9
Malaysia	108,139.7	26.0	307,582.2	74.0	415,721.9
Myanmar	7,207.7	48.3	7,717.4	51.7	14,925.1
Philippines	23,675.6	21.2	88,076.0	78.8	111,751.6
Singapore	205,670.9	26.5	569,481.7	73.5	775,152.6
Thailand	111,450.8	24.3	347,453.5	75.7	458,904.4
Vietnam	34,298.1	17.2	165,284.0	82.8	199,582.1
ASEAN	598,242.2	25.0	1,790,350.0	75.0	2,388,592.3

Source: ASEAN Merchandise Trade Statistics Database (compiled/computed from data submission, publications and/or websites of ASEAN Member States' national ASEAN Free Trade Area (AFTA) units, national statistics offices, customs departments/agencies, or central banks)

with disputes, and if this does not work, the matter is to be dealt with at the level of ASEAN economic ministers or at the leaders' summit meeting level.)[119]

But AFTA and related initiatives did not produce a noticeable increase in intra-ASEAN trade: as a proportion of total ASEAN trade, this remained around 16–17 per cent during the 1980s.[120] From 1991 to 1995, trade among the ASEAN six grew at an annual rate of 21.6 per cent, totalling US$137 billion, or 23 per cent of their total trade. This compares with the ASEAN six's trade with the world which grew at a slower annual rate of 15 per cent over the same period. But if transshipment through Singapore is discounted, the level of intra-ASEAN trade falls to about 12 per cent.[121] In 2011, intra-ASEAN trade accounted for 25 per cent of the ASEAN members' total trade (see Table 5.4). Moreover, AFTA, which was to lead the way to a more comprehensive ASEAN Economic Community (AEC) by 2015, remained plagued by fears among ASEAN members concerning the unequal distribution of gains. These fears were aggravated by the differing levels of development among the ASEAN six and the new ASEAN members, even though the latter were allowed extensions beyond the 2003 deadline to bring down their tariffs to the required 0–5 per cent level.

Another form of economic cooperation in Southeast Asia which developed rapidly in the early 1990s was technically outside the formal ASEAN framework. Variously called 'natural economic territories' (NETs), 'subregional economic zones' or 'growth triangles', these represented a 'market-driven' approach to regional economic cooperation. The NETs brought together geographically contiguous areas (as opposed to the entire national territory of AFTA members) within two or more states with natural economic complementarities. In Southeast Asia, at least three such areas have emerged: the Singapore–Johor–Riau (SIJORI) triangle; the Indonesia–Malaysia–Thailand Growth Triangle (IMT-GT); and the Brunei, Indonesia, Malaysia, Philippines East ASEAN Growth Area (BIMP-EAGA) involving Sabah, Sarawak and Labuan in Malaysia, North Sulawesi, East Kalimantan and West Kalimantan in Indonesia, the Mindanao region of the Philippines and Brunei. A somewhat different category of subregional cooperation is the Greater Mekong Growth Area, involving China's Yunnan province, Laos, Cambodia, Vietnam, Thailand and Burma. These NETs join similar concepts in Northeast Asia, including the Southern China Growth Triangle and the Tumen River Area Development Programme.

The emergence of these NETs could foster greater regional peace and stability within ASEAN. Singapore's former Foreign Minister, and a founding father of ASEAN, S. Rajaratnam, argued that

> [j]ust as the European Community has integrated a number of isolated national states into a cohesive economic and security organisation, I believe that the Johor–Riau–Singapore triangle will also act as a catalyst regional body.[122]

Several of the NETs straddle territory that has been or is currently under dispute: for example, the NETs linking Borneo and Mindanao, the border territories of Malaysia and Thailand and Indonesia and Malaysia (part of the IMT-GT area). Malaysia's former Deputy Prime Minister, Anwar Ibrahim, claimed, '[i]nstead of talking about border disputes, we are now promoting economic cooperation through growth triangles and other cross-border linkages'.[123]

But progress in implementing these NETs remained a hostage to interstate security relations. The unresolved dispute between Malaysia and the Philippines over Sabah still undermines the implementation of the BIMP-EAGA concept. Moreover, the NETs in some cases caused tensions over the unequal distribution of benefits.[124] Singapore was seen by sections within Malaysia and Indonesia as being the major beneficiary of the NET. Indonesia felt concerned that Singapore, occupying only 3 per cent of the land area within SIJORI, accounted for about half of its population and 90 per cent of its income.[125]

Advocates of regional economic interdependence argue that the NETs and other forms of regional economic interdependence reduce the incentives for states to resort to force in resolving interstate disputes because of the risk of severely disrupting each state's economy.[126] But as the Asian financial crisis of 1997 and its aftershocks demonstrated, economic interdependence could also serve as a transmission belt for spreading security problems through the region. The crisis also showed that any pacific effects of interdependence are less likely to hold if there exist significant economic disparities among states (as between Singapore and its neighbours) and that the potential political gains of interdependence would be particularly vulnerable to economic downturns, especially if the impact of the downturn was felt unevenly within a group of states.

While the Asian crisis was not strictly 'Southeast Asian' in scope (apart from South Korea, it acquired the attributes of a global crisis affecting countries as far apart as Russia and Brazil), the 'contagion' effect of the crisis was most seriously felt in Southeast Asia. The crisis confronted the regional concept and regionalism of Southeast Asia with a number of challenges, undermining intra-ASEAN relations, aggravating latent bilateral tensions and damaging ASEAN's credibility as an instrument of regional cooperation. The crisis directly affected four ASEAN member countries: Thailand, Indonesia, Malaysia and the Philippines. At its worst during the first weeks of January 1998, the baht had fallen by 40 per cent, the rupiah by 80 per cent, the ringgit by 40 per cent, and the peso by 30 per cent against the dollar from their values on 1 July 1997.[127] The depreciation of these currencies placed pressure on Singapore, the regional trade centre, to follow suit. Brunei Darussalam earns petrodollars from its exports of oil and gas, and major imports of food come from ASEAN countries with devalued currencies; but the Brunei dollar was also devalued since it is tied to the Singapore dollar. The new members of ASEAN, Vietnam, Laos, and Burma – and the one future member, Cambodia – were also affected, as most of their foreign direct investments come from the older member countries of ASEAN.[128] In terms of capital outflow, more than \$30 billion fled Indonesia, Malaysia, the Philippines and Thailand in 1997 and 1998. Thailand was one of the countries worst hit by the crisis and it accepted a US\$17.2 billion (HK\$133.12 billion) rescue package from the International Monetary Fund in August 2007.[129]

The Asian crisis severely curtailed growth rates in Southeast Asia. The World Bank, which in 1993 had coined the term 'the Asian miracle', dubbed the crisis 'the biggest setback for poverty reduction in East Asia for several decades'.[130] The study by the UN's International Labour Organisation (ILO) showed that between August 1997 and December 1998, unemployment in Indonesia rose from 4.3 million to 13.7 million. In Thailand, the numbers exploded from 0.7 million in February 1997 to 1.9 million in December 1998, in Malaysia from 224,000 unemployed in December 1997 to 405,000 in December 1998.[131] Indonesia suffered the sharpest increases in unemployment and poverty.[132]

Although the crisis's impact on the region's countries was far from uniform, the dimensions of the regional interdependence could be seen from common factors and 'contagion effect' which underpinned the crisis throughout the region.[133] The crisis in Thailand, Korea, Indonesia and Malaysia made investors nervous and created the fear that other countries in the region had similar problems. To the serving Secretary-General of ASEAN, Rodolfo Severino, this was a reminder of the common vulnerability of Southeast Asian economies. 'The first lesson is that the countries in a region, certainly in Southeast Asia', claimed

Severino, 'are more inter-connected and more interdependent than previously thought'. In his view, 'what one country does with its economy and even with its politics almost invariably affects its neighbors'.[134]

The Asian economic crisis prompted ASEAN to take steps to strengthen economic cooperation. Stung by criticism of its failure to take timely action to deal with the crisis, the AFTA timetable was moved forward for the original six members from 2003 to 2002. Recognising that trade liberalisation was not enough, ASEAN initiated financial cooperation by holding the first meeting of ASEAN finance ministers to coordinate financial supervision and to strengthen ASEAN's investment climate, including a common commitment of all ASEAN members to 100 per cent foreign equity ownership.[135] These responses not only confirmed ASEAN's constitutive norm of 'open economies', but also indicated a deepening of multilateralism. Another step was the institution of an ASEAN Surveillance Process (ASP) involving peer review and frank exchange of views and information on important finance matters. The process, established at the special meeting of the ASEAN Finance Ministers on 4 October 1998, was intended to prevent future crises through the conduct of an early warning system and regional economic surveillance exercise. To this end, it would involve 'a peer review process and the exchange of views and information among the ASEAN Finance Ministers on macroeconomic and finance matters'.[136] The process also led to the creation of new institutions, including a forum of ASEAN Finance and Central Bank Deputies and a special working group, an ASEAN Surveillance Coordinating Unit (ASCU) based at the ASEAN Secretariat and the ASEAN Surveillance Technical Support Unit (ASTSU) based at the Asian Development Bank in Manila (later transferred to Jakarta).[137]

The creation of the ASP not only involved the creation of new institutions, thereby marking a departure from the ASEAN Way of informality. It also signalled a minor erosion of the non-interference doctrine. Although the term Surveillance Process, preferred over the Asian Development Bank's initial proposal for a more intrusive ASEAN Surveillance Mechanism, indicated limits to any shift in this regard, the challenge to non-interference did become serious as a result of other repercussions of the Asian crisis, as will be discussed in the final section of this chapter. The next stage in ASEAN's efforts to manage economic interdependence would come in the shape of an ASEAN Economic Community (AEC), as one of the three official pillars of ASEAN along with the ASEAN Political-Security Community and the ASEAN Socio-Cultural Community (more on this in Chapter 7)

The AEC, which is officially set to come into existence by 2015 seeks to turn ASEAN into 'a single market and production base with five core elements: (i) free flow of goods; (ii) free flow of services; (iii) free flow of investment; (iv) freer flow of capital; and (v) free flow of skilled labour.'[138] The realisation of the AEC faces several obstacles, which makes it unlikely that all its elements, such as removal of non-tariff barriers and the free movement of skilled labour, would be in place by 2015. Progress among the ASEAN member countries in meeting their commitments to the AEC has been uneven, which itself reflects wide development gaps among its members, and opposition from domestic interest groups in member states. On the positive side, 99 per cent of the total tariff lines among the ASEAN-6 (the original five ASEAN members and Brunei) had been reduced to zero by 2010, while tariffs among

Table 5.5 Growth rates in Southeast Asia, 1997–2003

Year	1997	1998	1999	2000	2001	2002	2003
GDP growth %	4	−7.5	3.1	6.0	2.0	3.8	4.6

Source: Asian Development Bank, *Asian Development Outlook*, various years.

the rest, the newer ASEAN members, had fallen to 0–5 per cent by 2010. Despite the challenges, the AEC is believed to deepen economic interdependence among the ASEAN members.

ASEAN as a 'defence community'

As noted in Chapter 2, since ASEAN's creation in 1967 its members developed a range of defence ties, albeit on a bilateral basis. These include (1) border region cooperation, (2) intelligence sharing, (3) joint exercises, (4) exchange activities between military education and training institutes, (5) frequent senior-level official visits, (6) provision of combat training facilities and (7) cooperation in the defence industrial sector. While intra-ASEAN bilateral security and defence cooperation in the formative years of ASEAN revolved primarily around border cooperation and intelligence sharing, cooperation in the 1980s and 1990s featured joint exercises, training and, to a lesser extent, defence industrial cooperation. Bilateral army exercises, initially resisted because they might allow the 'territorial familiarisation' of the host nation by the security forces of the guest country, were instituted during the late 1980s, especially between Indonesia and Singapore and between Malaysia and Singapore.[139]

In addition, ASEAN countries have been involved in cooperation in the area of training and exchange of facilities. Singapore has maintained army training camps in Thailand and Brunei and, until the withdrawal of US forces there, fighter aircraft units at Clark Air Force Base in the Philippines. In March 1989 a 10,850 hectare air weapons testing range in Sumatra jointly developed by Indonesia and Singapore became operational. ASEAN members allowed and encouraged participation of students from other ASEAN countries in military education and officer training programmes at their national institutions. ASEAN armed forces have also developed ties in tactical areas, such as commando training by Thai troops in Singapore, special forces training by Malaysian troops in Indonesia, and jungle warfare training in Malaysia by trainees from other ASEAN states, including Singapore.

A more modest form of defence cooperation relates to defence industries. In 1978, General Maradan Panggabean, Indonesia's Coordinating Minister for Security and General Policies, suggested the establishment of an ASEAN arms factory.[140] In the aftermath of Vietnam's invasion of Cambodia, Thailand explored the possibility of an ASEAN 'war reserve contingency pool'. In 1988, Singapore and Thailand approved a project to co-produce a range of small arms. There has not been any attempt at joint procurement of weapons, however, despite some degree of standardisation in the 1980s. For example, all ASEAN states except Brunei acquired F-5 fighter and C-130 transport aircraft, while three (Singapore, Malaysia and Indonesia) acquired A-4 attack aircraft. Later, the F-16 entered service in the air forces of Singapore, Indonesia and Thailand. But this was not due to any conscious policy or design. Opportunities for joint procurement which might have resulted in significant cost savings were ignored. For example, joint procurement was ignored during the purchase of a multi-role fighter aircraft by Singapore, Indonesia, Thailand and Malaysia; in the event, the first three separately acquired the F-16A/B from the USA, while Malaysia purchased the MiG-29 from the Soviet Union and the F-18 from the USA. Barriers to joint procurement have included differences in military spending levels, as well as differing geographical conditions, doctrine and overall military strategy, leading to divergent procurement needs. Similarly, lingering political suspicions affected the prospect for greater cooperation in defence production. For example, the fear that an ASEAN arms manufacturing scheme might create a leading role for Singapore, which would in turn give the island republic undue leverage over its neighbours, may have been a constraining factor in intra-ASEAN cooperation in defence production.

The end of ASEAN–Indochina polarisation has meant that military cooperation among the ASEAN states (see Table 5.6) could no longer provoke Hanoi. ASEAN has yet to embrace defence multilateralism, however. Singapore and Malaysia embarked on a bilateral security dialogue, the Malaysia–Singapore Defence Forum, and signed a memorandum of understanding on defence industrial cooperation that was intended to involve co-production as well as joint marketing of defence equipment.[141] Bilateral defence industrial cooperation was also evident in the case of an agreement between Indonesia's PT Pindad and Singapore's Chartered (Firearms) Industries allowing the former to produce Singapore's 40 mm automatic grenade launcher.[142] Malaysia and the Philippines set aside their long-standing dispute over Sabah to sign an agreement covering an exchange of defence-related information, logistic support and training.[143] Singapore and the Philippines launched their first ever army exercise, codenamed 'Anoa-Singa', in 1993.[144] Malaysia signed a memorandum of understanding with Indonesia to import six Indonesian-built CN-235 transport aircraft in return for Indonesia's purchase of 20 Malaysian-built SME MD3-160 acrobatic trainer aircraft.[145]

Nonetheless, the ASEAN norm against multilateral military cooperation enunciated at the Bali summit has clearly survived into the post-Cold War period. In the words of Malaysia's then Defence Minister, Najib Tun Razak:

> Asean doesn't need a military pact. Asean military forces are familiar with each other on a bilateral basis. To me, that's good enough. Because when you have a pact, people will ask: Who is it directed at? So it raises a lot of questions. So rather than alarming anyone or sending a wrong signal, it is better for us to continue on the same basis because we have been so successful.[146]

In a similar vein, while serving as the Chief of the Malaysian Armed Forces, General Hashim Mohammed Ali stressed the advantages of continuing with bilateral cooperation because of the flexibility it affords. In his view, bilateralism

> allows any Asean partner to decide the type, time and scale of aid it requires and can provide. The question of national independence and sovereignty is unaffected by the decision of others as in the case of an alliance where members can evoke the terms of the treaty and interfere in the affairs of another partner.[147]

Not surprisingly therefore, steps towards defence multilateralism within ASEAN, even after the settlement of the Cambodia conflict and Vietnam's entry into the grouping, have been modest. A number of developments in the mid-1990s attest to this.[148] For example, in 1995 Singapore and Indonesia offered fellow ASEAN members access to their jointly developed Air Combat Manoeuvring Range (ACMR) in Sumatra. Further, around this time, ASEAN reportedly set up a special working group to discuss defence cooperation. On the other hand, a proposal to create a regional association of national defence industries of ASEAN states failed due to political and financial problems. An invitation from Thailand to its five ASEAN neighbours (as well as Australia, New Zealand and the USA) to participate in a new multilateral exercise also fell through, although Singapore in 1994 became the first

Table 5.6 ASEAN military cooperation, 1977–97: bilateral military exercises

Countries involved	Name of exercise	Year started	Frequency
Indonesia/Brunei (Navy)	Helang Laut	?	Biennial
Indonesia/Malaysia (Army)	Kekar Malindo	1977	Annual
	Tatar Malindo	1981	Intermittent
	Kripura Malindo	1981	Intermittent
Indonesia/Malaysia (Air)	Elang Malindo	1975	Annual
Indonesia/Malaysia (Navy)	Malindo Jaya	1973	Annual?
Indonesia/Malaysia (Combined Forces)	Darsasa Malindo	1982	Intermittent (twice since 1982)
Indonesia/Singapore (Army)	Safakar Indopura	1989	Annual
Indonesia/Singapore (Air)	Elang Indopura	1980	Annual
Indonesia/Singapore (Navy)	Englek	1974	Biennial
Indonesia/Thailand (Air)	Elang Thainesia	1981	Annual
Indonesia/Thailand (Navy)	Sea Garuda	1975?	Intermittent
Indonesia/Philippines (Navy)	Philindo/ Corpatphilindo	1972	Intermittent
Malaysia/Singapore (Army)	Semangat Bersatu	1989	Intermittent
Malaysia/Singapore (Navy)	Malapura	1984	Annual (suspended)
Malaysia/Thailand (Air)	Air Thamal	1981	Annual
Malaysia/Thailand (Navy)	Thalay	1980	Intermittent?
Malaysia/Brunei (Navy)	Hornbill (and others)	1981?	Intermittent
Malaysia/Brunei (Army)	Malbru Setia	1993	Intermittent?
Malaysia/Philippines (Navy)	Sea Malphi	?	Intermittent?
Singapore/Thailand (Air)	Sing-Siam	1981	Initially intermittent, but biennial since 1996
Singapore/Thailand (Navy)	Thai-Sing	1983	Annual
Singapore/Brunei (Navy)	Pelican	1979	Annual
Singapore/Brunei (Army)	Termite/Flaming Arrow/Juggernaut	1985	Annual
Singapore/Brunei	Maju Bersama	1995	Annual
Singapore/Philippines	Anoa-Singa	1993	Annual?
Singapore/Philippines (Navy)	Dagat Singa (Sea Tiger)	1996	Annual

Sources: Donald Weatherbee, 'ASEAN Security Co-operation and the South China Sea', Paper presented to the Pacific Forum Symposium on National Threat Perceptions in East/Asia Pacific, Waikoloa, Hawaii, 6–8 February 1982; Personal interviews in Kuala Lumpur, Malaysia, 16 August 1989; Personal interview with the Defence Attaché of the Philippines, Jakarta, 10 August 1989; Robert Karniol, 'Singapore, Thailand to Improve Defence Links', *Jane's Defence Weekly*, vol. 26, no. 6 (1996), p. 12; B.A. Hamzah, 'ASEAN Military Cooperation Without Pact or Threat', *Asia Pacific Community*, no. 22 (Fall 1983), pp. 42–3; K.U. Menon, 'A Six Power Defence Arrangement in Southeast Asia', *Contemporary Southeast Asia*, vol. 10, no. 3 (December 1988), p. 314; *Asian Defence Journal, Asia-Pacific Defence Reporter, Bangkok Post, China News, Indonesia Observer, Jane's Defence Weekly, New Straits Times, Pioneer, Star, Straits Times, Sunday Times (Singapore)*.

outside country to be allowed the right to observe fully the Cobra Gold bilateral exercise between the USA and Thailand. Similarly, Malaysia's suggestion to establish an ASEAN peacekeeping force, based on the Nordic Battalion model (which consists of soldiers from Scandinavian countries), received only limited support, partly because of fears that it would be seen as an attempt by ASEAN to form a military alliance, and that it would not be politic to deploy such a force in intra-ASEAN conflicts (more on this in Chapter 7).

Defence cooperation between the old and the new members of ASEAN proceeded on a bilateral basis. The Indochinese states were drawn into the web of bilateral defence co-operation with ASEAN, and Vietnam established defence links with the Philippines, Indonesia and Thailand, although an offer by Thailand to establish a 'hot line' between Hanoi and Bangkok, and to exchange equipment and hold bilateral naval exercises, was turned down by Hanoi, attesting to lingering mutual suspicions and also pending progress in resolving its overlapping territorial claims in the Gulf of Thailand. The Philippines has offered training facilities for Vietnamese officers at its military academy and has indicated a desire to cooperate on maintaining and reconditioning defence equipment.

As noted, the establishment of the ADMM and the ADMM Plus has created a new platform for regional defence cooperation. But neither constitutes an alliance, and thus do not represent a violation of the ASEAN norm of 'no military pacts', or multilateral defence cooperation geared to a common external threat. Established in 2006 by the ten ASEAN members, the ADMM was expanded in 2010 to an ADMM Plus, to serve 'as a platform for the defence establishments of ASEAN and their key security partners to strengthen the region's capacity and effectiveness in addressing common security challenges'.[149] Originally slated to meet once in three years (later reduced to once in two years), the membership of the ADMM Plus is the same as that of the East Asia Summit (EAS). Its initial scope of co-operation includes humanitarian assistance and disaster relief, maritime security, military medicine, counter-terrorism and peacekeeping operations (PKO). In essence, it is a forum for exchange of views on regional and international security issues and is primarily a confidence-building exercise. The same can be said of the Shangri-la Dialogue (SLD), which is seen by some as a competitor to the ADMM Plus. Organised annually by the International Institute for Strategic Studies (IISS) in Singapore since 2002, the SLD has been hailed as Asia's preeminent gathering of senior defence officials. But it is really a confidence-building exercise. It tries to cover a broad range of issues, including non-traditional ones and, unlike the ADMM and ADMM Plus, allows participation by non-official experts in parts of its discussions. Its ownership by the IISS, an 'outside' think-tank headquartered in London (but with regional offices, including one in Singapore) is a significant source of resentment among some circles in Southeast Asia. China's refusal to enhance the level of its representation (only once between 2002 and 2011 did China send its defence minister to the meeting) also undermines the significance of the SLD.

ASEAN states continue to see threat-oriented cooperation as normatively undesirable and unduly provocative to potential adversaries (Vietnam in the past, China now). This does not preclude collective action against external or internal threats in time of need. Najib Razak once claimed that, given the degree of interoperability achieved among the ASEAN forces as a result of bilateral exercises, 'there is nothing to prevent ASEAN from acting collectively if there is the political will to do so. . . . If there is a need to have an ASEAN military force, it could be done almost overnight.'[150] But bilateral defence cooperation has proved more useful and served as a confidence-building measure. Whether or not this will change depends very much on the progress of intra-ASEAN counter-terrorism cooperation as well as the ASEAN Security Community initiative, to be discussed in Chapter 7.

Sovereignty, non-interference and regional problem solving

In the areas of dispute settlement, if not in the area of defence cooperation, ASEAN's norms had come under considerable stress in the first decade of the post-Cold War era. The norm concerning non-use of force had been severely tested, especially in the case of relations between Singapore and Malaysia. While these ASEAN members avoided outright military confrontation, their bilateral tensions did disrupt military ties and the two states also appear to have been engaged in a bilateral arms race. There have been other challenges to ASEAN's norms from both domestic and international developments.

The foremost among these challenges concerns the doctrine of non-interference. Indeed, the tensions between the principle of sovereignty and the call from some ASEAN quarters for revising the doctrine of non-interference turned out to be one of the central challenges to ASEAN regionalism in the latter half of the 1990s. As discussed in the previous chapter, the non-interference principle had already come under some stress over the admission of Burma and Cambodia into ASEAN, but it was the Asian economic crisis, itself described by the Filipino President, Joseph Estrada, as the 'greatest challenge [to ASEAN] since its founding',[151] which posed a particularly serious test to the doctrine as an approach to managing intra-regional relations.

The Asian crisis had been widely recognised, even within the grouping itself, as a major blow to ASEAN's credibility. Malaysia's Prime Minister, Mahathir Mohamad, admitted that ASEAN's response to the economic crisis had 'created the impression of an ASEAN in disarray, its members at odds with each other'.[152] President Estrada of the Philippines agreed; in his view, 'doubts have been raised about the ASEAN spirit, about our solidarity, about our credibility'.[153] At issue was not only ASEAN's economic response to the crisis, but also the bilateral tensions that had surfaced among member states, such as that between Malaysia and Singapore.

The debate over the non-interference doctrine intensified when it was blamed for ASEAN's incapacity to respond effectively to the crisis, especially in alerting Thailand to its economic woes. While outside commentators were quick to point out this shortcoming,[154] it was the Foreign Minister of the new Thai government, Surin Pitsuwan, who emerged as the strongest critic of the doctrine. As he put it, 'it is time that Asean's cherished principle of non-intervention is modified to allow it to play a constructive role in preventing or resolving domestic issues with regional implications'. Elaborating, he added: 'when a matter of domestic concern poses a threat to regional stability, a dose of peer pressure or friendly advice at the right time can be helpful'.[155]

In place of a strict adherence to non-interference as an ASEAN norm, Surin proposed the idea of 'flexible engagement'. Calling this a 'more flexible interpretation of the certain fundamental approaches' undertaken by ASEAN, Surin argued that ASEAN members needed more 'openness' in dealing with one another. This implied that ASEAN members should not refrain from commenting on each other's domestic policies when they have regional implications. Indeed, Surin's deputy, Sukhumbhand Paribatra, stated that the flexible engagement approach, towards Burma at least, meant speaking frankly about its domestic situation: 'True friends speak frankly to each other. We don't talk sweet.'[156]

Though mooted in the context of the economic crisis, the concept of 'flexible engagement' must be viewed in the broader context of ASEAN's handling of intra-regional problems. To some degree, it was intended to address newly emerging transnational issues facing ASEAN, including the problems of human rights, environmental degradation and refugees. These problems require an approach that goes beyond ASEAN's traditional policy of non-intervention, no matter how useful the latter might have been to ASEAN during its formative years. Flexible engagement could be a necessary reform to the time-honoured ASEAN Way. It could be used as a means of improving regional transparency, and could provide early warning and develop policy approaches to deal with transnational economic and social problems.

Some of these transnational issues related directly to Thailand's own predicament. The concept of flexible engagement reflected the new Thai government's attempt to distance itself from its predecessor's policy, endorsed by ASEAN as a whole, of 'constructive engagement' towards Burma, which conflicted with the new Chuan Leekpai government's democratic credentials and which had been costly in terms of disrupted economic ties with the EU. Flexible engagement also reflected Thailand's need to put pressure on the regime in Burma over the influx of refugees, numbering about a million, into Thai territory.

Like the idea of 'constructive intervention' proposed earlier by the now deposed Malaysian Deputy Prime Minister, Anwar Ibrahim, flexible engagement was also intended to move ASEAN towards a more proactive role. Indeed, the Foreign Minister of the Philippines, Domingo Siazon, emphasised this aspect when he contrasted 'flexible engagement' with ASEAN's previous approach of 'benign neglect' of each other.[157] This view was contested by other ASEAN members, especially by Malaysia's Foreign Minister, Abdullah Badawi, who argued that non-interference had not in the past prevented governments from speaking candidly about each other's domestic issues if and when appropriate.[158] But it attracted support from Siazon who, as the only ASEAN minister to have openly sided with Surin, likened flexible engagement to the EU's policy, 'where you actually address each other's problems openly and sometimes even confront each other, but in the process, lead to a better synthesis and have a better product'.[159] Using a cautious tone, Siazon noted that: 'when the situation is opportune, more pro-active Asean policy among its members may be felicitous and it may not be sufficient just to have a policy of non-intervention'.[160]

But Thailand's other neighbours were far less receptive, some even openly hostile, to the flexible engagement concept.[161] Some even suspected, perhaps correctly, that the proposal was an attempt by Thailand to assume a leadership position in ASEAN (especially in the wake of the leadership vacuum left by the exit of Indonesia's Suharto), similar to the days of the Cambodia conflict when Thai security concerns were driving ASEAN's political agenda. The ensuing debate exposed divisions within ASEAN over one of its most basic norms. Malaysia issued one of the bluntest rejections of flexible engagement, with Foreign Minister Badawi insisting that quiet diplomacy consistent with the ASEAN Way was still the best way, 'befitting a community of friends bonded in cooperation' and that maintaining this practice was 'critical to our collective being', while the opposite course, 'criticising loudly, posturing adversarially and grandstanding' would 'bring less results and does more harm than good'.[162]

Singapore's Foreign Minister, S. Jayakumar, also defended the non-interference doctrine as practised within the ASEAN context. Reminding fellow members that 'Asean countries' consistent adherence to this principle of non-interference' had been 'the key reason why no military conflict ha[d] broken out between any two member countries since the founding of ASEAN', Jayakumar argued that 'the surest and quickest way to ruin is for ASEAN countries to begin commenting on how each of us deals with these sensitive issues' such as race, religion, language.[163] Brunei, with a concern for regime security which could be undermined by a policy that encouraged other ASEAN members to comment on its political situation, also rejected flexible engagement. Any departure from non-interference was especially alarming to Vietnam and Burma, whose governments were most fearful that a policy of flexible engagement would be detrimental to their internal stability and regime survival. This view was shared by Laos as well.

Apart from the issue of regime security, the reluctance of Thailand's ASEAN partners to endorse any departure from the norm of strict non-interference had to do with a fear that such a move would rekindle bilateral disputes and lead to regionalisation of issues that are best settled bilaterally. Flexible engagement would needlessly transform bilateral issues into an ASEAN issue.[164] Moreover, there was also a concern that it could lead to unwarranted interference by external powers in ASEAN affairs, e.g. in the name of a more proactive policy on human rights and democracy, thereby undermining ASEAN's other norm concerning regional autonomy.

ASEAN foreign ministers, at their annual meeting in Manila in July 1998, decided to stick to the old principle of non-interference.[165] Instead of flexible engagement, the evidently less intervention-oriented notion of 'enhanced interaction' at the suggestion of Ali Alatas was adopted as a policy framework to deal with transnational issues within the region.[166] But while non-interference survived, the attempts to tinker with it would not fade away for several reasons.

One was the impact of democratisation (already noted earlier as a factor behind the Thai push for flexible engagement) and the growing salience of human rights and democracy on the ASEAN agenda. Although partly responding to pressures from outside (including the Western countries), this is also the result of the growing realisation of some ASEAN members that meaningful cooperation between ASEAN and the international community would require narrowing the gap between them on the understanding of human rights and democracy. As Surin Pitsuwan commented, 'the issues of democracy and human rights are those we have to increasingly deal with in our engagement with the outside world'.[167] One of the effects of democratisation is the unravelling of ASEAN's earlier efforts to develop a common position on human rights and democracy to counter pressures from the West. This effort had led ASEAN foreign ministers to issue a statement in July 1993 adopting what may be called a 'relativist' position on human rights. The statement, issued not long before the Vienna World Conference on Human Rights, had called for viewing economic, social, civil and cultural rights as being 'indivisible' and of 'equal importance', thereby implying a rejection of what they saw as the West's excessive focus on political rights. It also called for the promotion of human rights to pay 'due regard for specific cultural, social, economic and political circumstances' of individual countries, thereby rejecting the notion of universal human rights advocated by the West.[168] The ASEAN statement reflected the belief of some members, especially the Singaporean elite, about the existence of a set of Asian values which stressed a communitarian ethic over Western-style individualism. As with human rights, many ASEAN policymakers and scholars also rejected what they saw as the Western understanding of, and efforts in promoting, democracy in the region. They rejected the suitability of Western-style liberal democracy for the region and warned that Western efforts to promote democracy would undermine the foundations of regional order in Southeast Asia based on the inviolability of state sovereignty and the doctrine of non-interference in the internal affairs of members.

The ASEAN 'consensus' on human rights and democracy,[169] widely perceived to be a justification for authoritarian rule in the region, unravelled quickly after the Asian financial crisis. As their societies have democratised further, Thailand and the Philippines have come closer to a 'universalistic' understanding of human rights and democracy, a fact noted with some apprehension by officials in Burma in an assessment of ASEAN's future prospects.[170] In a first such move by an ASEAN member, Thailand under the new Chuan

Leekpai government actually seemed to make democracy promotion in the region part of its foreign policy agenda. Although this was not aggressively pursued, Asada Jayanama, a senior Thai diplomat, stated,

> We want to encourage Indonesia to move towards democratisation because then we'll have three important democratic countries in Southeast Asia: Indonesia, Thailand and the Philippines. That will change the picture.[171]

Pitsuwan hoped that Thailand's democratic system 'will be an inspiration to freedom and democracy-loving peoples in other countries, without interfering in their internal affairs'. He explained his sovereignty-eroding 'flexible engagement' idea as a reflection of Thailand's 'commitment to freedom and democracy'.[172]

It is therefore no coincidence that the two most open societies in ASEAN, Thailand and the Philippines, also emerged as the strongest advocates of a more interventionist ASEAN, while Vietnam and Burma, the two least democratic systems in ASEAN, remain most opposed to rethinking non-interference. Moreover, the advent of a more democratic regime in Indonesia (starting with the interim Habibie government) strengthened the hand of pro-democracy, and therefore pro-interventionist, forces within ASEAN. Indeed, support from new leaders in the Philippines and Indonesia for the police treatment of Malaysia's sacked Deputy Prime Minister Anwar Ibrahim, which greatly angered Mahathir, about unwarranted interference in Malaysia's internal affairs, was indicative of this trend.[173]

Apart from democratisation, environmental disasters also challenged ASEAN's norm of non-interference. The environmental challenge to ASEAN was highlighted during the Indonesian forest fires of 1997, when fires on the islands of Sumatra and Kalimantan, according to some estimates, destroyed between 750,000 and 1.7 million hectares of forest. The transnational fallout of environmental degradation was most starkly evident in the form of a haze that covered much of Indonesia and neighbouring Singapore and Malaysia. The Economy and Environment Programme for Southeast Asia (EEPSEA) put the economic cost of the 1997 haze at US $1.4 billion (although other estimates have put the total cost of the forest fires and the ensuing haze to the Southeast Asian region at US $5–6 billion).[174] As the haze worsened, prompting anger from Singapore and Malaysia, President Suharto was forced to issue an unprecedented apology to his affected neighbours for not having kept his domestic environmental situation under control. While efforts to address forest fires through the ASEAN framework have not been encouraging, the controversy over the issue suggests that ASEAN members now demanded better environmental management from fellow member states and face the need to devise common responses that might involve compromising on the doctrine of non-interference.

The East Timor crisis following the UN-supervised referendum on 30 August 1999 further attested to ASEAN's reluctance to dilute its non-interference doctrine. ASEAN was not only unwilling to criticise Indonesia for the atrocities committed by Timorese militias organised and supported by the Indonesian military, members were also not ready to send troops in support of the Australian-led multinational force that went in there on 20 September 1999. At a meeting with Surin Pitsuwan, Indonesian President Jusuf Habibie told him that he preferred ASEAN forces to Western troops in East Timor (Habibie wanted anyone but an Australian; Scandinavian forces and commander were acceptable).[175] But logistical problems (lack of combat-ready forces and transport to deploy within days) and political barriers kept ASEAN from having a leading role in the crisis. ASEAN's political dilemma on the crisis was well summed up by *Sai Gon Giai Phong (Liberated Saigon)*, a paper published by the Communist Party of Ho Chi Minh City, Vietnam, which wrote on 20 September 1999:

> Asian countries, especially ASEAN countries, seemed to be very cautious about the situation in East Timor despite the fact that Indonesia wanted to have a majority of Asian troops in the multinational force. This cautious attitude proves the respect held by ASEAN countries for both international and ASEAN principles, that is, 'no intervention into the internal affairs of other countries', and the respect they hold for Indonesia's sovereignty in East Timor since at this point in time East Timor is still an integral part of Indonesia. Right now the public is concerned about the situation in East Timor, especially the objectivity of the multinational force preparing to arrive in East Timor.[176]

Despite the East Timor experience and having been rejected by his ASEAN peers in 1998, Surin maintained in 2001: 'everyone has tried to disown it [his doctrine of 'flexible engagement'], but it has survived'.[177] His idea had already done much to 'lessen the salience of state sovereignty' in ASEAN.[178] To some extent, he was right. One example of a mild shift in ASEAN's policy was the discussion of Burma's internal affairs at an official ASEAN meeting. During the APEC summit in Brunei in 2000, ASEAN leaders, at the behest of the Sultan of Brunei and with the backing of Malaysia's Mahathir Mohamad and Singapore's Goh Chok Tong, organised a special informal session with the leader of the Burmese Junta at which the latter was asked to give a 'progress report' on his country's political situation. This to Surin was the 'first ever talking about issues of internal nature in ASEAN'.[179] The subsequent, but short-lived release of Burmese opposition leader Aung San Suu Kyi in May 2002 could be due partly to ASEAN pressure. Indonesia was becoming now more receptive to comments by regional neighbours on its domestic affairs, which would be one of the bases of its proposal for an ASEAN security community.

While the debate on flexible engagement ended with the reaffirmation of the traditional ASEAN Way of quiet and 'polite' diplomacy over open debate and mutual criticism, related aspects of the ASEAN Way continued to be questioned. Tommy Koh, the eminent Singaporean diplomat, articulated the need to move beyond the ASEAN Way, noting the tendency of East Asian leaders to pursue cooperation by 'building trust, by a process of consultation, mutual accommodation and consensus' while displaying a 'general reluctance to build institutions and to rely on laws and rules'. The economic crisis, Koh contended, showed the need to supplement the ASEAN Way by institutions.[180] Some officials in ASEAN member states saw the emergence of an ASEAN troika system for crisis management and the establishment of an ASEAN financial surveillance process as examples of such institutionalisation.[181] The Philippines' Domingo Siazon even raised the possibility of an EU-style ASEAN. Although the ASEAN Surveillance Process developed after the Asian financial crisis was watered down from a more intrusive system because ASEAN did not want to be 'dictated' to by the Western countries and their mechanisms and wished to follow its own style,[182] the ASP, in Siazon's view, was already a step 'towards institutionalising closer co-ordination of national economic policies and performance and fostering rule-based transparency in governance'.[183] Even the more conservative elder statesman of ASEAN, Ali Alatas, would concede that the troika represented an attempt by ASEAN countries to move beyond non-interference, accepting that ASEAN could have a role in Indonesia's domestic crisis within the framework of enhanced interaction if the domestic situation in Indonesia has a 'genuine spill-over effect and poses a clear danger to its neighbours'.[184] A senior Singaporean Foreign Ministry official also acknowledged changes in ASEAN's attitude towards non-interference. ASEAN had avoided discussing contentious issues ('sweeping problems under the carpet') out of deference to this norm, and thereby creating 'confidence in the principle of sovereignty'. But ASEAN's practice of sweeping problems under the carpet was changing, at least at the 'level of practice, if not principle'.[185]

Overall, the environmental and economic crises in ASEAN in the late 1990s showed that the key goals of ASEAN regionalism, including the management of intra-regional disputes, the forging of common understanding of and approaches to regional problems that are central to the development of a security community, may no longer be guided by a consensus on strict adherence to sovereignty and its corollary, the doctrine of non-interference. The pressures to revise ASEAN's norms such as non-interference had paradoxical effects. On the one hand, they marked the erosion of the traditional bases of ASEAN's approach to regional order. But they also carried the promise of helping the revitalisation of ASEAN and furthering its development as a security-community-building regional institution. The debate over non-interference raised serious questions about ASEAN's capacity to adapt to the changing domestic, regional and global circumstances affecting its members and to move, in the foreseeable future at least, towards a deeper approach to regionalism characteristic of mature security communities. This is a challenge that would be further evident when ASEAN moved towards an 'ASEAN security community'.

Notes and references

1   'A New Call for Unity', *Asiaweek*, 22 October 1982.
2   Noordin Sopiee, 'ASEAN and Regional Security', in Mohammed Ayoob (ed.), *Regional Security in the Third World* (London: Croom Helm, 1986), p. 229. It should be noted that Sopiee's analysis was entirely atheoretical and had no discussion of, and not even a footnote to, Deutsch's original work. But the label security community had been applied to ASEAN as early as 1977, when Richard Mansbach speculated that ASEAN 'may become a kind of regional "core", the importance of which is widely recognised in the establishment of a "security community" in which resort to violence becomes unthinkable'. Richard W. Mansbach, 'Southeast Asia in the Global System', in *Southeast Asia in Transition: Regional and International Politics* (Seoul: The Institute of Far Eastern Studies, Kyung Nam University, 1977), p. 17.
3   As this author had argued in 1992, while

> ASEAN has indeed become a security community in the sense that its members do not foresee the prospect for resorting to armed confrontation among themselves to resolve existing bilateral disputes . . . the fact that a number of disputes have persisted and defied political and diplomatic solutions casts a shadow over ASEAN's image as a security community. . . . ASEAN's future as a regional security community faces two major challenges: firstly, overcoming several lingering intra-ASEAN disputes that are potentially disruptive of regional peace, and secondly, reaching a consensus on how to approach the task of eventual reconciliation with Vietnam and thereby move the subregional (ASEAN) 'security community' to a regional (Southeast Asian) entity.

(Amitav Acharya, 'The Association of Southeast Asian Nations: "Security Community" or "Defence Community" ', *Pacific Affairs*, vol. 64, no. 2 (Summer 1991), pp. 159–78).
4   Michael Vatikiotis, 'Border Burdens', *Far Eastern Economic Review*, 6 March 1997, p. 34.
5   Ingrid Wessel and Georgia Wimhofer, eds., *Violence in Indonesia*, Hamburg, Abera-Verl, 2001.
6   US Department of State, Country Reports on Human Rights Practices, Burma, 31 March 2003, available http://www.state.gov/g/drl/rls/hrrpt/2002/18237.htm.
7   It is possible for a country to be involved in two or more state-based armed conflicts in a given year and thus accumulate more than one conflict-year for each calendar year. Myanmar for example was embroiled in six different intra-state conflicts.
8   Singapore had operated a British-built lighthouse on the island, claiming it on the basis of control exercised since the 1840s, while Malaysia claimed the island as belonging to the state of Johor. An understanding between the two countries in December 1981 stipulated that the dispute should be

resolved through an exchange of documents. In 1989, Singapore proposed arbitration by the ICJ to settle the dispute, and Malaysia agreed to this proposal. The ICJ ruled in May 2008 to recognise Singapore's sovereignty over Pedra Branca, although it gave the adjoining Middle Rocks to Malaysia and left undecided the status of South Ledge. (These other islands are much smaller than Pedra Branca.) The decision cannot be appealed and both sides agreed to respect it. 'Decision resolves 28-year-old dispute', *The Star Online*, 24 May 2008. Available at thestar.com.my/services/ printerfriendly.asp?file=/2008/5/24/nation/21353526.asp&sec=nation (accessed 30 May 2008).

 9 Commodore Ahmad Ramli Nor, 'ASEAN Maritime Cooperation', paper presented to the Defence Asia '89 Conference on 'Towards Greater ASEAN Military and Security Cooperation: Issues and Prospects', Singapore, 22–25 March 1989, pp. 2–6. Malaysia and Thailand have announced an agreement for the joint exploitation of maritime resources in their disputed maritime jurisdiction.

10 Amitav Acharya, 'Arms Proliferation Issues in ASEAN: Towards a Conventional Defence Posture?', *Contemporary Southeast Asia*, vol. 10, no. 3 (December 1988), p. 246.

11 *Straits Times*, 18 February 1992.

12 Michael Vatikiotis, 'Border Burdens', *Far Eastern Economic Review*, 6 March 1997, p. 34.

13 *Straits Times*, 27 November 1986.

14 *Straits Times* (Weekly Overseas Edition), 2 September 1989.

15 See: *Malaysia*, EIU Country Report, 1st Quarter 1997, p. 14.

16 *Bangkok Post*, 21 September 1998, p. 11.

17 *International Herald Tribune*, 18 September 1998, p. 6.

18 *Straits Times*, 19 October 1998, p. 16.

19 Singapore played down the significance of the phrase to say that Mahathir had used the phrase several times before and 'seems to have a fondness for skinning cats'.

> He has used this phrase 'we can skin a cat in many ways' on several other occasions. For example: In an interview with Asia Incorporated of 4 May, in answer to a question 'If you had to describe Malaysia's approach to globalisation in one sentence, how would you do it?', and he replied, 'Firstly, listen to everyone . . . Number two, always accept that there are many ways to skin a cat, many ways to do things in order to achieve results.' Similarly at the PEBC conference in Kuala Lumpur, when asked to explain Malaysia's approach in dealing with the 1997 Asian Financial Crisis, he said: 'People know that there are many ways to skin a cat. We have chosen the unorthodox way and the cat has been neatly skinned.' (NST, 7 May 02)

'Transcript of Remarks on Malaysia–Singapore Relations by Minister for Foreign Affairs, Prof S. Jayakumar in Parliament, 16 May 2002'. Available app-stg1.mfa.gov.sg/2006/press/view_press. asp?post_id=1262 (accessed 1 June 2008).

20 In 2001, Joey Long, a Singaporean scholar who has studied the issue more thoroughly than most, dismissed the 'prevailing scholarship' holding that 'water may be a determinant factor sparking violent conflict between Singapore and Malaysia' 'is too alarmist', because Singapore had 'the means to achieve a measure of water self-sufficiency and is not vulnerable to Malaysia's use of the water link as leverage'. 'Consequently', he argued, 'scholars should begin to regard the water issue between Singapore and Malaysia as desecuritised.' Joey Long, 'Desecuritizing the Water Issue in Singapore–Malaysia Relations', *Contemporary Southeast Asia*, vol. 23 (2001). According to another analyst, 'Military repercussions cannot be ruled out in the event of a sudden disruption of water supplies from Malaysia, but this threatening situation may be overexaggerated.' Lee Poh Onn, 'Water Management Issues in Singapore', paper presented at the Conference on Water in Mainland Southeast Asia, organised by the International Institute for Asian Studies, Netherlands, and the Center for Khmer Studies, Cambodia, Siem Reap, Cambodia, 29 November–2 December 2005. Mahathir himself rejected the possibility of war between the two nations over water in April 2002 when he said, 'We must be careful in handling a problem such as this because we don't want to be at war with Singapore . . . That's why, when handling national affairs, we have to be extremely careful and wise. . . .' (Bernama, 14 April 02) Cited in transcript of remarks on Malaysia–Singapore Relations by Minister for Foreign Affairs, Prof S. Jayakumar in Parliament, 16 May 2002. Available app-stg1.mfa.gov.sg/2006/press/view_press.asp?post_id=1262 (accessed 1 June 2008).

21 Long, 'Desecuritizing the Water Issue'.

22 'Pedra Branca Ruling'.

23 'Malaysia and Singapore: A New Detente', *BusinessWeek*, 6 September 2006, available at www.businessweek.com/magazine/content/04_36/b3898081.htm (accessed 1 June 2008).

24 Ministry of Foreign Affairs, Singapore, 'Remarks by Minister for Foreign Affairs, Prof S. Jayakumar, in Parliament in reply to questions on Singapore–Malaysia Relations', 6 February 2004. Available at app.info.gov.sg/data/art_RemarksByMinisterForForeignAffairsProfSJayakumar InParliamentInReplyToQuestionsOnSingapore-malaysiaRelations_060204.html (accessed 7 June 2008).

25 This issue surfaced in December 2002 when Singapore started reclaiming land to extend its territory on its own side of the maritime boundary in the Strait of Johor. Malaysia, citing the impact on navigation routes, environmental damage and loss of income of its fishermen, referred the matter to the International Tribunal on the Law of the Sea in October 2003, seeking an injunction against Singapore to stop the reclamation. Although it failed to secure an injunction, the court directed Singapore to a token compensation to Malaysian fishermen and respect for Malaysian environmental concerns. To quote Tommy Koh, the noted Singaporean diplomat, 'It is not certain that the land reclamation case would have been settled amicably if Dr Mahathir were still the Prime Minister.' Tommy Koh and Jolene Lin, 'The Land Reclamation Case: Thoughts and Reflections', *Singapore Yearbook of International Law*, vol. x, 2006, pp. 1–7. Available at www.ips.org.sg/pub/ pa_tk_The%20Land%20Reclamation%20Case%20Thoughts%20and%20Reflections%20_2007. pdf (accessed 7 June 2008).

26 *Straits Times*, 5 August 1998, p. 16.

27 Cited in Lee Poh Onn, 'Water Management Issues in Singapore', Paper presented at Conference on Water in Mainland Southeast Asia, 29 November–2 December 2005, Siem Reap, Cambodia. Organised by the International Institute for Asian Studies, Netherlands, and the Center for Khmer Studies, Cambodia. Available at www.khmerstudies.org/events/Water/Lee%20Nov%202005.pdf (accessed 1 June 2008).

28 Moreover, Indonesia wants to go after some 18,000 Indonesians living in Singapore who are worth more than US$1 million, with an aggregate wealth of US$87 billion. 'Singapore, Indonesia Finally Settle Extradition Treaty', *Asia Sentinel*, 24 April 2007. Available at www.asiasentinel.com/index. php?option=com_content&task=view&id=462&Itemid=31 (accessed 9 June 2008).

29 BBC News, 12 February 2001.

30 BBC News, 30 January, 2003.

31 The Preah Vihear temple is located on a cliff on the Thai–Cambodian border. In 1962, the ICJ awarded the temple itself to Cambodia, but left the question of the demarcation of their adjacent border area unresolved. Thailand had disputed the colonial era French-imposed borderline. Cambodia, with support from the Thai government, had successfully secured the UNESCO listing of the temple as a world heritage site in 2007. But the Thai constitutional court in 2008 declared its government's support for the Cambodian application to UNESCO unconstitutional. Alleging that Cambodians were moving freely in the territory claimed by Thailand, as well as in the temple itself, the Thai military – which had deposed the government of Thaksin Shinawatra in a coup in 2006 – quickly deployed troops to the temple area where they faced Cambodian troops. While Thai anti-Thaksin political parties and the military used the constitutional court's verdict to seek the ousting of the Samak government, the crisis was also aggravated by the fact that Cambodian Prime Minister Hun Sen was facing national elections and could only benefit by the stirring of domestic nationalism. Following bilateral talks between the Foreign Ministers (ASEAN mediation was then rejected by Thailand, although ASEAN urged restraint on both sides) and once the Cambodia elections were over, the two sides withdrew most of their troops, leaving only a token force. But tensions again flared in February and April 2011, leaving an estimated 26 people dead and 'tens of thousands' displaced. Indonesia, as the Chair of ASEAN, mediated in the dispute.and proposed an agreement in May 2011 to deploy military and civilian monitors to the site. Cambodia accepted, but the deployment was blocked due to objections by the Thai military. Cambodia then asked the ICJ to clarify its 1962 ruling about the ownership of the areas adjacent to the temple. The ICJ ordered a provisional demilitarised zone in the area. It is not certain that the ICJ verdict in November 2013, which awarded the temple to Cambodia but did not clarify the status of the surrounding areas, would settle the conflict permanently. 'Q&A: Thailand-Cambodia temple dispute,' 14 September 2011 Available at http://www.bbc.co.uk/news/world-asia-pacific-12378001, (date accessed 1 September 2013) Murray Hiebert and Amy Killian, 'Thailand, Cambodia Spar at UN Court over Preah Vihear Temple,' Apr 23, 2013, Available at: http://csis.org/publication/ thailand-cambodia-spar-un-court-over-preah-vihear-temple (date accessed 1 September 2013).

32 FBIS-EAS-90–159, 16 August 1990, p. 34.

33 *Malaysia*, EIU Country Report, 1st Quarter 1997, p. 17.

34   *Star*, 17 June 1995, p. 2.
35   *Malaysia*, EIU Country Report, 1st Quarter 1997, p. 17.
36   *Straits Times*, 1 March 1995, p. 13; 'Malaysia–Indonesia's Disputed Claim', *Asian Defence Journal* (April 1995), p. 79.
37   Acharya, *Constructing a Security Community in Southeast Asia.*
38   Surin Pitsuwan, 'The ASEAN Heart of Asia,' *Jakarta Post,* 15 June 2011. p.7.
39   It is useful to remind ourselves that the Thai–Cambodia dispute over Preah Viehar was not 'settled' by the ICJ ruling in 1962.
40   The Spratly Islands dispute involves China, Taiwan and four ASEAN members: Vietnam, the Philippines, Malaysia and Brunei. The claims of the last three differ from the rest in significant ways. First, unlike China, Vietnam and Taiwan, they do not claim the entire Spratlys chain, but only certain islands. Manila has the largest claim of the three on the Spratlys, covering some 60 islets, rocks and atolls collectively called Kalayaan (this does not include Spratly Island itself). Malaysia's total claim includes three islands and four groups of rocks. Brunei claims only the Louisa Reef, although a 200 mile (320 km) EEZ around the Reef would extend to the southern Spratlys. Unlike China and Vietnam, the rest of the ASEAN parties base their claim not so much on historical grounds, but on the international law of the sea, including its provisions regarding the natural prolongation of the continental shelf (although the Philippines' claim is based on the argument that the islands were 'discovered' by a Philippine businessman in 1947).
41   J. Soedjati Djiwandono, preface to special issue on 'South China Sea: Views from ASEAN', *Indonesian Quarterly*, vol. 18, no. 2 (1990), p. 102.
42   Ambassador Hasjim Djalal, 'Territorial Disputes at Sea: Situation, Possibilities, Progress', paper presented to the Tenth Asia-Pacific Roundtable, Kuala Lumpur, 5–8 June 1996, pp. 2–3.
43   James A. Morse, 'ASEAN Focuses Concern on Spratly Islands Issue', *Wireless File* (East Asia and Pacific), United States Information Service, 23 July 1992, pp. 2–3.
44   Amitav Acharya, 'The ARF Could Well Unravel', in Derek Da Cunha (ed.), *The Evolving Pacific Power Balance* (Singapore: Institute of Southeast Asian Studies, 1996), pp. 63–9.
45   Hans Indorf, *The Spratlys: A Test Case for the Philippine Bases* (Manila: Centre for Research and Communication, 1988), p. 14.
46   Larry A. Niksch, 'The South China Sea Dispute', CRS Report for Congress, 95–934 F (Washington, DC: Congressional Research Service, The Library of Congress, 29 August 1995), p. 2.
47   Cited in Moses Manoharan, 'Indonesia Force Modernization', Reuter dispatch, 9 February 1993.
48   'Malaysia: Preparing for Change', *Jane's Defence Weekly*, 29 July 1989, p. 159.
49   David Hague, 'ASEAN: China flexes its muscles', *Sydney Morning Herald*, 28 July 1994.
50   Carlyle Thayer, *Beyond Indochina*, Adelphi Paper no. 297 (London: International Institute for Strategic Studies, 1995), p. 34.
51   Gary Klintworth, 'South East Asia–China Relations Continue to Evolve', *Asia-Pacific Defence Reporter* (February–March 1997), p. 26.
52   The futility of the China–Philippine agreement was amply demonstrated in 1997 when a Philippine reconnaissance mission discovered three Chinese frigates near islands occupied by Philippine troops, and a newly built Chinese structure on a neighbouring island. This prompted a diplomatic protest by Manila, which also informed its fellow ASEAN members of the situation and announced a plan to construct more bases in the area.
53   *Bangkok Post*, 23 August 1997, p. 5. Jusuf Wanandi, 'ASEAN's China Strategy: Towards Deeper Engagement', *Survival*, vol. 38, no. 3 (Autumn 1996), p. 123.
54   'Questions Raised over Speed of Move towards Conflict Resolution', *Straits Times*, 24 July 1999, p. 30.
55   This prompted officials and legislators in Manila to speak of a collusion between Kuala Lumpur and Beijing, since the construction was believed by the Philippines to have started after a visit by the Malaysian Foreign Minister to Beijing in May 1999. *Straits Times*, 30 June 1999, p. 16.
56   *Straits Times*, 23 July 1999, p. 32.
57   Cited in *New York Times*, 16 October 2002. See also S. P. Seth, 'US not likely to forfeit role in Asia', publish.gio.gov.tw/FCJ/past/02110862.html.
58   Personal interview, Beijing, June 2002.
59   *Washington Times*, 29 July 2002.
60   Isagani de Castro, 'Big brother' China woos ASEAN', *Asia Times*, 6 November 2002. Available at www.atimes.com/atimes/Southeast_Asia/DK06Ae02.html.

61 Geoff Dyer, 'Beijing's elevated aspirations,' FT.Com, November 10, 2010, http://www.ft.com/intl/cms/s/0/1cfa57c4-ed03-11df-9912-00144feab49a.html#axzz1cqPZnXCa

62 This was a revised version of a map originally drawn in 1947 by the Republic of China, but which had been adopted by the PRC after it came to power in 1949. Importantly, this map did not resolve the ambiguity surrounding China's claims. China has not clarified what it is claiming whether all the waters, rocks, islands and other features within the 9-dash lines. Also the basis of China's claim under international law, specifically the UN Law of the Sea (UNCLOS), has not been clarified. Instead, China's 'indisputable sovereignty' over the South China Sea is asserted on the basis of 'historic rights'. Carlyle A. Thayer, 'South China Sea and Regional Security,' *Thayer Consultancy Background Brief*, July 20, 2013. Some Chinese commentators argue that those rights, including the 9-dash map, had never been questioned until after the advent of the UNCLOS in 1982.

63 Dario Agnote, 'ASEAN needs "more effective" code with China on sea row,' Kyodo News, http://www.abs-cbnnews.com/focus/07/10/13/asean-needs-more-effective-code-china-sea-row, accessed 20 August 2013; Carlyle A. Thayer, 'South China Sea and Regional Security,' *Thayer Consultancy Background Brief*, July 20, 2013.

64 ASEAN Secretariat, 'Recent Developments on the Implementation of the Declaration on the Conduct of Parties in the South China Sea,' Jakarta, 2 April 2012.

65 Cited in Carlyle A. Thayer, 'ASEAN'S Code of Conduct in the South China Sea: A Litmus Test for Community-Building?,' *The Asia-Pacific Journal: Pacific Focus,* http://www.japanfocus.org/-Carlyle_A_-Thayer/3813#sthash.GqQYRk8N.dpuf, accessed 20 August 2013.

66 Thayer, 'ASEAN'S Code of Conduct in the South China Sea'.

67 Thayer, 'ASEAN'S Code of Conduct in the South China Sea'.

68 This observation may be more true of Cambodia than other new members, such as Vietnam and Myanmar. After all, this is not the first time that Cambodia's engagement with ASEAN has been problematic. In July 1997, Hun Sen's 'coup' against co-premier Norodom Ranarridh led ASEAN to postpone Cambodia's imminent accession to ASEAN. Hun Sen also alarmed fellow ASEAN members, especially his Thai neighbour, by hosting fugitive former Thai Prime Minister Thaksin Shinawatra and even appointing him as a personal advisor in November 2009. This went against the established ASEAN principle that granting support to a fugitive from a member state would constitute an act of interference in the internal affairs of that member state. Will Cambodia go all the way in deferring to China, or acting as a 'proxy' for Beijing? Such a policy would not only impose costs for Cambodia, such as isolating it from its neighbours, but would also go against the traditional grain of its foreign policy. As Norodom Sihankouk, when he was still the king of Cambodia, once told this author, Cambodia does not want to be a supplicant to a great power and that his country would always need to be watchful about China's intentions because of China's size and proximity to Cambodia.

69 'Clarification on Non-Issuance of the 45th AMM Joint Communiqué', 26 July 2012. http://www.cambodianembassy.jp/index.php?option=com_content&view=article&id=228%3Aclarification-on-non-issuance-of-the-45th-amm-joint-communique&catid=1%3Alatest-news&Itemid=64&lang=en

70 http://www.asean.org/documents/44thAMM-PMC-18thARF/44thAMM-JC.pdf

71 Thayer, 'ASEAN'S Code of Conduct in the South China Sea'.

72 ASEAN Secretariat, 'Recent Developments on the Implementation of the Declaration on the Conduct of Parties in the South China Sea.'

73 Carlyle A. Thayer, 'ASEAN's Code of Conduct (Unofficial),' *Thayer Consultancy Background Brief,* July 11, 2012.

74 Cited in Agnote, 'ASEAN needs "more effective" code with China on sea row.'

75 'Remarks by Foreign Minister Yang Jiechi at the ARF Foreign Ministers' Meeting,'

76 William Wan, 'Clinton issues challenges on North Korea, South China Sea,' *Washington Post,* 23 July 2011. http://www.washingtonpost.com/world/asia-pacific/clinton-issues-challenges-on-n-korea-south-china-sea/2011/07/23/gIQA7805UI_story.html

77 'South China Sea Tensions a Threat to Peace: Clinton,' *Jakarta Globe*, 23 July 2011.

78 Ron Huisken, *Limitations of Armaments in Southeast Asia: A Proposal*, Canberra Papers on Strategy and Defence no. 16 (Canberra: Australian National University, Strategic and Defence Studies Centre, 1977).

79 See: Tim Huxley, 'South-East Asia's Arms Race: Some Notes on Recent Developments', *Arms Control*, vol. 11, no. 1 (May 1990), pp. 69–76.

80 Opening address by Dr Yeo Ning Hong, Minister for Defence, Singapore, at the First Asia-Pacific Defence Conference, Singapore, 26 February 1992, pp. 2–3.

81 Cited in *International Herald Tribune*, 29 October 1992.

82 US Arms Control and Disarmament Agency. *World Military Expenditures and Arms Transfers 1995* (Washington, DC: US Government Printing Office, 1996). Taken from Acharya, *Constructing a Security Community in Southeast Asia.*

83 Robert Hartfiel and Brian Job, *Raising the Risks of War: Defence Spending Trends and Competitive Arms Processes in East Asia*, Vancouver: University of British Columbia Institute of International Relations Working Paper No. 44, March 2005, available at www.iir.ubc.ca/Papers/Hartfiel-Job-WP44.pdf (accessed 30 September 2007).

84 Richard A. Bitzinger and Curie Maharani, 'Arms, Money, and Security: Southeast Asia's Growing Importance as an Arms Market', RSIS Commentaries, 8 April 2008, p. 2.

85 Anthony Spellman, 'Rapid Deployment Forces on Horizon for Malaysia, Singapore', *Armed Forces Journal International* (April 1991), p. 36.

86 John Bushell, 'ABRI Significant Force, But No Power Projection Capability', *Asia-Pacific Defence Reporter* (November 1991), pp. 30–31.

87 'Military Draws up Plans to Trim down Troops', *Manila Chronicle*, 28 November 1990, pp. 1, 9.

88 Bitzinger and Maharani, 'Arms, Money, and Security: Southeast Asia's Growing Importance as an Arms Market', p. 2.

89 Hideaki Kaneda, 'Southeast Asia's Growing Arms Race', *Taipei Times*, 12 June 2006, p. 8, available at www.taipeitimes.com/News/editorials/archives/2006/06/12/2003313130 (accessed 2 June 2008).

90 Bitzinger and Maharani, 'Arms, Money, and Security', p. 2.

91 Richard A. Bitzinger, *The China Syndrome: Chinese Military Modernization and the Rearming of Southeast Asia*, Working Paper No. 126 (Singapore: Rajaratnam School of International Studies, May 2007), p. 9.

92 These estimates are in constant (2009) US dollar terms. In current (2010) dollar terms, SIPRI Data puts the defence spending of ASEAN countries at US$ 28.7 billion in 2010. *World Armaments and Disarmament: SIPRI Yearbook, 2011* (Oxford University Press for Stockholm International Peace Research Institute, 2011). Available at: http://www.sipri.org/yearbook/2011/04/04A. In May 2011, Indonesian Defence Minister Purnomo put the ASEAN countries' defence spending at US$ 25 billion. 'Indonesia, Malaysia agree to promote ASEAN defence industry collaboration,' 20 May 2011, Available at: http://www.investors.com/NewsAndAnalysis/Newsfeed/Article/131651749/201105200224/Indonesia-Malaysia-agree-to-promote-ASEAN-defence-industry-collaboration.aspx.

93 'Singapore first among ASEAN to make list of top 10 biggest arms importers,' http://jacob69.wordpress.com/2010/03/30/singapore-first-among-asean-to-make-list-of-top-10-biggest-arms-importers-and-then-theres-the-iron-dome/

94 http://www.channelnewsasia.com/stories/singaporelocalnews/view/1138171/1/.html

95 Kaneda, 'Southeast Asia's Growing Arms Race'.

96 'Southeast Asia, Australasia and the Southwest Pacific', London: International Institute for Strategic Studies. Available at www.iiss.org.uk/programmes/south-east-asia (accessed 10 December 2006).

97 Bitzinger and Maharani, 'Arms, Money, and Security', p. 3.

98 Barry Buzan, *An Introduction to Strategic Studies: Military Technology and International Relations* (London: Macmillan, for the International Institute for Strategic Studies, 1987), p. 69.

99 See: Robert S. McNamara, 'The Dynamics of Nuclear Strategy', *Department of State Bulletin*, vol. lvii, 9 October 1967. For a critique of the 'action–reaction' model and alternative explanations of the arms race, e.g. taking into account domestic politics, see: George Rathjens, 'The Dynamics of the Arms Race', *Scientific American* (April 1969); Sam C. Sarkesian, *The Military–Industrial Complex: A Reassessment* (Beverly Hills, CA: Sage, 1972).

100 Deputy Supreme Commander Admiral Prida Karasut as paraphrased in *Bangkok Post*, 14 November 1992, pp. 1, 3.

101 FBIS-EAS-92–076, 20 April 1992, p. 27.

102 Bitzinger, 'The China Syndrome', p. 9.

103 Bitzinger and Maharani, 'Arms, Money, and Security', p. 2.

104 The editorial comments by a Thai newspaper, the *Nation*, are revealing: 'There is a whole nexus from the rank of lieutenant colonel up to the generals who have mastered the art of earning private revenues together with the arms procurers, the agents and the suppliers.' 'Military Spending Practices Criticized', FBIS-EAS-93–023, 5 February 1993, p. 50.

105 'RI's defense spending ranks low in SE Asia,' Available at: http://www.thejakartapost.com/news/2010/12/01/ri%E2%80%99s-defense-spending-ranks-low-se-asia.html

106 Tim Huxley and Susan Willett, *Arming East Asia*, Adelphi Paper no. 329 (London: International Institute for Strategic Studies, 1999), p. 10.

107 See: Desmond J. Ball, 'Arms and Affuence: Military Acquisitions in the Asia/ Pacific Region', *International Security*, vol. 18, no. 3 (Winter 1993–94), pp. 78–112; Amitav Acharya, *An Arms Race in Post-Cold War Southeast Asia? Prospects for Control*, Pacific Strategic Papers, no. 8 (Singapore: Institute of Southeast Asian Studies, 1994).

108 *Los Angeles Times*, 31 May 2008. See also Cris Sholto Heaton, 'Is there an Arms Race in Asia?', *MoneyWeek*, 3 August 2007.

109 Malaysia's response to the Lee Kuan Yew proposal was that the prevailing bilateral relations between the two countries were good enough not to warrant such measures. But the Malaysian defence minister acknowledged that Lee's offer served to 'reassure Singapore's neighbours that its arsenal was not offensive in nature'. 'Defense Minister Interviewed on Arms Control', FBIS-EAS-91–151, 6 August 1991, p. 41.

110 *The Age*, 10 April 1992.

111 Stuart Drummond, 'ASEAN: National Policies Versus Economic Cooperation', *Round Table*, no. 295 (1985), p. 263.

112 'Summary Record: New Directions for ASEAN Economic Cooperation', in *Proceedings of the Second ASEAN Roundtable*, Kuala Lumpur, 20–21 July 1987, p. 8.

113 Apart from trade liberalisation and collective bargaining, ASEAN's economic cooperation in the 1970s and 1980s included measures to promote industrial development and energy and food security. ASEAN industrial development cooperation had three main aspects. The first was ASEAN Industrial Projects, launched in 1978. These included an ammonia-urea project in Indonesia, a urea project in Malaysia, a rock salt, soda ash project in Thailand, a copper fabrication plant in the Philippines, and a Hepatitis B vaccine project in Singapore. The second was the ASEAN Industrial Complementation Scheme, whose basic agreement was signed in June 1981. The scheme was aimed at promoting industrial development in the region by permitting the private sector to agree in advance to industrial specialisation, thereby eliminating 'unnecessary competition among ASEAN countries'. It provided for vertical and horizontal specialisation. But the number of industrial projects suitable for component production was limited, and getting ASEAN members to agree on a scheme has proved to be difficult. Hence the rationale for the third element in ASEAN industrial cooperation, called the ASEAN Industrial Joint Venture Scheme. Launched in 1980, this scheme aimed at encouraging private sector participation in intra-ASEAN industrial cooperation. AIJV schemes required participation by only two private sector partners. In order to promote food and energy security programmes, ASEAN members agreed in 1977 to an ASEAN emergency petroleum-sharing scheme comprising the national oil corporations of the member countries. An ASEAN Food Security Reserve System was established in 1979 'to provide mutual support in the time of emergencies as well as an early warning system for such emergencies'. An ASEAN Emergency Rice Reserve of 50,000 tonnes was set up. On these initiatives, see: Chn'g Meng Kng, 'ASEAN Economic Cooperation: The Current Status', *Southeast Asian Affairs 1985* (Singapore: Institute of Southeast Asian Studies, 1985), pp. 31–53; Hans Christoph Rieger and Tan Loong-Hoe, 'The Problems of Economic Cooperation in ASEAN', in *Regional Cooperation: Recent Developments*, Report no. 13 (London: Commonwealth Secretariat, 1987); Marjorie L. Suriyamongkol, *Politics of ASEAN Economic Co-operation* (Singapore: Oxford University Press, 1988). For a review of the main literature on ASEAN economic cooperation, see: Hans Christoph Rieger, 'Regional Economic Cooperation in the Asia-Pacific Region', *Asia-Pacific Economic Literature*, vol. 3, no. 2 (September 1989), pp. 5–33.

114 Much of the total intra-ASEAN trade volume was accounted for by bilateral trade between Singapore and Malaysia and between Malaysia and Indonesia. In addition, about 65 per cent of intra-ASEAN trade was fuel trade (mineral fuels, lubricants and related materials). M. Hadi Soesastro, 'Prospects for Pacific-Asian Regional Trade Structures', in Robert Scalapino *et al.* (eds), *Regional Dynamics: Security, Political and Economic Issues in the Asia-Pacific Region* (Jakarta: Centre for Strategic and International Studies, 1990), p. 391.

115 Hans Indorf, *Impediments to Regionalism in Southeast Asia* (Singapore: Institute of Southeast Asian Studies, 1984), p. 57.

116 For an overview of ASEAN's role in GATT, see: M. Hadi Soesastro, 'ASEAN's Participation in GATT', *Indonesian Quarterly*, vol. 15, no. 1 (January 1987), pp. 107–27.

117 Ernst B. Haas, 'War, Interdependence and Functionalism', in Raimo Vayrynen (ed.), *The Quest for Peace: Transcending Collective Violence and War among Societies, Cultures and States* (Beverly Hills, CA: Sage, 1987), p. 122.

118 Address before the Eighth Pacific Economic Cooperation Conference, Singapore, 20–22 May 1991.

119 Richard Stubbs, 'Signing on to Liberalization: AFTA and the Politics of Regional Economic Cooperation', Manuscript (1999), pp. 297–318.

120 M. Hadi Soesastro, 'Prospects for Pacific-Asian Regional Trade Structures', in Robert Scalapino *et al.* (eds), *Regional Dynamics: Security, Political and Economic Issues in the Asia-Pacific Region* (Jakarta: Centre for Strategic and International Studies, 1990), p. 391.

121 *The New ASEANs: Vietnam, Burma, Cambodia and Laos* (Canberra: Department of Foreign Affairs and Trade, 1997).

122 *Straits Times*, 17 June 1992, p. 2.

123 Fauziah Ismail, 'Malaysia: Use ASEAN Spirit as Basis – Anwar', *Business Times* (Malaysia), 7 June 1994.

124 Sree Kumar and Sharon Siddique, 'Beyond Economic Reality: New Thoughts on the Growth Triangle', in *Southeast Asian Affairs 1994* (Singapore: Institute of Southeast Asian Studies, 1994), pp. 47–56; Amitav Acharya, 'Security Implications of Transnational Economic Activity: The Growth Triangles of Southeast Asia', Paper presented to the Fourth Southeast Asia Roundtable on Economic Development, Kuala Lumpur, 27–28 June 1994.

125 Sandra Burton, 'Growing by Leaps – Triangles', *Time*, 17 January 1994, pp. 26–8.

126 Robert A. Scalapino, 'Challenges to the Sovereignty of the Modern State', in Bunn Nagara and K.S. Balakrishnan (eds), *Proceedings of the Seventh Asia-Pacific Roundtable, The Making of a Security Community in the Asia-Pacific* (Kuala Lumpur: ISIS Malaysia, 1994), p. 50.

127 Suthad Setboonsarng, 'ASEAN Economic Cooperation: Adjusting to the Crisis', *Southeast Asian Affairs*, 1998.

128 Ibid.

129 'Number of Asian Poor Set to Double', www.geocities.com/Yosemite/7915/9811/ Asia_Poverty-Dbl.html.

130 Frank Ching, 'Social Impact of the Regional Financial Crisis' in 'Policy Choices, Social Consequences and the Philippine Case', available www.asiasociety.org/ publications/update_ crisis_ching.html (accessed 27 May 2006).

131 Kerstin Marx, 'Asia: Crisis causes massive unemployment', Third World Network, available at www.twnside.org.sg/title/mass-cn.htm

132 Chalongphob Sussangkarn, Frank Flatters and Sauwalak Kittiprapas, 'Comparative Social Impacts of the Asian Economic Crisis in Thailand, Indonesia, Malaysia and the Philippines: A Preliminary Report', *TDRI Quarterly Review*, vol. 14, no. 1, March 1999, pp. 3–9.

133 'The Asian Crisis: A View from the IMF', Address by Stanley Fischer, First Deputy Managing Director of the International Monetary Fund at the Midwinter Conference of the Bankers' Association for Foreign Trade, Washington, D.C., 22 January 1998.

134 'No Alternative to Regionalism', (interview of Rodolfo Severino, Jr. by Panorama in August 1999), available at www.aseansec.org/2829.htm.

135 'Statement on Bold Measures', 6th ASEAN Summit, Hanoi, 16 December 1998, available www.aseansec.org.id (accessed 2 December 1999).

136 'Economic Cooperation', in *Annual Report 1998–1999*, Association of Southeast Asian Nations, available www.asean.org.id (accessed 2 December, 1999).

137 'ASEAN Finance Cooperation', available at www.aseansec.org (accessed 2 December 1999).

138 *ASEAN Economic Community Factbook* (Jakarta: ASEAN Secretariat, 2011), Xiii. Available at http://www.aseansec.org/wp-content/uploads/2013/07/ASEAN_AECFactBook.pdf (accessed 2 September 2013)

139 For a detailed examination of these initiatives and other defence-related interactions among the ASEAN states, see: Amitav Acharya, 'Defence Cooperation and Transparency in South East Asia', in Gill Bates and J.N. Mak (eds), *Arms, Transparency and Security in Southeast Asia*, SIPRI Research Report no. 13 (Oxford: Oxford University Press, 1997), pp. 49–62.

140 *New Straits Times*, 6 July 1978.

141 *Jane's Defence Weekly*, 28 January 1995, p. 16; *Asian Defence Journal* (March 1995), pp. 15–17.

142 *Jane's Defence Weekly*, 28 May 1994, p. 23.

143 *Jane's Defence Weekly*, 8 October 1994, p. 2.

144 *Asian Defence Journal* (July 1994), p. 85.

145 Ibid., p. 82; *Asian Defence Journal* (April 1995), p. 79.

146 Ismail Kassim, 'Malaysia Beefs up Armed Forces for a New Role', *Straits Times*, 24 July 1994, p. 7.

147 Hashim Mohammed Ali, 'Regional Defence from the Military Perspective', *ISIS Focus*, no. 58 (January 1990), pp. 41–2.

148 The discussion in this paragraph draws heavily on Amitav Acharya, 'Defence Cooperation and Transparency in South East Asia', in Gill Bates and J.N. Mak (eds), *Arms, Transparency and Security in Southeast Asia*, SIPRI Research Report no. 13 (Oxford: Oxford University Press, 1997), pp. 57–8.

149 http://www.aseansec.org/25303.htm, Accessed 18 August 2013.

150 Interview with *Jane's Defence Weekly*, 18 December 1993, p. 32.

151 Reuters, 15 December 1998.

152 Ibid.

153 For further discussion, see Roger Mitton and Alejandro Reyes, 'Hurting in Hanoi', *Asiaweek*, 25 December 1998, pp. 28–38.

154 In the view of *The Economist* magazine, for example, had ASEAN not been so committed to non-interference, Thailand's neighbours might have provided more timely warning to Bangkok to attend to its domestic troubles before it became a regional contagion. But 'any persuasion from fellow ASEAN members [to Thailand] to set a new course was so discreet that it was easy to ignore'. 'The Limits of Politeness', *The Economist*, 28 February 1998, p. 43.

155 *Bangkok Post*, 13 June 1998, p. 5.

156 *Straits Times*, 13 July 1998, p. 17.

157 *Straits Times*, 23 July 1998, p. 30.

158 Abdullah Ahmad Badawi, 'Statement by the Minister of Foreign Affairs of Malaysia at 31st ASEAN Ministerial Meeting', 24 July 1998.

159 Ibid.

160 *Straits Times*, 5 July 1998, p. 26.

161 *Straits Times* (Internet Edition), 27 June 1998.

162 Abdullah Ahmad Badawi, 'Statement by the Minister of Foreign Affairs of Malaysia at 31st ASEAN Ministerial Meeting', 24 July 1998.

163 *Straits Times*, 23 July 1998, p. 30.

164 Abdullah Ahmad Badawi, 'Statement by the Minister of Foreign Affairs of Malaysia at 31st ASEAN Ministerial Meeting', 24 July 1998.

165 *Straits Times* (Editorial), 5 August 1998, p. 34.

166 *Straits Times*, 25 July 1998, p. 23.

167 Ibid.

168 Joint Communiqué of the Twenty-Sixth ASEAN Ministerial Meeting, Singapore, 23–24 July 1993, p. 7.

169 Even then, there were intra-ASEAN differences over human rights. See: Carolina Hernandez, 'ASEAN Perspectives on Human Rights and Democracy in International Relations: Problems and Prospects', Working Paper 1995–1, Centre for International Studies, University of Toronto, 1995.

170 Cited in Barry Wain, 'Asean's Split Personality', *Asian Wall Street Journal*, 24 December 1998.

171 'Interview/Asada Jayanama: Is Thai Diplomacy Abreast With the Times?', Dow Jones Interactive, ptg.djnr.com/ccroot/asp/pu. Accessed 31 August 2000, p. 3.

172 Surin Pitsuwan, 'The Role of Human Rights in Thailand's Foreign Policy', statement at the seminar on Promotion and Protection of Human Rights by Human Rights Commissions, Bangkok, 2 October 1998. Text available at www.hk-consulate.go/th/speech.htm. Accessed 28 August 2000, p. 5.

173 *Straits Times*, 21 October 1998, p. 1.

174 Straits Times Interactive, 18 March 1998.

175 Habibie asked Surin to convey to their fellow ASEAN members: 'please come in large numbers to help'. This to Surin constituted an example in which the 'ASEAN countries had to go into the

territory of another ASEAN country to calm things down'. Personal interview with Surin Pitsuwan, Bangkok, 10 May 2002. Habibie had told the author the same in a conversation on the margins of a High Level Expert Group Meeting of the InterAction Council in Seoul during 14–15 March 2001. Later, Habibie's chief foreign policy advisor, Dewi Fortuna Anwar, confirmed this account to the author: Habibie had told Surin that if an international force was to be deployed in East Timor, then it 'should be mostly Asian and it should be led by an ASEAN country'. Personal interview with Dewi Fortuna Anwar, Bangkok, 10 May 2002.

176 'East Timor: Support Steady Despite "Daunting Unknowns" ', United States Information Agency, 21 September 1999.

177 Personal interview with Surin Pitsuwan, Singapore, 27 September 2001.

178 Personal interview with Surin Pitsuwan, Bangkok, 10 May 2002.

179 Personal interview with Surin Pitsuwan, Bangkok, 10 May 2002.

180 Tommy Koh, 'What E. Asia Can Learn from the EU', *Straits Times*, 10 July 1998, p. 48.

181 Personal interview with Ambassador Tommy Koh, Singapore, August 2001. The troika was first proposed by Thai Prime Minister Chuan Leekpai (as another Thai initiative reflecting the Chuan government's initiative to dilute the non-interference doctrine) at the 3rd ASEAN Informal Summit in Manila on 28 November 1999. The troika is to comprise the Foreign Ministers of the present, past and future chairs of the ASEAN Standing Committee. But in certain situations, the composition of the ASEAN troika could be adjusted subject to the consent of the ASEAN Foreign Ministers. The mission of the troika has been left somewhat unclear, perhaps deliberately so. But what is clear is that its function is not to make decisions, but rather to 'support and assist' the ASEAN Foreign Ministers. Neither can the troika deal with matters beyond the issues assigned to it by the ASEAN Foreign Ministers. And it has been stated clearly that 'In carrying out its tasks, the ASEAN Troika shall refrain from addressing issues that constitute the internal affairs of ASEAN member countries.' ('The ASEAN Troika', www.aseansec.org.)

182 Personal interview with Termsak Chalermpalanupap, Special Assistant to the Secretary-General, ASEAN, Bangkok, 16 January 2001.

183 *Straits Times*, 19 August 1998, p. 21.

184 Personal interview with Ali Alatas, Jakarta, 27 September 2000.

185 Personal interview with Bilahari Kaushikan, Permanent Secretary, Ministry of Foreign Affairs, Singapore, Paris, 11 March 2002.

6 ASEAN and Asia-Pacific security

Limits of the ASEAN Way?

Security communities are basically inward-looking constructs. The concept of security community describes the absence or the peaceful management of conflict among a group of states. It does not tell us how such a community may relate to external pressures, such as shifts in balances of power or changes affecting the norm of sovereignty, at the global level. States within a security community rule out war against each other, but they may not do so with respect to states outside the grouping. As noted in Chapter 2, security communities may develop collective security and collective defence provisions. These provisions may be construed as important indicators of the identity-building process in security communities, but those in a nascent stage need not have such features. Similarly, the norms through which members of a security community relate to each other may not be the same as those which govern their relationships with non-members. For example, if we regard the EU as a security community, it does not mean that the EU has abandoned war as an instrument *vis-à-vis* non-EU members. Similarly, while ASEAN members had come to view the use of force against each other as a remote possibility by the 1980s, they had not developed such expectations *vis-à-vis* other countries in Southeast Asia, especially Vietnam.

As with any social group having common interests, security communities have common expectations concerning outside actors and the norms governing their *collective* conduct towards such actors. Because external events and external relations can have important implications for states belonging to a security community, the latter must ensure that such events do not create or exacerbate the potential for conflict in their intra-mural relations. For example, common perceptions of external threats will induce greater unity and cohesion within a security community. The behaviour of the major world powers can have a significant bearing on the fate of security communities and affect relationships among their members. It is not easy to isolate intra-mural relationships within a security community from the relationships between it and outside actors and events. A regional security community, in order to ensure that it remains free of violent intra-mural conflict, must also manage its relations with extra-regional actors, including the major powers, with a view to preventing any conflict-causing or destabilising effect of the latter on the community. The fortunes of regional organisations throughout the world have risen and fallen depending on how they have related to extra-regional actors.

Since security communities have already succeeded in ensuring, or nearly ensuring, conflict avoidance and pacific settlement of intra-mural disputes, they are likely to be seen as a credible model for launching similar processes beyond their walls. In other words, the very norms that have underpinned relations within security communities could be extended to govern relations between the community and outside actors, with the hope that the latter may be socialised into a relationship that develops the qualities of a wider security community. Moreover, successful security communities are likely to have a significant demonstration effect. The EU has provided encouragement for regional cooperation in many other parts of the world, even if its model of 'regional integration' has proved hard to replicate elsewhere. The CSCE/OSCE concept has proved attractive for confidence-building measures within other regional organisations or in bilateral relationships. (One notable example is China's border agreements with Russia and four Central Asian republics as well as India, which incorporates many elements of the OSCE model.)

It is hardly surprising that towards the late 1980s and early 1990s ASEAN's model of security cooperation came to be seen as the basis for constructing a wider security framework, if not a security community *per se*, in the Asia-Pacific region. The initial impetus for such a forum did not come from ASEAN. It was the outside powers, especially Russia, Australia and Canada, which had come up with proposals for Asia-Pacific security cooperation based partly on the CSCE/OSCE idea. ASEAN, however, while rejecting 'imported' models of multilateralism, presented itself as the anchor for a new security arrangement to be based, as far as possible, on its model and in which it could play a leadership role.

Evolution of the ARF

The end of the Cold War confronted ASEAN with new challenges as well as opportunities for trying to reshape regional order. The end of the US–Soviet and Sino-Soviet rivalries had contributed to a substantial reduction in regional tensions and the prospect for competitive external intervention in Southeast Asia. However, ASEAN members became concerned about a 'power vacuum' in the region, which might lead to new kinds of conflicts and rivalry involving external powers. These concerns stemmed from the reduction of Soviet and US forces in the region. In January 1990, Moscow had announced its intention to remove all but a small segment of its naval and air units stationed in Cam Ranh Bay. While this initiative eased ASEAN's concerns about the security of sea lanes, it also meant the removal of a useful counterweight to China, especially for those ASEAN members traditionally suspicious of China.[1] The Soviet withdrawal also had the effect of reducing the utility of the Philippine bases for the USA, at a time when it was already losing interest in renegotiating the terms of tenure dictated by a nationalist Philippine Senate. Coming in the wake of the reduction of Soviet forces along the Sino-Soviet border, and a build-up of Chinese naval power, the Soviet departure from Cam Ranh appeared to enhance Beijing's ability to dominate the regional maritime environment.[2]

ASEAN members were most worried about trends in US force reductions. In 1992, under a new strategic plan for the region, called the East Asia Security Initiative (EASI), the USA had announced a 12 per cent cut in its forces in Asia, from 135,000 troops to approximately 120,000 by the end of that year. But the rejection by the Philippine Senate of a new bases treaty with the USA also implied additional cuts in the US military presence.[3] Theoretically, the USA could compensate for the loss of Philippine bases by increased access to other facilities in the region (such as in Singapore), and could carry out all conceivable contingency missions in the region with the help of its remaining Pacific forces (plus reinforcements from Alaska and continental USA).[4] But some Pentagon officials expressed fears that cutbacks necessitated by the loss of Philippine bases 'would eliminate real combat capability' and 'may initiate destabilising actions by regional powers'.[5]

Moreover, these developments raised fears in some ASEAN member states regarding a possible scramble among 'regional powers' seeking to step into the 'vacuum'. Among the regional powers, China, Japan and, to a lesser extent, India were generally identified as the three leading contenders for influence, presumably because of their capability to project power into the Southeast Asian region.[6] While perceptions of the next regional hegemon differed within ASEAN, with Indonesia and Malaysia more fearful of China, while Singapore showed a greater anxiety about Japanese remilitarisation, Prime Minister Goh Chok Tong of Singapore warned that the reduction of the US presence would give rise to a contest for regional leadership among China, India and Japan.[7] Furthermore, ASEAN members feared threats from any serious escalation of the US–Japan trade dispute, which could threaten the US–Japan security relationship.[8] The state of Sino-US relations was also seen within ASEAN as a key factor in Southeast Asian security. The growing friction between the USA and China over human rights and Washington's threat of economic sanctions against China would make the latter 'angry and resentful' and could 'have serious long-term consequences for Asia-Pacific peace and stability'.[9]

These concerns of ASEAN members confirm that states facing a common security challenge, in this case strategic uncertainty rather than the emergence of a commonly perceived threat, could encourage a new multilateralism, including a security community. Another important trigger for the latter, also evident in the case of ASEAN's attitude towards the ARF, was interdependence, in both the economic and security arenas, between Southeast Asia and the wider Asia-Pacific region. The economic links between Southeast Asia and Northeast Asia have been matched by a growing security interdependence, as evident in the growing salience of problems such as the territorial disputes in the South China Sea or the potential for regional hegemony by China and Japan, both of which transcend subregional dimensions. As a consequence, bilateral and subregional approaches were deemed inadequate for ensuring regional stability. A region-wide framework was more necessary than ever (see Table 6.1).

Such material conditions as the changing balance of power or economic interdependence do not in themselves explain ASEAN's decision to involve itself in Asia-Pacific multilateral security debates. Ideas emanating from outside the region also had an important influence. These included the related principles of 'common security' and 'cooperative security', as described in Table 6.1. Proponents of these ideas saw multilateralism as a more *desirable* long-term alternative to balance of power security arrangements and deterrence-based security strategies.[10] The crucial role played by the CSCE in easing the Cold War in Europe provided an initial impetus for proposals for similar arrangements in the Asia-Pacific based on corresponding ideas about common security. Indeed, the initial proposals for Asia-Pacific multilateralism envisaged a process roughly akin to the CSCE. For example, the genesis of the ARF may be traced to Mikhail Gorbachev's Vladivostok speech in 1986, in which he had called for a 'Pacific Ocean conference similar to the Helsinki [CSCE] conference'.[11] In 1990, the Australian External Minister Gareth Evans had envisaged 'a future Asian security architecture involving a wholly new institutional process that might be capable of evolving, in Asia just as in Europe, as a framework for addressing and resolving security problems'.[12] Another idea about multilateralism in Asia-Pacific security was the Canadian notion of 'cooperative security', outlined in a proposal by External Affairs Minister Joe Clark in July 1990.[13] In contrast to the still-born Soviet and Australian proposals, the Canadian government managed to sponsor a two-track and subregional dialogue process under the auspices of the North Pacific Cooperative Security Dialogue (NPCSD) involving China, North Korea, South Korea, Japan, Russia, the USA and Canada. This initiative furthered the development of the idea of cooperative security as an approach to regional order.[14]

The initial response of ASEAN policymakers to such proposals was marked by a certain amount of ambivalence. To be sure, at their first post-Cold War summit held in Singapore in

Table 6.1 Proposed frameworks of multilateralism, 1990–92

Proposer	Type of multilateralism	Scope	Institution	Process
Soviet Union/ Australia[a]	'Common Security'; CSCE model	Comprehensive; focus on CSBMs and nuclear arms control	New; Asia-Pacific wide	Broad-brush; government-led
Canada	'Cooperative Security'	Comprehensive; with a strong focus on non-military threats[b]	New; Northeast Asia only	Evolutionary; two-track
ASEAN/Japan	'Security Dialogue'	Comprehensive but with minimal focus on EHD[c] issues	Existing; limited to enhanced PMC[d] members and special invitees	Intergovernmental
USA	'Flexible Multilateralism'	Conventional threats; focus on some interstate conflicts	No new standing institution envisaged; maintain existing alliances	Case-by-case approach; intergovernmental

Source: Amitav Acharya, David Dewitt and Paul Evans, 'Overview: The Agenda for Cooperative Security in the North Pacific', a briefing paper prepared for the Conference on Cooperative Security in the North Pacific, held in Vancouver 21–24 March 1993 (published in David Dewitt, 'Common, Comprehensive, and Cooperative Security', *Pacific Review*, vol. 7, no. 1 (1994), p. 261; subsequently modified by Acharya).

Notes:
a Australia subsequently distanced itself from the Russian-proposed OSCE-style institution and called for both regional bilateral and multilateral arrangements for an 'Asian Security System'.
b Includes economic underdevelopment, trade disputes, overpopulation, irregular migration and refugee movements, environmental degradation, political oppression, human rights abuses, terrorism and the illicit trade in drugs.
c Environment, human rights and democracy.
d Enhanced PMC refers to the six ASEAN members (before 1995) plus Japan, Canada, the USA, Australia, South Korea, the EC, New Zealand, Russia, China, Vietnam, Laos and Papua New Guinea.

January 1992, ASEAN members authorised the grouping to deal with security issues and organise regional security dialogues both within Southeast Asia and at the Asia-Pacific level.[15] But they were not ready immediately to endorse a CSCE-type forum for the Asia-Pacific. Although ASEAN itself was a subregional model of cooperative security, it was the call for a more structured and formalistic security forum like the CSCE that generated misgivings. Many ASEAN government leaders and academic specialists believed in the early 1990s that the idea of cooperative security and the CSCE model would not work in Asia. They argued that the conditions which had facilitated the CSCE, i.e. a rigid bipolarity and a well-defined alliance framework, had been absent from Asia. The existence of numerous territorial disputes, a culturally rooted aversion to formal confidence-building and transparency measures among Asian policymakers, and the proven worth of the bilateral alliances of the USA meant that regional order in the Asia-Pacific region was more elusive, and less amenable to multilateral approaches. ASEAN leaders argued that the Asia-Pacific was too complex and diverse a region for CSCE-type arrangements. Moreover, they were fearful that if ideas originating from outside the region were to define the regional security framework, it would compromise ASEAN's norm of 'regional solutions to regional problems'. As Lee Kuan Yew argued, such an outcome could lead ASEAN to 'lose its identity'.[16]

Ironically enough, the very same concern would eventually lead ASEAN to view multilateralism in a more favourable light. In order to defend its norm of regional autonomy, ASEAN had to seize the initiative from outside countries in seeking to shape regional security. Added to this concern was a sense that playing a major role in launching a regional security framework could be an important way of underscoring the continued and broader relevance of ASEAN's norms. While a formal CSCE-type institution was seen by the ASEAN members to be impractical in the Asia-Pacific region, it was easier for them to accept proposals for looser and more consultative mechanisms for promoting an exchange of views on security issues within the region.[17] After all, this approach would correspond to the ASEAN Way. Moreover, a multilateral security framework could be a useful 'insurance policy' for ASEAN should the US regional military presence decline to a level where it could no longer provide a credible security guarantee within a balance of power framework.

At the same time, ASEAN members, influenced by research and debates organised by their think-tanks and provoked by similar ideas suggested by Foreign Minister Tavo Nakayama, came up with a model of an 'indigenous' forum which could form the basis for security discussions. This *existing* ASEAN mechanism was the ASEAN Post-Ministerial Conferences (ASEAN-PMC). The ASEAN-PMC was a series of annual meetings between ASEAN Foreign Ministers and their counterparts from countries that had the status of 'dialogue partner'. These meetings had been initiated gradually since the mid-1970s. The original members of the PMC included the USA, Australia, New Zealand, Canada, the EU and Japan. (South Korea was added to the list of official dialogue partners later, followed by China and India.) While the focus of the ASEAN-PMC had been primarily economic, political issues (such as the Cambodia conflict) formed part of its agenda in the 1980s. By using the PMC as the initial vehicle for multilateral security discussions, ASEAN could satisfy two of its important norms: the need for an indigenous approach and the ASEAN Way of dialogue, which was already the hallmark of the PMC. In such a forum, the ASEAN members would have a controlling influence over the agenda of discussions. ASEAN would thus occupy a central place in the development of any future regional security institutions.[18]

The ASEAN Foreign Ministers Meeting in July 1992 and the ASEAN-PMC meetings in Manila were a crucial turning point in ASEAN's decision to play a direct and important role in Asia Pacific security multilateralism under an expanded PMC framework. During these meetings, security issues were discussed extensively; in a significant move, China was invited to participate in some of these discussions as a 'guest' of ASEAN.[19] The following year, in May 1993 in Singapore (which played a crucial role as the chair of the ASEAN Standing Committee), the ASEAN-PMC members held a 'Special Senior Officials' Meeting' (SOM) to discuss regional security issues. Its recommendations to invite China, Laos, Papua New Guinea, Russia and Vietnam to meet ASEAN and its dialogue partners within the framework of the ASEAN Regional Forum in Bangkok in the following year were approved by the ASEAN Foreign Ministers at their meeting in Singapore in July 1993.

Helping to secure the acceptance of the idea of cooperative security were existing and emerging second-track processes of multilateral dialogue in the Southeast Asia and Asia-Pacific regions. In 1993 the most prominent ASEAN-wide body, the ASEAN Institutes of International and Strategic Studies (ASEAN-ISIS; for further discussion of its membership and role see Chapter 7, 'Towards participatory regionalism'), released a report suggesting a number of confidence-building measures.[20] Moreover, in June 1993 in Kuala Lumpur, about a year before the launching of the ARF, a group of think-tanks in the Asia Pacific region established the Council for Security Cooperation in the Asia Pacific (CSCAP)[21] with the objective, as one of its founding members put it, of creating a 'more regularized, focused and inclusive' non-governmental process on Pacific security issues.[22]

While ASEAN's decision to support the development of a multilateral security forum in the Asia Pacific region conformed to its norms of regional autonomy and the ASEAN Way, it also represented an important reinterpretation of its norm concerning regional autonomy as expressed through the ZOPFAN framework. While maintaining its official adherence to ZOPFAN,[23] ASEAN members faced increasing questions about its continued relevance. These included whether ZOPFAN was still a practical and desirable notion. Apart from the fact that ZOPFAN had never been, and was unlikely to be, accepted by outside powers, continued adherence to the ZOPFAN ideal also begged the question whether Southeast Asia as a region could somehow be insulated from the interests and interactions of major external powers. Intra-ASEAN differences over ZOPFAN, evident in the early stages of ASEAN, found their way into post-Cold War deliberations over its relevance.[24] In contrast to the attitudes of Singapore and Thailand, Indonesia was clearly reluctant to abandon ZOPFAN as a framework for regional security. Foreign Minister Ali Alatas viewed ZOPFAN as 'an evolutionary process', representing 'the regional, multilateral framework within which it is hoped to promote national and regional resilience and to seek the disentanglement of the region from the contending strategic designs of the great powers'.[25] But a closer reading of the positions of Malaysia and Indonesia would suggest that neither viewed the implementation of ZOPFAN in its original form as a feasible response to the challenge of post-Cold War regional order. Malaysia appeared to move away from ZOPFAN by promoting the Treaty of Amity and Cooperation signed at the Bali summit in 1976 as being the more appropriate instrument for ASEAN's dealings with the Indochinese states and external powers.[26] Similarly, Indonesia accepted the need for adjustments to the ZOPFAN concept in light of a changing regional strategic environment.[27] As Ali Alatas conceded, Southeast Asian countries 'can't keep the four powers [the USA, Japan, China and the Soviet Union] out of the region'. The implication was that regional security would be best ensured not through excluding the Great Powers as envisaged in ZOPFAN, but through 'equilibrium among them and between them and Southeast Asia'.[28] This revision formed a major conceptual rationale for ASEAN's participation in the ARF. ASEAN members continued to

Table 6.2 Major Asian institutions and dialogues influenced by the Cooperative Security Norm

Name	Established	Purpose and Role
ASEAN Regional Forum	1994	A cooperative security organisation, partly inspired by the OSCE, but with Asian characteristics. Its primary goal is confidence-building, preventive diplomacy and conflict resolution, but political differences and sovereignty concerns have kept it from undertaking the latter two functions. Lately, it has shifted focus towards transnational security issues, especially disaster management and terrorist financing.
Asia Pacific Economic Cooperation Leaders' Meeting	1993	Although APEC was established in 1989 at the ministerial level to promote trade liberalisation, its leaders' conclave, held annually since 1993, has discussed a range of security issues, such as the East Timor violence in 1999 and the 9/11 attacks in 2001. Some say that the summit and its focus on security has become the main rationale for APEC; and if so, its future may be clouded by the emergence of the East Asian Summit, which has a smaller membership (including India, which is not an APEC member).

(Continued)

Table 6.2 (Continued)

Name	Established	Purpose and Role
East Asia Summit	2005	A leaders' forum comprising 18 members, including the ten ASEAN members, China, Japan, South Korea, US, Russia, India, Australia and New Zealand. Its expansion to include non-East Asian countries, especially the US, was the result of a fear by some ASEAN members that China might otherwise dominate the forum. The summit level meeting is not limited to discussion of security issues: its agenda includes energy, environment, Avian Flu, poverty eradication, natural disaster mitigation, and finance. But in recent years, it has attracted attention for its discussion of the South China Sea conflict, despite China's effort to keep this issue out of the EAS agenda.
The ASEAN Defence Ministers Meeting (ADMM) Plus	2010	It grew out of the ASEAN Defence Ministers' Meeting, which has been in existence since 2006. Originally slated to meet once in three years (now reduced to once in two years), its membership is the same as the EAS. Its initial scope of cooperation includes humanitarian assistance and disaster relief, maritime security, military medicine, counter-terrorism and peacekeeping operations (PKO), but in essence, it is a forum for exchange of views on regional and international security issues and is primarily a confidence-building exercise.
Shanghai Cooperation Organization (SCO)	2001	An outgrowth of the Shanghai Five (China, Russia, Kazakhstan, Kyrgyzstan, Tajikistan) created in 1995 to demilitarise the border between China and the former Soviet Union. The SCO was created in 2001 with the addition of Uzbekistan. Although a multipurpose grouping, it has focused on confidence-building measures and measures to combat the 'three evils' of terrorism, extremism, and separatism. It has undertaken joint military exercises as well as intelligence sharing and other forms of counter-insurgency cooperation.
Shangri-La Dialogue	2001	Brings together annually in Singapore the defence ministers from Asia Pacific countries. Organised by the London-based International Institute for Strategic Studies, it serves as a forum for a public exchange of views, as well as private consultations among senior regional defence officials on security issues of common interest. It has been especially important in debating the rise of China, maritime security and the US military presence in the region.
South Asian Association for Regional Cooperation (SAARC)	1985	SAARC's constitution excludes contentious issues from its agenda, although this has not prevented discussion of such issues on the margins of SAARC summits. SAARC has also undertaken cooperation on non-traditional security issues, such as terrorism, transnational crime, and energy security.
Six Party Talks (SPT)		Initiated in 2003 the SPT is an example of *ad hoc* multilateralism in Asia. The SPT process envisaged the creation of a security framework for Northeast Asia, but this has lagged because of the breakdown of the SPT process in 2007.

*In addition, Asia has a multitude of semi-official and second-track security dialogues, some performing important functions as sounding boards for new ideas about security, such as the ASEAN-Institute of Strategic and International Studies (ASEAN-ISIS), the Asia-Pacific Round Table (APRT, held in Kuala Lumpur annually) and the Council for Security Cooperation in Asia Pacific (CSCAP).

work on a Southeast Asia Nuclear Weapon-Free Zone (SEANWFZ) Treaty (eventually signed on 15 December 1995) as a limited step towards the realisation of the ZOPFAN concept,[29] but in general, ASEAN came to accept the principle of 'inclusiveness' underlying the idea of cooperative security as an important new norm. This meant accepting a dilution of its existing norm of regional autonomy.

The ARF and the ASEAN Way

The first working session of the ARF convened in Bangkok on 25 July 1994 with 18 founding members, including Malaysia, Indonesia, Brunei, Singapore, Thailand, the Philippines, the USA, Canada, Japan, South Korea, Australia, New Zealand, the EU, Russia, China, Papua New Guinea, Vietnam and Laos. The ARF became the first truly 'multilateral' security forum covering the wider Asia-Pacific region. It is the only 'regional' security framework in the world today in which all the major players of the international system (including the USA, Russia, Japan, China and the EU) are represented. By anchoring the ARF, ASEAN sought to create a regional order based not only on its own norms, but also on the relatively new norm of inclusiveness, which is central to the idea of cooperative security.[30] Inclusiveness demands that the ARF not be a dialogue only among the like-minded; it must engage all principal regional actors with different and perhaps conflicting perspectives on regional security issues.[31] Thus, as Gareth Evans, Australia's Foreign Minister at the time of the ARF's creation, pointed out, the purpose of the ARF was to build 'security with others rather than against them'.[32] Underlying this vision was a belief that the balance of power approach to regional order needed at least to be supplemented by a cooperative security approach. Malaysia's Foreign Minister, Abdullah Badawi, denounced the 'deterrence' approach as outmoded. The concept of an ARF, he contended, 'requires the development of friendship rather than the identification of enemies. The nature of security problems in the Asia-Pacific is such that they do not lend themselves amenable for management through the old method of deterrence by countervailing force'.[33]

The ARF did not and does not include Taiwan (which is also a Spratly claimant). Although Taiwan had been allowed into a multilateral intergovernmental economic regime such as the Asia-Pacific Economic Cooperation (APEC) forum, China drew a firm distinction between security multilateralism and economic regionalism in opposing Taiwanese membership of the ARF. Beijing also scuttled Taiwan's full-scale participation in the CSCAP, arguing that the CSCAP is not as 'non-governmental' as it claims to be, since it allows participation by government officials in a non-official capacity. In 1994, the USA expressed opposition to the early inclusion of North Korea in the ARF framework.[34]

Since then, the ARF has also seen a steady expansion of its membership, with India and Burma joining in 1996, Mongolia in 1999, North Korea in 2000, Pakistan in 2004, Timor Leste in 2005, Bangladesh in 2006 and Sri Lanka in 2007. While consistent with the norm of inclusiveness, this also creates the problem of coordination within the grouping.

The imprint of the norms of ASEAN was amply evident in the initial development of the ARF. Its first meeting held in Bangkok in July 1994 agreed to 'endorse the purposes and principles' of the Treaty 'as a code of conduct governing relations between states and a unique diplomatic instrument for regional confidence building, preventive diplomacy and political and security cooperation'.[35] Moreover, the informal process-driven approach of ASEAN guided the ARF's evolution.[36] From the outset, the ASEAN members sought to 'dominate and set the pace' of the ARF, and occupy 'the driver's seat' while recognising 'the concerns and interests of outside powers'.[37] ASEAN's diplomatic centrality was evident not just in the name 'ASEAN' (as opposed to 'Asian') Regional Forum, it was also reflected in the fact that ARF annual sessions were to be held in ASEAN countries (although this was different for the ARF's 'inter-sessional support groups' – essentially working committees dealing with specific issue areas – which were chaired by an ASEAN member along with one non-ASEAN state and could be held outside an ASEAN member country).

The ARF's aversion to rigid institutionalism was remarked upon by Singapore's Foreign Minister who noted that the ARF did not have 'a master plan or a rigid road map', nor did it 'want to force the pace'. It started with a minimal institutional structure consisting primarily of its annual Foreign Ministers' conclave, as well as the senior officials meeting (ARF-SOM) that precedes it by a few months. In between these, the only other intergovernmental meetings were those of the inter-sessional groups which were instituted following a decision at the 1995 ARF meeting. No ARF secretariat was created; but the ASEAN Secretariat in Jakarta would establish an ARF unit.

Further evidence of the impact of the ASEAN Way on the ARF process was its cautious and incremental approach, evident from a document entitled 'The ASEAN Regional Forum: A concept paper' circulated by ASEAN at the second ARF meeting held in Brunei on 1 August 1995. The paper, which was meant to serve as a blueprint for the ARF (although it was not formally adopted by the ARF in its entirety), envisaged three categories of security cooperation: confidence building measures (CBMs), preventive diplomacy and conflict resolution (later changed to 'elaboration of approaches to conflicts').[38] While this three-fold categorisation was itself incremental (with CBMs to be followed by preventive diplomacy initiatives which would then be followed by approaches to conflicts), each of these categories contained measures with a two-stage implementation schedule. The first category included measures that could be carried out in the short term, while the second category contained measures that required a longer-term consideration and approach. The short-term measures envisaged by the concept paper consisted of dialogues on security perceptions, including voluntary statements of defence policy positions, and publication of defence white papers or equivalent documents. Measures in the long-term implementation category ranged from simple transparency measures (including information and communication CBMs) to somewhat more ambitious CBMs including prior notification of military deployments with region-wide significance. The concept paper also sought to make use of existing global CBMs such as the UN Register on Conventional Arms by calling for the exploration of a regional version. The concept paper adopted a broad view of CBMs aimed at dealing with both military and non-military issues. Indicative were its proposals concerning information exchanges and training on drug trafficking and the development of a mechanism to mobilise relief assistance in the event of natural disasters. A relatively novel and interesting proposal contained in the paper was the call to arms manufacturers and suppliers to reveal the destination of their arms exports. The paper recommended several transparency measures, including coordination of existing security studies activities and the establishment of a regional security studies centre.

But Chinese reservations forced a change in the wording of the concept paper from 'conflict resolution' in the original ASEAN-developed draft to the vague and almost comical expression of 'elaboration of approaches to conflicts'. China was adamant that the ARF cannot have a managerial role in dispute settlement. China initially opposed the inclusion of the South China Sea dispute on the ARF's agenda, arguing that the ARF was not a suitable forum for handling contentious issues.[39] While it relented on this issue in 1995, by agreeing to direct talks with ASEAN on the conflict outside the ARF framework, Beijing held that the ARF itself was 'not an appropriate place' to resolve the dispute and that 'the most effective way to handle this dispute is through bilateral negotiations'.[40]

Reviewing the ARF's cooperative security agenda reveals both the utility and dangers of the ASEAN Way. On the one hand, the ASEAN Way of informalism, incrementalism and emphasis on non-binding agreements and voluntary compliance has been useful in adopting an initial set of CBMs. On the other hand, as Desmond Ball has argued, the measures adopted so far 'do not impinge on core national interests – i.e. territorial claims and other sovereignty issues, defence capabilities and operations, or internal political processes (which might be affected by more transparent policymaking)'.[41]

From confidence-building to preventive diplomacy

The second meeting of the ARF held in Brunei on 1 August 1995 approved a number of CBMs, including exchanging annual defence postures on a voluntary basis, increasing dialogues on security issues on a bilateral, subregional and regional basis, maintaining senior-level contacts and exchanges among military institutions, and encouraging participation of the ARF members in the UN Conventional Arms Register. The establishment of an Inter-sessional Support Group (ISG) on CBMs, which was agreed at the Brunei meeting, provided an additional forum for the ARF member countries to develop and exchange ideas about confidence building. At subsequent ARF meetings, the CBM agenda was further advanced with agreement to expand the scope of defence policy papers submitted voluntarily by ARF members to include their defence contacts and exchange programmes.[42] Another key area of agreement was to open up the ARF-SOM to defence representatives and encourage their greater participation in inter-sessional activities. Contact CBMs were augmented by agreement to develop exchanges and meetings among national defence colleges. The first meeting of the heads of national defence colleges was held in October 1997. At an ARF meeting on CBMs in November 1997, a US proposal for compiling a list of CBM publications written in ARF countries and a list of CBM experts in those countries was approved.[43] On the other hand, important CBM proposals, such as the idea of a regional arms register, made little headway. Moreover, the ARF has been unable to move much beyond simple transparency measures and information exchanges to more ambitious 'constraining measures'. As noted earlier, some ARF members had voiced objections that such 'Western' measures were unsuited to the Asian milieu.

The fourth ARF meeting in 1997 decided that the CBM agenda had progressed sufficiently (an assumption questioned by critics) to warrant serious consideration of the next stage in the ARF's evolution, namely preventive diplomacy (PD), especially if there was an overlap between CBMs and PD.[44] But the ARF's PD agenda was to be stymied by both definitional issues and the problem of operationalising it. An initial concern of China was to ensure that PD did not involve the use of force, or 'preventive deployment', and that it was limited to interstate, rather than intra-state conflicts.[45] But even after this was accommodated[46] – although Chinese concerns about 'preventive deployment' remained following the NATO intervention in Kosovo in 1999 – China continued to seek to delimit the scope of PD (see the box below).

Defining preventive diplomacy

Chinese modifications to the definition of preventive diplomacy offer a good indication of contestations and compromises that helped to get Beijing involved in security multilateralism. In a document dated 6 November 1999, ASEAN, drawing upon the proposed definition worked out by a CSCAP Bangkok meeting in March 1999, offered the following definition of PD:

> consensual diplomatic and political action with the aim of:
>   preventing severe disputes and conflicts from arising between States which pose a serious threat to regional peace and stability;
>   preventing such disputes and conflicts from escalating into armed confrontation; and preventing such disputes and conflicts from spreading geographically.

On 1 February 2000, China offered an 'amended' definition which defined PD as:

> peaceful diplomatic actions undertaken by *sovereign* states to prevent *armed conflicts* between states in the region with the consent of all states *directly involved* in a dispute. (author's emphasis)

The intent was clear: China wanted PD to be strictly between 'sovereign states', applicable strictly to 'armed conflicts' (rather than more broadly to 'disputes and conflicts'), and involving only parties 'directly involved'. These restrictions meant the ARF's PD role would not apply to Taiwan and ensured that the ARF would not sanction interference by third parties such as the US in conflicts such as Taiwan or the South China Sea. In the end, the Concept Paper on PD dated 5 April 2000 (drafted by Singapore), accepted the language proposed by Beijing:

> PD is consensual diplomatic and political action taken by sovereign states with the consent of all directly involved parties:
>   To help prevent disputes and conflicts from arising between States that could potentially pose a threat to regional peace and stability;
>   To help prevent such disputes and conflicts from escalating into armed confrontation; and
>   To help minimise the impact of such disputes and conflicts on the region.

China had also recommended the deletion of 'preventing such disputes and conflicts from spreading geographically' from the original ASEAN definition, on the ground that this belonged to the third stage of the ARF, known as 'elaboration of approaches to conflicts', and hence was premature at the PD stage. The Singapore Concept Paper rephrased it: 'To help minimise the impact of such disputes and conflicts on a region'. Another of China's proposed amendments was to delete the phrase: 'preventing severe disputes and conflicts from arising between States which pose a serious threat to regional peace and stability', altogether, because as the Chinese put it, 'conflicts usually refer to armed actions, hence are not at the same level with disputes', disputes cannot be prevented from arising, and including disputes would render the ARF's mandate too 'ambitious'. But the Singapore-drafted Concept Paper kept reference to 'disputes'.

> *Source:* Documents prepared for, and circulated at, the ARF Inter-sessional Support Group Meeting of Confidence Building Measures (ISG on CBMs), Tokyo, 13–14 November 1999; ISG-CBMs, Singapore 5–6 April 2000; ISG-CBMs, Seoul, 1–3 November 2000; ISG-CBMs, Kuala Lumpur, 18–20 April, 2001. These documents were made available to the author by an ARF member state on a highly confidential basis.

The author stands by their accuracy. 'The ARF Concept Paper on the Concepts and Principles of Preventive Diplomacy', prepared by Singapore for the 5–6 April 2000 ISG-CBMs meeting, is available at www.aseanregionalforum.org/LinkClick.aspx?fil eticket=XHzV3KDf5bM%3d&tabid=89&mid=453 (accessed 6 June 2008).

But the ARF has faced major obstacles in moving to a preventive diplomacy role. In 2001, the ARF meeting in Hanoi adopted four steps to PD, including confidence building efforts, norms building, enhancing channels of communication and the role of the ARF chair.[47] Drawing upon the Bangkok CSCAP meeting of 1999, it identified eight principles of PD:

1   It is about diplomacy. It relies on diplomatic and peaceful methods such as diplomacy, negotiation, enquiry, mediation and conciliation.
2   It is non-coercive. Military action or the uses of force are not part of PD.
3   It should be timely. Action is to be preventive, rather than curative. PD methods are most effectively employed at an early stage of a dispute or crisis.
4   It requires trust and confidence. PD can only be exercised successfully where there is a strong foundation of trust and confidence among the parties involved and when it is conducted on the basis of neutrality, justice and impartiality.
5   It operates on the basis of consultation and consensus. Any PD effort can only be carried out through consensus after careful and extensive consultations among ARF members, with due consideration for the need for timeliness.
6   It is voluntary. PD practices are to be employed only at the request of all the parties directly involved in the dispute and with their clear consent.
7   It applies to conflicts between and among states.
8   It is conducted in accordance with universally recognised basic principles of international law and interstate relations embodied, inter alia, in the UN Charter, the Five Principles of Peaceful Co-existence and the TAC. These include respect for sovereign equality, territorial integrity and non-interference in the internal affairs of a state.

The June 2003 ARF meeting in Phnom Penh agreed to continue work on CBMs 'as the foundation of the ARF process' while noting that the ARF had 'initiated exploratory work on preventive diplomacy' and should now begin implementing some measures of PD such as enhancing the role of the ARF chair through interaction with other regional and international organisations.[48] In 2005, the ARF ISG on CBMs was renamed the ARF Inter-sessional Support Group on Confidence Building Measures and Preventive Diplomacy (ISG on CBMs & PD). But China has remained cautious, arguing that confidence building should remain the primary function of the ARF, despite some overlap between its two functions.

In functional terms, the ARF's agenda has expanded. In October 2000, an ARF meeting addressed issues of transnational crime through coordination and cooperation among ARF countries. In addition to 'piracy, illegal migration and illicit trafficking of small arms', other issues of transnational crime including 'drug trafficking, computer crime, money laundering and terrorism', were brought into the ARF's agenda.[49] The 9/11 terrorist attacks led the ARF to shift its focus from conventional interstate confidence-building and preventive diplomacy issues to cooperation against non-traditional or transnational issues. At its annual ministerial meeting in July 2002 the ARF adopted a series of measures targeting terrorist financing. These measures included: freezing terrorist assets; implementation of international standards; international cooperation on the exchange of information and outreach;

technical assistance; and compliance and reporting. The ARF also formed an Inter-Sessional Group on Counter-Terrorism and Transnational Crime (co-chaired by Malaysia and the US). At the 10th ARF meeting in Cambodia in June 2003, Singapore's Foreign Minister, S. Jayakumar, urged the ARF to 'go beyond regional matters to global issues'.

> Previously, the ARF was mostly preoccupied with country or region-specific issues such as territorial disputes in the South China Sea . . . [now it has to handle] issues which are less country-specific and more global and transnational in nature.[50]

That ARF meeting added maritime security to its agenda because 'Southeast Asia and Asia-Pacific contain vital sea-lanes', and therefore 'all countries have a stake in the safety and integrity of these sea-lanes'.[51] The 3rd ARF Inter-Sessional Meeting on Counter-Terrorism and Transnational Crime in Bangkok in April 2005 reached agreement on the sharing of intelligence among ARF countries, albeit 'based on bilateral arrangement in light of sensitivities' and with need to 'respect national laws of respective countries'.[52] The ARF has also considered disaster relief, including cooperation in 'risk identification and monitoring, disaster prevention and preparedness, emergency response and disaster relief, and capacity-building'.[53]

A good deal of the ARF's agenda of cooperative security focuses on 'capacity building and information sharing, including intelligence exchanges on terrorism'.[54] Institutionally, the ARF has developed and expanded the number and type of meetings. The major events in the ARF calendar are the annual meeting of foreign ministers held immediately after the ASEAN Ministerial Meeting (AMM), and ASEAN Post-Ministerial Conferences (ASEAN-PMC). These meetings are preceded in May by the ARF Senior Officials' Meeting (ARF-SOM), which prepares the ground for decisions at the ARF ministerial. In 1996, the ARF introduced Inter-sessional Meetings (ISM) and Inter-sessional Support Group (ISG) meetings, the former involving strictly official participation, to continue discussion on key agenda items between the ministerials. The first, and perhaps the most important, ISG covered confidence-building measures (ISG on CBMs, later covering preventive diplomacy as well). It was instrumental in developing the ARF's agenda on confidence-building measures and the definition and scope of preventive diplomacy. Other inter-sessional meetings have included search and rescue coordination and cooperation, and peacekeeping operation, disaster relief and counter-terrorism and transnational crime.

The total number of ARF meetings (inter-governmental or Track-I, including the annual events such as the ARF ministerial and the ARF-SOMs, ISMs and ISGs) has increased steadily from one in 1994 and 1995, to nine in 1998 and 14 in 2000. In 2007, there were 19 such Track-I ARF meetings. (In addition, there are a number of semi-official or Track-II meetings, averaging about six per year, organised by the Council for Security Cooperation in Asia Pacific (CSCAP), a grouping of regional think-tanks, on the subjects of confidence-building (including preventive diplomacy), transnational crime, maritime security, and terrorism; CSCAP organises its own working groups on these subjects.) The Track-I meetings and activities of the ARF fall into four broad categories: seminars/workshops, experts' group meetings, training programmes and non-operational exercises. Seminars and workshops are the main activity. Since 1997, ARF members have organised some 50 seminars and workshops (mostly since 2000) on a wide range of areas including traditional issues (CBMs and PD, production of defence policy documents, maritime security, missile defence, and proliferation of weapons of mass destruction) and non-traditional security issues (e.g. disaster relief, tropical hygiene and infectious diseases, shipboard generated waste, narcotics control, energy security, alternative development, Severe Acute Respiratory Syndrome (SARS) and avian flu, small arms and light weapons, economic security, and anti-piracy). A number of seminars or workshops have been held on peacekeeping, humanitarian assistance, law of armed conflict, and civil–military relations and cooperation. Terrorism has also been emphasised since 9/11, with seminars on the prevention of terrorism, financial measures against terrorism, and managing the consequences of a major terrorist attack. ARF meetings have shared and discussed updates on terrorist organisations, terrorist activities, national, bilateral and multilateral counter-terrorism measures, and border security arrangements regarding the movement of people and goods.[55] They have organised capacity-building meetings on counter-terrorism; in 2003, Singapore held a series of training workshops for ARF members covering aviation security, intelligence analysis, post-blast investigation and bomb and explosives identification.[56] In 2008, Australia and Indonesia co-organised a desktop exercise on disaster relief in Jakarta.

The training activities organised under the ARF's auspices by member states have covered maritime security, combined humanitarian assistance response and peacekeeping operations, in addition to an ARF professional development programme, and an ARF professional training programme on China's security policy (described thus, but perhaps just a seminar). Another category are experts' meetings, on subjects including peacekeeping, export licensing, transnational crime, disaster relief, and maritime issues. A limited number of non-operational exercises have been held, including a maritime security shore exercise.[57]

The first of the annual meetings of heads of defence colleges and institutions was held in 1997. A proposal drafted by Brunei in July 2002 as the ARF chair suggested 'accepting military and defence officials as members of the forum in addition to foreign ministers; reinforcing information-sharing, security cooperation and financial measures among participating countries to crack down on international terrorism; allowing the ASEAN secretariat to strengthen the ARF Chairman's role'.[58] ARF defence officials met for the first time in 2002, and from 2003, two such talks are held annually, called 'ARF defence officials' dialogue' (at the level of defence senior officials held in May before the ARF senior officials' meeting) and 'ARF defence officials' meeting' (just before the ministerial meeting). In an important development, the first annual ARF Security Policy Conference (ASPC), chaired by Indonesia and hosted by China in Beijing, took place on 4–6 November 2004. China's interest in this forum could be a response to the Shangri-la Dialogue organised annually since 2002 by the London-based think-tank, the International Institute for Strategic Studies, which China had initially distanced itself from by sending junior officials (possibly due to Taiwanese sponsorship of the event in its initial years). The ASPC meetings have exchanged national 'views on regional defence and security outlook', taken note of both traditional and non-traditional threats to the region, such as terrorism, epidemics, environmental degradation, energy security and food security, discussed cooperation on disaster relief, and taken note of outcomes of related ASEAN and ARF seminars and meetings on regional security cooperation.[59]

The ARF has continued to focus on non-traditional security issues. For example, in July 2009, it adopted the ARF Work Plan for Counterterrorism and Transnational Crime, focusing on capacity-building measures, technical support, and information exchange through workshops, technical assistance, training courses, and multilateral exercises.[60] Since 2009, the ARF has held a number of exercises on humanitarian assistance and disaster relief. The first such exercise was held May 4–8 2009, with the US and the Philippines co-sponsoring the event and simulating response to a typhoon. Civilian-led but supported by the military, this Voluntary Demonstration of Response (VDR) exercise was dubbed a 'first-ever field exercise for ARF'.[61] In May 2013, the ARF held its third Disaster Relief Exercise in Thailand using a scenario of an 8.9-magnitude earthquake and typhoon. This was called 'by far the most inclusive simulation exercise in the Asia Pacific region,' involved participation from the ARF members as well as the ASEAN Coordinating Centre for Humanitarian Assistance on disaster management (AHA Centre), the United Nations Office for the Coordination of Humanitarian Affairs (UNOCHA) and the Red Cross and Red Crescent.[62] Moreover, in a bid to speed up its response to regional problems, the ARF in July 2009 adopted rules for 'Friends of the ARF Chair' (FOC). This group will consist of three foreign ministers who would assist the ARF chair to deal with regional and international issues, although its role is advisory in nature.[63]

Limits and benefits of the ARF

Whether the ARF, modelled in part after the ASEAN Way, will be an effective instrument of regional order in the Asia Pacific region has attracted much debate and scepticism. Critics see it as a 'talk-shop'.[64] A *Bangkok Post* analysis of the first ARF meeting in Bangkok was suggestively titled 'a casual approach to deadly serious security issues'.[65] Michael Leifer described the ARF as a 'highly imperfect diplomatic instrument for coping with the new and uncertain security context'.[66] In his view,

> the prerequisite for a successful ARF may well be the prior existence of a stable balance of power. The central issue in the case of the ARF is whether, in addition to diplomatic encouragement for a culture of cooperation driven partly by economic interdependence, the region shows the markings of a stable, supporting balance or distribution of power that would allow the multilateral venture to proceed in circumstances of some predict-ability. The ARF's structural problem is that its validity seems to depend on the prior existence of a stable balance, but it is not really in a position to create it.[67]

ASEAN members and security analysts also speak of the need for a 'balance' of power as a fundamental prerequisite for regional order. As Ali Alatas put it, regional security requires an 'equilibrium among them [the major powers] and between them and Southeast Asia'.[68] Singapore's leaders have been even more outspoken about the importance of maintaining a balance of power. But a careful reading of this position would suggest that a distinction is made between balance of power as an *outcome* and balance of power as an *approach*.[69] The balance of power as an actual situation of the distribution of power and influence is certainly desirable. But this does not mean that such an outcome should be or can only be achieved through a balance of power 'policy' involving a 'competitive manipulation of power rela-tionships' and the use of mechanisms such as deterrence, alliances and military build-ups. While these have their place in ASEAN countries' security strategies, for a variety of reasons, their support for and participation in an outright balancing strategy is a qualified one.

The first of these reasons is a concern that one of the principal traditional mechanisms of achieving a balance of power, its alliances with outside powers, is of doubtful value. This itself is rooted in ASEAN's misgivings about the potential unreliability of major power security guarantees that are integral to a balance of power mechanism. The ASEAN states recognise the continuing political and strategic value of US alliances in the post-Cold War era, including their impact in restraining the future security posture of Japan and their role in providing the necessary legal and political basis for a continued strong US mili-tary presence in the region. But these alliances had lost some of their original purpose and credibility, especially in dealing with low-level (but more likely) security threats in Southeast Asia such as domestic instability or interstate territorial disputes. A classic example is the US refusal to accept Manila's claim that the scope of their mutual defence treaty covers its positions in the Spratly Islands, and this further attests to the uncertain nature of their alliance relationship.[70] A US-led balance of power approach may not be relevant to the task of preventing and managing small-scale regional conflicts, such as the resurgence of instability in Cambodia, border clashes in Southeast Asia, or armed conflict over the South China Sea islands.

Moreover, the ASEAN states share the view that a highly adversarial Sino-US relationship with a containment strategy will threaten regional stability. Lee Kuan Yew, perhaps the most outspoken critic of a containment strategy, argues that a strong and belligerent US response to Chinese power will stoke nationalist and hardline sentiments in China, with the consequence that 'the medium and small countries of the region have to live with the results of an aroused and xenophobic China'.[71]

ASEAN's support for the ARF is also based on its distrust of a possible Asian concert system, a framework in which the major powers themselves develop a mechanism to regulate their own interactions.[72] A concert model implies Great Power primacy in maintaining regional order. This would not be acceptable to ASEAN. An Asian concert would effectively marginalise ASEAN. While ASEAN members agree that cooperation among Great Powers is beneficial to ASEAN's own community-building efforts, ASEAN seeks a more equal relationship among the regional countries. In short, ASEAN wants a community-guided concert, not a concert-guided community.

On the other hand, a multilateral forum like the ARF may be able to help create a 'situation of equilibrium' among the major powers through the creation of norms and habits of cooperation. To some extent, the ARF is as much about engaging the USA as engaging China. By engaging the USA multilaterally in the region's security affairs, ASEAN seeks to discourage it from resorting to a policy of pre-emptive containment of China. It also hopes that the continued engagement of the USA will preclude the emergence of an independent Japanese security role, which would be destabilising for ASEAN. Moreover, acting collectively through a multilateral forum, ASEAN may shape the development of ideas and principles that might persuade the region's major powers to view diplomacy and 'rules of acceptable conduct', rather than arms races and alliances, as the principal means of deterring aggressive behaviour while preserving regional equilibrium and preventing a concert of powers. Additionally, the norms developed by the ARF may constrain the use of force in intra-regional conflicts. The ARF increases the costs of the use of force to settle interstate disputes. Gareth Evans has argued that the ARF has already helped to diffuse the South China Sea problem in 1995.[73] The ARF members, China included, will violate the multilateral norms of the ARF at considerable risk of political isolation. As Michael Green, a George W. Bush administration official, puts it, the ARF helps regional actors to 'demand standards of behaviour from China in ways that would simply not be as effective on a bilateral basis'.

Sceptics of the ARF argue that in dealing with Chinese power at least, ASEAN 'will have to decide whether to place their trust primarily in the ARF, or whether to place it in a US-led balance of power'.[74] But ASEAN countries evidently do not see the need to *choose* between the two, but rather seek to use multilateralism to moderate and maintain a stable balance of power.

To this end, ASEAN was vindicated by the shift in the attitude of the USA and China towards the ARF. When ideas about multilateralism began to circulate in the late 1980s, they were greeted with open hostility from the Bush administration whose officials quickly dubbed multilateralism a 'solution in search of a problem'.[75] Even more importantly, Washington viewed a new multilateral security institution in the Asia Pacific region as a threat to its existing alliance system which had proved its worth during the Cold War period. It was contended that '[w]hile the United States would adjust the form of its security role in the region [in the post-Cold War era], it intends to retain the substance of its role and the bilateral defence relationships which give it structure'.[76]

But the US policy towards the ARF soon became noticeably positive. The shift was helped by a realisation that countries in the region viewed multilateralism not as a substitute for US military supremacy and its bilateral alliances, but as a necessary complement to the latter. The new US attitude was first signalled during the later stages of the Bush administration, when Secretary of State James Baker expressed support for flexible and *ad hoc* multilateral efforts to deal with specific security issues.[77] The Clinton administration was more explicit in its support of multilateralism, identified as one of the ten major goals of the new US policy in Asia.[78] Current US policy on multilateralism envisages a concentric circle of security institutions, which includes (1) its existing bilateral alliances, (2) the newly developed security consultations within the ASEAN-PMC and the ARF, and, where appropriate, (3) multilateral action by the most concerned and relevant actors to resolve specific security problems such as in the Korean Peninsula. Within such a multi-layered approach, the various elements are seen to be complementary, rather than mutually exclusive. As a US official put it, '[t]hese arrangements can function like overlapping plates of armor . . . covering the full body of our common security concerns'.[79]

Like the USA, China initially opposed multilateralism in Asia-Pacific security relations. It was fearful that the ARF could be manipulated by larger powers such as the USA to apply pressure on China to compromise on its territorial claims and constrain its legitimate geopolitical role. Moreover, China was suspicious that the ARF might develop into a tool in the hands of the Western powers for interfering in the domestic affairs of the Asian member states. Furthermore, the possibility that the ARF could develop into an anti-Chinese bandwagon of its smaller neighbours was, and remains, unsettling to many Chinese strategists who see engagement in multilateral security cooperation as a novel enterprise with no precedent in Chinese history. One study of Chinese attitudes towards multilateralism in 1994 (the year the ARF was established) concluded:

> The Chinese expect that bilateral relations and the balance of power among the major powers will continue to be the primary factors affecting stability in the Asia-Pacific, not a multilateral security structure. The majority of Chinese specialists portray multilateralism as largely irrelevant – or potentially damaging – to efforts aimed at solving or managing most of the key disputes in the Asia-Pacific region.[80]

But China too came to take a more supportive role in multilateralism and the ARF. Initially, this was due to a fear of regional isolation. But later China also saw some positive benefits from multilateralism. Chen Jian, the Chinese Assistant Foreign Minister, stated that China would support the ARF 'as a new approach to regional security, an approach different from Cold War mentality, an approach which seeks to strengthen peace through dialogue and cooperation'.[81] China supports the ASEAN Way of seeking cautious and incremental progress in the ARF's security agenda, in contrast to the fast-track approach favoured by the ARF's Western members. While it has opposed a role for it in conflict resolution, China does accept that the ARF 'can only move in a progressive way and make incremental progress' which includes preparing 'the groundwork for future cooperation'.[82] China has come to acknowledge the usefulness of the ARF as the only multilateral venue available to it where it can discuss and share its security concerns and approach with Asia-Pacific countries. In fact, the opportunity provided by these for voicing China's own security concerns regarding US security policy in the region, such as the strengthening of the US–Japan (and US–Australia) security relationship in the later 1990s, may have been a major factor behind its more positive attitude towards multilateralism.

Chinese Views on the Impact of the ARF on Chinese Interests and Policy

A. Responses to questions about why China joined the ARF and what impact the ARF is having on Chinese policy

1 'China joined the ARF mainly because it did not want to be left out. Now it sees benefits.'
2 The ARF helps China in three ways: (1) to 'learn directly from others what are the key problems in the region, not only between China and its neighbours, but also generally'. This is 'better than China's inward-looking view of the region as before'; (2) to 'learn about international arrangements, including the experience of other international organisations, in Europe'. Multilateralism is 'helping to internationalise Chinese diplomacy'; (3) 'During the ARF process, China has realised that even if China faces great pressure on certain issues, such as the Spratlys, China is also gaining a broad sense of regional security, helping China to broaden its views on security.'
3 China's message has 'gone through that it wants to be a responsible country' (read power). The ARF has helped to 'spread the message'.
4 'The ARF is a constructive way to elaborate our policies.'
5 'The ARF is a way of China engaging ASEAN.'
6 'Through the ARF process China opened to the region.'
7 The ARF makes 'China feel more comfortable about its environment'.
8 'Because of the ARF, Chinese foreign policy is more open, China is more active in regional affairs.'
9 The ARF has helped to 'remove mistrust about China, misunderstanding between China and other countries'.
10 'Removing mistrust could be done bilaterally, but multilateralism is more useful. Multilateralism provides a bigger stage' for China to do so.
11 'Asia Pacific countries are more willing to speak their mind about their fear of China in multilateral forums than through bilateral channels.'
12 The ARF will make alliances 'less attractive' (thereby reducing US policy options in the region).
13 The ARF 'opened a new window' for Chinese Foreign Ministry officials. 'It told them how the outside world looks at China'. And 'when you know how the outside world thinks of China', it helps China to develop more sensitive policies.
14 The ARF was a 'learning process' which will change Chinese behaviour in the long term. China is 'learning a new form of cooperation, not across a line [in an] adversarial style, but [in a] cooperative style'.

B. Responses to questions about the impact of the ARF on the regional strategic environment.

1   The ARF is 'slowing changing mind-sets', 'increasing transparency, confidence'. It has increased the regional countries' 'political willingness to be with others'.
2   The ARF is an 'education process' for the region.
3   'The ARF transforms people's security conception and perceptions.'
4   'Because of the ARF, China is more willing to settle its disputes by peaceful means.' (This comment, from a Foreign Ministry official who deals regularly with the ARF (hence is more 'socialised' than most), was in response to a question asking if the ARF makes it less likely for China to use force to settle regional disputes. A more qualified response came from a think-tank scholar who argued 'learning will lead indirectly to China becoming more likely to use peaceful means of settling its disputes'. He was much less willing to rule out the use of force. But he did make an important distinction: Security issues that do not have strong domestic impact will be more amenable to peaceful Chinese behaviour. This may include Korea and exclude Taiwan and, insisted the scholar, the South China Sea. As one Chinese analyst put it, multilateralism is being viewed by China as a serious 'learning' process and not just a lot of idle chat in a 'teahouse'.)

Source: Interviews conducted during three research trips to China since the formation of the ARF in 1994 as well as two sessions of the Canada–China Seminar on Multilateralism and Cooperative Security (CANCHIS) held in 1997, 1998, 1999 and 2000. The aim of these interviews was to monitor continuity and change in Chinese thinking on multilateralism. Approximately 25 people were interviewed, including officials from the Ministry of Foreign Affairs, Ministry of Defence, The People's Liberation Army and researchers at a number of Beijing think-tanks.

Japan and India have also been supportive of the ARF. Japan's policymakers viewed the Nakayama proposal as a key catalyst of the ARF's formation. After that, Japan 'applied itself as a loyal supporter to the ASEAN-led process to establish the ARF, and participated enthusiastically in its inaugural meeting in 1994'.[83] Participation in the ARF was seen as a cornerstone of Japanese Asia policy. Japan organised a semi-official meeting on the ARF in May 1994 to brainstorm its contribution to the forum and in 1995 co-chaired with Malaysia the first inter-sessional support group of the ARF dealing with confidence-building measures. Tokyo contributed ideas to the development of some of the early ARF measures on CBMs such as annual defence white papers. It also played a 'mediating role' between Western members of the ARF, such as the US, Australia and Canada, which pushed for the rapid institutionalisation of the ARF, and Asian members such as China and ASEAN, which preferred to move at a slower pace and in keeping with the 'ASEAN Way' with an emphasis on informal mechanisms, a modest level of legalisation and in conformity with the voluntary participation principle.[84] Although Tokyo's interest in the organisation dwindled somewhat after it could not push its security concerns of immediate importance, such as the Chinese nuclear test and North Korea missile and nuclear tests, into the ARF's agenda,[85] and the Koizumi government seemed to lay more emphasis on the US–Japan security alliance, Japan continued to remain an active force in the ARF.

India joined the ARF somewhat late, in 1996, after overcoming an initial ASEAN reluctance. The ARF marked a turning point in India's engagement in wider Asian regionalism. After being a key player in Asian regionalism in the 1940s and 1950s, India paid scant attention to the regionalism developed by ASEAN. Its domestic security and economic problems, defeat by China in the 1962 war, and preoccupation with rivalry with Pakistan ensured India's loss of interest in Southeast Asia. For ASEAN's founding members, India's growing alignment with the Soviet Union, including its recognition of the Soviet-backed and Vietnamese-installed Heng Samrin regime in Cambodia in the 1980s was deeply alienating. But the end of the Cold War and India's economic reforms in the 1990s, combined with a growing concern about China engendered renewed interest on the part of ASEAN in engaging India. India was made a sectoral dialogue partner of ASEAN in 1992, and a full dialogue partner in 1995. In 1996, India joined the ARF, primarily at Singapore's initiative, despite some lingering Indonesian misgivings. These developments were seen in Delhi as 'a conscious acknowledgement [by ASEAN] of India's look-east policy' and 'the acceptance of India's role and position in the Asia-Pacific region'.[86] India's participation in the East Asian Summit will be discussed later. India has been active in CBMs, maritime security and counter-terrorism initiatives and meetings of the ARF. According to the Indian External Affairs Ministry

> We see in the ARF, an experiment for the fashioning of a new pluralistic, cooperative security order in tune with the diversity of the Asia-Pacific region and in consonance with the transition away from a world characterised by poles built around military alliances. We remain ready to contribute to it. Though the ARF covers a broader region, India believes that it is built around the nucleus of ASEAN and is ASEAN driven.[87]

In conclusion, the ARF's contribution to regional order may well lie in the socialising impact of multilateralism on the balancing behaviour of major Asia-Pacific powers. Those who argue (like Professor Leifer) that the region needs a prior and stable balance of power for an effective ARF should also be reminded that it needs an ARF for ensuring a balance of power that does not stimulate competition leading to war. Multilateralism in the manner of the ARF mutes and moderates balancing tendencies and helps, pending the transformation of balancing behaviour, preservation of regional stability.

The East Asia Summit and ASEAN

Next to the ARF, perhaps the most significant development in multilateral security cooperation in Asia Pacific is the East Asia Summit (EAS), held for the first time in Kuala Lumpur in 2005 with the participation of the leaders of the ten ASEAN members plus Japan, China, South Korea, Australia, New Zealand and India. The purpose of the EAS, as the Kuala Lumpur summit declaration put it, would be to serve as a forum for dialogue on 'broad strategic, political and economic issues of common interest and concern' (EAS 2005 Declaration). The advent of the EAS and of East Asian regionalism more generally represented a new stage in the evolution of Asian regionalism and ASEAN. Until 1997, regional institutions in Asia were organised either on a subregional (ASEAN, South Asian Association for Regional Cooperation (SAARC), and Shanghai Cooperation Organization (SCO)) or a transpacific (APEC, ARF) basis. The emergence of the APEC reflected growing transpacific economic interdependence, while the ARF responded to the end of Cold War divisions. and the impact of norms of cooperative security promoted by Canada and Australia. But these institutions, as well as ASEAN itself, were undermined by the 1997 crisis for their failure to deal with its economic and political repercussions. Not surprisingly therefore, the region's post-crisis multilateralism came to include creating an East Asian (as opposed to Asia-Pacific) framework. The first to emerge was the ASEAN Plus Three (APT) grouping in 1997, comprising the ASEAN members, China, Japan and South Korea. A later addition would be the East Asia Summit, an annual gathering of the leaders of the ten ASEAN members, plus China, Japan, South Korea, India, Australia and New Zealand, which held its inaugural session in December 2005.

The contemporary move towards an East Asian institution began in 1990 when the then Malaysian Prime Minister, Mahathir Mohamad, proposed an East Asian Economic Grouping (later renamed the East Asian Economic Caucus). His proposal was spurred by a fear of regional trade blocs in Europe and North America. The EU was about to become a single market, and the North American Free Trade Agreement was emerging. If East Asia did not do anything, reasoned Mahathir, it would be marginalised. Adding to the concern was the crisis over the Uruguay Round of the General Agreement on Tariffs and Trade (GATT), which was facing a breakdown.

But the EAEG proposal stalled in the face of stiff American opposition. In his memoirs, US Secretary of State James Baker confesses to having done his best to 'kill' the proposal, 'even though in public [he] took a moderate line'.[88] US pressure contributed to Japan's reluctance to assume leadership of the grouping, as Mahathir had envisaged. Moreover, the fear of regional trading blocs that inspired Malaysia's proposal proved to be unfounded. The GATT Uruguay Round was successfully completed, thereby undercutting a rationale for an East Asian grouping.

After the collapse of regional currencies that marked the outbreak of the 'Asian economic crisis' in mid-1997, however, East Asian regionalism got a new lease of life. The seemingly very different responses from Washington to the Thai Baht collapse and the Peso crisis in Mexico fuelled perceptions of US apathy towards the region. Washington's response to the Peso crisis was prompt and generous, while in the case of Thailand it simply let the IMF take the lead and provided little direct financial aid. This, coupled with the manner in which Washington abruptly and totally rejected Japan's proposal for an Asian Monetary Fund as a bulwark against future crises 'antagonized opinion leaders of the region'.[89]

The crisis spurred the APT. Limited to the ten ASEAN members and Japan, China and South Korea, the APT focused on regional financial cooperation, which had not been undertaken within the APEC framework. Stubbs finds the sources of the APT to lie in the region's shared historical experiences, common cultural traits, 'a distinctive set of institutions and a particular approach to economic development' and a 'distinctive form of capitalism' rooted in business networks.[90] It gave ASEAN a fresh start, proving to the world that the grouping has not lost all sense of purpose and relevance stemming from its perceived failure to offer an effective response to the crisis.

At the behest of South Korean leader Kim Dae Jung, APT leaders set up an East Asia Vision Group (EAVG), to consider pathways towards regional cooperation. Its report, released in 2001 and entitled 'Towards an East Asian Community: a Region of Peace, Prosperity and Progress' stressed the need for 'fostering the identity of an East Asian community' as well as 'promotion of regional identity and consciousness'. It also called for an East Asia Summit.[91] Following the EAVG's report, East Asian governments formed another group called the East Asian Study Group (EASG). This was an intergovernmental level group whose objective was to study the EAVG report and make concrete and practical recommendations. This group's report, released in November 2002, proposed two kinds of measures:

17 short-term ones which can be implemented immediately, and nine medium-term/long-term measures that required further study.[92] Among the first category were proposals for forming an East Asian Business Council, an East Asian Investment Information Network, Network of East Asian Think Tanks, and an East Asian Forum that brings together government officials and civil society organisations. Other proposals in this category included strengthening mechanisms for cooperation on non-traditional security issues such as illegal migration, drug trafficking, and human smuggling. Among the medium-term/long-term proposals that required further study was the idea of forming an East Asian Free Trade Area, a regional financing facility, and an East Asian investment area that would expand the existing ASEAN investment area. Most importantly, the report endorsed the proposal to develop the APT Summit into an East Asian Summit.

A major impetus for an East Asian Summit and the vision for an East Asian Community was the accelerating East Asian regional economic interdependence. Intra-regional trade in East Asia in 2003 accounted for 54 per cent of the region's total trade, compared with 35 per cent in 1980. Intra-East Asian trade today is higher than that in the NAFTA region (46 per cent), 'very much comparable to intra-regional trade in the European Union before the 1992 Maastricht treaty'.[93] Although East Asian nations, with the notable exception of China, rely on investment from outside East Asia, the share of intra-regional foreign direct investment jumped from 24 per cent in the latter half of the 1980s, to 40 per cent in 1995–97.[94] On top of economic linkages, the East Asian Community idea has been strengthened by a string of regional crises since the financial meltdown in 1997. The outbreak of SARS in 2003 and the Indian Ocean Tsunami in 2004 have fostered a sense of shared vulnerability of the region to complex transnational disasters, which come with little warning and respect no national boundaries.

ASEAN's motivations in supporting East Asian regionalism had at least five major elements. First, East Asian regionalism provides ASEAN with an important additional layer of engagement between the region's pre-eminent rising power, China, and its neighbours. This may create the possibility of placing China in a 'golden cage', or China developing a form of what Ikenberry calls 'institutional self-binding',[95] whereby a great power adopts a structure of restraint towards its weaker neighbours in exchange for the latter's collective recognition of its own economic and security interests and leadership. East Asian regionalism may be a better mechanism for such Chinese self-binding than ARF or APEC, where the presence of the US makes China nervous about making concessions which may be perceived as a sign of weakness and not even be reciprocated by Washington. Indeed, China has in the past seen US policies of engagement through the ARF as a form of 'soft containment'.

Second, East Asian regionalism offered a psychological cushion to ASEAN against US dominance. This may be seen as a form of 'institutional balancing' (different from 'institutional binding' proposed by Ikenberry), whereby a group of states use a regional institution to counter the dominance of a great power that remains outside the grouping. The very existence of East Asian institutions forces the US to weigh the diplomatic and political costs of action in a future regional crisis that may be construed as grossly unsympathetic or hostile by regional actors, for example the latter's resentment against the US in the wake of the 1997 crisis.

Third, East Asian regionalism serves as a framework for undertaking certain functional tasks which other regional groupings may be less suited or inclined to perform. Financial cooperation is one of them, and has already been undertaken by the APT. East Asian regionalism has also proven useful in addressing non-traditional security threats, such as pandemics. The regional response to the SARS crisis was undertaken through an East Asian framework and this may prove useful again should there be a massive outbreak of bird flu. The focus on energy security at the second EAS in Cebu is also noteworthy given the membership in the EAS of both India (not an APEC member) and China, two of the biggest consumers of energy resources.

Fourth, East Asian regionalism may be a better platform for promoting normative change in the region, especially the much-needed dilution of the non-interference doctrine. In ARF or APEC, such dilution is less likely, because of the likelihood that any such effort would be forcefully championed by their Western members such as the US or Australia, and invite suspicion and rejection by the more tradition-bound East Asian nations such as China and Vietnam. The level of comfort for discussing political issues that impinge on non-interference might be greater within an East Asian context and forum.

Finally, East Asian regionalism, especially its summit, provides a forum for interactions between China and Asia's two other rising powers: India and Japan. This ensures not only that the EAC will not be dominated by China, which is a concern of some of its detractors. But the simultaneous engagement of China, Japan and India through the EAS also offers the region's weaker states a greater scope for autonomy. Weak states are known for their tendency to play great powers against one another to secure a margin of freedom for their own actions and to secure material benefits. While pushed to its extreme this may be destablising, some amount of competitive bidding by the Asian powers for influence over ASEAN may be good for the latter, especially if the benefits offered include geopolitical restraint and economic assistance. Indeed, this has already happened.

East Asian regionalism also faces some powerful obstacles. The first is contested regional definition. The Kuala Lumpur summit defined East Asia in 'political rather than geographical terms'.[96] The broadening of the summit to include India, Australia and New Zealand, at the behest of Japan and Singapore,[97] and justified as a way of underscoring the 'open' and 'inclusive' nature of the grouping, became a source of considerable controversy. Ironically, Mahathir himself disowned the summit for its inclusion of these non-East Asian countries, especially Australia. He accused Canberra of being America's 'deputy sheriff ' that would 'represent not the east but the views . . . of America'.[98]

Such political differences over regional definition cloud the future institutional development of the East Asian regionalism. China had opposed moves to include Australia, New Zealand and India in the lead-up to the summit. Whereas the move to broaden the summit was undertaken by Japan and Singapore partly due to their fears of Chinese dominance, Beijing saw this move as a Japanese ploy to weaken Chinese influence in East Asia. While Japan and India want the summit to be the basis for the development of the East Asia Community, Beijing would prefer to develop such a community through the APT process, which does not include Australia, New Zealand and India.[99]

A second issue for East Asian regionalism is duplication of tasks between East Asian and Asia Pacific institutions. Although, as noted, financial cooperation undertaken by the APT, including the system of bilateral currency swaps, is distinctive to East Asian regionalism, East Asian institutions are also supposed to tackle non-traditional security issues, such as terrorism, natural disasters, and environmental degradation, that also fall within the mandate of APEC and ARF. The EAS intends to deal with strategic issues through dialogue and cooperation, which is the main purpose of the ARF. The EAS also seeks to promote economic development, energy security, financial stability and economic integration. APEC has focused on trade, but some see its future being contingent on taking a stronger role in economic development and energy security. There are now three frameworks for FTAs in the region: Asia-Pacific wide (APEC-based), EAS-wide (pushed by Japan) and APT-wide (backed by China). Both EAS and APEC have summit level meetings which overlap to a great extent, with the notable exception of the absence of the US from the EAS.

Another challenge for East Asian regionalism concerns the 'leadership' role of ASEAN. The Kuala Lumpur summit's declaration made it clear that ASEAN will be the 'driving force' of the summit. It will be hosted and chaired by an ASEAN member state which assumes the ASEAN chairmanship and will be held back to back with the annual ASEAN summit. ASEAN's leadership of the EAC is consistent with its role as the hub of wider regional cooperation mechanisms such as the ARF and APT. Defending ASEAN's leadership of East Asian regionalism, Singapore's former Prime Minister Goh Chok Tong argues: 'ASEAN does not threaten anybody and the big countries in the region will want ASEAN to play that facilitating role'.[100] But critics feel that ASEAN's capacity for leadership is undermined by severe internal weaknesses, which include the challenge of economic competition from China, intra-mural political bickering, and domestic political problems in member states. ASEAN is leading the EAC process mainly by default, because neither of the region's two major powers, China and Japan, is in a political position to do so. 'Cooperation in East Asia', argues Japanese scholar Takashi Shiraisi, 'cannot work if the prime mover is either of the two countries'.[101]

And this leads to what might be the most serious challenge to the East Asian Community idea: the spiral of mistrust between China and Japan. Recent Sino-Japanese tension reverses decades of reconciliation which might otherwise have served as the basis for a genuine East Asian Community. In many ways, China and Japan have complemented each other as benefactors to the region. In the 1980s and 1990s, outward Japanese investment contributed to common prosperity in East Asia. The Chinese economy has increasingly assumed the role of regional integrator. In the 1997 crisis, aid offered by Japan was an important psychological factor behind Malaysia's ability to withstand the crisis, while China's pledge not to devalue its currency helped to stave off any further aggravation of the crisis. The SARS crisis moved China closer to the region after Beijing made up for its earlier secrecy over the outbreak by cooperating closely with neighbours in containing the pandemic. And Japan was the largest Asian provider of humanitarian economic aid in response to the Indian Ocean Tsunami.

But while their economic and functional ties with the region were largely complementary, the political and strategic roles of China and Japan in East Asia became increasingly competitive. Japan was alarmed by Chinese nuclear tests and military expansion in the 1980s and 1990s. Responding, it strengthened its alliance with the US, which in turn fuelled Chinese perceptions of renewed Japanese militarism. Japan's prolonged economic stagnation at a time of China's meteoric rise fuelled Japanese insecurity. North Korea's missile tests and nuclear programme aggravated Japan's insecurity and moved Tokyo closer to Washington's strategic agenda. The George W. Bush administration's war on terror offered an opportune framework for Japan to carry out political and constitutional changes which in reality have their basis in its concerns about the rise of China. These changes, which permit an expansive role for Japan's military are interpreted by neo-nationalist elements in China as a further sign of Japanese militarism. These forces have also exploited anti-Japanese sentiments over the visits to the Yasukuni Shrine by the then Prime Minister Koizumi and the publication of Japanese textbooks that glossed over Japanese wartime atrocities in East Asia. Anti-Japanese demonstrations in China, sometimes tolerated by the authorities in Beijing, produced a nationalist backlash in Japan. As a result, Sino-Japanese competition and mistrust creates a kind of unstable core at the heart of the EAC concept. It remains to be seen whether there will be any genuine improvement under the post-Koizumi governments.

Another uncertainty about East Asian regionalism is the role of the US. Washington has had a history of anxiety attacks over East Asian regionalism. Within the US policy-making community, a sharply negative view of East Asian regionalism has emerged. Some see it as driving a wedge between the US and East Asia, or as an instrument for Chinese strategic gain at the expense of the US. Thus, Fred Bergsten worries that the EAS might cause a 'fundamental split between East Asia and the U.S.'.[102] Richard Armitage, Deputy Secretary of State under the first George W. Bush administration, described East Asian regionalism as a 'thinly-veiled way to make the point that the US is not totally welcomed in Asia. . . . What worries me about the EAC idea is that it is the beginning of an erosion of the US military alliances in the region. It seems that China is quite willing to be involved in fora that do not include the US.'[103] Dana Dillon of the Heritage Foundation wishes that: 'With artful management of the process by engaged American diplomats, the U.S. can either neutralise EAS into another Asian talk-shop, like the ASEAN Regional Forum, or use it to help harness China's economy while muzzling its military'.[104] Underlying such perspectives is a tendency, familiar in the US policy-making community, to view Asian (especially East Asian) multilateralism and US strategic and economic interests in the region in zero-sum terms.

As part of James Baker's attempt to 'kill' Mahathir's EAEG proposal, a demarche to the ASEAN Secretary-General in 1993 from Washington warned that it would be 'concerned about anything that raises questions about United States commitment to the region and exclusion from the region'.[105] The George W. Bush administration viewed the approaching EAS with a mixture of feigned disinterest and ignorance. Eric John, Deputy Assistant Secretary of State for East Asia and the Pacific, told a US congressional hearing: 'Nobody knows what the East Asia summit is other than leaders coming together'.[106] John described the summit as too much of a 'black box' for Washington even to realise what it is missing out on. 'I would hesitate to push for an invitation to an organization we don't know what it does.'[107]

Interestingly, even some friends of Washington did not believe US participation in the EAS was either necessary or desirable. Hitoshi Tanaka, a former Japanese Deputy Foreign Minister, contended that the US is not 'committed to the East Asia community building' and hence should not be regarded as 'a member of the East Asian Community'.[108] Singapore's former Prime Minister Goh Chok Tong argued that 'East Asia cannot be extending to countries in the Pacific, for then even the political definitions would get stretched beyond belief'. In Goh's view, the region's 'engagement with the US could be through the APEC and the ARF'.[109]

Following ASEAN's decision to include India, Australia and New Zealand in the inaugural EAS in Malaysia in 2005, there was expectations that the US might join the EAS. These specualtions were fuelled by the Obama administration's move, soon after entering office in January 2009, in strengthening its relations with ASEAN. Among other things, the Obama administration pledged to reverse its predecessor George W. Bush administration's perceived neglect of ASEAN, as indicated in the periodic failure of Secretary of State Condoleeza Rice to show up at the annual meetings with ASEAN involving the US. In contrast, not only did Hillary Clinton paid a visit to the ASEAN Secretariat in Jakarta part of her itinerary during her first overseas trip as the new Secretary of State, the new administration also signed ASEAN's Treaty of Amity and Cooperation, and appointed an ambassador to ASEAN, based first in Washington, D.C. and subsequently in Jakarta. After mulling over its options, such as whether to strengthen APEC into a fully fledged economic and security grouping, or encourage the creation of a new umbrella grouping proposed by the then Australian Prime Minister Kevin Rudd in 2009 (called the 'Asia-Pacific Community'), or to join the EAS,[110] the Obama administration finally went for the latter option. The US formally joined in the EAS in 2011 (although Secretary of State Clinton attended the 2010 EAS in Hanoi in October 2010). On 19 November 2011, President Obama joined seventeen other Asian leaders in Bali for the sixth East Asia Summit. This was the first time that all the great powers with a direct

Table 6.3 US engagement with ASEAN under Obama: highlights

- Secretary Clinton's first overseas tour to ASEAN Secretariat in Jakarta in February 2009
- Signing of ASEAN's Treaty of Amity and Cooperation in July 2009
- President Obama's meeting with ASEAN Leaders in November 2009 and September 2010
- Arrival in Jakarta of David Lee Carden as the United States' first resident Ambassador to ASEAN in April 2011. Previously, he was the US Ambassador for ASEAN Affairs, a position created in 2008, was based in Washington, D.C.
- President Barack Obama's participation in the 6th EAS in November 2011

role in Asia-Pacific security were represented in the same summit level regional grouping (India is not part of the APEC and hence its leader does not attend the annual APEC Leaders' Meeting).

In a speech delivered to the Council on Foreign Relations in Washington D.C. on 8 September 2010, Clinton set up an ambitious goal for the US engagement in the EAS. The US, she declared, would be 'encouraging its development into a foundational security and political institution for the region, capable of resolving disputes and preventing them before they arise.'[111] (This was bound to concern China, which had opposed similar efforts to introduce preventive diplomacy and conflict resolution through the ARF a decade ago.) But questions remained about what US participation might mean for the East Asia Summit or the broader regional architecture.[112] Among these were concerns that Washington might try to force a new EAS agenda focused on geopolitics or that it will seek to dilute, if not supplant, ASEAN's central role. Another worry was that the EAS could become a forum dominated by the US–China rivalry, however, Washington appeared sensitive to the fact that it was a new face at the table. Similarly, while the US might have seen the EAS as a useful way to counter China's growing influence in the region, it would be unlikely to seek a confrontation in Bali. For example, on the South China Sea issue, Washington had lately shown a preference for framing this as an issue about principles rather than singling out China for criticism.

There has also been speculation that the US and other non-ASEAN EAS members might seek to drop the soft institutional approach of 'the Asean Way' and reduce ASEAN's control over the EAS agenda and membership. There is no doubt that Washington would prefer to see less scripted interactions at the EAS, where leaders would be freer to raise and discuss issues. The US would also like to see regional groups develop stronger secretariats and become more formally institutionalised over time. This notwithstanding, the talk out of Washington was about being respectful to ASEAN and proceeding carefully.

It remains to be seen whether US interest in the EAS is sustainable over time. The EAS is only a summit, not yet a fully fledged institution. Washington may now be happy to engage with ASEAN and other EAS members to gradually shape the future agenda and priority issues, but it would also want to see the EAS develop into a 'results-oriented' institution. As was the case with its participation in the ARF, US frustration could grow if the EAS does not start to develop actionable goals and follow up its commitments. Another question concerns economics, trade and finance. Here, Washington seems to give clear priority to the Trans-Pacific Partnership (TPP) framework which was started by the Obama administration with the initial negotiations involving itself, Australia, Brunei, Chile, Malaysia, New Zealand, Peru, Singapore, and Vietnam. Japan and Canada have since announced their participation. The TPP is theoretically open to all APEC members; however by seeking to create a high quality and trade agreement with demanding rules and standards, it may end up excluding many regional players. It does not yet include China mainly because, as some would have it, the US views it with suspicion. The TPP has created a potential divide and competition in Asia–Pacific economic regionalism, leading to the emergence of a competing framework in the form of the Regional Comprehensive Economic Partnership (RCEP) that excludes the US. The RCEP envisages a free trade agreement involving the ten ASEAN members plus Australia, China, Japan, South Korea, India, and New Zealand. US officials argue that they do not see the EAS as an appropriate policy space for discussing economic, trade and finance issues. Though this attitude may or may not change, it reflects a deeper, underlying tension, namely whether the most appropriate model for regional integration is one that is a trans-Pacific or East Asian.

ASEAN–US security ties

Yet, the US remains critical to the security strategies of some ASEAN members. This requires careful understanding because defence ties between ASEAN and the US are often seen by critics to be a sign of the limited impact of multilateralism. Several ASEAN countries, including Singapore, Malaysia, Indonesia, Thailand and the Philippines, have strengthened their security ties with the US.

In 1989, Singapore announced an offer to provide military facilities to the USA. The USA and Singapore signed a memorandum of understanding in November 1990 which provided for the deployment of US aircraft (on a rotational basis) and military personnel in Singapore. This was followed by an agreement on 3–5 January 1992 to relocate a major naval logistics facility responsible for port calls and resupply for US navy ships and coordinating warship deployments in the Pacific region from Subic Bay to Singapore.[113] Somewhat more quietly, Malaysia and the USA have been cooperating on military matters within the framework of agreement on Bilateral Training and Education Cooperation signed in January 1984 (the agreement had been kept secret at Malaysia's request). During the 1980s, the frequency of joint exercises between the two countries, involving naval, air and ground forces, had reportedly reached an average of one exercise per month,[114] although many of these were quite small.[115] Malaysia also offered maintenance facilities to US military transport aircraft at Subang Airport, and ship repair as well as sports and recreational facilities to the US Navy at Lumut on a commercial basis.[116] Brunei followed Singapore in signing a memorandum of understanding that allows several US warship visits and joint training with Bruneian forces.[117] Indonesia concluded a maritime search and rescue agreement with the USA in July 1988 and offered port call facilities to the USA in Surabaya, Medan, Jakarta and other ports, and facilities for ship repair to the US Navy at Surabaya on a commercial basis. In the 1990s, there were other forms of access to Indonesian facilities by US forces, and the conduct of joint military exercises between the two countries, although such ties remained sensitive and low-key.[118] Thailand, whose military cooperation with the USA dates back to 1950, signed a new agreement with the USA in 1990 covering interoperability of its tactical command and control systems and extended an earlier agreement providing for US help in developing a modern logistics support system for Thailand. Moreover, Thailand allowed the use of its airports for refuelling and maintenance of US military aircraft during the 1990–91 Gulf War.[119] The bilateral security agreement signed between Indonesia and Australia on 18 December 1995 (revoked in 1999 by Indonesia in apparent retaliation against Australian policy towards East Timor) could also be viewed in a similar light. While the agreement was mainly a CBM between Jakarta and Canberra and its strategic value was limited by the fact that it only provided for consultations in the event of a crisis, it reversed Jakarta's long-standing opposition to security pacts of any kind with outside powers.[120]

Growing concern about the rise of China, the war on terror following the 9/11 attacks and the Bali bombings saw new forms of security cooperation between the US and key ASEAN countries. (Specifics of US counter-terrorism cooperation with ASEAN countries will be discussed in Chapter 7.) After having left its bases on Philippines soil, the US resumed a close security relationship with the Philippines, partly induced by Manila's concerns about China in the Spratlys, by signing a Visiting Forces Agreement in 1998 and has since conducted 'dozens of joint military exercises, training tens of thousands of U.S. and Philippine soldiers' (such as the 'Talon Vision/PHIBLEX') aimed at improving interoperability and readiness, and building professional relationships among the two military forces.[121] The two countries set up a defence policy board as 'a new bilateral defense consultative mechanism' in November 2001.[122] The Philippines was designated 'a major non-NATO ally' by the George W. Bush administration in October 2003. The US initiated the Philippine defence reform programme, 'a broad-based, multi-year cooperative defense reform effort designed to address systemic organizational deficiencies, correct root causes of strategic and operational shortcomings and achieve long term, sustainable institutional improvements in management, leadership and employment of the Armed Forces of the Philippines (AFP)'.[123]

The plan for a US–Singapore 'Strategic Cooperation Partnership' was announced in October 2003. The 'Strategic Framework Agreement for a Closer Cooperation Partnership in Defence and Security' was signed in July 2005, providing for an annual strategic dialogue, joint military exercises and training covering regional threats as well as peacekeeping missions, and expanding Singapore's access to US defence technology. Two accompanying agreements were also concluded, one providing for sharing of military expertise and defence capabilities to deal with non-conventional threats, and the other updating and extending the agreement over US access to military facilities in Singapore signed in 1990, which was due to expire in 2005. The US–Singapore strategic relationship is geared to security concerns rather than just to the war on terror, including a desire to preserve the balance of power in the Asia-Pacific.[124]

US security relations with Malaysia also progressed in the post 9/11 period. In a May 2002 speech in Washington, D.C., Malaysian Defence Minister Najib Tun Razak described US–Malaysia defence cooperation as a 'very well-kept secret', describing Malaysia as 'a steady, reliable friend of the United States' engaged in 'security cooperation [with the US] across a range of fronts'. The US and Malaysia conducted 14 exercises and training events in Peninsular Malaysia in 2007.[125]

The annual US–Thailand exercise Cobra Gold, once a bilateral affair, became the 'premier multilateral exercise' of the US Pacific Command, involving countries such as Singapore as participant and even China as observer. In 2006, for example, aside from the five main participating countries, Thailand, the United States, Singapore, Japan and Indonesia, several others were invited 'to participate in various roles during the exercise'. These included Australia, Bangladesh, Brunei, Canada, China, Fiji, France, Germany, India, Italy, Korea, Malaysia, Mongolia, Nepal, Papua New Guinea, the Philippines, Russia, Sri Lanka, Tonga, the United Kingdom and Vietnam.[126] The goal of Cobra Gold has been officially described by the US as 'building regional competencies to respond to a wide range of transnational security threats and humanitarian relief contingencies'.[127] Thailand was also designated as a 'major non-NATO ally' of the US.

A turnaround has also occurred in US–Indonesia defence relations, which had virtually ground to a halt since the East Timor crisis in 1999. In November 2005, the Bush administration, citing 'national security interests', waived restrictions imposed by Congress on the provision of foreign military financing (FMF) and defence exports to Indonesia. There were no further legislative restrictions on military relations specific to Indonesia. A joint statement by President Bush and President Yudhoyono in May 2006 noted that 'normal military relations would be in the interest of both countries'. In 2006, the US resumed International Military Education and Training (IMET) aid, enabling some 40 Indonesian military officers to be trained in the 2006–07 fiscal year. The same year the US also lifted the ban on sale of non-lethal weapons under the Foreign Military Sales (FMS) programme. In resuming arms sales and normal defence relations, the Bush administration stressed Indonesia's importance as 'the world's third largest democracy', and as 'the world's most populous majority-Muslim nation', its 'unique strategic role in Southeast Asia', and its role as 'a voice of moderation in the Islamic world'. Indonesia was also cited for its 'key role in guaranteeing security in the strategic sea lanes in Asia' and as 'a leading member of the Association of Southeast Asian Nations'. The US also noted 'significant progress in advancing its democratic institutions and practices in a relatively short time'.[128] IMET funds to Indonesia jumped from $938,000 in financial year 2006 to $1.5 million for financial year 2009 (74 students). The US and Indonesia have conducted a number of exercises, such as Garuda Shield 2007, their first joint brigade-size manoeuvre since 1997, and Naval Engagement Activity (NEA) with marines. Indonesia was invited to participate in the Cobra Gold exercise for the first time in 2006.[129] Not all of these relate to the war on terror. In appealing to the US Congress to l ift military sanctions against Indonesia, Admiral William Fallon, Commander of the US Pacific Command, argued: 'We cannot afford to cede influence to other regional powers, such as China, with this important country.'[130]

During the Cold War, Singapore, Thailand and the Philippines saw ASEAN regionalism as a supplement to their bilateral defence links with the US, while Singapore and Malaysia (through FPDA) and Brunei might have seen their defence ties with UK in a similar light. Singapore also saw the US as a regional security guarantor after the British withdrawal from the region in the 1970s. But this situation has changed. While ASEAN countries in general do not see multilateralism as a substitute for their external security linkages in the short term, this does not mean they are willing to sacrifice regional cooperation and a measure of security autonomy for the sake of close ties with the US and its agenda of balancing Chinese power or fighting the war on terror (see the further discussion in Chapter 7 under counter-terrorism cooperation). Because the ASEAN states cannot individually or collectively aspire to defence self-reliance, a policy of military balancing would amount to increased dependence on external security guarantees. Moreover, ASEAN members view their external security linkages and the regional security understandings and norms as increasingly 'convergent' and complimentary. This view is supported by US defence officials, such as the former chief of the US Pacific Command, Admiral Dennis Blair, who used the concept of 'security community' as the basis of a policy initiative to make US military activities in the region, such as the Cobra Gold exercises, more inclusive.[131]

It is not the case that ASEAN members view multilateral security dialogues and cooperation as mere supplements to their external defence ties. Instead, a transition may even be taking place, whereby external defence guarantees (whose credibility cannot be taken for granted) are seen as a means of last resort and hence a supplement to regional security understanding and cooperation.

ASEAN and the Great Powers

Therein lies a major rationale for ASEAN-led security multilateralism in the Asia-Pacific. It not only helps to enhance the prospects for a more predictable and constructive relationship among the major powers, but also enables ASEAN to dilute Great Power dominance in Southeast Asia, in keeping with the original ASEAN norm of regional autonomy. A key element of this ASEAN strategy is the co-engagement of China, the United States, Japan and India.

The rise of China has led to prospects that ASEAN might either resort to balancing against, or bandwagoning with, China, the two postures commonly found in a realist understanding of responses to rising powers. But a balancing posture would compromise ASEAN's previous policy of engaging China through multilateral institutions such as the ARF, while bandwagoning would mean accepting regional institutions dominated by China. Either development would threaten ASEAN's own security community building project and jeopardise ASEAN-led multilateralism in Asia.

China presents the greatest challenge to ASEAN. In terms of size, economic resources and military strength, China dwarfs Southeast Asia and has the potential to deeply affect the autonomy of ASEAN. China's GDP is more than double that of ASEAN (in 2003 US$1.43 trillion for China compared with US$746.8 billion for ASEAN).[132] So is its defence expenditure.[133] The gap is likely to grow wider. In 2001, a Rand Corporation assessment warned that the gap in military capabilities between the ASEAN countries and China was likely to grow over the next 10 to 15 years due to the impact of the Asian financial crisis, including cutbacks in defence modernisation of ASEAN states due to the crisis while China's remained unfettered.[134]

Some analysts have spoken of the likely emergence of a Chinese sphere of influence in Southeast Asia, such as a 'centre–periphery relationship'.[135] Aside from the sheer growth of Chinese power, China's building of dams in the upper reaches of the Mekong River gives it an ability to control the flow of water to other riparian states, especially Laos, Cambodia and Vietnam.[136] China's links with Burma, such as the sale of military equipment, military training programmes, and the stationing of Chinese military personnel to train and operate sophisticated electronic communication and surveillance equipment,[137] are also of concern to ASEAN members. While some of these reports may have been overstated,[138] they have nonetheless shaped ASEAN's opposition to Western sanctions against the repressive military junta in Burma and its decision to admit Burma as a full member in 1997.

Long-term concerns about Chinese military build-up remain in Southeast Asia.[139] Chinese power projection is constrained by a number of factors: limited range of force projection assets and long-range strike capabilities, and lack of combat experience and training.

Table 6.4 Accession to the Treaty of Amity and Cooperation (Selected countries)

Country	Date
China	2003
India	2003
Japan	2004
Russia	2004
New Zealand	2005
Australia	2005
France	2007
United States	2009
European Union	2012

According to a Pentagon estimate of 2002, China has the ability to pursue a 'limited harassment' of ASEAN by sea and air.[140] It might be able to seize most islands in the disputed areas in the South China Sea, but holding on to them would be difficult.[141] The main goal of China's military build-up has been to 'diversify its options for use of force against potential targets such as Taiwan and to complicate United States intervention in a Taiwan Strait conflict'.[142] But forces being developed against Taiwan could also be used in Southeast Asia, especially as China expands it naval and air capabilities.

Political relations between China and ASEAN have improved in the past decade, thanks partly to their convergent approach to three of Southeast Asia's major recent challenges: the 1997 currency crisis, the threat of terrorism, and the SARS outbreak. ASEAN appreciated China's pledge not to devalue its currency in the wake of the Asian crisis in 1997. The Spratlys issue, as noted, has been pushed into the backburner.

At the same time, China's increasingly powerful economy is seen both as an economic threat to Southeast Asia and as a source of Chinese influence over the region. Singapore's Goh Chok Tong, described China's economic transformation as 'scary', and the region's 'biggest challenge', according to Goh, is 'to secure a niche for ourselves as China swamps the world with her high quality but cheaper products'.[143]

At the top of ASEAN's economic concerns about China is the issue of investment diversion. Total FDI flows to China were US$3.4 billion in 1990, US$28 billion in 1993, and US$44 billion in 1997, and the figure has remained at around US$40 billion since. In comparison, FDI to ASEAN-5 was US$12.4 billion in 1990, US$27 billion in 1997 and US$11.4 billion in 2001. In 1990, according to UNCTAD estimates, ASEAN received 52.6 per cent of the total FDI to Asia, while China received 14.4 per cent. In 2001, in a dramatic reversal of the trend, these figures stood at 14.7 per cent and 55.5 per cent respectively.[144]

Partly to counter China's economic challenge, ASEAN developed a multilateral approach to economic relations with China. The China–ASEAN free trade area (proposed by Beijing itself) is billed as the largest free trade zone in the world covering a total population of 1.7 billion people and a combined GDP of about US$2 trillion. It aims at reducing and eliminating tariffs by 2010 for China and the ASEAN-6, and by 2015 for Cambodia, Laos, Burma and Vietnam. The FTA could bolster ASEAN's and China's GDP by 0.9 per cent and 0.3 per cent respectively. It would also increase ASEAN's exports to China by 48 per cent and China's exports to ASEAN by 55 per cent.[145]

An FTA with China with its large domestic market will create more trade and investment opportunities for ASEAN member states. A China–ASEAN FTA sets a model for similar concessions for ASEAN from future FTAs with Japan, Korea and India. It would make ASEAN more attractive as an FDI destination. For China, while ASEAN's market of 500 million people and rich natural resources are important considerations behind its drive for an FTA with ASEAN, trade liberalisation also offers potential political benefits.

Despite their desire to cultivate Beijing, and their weaker economic and strategic position, the core ASEAN countries are unlikely to bandwagon collectively with China. Except in the case of Burma, there is no substantial military relationship between China and any of the original members of ASEAN. Defence relations between China and ASEAN members remain rudimentary and are aimed at confidence-building, rather than fighting a common enemy (except non-traditional challenges). Following China's accession in October 2003 to the ASEAN Treaty of Amity and Cooperation and the China–ASEAN Joint Declaration on Strategic Partnership for Peace and Prosperity, a five-year (2005–2010) Plan of Action adopted in December 2004 called for closer security cooperation in areas such as confidence and trust in defence and military fields; dialogue, consultation and seminars on

defence and security issues; cooperation on military personnel training; joint military exercises; and peacekeeping operations.[146] At the same time, ASEAN countries remain wary of
Chinese geopolitical moves. While the arms build-up in Southeast Asia is by no means
solely geared to countering China, the possibility of China developing an expansionist security approach is an important factor for Malaysia, Singapore and the Philippines.[147] Security
relations between China and Vietnam have improved with border agreements (a land border
agreement in 1999 and an agreement on the delimitation of the Tonkin Gulf and an agreement on Fishery Cooperation in December 2000).[148] China and Vietnam have conducted
joint maritime patrols in the Gulf of Tonkin. But Vietnam and China are not in a bandwagoning relationship. Recent joint statements involving China and Singapore, and China and the
Philippines have included modest proposals for defence exchanges.[149]

To the extent possible, ASEAN would avoid taking sides in the US–China rivalry. ASEAN
countries do not support an independent Taiwan, but they will not necessarily acquiesce
in an unprovoked Chinese military takeover of Taiwan. However, there is little chance of
Southeast Asia subjecting itself to a 'Chinese Monroe Doctrine' in which Beijing denies the
region to 'outside' powers such as the US. Although Sino-ASEAN relations seem unequal
at present, ASEAN is not without bargaining power in its dealings, especially its collective
dealings, with China. China needs ASEAN's acquiescence and cooperation to realise its
leadership ambitions in Asia and the world. Its relationship with ASEAN is a test case of
Beijing's credibility as an engaged and constructive world power. While Beijing remains
wary of ASEAN's pressure on the South China Sea dispute and the pro-US defence orientation of many ASEAN members, there are also reasons for Beijing to view Southeast Asia
as a relatively 'safe' and 'benign' area within which to cultivate positive and mutually
beneficial relationships. Beijing is also mindful that an adverse relationship with Southeast
Asia could move many of the countries in the region towards closer alignment with China's
competitors, such as Japan and the US. This offers an opportunity to ASEAN states to extract
strategic restraint from China and develop cooperative security strategies.

ASEAN seeks to ensure China's enmeshment in a system of regional order in which the
costs of any use of force in dealing with problems with its neighbours will be outweighed by
benefits. The key element of this approach is the ARF.[150] If China is to turn away from this
framework and view and use regional institutions as an instrument of leverage, they will
certainly unravel. But it will also cost significant diplomatic and strategic influence.

ASEAN's co-engagement policy towards the Great Powers is also evident in its approach
to relations with India and Japan. While ASEAN has always been supportive of Japan's
engagement, its invitation to India is a new development. Closer ASEAN–India cooperation,
originally reflected in ASEAN's decision to accept India as a full dialogue partner and let
India into the ARF, led ASEAN subsequently to invite India to hold a summit meeting with
ASEAN, the first of which was held in Cambodia in 2002.[151] ASEAN's interest in India has
economic, strategic and cultural dimensions. The primary catalyst was economic. ASEAN's
trade with India jumped five times from US$2.5 billion in 1993–94 to US$13.25 billion in
2003–04, still a far cry from China–ASEAN trade, but of growing importance.[152] The strategic rationale was offered by Singapore's Prime Minister Goh Chok Tong, for whom ASEAN
countries 'welcome India's participation' in ASEAN because:

> We do want another big country to be actively engaged with Asean. Otherwise, Asean
> would be, in a sense, overwhelmed by their [sic] Northeast Asian countries – China,
> Japan. So, if we have another wing in terms of constructive engagement, and that is
> India, it will make for a more stable Asean.[153]

And in 2005, Singapore's Foreign Minister George Yeo commented that the rise of China and India is returning Southeast Asia to its 'historic position and role' as a crossroads in East–West trade. ASEAN's destiny lies in exploiting its geographical position to cement its interdependence with both giants.[154]

It should be noted that while ASEAN has helped India to return to Asian regionalism, India's role in Southeast Asia today is quite different from that in the 1940s and 1950s. Then, India was the leader of Asian regionalism; now, it is following ASEAN's lead. Second, while India's role in the earlier phase of Asian regionalism was dominated by political and strategic concerns, especially Nehru's bid to gain acceptance of Communist China in Asia and weaken US-led SEATO, economic motives play a large part in contemporary Indian interest in Asian regionalism. In either case, ASEAN retains an important influence over the terms of India's engagement.

As ASEAN–India ties have strengthened, there has been much talk about an emerging Sino-Indian rivalry in Southeast Asia. To some extent, this is evident in Burma. And in Southeast Asia, memories of Sino-Indian diplomatic competition (perceived if not real) in the 1950s (Indian premier Jawaharlal Nehru and Chinese premier Chou En-lai at the 1955 Asia-Africa Conference in Bandung, Indonesia) are still present. In relating to Southeast Asia, China has some important advantages over India. Many leaders in Southeast Asia are ethnically Chinese. China has a head start over India in economic reform and hence its economic influence in Southeast Asia is substantially stronger. Its trade with ASEAN is substantially larger than India's ASEAN trade. The attraction of India in Southeast Asia is somewhat negative, linked to a desire among ASEAN members not to put all their economic eggs in a single basket. Just as in geopolitics, the policy is to avoid becoming too dependent economically on China. But India is not without some cards. It has no territorial disputes with Southeast Asia like the Spratlys; India's growing security ties with the US are a plus for ASEAN, which is mainly pro-US; and India's naval power in Western Southeast Asian waters is more substantial than China's.

While ASEAN members such as Singapore hope that drawing India into its multilateral sphere will balance China's diplomatic and strategic influence, the concept of 'balancing' must be a qualified one. Justifying the participation of India, New Zealand and Australia in the East Asian Summit, Lee Kuan Yew commented:

> We agreed that we should also invite India, Australia and New Zealand and keep the center in ASEAN; also, India would be a *useful balance* to China's heft. This is a getting-together of countries that believe their economic and cultural relations will grow over the years. And this will be a restoration of two ancient civilizations: China and India. With their revival, their influence will again spread into Southeast Asia. It would mean great prosperity for the region, but could also mean a tussle for power. Therefore, we think it best that from the beginning, we bring all the parties in together. It's not Asians versus whites. Everybody knows Australia and New Zealand are close to the U.S. There shouldn't be any concern that this is an anti-American grouping. It's a *neater balance*.[155]
> (emphasis added)

This is, of course, a typical Singaporean position and language, reflecting its faith in the 'balance of power' to a degree not necessarily shared by other ASEAN members. But it underscores that the regional tendency is to use the term balancing in terms of their diplomatic ability to engage major powers, rather than in confrontational military terms.

One major and potentially ambiguous consequence of ASEAN's co-engagement strategy is a degree of competitive bidding it has engendered among the engaged powers. It has been argued that the Chinese charm offensive in Southeast Asia and its offer of regional economic integration reflected its own competitive instincts *vis-à-vis* the US and Japan. China

> did not want to stand by and watch ASEAN continue to weaken after the financial crisis. China's concern was that once ASEAN lost its capacity for independent action, it would turn to the United States.[156]

Realists warn that China is using its free trade deal with ASEAN to replace Japan as the primary driving force for regional economic growth and integration. At the same time, competing with Chinese influence in Southeast Asia has been one (but by no means the only or the most important) factor behind Japanese and Indian approaches to the region. For example, Japan closely followed China's proposal for an FTA with ASEAN with agreements of its own for economic partnership with ASEAN in 2002 and 2003. When China signed ASEAN's Treaty of Amity and Cooperation (TAC) in 2003, Japan was criticised by some domestic groups for being upstaged by China. Japan followed suit the following year. This prompted the comment that Japan's main motivation for signing the TAC, and its decision to offer a closer economic relationship agreement with ASEAN, were a desire 'not to fall too far behind China, which had signed TAC in 2003 and offered a FTA with ASEAN even earlier'.[157] India appears to be engaged in a similar bid for ASEAN. Its free trade proposal with China, as India's Ministry of External Affairs explained, 'was an effort to "upgrade" India's political partnership with ASEAN and "to bring it at par with" those with China and Japan'.[158] And India has consciously tried to cultivate the regime in Burma, largely in response to the growing Chinese influence there. However, Sino-Japanese competition in Southeast Asia should not be overstated. Japan's interest in Southeast Asia predates China's rise by a considerable margin, and is not a replay of any Cold War geopolitical rivalry. For example, Japan's support for ARF had nothing to do with China's influence or potential influence over the grouping. And India's own historical, economic and cultural links with Southeast Asia are important factors behind its engagement with ASEAN.

Moreover, competition with China by Japan and India is not without benefits for ASEAN's quest for regional order. It might check the occasional tendency in Japan to pursue strategic relations with the US at the expense of ASEAN or Asian multilateralism, as seemed likely for a while under the Koizumi government.[159] At the same time, none of these powers are in a position to supplant ASEAN as the 'driver' of Asian regionalism. ASEAN remains understandably keen to preserve its central role in Asian regionalism, assuming that being the institutional hub gives it a degree of influence over regional affairs that it could not otherwise muster through economic or military means. Although there are signs of growing dissatisfaction with the leadership of ASEAN in Asian regional institutions, moving away from ASEAN leadership is not going to be easy. Asia as a region has been traditionally inhospitable to Great Power-led regional institutions. Examples of such failure include the Indian-sponsored Asian Relations Organisation, the US-led South East Asia Treaty Organisation, and the Japanese and Australian backed Asia and Pacific Council. Neither China nor Japan would be acceptable as an outright leader of an Asian regional institution, not the least because of their mutual rivalry.

It is in this context that one should assess ASEAN countries' response to the US 'pivot' or 'rebalancing' strategy. The new strategy was announced by the Obama administration amidst its growing concern about China's military build-up and the impending US withdrawal from Iraq (later Afghanistan). The origin of the US pivot strategy is usually traced to US

President Obama's address to the Australian Parliament on 17 November 2011.[160] In this speech, Obama asserted that:

> With most of the world's nuclear power and some half of humanity, Asia will largely define whether the century ahead will be marked by conflict or cooperation . . . As President, I have, therefore, made a deliberate and strategic decision—as a Pacific nation, the United States will play a larger and long-term role in shaping this region and its future . . . I have directed my national security team to make our presence and mission in the Asia Pacific a top priority . . . As we plan and budget for the future, we will allocate the resources necessary to maintain our strong military presence in this region . . . we are already modernizing America's defense posture across the Asia Pacific. It will be more broadly distributed—maintaining our strong presence in Japan and the Korean Peninsula, while enhancing our presence in Southeast Asia. Our posture will be more flexible—with new capabilities to ensure that our forces can operate freely . . .[161]

The term 'pivot' soon came to be used interchangeably with 'rebalancing' mainly because the latter conveyed the adjustments more accurately and less controversially (without implying any major retreat from Europe or the Middle East, for example). Moreover, administration officials were careful to stress that the pivot was not just from Middle East to Asia, but also from Northeast Asia to Southeast Asia.[162] Under 'rebalancing', the US navy would shift from a 50/50 split between the Pacific and the Atlantic to a 60/40 split by 2020, including six aircraft carriers. The aim of rebalancing is to 'maintain a nuanced balance' against China while averting 'the potential for a . . . slippery slope toward growing confrontation with China'.[163] While the new US strategy faces budgetary challenges it also has significant bipartisan support. Although the rebalancing strategy was initially regarded as a mainly military redeployment posture, US officials soon came to present it as a more comprehensive posture including its engagement in multilateral institutions.

ASEAN countries have generally welcomed the US rebalancing policy as a useful indicator of the overall US engagement in the region at a time when China has grown increasingly assertive. However, there are fairly strong and widespread doubts in Southeast Asia as to whether the US can deliver on its rebalancing strategy, and sustain it over the long term, especially in view of its budgetary crisis and the long-term 'decline' of US power. Another concern is that rebalancing might provoke a strong Chinese reaction and spur US–China rivalry that might draw in ASEAN. Thus, Indonesia's Foreign Minister Marty Natalegawa has warned that 'too much rebalancing may be as bad as too little', an implicit warning to the US not to provoke China too much.

What about China's role in the evolving great power relationship in Asia? China's attitude and role is a central factor in shaping the future of ASEAN-led multilateral cooperation in Asia. Post-Cold War multilateralism in Asia was to a large extent inspired by the desire among its protagonists – ASEAN, Canada, Australia – to engage China. After a brief period of hesitancy, China has embraced ASEAN-based institutions, such as the ASEAN Regional Forum (ARF), ASEAN Plus Three (APT), and the East Asia Summit (EAS). But doubts have arisen over China's participation in these institutions. How they are answered will make the critical difference between their continuation and irrelevance.

First, some observers note that China's earlier enthusiasm for ASEAN-based institutions have waned, partly due to the escalation of the South China Sea dispute, in which China feels under pressure from ASEAN and the United States. While China remains actively engaged in them, there may be some sections in Chinese policymaking circles (officials as well as experts) who see multilateralism as a challenge to Chinese national interests. No one predicts a Chinese withdrawal from these institutions. But if China decides to downgrade its participation (how such a step might look is worth considering), these institutions would diminish their relevance.

Second, and closely related to the above, are the implications of the US entry into EAS, and more generally the Obama administration's 'pivot' or 'rebalancing' strategy, for China's participation in multilateralism in the Asia–Pacific. China regards the 'rebalancing' with much suspicion as a softer form of 'containment'. What sort of adjustment this might lead to in China's policy towards ASEAN-led institutions will be important in shaping the future of Asia–Pacific multilateralism.

Third, nearly two decades since it joined the ARF in 1994, China's position and purpose in Asia–Pacific multilateral institutions remains unclear. Initially, Beijing called for security multilateralism to remain focused on confidence-building, rather than embrace the more expansive, if not intrusive, tasks of preventive diplomacy and conflict resolution. Has this changed, or will it ever change. The status quo contributes to the perception of stagnation and ineffectiveness of the ASEAN-based institutions. It is not clear whether this is something China really wants to see? If not, what sort of strengthening might China want to undertake in them? In a related sense, does Beijing have a preference for some type of institutions over others? For example, analysts have suggested that Beijing would prefer to strengthen the APT over the EAS.

Conclusion

This chapter has addressed two questions: the extent to which the development of wider Asian multilateralism upheld the norms of ASEAN and the impact of the burdens imposed on ASEAN by its 'driver's' role in the ARF and in East Asian regionalism. ASEAN's role in promoting the ARF reflected its growing self-confidence about the relevance of its norms of regional cooperation. The ARF embraced ASEAN's norms, the Treaty of Amity and cooperation, and the ASEAN Way of institution building. While compromising on ZOPFAN, one aspect of its norm of regional autonomy, ASEAN was able to salvage it by assuming a central role in the development of the ARF.

To be sure, the ASEAN Way is not easily duplicated in the wider Asia–Pacific or East Asian milieu. The advent of the ARF represents a significant broadening of ASEAN's hitherto inward-looking and subregional political and security agenda. But the critics of the ARF may be too quick to pronounce judgment on ASEAN-led multilateralism. Multilateralism may turn out to be much more than an 'adjunct' to balance of power mechanisms. In the short term, the ARF may help shape the balance of power by providing norms of restraint and avenues of confidence-building among the major powers. In the long term, the ARF and East Asian regionalism may even enable states to transcend the balance of power approach. The latter possibility, if remote, does exist and cannot be ignored in any serious consideration of prospects for regional security in the Asia-Pacific region.

'The significance of our efforts', wrote Adam Malik in 1975 in a perceptive commentary on the future of regionalism in Southeast Asia, lies in 'working for peace in Southeast Asia that is not only founded on the stability of a balance but is sourced in a sense of shared aspirations and common destiny.'[164] The statement neatly reflects ASEAN's achievements and dilemmas in anchoring a new multilateral security framework for the Asia-Pacific region. ASEAN's faith in the balance of power approach has been shaken over the past decades by the declining credibility of external security guarantees and a realisation of the dangers and uncertainties inherent in the system. At the same time, the ideal of cooperative security and collective identity building to be attained through a multilateral framework remains a distant, if not altogether elusive, goal. As a result, ASEAN countries have been obliged to reconcile their quiet adherence to the mechanisms of a balance of power system with an enthusiastic promotion of the East Asian regionalism. This posture is not likely to disappear for some time; but it does not preclude the development of a security community in the wider East Asian and Asia-Pacific region.

Some analysts see Asia's emerging multipolarity as a dangerous development, especially compared to Cold War bipolarity. One strand of theory, neo-realism, argues that multipolar systems tend to be more prone to war than bipolar systems. Having only two main actors holding each other in check allows for a simpler and more predictable pattern of alliances and interactions, whereas a multipolar environment would be more complex and chaotic. They contrast Europe's nineteenth- and early-twentieth century multipolarity – a highly unstable period culminating in two world wars – with the 'long peace' of the post-World War Two bipolar era. From this perspective, Asia's emerging multipolarity might mean Europe's past could be Asia's future. Others, especially liberal and constructivist theorists, do not see any necessary correlation between bipolarity and conflict, and some even argue that multipolar interactions can induce stability by creating more opportunities for alignments and interactions. After all, rising powers with aggressive intentions would have to contend with more than one potentially countervailing power.

This debate remains unsettled to date, but has implications for ASEAN's long-term future. ASEAN was to some extent the product of a bipolar era, with the US and the USSR shaping the regional balance of power through their forward military presence and alignments (US with Japan, South Korea, Thailand and the Philippines, Republic of China, Australia and New Zealand; and the USSR with Communist China – before the Sino-Soviet split – Vietnam, and India). Moreover, ASEAN emerged at a time when the three indigenous Asian powers, Japan, China and India, were all unwilling or unable to assume serious regional leadership. India had lost influence in Southeast Asia following the 1962 defeat at the hand of China, and was otherwise distracted by domestic problems and its rivalry with Pakistan. Mao's China was mired in its Cultural Revolution, and was viewed with intense suspicion by its neighbours because of its support (until the late 1970s) for communist insurgencies in Southeast Asia. Japan, although re-emerging by the 1960s from its World War Two defeat with an increasingly powerful economy, was not seen as an acceptable regional leader due to persisting memories over its wartime role, as well as fears over its economic dominance. Realising this, Japanese governments abstained from seeking or taking on any major independent regional political role.

Such a situation gave ASEAN a double opening. First, the Cold War stalemate between the US and the USSR gave ASEAN a margin of freedom to pursue its own economic and security goals (which included a relatively non-aligned posture through its Zone of Peace, Freedom and Neutrality framework) without being molested by superpower intervention. At the same time, the predicaments of China, India and Japan gave ASEAN the space to develop its own brand of regionalism, the ASEAN Way, without being overshadowed by the traditional Asian great powers.

While the rise of China and India and the gradual erosion of anti-Japanese sentiments in Southeast Asia (although not necessarily in China and Korea) do not automatically translate into a capacity for them, either individually or collectively, to lead regional institutions,[165] it does give them a much greater ability to shape regional order. It narrows ASEAN's margin of autonomy and challenges its capacity to 'lead' Asian regional institutions. Some Southeast

Asians wonder whether the re-emergence of China and India will return Southeast Asia to its historical predicament as an appendage of the two historically important civilizations and marginalise it politically and economically. Moreover, with five great powers engaged in the competition and balancing, ASEAN might find itself facing difficult dilemmas in deciding and coordinating how to engage them individually and collectively over different issue areas.

Another future for ASEAN – an equally unpromising one at that – would be a coming together of the great powers into some sort of a concert, akin to the European Concert of Powers established after the Napoleonic wars in the nineteenth century. Such a concert, a subset of which could be a Sino-US condominium, would entail their joint management of regional political and security affairs, aside from economic dominance. As a well-known saying in Southeast Asia goes, 'when the elephants fight, the grass suffers, when the elephants make love, the grass also suffers.' An Asian concert of powers involving China, the US, Japan and India would marginalise the weak, as the European Concert did in the nineteenth century. That would make ASEAN centrality and leadership a thing of the past.

These developments need not doom ASEAN, but they will severely test its political maturity and foresight. Coping with the global and regional power shift would require a measure of cohesion and purpose in dealing with the great powers of the region that would determine whether ASEAN could retain its centrality or sinks into irrelevance.

Notes and references

1 *Jakarta Post*, 9 September 1989.
2 *Straits Times*, 28 August 1992, p. 4.
3 In addition to the 11 per cent cuts from an original strength of 135,000 personnel (including 25,000 on board ships) envisaged under EASI-I, 8,100 personnel were withdrawn from the Philippines. A further reduction of about 10 per cent was planned for the second phase of EASI (1993–95). Susumu Awanohara, 'America's Easi Options', *Far Eastern Economic Review*, 3 September 1992, p. 23.
4 'Too Committed to Withdraw from Asia', Interview with Admiral Charles Larson, Commander-in-Chief, US Pacific Command, *Asia-Pacific Defence Reporter* (August–September 1992), p. 33.
5 William T. Pendley, 'US Security Strategy in East Asia for the 1990s', *Strategic Review*, vol. 20, no. 3 (Summer 1992), pp. 12–13. Mr Pendley served as the Deputy Assistant Secretary of State for East Asia and Pacific Affairs under the Bush administration.
6 The former Foreign Minister of Indonesia, Mochtar Kusuma-Atmadja, referred to these countries as 'the emerging powers in Asia with hegemonistic ambitions'. See his 'Some Thoughts on ASEAN Security Co-operation', *Contemporary Southeast Asia*, vol. 12, no. 3 (December 1990), p. 168.
7 *Straits Times*, 10 February 1990.
8 Interview with *Far Eastern Economic Review*, 'Live and Let Live', 11 July 1991, p. 13.
9 Lee Kuan Yew in *Straits Times Weekly Overseas Edition*, 14 November 1992, p. 24.
10 For a critique, see: Geoffrey Wiseman, 'Common Security in the Asia-Pacific Region', *Pacific Review*, vol. 5, no. 2 (1992).
11 For an analysis see: Amitav Acharya, 'The Asia-Pacific Region: Cockpit for Superpower Rivalry?', *World Today*, vol. 43, nos 8–9 (August–September 1987), pp. 155–58.
12 Cited in ibid.
13 Although the initial articulation of this concept seemed to mirror a number of key aspects of 'common security', Canadian scholars subsequently argued it to be a distinct notion. Among the similarities between the two notions is their common rejection of deterrence-based security systems and a related emphasis on collective problem-solving mechanisms over balance of power approaches. In addition, both approaches defined 'security' broadly and comprehensively to incorporate both military and non-military issues. Canadian statements on 'cooperative security' have consistently included issues ranging from arms proliferation and peacekeeping to illegal immigration, drug trafficking, environmental degradation, refugees and population growth. But

a more distinctive aspect of 'cooperative security' was its recognition of the need for a more gradualist approach to institution building, in contrast to the broad-brush approach of 'common security'. While allowing for the creation of new multilateral institutions, the Canadian protagonists of cooperative security stressed the need to retain the existing bilateral alliances involving the USA as a useful complement to the former. David B. Dewitt, 'Common, Comprehensive and Cooperative Security', *Pacific Review*, vol. 7, no. 1 (1994), pp. 1–15; Stewart Henderson, 'Zone of Uncertainty: Canada and the Security Architecture of Asia-Pacific', *Canadian Foreign Policy*, vol. 1, no. 1 (Winter 1992/93).

14 The NPCSD was organised on two tracks, a governmental track involving discussions among policy planning staff (Track-I), and a non-governmental track involving both academic and official experts (with the participating officials acting in their private capacity, although this distinction was quickly blurred). The North Pacific scope of the NPCSD was based on the premise that the Asia Pacific region was 'simply too vast and diverse to fit into any one conceptual mould'. But while a subregional framework for multilateralism seemed more practical than the macro-regional framework envisaged by the Australian and Soviet proposals, it also excluded ASEAN and Australia, the other key players in the regional security debate. The Canadian initiative did, however, have one useful effect on ASEAN. The NPCSD, being probably the first multilateral security consultation (even if semi-official) within the region with explicit government backing, might have added a sense of urgency to ASEAN's own ideas about regional security consultations. Certainly, it impressed on ASEAN the need to respond to the growing number of proposals from 'outsiders' which, if pursued, would deeply affect security management in ASEAN's own geostrategic environment. The other contribution of the NPCSD was in developing the so-called 'Track-II' channel which turned out to be the more developed segment of the two-track approach. The series of NPCSD workshops held during the period 1991–93 generated considerable policy-relevant debate and increasingly sophisticated ideas about the objectives and instruments of multilateralism. Amitav Acharya, David Dewitt and Paul Evans, 'Overview: The Agenda for Cooperative Security in the North Pacific', in David Dewitt and Paul Evans (eds), *The Agenda for Cooperative Security in the North Pacific* (Toronto: York University Centre for International and Strategic Studies, 1992), Appendix II.

15 For an extensive discussion of the implications of the 1992 ASEAN summit, see: Amitav Acharya, *A New Regional Order in Southeast Asia: ASEAN in the Post-Cold War Era*, Adelphi Paper no. 279 (London: International Institute for Strategic Studies, 1993).

16 Excerpts from Lee Kuan Yew's interview with the Australian, published in *Straits Times*, 16 September 1988. See also: Michael Vatikiotis, 'Yankee Please Stay', *Far Eastern Economic Review*, 13 December 1990, p. 32.

17 *Straits Times*, 10 July 1991.

18 Whether the idea of using the ASEAN-PMC as a vehicle for regional security dialogue was an ASEAN idea is a matter of some debate. The controversy stems from the fact that the first official-level proposal for using the PMC for security discussions was made by the Foreign Minister of Japan, Taro Nakayama. Speaking at the ASEAN Foreign Ministers Meeting in Kuala Lumpur in July 1991, Nakayama stated that the ASEAN-PMC could be used for 'a process of political discussions designed to improve the sense of security among us'. Cited in Michael Vatikiotis, 'The New Player', *Far Eastern Economic Review*, 1 August 1991, p. 11. There is some controversy about who was first to conceive the idea of using the ASEAN-PMC as a vehicle for regional security dialogues. While the Japanese Foreign Minister was the first senior government leader to propose the idea formally, this should not detract from the role of ASEAN-ISIS in developing and debating the idea initially. It is fair to say that the idea originated in non-governmental discussions in which members of ASEAN-ISIS played an important role. Indeed, the proposal for security dialogue (including the idea of using the ASEAN-PMC for security consultations) contained in the ASEAN-ISIS report 'A Time for Initiative' was discussed at an ASEAN-ISIS meeting in Jakarta on 2–4 June 1991, well before the Nakayama proposal was made at the ASEAN-PMC on 22 July 1991. See: Pauline Kerr, 'The Security Dialogue in the Asia-Pacific', *Pacific Review*, vol. 7, no. 4 (1994), p. 402. Moreover, the ideas proposed by ASEAN-ISIS were further discussed at a conference organised by the Foreign Ministries of the Philippines and Thailand in Manila on 5–7 June 1991, entitled 'ASEAN and the Asia-Pacific Region: Prospects for Security Cooperation in the 1990s'.

    ASEAN-ISIS sources generally attribute the Nakayama initiative to a senior Japanese Foreign Ministry official, Yukio Satoh, who participated in the Manila meeting in June 1991. According to

Lam Peng Er, a Singaporean expert on Japanese foreign policy, 'Apparently, Satoh informed his ministry about the discussions and it was refined and repackaged as "Nakayama's Initiatives".' Moreover, Lam argues that 'proposals from Tokyo about the ARF should be more accurately known as "Satoh's Initiatives"'. Lam Peng Er, 'Japan and Conflict Management in Pacific Asia', Paper presented to the Conference on 'Japan and Regionalism: The Bases of Trust and Leadership', organised by the Faculty of Asian and International Studies, Griffith University, Brisbane, Australia, 8–9 January 1998, p. 12.

19 Jane A. Morse, 'U.S. Pleased with ASEAN's Attention to Regional Security', *Wireless File (East Asia, and Pacific)* (Singapore: United States Information Service), 24 July 1992, p. 8; *Asian Wall Street Journal*, 23 July 1992.

20 Earlier, in a landmark June 1991 report entitled 'A Time for Initiative', which articulated ideas already mooted and discussed in ASEAN-ISIS circles for some months, ASEAN-ISIS proposed that the annual meetings of ASEAN Foreign Ministers with their dialogue partners should be followed by a 'Conference on Stability and Peace in the Asia Pacific'. The meeting, to be held at 'a suitable retreat . . . for the constructive discussion of Asia Pacific stability and peace' would comprise such states as China, Russia, North Korea and Vietnam on a regular basis, while other governments could be invited from time to time depending on the nature of the issues on the conference agenda. See: 'A Time for Initiative', *ISEAN-ISIS Monitor*, no. 1 (July 1991), pp. 2–3. See also: Lau Teik Soon, 'Towards a Regional Security Conference: Role of the Non-Government Organizations', Working Papers no. 1 (Department of Political Science, National University of Singapore, 1991). ASEAN Institutes for Strategic and International Studies (ASEAN-ISIS), *Confidence Building Measures in Southeast Asia*, Memorandum no. 5 (December 1993).

21 The founding members of CSCAP included: five think-tank members of ASEAN-ISIS, plus the Strategic and Defence Studies Centre, Australian National University, Australia; the University of Toronto–York University Joint Centre for Asia Pacific Studies, Canada; the Japan Institute for International Affairs, Japan; the Seoul Forum for International Affairs, South Korea; and Pacific Forum/CSIS, USA. Subsequently, government-affiliated think-tanks from North Korea and Vietnam became members. China became a member in 1996 after winning concessions from the CSCAP members regarding Taiwan's participation (under the compromise formula, Taiwan would not be a formal member of CSCAP, but Taiwanese representatives, who must be approved by China, could participate in CSCAP meetings as individuals at the invitation of CSCAP co-chairs). Another condition imposed by China is that Taiwan Strait security issues must not be discussed within CSCAP. China had opposed Taiwanese membership in CSCAP by drawing a spurious distinction between CSCAP, which it claimed was not a strictly non-governmental group, and non-governmental Pacific economic groupings such as the Pacific Economic Cooperation Council (PECC), of which Taiwan was a full member. Finally, India was accepted as an associate member. Despite the problem with Taiwanese membership, CSCAP can claim to be more inclusive than the ARF.

22 Paul Evans, 'The Dialogue Process on Asia Pacific Security Issues: Inventory and Analysis', *Studying Asia Pacific Security – The Future of Research, Training and Dialogue* (Toronto: University of Toronto/York University Joint Centre for Asian Pacific Studies 1994), p. 314.

23 *New Straits Times*, 3 February 1988.

24 *Straits Times* (Editorial), 1 February 1992.

25 Keynote address by Ali Alatas to the United Nations Regional Disarmament Workshop for Asia and Pacific, in *Disarmament* (New York: United Nations Department for Disarmament Affairs, 1991), p. 14.

26 Bilveer Singh, *ZOPFAN and the New Security Order in Asia-Pacific* (Petaling Jaya: Pelanduk Publications, 1991), p. 98.

27 *Straits Times*, 31 December 1990.

28 Interview with *Far Eastern Economic Review*, 'Live and Let Live', 11 July 1991, p. 13.

29 Amitav Acharya and J.D. Kenneth Boutin, 'The Southeast Asia Nuclear Weapon-Free Zone', *Security Dialogue*, vol. 29, no. 2 (June 1998), pp. 219–30.

30 David B. Dewitt, 'Common, Comprehensive and Cooperative Security', *Pacific Review*, vol. 7, no. 1 (1994).

31 Peter Ho Hak Ean, 'The ASEAN Regional Forum: The Way Forward', Paper presented to the Third Workshop on ASEAN–UN Cooperation in Peace and Preventive Diplomacy, Bangkok, 17–18 February 1994.

32 *Straits Times*, 4 August 1994, p. 2.

33 'ARF: S'pore proposes a gradual approach', *Straits Times*, 23 July 1994, p. 1.

34 *Business Times (Malaysia)*, 30 July 1994; 'N. Korea not yet ready for security forum, U.S. says', Kyodo News Service, Japan Economic Newswire, 29 July 1994.

35 'Chairman's Statement: The First Meeting of the ASEAN Regional Forum (ARF), 25 July 1994, Bangkok', p. 2.

36 Desmond Ball, 'A Critical Review of Multilateral Security Cooperation in the Asia-Pacific Region', Paper presented to the Inaugural Conference of the Asia-Pacific Security Forum on the Impetus of Change in the Asia-Pacific Security Environment, Taipei, 1–3 September 1997, pp. 16–17.

37 Yang Razali Kassim, 'Minister: Asean will always have driver's seat in forum', *Business Times*, 25 July 1994, p. 3.

38 'The ASEAN Regional Forum: A Concept Paper' (ASEANSEC).

39 *Sydney Morning Herald*, 28 July 1994.

40 Amitav Acharya, 'The ARF Could Well Unravel', in Derek Da Cunha (ed.), *The Evolving Pacific Power Balance* (Singapore: Institute of Southeast Asian Studies, 1996), pp. 63–9.

41 Ball, 'A Critical Review of Multilateral Security Cooperation in the Asia-Pacific Region', p. 16.

42 For a detailed review of the evolution of CBMs in the Asia-Pacific region with particular reference to the ARF, see: Amitav Acharya, *The ASEAN Regional Forum: Confidence-Building* (Ottawa: Department of Foreign Affairs and International Trade, 1997). This was circulated as an official Canadian document at the Beijing ARF ISG meeting on CBMs in March 1997.

43 Glen Sheppy, 'ARF Meeting of the Inter-Sessional Support Group on Confidence-Building Measures', *CANCAPS Bulletin*, no. 15 (November 1997), pp. 13–14.

44 Glenn Sheppy, 'ARF IV: Moving Beyond a "Talk Shop" ', *CANCAPS Bulletin*, no. 14 (August 1997), p. 12.

45 Amitav Acharya, 'Preventive Diplomacy: Concept, Theory and Strategy', in Desmond Ball and Amitav Acharya (eds), *The Next Stage: Preventive Diplomacy and Security Cooperation in the Asia-Pacific Region* (Canberra: Strategic and Defence Studies Centre, Australian National University, 1999), pp. 93–115.

46 The working definition of preventive diplomacy was hammered out at a back-to-back CSCAP Seminar on Preventive Diplomacy and an ARF ISG on CBMs, held in Bangkok on 28 February–2 March, and 3–5 March, 1999 respectively. The author participated in the CSCAP Seminar as a Canadian delegate and was part of a drafting committee on the definition of PD, which included members of the Chinese, Australian, Japanese, Indonesian and US CSCAP Committees. The definition of PD was adapted after modifications, from a 1996 essay by the author, which defined PD as:

> Action (diplomatic, political, military, economic and humanitarian) taken by governments, multilateral (the UN as well as regional groups) organisations and international agencies (including non-governmental actors) with the aim of:
>   preventing severe disputes and conflicts from arising between and within states;
>   preventing such disputes and conflicts from escalating into armed confrontation;
>   limiting the intensity of violence resulting from such conflicts and preventing it from spreading geographically;
>   preventing and managing acute humanitarian crises associated with (either as the cause or the effect) such conflicts.

At the Bangkok CSCAP meeting, the Chinese member of the drafting committee (a retired ambassador) vigorously objected to defining the scope of PD as including disputes and conflicts 'between and within states', saying that it was sure to be rejected by the Chinese government. Moreover, reference to any military action was deleted in favour of 'consensual diplomatic and political action'. The definition worked out by the CSCAP was adopted by the ARF ISG on CBMs, and was then reviewed by the member states before being part of the Singapore-drafted concept paper in 2000. The earlier essays by the author are: Amitav Acharya, 'Preventive Diplomacy: The Concept and Its Evolution in the Asia Pacific Region', in *Proceedings of the Eighth Asia Pacific Roundtable* (Kuala Lumpur: Institute of Strategic and International Studies, 1996); and Acharya, 'Preventive Diplomacy: Concept, Theory, and Strategy', paper presented to the International Conference on 'Preventive Diplomacy for Peace and Security in the Western Pacific', jointly sponsored by the 21st Century Foundation and the Pacific Forum CSIS, Taipei, Taiwan, 29–31 August 1996. Both these papers appear as chapters in Desmond Ball and Amitav Acharya, (eds.),

The Next Stage: Preventive Diplomacy and Security Cooperation in the Asia-Pacific Region (Canberra: Strategic and Defence Studies Centre, Australian National University, 1999).

47 'ASEAN Regional Forum: Concept and Principles of Preventive Diplomacy', 25 July 2001 (ASEANSEC).

48 'Chairman's Statement: The Tenth Meeting of the ASEAN Regional Forum', 18 June 2003 (ASEANSEC).

49 'Co-Chairman's Summary Report of the ARF Experts' Group Meeting (EGM) on Transnational Crime', 30–31 October 2000 (ASEANSEC).

50 *Straits Times*, 19 June 2003.

51 Ibid.

52 'Co-Chairs' Summary Report of the Third ASEAN Regional Forum Inter-Sessional Meeting on Counter-Terrorism and Transnational Crime', 6–8 April 2005 (ASEANSEC).

53 'Co-Chairs' Summary Report of the Meeting of the ASEAN Regional Forum Inter-Sessional Support Group on Confidence Building Measures and Preventive Diplomacy', 1–3 March (ASEANSEC).

54 'Co-Chairs' Summary Report of the Meeting of the ASEAN Regional Forum Inter-Sessional Support Group on Confidence Building Measures', 26–28 October 2004 (ASEANSEC).

55 'Report of the ARF Inter-Sessional Meeting on Counter-Terrorism and Transnational Crime', 21–22 March 2003 (ASEANSEC).

56 'Co-Chairs' Summary Report of the Meeting of the ASEAN Regional Forum Inter-Sessional Support Group on Confidence Building Measures', 26–28 March 2003 (ASEANSEC).

57 Source: www.aseanregionalforum.org/PublicLibrary/ARFActivities/ListofARF TrackIIActivities/tabid/95/Default.aspx (accessed 15 June 2008).

58 *Daily Yomiuri* (Tokyo), 22 July 2002, p. 1.

59 'Chairman's Summary Report of the 5th ARF Security Policy Conference', Singapore, 8 May 2008. Available www1.apan-info.net/DesktopModules/Bring2mind/DMX/Download.aspx?TabId =3368&DMXModule=11167&Command=Core_Download&EntryId=14673&PortalId=59 (accessed 13 June 2008).

60 'ASEAN: Regional Forum Adopts Counterterrorism Work Plan; Rules for Emergency Group Also Approved,' Available at: http://www.loc.gov/lawweb/servlet/lloc_news?disp3_l205401481_ text (accessed 1 September 2013).

61 U.S. Department of State, 'ASEAN Regional Forum (ARF) to Hold First Disaster Relief Exercise in the Philippines,' Media Note, 6 April 2009, Available at http://www.state.gov/r/pa/prs/ps/2009/04/121338.htm (accessed 1 September 2013)

62 ASEAN Secretariat, 'ASEAN Regional Forum Gears Up for a Stronger Civil Military Coordination and Disaster Relief Operation,' 13 May 2013 Available at: http://www.asean.org/news/asean-secretariat-news/item/asean-regional-forum-gears-up-for-a-stronger-civil-military-coordination-and-disaster-relief-operation (accessed 1 Sept 2013).

63 'Asian security forum to adopt rules for quick-reaction group,' Available at http://aseanregionalforum. asean.org/index/31-asian-security-forum-to-adopt-rules-for-quick-reaction-group.html (accessed 1 September 2013)

64 'China Looks Abroad', *The Economist*, 29 April 1995, p. 17.

65 *Bangkok Post* Weekly Review, 5 August 1994, p. 7.

66 Michael Leifer, *The ASEAN Regional Forum*, Adelphi Paper no. 302 (London: International Institute for Strategic Studies, 1996), p. 55.

67 Ibid., pp. 57–8.

68 Interview with *Far Eastern Economic Review*, 'Live and Let Live', 11 July 1991, p. 13.

69 This distinction is not conceptually new in the theoretical literature on international relations, although it is often ignored in policy-oriented discourse. Most scholars of balance of power distinguish between balance of power as 'a mere factual description of the distribution of political power in the international scene' and balance of power as 'a theoretical principle acting as a guide to foreign policy-making . . . so that the preponderance of any one state may be avoided'. Ernst B. Haas, 'The Balance of Power: Prescription, Concept or Propaganda', in Robert L. Pfaltzgraff, Jr (ed.), *Politics and the International System* (Philadelphia: J.B. Lippincott, 1969), p. 386. Two of the four meanings of the term balance of power mentioned by Morgenthau are that (1) 'as a policy aimed at a certain state of affairs', and (2) 'as an actual state of affairs'. Hans Morgenthau, *Politics among Nations*, 3rd edition (New York: Knopf, 1960), p. 167. Inis Claude also called for

the separation of balance of power as a 'situation' from balance of power as a 'policy'. Inis L. Claude, *Power and International Relations* (New York: Random House, 1962), pp. 13–25. Elsewhere, Claude warns against abuse of the concept:

> too often they fail to distinguish between balance of power as a situation of equilibrium and as a system of states engaged in competitive manipulation of power relationships among themselves. This means that we cannot be certain whether we are being asked to welcome a result or to accept the claim that a certain mechanism is reliably conducive to that result. It sometimes appears that this vagueness is designed to encourage the fallacy that might be described as a 'solution by labelling': the assumption that a scheme designated as a balance of power system necessarily produces and maintains a balance of power.

(Inis L. Claude, 'The Balance of Power Revisited', *Review of International Studies*, vol. 15 (1989), p. 77.)

70   The traditional US position has been that the scope of the US–Philippine Mutual Defense Treaty commits the USA to the defence of the 'metropolitan territory' of the Philippines and does not include the Philippine positions in the Spratlys. But in a letter to the Philippine Foreign Minister in January 1979, US Secretary of State Cyrus Vance stated that an attack on the Philippine armed forces 'would not have to occur within the metropolitan territory of the Philippines or island territories under its jurisdiction in the Pacific in order to come within the definition of Pacific area in Article V of the US–Philippine Mutual Defense Treaty'. Larry A. Niksch, *The South China Sea Dispute*, CRS Report for the Congress 95–934 F (Washington, D.C.: Congressional Research Service, Library of Congress, 29 August 1995), p. 6.

71   *Straits Times Weekly Edition*, 20 November 1993, p. 5.

72   Amitav Acharya, 'A Concert of Asia?', *Survival*, vol. 41, no. 3 (Autumn 1999), pp. 84–101.

73   Gareth Evans, 'Asia Pacific in the Twenty-First Century: Conflict or Cooperation', *World Today*, vol. 52, no. 2 (February 1996), p. 52.

74   'East Asia after the Taiwan Crisis', *Strategic Comments*, vol. 2, no. 3, 12 April 1996, p. 2.

75   'Asian Security in the 1990s: Integration in Economics: Diversity in Defense', speech by Richard Solomon, Assistant Secretary of State for East Asian and Pacific Affairs, at the University of San Diego, 30 October 1990, excerpts published US Department of State Dispatch, 5 November 1990.

76   *Straits Times*, 7 August 1991.

77   James A. Baker, 'America in Asia: Emerging Architecture for a Pacific Community', *Foreign Affairs*, vol. 70, no. 5 (Winter 1991/92), p. 5.

78   Susumu Awanohara, 'Group Therapy', *Far Eastern Economic Review*, 15 April 1993, pp. 10–11.

79   Statement by the US Secretary of State Warren Christopher at the ASEAN Post-Ministerial Conference, Singapore, 26 July 1993, p. 3.

80   Banning Garrett and Bonnie Glaser, 'Multilateral Security in the Asia-Pacific Region and its Impact on Chinese Interests: Views from Beijing', *Contemporary Southeast Asia*, vol. 16, no. 1 (June 1994), p. 14.

81   Chen Jian, 'Challenges and Responses in East Asia', speech by HE Chen Jian, Assistant Foreign Minister of China, at First CSCAP General Meeting, Singapore, 4 June 1997, p. 11.

82   Ibid., p. 9.

83   Kuniko Ashizawa, 'Australia–Japan–U.S. Trilateral Security Dialogue and the ARF: Extended Bilateralism or a New Minilateral Option?' (draft paper, 2008), pp. 14–16. See also, Takeshi Yuzawa, 'The Evolution of Preventive Diplomacy in the ASEAN Regional Forum: Problems and Prospects', *Asian Survey*, vol. 46, no. 5 (2006), pp. 785–804.

84   For details, see: Takeshi Yuzawa, *Japan's Security Policy and the ASEAN Regional Forum: The Search for Multilateral Security in the Asia-Pacific* (London: Routledge, 2007).

85   Ibid., p. 158.

86   'India and the ARF' (New Delhi: Ministry of External Affairs). Available meaindia.nic.in/onmouse/ arf1.htm (accessed 7 July 2008).

87   Ibid.

88   James A. Baker III, with Thomas M. DeFrank, *The Politics of Diplomacy: Revolution, War, and Peace, 1989–1992* (New York: G.P. Putnam's Sons, 1995).

89   Richard Stubbs, 'ASEAN Plus Three: Emerging East Asian Regionalism?', *Asian Survey*, vol. 42, no. 3 (2002), p. 449.

90   Ibid.

91 *Towards an East Asian Community: Region of Peace, Prosperity and Progress*, East Asia Vision Group Report, 2001.
92 Final Report of the East Asia Study Group, 4 November 2002.
93 'Towards a Borderless Asia: A Perspective on Asian Economic Integration', speech by Haruhiko Kuroda, President Asian Development Bank, at the Emerging Markets Forum, 10 December 2005, Oxford, UK Available www.adb.org/Documents/Speeches/2005/ms2005088.asp#_ftn3 (accessed 14 May 2006).
94 Takashi Isogai and Shunichi Shibanuma, 'East Asia's Intra-and Inter-Regional Economic Relations; Data Analyses on Trade, Direct Investments and Currency Transactions', Bank of Japan Working Paper, 2000. Available: www.boj.or.jp/en/ type/ronbun/ron/wps/kako/iwp00e04.htm (accessed 14 May 2006).
95 G. John Ikenberry, *After Victory: Institutions, Strategic Restraint, and the Rebuilding of Order after Major Wars* (Princeton, NJ: Princeton University Press, 2001).
96 *Straits Times*, 5 November 2005.
97 *Agence France Presse*, 6 September 2005.
98 ABC Online, 7 December 2005.
99 *Yomuri Shimbun* (Tokyo), 25 November 2005.
100 *Straits Times*, 5 November 2005.
101 Takashi Shiraishi, 'Insights into the World/ East Asian Community Won't Hurt U.S. Interests', *Daily Yomiuri*, 4 September 2005.
102 Cited in 'Asia Craves EU-Style Integration, Lacks Clarity', Andy Mukherjee, Bloomberg.com.
103 Bernard Gordon, 'The FTA Fetish', *Wall Street Journal*, 17 November 2005, p. A.16.
104 Dana Robert Dillon, 'Watching the East Asian Summit', *The Heritage Foundation Policy Research and Analysis*, 18 August 2005, p. 1.
105 Cited in Termsak Chalermpalanupap, 'Towards an East Asian Community: The Journey Had Begun'. Available: www.aseansec.org. 13203.htm
106 *Bernama Daily Malaysian News*, 3 October 2005.
107 *Agence France Presse*, 23 October 2005.
108 *Kyodo News*, 9 November 2005.
109 *Financial Express*, 9 November 2005.
110 Amitav Acharya, 'Competing Communities: What the Australian and Japanese Ideas Mean for Asia's Regional Architecture,' *PacNet*, No. 70, 27 October 2009.
111 Text at http://voices.washingtonpost.com/checkpoint-washington/2010/09/clinton_declares_an_american_m.html, accessed 18 August 2013.
112 The following section draws from David Capie and Amitav Acharya, 'East Asia Summit: US Participation Signals a New Beginning,' *The Straits Times,* 19 November 2011.
113 Michael Vatikiotis, 'Permanent Presence', *Far Eastern Economic Review*, 16 January 1992, p. 22.
114 *Straits Times*, 17 April 1992.
115 Notable joint activities include the annual *Mekar* exercises involving the US Navy and the Malaysian air and naval forces; and reported exercises involving US ground forces in the Malaysian jungle warfare facility at Ulu Tiram. Jeffrey D. Young, *U.S. Military Interaction with Southeast Asian Countries* (CRS Report no. 92–241F) (Washington, D.C.: Congressional Research Service, Library of Congress, 1992), p. 12.
116 *Straits Times*, 10 April 1992; *Straits Times*, 14 April 1992.
117 *Straits Times*, 25 July 1991.
118 Jeffrey D. Young, *U.S. Military Interaction with Southeast Asian Countries* (CRS Report no. 92–241F) (Washington, D.C.: Congressional Research Service, Library of Congress, 1992), p. 14.
119 *Straits Times*, 10 April 1992.
120 Cameron Stewart, 'Alliance Secures Coastline Defences', *Australian*, 15 December 1995, p. 5. While the Australian government strongly denied that the treaty was directed against any 'third party', the strategic orientation of the Indonesia–Australia agreement, before the East Timor crisis in 1999, was evident in their subsequent decision to cooperate in defending Indonesia's oil-rich Natuna Islands, an area that lies inside jurisdictions claimed in the past by Beijing. Alan Dupont argued that the Australia–Indonesia security treaty was 'predicated on the notion of shared security interests rather than defence against common threats'. Alan Dupont, 'The Australia–Indonesia Security Agreement', *Australian Quarterly*, vol. 68, no. 2 (1996), pp. 49–50. It would appear that the treaty was of greater significance to Australia than to Indonesia. As an Australian commentator

observed, it was Australia's first Asian security treaty for 25 years (the previous one had been the Five Power Defence Arrangements); its first 'reciprocal security treaty' with an Asian country; and its first security treaty with a country with which it had in the past been involved in direct physical combat (during the *Konfrontasi*). In terms of its strategic importance, the treaty was said to be next to the Australia–US alliance under the ANZUS Treaty. Ibid., p. 52.

121 'Facts about the U.S.–Philippines Visiting Forces Agreement', US Embassy, Manila, 20 January 2006. Available: manila.usembassy.gov/wwwhr711.html (accessed 14 June 2008).

122 Sonny Africa, 'US Military Presence in Southeast Asia: Safeguarding Regional Interests,' Available at info.ibon.org/index.php?option=com_content&task=view&id=46&Itemid=50 (accessed 4 June 2008).

123 Statement of Admiral William J. Fallon, U.S. Navy Commander U.S. Pacific Command, Before the Senate Armed Services Committee on the U.S. Pacific Command Posture, 8 March 2005. Available: www.shaps.hawaii.edu/security/us/2005/20050308_fallon.html (accessed 14 June 2008).

124 Amitav Acharya, *Singapore's Foreign Policy: The Search for Regional Order* (Singapore: World Scientific, 2007).

125 Ambassador James Keith, 'U.S.–Malaysia Security Relations and the East Asian Region', Speech at the Armed Forces Defense College, Kuala Lumpur 16 April 2008. Available: malaysia.usembassy.gov/speeches/ambspeech_041608.pdf (accessed 14 June 2008).

126 U.S. Pacific Command Public Affairs, 25 May 2006. Available: www.pacom.mil/news/news2006/060420cobragold.shtml (accessed 15 June 2008).

127 Statement of Admiral William J. Fallon, U.S. Navy Commander U.S. Pacific Command, Before the Senate Armed Services Committee on the U.S. Pacific Command Posture, 8 March 2005. Available: www.shaps.hawaii.edu/security/us/2005/20050308_fallon.html (accessed 14 June 2008).

128 U.S. Department of State, Office of the Spokesman, 4 January 2006. Available: news.findlaw.com/wash/s/20060105/20060105140725.html (accessed 14 June 2008).

129 'Guide to U.S. Security Assistance to Indonesia and East Timor' (revised April 2008). Available: www.etan.org/news/2007/milglossary.htm

130 Statement of Admiral William J. Fallon, U.S. Navy Commander U.S. Pacific Command, Before the Senate Armed Services Committee on the U.S. Pacific Command Posture, 8 March 2005, p.23. Available: www.shaps.hawaii.edu/security/us/2005/20050308_fallon.html (accessed 14 June 2008).

131 Admiral Dennis C. Blair, 'Security Communities Are the Way Ahead for Asia', *International Herald Tribune*, 21 April 2000.

132 In 1995, China's GDP of US$700 billion was only marginally higher than ASEAN's combined GDP of US$652 billion. By 2003, however, China's GDP had increased to US$1,409.9 billion, more than twice that of ASEAN (US$ 685.9 billion). Per capita income in China in 1995 was US$342, compared with US$1,359 for ASEAN as a whole. In 2003, China's had jumped to US$1,100, slightly lower than the per capita income of ASEAN at US$1,265. Thitapha Wattanapruttipaisan, *Watching Brief on China and ASEAN: Part One: The Rise of China as an Economic Power*, Paper Number 05/2005 (Jakarta: Studies Unit, ASEAN Secretariat, 28 February 2005). Available: unpan1.un.org/intradoc/groups/public/documents/APCITY/UNPAN024774.pdf (accessed 17 June 2008).

133 According to Stockholm International Peace Research Institute (SIPRI), China's defence spending in 2000 (in constant 2005 US dollars) was 23.7 billion, while that of ASEAN (excluding Vietnam, Burma and Laos for which SIPRI data are not available) was 11.7 billion (also in constant 2005 US dollars). In 2007, China's spending jumped to 58.2 billion, while that of ASEAN (again excluding Vietnam, Burma and Laos), was 17.7 billion, both figures in constant 2005 US dollars. Source: *SIPRI military expenditure database*, Available: milexdata.sipri.org/result.php4 (accessed 18 June 2008). In March 2007, China announced that it would increase its annual defence budget by 17.8% over the previous year, to $45 billion. 'China's Defense Budget'. Available: www.globalsecurity.org/military/world/china/budget.htm (accessed 17 June 2008). But Washington claimed that the real Chinese defence budget for 2007 was at least double the stated amount. 'China to raise military spending', BBC News: news.bbc.co.uk/2/hi/asia-pacific/7276277.stm (accessed 17 June 2008).

134 Richard Sokolsky, Angel Rabasa and C. Richard Neu, *The Role of Southeast Asia in U.S. Strategy Toward China* (Santa Monica, CA: The Rand Corporation, 2001), pp. 53–6.

135 S.D. Muni, *China's Strategic Engagement with the New ASEAN*, IDSS Monographs, no. 2, 2002, pp. 21 and 132.

136 Ron Moreau and Richard Ernsberger Jr., 'Strangling the Mekong', *Newsweek*, 19 March 2001, Atlantic edition, p. 26; for details of the Chinese dams, see: Muni, *China's Strategic Engagement with the New ASEAN*, p. 84.

137 Andrew Selth, 'The Burmese Army', *Jane's Intelligence Review*, vol. 7, no. 11, 1 November 1995, p. 515.

138 Andrew Selth, 'Burma: A Strategic Perspective' Asia Foundation Working Paper 13, May 2001 (originally presented at the conference on 'Strategic Rivalries in the Bay of Bengal: The Burma/ Myanmar Nexus', Washington D.C., 1 February 2001). Available: www.asiafoundation.org/pdf/ WorkPap13.pdf

139 Malaysia's former armed forces chief, General Hashim Mohammed Ali, noted in March 1992 that while India was constrained by domestic problems and Japan by constitutional limitations, China continued to increase its defence spending and had threatened the use of force to support its territorial claims in the South China Sea: *Sunday Times* (Singapore), 29 March 1992. Indonesia's armed forces commander, General Try Sutrisno, expressed similar concerns about China: *Straits Times*, 6 October 1992.

140 Ibid.

141 CNN International, 17 July 2002.

142 Ibid.

143 *International Herald Tribune*, 21 August 2001, p. 9.

144 *Foreign Direct Investments to China and Southeast Asia: Has ASEAN Been Losing Out?*, 2002. Available: www.mti.gov.sg/public/PDF/CMT/NWS_2002Q3_FDI1.pdf?sid=92&cid=1418 (accessed 16 May 2003).

145 Ibid.

146 Jing-dong Yuan, *China–ASEAN Relations: Perspectives, Prospects and Implications for U.S. Interests* (Carlisle, PA: Strategic Studies Institute, US Army War College, October 2006), p. 15.

147 For further details, see: Mely Caballero Anthony, 'U.S.–Philippines Relations post September 11: Security Dilemmas of a Front-Line State in the War on Terrorism', *IDSS Commentaries*, October 2002.

148 *People's Daily*, 25 January 2002.

149 Carlyle A. Thayer, 'China Consolidates its Long-term Bilateral Relations with Southeast Asia', *Comparative Connections*, 2nd Quarter, 2000.

150 Amitav Acharya, 'ASEAN and Conditional Engagement', in James Shinn (ed.), *Weaving the Net: Conditional Engagement with China* (New York: Council on Foreign Relations, 1996), pp. 220–48.

151 Sujit Chatterjee, 'India, ASEAN agree to create Free Trade Area', *Indian Express*, 9 January 2003.

152 'Enhancing India–Asean Trade', 14 April 2005. Available: www.ibef.org/artdisplay.aspx?cat_ id=402&art_id=5806 (accessed 2 July 2008).

153 BBC London, East Asia Today, 5 November 2002, 2200 hours (Source: Foreign Broadcast Monitor, Ministry of Information and the Arts, Singapore, 6 November 2002, pp. 7–8).

154 George Yeo, Minister for Foreign Affairs, Singapore, speech at the Global Leadership Forum in Kuala Lumpur, 6 September 2005. Available: www.mfa.gov.sg/internet/ (accessed 23 June 2008).

155 Interview with *Time Asia*, 5 December 2005. Available: www.time.com/time/asia/covers/ 501051212/lky_intvu.html (accessed 7 December 2006).

156 Lai Foon Wong, 'China–ASEAN and Japan–ASEAN Relations during the Post-Cold War Era,' *Chinese Journal of International Politics*, vol. 1 (2007), p. 400.

157 Ibid., pp. 385, 393. The Japan–ASEAN Free Trade Agreement was ratified by the Japanese parliament on 21 June 2008. The agreement, 'the first multinational free trade agreement for Japan', will abolish tariffs on 93 per cent of Japanese imports from ASEAN within 10 years, while the six original ASEAN members – Brunei, Indonesia, Malaysia, the Philippines, Singapore and Thailand – will remove all tariffs on 90 per cent of their imports from Japan within 10 years. 'Japan ratifies free trade pact with ASEAN'. Available afp.google.com/article/ALeqM5gjudm TCBTUOIFDObl_xKPOjSBUUQ (accessed 23 June 2008); 'Japan's Parliament approves free trade with ASEAN', Radio Australia. Available: www.radioaustralia.net.au/news/stories/200806/ s2281707.htm?tab=asia (accessed 22 June 2008).

158 Jonathan Holslag, 'Keeping the Ends up: China and India's Scramble for Trade Agreements in Asia', *Asia Paper*, vol. 3, no. 4 (Brussels: Institute of Contemporary China Studies, 10 January 2008).

159 Giving priority to the US–Japan alliance is not rare for Japanese governments, but Koizumi and Foreign Minister Taro Aso seemed especially keen to stress relations with the US. Moreover, their relative emphasis on non-Asia policy initiatives, such as Aso's 'Arc of freedom and prosperity initiative', moved Japan closer to the US in the global arena, and a bit further from Asia, as did Japan's participation in the US-led Iraq war and the war on terror. And neither Koizumi nor Aso appeared to pursue enthusiastically their signature initiatives for Japan–Asia (except for Japan–ASEAN), or, more importantly, sought to mend the deteriorating relations with the most important Asian neighbours, China and South Korea. Personal communication with Kuniko Ashizawa, Oxford Brookes University, 2 July 2008.

160 Mark E. Manyin, et al., *Pivot to the Pacific? The Obama Administration's 'Rebalancing' Toward Asia*, CRS Report for Congress 7–5700 (Washington D.C: Congressional Research Service, 28 March 2012). It was also articulated in a Pentagon policy document, *Sustaining US Global Leadership: Priorities for 21st Century Defense*. Ron Huisken, 'Pacific pivot: America's strategic ballet,' *East Asia Forum*, 1 May 2012 http://www.eastasiaforum.org/2012/05/01/pacific-pivot-america-s-strategic-ballet/. Accessed 18 August 2013. Another initial outline can be found in Hillary Clinton, 'America's Pacific Century', *Foreign Policy* (November 2011); Thomas Donilon, 'America is Back in the Pacific and will Uphold the Rules', *Financial Times*, 27 November, 2011.

161 President Barack Obama, Remarks By President Obama to the Australian Parliament, November 17, 2011, accessed in http://www.whitehouse.gov/the-press-office/2011/11/17/remarks-president-obama-australian-parliament.

162 Intervew with Kurt Campbell, Assistant Secretary of State for East Asian and Pacific Affairs, U.S. Department of State, 'The Obama Administration's Pivot to Asia,' http://www.foreignpolicyi.org/files/uploads/images/Asia%20Pivot.pdf., accessed 18 August 2013

163 The Brookings Institution, 'Understanding the U.S. Pivot to Asia,' 31 January 2012, Washington, D.C.: The Brookings Institution. Available at http://www.brookings.edu/events/2012/01/31-us-asia. (Accessed August 3, 2012), 9.

164 Adam Malik, 'Regional Cooperation in International Politics', in *Regionalism in Southeast Asia* (Jakarta: Centre for Strategic and International Studies, 1975), p. 168.

165 Amitav Acharya, 'Can Asia Lead? Power ambitions and global governance in the twenty-first century,' *International Affairs*, vol. 87, no.4 (2011), 851–69.

7 The 'ASEAN security community'

Idea shaping reality?

During the Cold War and before the Asian financial crisis, security challenges to ASEAN members came primarily from internal instability, regime insecurity, superpower rivalry, the changing balance of power spurred by superpower retrenchment after the Cold War, and interstate rivalries and conflicts in Southeast Asia. Responding to such challenges legitimised the non-interference norm. Some of these challenges would not disappear. But the dangers which confronted ASEAN in the later part of the 1990s and at the dawn of the new millennium were different in nature. These are better described as non-traditional or transnational dangers. They included terrorism, the outbreak of Severe Acute Respiratory Syndrome (SARS), the 2004 Indian Ocean Tsunami and the regional haze problem caused by forest fires in Indonesia.

In the immediate aftermath of the Asian financial crisis, ASEAN had stuck to a Westphalian view of sovereignty. It avoided any meaningful dilution of non-interference. But as non-traditional dangers proliferated, pressures for normative and institutional change could no longer be resisted. They compounded the burdens imposed on ASEAN due to membership expansion and the extension of its security framework to the Asia-Pacific region.

As Chapter 1 notes, increased demands of socialisation and the need to cope with transnational challenges may pose serious challenges to security community building. Deeper and newer institutional responses would be needed to maintain the community, or to prevent its slide into decadence. This was ASEAN's key challenge at the dawn of the new millennium. This chapter examines post-1997 challenges to ASEAN and its response to them, the core element of which was the development of an 'ASEAN security community' and the ASEAN Charter.

Transnational challenges

The new transnational dangers facing ASEAN have three important features. First, the terrorist challenge and the SARS pandemic arose suddenly and unexpectedly. Second, they were often linked to the effects of globalisation. Third and more important, they obeyed no national boundaries. National responses to such challenges were inadequate; regional and international cooperation seemed not only preferable, but also imperative. While the Asian economic crisis of 1997 had given ASEAN members a foretaste of such challenges, the new transnational dangers presented themselves with greater intensity at the dawn of the new millennium.

Terrorism: the Bali bombings

The 9/11 attacks on the US brought terrorism to the forefront of ASEAN's security agenda. Whether the severity of the threat facing ASEAN members justified this would be a matter of debate. But ASEAN and Southeast Asia were drawn into the US-led global war on terror for two reasons.

First, in conjunction with the deployment of US troops to the southern Philippines in January 2002 to participate in counter-insurgency operations, the United States labelled the region as 'the second front' in the global war on terror. Southeast Asia earned this labelling for two ostensible reasons – the existence of a terrorist network (Jemaah Islamiyah or JI) and the perceived links between this, the global terrorist network Al-Qaeda, and the insurgency carried out by the Moro Islamic Liberation Front (MILF) in the southern Philippines.[1]

The terrorist bombings in Bali that killed over 200 people on 12 October 2002 (followed by another attack on Bali a year later) were a more important reason in bringing terrorism to the forefront of ASEAN's security concerns. Prior to the 2002 bombings, Al-Qaeda had generally shied away from easy 'soft' targets in favour of attacks on 'hard' targets that represent US power such as the *USS Cole*, the World Trade Center and the Pentagon. After the Bali bombings, it appeared that terrorists would turn to soft targets. Southeast Asia, with its porous borders and existing internal conflicts in Indonesia, southern Thailand and the southern Philippines, seemed to offer an especially attractive region for such targets.

Hence, an ASEAN spokesman would note that 'today's international terrorism is probably the most serious security threat in the region since the Indochina conflict'.[2] Within ASEAN, however, perspectives differed as to the extent of danger posed by terrorism to the region. Singapore's was largely in tune with the US. Both saw terrorism as a severe existential threat not only to its national security but also to the stability of Southeast Asia. Singapore's Deputy Prime Minister Tony Tan found terrorism to be the most 'immediate security threat' facing the region.[3] Neither Malaysia nor Indonesia saw terrorism as an existential threat in the manner of Singapore, Australia or the United States. For domestic reasons, they were also wary of what they saw as the US attempt to associate terrorism with Islam. For Singapore, which discovered a terrorist cell in December 2001, and had placed 31 people under detention during the following year under its Internal Security Act, there was a clear and indivisible nexus between terrorism and radical Islam. A senior Singapore official noted that while 'It may not be politically correct to focus on the relationship between Islam and terrorism', the 'common thread that seemed to united JI members was their desire for spiritual revival . . . What they were . . . taught was that to be a good, genuine Muslim, you would have to hate the West, bring down secular, pro-Western governments in the region and pave the way for an Islamic regional government.'[4] By contrast, the Malaysian Prime Minister, Dr Mahathir Mohamad, often angrily refuted reports linking Malaysian political and religious organisations to the global Al-Qaeda network.[5] The Thaksin Shinawatra government in Bangkok chose to regard violent incidents in southern Thailand as 'the work of the thugs and gangsters'.[6] It denied the possibility of the southern provinces being used as training bases and staging sites for terrorist attacks by regional extremist networks such as the JI.[7]

Against this backdrop, it was hardly surprising that differences would emerge over counter-terrorism strategies and the resources channeled towards fighting this danger. The Philippines viewed terrorism mainly as a form of heightened insurgency carried out by the MILF in the southern Philippines, which must be defeated through military means. Singapore saw itself as a tempting target of Islamic terrorists because of its wealth, the concentration of its national infrastructure within a limited geographic space, and its close security links with the US (which had become closer since 9/11), and developed a homeland security approach stressing infrastructure protection and heightened surveillance.[8] Newly democratic Indonesia refused to ban the JI organisation or adopt legislation, similar to the Internal Security Acts (ISAs) of Singapore and Malaysia, to fight terrorism. Members of the Indonesian parliament and civil society organisations vigorously opposed such a move, drawing parallels with the repressive laws and practices of the Suharto regime.

The main regional extremist network in Southeast Asia, JI, was found to have a transnational organisational structure, with four *mantiqs* (regions): (1) Singapore and Malaysia; (2) Indonesia; (3) Sabah, Sulawesi and the southern Philippines; and (4) northern Australia. It had links with the MILF in the southern Philippines, which allowed it to maintain training camps within its own training facility in MILF's Camp Abu Bakar. A regional 'caucus' of leaders of various Southeast Asian terror organisations, called *Rabitatul Mujahidin* and comprising the JI, the MILF, as well as rebel groups in Aceh, Burma (the Rohingyas), Sulawesi, and southern Thailand, was formed with a view to 'co-operate and share resources for training, procurement of arms, financial assistance and terrorist operations'.[9]

The JI developed its 'closest' transregional 'relationship' with Al-Qaeda.[10] Terrorism experts pointed to the JI's recruitment in Afghanistan in the 1990s and the support it enjoyed from Al-Qaeda when it planned to attack US targets in Singapore. After being expelled from Afghanistan by the US invasion in December 2001 and unable to penetrate the closed and heavily policed homelands of the repressive Gulf states, Al-Qaeda turned its attention to the more friendly and open grounds of Southeast Asia.

Some of these reports were unquestionably exaggerated.[11] Moreover, the regional and extra-regional networking by Southeast Asian extremist groups notwithstanding, terrorism in Southeast Asia was never a single overarching phenomenon. Terrorist groups differ in terms of motivations, targets and tactics. Some groups seek to punish rival ethnic groups in a situation of ethnic hatred and conflict – an example being the Majelis Mujahidin Indonesia (MMI) in Ambon, Indonesia. The goal of replacing existing regimes with ones based on Islamic principles was an important underlying factor driving other Southeast Asian extremist groups. There are also those that seek independence or autonomy from existing nation states. These are classical separatist movements which were now branded as terrorist by governments and analysts partly with a view to de-legitimising them – examples include the MILF and Abu Sayaaf in the southern Philippines (in China, the Uighurs would be in a similar situation).

ASEAN's response to the threat of post 9/11 terrorism came in the form of 'The ASEAN Declaration on Joint Action to Counter Terrorism' adopted by the seventh ASEAN Summit in Brunei Darussalam in November 2001. The declaration condemned 'acts of terrorism in all its forms and manifestations, committed wherever, whenever and by whomsoever', as a 'profound threat to international peace and security'.[12] It called for measures to combat terrorism such as cooperation among law enforcement agencies, exchange of information and intelligence on terrorist organisations, their movement and funding, sharing of 'best practices' among counter-terrorism agencies, and regional capacity building programmes for investigating, detecting, monitoring and reporting of terrorist acts. It was careful to stress that any such 'cooperative efforts [to fight terrorism] . . . should [be] in line with specific circumstances in the region and in each member country'. The early signing of or accession to all relevant international anti-terrorist conventions, including the International Convention for the Suppression of the Financing of Terrorism, and compliance with measures taken at the UN level, was urged on ASEAN members, as was cooperation between the pre-existing

ASEAN Ministerial Meeting on Transnational Crime (AMMTC) and other relevant ASEAN bodies in countering terrorism.

A special AMMTC held in Kuala Lumpur in May 2002 identified six strategic areas of counter-terrorism cooperation: information exchange, cooperation in legal matters, cooperation in law enforcement matters, institutional capacity-building, training and extra-regional cooperation. In implementing this work programme, ASEAN member countries carried out training programmes and projects on counter-terrorism, which would include courses on psychological operation/warfare for law enforcement officials and on intelligence procuring, bomb/explosive detection, post-blast investigation, airport security and travel document security, immigration matters and cross-border controls. Another aspect of counter-terrorism cooperation was to establish regional databases on national laws, regulations, and bilateral and multilateral treaties or agreements of members. These efforts culminated in the adoption of an ASEAN Convention on Counter Terrorism on 30 January 2007. Avoiding a definition of terrorism that would have proved contentious (and has eluded the UN), the convention identified criminal acts of terrorism in terms of offences listed under 14 international conventions, and established guidelines for setting up jurisdiction in cross-border acts of terrorism within ASEAN (acts committed within a country by one of its own nationals arrested in its own territory are to be generally excluded). The convention upholds the principles of sovereign equality, territorial integrity and non-interference, perhaps more explicitly than other ASEAN conventions.[13]

Developing a common approach to terrorism in ASEAN has had its limits, reflecting, as discussed, differing national perceptions of the severity of the terrorist challenge, as well as differing political conditions in, and capabilities of, ASEAN member states. Bilateral and trilateral measures seemed more feasible. One of the early developments after the Bali bombings was a trilateral pact signed on 7 May 2002 between the Philippines, Indonesia and Malaysia. It provided for joint operations to hunt suspected terrorists, the setting up of hotlines and sharing of airline passenger lists aimed at suppressing not terrorism alone, but also piracy as well as money laundering. Thailand and Cambodia joined this agreement subsequently, but not Singapore, reflecting political differences. One critic dismissed the agreement as 'longer on form than on substance';[14] in reality, the issue was not substance, but implementation.

ASEAN members looked beyond Southeast Asia to garner support in combating terrorism. Cooperation with the US and Australia proved especially important, although, with the exception of Singapore and the Philippines, this was more as a result of intense pressure from the Bush administration and Canberra (where the government of John Howard had infamously called itself to be a faithful ally, a 'deputy sheriff' to the US in the region) than proactive enthusiasm on their own part. Singapore was the first Asian country to join the controversial US Container Security Initiative (CSI) and later the Proliferation Security Initiative (PSI), designed to prevent the smuggling of terrorists or weapons in ocean-going cargo containers into the USA and to interdict vessels suspected of carrying illegal nuclear materials. Alongside bilateral agreements with a number of ASEAN members (see Table 7.1), the US persuaded ASEAN to agree to a US–ASEAN Joint Declaration for Cooperation to Combat International Terrorism in August 2002 to serve as 'a framework for cooperation to prevent, disrupt and combat international terrorism through the exchange and flow of information, intelligence and capacity-building'. The particular focus of this declaration was to promote intelligence and information sharing on terrorist financing and to develop close liaison among law enforcement agencies.[15] The agreement did not provide for any operational measures, such as the US counter-terrorism 'exercises' with the Philippines.

Table 7.1 Selected Bilateral Anti-Terrorism Agreements/Declarations between ASEAN Member Countries and the US and Australia

US–Philippines, February 2002

US–Singapore, 31 July 2002

US–Malaysia Anti-Terrorism Pact, 14 May 2002

US–Vietnam, 21 June 2005

US–Indonesia, 2 August 2002

US–Thailand, 14 December 2001

Japan–Indonesia Joint Announcement on Fighting against International Terrorism, 24 June 2003

Australia–Indonesia MoU on counter-terrorism, 7 February 2002

Joint Declaration on Comprehensive Partnership between Australia and the Republic of Indonesia, 4 April 2005

Agreement between the Republic of Indonesia and Australia on the Framework for Security Cooperation, 13 November 2006

Australia–Malaysia MoU on combating terrorism, 2 August 2002

Australia–Philippines MoU on combating terrorism, 4 March 2003, July 2003

Australia–Thailand MoU on counter-terrorism, 3 October 2002

Australia–Cambodia MoU on counter-terrorism, 18 June 2003

Australia–Brunei MoU on counter-terrorism, 15 February 2005

The close cooperation between some ASEAN members and outside powers did not obscure important differences with the US over strategic perspective and approach. An analyst at the conservative Heritage Foundation in the USA complained that Thailand and Indonesia were using regional cooperation 'as diplomatic camouflage to minimize American pressure and non-provocative security measures to avoid attention from the terrorists'.[16] ASEAN members did not generally feel comfortable with the US invasion of Iraq and regarded it as a distraction from the fight against terrorism. Thailand provided the US with access to its military bases, but did not join the 'coalition of the willing'. The Philippines joined the coalition and supported the war, eager not to imperil its access to desperately needed military aid to modernise its armed forces and fight the rebellion in the south. Singapore joined the 'coalition of the willing' in Iraq (failure to do so might have jeopardised its bilateral trade agreement with the US which was reaching critical final stages), and as discussed in Chapter 6, agreed to a major strategic partnership with the US in 2003, with an agreement signed in 2005. But a telling aspect of the agreement was the designation of Singapore as a 'Major Security Cooperation Partner', compared with the 'major non-NATO ally' status given to Thailand and the Philippines. The Defence Minister of Singapore would describe US–Singapore ties as a 'special relationship' binding two nations who are 'more than just friends' but not allies. Apart from reflecting that unlike the latter, Singapore was outside the network of Cold War-era bilateral alliances, this was politically a less provocative designation to Indonesia and Malaysia.[17] Malaysia withheld overflight rights which it had sanctioned during the attack on the Taliban. The US provided US$12 million to Malaysia to support the construction of coastal radars in Eastern Sabah to boost Malaysian efforts to check movement of terrorist groups through the Sulu Sea to and from the southern Philippines. (and the Philippines and Indonesia are involved in similar efforts with the US). Nevertheless, both Malaysia and Indonesia, which normalised its defence ties with the US in 2005–06 and received US military aid, criticised the Iraq invasion, prompted partly by rising anti-Americanism which was especially rife in Indonesia.

Australia's eagerness to join the war on terror in Southeast Asia led to a joint declaration with ASEAN on counter-terrorism in July 2004 and several bilateral agreements. Its co-operation with Indonesia led to the creation of a 'law enforcement' centre in Semarang, At a time when US–Indonesian cooperation was stymied due to lingering East Timor sanctions, even though the two countries signed a security memorandum of understanding (MoU) in 2002, Australia's assistance to Indonesia was an effective substitute and led to extensive cooperation with Indonesian security forces.

More controversial was the US-mooted Regional Maritime Security Initiative (RMSI). Malaysia and Indonesia objected to a remark made by the then head of the US Pacific Command, Admiral Thomas B. Fargo, at a congressional hearing on 31 March 2004 which suggested 'the possibility that [US] Navy and Marines units might patrol the Strait of Malacca', including areas 'within their territorial waters'. Although the US would subsequently call this a misinterpretation, the ensuing misgivings about the possibility of unilateral interdiction in the Straits by the US military prompted Malaysia and Indonesia (Singapore welcomed the US role) to step up their own security measures. In addition, Malaysia, Indonesia, and Singapore established a Malacca Straits Security Joint Working Group and carried out coordinated patrols, and an 'eyes in the sky' programme of aerial surveillance of the Straits and intelligence sharing.[18]

As the above discussion shows, the involvement of outside powers in counter-terrorism was the result of both push and pull factors. For the Philippines, cooperation with the US was strongly motivated by a lack of resources to fight the Mindanao rebels, to gain US military equipment to modernise the Philippine military and bolster the regime security of President Arroyo. For Singapore, it was the prospect of cementing existing security ties with the US that had been a traditional cornerstone of its security policy and of reaping the benefits of a free trade deal. Indonesia and Malaysia played to their traditional sentiment for autonomy from Great Power intrusion into the region. The US 'threat' to patrol the Straits unilaterally might have succeeded in jolting Malaysia and Indonesia into action (if indeed this was the US motive), but the result was cooperation acceptable to all sides. Indonesia and Malaysia accepted US financial, information and technical support in securing the Straits of Malacca jointly with Singapore and in enhancing their surveillance of the Sulu Seas in cooperation with the Philippines, motivated by a pragmatic desire to avail of resources that were easily forthcoming without compromising their sovereignty. Non-interference, including that by outside powers, remained important and explained the limited nature of intrusive collaboration with the US or Australia.

A study of ASEAN counter-terrorism cooperation by an Indonesian researcher finds that such cooperation 'remains nascent and qualified,' Yet, it also concludes that 'Increasing cooperation on counter-terrorism with ASEAN at the operational level – between state executives and law enforcement agencies provides a further illustration of the association's ability to act as a security community.'[19] Overall, ASEAN's record on counter-terrorism cooperation has been more visible in the normative domain than in the operational one. To cite the Indonesian researcher: Despite the many differences between ASEAN member states, the issue of terrorism has created the need for greater institutional cooperation because of its transnational character. Within the region, terrorists have created networks that cooper-ate in areas of funding, training, providing sanctuary and on operations. These cross-border links within Southeast Asia, have led the ASEAN states to the realisation that they face a common threat. The nature of this challenge has strengthened the awareness of their security interdependence. Dealing with terrorism has also created both compelling reasons and new opportunities to develop security cooperation to a much higher level than in the past.[20]

The Severe Acute Respiratory Syndrome pandemic[21]

An atypical form of pneumonia with a mortality rate of around 10 per cent, Severe Acute Respiratory Syndrome (SARS) first appeared in November 2002 in China's Guangdong province. In the East Asia region, it most seriously affected China, Hong Kong, Taiwan, Singapore and Vietnam, with the crisis reaching severe proportions between February and July 2003. Within ASEAN, Singapore was the hardest hit, reporting over 200 cases and suffering the highest number of deaths (27 by 10 May 2003) outside of China, Hong Kong and Taiwan.[22] At the height of the crisis, close to 1,000 people were in quarantine in Singapore; air travel arrivals in the month of April 2003 dropped by half compared with April 2002, and retail sales dropped by almost 50 per cent in the same period. Singapore's Prime Minister, Goh Chok Tong, estimated a $1.5bn loss to the national economy in 2003 alone due to a sharp drop in tourist arrivals.[23]

In responding to SARS, ASEAN agreed at an 'unprecedented pace' (in the words of ASEAN Secretary-General Ong Keng Yong) to convene a special meeting to which China and Hong Kong were also invited under the ASEAN Plus Three (APT) framework.[24] The use of the APT framework was appropriate since China's cooperation was vital to this effort to combat SARS. ASEAN's refusal to criticise China for its initial secrecy over SARS, and its move to solicit cooperation with Beijing, pleased Beijing. The APT Health Ministers Special Meeting held on 26 April 2003 in Malaysia, followed by a meeting of their leaders in Bangkok on 29 April, underscored the urgency of the crisis. These meetings took the important decision to keep national borders open; avoiding 'blanket bans' (although China banned travel by its nationals to Malaysia) in favour of an 'isolate and contain' strategy to enable those not affected by SARS to travel freely within the region. Subsequent meetings worked out further measures of cooperation: the May 2003 Aviation Forum on SARS in the Philippines dealt with the screening for departing and arriving passengers and standardised health declaration cards, while in June 2003, China and ASEAN worked out the Entry–Exit Quarantine Action Plan for Controlling the Spread of SARS. Other notable actions by the APT included members taking the lead in drafting the common resolution on SARS adopted by the 56th World Health Assembly at its May 2003 session in Geneva, and Malaysia hosting the WHO Global Conference on SARS in Kuala Lumpur in June 2003 to review the epidemiological, clinical management and laboratory findings on SARS, and discuss global control strategies.

Through all these meetings, the countries concerned had worked out a range of measures to combat SARS, such as information sharing, including exchange of mobile phone numbers of health officials, contact tracing and follow-up procedures, close and continuous contact among health officials in ASEAN, China and Hong Kong, a 'hotline' among the Health Ministers and their senior officials to facilitate communication in emergencies, harmonising pre-departure screening procedures and promoting public awareness and education on SARS.[25] ASEAN countries that did not have a SARS problem and were thus reluctant to impose health screening measures were prevailed upon to do so, on the grounds that without those measures, an ASEAN containment strategy would be jeopardised. By the end of May, three of the affected countries in ASEAN exited the WHO Affected Countries' List. Vietnam on 28 April was followed by the Philippines on 20 May. Singapore, which reported the last case of local infection of SARS in the region on 11 May, exited on 30 May. An APT Health

Ministers' Meeting in Cambodia on 10–11 June declared ASEAN to be a 'SARS Free Region', a statement endorsed by the WHO. The meeting agreed to an action plan to respond to future outbreaks of SARS and other infectious diseases, covering guidelines for international travel; the creation of an ASEAN SARS Containment Information Network; capacity building on alert and response through early warning system (including the establishment of an ASEAN Centre of Excellence for Disease Control), and public education. While 'congratulating' China 'for its very strong political commitment in containing SARS', the meeting asked for more transparency from Beijing on the actual dates of when cases were isolated and how the patients had become infected (either through community-based or hospital-based transmission), suggesting that not everything about China's response was satisfactory, despite the desire not to publicly criticise or ostracise that country.[26] And while SARS had receded in November 2003, the APT launched a new hotline on communicable diseases.

The Indian Ocean Tsunami[27]

A powerful Tsunami triggered by an earthquake off the west coast of Sumatra and measuring 9.15 on the Richter scale devastated large coastal areas of South and Southeast Asia on 26 December 2004. The disaster killed at least 200,000 people, making it one of the deadliest natural calamities in modern history. A number of countries in Southeast Asia and beyond were affected, including Sri Lanka, India, the Maldives, Somalia and South Africa. Foreigners, most of them tourists, were among those killed; countries such as Sweden and Germany lost over 500 citizens in the disaster. Indonesia was the hardest hit – the epicentre of the earthquake that triggered the deadly waves was located off the coast of Sumatra, and whole coastal regions were destroyed. At least 128,000 people died, while about 37,000 others remained missing in Indonesia. In India, more than 10,000 people lost their lives, mostly from Tamil Nadu and the Nicobar and Andaman islands. India, while rejecting foreign aid for itself, provided assistance to other affected countries, especially Sri Lanka. More than 5,300 people were killed in Thailand, of whom 2,200 were foreigners from 36 countries. The number of people still missing exceeded 2,800. Malaysia was shielded by Sumatra, and therefore spared the widespread devastation. Nonetheless, at least 68 people were confirmed dead.

A month after the Tsunami, the major providers in a total $7 billion plus of pledged government aid (excluding private donations – considerable in the UK, the US and Germany – but including both short-term and long-term aid) to the Tsunami affected countries were: Australia $764m, Germany $647m, Japan $500m, United States $350m, Canada $343m and Norway $183m. Aid from the European Union was $628m, bringing to $2bn the total amount given by the bloc (the EU plus its member states). The United States, Australia, India and Japan led in military humanitarian assistance. US deployments involved some 12,600 personnel, 21 ships, 14 cargo planes and more than 90 helicopters. Britain sent military transport planes to deliver aid, while Australia deployed about 350 military personnel, 4 military helicopters, a troop transport ship, and a military health support team. India 'staged its biggest relief operation ever' in Sri Lanka, the Maldives and Indonesia, involving at least 16,000 troops, 32 navy ships, 41 aircraft including at least 16 helicopters, and medical teams. Germany's contribution included a mobile hospital to Aceh and a military ship with two helicopters, aid supplies, water treatment equipment and an operating theatre.[28] Japan fielded three warships and vessels, and troops.[29]

While the main relief efforts came from countries outside the region, Singapore's contribution was estimated at nearly $150m, 'making it by far the Republic's largest humanitarian exercise'. Out of this, $70m was in direct government aid, including $5m for immediate relief; $16.5m for reconstruction; and $44m to deploy assets and personnel in affected countries. In addition, the Singapore Red Cross had raised $75m by February 2005.[30] Malaysia deployed a contingent of 250 police to Aceh and provided engineering expertise in areas designated by Indonesia for assistance. Singapore provided US$30m from government and private donations and was also among the first countries to send a 900-strong contingent to Aceh, deploying aircraft, landing ships and helicopters. It opened up its air and naval facilities to all countries helping in the massive relief and reconstruction effort. Brunei offered financial support, and Thailand declined a Japanese offer of financial assistance worth US$20m and instead recommended that it be sent to those countries Tokyo deemed needier. Laos raised US$55,000 for countries hit by the Tsunami and the Philippines sent medical missions that had the added task of locating Filipino victims.[31]

In January 2005, a Special ASEAN Leaders' Meeting in Jakarta discussed coordination of international relief efforts and the creation of a regional early warning system. ASEAN's proposed resolution on 'Strengthening Emergency Relief, Rehabilitation, Reconstruction and Prevention on Aftermath of the Indian Ocean Tsunami Disaster' was adopted by consensus by the UN General Assembly on 19 January 2005. This called for utilising military and civilian personnel in disaster relief operations, and establishing an ASEAN Humanitarian Assistance Centre and an ASEAN Disaster Information Sharing and Communication Network. This was followed by a ministerial meeting in Phuket, one of the affected towns in Thailand, on 29 January 2005 to consider tsunami early warning arrangements, which, had a system existed, might have saved many lives lost in the disaster. Such a system would not be entirely new, but built on existing institutions and mechanisms, including upgraded national systems, which could be linked to subregional and regional systems for early warning on earthquakes and other natural disasters. This required cooperation with international agencies, not only on an intra-ASEAN basis. Efforts to create a tsunami early warning and mitigation system were initiated by UNESCO, which usually coordinates such mechanisms. Since 2005, UNESCO has organised several meetings to coordinate development of an Indian Ocean Tsunami Warning and Mitigation system (IOTWS). The IOTWS would be a coordinated network of national systems and capacities, based on existing institutions and would complement existing warning frameworks, including early warning systems for other disasters. Member states would have the responsibility for issuing warnings and disseminating them within their respective territories. Disagreements over a single regional headquarters had led to a proposal for seven, based in Australia, India, Indonesia, Malaysia, Thailand, Iran and Pakistan.[32] In the meantime, the Thai government reportedly asked the non-profit group, Asian Disaster Preparedness Centre in Thailand 'to serve as a regional center or focal point for a multi-nodal tsunami early warning arrangement in the region'.[33] Indonesia has developed its own national early warning capability. There is now an ASEAN Coordinating Centre for Humanitarian Assistance in Disaster Management established in 2011.

The haze from Indonesia

According to a report by the International Development Research Centre of Canada, published in 1999, the 1997 haze caused by forest fires in Indonesia's Sumatra and Kalimantan provinces, constituted 'certainly one of the century's worst environmental disasters'. It had destroyed an 'area the size of Costa Rica' while 'The lives and health of

70 million people were jeopardised and species already endangered, such as orangutans, rhinos, and tigers, were pushed closer to extinction.' The study 'conservatively' assessed the cost of the haze at US$4.5 billion, 'more than the *Exxon Valdez* oil spill and India's Bhopal chemical spill combined'.[34] Although there had not been a recurrence of the haze until 2006, this was mainly due to 'favourable climate conditions'.[35] The report had concluded that a recurrence of the haze could not be ruled out.

The worst haze to hit Southeast Asia since 1997 occurred in the second half of 2006 and was particularly severe in October, when satellite images showed some 561 'hotspots' in south Kalimantan alone. Malaysia and Singapore were also severely affected, with Malaysian political parties demonstrating outside the Indonesian embassy in Kuala Lumpur and the Prime Minister of Singapore writing to the Indonesian President to express his 'disappointment' about the reappearance of the problem and arguing that ASEAN's credibility, alongside investor confidence and Indonesia's international standing, was at stake.[36] This letter prompted an apology from President Yudhoyono and assurances of action including ratifying the ASEAN Agreement on Transboundary Haze Pollution signed in 2002.[37] Indonesia was criticised for not doing enough to prevent the haze, despite having mobilised its military, and more specifically for not having ratified the ASEAN Agreement. Such criticism from its neighbours, in turn, brought a nationalist backlash from Indonesian lawmakers, with a member of the Indonesian parliamentary commission on the environment saying that the region and the world owed Indonesia for the oxygen the country produces and blaming Singapore and Malaysia for not being 'good neighbours' (presumably for not controlling illegal logging in Indonesia by companies based there, which was a major reason for the haze).[38]

The ASEAN Agreement had come into force after being ratified in 2003 by the required five members: Brunei Darussalam, Malaysia, Burma, Singapore and Vietnam. It was praised at its signing by the UN Environment Programme as the 'first international treaty addressing transboundary air pollution outside of Europe' and as a 'legally binding' instrument. While the Agreement carries no 'punitive measures', it imposes national obligations on member states to punish illegal loggers, take speedy action against outbreaks of fire, establish early warning systems, exchange information and technology and provide mutual assistance, and establishes a number of mechanisms and institutions including an ASEAN Coordinating Centre to facilitate such common responses.[39]

Indonesia hosted an Environment Ministerial Meeting on Transboundary Haze Pollution on 13 October 2006 to discuss the haze problem, and at that meeting Malaysia proposed the creation of a special fund to fight it. The meeting 'respectfully' urged Indonesia to ratify the ASEAN Agreement, and established a ministerial steering committee to oversee plans to tackle the problem.[40] Indonesia had cited a lack of resources in dealing with the problem, and had to rely on Russian helicopters to douse the fires. Subsequently, Jakarta claimed to have stepped up efforts to tackle the haze problem. In April 2008, the Indonesian Environment Minister claimed that there had been a decline in the number of hotspots in Sumatra and Kalimantan in 2007 by 51 per cent compared with 2006. Indonesia has committed to reducing the number of hotspots by 50 per cent in 2009, 75 per cent in 2012 and 95 per cent in 2025, with 2006's data as reference.[41] An ASEAN Transboundary Haze Pollution Control Fund was established to implement the Agreement, and an ASEAN Coordinating Centre for Transboundary Haze Pollution Control will implement operational activities associated with the Agreement. In April 2008, however, the Indonesian national legislature refused to ratify the ASEAN Transboundary Pollution Agreement, with some lawmakers arguing that national action by Indonesia will be enough and blaming the haze on logging companies from Malaysia and Singapore.[42]

The haze returned in June 2013 with southern Malaysia and Singapore as the most severely affected areas, where the pollution index reached an all-time high. Malaysia declared a state of emergency in some areas of its Johore state. As before, the haze was once again blamed on land-clearing by palm oil companies, some of which are owned or registered in Malaysia and Singapore. The President of Indonesia offered another apology, and environment ministers from Malaysia, Brunei, Indonesia, Singapore and Thailand met in July 2013 to address the problem, and agreed to launch a joint haze monitoring system that would include sharing of maps among palm oil companies, thus allowing for a more accurate identification of companies to blame for the haze. The Indonesian government also promised to speed up and ratify the ASEAN transboundary pollution treaty.[43]

Democratisation and ASEAN: Indonesia and Burma

Another type of challenge to ASEAN since the Asian financial crisis would influence its normative and institutional direction. This was the challenge of domestic political change, notably the successful, if painstaking, transition to democracy in Indonesia following the downfall of Suharto, and the continuing suppression of political reform in Burma. Thanks to these developments, and the periodic setbacks in the Philippines and Thailand, democracy and human rights acquired regional importance and implications. As noted in Chapter 1, like transnational dangers, domestic political transitions can create pressures for change in regional security communities by challenging the community's core norms and creating new leadership structures. The demise of the Suharto regime pushed Jakarta to propose new initiatives for reforming ASEAN in order to reaffirm its post-Suharto leadership role and to some extent project its new democratic credentials (for domestic and international legitimacy). The Burmese issue, by contrast, became a major burden on ASEAN in terms of its relations with the international community and increased the pressure on its non-interference doctrine.

In the immediate aftermath of the downfall of the Suharto regime and the democratic transition in Indonesia, Indonesia's neighbours, especially Singapore, were apprehensive that the exit of the 'father of ASEAN' might lead, at worst to a return to Sukarno-era nationalism, or at best, to diminished interest in, and commitment to, the ASEAN idea on the part of Jakarta.[44] These fears proved unfounded. But the democratic transition in Indonesia did affect ASEAN.

Despite an initial sign of an unwitting neglect of ASEAN on the part of the Habibie and Wahid government in Jakarta,[45] Jakarta signalled a more activist attitude towards ASEAN. It also took a more open attitude towards non-interference. To quote Adian Silalahi, Director General for ASEAN, Indonesian Foreign Ministry: 'We still adhere to those principles [of ASEAN], but I believe that on this issue [non-intervention] we are more open now . . . Indonesia is more open, more flexible because of the democratization process.'[46] In July 2004, President Megawati Sukarnoputri, in opening the 37th ASEAN Ministerial Meeting in Jakarta, urged ASEAN members to have 'open and honest dialogue', even in addressing their internal problems which if not resolved could have a severe impact on the region.[47] And Indonesian Foreign Minister (under both Megawati and Susilo administrations), Hassan Wirayuda coined the term 'intermestic' to describe issues that straddle international and domestic affairs, and which emerged as one of the key challenges for Indonesia in ASEAN.[48] Moreover, Indonesia continued to take an interest in the issue of political reform in Burma. What is more important, it was no longer the Presidency and the foreign ministry, but also the Indonesian parliament and NGO groups who had their voices expressed in pressuring

Burma to liberalise its polity, thereby continuing a trend that was evident during the arrest of Anwar Ibrahim earlier. Democratisation in Indonesia opened up space for foreign policy debate, if not decision-making, to groups who had been previously kept out of it.[49]

ASEAN and Myanmar, 2000–06: Shift from non-interference?

18 February 2000: Malaysian Foreign Minister Syed Hamid Albar says that 'it is up to the Myanmar government to resolve its internal situation . . . The political system that they have is for them to determine.' Noting that Myanmar is 'stable and peaceful', Syed Hamid said that the country's entry into ASEAN has brought positive results.

29 August 2000: Thai Foreign Minister Surin Pitsuwan expresses his concern that the recent stand-off between Aung San Suu Kyi and the military regime in Myanmar 'may affect the image of ASEAN as a whole'.

7 September 2000: In Hanoi, which holds the rotating chair of ASEAN, Foreign Ministry spokesman Le Dung states that ASEAN 'has never issued a position on Myanmar's affairs'.

19 July 2001: Syed Hamid hails what he sees as 'signs, indications of reconciliation' between the opposition and the military regime in Myanmar. 'We have to allow Myanmar to evolve itself into a system that is acceptable.'

6 May 2002: ASEAN countries applaud the military junta's decision to release Suu Kyi from house arrest. Malaysian Prime Minister Mahathir Mohamad called for patience in engaging with Myanmar: 'I don't think anything can be achieved overnight. It has taken us a long time, but we have to be patient.'

3 June 2003: Responding to the news that Suu Kyi has been arrested again by the military regime, ASEAN Secretary-General Ong Keng Yong said that the grouping will ask Rangoon to provide more information on her detention. He stated that 'we should let the Myanmar authorities come and use ASEAN channels to tell us what is happening'. At the same time, Ong noted that 'you cannot go in and tell your family member you cannot do this, you cannot do that'.

16 June 2003: According to Secretary-General Ong, ASEAN Foreign Ministers 'had a good exchange of views on Myanmar and (the ministers) conveyed the request . . . to the Myanmar government that (we) would like to see an easing of tensions and early release of Aung San Suu Kyi'.

18 June 2003: Philippines Foreign Secretary Blas Ople thinks ASEAN's long-standing policy of 'constructive engagement' with Myanmar may be reviewed if there is no tangible progress on political reform.

20 July 2003: Mahathir warns in an interview that Myanmar may face expulsion from ASEAN if Suu Kyi is not released soon. According to him, 'in the end, it may have to be that way'.

22 March 2005: The Minister in the Malaysian Prime Minister's Office, Nazri Abdul Aziz, says 'we will ask for Myanmar's turn to be the chairman of ASEAN to be suspended and given to other countries until democratic reforms are carried out'.

13 June 2005: ASEAN Secretary-General Ong argues that: 'If Myanmar chairs ASEAN, then there will be constant international attention on this situation in Myanmar, and there will be a certain amount of pressure in moving the national reconciliation and democratisation process . . . But if they are out of the chair, then for the next one or two years, they won't be on the radar scope.'

26 July 2005: Laos Foreign Minister Somsavat Lengsavat announces Myanmar's decision to give up the ASEAN chairmanship.

29 September 2005: Malaysia's Deputy Prime Minister Najib Razak concedes that 'the policy of constructive engagement has shown some dividends but not as much as we had hoped'.

2 March 2006: Singapore Foreign Minister George Yeo tells Parliament that 'we will have to distance ourselves a bit [from Burma] if it is not possible for them to engage us in a way which we find necessary to defend them internationally'. ASEAN's efforts had little impact on Rangoon, so long as China and India kept their 'gates' open to Burma.

Sources: Agence France Presse, 18 February 2000; Reuters News, 29 August 2000; *The Nation*, 2 September 2000; Agence France Presse, 7 September 2000; Reuters News, 19 July 2001; Agence France Presse, 6 May 2002; *Kyodo News*, 6 May 2002; Agence France Presse, 3 June 2003; Associated Press, 16 June 2003; Bernama Daily Malaysian News, 16 June 2003; Agence France Presse, 18 June 2003; Agence France Presse, 20 July 2003; *Jakarta Post*, 29 June 2004; Agence France Presse, 22 March 2005; Associated Press, 13 June 2005; En-lai Yeoh, Associated Press, 29 September 2005; Agence France Presse, 3 March 2006.

In the meantime, Burma continued to offer the most severe test of ASEAN's non-interference doctrine, and perhaps ASEAN's international credibility and standing. Three events were especially important: the issue of Burma's chairmanship of ASEAN in 2006, the 'saffron uprising' in August 2007, and the cyclone *Nargis* in May 2008.

Until the issue of Burma's chairmanship of ASEAN came up in 2005, ASEAN collectively had indicated little shift in its non-interference doctrine, despite holding brief discussions with the regime on the issue on the margins of ASEAN meetings, and individual ASEAN leaders had shown signs of exasperation with Burma's stalled reform process. (See the box above.) ASEAN initially wanted to go ahead with Burma's turn at chairing ASEAN and hosting the annual ASEAN Ministerial Meeting (AMM), but gave in to both international pressure and growing dissatisfaction among some of its members (including Malaysia and Indonesia) over the lack of progress in Burma's 'road map' to democracy. ASEAN meetings in 2005 discussed the issue of political reform and the progress of constitution-drafting in Burma with the Junta's representatives. Opinion within ASEAN was divided, with Malaysia's Mahathir going so far as to suggest the expulsion of Burma from ASEAN if it did not change its ways,[50] while the ASEAN Secretary-General, Ong Keng Yong of Singapore, urged the international community to accept Burma assuming the ASEAN chair for the putative benefit of keeping the regime engaged and using it as a leverage with the regime. In either case, however, the question of Burma's domestic political situation could no longer be kept under the carpet. In the end Burma was prevailed upon, despite the initial reluctance of the junta, to relinquish its rotational right to assume the chairmanship of ASEAN in 2006, which some in ASEAN saw as a minor defeat for the non-interference doctrine.

ASEAN's response to the uprising against the Burmese military junta led by Buddhist monks in August–September 2007 was in some ways more radical in tone. A statement issued by the grouping's Foreign Ministers at the UN headquarters in New York 'expressed their revulsion . . . over reports that the demonstrations in Burma are being suppressed by violent force and that there has been a number of fatalities'. It 'strongly urged Burma to exercise utmost restraint and seek a political solution'. Moreover, the Foreign Ministers 'called upon Burma to resume its efforts at national reconciliation with all parties concerned, and work towards a peaceful transition to democracy'.[51] However, there was no threat of sanctions or call for the suspension of Burma from ASEAN membership. By this time, as will be discussed shortly, while the ASEAN Security Community espousing commitment to a democratic ASEAN had been adopted three years ago, discussions about the ASEAN Charter had concluded with the decision not to have any explicit provision for suspension of a member as had been initially specified by the report of the Eminent Persons' Group on the ASEAN Charter. It is unlikely that ASEAN's pressure had any impact on the Burmese regime's self-styled reform process through the adoption of a new constitution (which had been boycotted by the opposition NLD and which would preserve a significant role for the military in the government, including monopoly over top government positions and guaranteed representation in the legislature), the preparations for which went ahead.

The disaster wrought by cyclone *Nargis* in May 2008 posed another dilemma over the Burmese government's refusal to allow direct international (mainly Western) humanitarian aid into the country. As tens of thousands of its citizens lay dead or dying, the junta refused rescue and rehabilitation efforts which could have been offered quickly by US naval forces (as well as Japanese and Indian forces) which were in the vicinity to participate in the annual Cobra Gold exercise with the Thai military. This was in a sense a situation different from the Indian Ocean Tsunami in December 2004, where Indonesia promptly accepted help from the international community, including aid from US naval forces as well as from India, China and other ASEAN countries. But the Burmese junta would have been especially fearful of the offer of help by US military forces. This would have compounded its fear of intervention for humanitarian purposes or 'humanitarian intervention' by the West which was advocated by the French Foreign Minister Bernard Koucher. The US, as well as the international NGO community did, however, reject the application of the UN's 'responsibility to protect' norm, because this was not a case of genocide – the community did not want any dilution of the norm. The junta proved more amenable to accepting aid from Asian neighbours, including China and India as well as ASEAN, which it knew would not use aid for meddling with its domestic politics.

Thai Foreign Minister Noppadon Pattama, asked if ASEAN would put pressure on the Burmese junta to accept international humanitarian aid, replied: 'There won't be any pressure, there would be persuasion to allow Burma to consider opening or giving more access to international humanitarian assistance.'[52] ASEAN finally agreed to coordinate and channel international relief to Burma at a meeting in Singapore on 19 May 2008. An ASEAN 'coalition of mercy' was sent to Burma to assess the damage and organise relief and rehabilitation, but the role of the ASEAN mission would be circumscribed by logistical constraints and the Burmese military's vigilance.

In short, while ASEAN's response to the political repression in Burma changed considerably, from benign and sometimes wilful indifference under the policy of 'constructive engagement' to voicing concerns and mild pressure, it did not significantly depart from the non-interference doctrine. Through the ASEAN Security Community (ASC) and the Charter, ASEAN tried to create new norms (such as common respect for and adherence to human rights and democracy) and institutions (such as an ASEAN Human Rights Body, and an ASEAN mechanism for peacekeeping and non-traditional security which can ostensibly provide disaster relief), to deal with situations like Burma. But political differences within the grouping have hampered such efforts, at least in the short term, too late for the brave monks of Burma who sacrificed their lives and freedom for the sake of enacting their own version of 'regime change'.

The dramatic events in Burma since 2011, which led to the release of opposition leader Aung San Suu Kyi, the holding of democratic by-elections leading to her being elected to the national parliament, and the limited release of political prisoners and restoration of press freedom, have rekindled hopes for the further evolution of human rights and democracy in Southeast Asia, traditionally seen as a bastion of authoritarian rule. The political situation in Burma, although hardly exceptional in Southeast Asia, has been a potent symbol of Southeast Asia's slide to authoritarianism after decolonisation. Burma was at the epicentre of debates over the 'cultural relativism' stance that ASEAN governments adopted during the Vienna World Conference on Human Rights in 1993. Burma has also been a reminder of how the Southeast Asian governments, as members of ASEAN, have neglected the importance of promoting human rights and democracy as part of their agenda of regional cooperation. A powerful symbol of this neglect was ASEAN's policy of 'constructive engagement' towards Burma, pursued in the aftermath of the 1988 military crackdown on pro-democracy forces there, which was widely criticised by the international community as shielding human rights abuses by the Burmese junta. That policy not only affected ASEAN's relations with Western nations, but also created an unfavorable international image for an otherwise respected grouping. The policy was also a reminder of the paradoxical impact of ASEAN's time-honoured non-interference doctrine, which has been credited for maintaining intra-mural peace, but causing the neglect of human rights and democracy in the region.

The political awakening of Burma is one of the most important and positive developments in Southeast Asian regional affairs. ASEAN has had a mixed record when it comes to promoting change in Burma. ASEAN should take some, but not too much, credit for the reforms in Burma. Since the early 2000s, after realising the failure and image costs of its constructive engagement policy, ASEAN gradually came to encourage Burma to step-up reform, albeit within the confines of its persisting, if slowly easing, non-interference principle. In ASEAN, Burma has had a framework for defining and pursuing its foreign policy which is an alternative to either self-destructive isolationism or an unsavory dependence on China. But while one should not dismiss ASEAN's role in shaping Burma's *foreign policy choices*, it is hard to prove that ASEA had a major impact in shaping Burma's *domestic developments*. Why the reforms are happening now in Burma is a matter of continuing speculation and debate. Sanctions did play a role. But the reforms in Burma are largely driven by domestic calculations and factors. A sense of growing frustration with the status quo; a desire for positive change among the elite, including sections within the armed forces, to break the country's isolation and catch up with its neighbours and the world at large; and, the personal image and approach of President Thein Sein are all factors that should be taken into account. A real reason behind the reforms could also be a calculated sense of regime security on the part of the military, which felt it could afford to step back a bit after having enacted a constitution that entrenches its hold on power for the long term. But relying on a new constitutional framework to legitimise continued military dominance can also have long-term unintended consequences, which may well put Burma on the path to genuine transformation.

Once the reforms are under way, however, ASEAN has a responsibility and a challenge to make a real contribution to the democratisation of Burma and its "return" to the international community. ASEAN might give the reformists in Burma vital diplomatic cover with which to reorient the country's domestic and foreign policy. ASEAN's policy challenges in Burma could include: keeping Burma on track with reform and ensuring that there will be no backsliding, through vigilance, persuasion and diplomatic efforts; helping with Burma's chairmanship of ASEAN in 2014, ensuring that it will be a successful meeting that enhances the country's reformist credentials; promoting democracy and human rights in the region as a whole so that Southeast Asia does not have another situation like Burma's long brush with military rule; and, lobbying for the right kind of international assistance to Burma which promotes sustainable development without turning it into an aid-dependent nation. In this respect, helping with capacity-building to effectively absorb and utilise aid would be especially crucial.

The ASC: from concept to reality

The idea of an ASEAN Security Community (ASC, renamed ASEAN Political Security Community, or ASPC, in the ASEAN Charter of December 2007) came from Indonesia.[53] Ostensibly, the proposal was aimed at resurrecting ASEAN which, in the words of Dr Rizal Sukma (of the Jakarta-based think-tank, Centre for Strategic and International Studies, and a key architect of the proposal), had been 'floating without a sense of purpose' since the 1997 economic crisis. It was also motivated by Jakarta's desire, as it was assuming the chairmanship of the ASEAN Standing Committee (July 2003–July 2004), to reaffirm its leadership in ASEAN, which was regarded with some doubt by its neighbours since the downfall of Suharto. As Dr Sukma would put it, if Indonesia did not push for closer security cooperation through the ASC now, 'it will need to wait for 10 years before its turn comes again'.[54]

Ideational influences were equally important. The original concept paper on the ASC, drafted by the Indonesian Foreign Ministry (Deplu), was surprisingly conceptual for a policy document, a feature which reflected the input of Indonesian academics such as Dr Sukma, who was clearly influenced by the academic literature on security communities. It defined a security community as a group whose 'member countries . . . have achieved a condition, as a result of flows of communication and the habit of cooperation, in which members share "expectations of peaceful change" and rule out "the use of force as means of problem-solving".'[55] In such a community, 'Member States regard their security as fundamentally linked to those of others and their destiny is bound by common norms, history, political experience, and geographic location.'[56] Distinguishing a security community from a security regime, it noted:

> Unlike a 'security regime', in which the renunciation of the use and the threat of the use of force are prompted only 'by the existence of a balance of power or a mutual-deterrence situation', ASEAN Security Community is based on a fundamental, unambiguous and long-term convergence of interests among ASEAN members in the avoidance of war.[57] (quotation marks as in the original document)

Conceptually, the ASC idea contained in the Deplu paper had two main elements. The first was its emphasis on non-use of force to settle disputes; the second was collective action to address common problems. On the first, it argued that: 'The principle of renunciation of the use of force and the threat of the use of force, which is already embedded in the Treaty of Amity and Cooperation (TAC), can serve as the foundation for an ASEAN Security Community.'[58] The non-use of force, a long-standing ASEAN goal, was consistent with the classical Deutschian notion of security communities. The second element contained in the Deplu paper was in response to new transnational dangers in the region, such as the Asian financial crisis, terrorism and the recently experienced SARS outbreak, which would presumably require a dilution of ASEAN's non-interference doctrine. Hence, 'ASEAN's efforts to combat international terrorism and its supporting elements – money laundering, small arms and light weapons trafficking, and other transnational issues have caused ASEAN to shift its priorities towards the need to increase cooperation in political and security areas.'[59]

But there was a tension between these two elements since ASEAN's record in avoiding war among its members was partly based on commitment to non-interference, and it was the same doctrine which needed to be adjusted, if not abandoned, to make it responsive to new threats facing the region. This in essence would be ASEAN's most important dilemma in realising the ASC idea.

The paper recommended a series of measures to implement the ASC, including 'innovative ways into conflict resolution', 'strengthening security and defence cooperation', and 'a more integrated security and defence institution' which would include an ASEAN Police and Defence Minister Meeting (APDMM), an ASEAN Centre for Cooperation on Non-Conventional Issues, an ASEAN Centre for Combating Terrorism, and an ASEAN Centre for Peace Keeping Training.[60] Dr Sukma would additionally call for an ASEAN Maritime Surveillance Centre.[61] Finally, the paper stated some of the key strategic issues relating to ASC, such as 'non-interference, national sovereignty, consensus-based decision-making, and the renouncement of the threat or use of force', which ASEAN needed to look into to realise the ASC.

Indonesian thinking on the ASC continued to develop as it assumed the chairmanship of the ASEAN standing committee from July 2003 to July 2004. Although nothing about the ASC was mentioned in the communiqué of the AMM in Cambodia on 16–18 June 2003, the concept was presented there by Indonesia to its ASEAN colleagues. A confidential explanatory paper of the Indonesian Foreign Minister offered further insights into Indonesian thinking. To reach the stage of a security community, ASEAN 'will already be at peace with itself and at peace with others in the immediate neighbourhood'. 'Such a condition', the paper added, would be based on a regional order which contained strong rules of good conduct and mechanisms for conflict prevention and resolution 'adequate and capable of overcoming various potential conflicts among its members'. A conflict-free ASEAN would mean '(1) the refusal by members to use or threaten to use armed force for resolving conflicts; (2) agreement on non-aggression; (3) absence of intra-regional threat perceptions (as well as perception of threats from outside the region); (4) creating "we feelings"; and (5) ASEAN becoming a democratic entity.'[62] It emphasised norm creation as central to regional order: 'Regional order based upon rules of good conduct will create "predictability" and "stability" in relations among the member states.' It also called for norm-setting with outside (extra-regional) powers through measures such as extending the scope for accession to the ASEAN Treaty of Amity and Cooperation by countries such as China and Papua New Guinea, the Declaration of the Conduct of Parties in the South China Sea between ASEAN and China and the accession to the TAC by other big powers such as Russia, India and Japan.[63]

Moreover, the document outlined an initial 'laundry list' of steps to achieve the ASC. Examples of mechanisms for addressing and resolving conflicts among members included negotiations and facilitation/mediation by the ASEAN High Council and the creation of an ASEAN Peacekeeping Operation. Other measures included those to promote 'political development' within the ASC through democracy, an ASEAN Human Rights Commission, good governance, mutual legal assistance, an ASEAN anti-terrorism pact and an agreement on non-aggression.[64]

Scepticism greeted the Indonesian proposal almost from the outset. In a confidential response, the Malaysian think-tank, ISIS Malaysia, noted that although the ASC proposal seemed to entail 'a more integrated political and security cooperation' that would include the establishment of mutual trust and the renunciation of force in resolving intra-regional conflicts, there was 'insufficient articulation of the ASC concept and what its adoption will entail'. Another major concern was whether the advent of an ASC would imply a 'common security perception stemming from a collective sense of security'. This was problematic because the ASEAN member states had 'different threat perceptions and security orienta-tions'. Hence, 'while the idea of a security community can be welcome in principle as a desirable goal . . . its utility and relevance should not be exaggerated.' In addition, the name 'ASEAN Community of Peace' would be preferred to the ASC, as the latter 'sounds very academic and Western . . . like an imported idea'.[65]

Malaysia also expressed concerns about the potential defence aspects of the ASC. Singapore did likewise, as some old hands in the Singapore foreign ministry were reminded of Indonesia's attempts to introduce defence cooperation into ASEAN at the Bali Summit of 1976. In October 2003, Malaysian Foreign Minister Syed Hamid Albar said that Malaysia had no objection to the establishment of the ASC provided it did not take the form of a military alliance. While there was a need to ensure regional security for economic progress to take place, 'We [ASEAN leaders] agree that it is not our goal to create a military bloc. Our focus for the ASEAN Security Community is on coming up with a caring society and human security.' In addition, he emphasised that there must be a 'certain level of comfort' before ASEAN members could act. Otherwise the idea of an ASEAN Security Community would be 'a mere talk shop'.[66]

Perhaps responding to such concerns, the Indonesian Foreign Ministry changed its phrase 'building a more integrated security and defence institution' found in the original Deplu paper to 'building a more integrated security cooperation' in an early August 2003 draft of what would be known as the Bali Concord II (to be signed at the forthcoming ASEAN Summit in Bali in October). It reaffirmed the Deplu paper's assertion that the ASC would be based on the principle of comprehensive security, which 'conceives security as having apart from military and defence dimensions, broad economic, social and cultural aspects as well as in the traditional and on-traditional aspects' (*sic*).[67] And the Indonesian defence ministry clarified that the concept of 'security' in the ASC was not to be defined in terms of military attack, but in terms of confronting terrorism, human trafficking, and money laundering.[68]

The final text of the Declaration of ASEAN Concord II (Bali Concord II), adopted by the ninth ASEAN Summit in Bali on 7 October 2003, formally endorsed the ASEAN Security Community idea (along with the ASEAN Economic Community and the ASEAN Socio-Cultural Community). Noting that the ASC was aimed at taking 'ASEAN's political and security cooperation to a higher plane', it did, however, recognise 'the sovereign right of the member countries to pursue their individual foreign policies and defence arrangements'. The 'principle of comprehensive security, . . . rather than . . . a defence pact, military alliance or a joint foreign policy', was affirmed as the basis of the ASC (*sic*). Finally, the declaration identified the key elements of the ASC to include 'norms-setting, conflict prevention, approaches to conflict resolution, and post-conflict peace building'.[69]

While endorsing the ASC, the Bali Concord II embodying the ASC also reaffirmed ASEAN's existing norms and approaches. It stressed peaceful settlement of intra-regional differences ('members shall rely exclusively on peaceful processes in the settlement of intra-regional differences'); confirmed the salience of non-interference ('Member Countries shall exercise their rights to lead their national existence free from outside interference in their internal affairs'); affirmed ASEAN's traditional reluctance to develop multilateral military cooperation, and restated ASEAN's fundamental principles ('The ASEAN Security Community shall . . . uphold ASEAN's principles of non-interference, consensus-based decision-making, national and regional resilience, respect for national sovereignty, the renunciation of the threat or the use of force, and peaceful settlement of differences and disputes'). It also endorsed 'existing ASEAN political instruments such as the Declaration on ZOPFAN, the TAC, and the SEANWFZ Treaty shall continue to play a pivotal role in the area of confidence building measures, preventive diplomacy and the approaches to conflict resolution'.[70]

The document did, however, identify some specific areas of cooperation over transnational challenges. Maritime affairs being transboundary in nature needed to be 'addressed regionally in an holistic, integrated and comprehensive manner'. Other areas of cooperation would include 'strengthening national and regional capacities to counter-terrorism, drug trafficking, trafficking in persons and other transnational crimes'. Keeping Southeast Asia free from 'all weapons of mass destruction was another goal'.[71]

As the chair of ASEAN's Standing Committee, Indonesia was asked to come up with a plan of action to implement the ASC.[72] Jakarta produced the first draft of the ASEAN Security Community in February 2004. It placed heavy emphasis on democracy and human rights and contained dozens of proposals for new mechanisms – such as a regional peacekeeping force, a non-aggression pact, an extradition agreement, a counter-terrorism convention, and an arms registry – making its fellow ASEAN members wonder as much about their sheer number as their content.[73] The following is a summary of the key elements of the initial Indonesian draft and how they fared through the painstaking negotiations before the final version was adopted in November 2004.

The ASEAN Security Community Plan of Action: Indonesian proposals (February 2004) versus the final version (November 2004)

1   Under the 'political development' section, the Indonesian draft urged that

   members shall promote political development in support of ASEAN leaders' commitment to strive for democracy *as an ASEAN shared value* . . . In order to better respond to the new dynamics within the respective ASEAN member countries, ASEAN shall nurture such common socio-political values and principles as democracy and *human rights*.

   In the final version, the references to democracy as a 'shared ASEAN value' and to democracy and human rights as exemplary of 'common socio-political values and principles' were dropped. The language was changed to:

   members shall promote political development in support of ASEAN Leaders' shared vision and common values to achieve peace, stability, democracy and prosperity in the region . . . In order to better respond to the new dynamics within the respective ASEAN Member Countries, ASEAN shall nurture such common socio-political values and principles.

2   The Indonesian draft contained a formulation

   ASEAN member countries shall not tolerate unconstitutional and undemocratic government changes.

   This appeared in the final version as

   ASEAN Member Countries shall not condone unconstitutional and undemocratic changes of government or the use of their territory for any actions undermining peace, security and stability of other ASEAN Member Countries.

It would appear that some member states wanted to give non-interference equal weight to commitment to democracy and human rights. Yet, significantly enough, the final draft retained the basic thrust of what may be the most important operating sentence of the political development section.

3   Under the list of 'Activities' designed to realise the ASC, the original draft called for

   Strengthening the systems of people's participation through regular and free elections.

   The final draft would only mention

   Strengthening democratic institutions and popular participation.

4   But a reference in the Indonesian draft to the 'Promotion of a just, democratic and harmonious environment' in ASEAN was retained. On human rights instruments, the initial Indonesian draft's call for establishing an 'ASEAN Regional Commission on Human Rights' was changed to 'Establishing a network among existing human rights mechanisms'. However, the ASEAN Charter approved three years later provided for a 'human rights body'.

5   The Indonesian proposals for 'Developing an ASEAN Charter of Rights and Obligations of Peoples' and 'ASEAN minimum standards of protection for migrant workers' were not to be found in the final draft of the ASC Plan of Action.

6   Among the new mechanisms proposed by Jakarta that were dropped in the final version were the ASEAN Peace Keeping Force (standby arrangement), ASEAN Maritime Forum, ASEAN Maritime Safety and Surveillance Unit, and ASEAN Non-Aggression Treaty. But several others from the original Indonesian draft were accepted, including an ASEAN Mutual Legal Assistance Agreement, ASEAN Extradition Treaty, and an ASEAN Convention on Counter Terrorism. Moreover, the final draft added two institutions, implied but not explicitly suggested in the Indonesian draft: an ASEAN Institute for Peace and Reconciliation and an ASEAN Humanitarian Assistance Centre.

   Sources: 'ASEAN Security Community Plan of Action', draft of 13 February 2004, prepared by Indonesia; 'ASEAN Security Community Plan of Action', final approved draft adopted at the Tenth ASEAN Summit, Vientiane, 29–30 November 2004. Available at www.aseansec.org/16826.htm (accessed 24 June 2008).

Especially controversial was the peacekeeping force idea. Singapore's Foreign Minister, S. Jayakumar, argued that it was 'probably not the right time now' for an ASEAN peacekeeping force. 'Perhaps sometime in the future, there may be scope for such an organisation.' ASEAN in his view was not set up as a security or defence organisation.[74] Echoing this, his Vietnamese counterpart, Nguyen Dy Nien, stated that it was 'too early' to consider setting up a peacekeeping force, adding: 'Each country has its own policy about politics and the military.'[75] Earlier, Thailand's Foreign Minister, Surakiart Sathirathai, had also opposed a peacekeeping force for ASEAN. Such a force was unnecessary because 'there is no conflict in the region which would need the mobilisation of such a force'.[76] This was disingenuous, because the experience of East Timor and the ongoing situation in Aceh were clearly the kind of conflicts that might have been better dealt with if peacekeeping cooperation existed in ASEAN.

Aside from practical issues such as differences in military doctrines, levels of military capability, and standards of weaponry, the obstacle to the peacekeeping force was the non-interference doctrine. Indonesia itself had suggested that the most likely area of deployment of an ASEAN peacekeeping force would be within ASEAN member states, especially those that faced serious internal conflicts such as the separatist conflict in Indonesia's Aceh province (which was yet to be resolved), the Mindanao region of the Philippines, and Thailand's southern provinces.[77] Indonesia had agreed to the presence of foreign peace monitors in Aceh under the aegis of the Geneva-based Henri Dunant Centre, which mediated in Jakarta's talks with the Acehnese rebels. It had invited troops from the Philippines and Thailand to participate in this mission. Jakarta in turn had sent military personnel to Mindanao to monitor the implementation of the 1996 peace settlement between Manila and the Moro Islamic Liberation Front. The Philippine government had accepted Malaysian diplomatic mediation in its peace talks with the MILF. But these steps were taken on a bilateral basis. Creating an ASEAN peacekeeping force, in the Indonesian view, would 'multilateralise' such cooperation.[78] And this was unacceptable to Singapore and Vietnam, as well as to Burma.

Some in ASEAN saw Indonesia's promotion of an ASEAN Security Community as a bid to reassert itself over the rest of the region. The finalisation of the ASEAN Security Community Plan of Action (ASCPA) took an unusual number of meetings, involving senior officials in Jakarta in February 2004, then ASEAN Foreign Ministers in early March at a special retreat in Ha Long Bay, Vietnam, followed by further senior official meetings in early May in Jakarta, mid-May in Jogjakarta, and early June in Jakarta. Moreover, ASEAN senior officials discussed the draft on the margins of ASEAN–Russia and ASEAN–China bilateral meetings in May and June respectively.[79] This suggests the sensitivities and difficulties involved in reaching agreement over the plan, which would go through several drafts. However, Indonesian Foreign Ministry spokesman Marty Natalegawa described Jakarta's draft criticisms as 'expected', considering its 'bold' approach in advocating such a plan. According to him, the proposals were designed to give Southeast Asians an 'ASEAN option' in security.[80]

The final version of the ASCPA, along with an annex of activities, was endorsed by ASEAN Foreign Ministers at their meeting in Jakarta during 29–30 June 2004, and given final approval by ASEAN leaders at their summit in Vientiane on 29–30 November 2004. The ASCPA has five components: political development; shaping and sharing of norms; conflict prevention; conflict resolution; and post-conflict peacebuilding. Perhaps the most interesting part of the political development section is the stipulation that 'ASEAN Member Countries shall not condone unconstitutional and undemocratic changes of government'.[81] This was to be tested by the Thai military coup in 2006, when ASEAN could do little but condone the military takeover.

The purpose of the 'shaping and sharing of norms' section is to promote 'a standard of common adherence to norms of good conduct', as well as to develop a 'we feeling' in the grouping.[82] The norms listed include non-alignment, fostering of peace-oriented attitudes of ASEAN member countries, conflict resolution through non-violent means, renunciation of nuclear weapons and other weapons of mass destruction and avoidance of an arms race in Southeast Asia, and renunciation of the threat, or the use, of force. However, there is a reference earlier in the document to the 'well-established principles' that were to guide the process of developing the ASC.

Moreover, according to an Indonesian Foreign Ministry document, the ASC would be founded upon the principles of non-intervention, consensus, national and regional resilience, sovereignty, avoidance of use of force in conflict situations and pacific settlement of disputes.[83] These are essentially the same as the core norms of ASEAN since its inception.

Another important set of proposals contained in the ASCPA concerns security cooperation.

These include non-intrusive confidence-building measures akin to that adopted by the ARF, such as exchanges among senior military officials, military academies, and staff colleges, periodic publication of strategic assessments and defence white papers; exchange of observers at military exercises; creation of an ASEAN arms register to be administered by the ASEAN Secretariat (the ARF has plans for a similar register), publication of an ASEAN members annual security outlook, voluntary briefing by ASEAN member countries on national security issues; and the development of an 'ASEAN early warning system based on existing mechanisms to prevent occurrence/escalation of conflicts'. Another important proposal was the call for an annual ASEAN Defence Ministers' Meeting, the first such meeting in ASEAN's history and important given the grouping's traditional reluctance to keep defence interactions at the bilateral level. This does not mean, however, that ASEAN is moving towards a military alliance. Indonesia was firm in denying this possibility of ASC leading to an ASEAN military pact or even a common foreign policy.[84] On the matter of dispute settlement, the ASCPA provided for the establishment of an ad hoc experts advisory committee (EAC) or an eminent persons group (EPG) that would assist the ASEAN High Council if and when the latter is convened to settle disputes among ASEAN members. And while the idea of a regional peacekeeping centre had been rejected earlier, the ASCPA encouraged cooperation among existing and planned national peacekeeping centres and called for establishing a network among such centres 'to conduct joint planning, training, and sharing of experiences'. This could conceivably lead to the establishment at a future date of 'an ASEAN arrangement' for the maintenance of peace and stability'.[85] Finally, the ASCPA mandated the drafting of an ASEAN charter.

The final shape of the ASC is a truncated version of the original Indonesia proposal. The alterations to the initial Indonesian draft plan of action attest to significant political contestations over the political norms of ASEAN, which in turn reflect differing political systems and security ideologies within ASEAN. How could a military dictatorship or an absolute monarchy or a communist regime endorse democracy as 'a shared ASEAN value' or 'regular and free elections'? What is remarkable, however, is that Indonesia still found it possible to retain at least some of its suggested rules and institutions for democracy and human rights; a considerable diplomatic effort by, and vindication for, Jakarta.

But the main problem with the ASCPA is the implementation of those ideas that have survived the intergovernmental negotiations. As the EPG on the ASEAN charter notes,

> ASEAN's problem is not one of lack of vision, ideas, or action plans. The problem is one of ensuring compliance and effective implementation.[86]

Since the ASCPA (changed to ASEAN Political-Security Community), there has been some progress towards implementing its recommendations. The most important ones are the convening of the first ASEAN Defence Ministers' Meeting in Kuala Lumpur in May 2006, and the signing of the ASEAN counter-terrorism convention in January 2007. The defence ministers' meeting, dubbed by an ASEAN spokesman as reflecting 'ASEAN's seriousness in carrying out the ASEAN Security Community plan of action',[87] includes consideration of non-traditional security threats such as transnational crimes and terrorism as well as maritime security and disaster relief efforts.[88]

The ASEAN Charter

The ASEAN Summit in Kuala Lumpur in December 2005 appointed an EPG to guide the development of an ASEAN charter as a step towards the development of an ASEAN

Table 7.2 Summary of the ASEAN Political and Security Community Blueprint

The APSC Blueprint is aimed at providing the roadmap and timetable to establish the ASEAN Security Community by 2015. It is guided by the ASEAN Charter and by the principles contained therein. Notably, the APSC and the ASEAN Charter subscribe to a *comprehensive approach to security*, which acknowledges the interwoven relationships between all dimensions of security political, economic, socio-cultural and environmental development. Therefore, the APSC on the one hand, promotes the renunciation of aggression and of the threat and use of force upholding, in this regard, the existing ASEAN mechanisms (ZOPFAN, the TAC and the Treaty on Southeast Asia Nuclear Weapon Free Zone); on the other, it also seeks to address non-traditional security challenges.

Based on these ideas the APSC pursues the following three goals:

1 A rules-based community of shared norms and values
2 A cohesive, peaceful, stable and resilient region with shared responsibility for comprehensive security
3 A dynamic and outward looking region in an increasingly integrated and interdependent world

To achieve these goals the ASEAN security blueprint outlines a number of specific activities that have to be undertaken by ASEAN members in the following areas:

1 A rules-based Community of Shared Norms and Values

Cooperation in Political Development

1.1 Promote understanding and appreciation of political systems, culture and history of ASEAN members
1.2 Lay the groundwork for an institutional framework to facilitate free flow of information for mutual support and assistance of ASEAN members
1.3 Establish programmes for mutual support and assistance among ASEAN members in the development of strategies for strengthening the rule of law and judiciary system and legal infrastructure
1.4 Promote good governance
1.5 Promotion and protection of human rights
1.6 Increase the participation of the relevant entities associated with ASEAN in moving forward ASEAN political development initiatives
1.7 Prevent and combat corruption
1.8 Promote principles of democracy
1.9 Promote peace and stability in the region

Shaping and Sharing ASEAN Norms

2.1 Adjust ASEAN institutional framework to comply with the ASEAN Charter
2.2 Strengthening Cooperation under the TAC
2.3 Ensure the full implementation of the DOC for the South China Sea
2.4 Ensure the implementation of the Southeast Asian Nuclear Weapon Free Zone Treaty and its Plan of Action
2.5 Promote ASEAN maritime cooperation

2 A Cohesive, peaceful, stable and resilient region with shared responsibility for comprehensive security

Conflict Prevention/Confidence-Building Measures

1.1 Strengthen Confidence-building measures
1.2 Promote greater transparency and understanding of defence policies and security perceptions
1.3 Build up the necessary institutional framework to strengthen the ARF process in support of the ASEAN Political Security Community
1.4 Strengthen efforts in maintaining respect for territorial integrity, sovereignty and unity of ASEAN members
1.5 Promote the development of norms that enhance ASEAN defence and security cooperation

(Continued)

Table 7.2 (Continued)

1.6 Conflict resolution and pacific settlement of disputes

1.7 Building up of existing modes of pacific settlement of disputes and consider strengthening them with additional mechanisms as needed

1.8 Strengthen research activities on peace, conflict management and conflict resolution

1.9 Promote regional cooperation to maintain peace and stability

1.10 Post conflict peace-building

1.11 Strengthen ASEAN humanitarian assistance

1.12 Implement human resources and capacity building programmes in post conflict areas

1.13 Increase cooperation in reconciliation and further strengthen peace-oriented values

Non-traditional security issues

1.1 Strengthen cooperation in addressing non-traditional security issues, particularly in combating transnational crime and other transboundary challenges

1.2 Intensify counter-terrorism efforts by early ratification and full implementation of the ASEAN Convention on Counter Terrorism

1.3 Strengthen ASEAN Cooperation on Disaster Management and Emergency response

1.4 Effective and timely response to urgent issues or crisis situations affecting ASEAN

Source: ASEAN Secretariat

community. The charter initiative was 'aimed at transforming ASEAN from being a non-binding political association to becoming an international organisation with a legal personality and a rule-based organisation with an effective and efficient organisational structure'.[89]

Unlike the UN and most regional organisations – such as the Organisation of American States, the African Union (formerly the Organisation for African Unity), the League of Arab States, and the Gulf Cooperation Council – ASEAN had begun life without a charter. Its later adoption of a charter is not without precedent, however, the Organisation for Security and Cooperation in Europe (OSCE) adopted its charter for European Security in November 1999, presumably because until then it had functioned as a conference, rather than as an organisation *per se*. ASEAN was founded with a declaration (the Bangkok Declaration) in 1967 and later a treaty (Treaty of Amity and Cooperation in Southeast Asia) in 1976, rather than a charter *per se*, in keeping with its well-known penchant for avoiding too much legalism and institutionalisation. Why the need for a charter now?

The most important considerations relate to the imperative for the deepening and legalisation of ASEAN. Since the end of the Cold War, ASEAN had gone through a process of widening including expansion of its membership to include all ten nations of Southeast Asia and incorporating new issue areas of cooperation such as environment, financial flows and counter terrorism. But this broadening had taken place without significant strengthening of ASEAN's institutions. In August 2005, Malaysian Prime Minister Abdullah Badawi hinted at two possible motives for having an ASEAN charter. The first was to create an international legal personality for ASEAN. The other was to provide 'the legal framework for incorporating Asean decisions, treaties and conventions into the national legislation of member countries'.[90] The latter is an especially critical innovation. ASEAN has in the past undertaken collective dealing and bargaining with external countries, but a common framework for applying ASEAN decisions at the national level, if realised, will be a significant step towards legalising and deepening ASEAN.

ASEAN is not, however, emulating the EU's degree of institutionalisation. George Yeo, the Foreign Minister of Singapore, argues that while there is much that ASEAN can learn from the EU, it is doubtful if 'ASEAN integration will ever reach even half the level of integration in Europe today'.[91] Tommy Koh, a member of the intergovernmental committee drafting the charter (following the EPG report), puts it differently: the EU served 'as an inspiration, but not a model' for ASEAN, including its charter.[92]

Within ASEAN, differences emerged over the charter between those who would like to use the opportunity afforded by it to pursue an ambitious agenda of legalisation and institutionalisation and those who would want to tread more conservatively. For example, Malaysian Prime Minister Badawi stated that the proposed ASEAN charter 'need not be an overly ambitious project'.[93] But Singapore's Prime Minister Lee Hsien Loong described the objective of the ASEAN charter as being to 'set a clear and ambitious long-term direction to ASEAN'.[94]

After holding a series of consultations with a cross-section of audiences, including NGOs, to gather ideas about the charter, the EPG submitted its recommendations in December 2006. Its major recommendations fell into five categories:

- Strengthening ASEAN's organisational structure and capacity. Its Secretary-General should have ministerial rank, with the authority to sign agreements on behalf of ASEAN in non-sensitive areas and to represent ASEAN in the UN (where it only has observer status). There should be four (instead of the current two) Deputy Secretary-Generals, and a professional staff. The ASEAN heads of government meeting should be held twice a year. Each of ASEAN's three communities – economic, security and socio-cultural – should have their own councils.
- Decision-making by majority voting. ASEAN should depart from the consensus principle, if necessary, in non-sensitive areas (i.e. excluding security and foreign policy issues). It could go for majority voting, either a simple majority or two-thirds or three-quarters majority. ASEAN could use 'ASEAN minus x' and 'two plus x' formulas to undertake cooperation if consensus cannot be reached over a particular issue.
- Compliance through sanctions. Compliance with ASEAN's objectives, principles, decisions, agreements and timetables, should be monitored. Members found to be in 'serious breach' of them will be taken to task. They may be deprived of their membership rights and privileges, or, in extraordinary circumstances, may even be expelled.
- Dispute settlement. There should be dispute settlement mechanisms in all areas of cooperation, especially economic and political areas. Currently, the ASEAN Free Trade Area has its dispute settlement mechanism, and the ASEAN Treaty of Amity and Cooperation (1976) provides for a high council to deal with disputes in political and security fields, although it has never been used.
- Creation of an 'ASEAN human rights body'.[95]

The EPG report listed a number of objectives and principles for ASEAN to be incorporated into the charter: a total of 19 objectives and 23 principles. Many were vague and overlapping. Presumably, this was an extended menu, and not all could find their way into the actual charter. Indeed, the EPG's report suffered a fate similar to Indonesia's proposals for the ASEAN Security Community: they were significantly diluted by the intergovernmental committee tasked to draft the actual provisions of the charter. When the ASEAN leaders formally adopted the charter on 20 November 2007, what emerged was a much more conservative document, belying hopes and expectations raised by the EPG report. Some of the institutional measures were kept, including twice-a-year summits and ASEAN Coordinating Council meetings (meetings of Foreign Ministers), with provision for ad hoc meetings and the creation of four Deputy Secretary-General posts; these staff, along with the Secretary-General, are not supposed to take instructions from their national governments. But the provisions for sanctions, majority voting, and dispute settlement procedures, all of which are important to the greater legalisation of ASEAN, were discarded or diluted. Decisions and actions over unresolved intra-ASEAN disputes and any breach of the charter or non-compliance by member states were to be decided by the ASEAN Summit, a political body of national leaders still committed to working through consensus, rather than a professional and specialised judicial or administrative mechanism. Hence, the charter, although not an insignificant political commitment to advancing ASEAN's institutional trajectory, makes a small break from the grouping's traditional preference for soft institutionalism, with its rules lacking in automaticity and subject ultimately not to an inviolable regional rule of law, but to political considerations and calculations.[96]

As with the ASC plan of action, human rights and democracy remain a contentious and uncertain area of cooperation in the charter. The Joint Communiqué of the 37th ASEAN Ministerial Meeting in Jakarta in June 2004 mentioned the 'promotion and protection of human rights' as one of the objectives of the charter, alongside other goals such as 'establishment of effective and efficient institutional framework for ASEAN'.[97] Democracy and human rights are mentioned three and seven times respectively in the charter. Its section on 'Purposes' includes a call 'To strengthen democracy, enhance good governance and the rule of law, and to promote and protect human rights and fundamental freedoms, with due regard to the rights and responsibilities of the Member States of ASEAN.' And Principles (h) and (i) call for 'adherence to the rule of law, good governance, the principles of democracy and constitutional Government' and 'respect for fundamental freedoms, the promotion and protection of human rights, and the promotion of social justice', respectively.[98] In the end, the terms of reference of the ASEAN Human Rights Body were not specified in the charter, but left to be decided by the ASEAN Foreign Ministers.[99] And democracy promotion remains problematic, as discussed in the previous section on the ASC.

The EPG report had called for ASEAN members to 'calibrate' the non-interference doctrine to deal with problems 'where common interest dictates closer cooperation'.[100] In the charter itself, principle (e) called for 'non-interference in the internal affairs of ASEAN Member States', while principle (f) stipulated 'respect for the right of every Member State to lead its national existence free from external interference, subversion and coercion', and principle (k) asked for 'abstention from participation in any policy or activity, including the use of its territory, pursued by any ASEAN Member State or non-ASEAN State or any non-State actor, which threatens the sovereignty, territorial integrity or political and economic stability of ASEAN Member States'.[101] These principles mirror the norms and practices enunciated by ASEAN at different stages in its history, including the 1976 Treaty of Amity and Cooperation in Southeast Asia. This suggests that one of the key purposes of the charter was to codify and consolidate the earlier principles and modalities of ASEAN that had evolved through many different stages and documents, rather than break significant new ground. The charter shows considerable path-dependency in ASEAN's normative evolution.

The ASEAN charter has been regarded as a 'work in progress'.[102] It is subject to review after five years since it came into force on 15 December 2008. It gives ASEAN a veneer of legal personality and sets the stage for further institutionalisation of the grouping. But, as with the ideas and measures contained in the ASC, the charter's ultimate challenge lies not in the 'lack of vision, ideas', but in 'ensuring compliance and effective implementation'.[103]

The ASEAN Charter, though seen as a welcome innovation and advance, has created some hurdles for ASEAN's effective functioning. A general problem is that the Charter creates a whole host of new rules ('rules for everything'). Yet, this has reduced flexibility and the autonomy of the ASEAN Secretary-General or for the member states, including foreign ministers who still play a central role in the management of ASEAN. A major issue arising in the post-Charter period concerns the relationship between the ASEAN Secretariat (ASEC) and the Committee of Permanent Representatives (CPR). The CPR comprises permanent ambassadors for each member country to ASEAN. The existing relationship between ASEC and the CPR is complex and tensions there have the potential to undermine the functioning of ASEAN across all pillars/sectors. The CPR model for ASEAN was copied from the EU. The CPR is supposed to function like a board of trustees, not micro-manage the day-to-day functions of the secretariat.[104] Yet, there is a perception that the CPR members have interpreted the Charter too liberally as granting them control and supervision over ASEC. In some instances, it has indulged in the micro-management of ASEC, particularly on organisational and personnel issues, even intervening in the employment and deployment of staff, affecting the work across all pillars.

Another challenge facing ASEAN concerns strengthening the ASEAN Secretariat. The ASEAN Charter created a number of provisions to strengthen ASEAN's institutional capacity generally, and the ASEAN Secretariat particularly. Despite the implementation of some of the EPG's recommendations, such as enhancing the status and authority of the Secretary-General, increasing the number of Deputy Secretary-Generals from two to four (two of whom are openly recruited based on merit), and the provision for openly recruited professional staff to manage the secretariat, it has become fairly clear that the member states, despite their declaratory commitment to greater institutionalisation and legalisation of ASEAN, do not want a strong secretariat. To compound matters, the member states pose many questions over ASEC's legitimacy on a wide range of actions. They seem to be more concerned with promoting a national agenda than a supranational one. Only the long-time professional staff members of the secretariat seem not to be pushing for a national agenda. While this is consistent with ASEAN's aversion to EU-style supranationalism, it also impedes the effective implementation of ASEAN's expanding range of tasks and functions. The key challenges to the effective functioning of the ASEC include whether ASEAN has the necessary resources to sustain its institutions; 'budget'; human resources, and relationship with national governments. The organisation structure of the ASEAN Secretariat does not enable ASEC to respond to changing developments and needs.

The figures indicate that there has been more than one meeting held at the secretariat for every day of the year, including weekends (table 7.3). The number of official meetings increased from 788 in 2008 to 1224 in 2010. These figures do not include attendance at conferences, meetings and briefings with stakeholders such as youth groups, business, academia, dialogue partners, as well as internal meetings, preparatory and coordination meetings, visits, consultations, and others. Each unit at the secretariat has three or more of these meetings per week. Many of these meetings require travel and the preparation of papers.

The consequences of a weak secretariat were highlighted in the context of the 2012 AMM in Cambodia which ended without issuing a communiqué. Apparently, three officials from the secretariat, including two Cambodians, had been sent to Phnom Penh to spend weeks before the Ministerial meeting. But they provided no forewarning of the coming crisis. This suggests either that the secretariat staff lacked the necessary analytic skills, or that valuable information was deliberately withheld for the sake of parochial national interests. It shows that ASEAN as an institution is yet to develop a mindset that rises above national positions and serves the common interest of the organisation when the situation calls for it.

Table 7.3 ASEAN Secretariat staff, workload and budget (2006–10)

Year	No. of official ASEAN meetings	No. of ASEAN Meetings at ASEC	Total No. of Meetings in ASEAN and ASEC	Change in the No. of Meetings in ASEAN and ASEC (%)	Change in the No. of Meetings with 2006 as the base year (%)	No. of ASEC staff	Increase in staff (%)	Change in No. of Staff with 2006 as the base year (%)	ASEC Budget (US$ millions)	Change in ASEC budget (%)
2006	738	n/a	738	n/a	0	200	n/a	0	8.49	0
2007	688	n/a	688	–7	–7	205	3	3	9.68	14.02
2008	438	350	788	15	7	234	14	17	7.83	–19.11
2009	619	577	1196	52	62	262	12	31	14.35	83.27
2010	702	522	1224	2	66	229	–13	15	14.33	0.14

Source: Pitsuwan, *ASEAN's Challenge.*

The problems surrounding ASEAN's institutionalisation in general and the ASEC in particular were amply highlighted by none other than the first post-Charter ASEAN Secretary-General, Surin Pitsuwan, himself. In a comprehensive and forceful report, entitled 'ASEAN's Challenge',[105] Pitsuwan specifically highlighted the 'high degree of confusion among the ASEAN organs which undermines ASEAN's community-building efforts.' As the report put it, 'ASEAN risks losing control and direction in the post-Charter negotiations of a number of instruments to define the roles and new measures, due to the tensions between the ASEAN organs.' Of special concern was the relationship between the ASEAN Secretariat and the CPR, and between the national secretariats and the ASEAN organs. He also stressed that ASEAN 'lacks the capacity and expertise' to create new mechanisms and agreements mandated by the Charter. He described ASEAN's engagement with the civil society as 'weak' and 'limited', which undermines ASEAN's aspirations to be a 'people-oriented organisation'. He called for greater openness and accountability in the operation of various ASEAN organs. He called for rectifying the 'conflict of interest' between the CPR and the ASEAN Secretariat. He asked the CPR to 'consult the Secretary-General directly on all decisions affecting the Secretariat and officially communicate its decisions to the Secretary-General,' and develop 'rules of procedures and mechanisms for resolving disputes between the different organs of ASEAN'. Among his other recommendations are broadening and deepening ASEAN's engagement with the civil society groups and other 'stakeholders', clarifying and strengthening the legal personality of the ASEAN Secretariat and its capacity to support ASEAN's dispute settlement mechanisms, reviewing the 'efficiency of ASEAN's decision-making mechanisms', and introducing voting for decision-making or routine and operation issues. The comprehensive nature and tone of this report clearly suggested that all was not well with the state of the ASEAN Secretariat, and that much more reform and strengthening was needed for ASEAN to realise its goals of establishing its three communities. In essence, these recommendations call for giving more authority to the Secretary-General and enhancing the capacity of the ASEAN Secretariat. The response of the CPR to these proposals was somewhat cool, especially concerning those proposals where it had to concede ground to the Secretary-General.

Another critical issue is the financing of ASEC/ASEAN. There is a severe shortage of funds for the routine management of the Secretariat's requirements. ASEAN's annual budget is about US$ 15 million. Increasing this amount runs into problems because of the huge wealth gaps among ASEAN members. ASEAN operates on the principle that member states contribute to the ASEAN budget on an equal basis. There could be additional contributions by members on a voluntary basis for specific needs. This sort of arrangement was justified in the past on the grounds that differential funding might lead to a hierarchy of powers. Members who make higher contributions may gain greater influence. Although there is no majority voting procedure in ASEAN as yet, which may mean members may seek voting power proportional to their share of the ASEAN budget, this does not mean that voting is totally absent. 'ASEAN votes, but seldom and not in public', is how one source familiar with ASEAN puts it. Moreover, there are subtle ways of exercising power, not just through voting. If one member, say a large member state like Indonesia, gives more money to ASEAN, it may demand more say over the management of ASEAN and influence its objectives, at least psychologically. Moreover, one former official questioned whether ASEAN is really underfunded. Sometimes in the past, it was not able to spend its entire budget. But this may be a question of efficient and timely use of resources, rather than the adequacy of funding.

ASEAN community building: Towards participatory regionalism?

The ASC is one of the three pillars of ASEAN's community-building initiative, the others being the ASEAN Economic Community (AEC) and the ASEAN Socio-Cultural Community. The AEC concept is an outgrowth of the ASEAN Free Trade Area and predated the ASC, having been proposed by Singapore Prime Minister Goh Chok Tong at the ASEAN Summit in Phnom Penh in November 2002. Endorsed by the Bali Concord II, the AEC aims at creating an 'ASEAN economic region in which there is a free flow of goods, services, investment and a freer flow of capital, equitable economic development and reduced poverty and socio-economic disparities in year 2020'. The AEC involves establishing 'ASEAN as a single market and production base, turning the diversity that characterises the region into opportunities for business complementation'. Moreover, the AEC comprises new mechanisms as well as existing economic initiatives including AFTA, the ASEAN Framework Agreement on Services (AFAS) and the ASEAN Investment Area (AIA). Also envisaged is regional integration in facilitating movement of business persons and skilled labour, and strengthening of the institutional mechanisms of ASEAN, such as the existing ASEAN Dispute Settlement Mechanism 'to ensure expeditious and legally binding resolution of any economic disputes'. Finally, the AEC recognises the reality of a two-tier ASEAN by pledging to 'accelerate the economic integration of Cambodia, Lao PDR, Burma and Viet Nam'.[106]

The AEC reflects ASEAN's concerns about a changing global and regional economic climate marked by increased competition from China and India. It is also aimed at giving 'ASEAN a bigger "voice" in the world stage and . . . strengthen the position of member states with regards to their participation in the World Trade Organisation (WTO)'.[107] But the AEC is unlikely to grow into a true customs union in the short term, involving removal of all trade barriers among the member states and the application of a common external tariff policy to non-member states. A major obstacle is the gap within ASEAN between its new members and some of the more developed older members, and the challenge of developing ASEAN's institutional structure to manage the complex integration process. What is more likely is an arrangement which includes a free trade area with some aspects of a common market (such as free movement of capital and labour). Bilateral trade arrangements signed by ASEAN members, such as Singapore, with outside countries also challenge AEC. As one Japanese analyst warns, 'Should ASEAN keep on proceeding on FTAs with non-ASEAN countries without solidifying internal integration, it may lose bargaining power as a union of states.'[108] And the political climate among the ASEAN members has to be conducive for the AEC to succeed: 'At the end of the day, it could very well be the political dimensions of forming an economic community that would pose the greatest challenge for ASEAN.'[109] In this sense, the fate of the ASEAN Economic Community to a large extent depends on the realisation of the ASEAN Security Community.

Security communities are based on a 'we feeling'. But who are 'we'? Regionalism in Southeast Asia has been primarily political, state-centric and elite-driven. The idea of an ASEAN Socio-Cultural Community is to bring regionalism down to the societal level, to foster people-to-people contacts, including 'interaction among ASEAN scholars, writers, artists and media practitioners to help preserve and promote ASEAN's diverse cultural heritage' with a view to 'fostering regional identity' and 'cultivating people's awareness of ASEAN'.[110] Other objectives are to protect and manage the region's environment and natural resources, to address poverty, promote equity and human development, develop human resources, and provide greater social protection.[111] Finally, it calls for engaging the civil society in 'providing inputs for policy choices'.[112]

The last element is especially important. A 'socio-cultural community' does not simply mean recognising extant social and cultural similarities among ASEAN member states and societies. It also requires allowing participation from non-elites and civil society groups. Until now, only think-tanks acting through the so-called Second Track or Track-II dialogues had provided any input into ASEAN's ideas and policies and acted as filtering mechanisms for new ideas about cooperation that were coming from outside the region (such as the idea of common and cooperative security). These Track-II processes are meetings (bilateral as well as multilateral) sponsored by think-tanks that bear explicitly and directly on policy-relevant issues. They have two main characteristics. First, the think-tanks involved are, in most cases, closely linked to their respective national governments, and rely on government funding for their academic and policy-relevant activities. As Stuart Harris puts it, Track-II diplomacy is dependent 'upon the consent, endorsement and commitment, often including financial commitment, of governments'.[113] Second, Track-II meetings involve participation by government officials alongside academics and other non-official actors, although officials usually participate in their private capacity. Although the participating officials seldom venture beyond the position of their respective governments, the principle of 'private capacity' enables governments to test new ideas without making binding commitments and, if necessary, back-track on positions.

The most prominent among them is the ASEAN Institutes for Strategic and International Studies (ASEAN-ISIS), a group of national think-tanks which are either created or supported by their governments. ASEAN-ISIS, formally set up in 1988 (although the network of institutions comprising it had existed for some time), played a major role in the development of Track-II mechanisms that supported official regionalism in ASEAN, especially in the regional security arena.[114] It is the oldest Track-II regional mechanism in Southeast Asia, and despite a proliferation of think-tanks dealing with a variety of issues (such as the Maritime Institute of Malaysia, the Institute of Policy Studies, Malaysia, and the Centre for Information and Development Studies, Jakarta) not affiliated with ASEAN-ISIS, those comprising the latter remain the most influential in policy circles. The official mission of ASEAN-ISIS is to 'encourage cooperation and coordination of activities among policy-oriented ASEAN scholars and analysts, and to promote policy-oriented studies of, and exchanges of information and viewpoints on, various strategic and international issues affecting Southeast Asia's and ASEAN's peace, security and well-being'.[115]

ASEAN-ISIS provided the impetus for the establishment of the ASEAN Regional Forum and the ASEAN Free Trade Area. It was instrumental in the creation of the Council for Security Cooperation in the Asia Pacific (CSCAP), which provided policy ideas into the ARF process. ASEAN-ISIS is the official sponsor of the Asia Pacific Roundtable for Confidence Building and Conflict Reduction held annually in Malaysia. But the line separating the 'official position' and the positions taken by many, if not all the think-tanks which comprise ASEAN-ISIS, is not always very wide. Moreover, a key principle of Track-II, the participation of government officials 'in their private capacity', has rarely been upheld in practice. Seldom have these officials been able to rise above national interests and concerns.

Beyond Track-II institutions, there have developed in Southeast Asia a number of private and semi-official vocational associations that bear the ASEAN name: such as the ASEAN Tourism Association, ASEAN Arts Festival, ASEAN Travel Agents Association, ASEAN Music Industry Association, ASEAN University Sports Council, ASEAN Federation of Furniture Manufacturers Association, and the ASEAN Chambers of Commerce and Industry (ACCI), to name a few. (Strangely enough, some of these groups are listed under 'External Relations' on the official ASEAN website.) Another institution created to forge socio-cultural contacts is the ASEAN Foundation,[116] whose functions include promoting ASEAN awareness at the societal level, managing student exchange programmes and scholarships, human resource development and dialogue on development cooperation strategies. The ASEAN University Network represents yet another semi-official networking in ASEAN whose functions include the development of 'ASEAN Studies' in the university curricula of member states. The Southeast Asia Ministers of Education Organisation (SEAMEO) acts as an umbrella organisation that coordinates the different scholarships on offer by the various universities within the region, in addition to offering a highly regarded English language training programme.

A very different type of collaboration in Southeast Asia may be called non-official regionalism; it consists of social movements groups and processes which challenge state dominance and present an alternative approach to regional issues. These include mainly NGOs, with a regional and transregional membership and focus.[117] For example, the Asia-Pacific Coalition for East Timor (APCET),[118] founded in 1994, campaigned against human rights violations and for independence for East Timor when it was under Indonesian rule. The Alternative ASEAN Network on Burma (ALTSEAN-Burma)[119] is a network of activists, NGOs, academics and politicians that has championed human rights and democracy in Burma and challenged ASEAN's policy of 'constructive engagement'. Bangkok-based Forum-Asia, one of the largest and most prominent NGOs in Southeast Asia, seeks to 'develop a regional response on issues of common concern in the region',[120] and promote alternative approaches to national security that stress the security of the people instead of national and regime security.[121] The Focus on the Global South, also based in Bangkok, and the Penang-based Third World Network, have organised campaigns against globalisation and the exploitation of labour and the environment by multinationals.

Of late, there has been closer networking among and between semi-official and non-official groups. ASEAN-ISIS organised the ASEAN People's Assembly (APA) for the first time in November 2000 on Batam island in Indonesia, immediately following an ASEAN Summit in next-door Singapore.[122] The assembly has now become a regular event and had held six sessions by 2007 (the first two in Batam and Bali respectively, the rest all in Manila, which like Bangkok is a haven for NGOs). The principle of 'open economies, open societies' debated at the inaugural APA illustrated one possible common ground between the NGO community which opposes economic globalisation while demanding political openness, and regional governments which had advocated open economies but not open societies. The agendas of these APA gatherings have been broad; that of the sixth APA held in Manila in October 2007 covered 'a range of issues and concerns affecting peoples of Southeast Asia, including terrorism and transnational security problems, peace and social conflict, media and press freedom, regional human rights mechanism, human security and human development, security sector reform and governance, and ASEAN Community building . . . and good practices in people-centered community building in various parts of Southeast Asia and beyond'.[123] The Fifth APA in Manila demanded that the ASEAN Charter should establish ASEAN as a 'people-centered organization' and include 'norms and principles that give priority to the protection of peoples and communities within the context of their human development and security interests'.[124] Notably, the sixth APA issued a statement to 'strongly condemn' the military junta in Burma for its crackdown on the Buddhist monks' uprising.[125]

A parallel development is the emergence of the Solidarity for Asian Peoples' Advocacy (SAPA), established in Bangkok in February 2006 with over 50 civil society organisations participating in the inaugural consultations. These groups included the Asian Partnership for Development of Human Resources in Rural Asia, Focus on the Global South, South East

Asian Committee for Advocacy (SEACA), Third World Network (TWN) and Forum-Asia. Forum-Asia acts as the coordinator of SAPA. While APA represents a moderate semi-official regionalism, SAPA is the culmination of a non-official regionalism contesting ASEAN's claim to be the standard-bearer of Southeast Asian regional identity.

While SAPA's concerns go beyond Southeast Asia and ASEAN, it has established a Working Group on ASEAN to provide and exchange information and analysis and coordinate activities 'targeted at ASEAN and its processes'. Its priorities for 2007 included the ASEAN Charter, to engage the EPG on the Charter and 'initiate a people's charter campaign'. It organises an ASEAN Civil Society Conference (ACSC). It has created a task force on an ASEAN Human Rights Mechanism with a view to 'strategize on a human rights agenda for ASEAN', and coordinate with national human rights institutions in ASEAN. Other goals are to campaign for the creation of an ASEAN Commission for Women and Children and an ASEAN Instrument for Migrant Workers.[126] Notably, SAPA was one of the four civil society organisations allowed to consult with the ASEAN Charter EPG's Civil Society Consultations on 17 April 2006 (the others being the ASEAN Inter-Parliamentary Organisation (AIPO), which called for the creation of an ASEAN parliament, and which did not want to be grouped together with CSOs; the Working Group for an ASEAN Human Rights Mechanism, which argued for the protection of internationally recognised human rights, and the Secretariat of APA, hosted by the Centre for Strategic and International Studies (CSIS) Indonesia, which in the end withdrew because APA was an assembly and not a network or organisation, and hence did not have the mandate to represent the many CSOs who attended the assemblies).[127]

On 8 August 2005, the members of ASEAN celebrated ASEAN Day for the first time. But the development of a broader and participatory regionalism in Southeast Asia and a 'people's ASEAN' is hardly imminent. This is not because there is any necessary tension between national and regional identities; the two can co-exist.[128] But it will be contingent upon the further development of popular participation and identification with ASEAN. In this respect, the findings of a survey by the *Straits Times* of Singapore in 2005 and headlined 'Asean's Quest for an Identity Gains Urgency', are interesting. The survey was conducted among a thousand English-speaking urban residents in Indonesia, Malaysia, Singapore, the Philippines, Thailand and Vietnam, and asked whether 'people in ASEAN identified with one another'. It showed that six out of ten polled agreed that they did.[129] To its critics, this meant that much more progress would have to be made in ensuring popular legitimacy for ASEAN. But six out of ten is also an impressive figure for an organisation that has been called illiberal and elitist.

Ironically, although only four out of ten Singaporeans identified with other ASEAN counties in the *Straits Times* poll, suggesting that 'Singaporeans are laggards when it comes to willingness to integrate', Singaporean officials have been most vocal in calling for an ASEAN identity. According to its Foreign Minister George Yeo, the people of ASEAN must 'internalize a greater sense of ASEAN citizenship'.[130] And its Prime Minister, Lee Hsien Loong, exhorts that ASEAN must 'find ways to promote among the peoples of ASEAN a deeper sense of belonging and community, and greater awareness of their common destiny . . . The fate of ASEAN ultimately lies in their hands.'[131]

ASEAN and human rights

The creation of the ASEAN Intergovernmental Commission on Human Rights (AICHR) in 2009 illustrates the proactive role of civil society in human rights norm diffusion in Southeast Asia. Since the early 1990s at least, a group of Southeast Asian NGOs have tried to persuade ASEAN to create a regional human rights mechanism, pointing to the fact that Asia is the only continent to lack a regional human rights body. In the late 1990s and early 2000s, the ASEAN governments began to seriously explore the idea of creating a regional human rights mechanism. The democratic transition in Indonesia after the fall of the Suharto regime in 1998 was a major catalyst of these efforts. Indonesia's leadership role in ASEAN helped to reorient ASEAN's stance on human rights. As part of a more general effort in ASEAN to revitalise its institutions, ASEAN started a process of consultations to create a human rights mechanism. This process involved not only ASEAN government officials, but also civil society groups. In a series of workshops on the idea of a regional human rights mechanism held since 2001, ASEAN invited NGOs to participate and offer their suggestions.[132] The ASEAN Charter under Article 14 spelt out the idea of an 'ASEAN Human Rights Body' After the Charter entered into force on 15 December 2008, a High Level Panel (HLP) drafted the Terms of Reference (ToR) for the ASEAN Human Rights Body on 21 July 2009. On 23 October 2009, the human rights body was officially named the ASEAN Intergovernmental Commission on Human Rights (AICHR) and officially inaugurated during the 15th Summit in Cha-am Hua Hin, Thailand.

Article 4 of the ToR states that the functions of the AICHR would be to:

1. Develop strategies to promote and protect human rights
2. Develop ASEAN Human Rights Declaration
3. Raise public awareness on human rights
4. Promote capacity building on implementation of international human rights treaties
5. Encourage ratification of human rights treaties
6. Promote implementation of ASEAN human rights instruments
7. Provide advisory role and technical assistance to ASEAN sectoral bodies
8. Engage in dialogue and consultation with ASEAN bodies and entities associated with ASEAN
9. Consult with other national, regional and international institutions and entities concerned with human rights
10. Obtain information from member states on human rights promotion and protection
11. Develop common approaches and positions on human rights matters
12. Prepare thematic studies on human rights
13. Submit annual report
14. Perform other tasks assigned by ASEAN Foreign Ministers Meetings.

While the AICHR has been hailed as a breakthrough in the search for a human rights mechanism in Southeast Asia, it has also been criticised by regional NGOs on several grounds.[133] The first is cultural relativism, as indicated in the language of Article 1.4, which lists the purpose of AICHR as being 'to promote human rights within the regional context; bearing in mind national and regional particularities and mutual respect for different histori-cal, cultural, and religious backgrounds, and taking into account the balance between rights and responsibilities.' This has led to concerns that 'regional particularities' or cultural relativism may justify human rights violations. A second concern is the salience of state sovereignty. Article 2 of the ToR reiterates the principles of states' independence and sover-eignty, non-interference, and respect for different cultures already found in Article 2 of the ASEAN Charter.

Third and most important, the AICHR's role (Article 3 of the ToR) is limited to being an intergovernmental 'consultative' body, which to its critics also suggests that it was never intended to be an independent watchdog. Its role is in the *promotion* of human rights, without any mandate for their *protection* in the first place. It has no authority to receive public complaint or investigate the suspected human rights violation in Southeast Asia. As one observer put it, during its first three years the AICHR 'had not really touched sensitive human rights issues' because of the ToR limiting its authority. As such, the AICHR is designed to rely on peer pressure.

Since its establishment, the AICHR has issued no fewer than twenty official press statements and organised a number of seminars and workshops that support its mandate to promote human rights. But it has offered no response to actual human rights violations in the region, such as the violence against Bersih 3.0 activists by police officers in Malaysia in April 2012, violence against the Rohingya people in Myanmar in June 2012, and the disappearance of a Lao human rights activist, Mr Sombath Somphone, in December 2012. As the human rights body in the region, civil society activists obviously expected that the AICHR would give a serious response in dealing with the cases. As one civil society representative maintains, 'There has not been any meaningful effort showed by the AICHR to push the ASEAN member states if human rights violations occurred in their territory, as well as, any political statement of the AICHR to respond to the situation' (*sic*).[134]

Despite its limitations, the AICHR nonetheless represents a shift in ASEAN's position on human rights. Moreover, its creation underscores a limited but important element of 'participatory regionalism' in Southeast Asia. As one study has argued, its creation shows that 'Non-governmental Organizations (NGOs) have been primarily responsible for lobbying for an ASEAN Human Rights Mechanism, as part of the push for political liberalization and respect for human rights.'[135] The ASEAN experience in AICHR shows that the regional level (which I consider as a subset of the category 'local'), including regional organisations and regional civil society groups, matters in norm diffusion; they can work together to develop new institutions that can advance the human rights awareness and agenda.

In 2010, a year after the creation of the AICHR, ASEAN launched another human rights body, the ASEAN Commission on the Promotion and Protection of the Rights of Women and Children (ACWC). The ACWC is different from the AICHR in an important respect. The twenty members of ACWC are drawn both from government agencies and rights groups, thereby attesting to its inclusive nature and its potential to act as a bridge between governments and civil society. The ACWC may thus be more in keeping with the aspirations of the regional civil society than the AICHR as currently constituted.

The ASEAN Human Rights Declaration[136] issued in November 2012 reflects the continued differences among the governments and the civil society in the understanding of human rights and approaches to its promotion. From the perspective of civil society groups, the Declaration is a missed opportunity that does not uphold the 'people's ASEAN' concept. They complain of lack of adequate consultations with the NGO community (only two consultations with the NGO community on the Declaration occurred in June and September 2011), and a lack of transparency. The Declaration's balancing of rights with duties is seen, in the words of a leading NGO representative,[137] as 'alien to international law of human rights' and 'philosophically different from the UDHR' (Universal Declaration of Human Rights). The Declaration's language to the effect that promotion of human rights should respect 'national and regional contexts' is a throwback to the "Asian values" debate. The Declaration imposes limitations on rights (such as those on national security grounds) that are too broad. Also it fails to protect the rights of indigenous people and self-determination is not mentioned. The issue of statelessness (or the right of every person to a citizenship) was in an initial draft of the Declaration, but was dropped from the final draft. (This would have been relevant to the Rohingyas of Myanmar.) Also dropped from the final draft was the right to association, and protection from false disappearance, meaning disappearance of political activists or journalists because they are kidnapped or murdered by security forces (this has been an issue in the Philippines, Indonesia and Laos). There had been some discussion of corporate accountability. Trade and investment in the region make this important, with implications for large-scale development projects, plantations, river dams, and infrastructure. But these were also dropped in the end. Hence the document reflects the lowest common denominator, and sets the standard lower than the international human rights standards that all ASEAN members have re-affirmed. Regional civil society groups fear that the Declaration could be used by regional governments to legitimise human rights abuses on the pretext of national law, regional particularities, and duties.

But the Declaration has its defenders, even among the civil society groups.[138] As one leader of a Southeast Asian NGO put it, the document is by necessity a consensus text, the outcome of political negotiation among different political systems. The Declaration while not legally binding, is nonetheless a 'living document', and 'the beginning, not the end' of a process of promoting human rights in the region. Among other things, it will help inspire a sense of ownership among ASEAN members on human rights. Thus, though it is 'not a perfect declaration,' it is 'not a disaster' either.

Conclusion

ASEAN's record on handling transnational challenges has been a mixed one. Its handling of the SARS crisis is perhaps the most creditable, while that of the haze problem, which is largely caused by human action and entirely preventable, has been the worst compared to other transnational challenges. The Asian financial crisis could not be entirely blamed on ASEAN; despite the culpability of national governments for economic mismanagement, the role of financial speculators and the nature of the global economy were partly to blame. Moreover, while ASEAN could have shown more unity (in terms of the Singapore–Malaysia and Singapore–Indonesia quarrels), in fairness, ASEAN was not created to deal with a financial crisis of such wide magnitude. Also, earthquakes could not be prevented or even predicted, but death tolls from the 2004 Tsunami could have been reduced with a proper early warning system. But ASEAN's response to the Tsunami was prompt and the role of Indonesia's neighbours, including Singapore and Malaysia, in offering humanitarian aid was generous. The lesson is that ASEAN's effectiveness in dealing with transnational challenges depends on the nature of the challenge and the responsibility and accountability of a particular member state within which the crisis originates. The Tsunami brought out mutual empathy and unity because it was a humanitarian disaster that is also a rare occurrence and could not be blamed on any particular country. The haze problem evoked Indonesian nationalism, thereby to some extent undermining ratification by Indonesia of the ASEAN anti-pollution agreement, although neighbourly pressure did prompt Jakarta to become more serious about tackling the problem. The SARS outbreak posed a real existential threat because of its unknown and unpredictable quality. The Asian financial crisis, though originating in Thailand, was actually a regional issue, as shown by the contagion. Despite ASEAN's immediate inability in dealing with the crisis, it brought about longer-term co-operation, especially in the financial area, and got ASEAN to shed some of its rigidity over the non-interference norm. In terms of ASEAN's norms, the financial crisis presented the most serious threat to this norm.

Overall, transnational challenges have not questioned the non-use of force norm. They might seem to have undermined the principle of 'regional autonomy' to some extent, especially in dealing with terrorism and large-scale natural disasters like the Tsunami and the Burmese cyclone in 2006, where assistance from extra-regional powers was critical. But that may be due to the very nature of transnational challenges, which ignore not only national boundaries, but also regional limits, and dealing with which requires resources that are often beyond the members of ASEAN, singly or collectively.

ASEAN's norm of non-interference evolved somewhat but remained influential in shaping ASEAN's response to transnational threats, which came at little notice and respected no national boundaries. There was no significant departure from this norm as demanded by reformist voices within the grouping. Indonesia's former Foreign Minister Ali Alatas, once a staunch defender of non-interference, would claim that through the initiatives such as the ASEAN Security Community and the Bali Concord II, it would be 'tacitly understood that the principles of respect for national sovereignty, non-interference and consensus-based decision-making should be applied in a flexible and selective manner'. He would see this as a vindication of his 'enhanced interaction' approach, suggested in 1998 in preference to Surin's more expansive 'flexible engagement' formula that was intended to 'help a member-country in addressing internal problems with clear external implications'.[139] Nonetheless, through the ASC and the ASEAN Charter, ASEAN did move its institutional reform agenda forward. Much would depend on the eventual implementation of the ASC's numerous proposed measures and the members' compliance with the ASEAN Charter provisions and more generally the development of a culture of compliance with ASEAN's agenda and instruments which the Charter seeks to inculcate. This will decide ASEAN's capacity to deal with the new challenges in the twenty-first century.

Notes and references

1 John Gershman, 'Is Southeast Asia the Second Front?' *Foreign Affairs*, vol. 79, no. 4 (July/August 2002), pp. 60–74.
2 Agence France Presse, 1 November 2002.
3 Agence France Presse, 6 September 2002.
4 Eddie Teo, 'The Emergence of Jemaah Islamiyah in Singapore', a speech at the Brookings Institution, 25 November 2002, p. 2.
5 http://news.bbc.co.uk/2/hi/asia-pacific/2340449.stm
6 *Time Asia*, 25 November 2002.
7 Ibid.
8 Agence France Presse, 28 February 2003.
9 Ministry of Home Affairs, Singapore, *The Jemaah Islamiyah Arrests and the Threat of Terrorism*, White Paper (Singapore: Ministry of Home Affairs, 7 January 2003), p. 7.
10 Ibid., pp. 4–5.
11 Amitav Acharya, *The Age of Fear: Power Versus Principle in the War on Terror* (Singapore: Marshall Cavendish and New Delhi: Rupa & Co., 2004).
12 'ASEAN Declaration on Joint Action to Counter Terrorism', 5 November 2001.
13 'ASEAN Convention on Counter Terrorism', 30 January 2007.
14 Dana Robert Dillon, 'The Shape of Anti-Terrorist Coalitions in Southeast Asia', The Heritage Foundation, 17 January 2003.
15 'ASEAN–United States of America Joint Declaration for Cooperation to Combat International Terrorism', Bandar Seri Begawan, Brunei, 1 August 2002.
16 Dillon, 'The Shape of Anti-Terrorist Coalitions in Southeast Asia'.
17 Ibid.
18 Richard P. Cronin, *The Second Bush Administration and Southeast Asia* (Washington, D.C.: The Henry L. Stimson Center, July 2007), p. 6.
19 Sartika Soesilowati, 'ASEAN's Response to the Challenge of Terrorism,' *journal.unair.ac. id (*Department of International Relations, FISIP, Airlangga University)*, Vol. 24, No. 3, (2011),

pp. 228–241 Available at http://journal.unair.ac.id/filerPDF/06%20sartika%20jurnal%20MKP%20 terorismenew%20_tyas_%20_editan%20niken_.pdf (accessed 1 September 2013)

20 Ibid.
21 This section draws from an earlier work: *Promoting Human Security in Southeast Asia: Ethical, Normative and Educational Frameworks in South-East Asia* (Paris: United Nations Educational, Scientific and Cultural Organisation, 2007).
22 'SARS in Singapore', 10 May 2003. Available goasia.about.com/cs/health/a/ SARS_Spore (accessed 10 June 2008).
23 news.bbc.co.uk/1/hi/business/3001717.stm (accessed 12 June 2008).
24 'The Impact of SARS on Asian Economy and ASEAN's Leaders' Response', Address by H.E. Ong Keng Yong, Secretary-General of ASEAN, Beijing, 13 May 2003.
25 Ibid.
26 Joint Statement of the Special ASEAN+3 Health Ministers Meeting on Severe Acute Respiratory Syndrome (SARS), Siem Reap, Cambodia, 10–11 June 2003.
27 Acharya, *Promoting Human Security in Southeast Asia.*
28 BBC News, 27 January 2005.
29 Xinhua News Agency, 8 January 2005.
30 *Straits Times*, 19 February 2005.
31 ASEAN's Response to the Tsunami Disaster – Issues and Concerns: A Special Report, Virtual Information Center, www.vic-info.org/. . ./$FILE/050509-SR-IssuesAndConcernsOn ASEANSpecialReport.doc (accessed 23 June 2008).
32 New Scientist Environment, 8 August 2005.
33 Asian Disaster Preparedness Centre, www.adpc.net/v2007/Programs/EWS/ BACKGROUND/ Default-BACKGROUND.asp (accessed 15 June 2008).
34 David Glover and Timothy Jessup (eds.), *Indonesia's Fires and Haze: The Cost of Catastrophe* (Ottawa: International Development Research Centre and Singapore: Institute of Southeast Asian Studies, 1999).
35 Ibid.
36 Channel News Asia (Singapore), 11 October 2006.
37 Following Lee's letter, the two leaders held a telephone conversation on 12 October 2006 in which the Indonesian President thanked Lee for his letter of disappointment and promised more action, while Lee thanked Yudhoyono for hosting an ASEAN meeting on the issue the next day. 'Telephone Call between Prime Minister Lee Hsien Loong and President Susilo Bambang Yudhoyono on Trans-boundary Haze Pollution', 12 October 2006, Ministry of Foreign Affairs, Singapore. Available at app.mfa.gov.sg/2006/press/view_press_print.asp?post_id=1856 (accessed 14 June 2008).
38 Gerald Giam, 'Haze Problem: Bilateral Pressure on Indonesia Works Best', *Singapore Angle*, 13 October 2006. Available www.singaporeangle.com/2006/10/ haze-problem-bilateral-pressure-on. html (accessed 14 June 2008).
39 UNEP Information Note, Geneva/Nairobi, 7 September 1999. Available www.grida.no/Newsroom. aspx?m=54&pressReleaseItemID=376 (accessed 14 June 2008); *Agence France Presse*, 10 June 2002; Environment News Service, 25 November 2003.
40 'Joint Press Statement: Sub-regional Ministerial Meeting on Transboundary Haze Pollution', Pekanbaru, Riau, Indonesia, 13 October 2006.
41 enews.mcot.net/view.php?id=3683 (accessed 14 June 2008).
42 Reuters UK, 14 March 2008.
43 'ASEAN welcomes Indonesia's commitment to ratify haze pact,' Channel NewsAsia, 17 July 2013, Available at: http://www.channelnewsasia.com/news/asiapacific/asean-welcomes-indonesia/747976.html
44 There is little evidence from Southeast Asia to suggest that democratisation actually increases the danger of regional war. Wars in Southeast Asia have been fought mostly between non-democracies; the two major examples being the war between North and South Vietnam, and the Vietnamese invasion of Cambodia in 1978, or between a semi-democracy and a state under authoritarian rule: Indonesia's *Konfrontasi* against Malaysia (which to some extent was inspired by Sukarno's need to divert attention from domestic troubles). This offers greater evidence of war initiation by authoritarian states. As noted in Chapter 5, Thailand under Chuan Leekpai had tried to promote democracy in ASEAN, ostensibly to create a new democratic bloc within the grouping, but this was not pursued to the detriment of regional peace. Moreover, democratic transitions in three out of the

four cases in Southeast Asia (Philippines 1986, Thailand 1991–92, Cambodia, 1993 and Indonesia, 1998) have not produced a single instance of a regime which would willingly undermine existing regional arrangements. There was no downgrading or change in the commitments of the Philippines and Thailand to ASEAN in the wake of democratic transitions, but instead, the solidarity shown by ASEAN leaders to President Cory Aquino might have enhanced the regime's dependence on ASEAN support and strengthened regionalism. The democratisation of Cambodia under the UN's auspices made it more suitable for membership in ASEAN, although it is debatable whether this move strengthened or weakened ASEAN. Hun Sen's tirade against ASEAN for postponing Cambodia's accession to ASEAN in 1997 in response to his 'coup' ceased when Cambodia was finally admitted in 1999 after undertaking necessary democratic changes.

45 Anthony Smith, 'Indonesia's Role in ASEAN: The End of Leadership', *Contemporary Southeast Asia*, vol. 21, no. 2 (1999), pp. 238–60; Amitav Acharya, 'Is There a Lack of Focus in Indonesia's Foreign Policy?', *Straits Times*, 2 October 2000.

46 Cited in *Jakarta Post*, 26 July 2000.

47 'ASEAN Harus Bisa Berdialog soal Masalah Dalam Negeri', *Kompas*, 1 July 2004. Available at 64.203.71.11/kompas-cetak/0407/01/utama/1122067.htm (accessed June 2008).

48 Rakaryan Sukarjaputra, 'Komunitas ASEAN 2015, Pertaruhan Besar Indonesia', *Kompas*, 16 August 2007. Available at www.kompascetak.com/kompas-cetak/0708/16/LaporanKhusus/3764442.htm (accessed 9 June 2008).

49 One of the most active voices in foreign policy issues was the DPR's (Dewan Perwakilan Rakyat, the lower house of the legislature of Indonesia) Komisi I (First Commission). It held working meetings with coordinating ministers in politics, law and security to offer various proposals on how to deal with Burma. Opinion in the committee was, however, divided, between those who wanted the government to take a strong and firm stance on Burma's military regime and those who, for geopolitical reasons (notably the potential for big powers like India and China to exploit Burma's domestic turmoil to their own advantage), wanted the Indonesian government to tread cautiously in pressuring Burma. 'Komisi I Berbeda Pandangan Soal Sikapi Myanmar', *Kompas*, 1 October 2007.

50 Associated Press, 16 June 2003; Agence France Presse, 18 June 2003; Agence France Presse, 20 July 2003.

51 'Southeast Asian Nations Express "Revulsion" at Myanmar's Violent Repression of Demonstrations', Ottawa, Canada, 27 September 2007. Available at www.indonesia-ottawa.org/information/details.php?type=news_copy&id=4765 (accessed 28 May 2008).

52 Agence France Presse, 19 May 2008.

53 The original version of the idea was contained in a concept paper prepared by the Indonesian Foreign Ministry. 'Towards an ASEAN Security Community', 9 May 2003. The paper came to be known as the 'Deplu Paper on the ASEAN Security Community'. Deplu stands for *Departemen Luar Negri* (Department of Foreign Affairs) in Bahasa Indonesia. A key policy intellectual behind the conceptualisation of the ASEAN Security Community idea and the drafting of the Deplu paper was Dr Rizal Sukma of the Centre for Strategic and International Studies, Jakarta. An elaboration of Dr Sukma's thinking can be found in a paper he presented on 3 June 2003 at a seminar organised by the Indonesian Mission to the UN in New York, at which I was the keynote speaker, underscoring Indonesia's interest in examining the academic roots of the security community concept. Rizal Sukma, 'ASEAN Cooperation: Challenges and Prospects in the Current International Situation', Paper presented at the seminar on ASEAN Cooperation: Challenges and Prospects in the Current International Situation, Permanent Mission of the Republic of Indonesia to the United Nations, New York, 3 June 2003, pp. 2–3. A report on this meeting including the text of Dr Sukma's paper is available at www.indonesiamission-ny.org/issuebaru/Mission/asean/photogallery.htm (accessed 28 May 2008).

54 *Straits Times*, 21 July 2003. Later, Sukma would list other reasons behind the Indonesian initiative: such as concerns over Singapore–Malaysia tensions, the need to dilute the non-intervention principle (non-intervention had made it difficult for deeper cooperation on internal matters with regional or transnational impact), and the need for a security pillar for ASEAN to complement the Singapore-proposed ASEAN Economic Community (there could not be an economic community without a political-security foundation). Rizal Sukma's presentation to the Seminar on The ASEAN Security Community, Singapore, 17 July 2003 (organised by the Institute of Defence and Strategic Studies, Institute of Policy Studies and Institute of Southeast Asian Studies).

55 'The Deplu Paper on ASEAN Security Community', p. 3.
56 Ibid., p. 3.
57 Ibid., pp. 3–4. Note that the phrases 'by the existence of a balance of power or a mutual-deterrence situation', and 'a fundamental, unambiguous and long-term convergence of interests among ASEAN members in the avoidance of war' in the Deplu paper are identical to the language used to differentiate a security regime from a security community in the first edition as well as the second of this book. See Amitav Acharya, *Constructing a Security Community in Southeast Asia*, first edition (London and New York: Routledge, 2001), pp. 17, 20. The Deplu paper used quotation marks for the first of the two borrowed phrases. An earlier draft of Bali Concord II, dated 25 August 2003 and circulated by Indonesia, also read: 'The ASEAN Security Community is based on a fundamental, unambiguous and long-term convergence of interests among ASEAN member countries in the avoidance of conflict and war through norm-setting, conflict-prevention, and post-conflict peace building.' *Bali Concord II* (Draft of 25 August 2003), given to the author by an Indonesian source. This author was not involved in the drafting of the Deplu paper, although he was invited to be the keynote speaker at the above-mentioned (footnote 53) special meeting convened by the Indonesian mission to the UN in June 2003, barely two weeks before Indonesia tabled the paper at an ASEAN meeting.
58 Deplu Paper on ASEAN Security Community, p. 4.
59 Ibid., p. 2.
60 Ibid.
61 Sukma, 'The Future of ASEAN', pp. 8–9.
62 Ibid., p. 1.
63 'Paparan Menteri Luar Negeri Pada Rapat Koordinasi Paripurna Tingkat Menteri Tangga', 22 July 2003, pp. 1–2.
64 Ibid., pp. 1, 3.
65 'The ASEAN Security Community Proposal, Comments from ISIS Malaysia', 1 August 2003.
66 *New Straits Times* (Kuala Lumpur), 6 October 2003, p. 20.
67 'Bali Concord II', Draft as of 21 August 2003, prepared by Indonesian Foreign Ministry, p. 4; *Straits Times*, 21 July 2003. Aside from comprehensive security, the Deplu Paper had also mentioned 'sharpening ASEAN cooperation in human security'. But this phrase was dropped from the final text of Bali Concord II.
68 Department Pertahanan RI, Jakarta, 'Konsep Asean Security Community Masih Digodok', 10 September 2003. Available at www.tempointeraktif.com/hg/luarnegeri/2003/09/10/brk,20030910-15,id.html (accessed 15 June 2008). A similar denial, quoting a *Jakarta Post* report of 8 August 2003, of the ASC developing into a 'defence or military alliance' but to a comprehensive effort to fight terrorism and separatism and other threats to regional harmony could be found in: 'Militer Terus Mengambil Inisiatif Politik', Kompas Cyber Media, 12 November 2003, available at www.prakarsa-rakyat.org/artikel/dinamika/artikel_cetak.php?aid=21 (accessed 15 June 2008).
69 Bali Concord II, Final Draft, 7 October 2003.
70 Ibid.
71 Ibid.
72 'Perubahan Institusional Perlu untuk Dukung Masyarakat ASEAN 2020', *Kompas*, 29 June 2004. Available www2.kompas.com/kompas-cetak/0406/29/ln/1116331.htm (accessed 12 June 2008).
73 'Wirajuda: Pertemuan Ha Long Bay Produktif', *Kompas*, 6 March 2004. Available http://64.203.71.11/kompas-cetak/0403/06/ln/895175.htm (accessed 9 June 2008); Barry Wain, 'Jakarta Jilted: Indonesia's neighbours are not very supportive of its vision of a regional security community', *Far Eastern Economic Review*, 10 June 2004.
74 'Wirajuda: Pertemuan Ha Long Bay Produktif'; *Straits Times*, 5 March 2004, p. 7.
75 *Straits Times*, 5 March 2004, p. 7; 'ASEAN Ministerial Meeting Retreat ends in Vietnam'. Available at english.people.com.cn/200403/05/print20040305_136556.html (accessed 2 July 2008).
76 Cited in Adrian Kuah, 'The ASEAN Security Community: Struggling with Details', *IDSS Commentaries*, 15 June 2004, p. 2.
77 *Asian Political News*, 21 June 2004.
78 On 15 June 2004, Indonesian officials insisted that the idea of a regional peacekeeping force was 'still alive', although the words 'developing a regional peacekeeping arrangement' were changed to 'developing an ASEAN arrangement for the maintenance of peace and stability', because 'some countries are still sensitive with the words'. Ibid. A year later five ASEAN members – Thailand,

Malaysia, Brunei, the Philippines and Singapore – would contribute forces alongside the EU mission to monitor the Helsinki Peace Accord on Aceh of August 2005.

79 Ministry of Foreign Affairs, Indonesia (Deplu), 'Briefing Pers Menteri Luar Negeri RI Ketua Panitia ASEAN KE-37', Jakarta, 30 June 2004. Available amm37.deplu. go.id/docs/briefingpers_menlu.pdf (accessed 9 June 2008).
80 Cited in Wain, 'Jakarta Jilted'.
81 'ASEAN Security Community Plan of Action', ASEANSEC. In his media briefing at the end of the AMM on 30 June 2004, Indonesian Foreign Minister Hassan Wirayuda stressed this principle in the following words: 'ASEAN will not permit change of government which has been done unconstitutionally and undemocratically'. Ministry of Foreign Affairs, Indonesia (Deplu), 'Briefing Pers Menteri Luar Negeri RI Ketua Panitia ASEAN KE-37', Jakarta, 30 June 2004. Available at amm37.deplu.go.id/docs/briefingpers_menlu.pdf (accessed 9 June 2008).
82 'ASEAN Security Community Plan of Action.'
83 ASEAN *Selayang Pandang* (Jakarta: Direktorat Jenderal Kerjasama ASEAN, Departemen Luar Negeri, Republik Indonesia, 2007), p. 152.
84 As a Foreign Ministry document puts it, ASC 'tidak ditujukan untuk membentuk suatu pakta pertahanan/aliansi militer, kebijakan luar negeri bersama'. Ibid., p. 29.
85 Deplu Paper on ASEAN Security Community, p. 5.
86 Report of the Eminent Persons Group (EPG) on the ASEAN Charter, p. 3.
87 M. C. Abad, quoted in 'ASEAN Defence Ministers to Commit to Security Community', Available at www.spacewar.com/reports/ASEAN_Defence_Ministers_To_Commit_To_Security_Community.html (accessed 25 July 2006).
88 Channel News Asia, 9 May 2006.
89 'Penyusunan Piagam ASEAN bertujuan untuk mentransformasikan ASEAN dari sebuah asosiasi politik yang longgar menjadi organisasi internasional yang memiliki (*legal personality*), berdasarkan aturan yang profesional (*rule-based organization*), serta memiliki struktur organisasi yang efektif dan efisien'. ASEAN *Selayang Pandang*, p. 30.
90 Amitav Acharya, 'Challenges for an Asean Charter', *Straits Times*, 24 October 2007.
91 'Speech by George Yeo, Minister for Foreign Affairs, at the Global Leadership Forum in Kuala Lumpur', 6 September 2005. Available app.mfa.gov.sg/pr/read_content.asp?View,4330 (accessed 10 June 2008).
92 Personal interview with Ambassador Tommy Koh, Singapore, 10 July 2007.
93 Abdullah Ahmad Badawi, 'Towards an ASEAN Community', 7 August 2004.
94 Speech by Prime Minister Lee Hsien Loong at the Third Asean Business and Investment Forum on 11 December 2005, Shangri-La Hotel, Kuala Lumpur. Available app.mfa.gov.sg/pr/read_content.asp?View,4394 (accessed 10 June 2008).
95 *Report of the Eminent Persons Group on the ASEAN Charter*, December 2006. This section is taken from my lecture to the Asia Inc Forum in Bandar Seri Begawan on 3 May 2007, also published as an op-ed, 'More Ambitious ASEAN Faces Crucial Test', *Borneo Bulletin*, 4 May 2007.
96 The Charter of the Association of Southeast Asian Nations.
97 'Joint Communiqué of the 37th ASEAN Ministerial Meeting', Jakarta, 29–30 June 2004.
98 The Charter of the Association of Southeast Asian Nations.
99 Ibid.
100 Report of the Eminent Persons Group on the ASEAN Charter, December 2006, p. 13.
101 The Charter of the Association of Southeast Asian Nations.
102 According to Ambassador Tommy Koh, the charter would not only make ASEAN a more 'rule based organisation' with 'more effective institutions', but also 'grow a new culture of taking obligations seriously' among its members. He said only 30 per cent of ASEAN's agreements were being implemented until then. The charter would also help improve ASEAN's 'very cumbersome and not very well coordinated organisational structure and decision-making process'; 'empower the secretariat', with two out of its four Deputy Secretary-Generals recruited from the open market; 'widen and deepen' ASEAN cooperation; 'enable ASEAN to continue to occupy the driver's seat in a regional forum such as APEC, ARF, and EAC'; 'make ASEAN a people-centred community, engage civil society'; and 'contribute to a bold and visionary ASEAN, with principles such as fundamental freedoms and human rights, constitutional government'. Koh argued that the ASEAN intergovernmental drafting committee did not want to 'make the perfect charter the enemy of the

good charter'. Tommy Koh, Remarks at the ISEAS Regional Outlook Forum, Shangri-La Hotel, Singapore, 8 January 2008 organised by the Institute of Southeast Asian Studies, Singapore.

103 Report of the Eminent Persons Group on the ASEAN Charter, p. 3.

104 The official functions of the CPR as stipulated by the Charter are to:

(a) support the work of the ASEAN Community Councils and ASEAN Sectoral Ministerial Bodies;

(b) coordinate with ASEAN National Secretariats and other ASEAN Sectoral Ministerial Bodies;

(c) liaise with the Secretary-General of ASEAN and the ASEAN Secretariat on all subjects relevant to its work;

(d) facilitate ASEAN cooperation with external partners; and

(e) perform such other functions as may be determined by the ASEAN Coordinating Council.

Source: http://www.aseansec.org/21069.pdf

105 Surin Pitsuwan, 'ASEAN's Challenge: Some Reflections and Recommendations on Strengthening the ASEAN Secretariat,' Submitted to H.E. Marty Natalegawa, Chair, ASEAN Coordinating Council, 12 December 2011.

106 'Declaration of ASEAN Concord II (Bali Concord II)', 7 October 2003.

107 Denis Hew, 'Towards an ASEAN Economic Community by 2020: Vision or Reality?', *Viewpoints*, Singapore: Institute of Southeast Asian Studies, 16 June 2003.

108 Naoko Munakata, 'Talking Regional, Acting Bilateral – Reality of "FTA Race" in East Asia', Research Institute of Economy, Trade and Industry. Available at www.rieti.go.jp/en/papers/contribution/munakata/01.html (accessed 16 June 2008).

109 Hew, 'Towards an ASEAN Economic Community by 2020'.

110 Declaration of ASEAN Concord II (Bali Concord II), 7 October 2003.

111 The ASEAN Socio-Cultural Community (ASCC) Plan of Action.

112 Ibid.

113 Stuart Harris, 'Policy Networks and Economic Cooperation in the Asia Pacific', *Pacific Review*, vol. 7, no. 4 (1994), p. 390.

114 The original members of the ASEAN-ISIS group included: Centre for Strategic and International Studies (Jakarta); Singapore Institute of International Affairs; Institute of Strategic and International Studies (Kuala Lumpur); Institute for Security and International Studies (Bangkok); and Centre for Integrative and Development Studies (Manila; subsequently, the Institute for Strategic and Development Studies, under the same director, took over the membership of ASEAN-ISIS). Brunei subsequently participated through officials of its foreign ministry. Of the ASEAN-ISIS members, ISIS-Bangkok is university based (Chulalongkorn University) while ISDS-Manila, though with the significant participation of the faculty at the University of the Philippines, is not formally part of the university. The CSIS in Jakarta used to have closer connections with the military than with the foreign ministry, as well as the private sector, from which it receives funding. In the wake of ASEAN's expansion, ASEAN-ISIS gained two new members, the Institute of International Relations, an arm of the Vietnamese Foreign Ministry, and the Cambodian Institute for Cooperation and Peace (more loosely tied to the government than its counterpart in Hanoi). Burmese and Laotian participation was expected following their admission to ASEAN in 1997. Burma and Brunei also participate through government research arms.

115 A Time for Initiative: Proposals for the Consideration of the Fourth ASEAN Summit (Jakarta: ASEAN-ISIS, 4 June 1991), p. 1.

116 www.aseansec.org, and http://www.aseanfoundation.org.

117 This section draws from Amitav Acharya, 'Democratisation and the Prospects for Participatory Regionalism in Southeast Asia', *Third World Quarterly*, vol. 24, no. 2 (2003), pp. 375–90.

118 www.asianexchange.org/Movements/94109509476240.php and http//www.iidnet. org/adv/timor/overview.htm.

119 www.asianexchange.org/Movements/94109392248271.php.

120 Forum-Asia Official Brochure, undated. Collected by the author at the headquarters of Forum-Asia in Bangkok.

121 Forum-Asia (1997), *The Security Syndrome: Politics of National Security in Asia*, Bangkok: Asian Forum for Human Rights and Development.

122 The topics at the inaugural ASEAN People's Assembly included human security, human rights, poverty reduction, resource and environmental management and the conflicts in Myanmar and East Timor.

123 'The Sixth ASEAN People's Assembly. ASEAN at 40: Realizing the People's Expectations'.
124 Available at www.asean-isis-aseanpeoplesassembly.net/pdf/Final%20Version-APA%202006%20 Chairman's%20Report%20(1).pdf (accessed 11 June 2008).
125 Available at www.asean-isis-aseanpeoplesassembly.net/pdf/APA_2007_Statement_on_ Myanmar_with_Signatures.pdf (accessed 11 June 2008).
126 Available at www.asiasapa.org/index.php?option=com_content&task=view&id=48&Itemid=76 (accessed 12 June 2008).
127 Available www.forum-asia.org/index.php?option=com_content&task=view&id=58&Itemid=47 (accessed 11 June 2008).
128 Peter Katzenstein, *A World of Regions: Asia and Europe in the American Imperium* (Ithaca, NY: Cornell University Press, 2005), pp. 76, 81.
129 *Straits Times*, 5 December 2005.
130 George Yeo, Speech to the Global Leadership Forum.
131 Lee Hsien Loong, Speech to the Asean 100 Leadership Forum, Singapore, 28 September 2005. Available at www.mfa.gov.sg/internet/ (accessed 24 June 2008).
132 An example of this process was that the High Level Panel (HLP) of officials drafting the terms of reference of the AICHR invited 'Civil society and human rights organizations in ASEAN Member States that wish to put forth their views about the ToR for the AHRB' to 'get in touch with the HLP or meet with individual HLP Members.' The HLP also held 'dialogue with representatives of ASEAN civil society and other relevant stakeholders (the informal Working Group for an ASEAN Human Rights Mechanism (WG AHRM), the Network of Four National Human Rights Institutions (4 NHRIs), the Solidarity for Asian People's Advocacy (SAPA), and the Women's Caucus for the ASEAN Human Rights Body) in 2008.' Termsak Chalermpalanupap, '10 Facts about ASEAN Human Rights Cooperation,' http://www.aseansec.org/HLP-OtherDoc-1.pdf
133 The following passages are taken from Forum-Asia, 'Hiding behind Its Limits: A Performance Report on the first year of the ASEAN Intergovernmental Commission on Human Rights (AICHR),' (Bangkok, SAPA Task Force on ASEAN and Human Rights, 2010), http://forum-asia. org/2010/Report%20on%20AICHR's%20first%20year%20_for_dist.pdf
134 Personal interview, 11 July 2013.
135 Yvonne Mewengkang, 'ASEAN Intergovernmental Commission on Human Rights (AICHR),' Substantial Research Paper (SRP), School of International Service, American University (Washington, D. C., March 2012); Li-ann Thio, 'Implementing Human Rights in ASEAN Countries: Promises to Keep and Miles to Go before I Sleep,' *Yale Human Rights and Development Law Journal 2*, no. 1 (1999), p. 73.
136 http://www.asean.org/news/asean-statement-communiques/item/asean-human-rights-declaration
137 Personal interview with a prominent human rights advocate in Southeast Asia. 29 November 2012.
138 Ibid.
139 Ali Alatas, 'Some Reflections on ASEAN Concord II', statement at the Regional Outlook Forum, Institute of Southeast Asian Studies, Singapore, 7 January 2004.

Conclusion
Remaking ASEAN

The concept of security community not only describes a condition of stable intra-mural peace and collective identity achieved by a given group of states, it also suggests a framework for analysing the process and dynamics of peaceful change leading to such a condition. I have used it as a conceptual framework to examine and assess ASEAN's evolution and role in regional security and its prospects for the future. In doing so, I have looked not only at the institutional role of ASEAN, which would be emphasised in a conventional institutionalist or neo-liberal framework, but also at the broader process of community building and identity formation that ASEAN has consciously engineered. Regional socialisation assumes particular importance because the existence and the continued survival of ASEAN would have been highly improbable on the basis of the traditional indicators of regionalism. The sheer diversity among the ASEAN members in terms of size, populations, cultural and linguistic differences, and political systems predisposes Southeast Asia against a viable form of regionalism. In this context, ASEAN could thrive only by developing a practical approach to socialisation, normative development and a conscious process of identity building.

ASEAN's approach to regional cooperation has differed not only from the conventional process of alliance building, in the sense of being inspired exclusively by a common external threat; it has also differed from integrationist models exemplified by the EU, which remains the most important example of a regional security community. In the North Atlantic area, a shared political culture of liberal democracy and an emerging trend towards close economic interdependence helped the founding of a security community. ASEAN lacked such background conditions at the time of its inception, and it continues to lack them today. Unlike Europe, the members of ASEAN did not share a liberal democratic political culture, although the common goal of regime survival against a common internal threat (i.e. communism) was an important triggering factor behind ASEAN. ASEAN's founders were largely inspired by the goal of developing a regional social community rather than an institutionally integrated economic and military bloc, which could overcome the divisions and separations imposed by colonial rule and lead to peaceful relations among the newly independent states of the region.

ASEAN's approach to community building was quite different from the path outlined by Deutsch. For Deutsch, a security community is the end product, or terminal condition, of a process of integration which is driven by the need to cope with the conflict-causing effects of increased transactions. The growing volume and range of transactions – political, cultural or economic – increases the scope for possible conflict among actors, forcing them to devise institutions and practices for peaceful adjustment and change.[1] But in the case of ASEAN, regional cooperation was undertaken in the absence of high levels of functional interdependence or interaction. ASEAN evolved as a sort of an 'imagined community', despite low initial levels of interdependence and transactions, and the existence of substantial political and situational differences among its members. In this sense, the vision of community preceded rather than resulted from political, strategic and functional interactions and interdependence.

Central to this process was a set of norms, among which non-interference, non-use of force, regional autonomy, the avoidance of collective defence and the practice of the 'ASEAN Way' were the most salient. Thirty years after the formation of ASEAN, Abdullah Badawi, the Malaysian Foreign Minister, saw 'the institution of norms of acceptable conduct and behaviour among its members' as one of 'ASEAN's great achievements'.[2] Despite an element of exaggeration, the statement has merit. While some of these norms were adapted from universal legal-rational principles, others had their sources in what ASEAN's founders claimed to be the unique socio-cultural practices of the region. Together they led to the emergence of what its members claimed to be a 'cultural-specific' and sociological approach to conflict management and decision making, called the 'ASEAN Way'. This turned out to be a key symbol of ASEAN, helping the grouping to overcome intra-mural tensions especially during the crucial early years of ASEAN, when the grouping was most vulnerable to such problems. Subsequently, the ASEAN Way was useful in attracting new members and persuading ASEAN's external dialogue partners to see things from an ASEAN perspective, as well as in muting substantive areas of disagreement.

The effects of ASEAN's norms

What has been the record of ASEAN in adhering to these norms? To help with the assessment of the effects of ASEAN's norms, Chapter 1 devised a framework with three sets of questions: (1) questions about dispute settlement; (2) questions about collective action; and (3) questions about collective identity.

The Cambodia conflict

Vietnam's invasion of Cambodia provided the most serious test of ASEAN's role in building regional order. It challenged the norms of non-interference and non-use of force, and dealt a blow to ASEAN's earlier hopes to develop a regional collective identity by securing Hanoi's incorporation into its regionalist framework. But while this served as the justification behind its effort to mobilise international opinion against Vietnam and isolate it, the norm of seeking a 'regional solution to regional problems' meant that ASEAN also had to search for a peaceful settlement of the dispute. ASEAN's management of the Cambodia conflict seriously tested aspects of the ASEAN Way, especially consensus seeking and avoidance of multilateral military cooperation. ASEAN faced considerable pressure to develop some form of collective military response, and thereby turn itself into a *de facto* alliance. But this was eschewed because of a desire to minimise provocations of Hanoi which might thereby provide further stimulus to the latter's alliance with the Soviet Union. While the principle of bilateralism in defence relations among the ASEAN members survived, somewhat more compromised were the ASEAN Way of consultations and consensus and the norm of regional autonomy. Differing perceptions of Vietnam within ASEAN, especially between the hardline camp of Thailand and Singapore and the moderate group of Indonesia and Malaysia (which saw Vietnam as less of a security threat than China), strained intra-mural solidarity. The latter group supported a *modus vivendi* with Hanoi that would check Chinese influence in the region. ASEAN as a group needed the help of China (as well as Western countries) in order to raise the cost for Hanoi of Vietnam's occupation of Cambodia. This brought strategic benefits to ASEAN as China promised in return not to support insurgencies in ASEAN. But ASEAN's deliberate and largely successful strategy of internationalising the crisis, while significantly raising the grouping's profile and securing it international acclaim, led to the Great Powers' assumption of a leading role in bringing the peace process to an end. This might be seen as a challenge to its norm of 'regional solutions to regional problems', but ASEAN did play an instrumental role in bringing peace to Cambodia, especially at a time when it was not a priority in the agenda of the superpowers, and eventually incorporating both parties to the conflict, Cambodia and Vietnam, into its fold.

ASEAN's expansion

Expansion of membership into 'ASEAN-10', a major development in ASEAN's post-Cold War evolution, initially posed a severe test to the organisation's norms. ASEAN hoped that expansion would enhance regional autonomy by increasing its bargaining power *vis-à-vis* external powers, would limit the scope for unwelcome Chinese influence in the peripheral states of Burma and Cambodia, would expand regional economic interdependence, and would limit the scope for regional disorder (including a spillover of domestic conflicts into neighbouring states) by promoting adherence to the doctrine of non-interference and the mechanisms of bilateral security cooperation. The decision to expand membership also reflected ASEAN's increasing self-confidence as an anchor of regional security. But against these putative gains one must consider the costs of an expanded membership. These included questions about the commitment of the new members to the norms of ASEAN, and dilution of the ASEAN Way. This was highlighted in July 2012 when the ASEAN Foreign Ministers failed to issue their customary joint communiqué because of disagreements partly induced by the pro-China stance of the ASEAN Chair, Cambodia, on the South China Sea conflict. In some respects, expansion provided a severe test of the norms that had underpinned the grouping's evolution. The principle of non-interference came under attack in Cambodia in 1997, where ASEAN was compelled to take a position in an essentially domestic conflict. Burma posed a more serious and continuing test, saddling ASEAN with the responsibility for managing its transition to an internationally acceptable form of governance. Expansion also imposed new economic and political burdens on ASEAN. Given the different levels of development between the new and the old members, it created the possibility of a two-tier ASEAN made up of haves and have-nots. It has also given ASEAN the challenging task of ensuring peaceful outcomes to the territorial and political disputes involving the new members. But on the plus side, Vietnam's entry into ASEAN has been easier than initially believed and a true success for the organisation.

Managing post-Cold War intra-regional relations

In the area of dispute settlement, the ASEAN Way of avoiding formal and legalistic approaches remains entrenched, although members are now less convinced of its utility and relevance, especially in the wake of the Asian economic crisis. The end of the Cold War in Asia was marked by an aggravation of conflicts in the maritime sphere, with the Spratlys dispute in particular becoming more militarised and contentious. While the major intra-ASEAN conflicts of the 1960s, such as the Sabah dispute between Malaysia and the Philippines, no longer threatened intra-mural peace, a number of bilateral disputes and tensions remain, especially between Malaysia and Singapore. The Spratlys conflict, though not strictly an intra-ASEAN problem, and despite ASEAN's 2002 declaration on a regional code of conduct and China's desire to maintain good relations with ASEAN, has seriously tested intra-ASEAN unity as well as ASEAN's relations with China. Disputes among ASEAN members have not led to outright war, although some – such as fishing disputes between Malaysia and the Philippines, or between Thailand and Cambodia, for example – have produced minor skirmishes. Territorial disputes and political rivalries between some ASEAN states (especially Singapore and Malaysia, and Malaysia and Thailand) undoubtedly form part of the rationale behind the move towards force modernisation, although this does not fit the pattern of a region-wide arms race. A host of non-interactive factors, including economic capacity, prestige and a shared need for greater self-reliance in the wake of superpower retrenchment from the region, are also important in explaining the arms build-up in the region.

ASEAN, the ARF and the Great Powers

The ARF introduced a new norm into the ASEAN process – that of 'cooperative security' – emphasising inclusiveness and dialogue among both like-minded and non-like-minded states, thereby modifying the traditional ZOPFAN framework, which had been somewhat exclusionary in so far as seeking involvement of outside powers in the management of regional order was concerned. But this need not mean abandoning the norm of regional autonomy, which was upheld, with ASEAN occupying what it called the 'driver's seat' role in the ARF and related East Asian institutions such as the APT and East Asian Summit (EAS). Under ASEAN's guidance, the development of these institutions has been, and is likely to remain, cautious, slow, non-legalistic and consensual, minimising formal and direct measures. The ASEAN Way faces considerable obstacles in guiding these institutions to become effective instruments of regional order. The norms of ASEAN were developed in the subregional context of Southeast Asia; they are not going to be easily transplanted into a larger and more complex security theatre such as the Asia-Pacific or even East Asia. While the ARF faces questions about its effectiveness and progress in moving towards a preventive diplomacy role, the East Asian Community idea, now partly realised through the EAS, itself faces questions about its own future owing to differences over membership, and the potential for Chinese dominance (or failing that, Chinese disinterest).The US entry into the EAS has sparked concerns about possible American dominance and Sino-US tensions within the EAS, which has the potential to undermine the entire multilateral project of ASEAN.

But multilateralism developed through these institutions remains critical to prospects for regional order. Critics of the ARF do not provide any concrete ideas about an alternative security architecture for the region, except for vague prescriptions about the need for a US-led balance of power system. The various possible ways of ensuring such an approach remain ill-defined and are marked by several uncertainties. Against this backdrop, multilateralism as embodied in the ARF remains an essential element of the post-Cold War security order in the Asia-Pacific region. Multilateralism is key to ASEAN states' ability to pursue the simultaneous engagement of China and the other major powers, such as Japan, India and the United States and thereby preclude the exclusive dominance of any of them in Southeast Asia, a long-standing ASEAN objective. This is impossible for any single ASEAN member to pull off alone. Moreover, while critics argue that viable multilateral security requires a prior balance of (military) power in the region, it is equally plausible to see multilateralism as a necessary instrument for ensuring that the rise of China is peaceful and that the relationship among the great powers of Asia does not degenerate into unbridled competition and rivalry.

Transnational dangers

While the main security challenges facing ASEAN until the Asian financial crisis were traditional threats, those facing it after the crisis and in the new millennium have been non-traditional security issues. And while traditional interstate conflicts were not able to seriously challenge ASEAN's addiction to non-interference, non-traditional security dangers have done a better job. Foremost among these were the SARS pandemic, terrorism and the Tsunami, as well as the Asian financial crisis in the longer term. Democratic transition in Indonesia and the lack of it in Burma also played a role, the former making Jakarta more amenable to flexible sovereignty, and the latter creating strains between ASEAN and the international community, as well as between ASEAN members, and thereby pushing ASEAN to speak on Burma's domestic politics, in violation of the stricter view of non-interference. Other norms have changed less. The norm against multilateral defence cooperation remains. Objections by Singapore and Vietnam to the Indonesian proposal for an ASEAN peacekeeping mechanism are a case in point. Although ASEAN defence ministers have met, in accordance with the Indonesian ASC proposals, this is not the beginning of an ASEAN military pact. ASEAN still espouses regional solutions, but in a sense that does not connote autarchy, but assertion of a role in regional affairs whenever and wherever possible.

To conclude, of ASEAN's norms, non-interference has been dented, but it persists to a degree that undermines ASEAN's capacity for effective responses to transnational dangers. The discussion and shaming of Burma and the criticism of Indonesia over the 2006 haze notwithstanding, non-interference thwarted ASEAN's ability to respond to the East Timor crisis and apply genuine pressure on Burma. It also makes it difficult, if not impossible over the long term, to develop a regional human rights body with real teeth. Despite the Singapore–Malaysia dispute over water, and the Singapore–Indonesia tensions in the wake of the Asian financial crisis, the norm of non-use of force to settle disputes, the most important condition for security communities, has endured. Challenges to the 'regional solutions to regional problems' norm are another matter. Any evaluation of this must not conflate it with self-reliance, but rather with the right not to be ignored or sidelined by outside powers or Great Powers within East Asia in the management of Southeast Asian affairs. ASEAN will always depend on outside powers for resources and political support, especially in addressing trans-national challenges that respect neither national nor regional boundaries and are too power-ful to be amenable to responses from any single state. ASEAN has not relied on outside powers to solve traditional interstate conflicts, although it has relied on the ICJ. On trans-national threats, lack of capacity has been a factor in seeking outside help, but lack of capa-city is not unique to ASEAN. ASEAN's challenge is not to achieve self-reliance, but to coordinate the seeking and channelling of outside support. At the same time, while economic interdependence with ASEAN remains fairly low relative to its linkages with East Asian and global economic players, thanks partly to its conformity with the ASEAN Way (including soft institutionalism, consultations and consensus, and the avoidance of highly legalistic procedures and mechanisms), in terms of its effects, apart from increasing the costs of conflict, it is also an important measure of the practice of multilateralism and the prospect for collective identity. In the meantime, ASEAN's norm of no military pacts remains more or less unchanged, despite recent developments including the ASEAN Political-Security

Community and the growing incidence of defence diplomacy carried out under the auspices of the Shangri-La Dialogue and the ASEAN Defence Ministers' Meeting Plus.

Institutional change

A mature security community requires mature institutions. The decision of the 2003 ASEAN summit to create an ASEAN Security Community (renamed as ASEAN Political-Security Community), alongside an ASEAN Economic Community and an ASEAN Socio-Cultural Community by the year 2020 represents an unprecedented and ambitious move in the history of regionalism in Southeast Asia. ASEAN is the only regional organisation to adopt officially an essentially academic notion, that of security community, as a policy instrument and final objective. The origin and evolution of this move show very clearly that it was inspired by the concept developed by Deutsch and refined and adapted to contemporary regional contexts by academic writers. Although the academic jargon found in the initial Indonesian articulation of the ASC was later dropped or diluted into more policy prose, the core aim of the ASC is the same as that of the academic concept: to rule out war as a means of problem-solving among the member states.

Indonesia's proposal for an ASC was meant to create new and more powerful institutions and strengthen existing ones further. But its and other efforts to institutionalise ASEAN have faced obstacles, of which three are especially noteworthy. The first is the reluctance of the more conservative members to create political and security institutions that threaten to dilute the non-interference norm. Institutional change is a good indicator of successful norm diffusion, or the borrowing and localisation of international norms. The difficulty ASEAN has faced in developing new and meaningful institutions in the area of human rights and democracy attests to the resilience of traditional norms of sovereignty in the face of emerging post-Westphalian principles such as humanitarian intervention. Even a less controversial institution like a regional peacekeeping force fell by the wayside in the development of the ASC.

A second issue is the non-use of existing and available legal frameworks and institutions, such as the High Council, and the treaty on transboundary pollution. Even if new rules and institutions are created, there is no guarantee that they will be used. ASEAN resists the application of automatic rules, such as the suggestion that a Foreign Ministers' meeting be convened within 48 hours of a regional crisis. A third obstacle to an institutionalised ASEAN is the recent decision by its leaders to assign the final determination and decisions about compliance and sanctions to political, rather than legal or administrative bodies. This is what happened to the ASEAN Charter, when the initial and bold proposals of the EPG for sanctions against non-compliance and other violations of ASEAN's rules were left to the ASEAN summits where political leaders are likely to soft pedal any move to impose penalties on fellow members on political grounds.

ASEAN's agenda for institutional change has also faced a challenge for intra-mural differences that defy the old–new member divide. For example, Singapore has been champion of strong economic institutions, but opposed institutionalisation in the political-security arena. Finally, some of the new mechanisms created under the ASEAN Charter have proven to be problematic. As Surin Pitsuwan's report, *ASEAN Challenge*, highlighted, these problems include poor coordination among ASEAN's different bodies, interference by the Committee of Permanent Representatives leading to loss of autonomy of the ASEAN Secretariat and the Secretary-General, and weak capacity (human and material resources) of the ASEAN Secretariat which undermines its ability to meet the growing demands placed on it by new and expanding areas of cooperation.

Democratising ASEAN

Unlike some regional groups such as the EU or the OAS, ASEAN has not championed democracy promotion or protection (for example as a condition for membership). But it might have taken a modest step by mentioning it in the APSC Plan of Action and the Charter. The APSC's provision that unconstitutional and undemocratic change of government will not be tolerated, if upheld in practice, is a critical step in making ASEAN more democratic. Equally significant is the creation of an ASEAN human rights mechanism, also enshrined in the Charter. On the other hand, contrary to some fears, democratisation of member states has not led to the weakening of ASEAN. In fact, the opposite might have been the case, especially in the case of Indonesia, which following democratic transition provided leadership in pushing for the ASC/APSC idea as a way of strengthening ASEAN. The idea of an ASEAN Socio-cultural Community aimed at developing a sense of regional identity among the citizens of ASEAN and accommodating the voices of civil society groups is a significant step, but like other pillars of the ASEAN community-building agenda, much depends on how far this broadening of ASEAN's official and highly elite-driven regionalism will actually go in practice. Consultations with NGOs by the ASEAN Charter EPG were encouraging, but in the end no formal mechanism has been created to give their input into the ASEAN decision-making process. The emergence of the ASEAN People's Assembly (APA), which is coordinated by regime-oriented semi-official think-tanks and the Solidarity for Asian People's Advocacy (SAPA), which is an initiative of non-official advocacy groups that are often at odds with state policy is important. Both these groups have not only engaged each other, but they have also engaged the ASEAN governments. Together, these three constitute elements of an emerging participatory regionalism, which is crucial to the future legitimacy and effectiveness of ASEAN.

Questions about regional identity

Most of the findings of the chapters as discussed above relate to the regulatory effects of ASEAN's norms, defined in terms of the degree of their compliance by ASEAN members individually and collectively in different issue areas. The foregoing analysis suggests that ASEAN's norms have had important regulatory impact. But security communities require the development of a common identity. Has the practice of norms helped the development of regional identity in Southeast Asia? What is not clear from the above discussion is the so-called constitutive effects of norms. By nature, these are difficult to measure. But the questions posed in Table 1.2 provide a helpful basis for judging constitutive effects.

The norms of ASEAN played a crucial role in the development of a regional identity. While the social and cultural diversity among ASEAN's members made it difficult to speak of a common cultural identity, socialisation processes developed around the ASEAN Way contributed to the development of a degree of what Deutsch would call the 'we feeling' in ASEAN. A fairly consistent pattern of adherence (notwithstanding occasional exceptions) to and practice of norms such as non-interference itself became part of the ASEAN identity. As Michael Leifer pointed out, ASEAN's consultative process, including the frequent meetings and other forms of multilateral interaction, gradually led to the development of 'an institutional culture' which helped ASEAN 'to avoid and control conflicts'.[3] It also fostered a common feeling of regional belonging and led to claims about institutional exceptionalism underpinning constructs such as the ASEAN Way.

Developing a regional collective identity was an important objective of ASEAN's founders. ASEAN's role in the Cambodia conflict and its development of multilateral security cooperation in the Asia-Pacific show a conscious attempt by the ASEAN members to differentiate ASEAN from a variety of competing actors and processes. During its formative years and during the Cambodia conflict, ASEAN juxtaposed itself against the ideological orientation, economic policies and security practices of the Indochinese segment of Southeast Asia. It claimed for itself an exclusive role in the promotion of regionalism in Southeast Asia. Similarly, ASEAN's economic regionalism was carefully distinguished from the EC/EU model. In the post-Cold War era, ASEAN has sought to define its approach to conflict management in opposition to the security institutions and practices in Europe. Such exceptionalism has become a key aspect of ASEAN security discourse, and has facilitated community building.

ASEAN's efforts to articulate the boundaries of Southeast Asia as a region, are evident from the pursuit of its 'One Southeast Asia' concept and its efforts to expand the scope for multilateralism and cover new issue areas previously excluded as indicated in the creation of AFTA, the institution of financial cooperation, and the emerging, if limited, policy coordination in dealing with transnational threats (terrorism, SARS and the haze). Yet, the constitutive potential of the 'One Southeast Asia' concept could be more superficial than the official proclamations on this subject would have us believe. The constitutive effects of ASEAN's norms in pushing its members to look beyond a strict adherence to sovereignty and non-interference have been limited. Developments in intra-regional relations also suggest that the ASEAN governments continue to emphasise the salience of state sovereignty in participating in cooperative regional ventures. As the debate about 'flexible engagement' showed, there is a great deal of reluctance and apprehension about compromising on this norm. Against this backdrop, while the realisation of ASEAN-10 might have created a sense of collective identity, this does not as yet amount to a fully-fledged 'constitutive' change moving the ASEAN members decisively away from their identity as sovereignty-bound actors. At the same time, state sovereignty is viewed more flexibly today in the ASEAN context and the impact of cooperation over a range of traditional and non-traditional security issues has moved ASEAN to some degree away from the strict sovereignty mindset that prevailed before the 1997 regional economic crisis.

Prospects for ASEAN

Before the Asian financial crisis, ASEAN's potential to become a regional security community had been widely acknowledged by scholars and policymakers from both within and outside the region. In 1992, Sheldon Simon argued that 'ASEAN may be a security community in the sense that no member would consider the use of force against another to settle disputes'.[4] Michael Leifer labelled ASEAN as a 'diplomatic community', rather than a security community. Nonetheless, he could 'claim quite categorically that ASEAN has become an institutionalized vehicle for intra-mural conflict avoidance and management. . . . ASEAN has been able to prevent disputes from escalating and getting out of hand through containing and managing contentious issues.'[5] David Martin Jones praised ASEAN's "collegial style and practice", and stated that ASEAN "was well established as a regional security actor," and might be "considered a security community."[6]

In the aftermath of the end of the Cold War, Kishore Mahbubani, a Singaporean diplomat, argued: 'We take it for granted. But the absence of war [among the ASEAN members] is a major achievement.'[6] Another long-time observer of ASEAN, Jusuf Wanandi, from Indonesia, even speculated: 'Since no more wars are expected to break out among its members, Asean may no longer be taken seriously by its members in the future.'[7] The absence of war among the ASEAN members since 1967 is certainly important. (It is interesting to note that not only has ASEAN itself been free from an intra-mural war, but no ASEAN country has fought an outright war with a non-ASEAN state since its inception in 1967.)

To be sure, ASEAN's record must be kept in perspective. For much of its history, it has been a relatively compact grouping, comprising a handful of states ruled by ideologically like-minded regimes facing the danger of communism. Moreover, one could argue that since the end of Sukarno's *Konfrontasi*, there had been no serious regional issue dividing the ASEAN members which could have conceivably led to war. But ASEAN did contribute to this situation by fostering a climate of socialisation and trust that might have suppressed Sukarno-like militant nationalist sentiments among the member states towards each other and led them to realise the benefits of cooperation over confrontation. Such instances of peaceful conflict management, even among a relatively small number of states, are rare in the developing world. Indeed, few other regional associations outside of the Euro-Atlantic context can claim this distinction.

ASEAN's security-community-building project faced a number of daunting challenges. While it had developed some of the attributes of a nascent security community by the early 1990s, such communities can decline as a result of both internal burdens and external challenges. To a large extent, the problems facing ASEAN in the late 1990s could be explained in terms of the burden imposed by membership expansion and the emergence of new sources of intra-regional and transnational conflict. To make matters worse, ASEAN might have overestimated its capacity to assume the role of 'driver' in the development of the ARFR, APT and EAS. These burdens now challenge the sanctity of ASEAN's norms and the credibility of the ASEAN Way, including the doctrines of non-use of force and non-intervention.

The idea of constructive intervention and flexible engagement, if pursued seriously, would constitute an especially significant challenge. Moreover, the ASEAN Way, especially the habit of consensus building, has already being seriously tested by the organisation's expansion to include Burma. ASEAN, which is already more institutionalised than the proponents of the ASEAN Way would have us believe, is abandoning some of its informality in favour of legalistic and formal measures. ASEAN is in many respects losing its uniqueness and becoming a 'regular' or 'normal' institution. This may in part be due to the fact that its agenda has become too complex to be handled through informal channels. In the past, ASEAN put too much emphasis on 'ritual' and style; now it has to deal with substantive issues, such as AFTA. While in the past the ASEAN Way meant avoiding grand designs or precise road maps, or setting formal agendas to keep things *ad hoc* and flexible, now ideas such as the ASEAN Economic Community and the ASEAN Political-Security Community attest to a more formal and regularised agenda.

Overall, the security burdens on ASEAN come from both internal and external sources. The internal burdens come from membership expansion and the emergence of new sources of interstate and transnational conflict. Externally, ASEAN's support for regimes like that in Burma alienates public and eventually official opinion in the West. The Asian economic crisis highlighted many of the challenges facing the norms of ASEAN and raised questions as to whether they can survive into the future. The downfall of the Suharto regime, resulting directly from its failed response to the crisis, deprived ASEAN of a long-time champion who had played the key role in the development of ASEAN and the ASEAN Way. The subsequent turmoil in Indonesia indicated a leadership vacuum in ASEAN, and contributed to the perception of an ASEAN without a clear sense of direction. The controversy surrounding the Thai call for 'flexible engagement', combined with the earlier debate in ASEAN about 'constructive intervention', and ASEAN's inability to offer a timely and collective response to the crisis over East Timor's separation from Indonesia in 1999, highlighted the problem ASEAN faces. At the time of its founding, the key norms of ASEAN, including the doctrine of non-interference, were derived from the UN Charter and were compatible with the norms of other international institutions. Today, however, the international community has increasingly accepted a less stringent view of sovereignty even as ASEAN resists any such shift. This disjunction between ASEAN's regional practice and the changing norms of sovereignty at the global level is a serious challenge to the organisation's credibility and international standing. It also relates to the possibility that changes to existing global norms could lead to the unravelling of a potential regional security community like ASEAN.

ASEAN has moved towards greater intra-regional interdependence and integration, thereby providing an additional set of disincentives to the use of force within the region.[8] But it has no comparable aspirations to become a 'democratic security community'. Unlike the EU, membership in ASEAN does not require a liberal democratic polity. Non-democratic regimes, such as those in Burma and Vietnam, have been welcomed into the ASEAN fold. But ASEAN has, through its security community plan of action and the ASEAN Charter, agreed that it will not tolerate unconstitutional and undemocratic changes in government and develop a regional human rights body. Complying with these obligations will be a key test of ASEAN's future credibility and progress. Its attitude towards the regime in Burma has changed. But a key challenge is that the idea of regional cooperation and community building, including mutual responsiveness and socialisation, remains narrowly confined to the intergovernmental level in ASEAN. This kind of regionalism does not necessarily translate into cooperation or development of 'we feeling' at the societal level, as Deutsch clearly envisaged. Hence, it is important to note that the network of indigenous non-governmental organisations which have promoted a semi-official and non-official regionalism gets encouragement, or at least tolerance, from ASEAN governments.

This leads to the prospects for a collective identity within ASEAN. As a result of membership expansion, the debate over the non-interference doctrine, and the divisions over human rights/democracy, ASEAN has faced several different sorts of intra-mural polarisation and factionalism. There is a liberal–conservative division based on the degree of commitment to human rights and democracy, with Thailand (under the Chuan Leekpai government, reversed by his successor Thaksin), the Philippines and later Indonesia (post-Suharto) in the former camp, and Vietnam, Burma, Malaysia and Singapore in the other. This divide also subsumes a pro-interventionist group which put forth ideas such as 'constructive intervention', 'flexible engagement', and the initial version of Indonesia's 'ASEAN Security Community' Plan of Action on the one hand, and a pro-sovereignty camp of the rest of ASEAN members who would keep the grouping firmly wedded to strict non-interference, quiet diplomacy and constructive engagement on the other. Then there is a 'North–South' divide, a two-tier ASEAN of 'haves' and 'have-nots', reflecting differing levels of development, a polarisation between the old and the new members. While any enlarged multilateral group can expect to have different coalitions pursuing separate agendas within its ambit, these emerging divisions within ASEAN are especially problematic in view of its traditional commitment to consensus-based agenda setting and decision making.

Constructing security communities is not a linear process. The norms that underpin a security community, like norms in general, are often contested although neither this nor their occasional violation make them irrelevant. The moral and functional import of norms changes over time. Non-interference once enjoyed a powerful legitimacy and political importance, not only for liberal Third World nationalists like India's Jawaharlal Nehru, but also for the developed countries (such as those that dominated the charter-making process of the UN) which made this norm into a governing principle for the international community. It continued to enjoy wide support in the Cold War period when the developing countries faced the twin dangers of neo-colonialism (in the context of the decolonisation process) and superpower intervention. Today, the very same norm stands discredited for sanctioning state repression as in Burma. The principles of non-interference and aspirations for regional autonomy remain important in avoiding war in Southeast Asia, but they have become functionally deficient in coping with transnational dangers such as financial volatility, environmental degradation or terrorism. While ASEAN remains wedded to these norms, there is no guarantee that this will not change, especially through the internal initiative of some of the ASEAN members themselves.

A nascent security community may decay into anarchy if it fails to cope with the burdens brought about by increased or new forms of interactions. After suffering a major blow from the Asian financial crisis, ASEAN has made a recovery, and is slowly reforming, and perhaps reinventing itself. The process of reform will not lead to the supranational path of the EU or to any substantial regional capacity for intervention. As before, ASEAN's relevance and credibility will depend primarily on its ability to keep intra-regional rivalries in check and prevent disputes among its members from turning into armed confrontation. Some ASEAN member governments fear that any departure from non-interference, which is crucial to address security challenges in their conventional sense, could ruin the grouping. But a flexible attitude towards sovereignty is also crucial to its ability to deal with current and future economic and political crises, and in dealing with transnational challenges – shadowy terrorist networks, pandemics, and natural catastrophes, that have confronted the grouping in the past decade. This is the essential normative paradox of contemporary Southeast Asian and Asian regionalism: the very norms and practices that have kept ASEAN and its offshoots internally viable have also limited their effectiveness in dealing with external and global challenges.

Hence, after four decades of progress in promoting peaceful intra-regional relations, ASEAN has not yet reached the stage of unfortified common borders or the high degree of economic interdependence characteristic of mature security communities. Intra-mural tensions, such as that between Singapore and Malaysia (although neither side has seriously contemplated using force in recent bilateral crises) detract from ASEAN's claim to be a security community in the Deutschian sense.[9] But if we use the more differentiated and evolutionary approach to security communities, ASEAN would fit the concept of a 'nascent' security community, especially when viewed in terms of the sustained effort of its members to 'coordinate their relations in order to: increase their mutual security; lower the transaction costs associated with their exchanges; and/or encourage further exchanges and interactions'.[10] Nascent security communities do not make war 'unthinkable' or abolish disputes and conflicts among their members. But the key test for such communities is whether its members manage their disputes without resort to force. In addition, ASEAN displays a sense of common identity which is not normally expected in a nascent phase (it is more likely in the ascendant period). Although ASEAN's progress towards the ascendant level looked more promising in the early 1990s than in the later part of that decade, such prospects appear somewhat better in recent years.

Though an 'imperfect union'[11] of weak Southeast Asian actors, ASEAN's achievements, especially relative to past political/security institutions in Asia are nonetheless substantial. Contemporary alternatives to it remain rather scarce. The ASEAN role in regional security is now being challenged by the growing geopolitical weight of China, Japan and India. Yet for historical and political reasons, none of these powers, nor the US, can replace ASEAN's normative framework. But if ASEAN is to move towards an ascendant future, its institutional reforms, such as those contained in the ASEAN Political-Security Community (along with the ASEAN Economic Community and the ASEAN Socio-cultural Community the ASEAN Political Security Community, as well as the ASEAN Charter, will make a vital difference. Implementing these frameworks will require further adjustments to its non-interference doctrine. A critical factor will be whether its treaties and institutions – old and new – will be used if and when needed.

ASEAN's irrelevance or even death has been predicted several times before. At birth in 1967, few people thought it would live to see another decade, given that the two previous attempts at regional cooperation in Southeast Asia, the Association of Southeast Asia and the MAPHILINDO (Malaysia, Philippines and Indonesia) concept, had ended within a few years after their creation. The Malaysia–Philippines dispute over Sabah in 1969, the aftermath of the US withdrawal from Indochina in 1975, the Vietnamese invasion of Cambodia in 1979, the end of the Cold War, and the outbreak of the Asian financial crisis in 1997, have all been seen as critical blows to ASEAN. But ASEAN survived, even a little strengthened each time. So there is precedent, and hope, that ASEAN would be around for some time.

But surviving is not the same as thriving. ASEAN might still keep plodding on, but would it still be a key player in regional peace, stability and prosperity in Asia – a role that it currently enjoys? This question becomes more difficult to answer.

The answer might well depend on three key challenges. First, what would be ASEAN's relations with the great powers? The biggest fear for ASEAN is that it will be swept aside by the rise of its two most powerful immediate neighbours, China and India, and the tide of great power competition that would draw in the US and Japan as well. ASEAN emerged at a time when India and China had just fought a war with each other and faced major domestic challenges, including Mao's Cultural Revolution in China. Japan in the late 1960s and 1970s was still on a recovery mode, politically if not economically. The field was thus open for ASEAN for anchoring regional cooperation.

How different is the situation today! China and India are racing to join Japan and US in the great power club, and seeking their rightful place at the top of world affairs. Japan, though stagnant economically, is reorienting itself – as a 'normal state' – to an active political and military role in Asia. Some things remain unchanged though. China, Japan and India do cancel each other out due to their mutual mistrust. All three and the US want ASEAN to accept its leadership in Asian regional cooperation.

Some imagine a concert of powers developing in Asia, wherein China, Japan, India and the United States could jointly manage regional security issues. This would marginalise ASEAN. As the saying in Southeast Asia goes, the grass suffers not only when the elephants fight, but also when they make love. But an Asian concert of powers would require the powers to overcome differences which are neither temporary nor trivial.

A second challenge is about ASEAN's future: what would be the state of inter-ASEAN relations? Here, the skirmishes on the Thai-Cambodian border do not inspire confidence. A degree of mistrust continues to cloud relationships between Singapore and Malaysia, Thailand and Burma, and Malaysia and Thailand. But this is a far cry from the 1960s and 1970s, and there is reason to hope that these intra-ASEAN conflicts would not doom the organisation. They would need, however, to be managed carefully, especially with the help of existing and new mechanisms that ASEAN is currently seeking to develop.

The third challenge is this: What would the domestic political configurations of ASEAN countries look like? Would ASEAN countries become more open and democratic? Indonesia has surely taken a major leap towards democracy. But we have seen a military takeover in Thailand in 2006. The military remains a key for political tone in Thailand & Burma. Domestic succession in many ASEAN countries remains uncertain and even volatile. Domestic turbulence can spill over borders and limit ASEAN members' ability to contribute to regional public good. As a regional group, ASEAN cannot shape the domestic politics of its members, but a collective commitment to participatory democracy and regionalism does help. The idea of a People's ASEAN has thus far only meant fostering cultural exchanges and cooperation, not promoting or defending democracy (although Indonesia's efforts through the Bali Democracy Forum are praiseworthy). ASEAN has made a tentative commitment to human rights, but this remains constrained by the resilience of the non-interference norm.

In essence, to stay relevant and perform effectively as 'the fulcrum of geopolitical stability in Asia', ASEAN must commit itself to four goals:

Centrality: The principle of ASEAN centrality implies that ASEAN must keep its seat at the 'driver's table' of the most important existing Asian regional institutions, especially the ARF, and the EAS, and that it should not allow itself to be sidelined, or marginalised by the initiatives from others, especially the great powers, to develop new or competing regional bodies covering Asia as a whole. The principle of ASEAN centrality is not an accident of history, but rooted in past historical political conditions favouring Asia's weaker states in developing regional cooperation.[12] In other words, ASEAN centrality owes itself not to the generosity of the big powers, but to two other long-term factors. First, none of these great powers – including the US, China, Japan and India –would be acceptable by the rest of the region as the sole driver of regionalism as each carries baggage from the past. Second, the two most important East Asian powers, China and Japan, do not find each other acceptable in such a role, and the prospect for a Sino-Japanese *rapprochement* in the manner of the postwar Franco-German reconciliation, which will provide the strongest challenge to ASEAN centrality, does not appear likely in the immediate future. But this does not mean ASEAN can take the principle for granted. It has come under scrutiny for giving ASEAN too much control. Critics of ASEAN centrality argue that ASEAN is unable to muster the resources and political will to exercise an effective leadership role in dealing with the big issues of the day. ASEAN needs to address such perceptions, with a proactive and robust system of dealing with regional crises and advancing common projects, without diluting its centrality – a major challenge for the organisation in the coming years.

Compliance: The second goal has to do with compliance. ASEAN has a whole host of old and new declarations, agreements, treaties, conventions, protocols, plans of action, blue-prints, concords, etc. to address a growing number of old and new challenges. But the key is to ensure members' compliance. ASEAN's sometimes well-deserved reputation as a talk shop stems not from a lack of cooperative instruments, but the failure to adhere to them. In other words, their poor 'usability'. ASEAN now has a programme of monitoring member states' compliance with the blueprints of its three communities, but it remains to be seen whether the mechanisms thus created are actually put into practice, such as conflict resolution mechanisms like the High Council and the 'good offices' role of the Secretary-General and the ASEAN Chair. At the same time, ASEAN must engage in capacity-building to implement and realise its various political and security objectives, as outlined in the Blueprint for the ASEAN Political-Security Community.

Conflict Resolution: ASEAN's practice of 'sweeping conflicts under the carpet' is no longer adequate by itself, if it ever was. As with domestic conflicts and terrorism, at least some interstate and regional conflicts require a resolution of their 'root causes' in order to be removed permanently as barriers to stability and cooperation. ASEAN should thus embrace the challenge of conflict resolution as well as preventive diplomacy. The ARF has sought these goals since inception, but the conflict resolution objective was renamed to a seemingly innocuous phrase: 'elaboration of approaches to conflicts', reportedly at China's insistence. ASEAN should now seek conflict resolution as part of its own agenda, by making existing regional arbitration mechanisms more juridical (with the help of a Council of third-party judges, for example), and introducing a certain amount of automaticity to their implementation.

Common/Cooperative Security: While this is a well-established principle of ASEAN and the ARF, sustaining it for the long term cannot be taken for granted. The key to this principle is 'inclusiveness' (inviting all relevant actors to the table and excluding none) and 'non-discrimination' or 'impartiality' (giving equal treatment to all actors, including the great powers, refraining from taking sides in the conflicts among them, and offering them a comforting atmosphere to sort out their differences). As China's power grows, there will be temptations for and opportunistic moves by individual ASEAN members to take China's side on critical territorial or strategic issues. There is no evidence as yet that either China or India is pursuing a 'divide-and-rule' approach towards ASEAN, but China may feel the temptation to do so in the future when its 'core interests' are at stake, by offering some ASEAN members substantial rewards for their exclusive friendship (such as economic and military aid, favourable stance towards their territorial claims, separate bilateral deals with individual claimants to the South China Sea, and political support for regimes facing international pressure over human rights/democracy). Resisting temptations for such a 'special relationship' with China (or India, or for that matter the US) and maintaining its 'honest broker' image and role in dealing with the great powers are vital for ASEAN to stay relevant in the multipolar Asian order. Such an approach should be consistent with the concept of 'dynamic equilibrium' introduced by Marty Natalegawa, the Foreign Minister of Indonesia and the chair of ASEAN in 2011.[13]

In conclusion, one could imagine ASEAN in the next few decades either as the wise counselor of Asia, or a marginalised relic of the past. By 2030 it could still be at its peak, functioning as a steady and calming influence on the rising powers of Asia: India and China. Or it might have lost its bearings, amidst the confusion of profound changes in the regional economic and military balance of power.

To avoid the latter fate, ASEAN's leaders must stay united, strengthen mechanisms for cooperation, steadfastly maintain its neutral broker image among the great powers and be attentive to their people's voices. By doing so, they will have a good chance of retaining ASEAN's driver's seat in Asian regional cooperation and turning Southeast Asia into a genuine pluralistic security community.

Notes and references

1 Karl Deutsch, 'Security Communities', in James Rosenau (ed.), *International Politics and Foreign Policy* (New York: Free Press, 1961), p. 99.
2 Keynote address by Haji Abdullah bin Haji Abdullah Badawi, Foreign Minister of Malaysia, at the Second ASEAN Congress, Kuala Lumpur, 20–23 July 1997.
3 Cited in Hoang Anh Tuan, 'ASEAN Dispute Management: Implications for Vietnam and an Expanded ASEAN', *Contemporary Southeast Asia*, vol. 18, no. 1 (June 1996), p. 67.
4 Sheldon Simon, 'The Regionalization of Defence in Southeast Asia', *Pacific Review*, vol. 5, no. 2 (1992), p. 122.

5 Michael Leifer, 'ASEAN as a Model of a Security Community?', in Hadi Soesastro (ed.), *ASEAN in a Changed Regional and International Political Economy* (Jakarta: Centre for Strategic and International Studies, 1995), p. 132.
6 *Straits Times*, 22 July 1997, p. 2.
   David Martin Jones, Political Development in Pacific Asia (Cambridge, UK: Polity Press, 1997), p. 183, 185.
7 Jusuf Wanandi, 'Key Test: How to Cope with Future Challenges', *Straits Times*, 26 July 1997, p. 49.
8 Hadi Soesastro, 'Economic Integration and Interdependence in the Asia Pacific: Implications for Security', Paper presented at the Eighth Asia Pacific Roundtable, Kuala Lumpur, 5–8 June 1994, p. 1; Robert A. Scalapino, 'Challenges to the Sovereignty of the Modern State', in Bunn Nagara and K.S. Balakrishnan (eds), *Proceedings of the Seventh Asia-Pacific Roundtable, The Making of a Security Community in the Asia-Pacific* (Kuala Lumpur: ISIS Malaysia, 1994), p. 50.
9 In a previous essay ('A Regional Security Community in Southeast Asia?', *Journal of Strategic Studies*, vol. 18, no. 3 (September 1995), pp. 175–200), I chose to characterise ASEAN as a 'security regime' rather than a 'security community'. But this assessment was based on the classic Deutschian notion, rather than the more differentiated interpretation provided by Adler and Barnett. The concept of security regime as developed in my earlier paper shares many features of the 'nascent' phase of pluralistic security communities as understood by Adler and Barnett.
10 Emanuel Adler and Michael Barnett, 'A Framework for the Study of Security Communities', in Emanuel Adler and Michael Barnett (eds), *Security Communities* (Cambridge: Cambridge University Press, 1998), p. 50.
11 On imperfect unions, see: Robert O. Keohane and Celeste A. Wallander, *Imperfect Unions: Security Institutions over Time and Space* (Oxford: Oxford University Press, 1999).
12 Acharya, *Whose Ideas Matter: Agency and Power in Asian Regionalism* (Ithaca: Cornell University Press, 2009).
13 'Dynamic equilibrium' is distinct from a 'balance of power' approach. Whereas the latter is based on adversarial alliances and coalitions, 'dynamic equilibrium' means engaging all major players to create a benign and stable regional architecture. Author's Personal Interview with Dr Marty Natalegawa, Jakarta, 5 July 2011. Hence, Indonesia is a little wary of the U.S. pivot/ rebalancing strategy. While greater US engagement in Southeast Asia is welcome, an excessive military rebalancing is viewed by Jakarta as having negative repercussions: as Indonesian officials put it, 'too much rebalancing would be as bad as too little'.

Select bibliography on ASEAN

Articles, book, chapters and conference papers

Acharya, Amitav (1991) 'Association of Southeast Asian Nations: "Security Community" or "Defence Community"?', *Pacific Affairs*, vol. 64, no. 2 (Summer), pp. 159–78.
—— (1995) 'A Regional Security Community in Southeast Asia?', *Journal of Strategic Studies*, vol. 18, no. 3 (September), pp. 175–200.
—— (1997) 'Ideas, Identity and Institution-Building: From the "ASEAN Way" to the "Asia-Pacific Way"?', *The Pacific Review*, vol. 10, no. 3, pp. 319–46.
—— (1999) 'A Concert of Asia?', *Survival*, vol. 41, no. 3 (Autumn), pp. 84–101.
—— (1999) 'Realism, Institutionalism, and the Asian Economic Crisis', *Contemporary Southeast Asia*, vol. 21, no. 1 (April), pp. 1–29.
—— (1999) 'Southeast Asia's Democratic Moment?', *Asian Survey*, vol. 39, no. 3 (May/June), pp. 418–32.
—— (2003) 'Democratisation and the Prospects for Participatory Regionalism in Southeast Asia', *Third World Quarterly*, vol. 24, no. 2, pp. 375–90.
—— (2003/4) 'Will Asia's Past Be Its Future?', *International Security*, vol. 28, no. 3 (Winter).
—— (2004) 'How Ideas Spread: Whose Norms Matter? Norm Localization and Institutional Change in Asian Regionalism', *International Organization*, vol. 58, no. 2 (Spring), pp. 239–75.
—— (2005) 'Do Norms and Identity Matter? Community and Power in Southeast Asia's Regional Order', *Pacific Review*, vol. 18, no. 1 (March), pp. 95–118.
—— (2007) 'ASEAN and 40: Mid-Life Rejuvenation?', *Foreign Affairs* (www.foreignaffairs.org) (15 August).
Alagappa, Muthiah (1991) 'Regional Arrangements and International Security in Southeast Asia: Going Beyond ZOPFAN', *Contemporary Southeast Asia*, vol. 12, no. 4 (March), pp. 269–305.
—— (1991) 'The Dynamics of International Security in Southeast Asia: Change and Continuity', *Australian Journal of International Affairs*, vol. 45, no. 1 (May), pp. 1–37.
—— (1993) 'Regionalism and the Quest for Security: ASEAN and the Cambodian Conflict', *Journal of International Affairs*, vol. 46, no. 2 (Winter), pp. 439–68.
Askandar, Kamarulzaman (1994) 'ASEAN and Conflict Management: The Formative Years of 1967–1976', *The Pacific Review*, vol. 6, no. 2, pp. 57–69.
Ball, Desmond. 'A Critical Review of Multilateral Security Cooperation in the Asia-Pacific Region', Presented to the inaugural conference of the Asia-Pacific Security Forum on 'The Impetus of Change in the Asia-Pacific Security Environment', Taipei, Taiwan, 1–3 September 1997.
—— 'Regional Maritime Security', Presented to the 'Conference on Oceans Governance and Maritime Strategy', Canberra, Australia, 18–19 May 1998.
Collins, Alan (2003) *Security and Southeast Asia: Domestic, Regional, and Global Issues* (Singapore: Institute of Southeast Asian Studies).
Djiwandono, J. Soedjati (1983) 'The Political and Security Aspects of ASEAN: Its Principal Achievements', *Indonesian Quarterly*, vol. 11, no. 3 (July), pp. 19–26.

Drummond, Stuart (1985) 'ASEAN: National Policies Versus Economic Cooperation?', *The Round Table*, no. 295 (July), pp. 263–71.

Emmerson, Donald K. (1987) 'ASEAN as an International Regime', *Journal of International Affairs*, vol. 41, no. 1 (Summer/Fall), pp. 1–16.

Evans, Paul M. (1996) 'Reinventing East Asia: Multilateral Cooperation and Regional Order', *Harvard International Review* (Spring), pp. 16–19, 68–9.

Frost, Frank (1980) 'The Origins and Evolution of ASEAN', *World Review*, vol. 19, no. 3 (August).

Garofano, J. (2002) 'Power, Institutions, and the ASEAN Regional Forum: A Security Community for Asia?', *Asian Survey*, vol. 42, no. 3, pp. 502–21.

Garret, Banning, and Bonnie Glaser (1994) 'Multilateral Security in the Asia-Pacific Region and its Impact on Chinese Interests: Views from Beijing', *Contemporary Southeast Asia*, vol. 16, no. 1 (June), pp. 14–34.

Hill, H. Monte (1978) 'Community Formation Within ASEAN', *International Organization*, vol. 32, no. 2 (Spring), pp. 569–75.

Hoang Anh Tuan (1996) 'ASEAN Dispute Management: Implications for Vietnam and an Expanded ASEAN', *Contemporary Southeast Asia*, vol. 18, no. 1 (June), pp. 61–80.

Hund, Markus (2002) 'From "Neighbourhood Watch Group" to Community? The Case of ASEAN Institutions and the Pooling of Sovereignty', *Australian Journal of International Affairs*, vol. 56, no. 1, pp. 99–122.

Huxley, Tim (1987) 'ASEAN's Prospective Security Role: Moving Beyond the Indochina Fixation', *Contemporary Southeast Asia*, vol. 9, no. 3 (December), pp. 194–207.

Ibrahim, Anwar (1997) 'Crisis Prevention', *Newsweek*, 21 July, p. 13.

Johnston, Alastair Iain (2003) 'Socialization in International Institutions: The ASEAN Way and International Relations Theory', in G. John Ikenberry and Michael Mastanduno (eds.), *International Relations Theory and the Asia-Pacific* (New York: Columbia University Press), pp. 107–62.

Jones, David Martin and Michael L.R. Smith (2007) 'Making Process, Not Progress: ASEAN and the Evolving East Asian Regional Order' *International Security*, vol.32, no.1 (Summer), pp. 148–184.

Jorgensen-Dahl, Arnfinn (1980) 'The Significance of ASEAN', *World Review*, vol. 19, no. 3 (August), pp. 55–9.

Karniol, Robert (1988) 'ASEAN's Need For Greater Defence Co-operation', *Jane's Defence Weekly*, vol. 10, no. 23 (10 December), pp. 1495–98.

Kerr, Pauline (1994) 'The Security Dialogue in the Asia-Pacific', *The Pacific Review*, vol. 7, no. 4, pp. 397–409.

Kuhonta, Erik (2006) 'Walking a Tightrope: Democracy versus Sovereignty in ASEAN's Illiberal Peace,' *Pacific Review*, vol. 19, no. 3 (September), pp. 337–58.

Kurus, Bilson (1995) 'The ASEAN Triad: National Interest, Consensus-Seeking, and Economic Co-operation', *Contemporary Southeast Asia*, vol. 16, no. 4 (March), pp. 404–20.

Kusuma-Atmadja, Mochtar (1990) 'Some Thoughts on ASEAN Security Cooperation: An Indonesian Perspective', *Contemporary Southeast Asia*, vol. 12, no. 3 (December), pp. 161–71.

Lau Teik Soon (1982) 'ASEAN and the Cambodian Problem', *Asian Survey*, vol. 22, no. 6 (June), pp. 548–60.

Leifer, Michael (1974) 'Regional Order in South-east Asia: An Uncertain Prospect', *The Round Table*, no. 255 (July), pp. 309–17.

—— (1992) 'Debating Asian Security: Michael Leifer Responds to Geoffrey Wiseman', *The Pacific Review*, vol. 5, no. 2, pp. 167–69.

—— (1999) 'The ASEAN Peace Process: A Category Mistake', *The Pacific Review*, vol. 12, no. 1, pp. 25–38.

Narine, Shaun (1998) 'Institutional Theory and Southeast Asia: The Case of ASEAN', *World Affairs*, vol. 161, no. 1 (Summer), pp. 33–7.

Peou, Sorpong (2002) 'Realism and Constructivism in Southeast Asian Security Studies Today', *The Pacific Review*, vol. 15, no. 1, pp. 1–20.

Rieger, Hans Christoph (1989) 'Regional Economic Cooperation in the Asia-Pacific Region', *Asia-Pacific Economic Literature*, vol. 3, no. 2 (September), pp. 5–33.

Shafie, Mohammed Ghazalie bin (1971) 'The Neutralisation of Southeast Asia', *Pacific Community*, vol. 3, no. 1 (October), pp. 110–17.

Simon, Sheldon W. (1992) 'The Regionalization of Defence in Southeast Asia', *The Pacific Review*, vol. 5, no. 2, pp. 112–24.

Singh, Bilveer (1993) 'The Challenge of the Security Environment in Southeast Asia in the Post-Cold War Era', *Australian Journal of International Affairs*, vol. 47, no. 2 (October), pp. 263–77.

Soesastro, M. Hadi (1987) 'ASEAN's Participation in the GATT', *Indonesian Quarterly*, vol. 15, no. 1 (January), pp. 107–27.

Stubbs, Richard (1999) 'War and Economic Development: Export-Oriented Industrialization in East and Southeast Asia', *Comparative Politics*, vol. 31 (April), pp. 337–55.

—— (2000) 'Signing on to Liberalization: AFTA and the Politics of Regional Economic Cooperation', *The Pacific Review*, vol. 13, no. 2, pp. 297–318.

—— (2002), 'ASEAN Plus Three: Emerging East Asian Regionalism?' *Asian Survey*, vol. 42, no. 3 (May/June), pp. 440–55.

Um, Khatharya (1991) 'Thailand and the Dynamics of Economic and Security Complex in Mainland Southeast Asia', *Contemporary Southeast Asia*, vol. 13, no. 3 (December), pp. 245–70.

van der Kroef, Justus M. (1985) 'Kampuchea: The Road to Finlandization 1983', *Asian Profile*, vol. 13, no. 3 (June), pp. 221–41.

Wanandi, Jusuf (1996) 'ASEAN's China Strategy: Towards Deeper Engagement', *Survival*, vol. 38, no. 3 (Autumn), pp. 117–28.

Wiseman, Geoffrey (1992) 'Common Security in the Asia-Pacific Region', *The Pacific Review*, vol. 5, no. 1, pp. 42–59.

Books, monographs, policy reports

Acharya, Amitav (1993) *A New Regional Order in Southeast Asia: ASEAN in the Post-Cold War Era* (Adelphi Paper no. 279) (London: International Institute for Strategic Studies).

—— (1997) *The ASEAN Regional Forum: Confidence-Building* (Ottawa: Department of Foreign Affairs and International Trade).

—— (2000) *The Quest for Identity: International Relations of Southeast Asia* (Singapore: Oxford University Press).

——(2009) *Whose Ideas Matter: Agency and Power in Asian Regionalism* (Ithaca: Cornell University Press).

Acharya, Amitav and Evelyn Goh (eds) (2007) *Reassessing Security Cooperation in Asia-Pacific* (Cambridge, MA: MIT Press).

Acharya, Amitav, Pierre Lizee and Sorpong Peou (eds) (1991) *Cambodia – The 1989 Paris Peace Conference: Background Analysis and Documents* (Millwood, NY: Kraus).

Acharya, Amitav, and Richard Stubbs (eds) (1995*) New Challenges for ASEAN: Emerging Policy Issues* (Vancouver: UBC Press).

Acharya, Amitav and Richard Stubbs (eds) (2009) *Theorising Southeast Asian Relations: Emerging Debates* (London: Routledge).

Alagappa, Muthiah (1987) *Towards a Nuclear-Weapons-Free Zone in Southeast Asia* (ISIS Research Note) (Kuala Lumpur: Institute of Strategic and International Studies).

—— (ed.) (2002) *Asian Security Order: Instrumental and Normative Features* (Stanford, CA: Stanford University Press).

Ali, Gen. H.A. 'Prospects for Defence and Security Cooperation in ASEAN', Presented to the Conference on 'ASEAN and the Asia-Pacific Region: Prospects for Security Cooperation in the 1990s', Manila, Philippines, 5–7 June 1991.

Anand, R.P., and Quisumbing, Purificacion V. (eds) (1981) *ASEAN: Identity, Development and Culture* (Quezon City: University of the Philippines Law Centre and East–West Centre Culture Learning Institute).

Antolik, Michael (1990) *ASEAN and the Diplomacy of Accommodation* (Armonk, NY: M.E. Sharpe).

ASEAN-Institutes for Strategic and International Studies (1993) *Confidence Building Measures in Southeast Asia* (Memorandum no. 5) (Jakarta: ASEAN-ISIS).

Ba, Alice (2009) *(Re)Negotiating East and Southeast Asia Region, Regionalism, and the Association of Southeast Asian Nations* (Stanford, CA: Stanford University Press).

Ball, Desmond, and Amitav Acharya (eds) (1999) *The Next Stage: Preventive Diplomacy and Security Cooperation in the Asia-Pacific Region* (Canberra: Strategic and Defence Studies Centre, Australian National University).

Broinowski, Alison (ed.) (1982) *Understanding ASEAN* (New York: St Martin's Press).

—— (ed.) (1990) *ASEAN into the 1990s* (Basingstoke: Macmillan).

Caballero-Anthony, Mely (2005) *Regional Security in Southeast Asia: Beyond the ASEAN Way* (Singapore: Institute of Southeast Asian Studies).

Centre for Strategic and International Studies (ed.) (1975) *Regionalism in Southeast Asia* (Jakarta: Centre for Strategic and International Studies).

Chan Heng Chee. 'The Interests and Role of ASEAN in the Indochina Conflict', Presented at the International Conference on Indochina and Problems of Security and Stability in Southeast Asia, Chulalongkorn University, Bangkok, Thailand, 19–21 June 1980.

Chin Kin Wah. 'ASEAN Institution-Building: The Fourth Wave', Presented at the Second ASEAN Congress, Kuala Lumpur, Malaysia, 20–23 July 1997.

Collins, Alan (2012) *Building a People-Oriented Security Community the ASEAN Way* (New York: Routledge).

Da Cunha, Derek (ed.) (1996) *The Evolving Pacific Power Balance* (Singapore: Institute of Southeast Asian Studies).

Dewitt, David, and Paul Evans (eds) (1993) *The Agenda for Cooperative Security in the North Pacific* (Toronto: Centre for International and Strategic Studies, York University).

Djalal, Ambassador Hasjim. 'Territorial Disputes at Sea: Situation, Possibilities, Progress', Presented at the 10th Asia Pacific Roundtable, Kuala Lumpur, Malaysia, 5–8 June 1996.

Djiwandono, J. Soedjati. 'Confidence-Building Measures and Preventative Diplomacy: A Southeast Asian Perspective', Presented at the Symposium on the Evolving Security Situation in the Asia Pacific Region: Indonesian and Canadian Perspectives, Jakarta, Indonesia, 26 June 1995.

Ellings, Richard J., and Sheldon W. Simon (eds) (1996) *Southeast Asian Security in the New Millennium* (Armonk, NY: M.E. Sharpe).

Emmers, Ralf (2003) *Cooperative Security and the Balance of Power in ASEAN and the ARF* (London: RoutledgeCurzon).

Emmerson, Donald K., and Sheldon W. Simon. 'Regional Issues in Southeast Asian Security: Scenarios and Regimes', Study presented at the Third Annual Workshop on Asian Politics, Defense Intelligence College/National Bureau of Asian Research, Monterey, CA, 18–19 March 1993.

Gill, Bates, J.N. Mak and Siemon Wezeman (1995) *ASEAN Arms Acquisitions: Developing Transparency* (Kuala Lumpur: Maritime Institute of Malaysia).

Gill, Ranjit (1987) *ASEAN: Coming of Age* (Singapore: Sterling Corporate Services).

Gordon, Bernard K. (1966) *The Dimensions of Conflict in Southeast Asia* (New York: Prentice Hall).

Haacke, Jürgen (2003), *ASEAN's Diplomatic and Security Culture: Origins, Development and Progress* (London: RoutledgeCurzon).

Haas, Michael (1989) *The Asian Way to Peace: A Study of Regional Cooperation* (New York: Praeger).

Hernandez, Carolina. 'Regional Security in ASEAN: A Philippine Perspective', Presented at the Asiatic Research Centre Conference on East Asian Security: Perceptions and Realities, Korea University, Seoul, Republic of Korea, 25–26 May 1984.

Hernandez, Carolina, and Ralph Cossa (eds) (1997) *Security Implications of Conflict in the South China Sea: Perspectives from the Asia-Pacific* (Manila: Institute for Strategic and Development Studies).

Ho Hak Ean, Peter. 'The ASEAN Regional Forum: The Way Forward', Presented to the Third Workshop on ASEAN–UN Cooperation in Peace and Preventive Diplomacy, Bangkok, Thailand, 17–18 February 1994.

Huisken, Ron (1977) *Limitations of Armaments in Southeast Asia: A Proposal* (Canberra Papers on Strategy and Defence no. 16) (Canberra: The Australian National University, Strategic and Defence Studies Centre).

Huxley, Tim (1985) *ASEAN and Indochina: A Study of Political Responses* (Canberra Studies in World Affairs no. 19) (Canberra: Australian National University, Department of International Relations).

—— (1986) *The ASEAN States' Defence Policies, 1975–81: Military Response to Indochina?* (Working Paper no. 88) (Canberra: Strategic and Defence Studies Centre, Australian National University).

Indorf, Hans H. (1984) *Impediments to Regionalism in Southeast Asia: Bilateral Constraints Among ASEAN Member States* (ASEAN Political Studies) (Singapore: Institute of Southeast Asian Studies).

—— (ed.) (1988) *Association of Southeast Asian Nations After 20 Years* (Washington, DC: Woodrow Wilson International Center for Scholars).

Jackson, Karl D., and M. Hadi Soesastro (eds) (1984) *ASEAN Security and Economic Development* (Research Papers and Policy Studies no. 11) (Berkeley, CA: Institute of East Asian Studies, University of California).

Jones, Lee (2011) *ASEAN, Sovereignty and Intervention in Southeast Asia* (New York: Palgrave Macmillan).

Jorgensen-Dahl, Arnfinn (1982) *Regional Organization and Order in Southeast Asia* (London: Macmillan).

Katsumata, Hiro (2010). *ASEAN's Cooperative Security Enterprise: Norms and Interests in the ASEAN Regional Forum* (New York: Palgrave Macmillan).

Koh, Tommy, Rosario G Manalo, and Walter Woon (ed.) (2009) *The Making of the ASEAN Charter* (Singapore: World Scientific).

Lau Teik Soon (ed.) (1973) *New Directions in the International Relations of Southeast Asia: Global Powers and Southeast Asia* (Singapore: Singapore University Press).

—— (1991) *Towards a Regional Security Conference: Role of the Non-Government Organizations* (Working Paper no. 1) (Singapore: Department of Political Science, National University of Singapore).

Leifer, Michael (1980) *Conflict and Order in Southeast Asia* (Adelphi Paper no. 162) (London: International Institute for Strategic Studies).

—— (1989) *ASEAN and the Security of South-East Asia* (London: Routledge).

—— (1995) *Dictionary of the Modern Politics of South-East Asia* (London: Routledge).

—— (1996) *The ASEAN Regional Forum* (Adelphi Paper no. 302) (London: International Institute for Strategic Studies).

Lo, Chi-kin (1989) *China's Policy Towards Territorial Disputes: The Case of the South China Sea Islands* (London: Routledge).

Luhulima, C.P. (1995) *ASEAN's Security Framework* (CAPA Reports no. 22) (San Francisco: Center for Asia Pacific Affairs, The Asia Foundation).

Mak, Joon Nam (1986) *Directions for Greater Defence Cooperation* (Kuala Lumpur: Institute of Strategic and International Studies).

Mak, J.N. 'The ASEAN Process ("Way") of Multilateral Cooperation and Cooperative Security: The Road to a Regional Arms Register?', Presented at the MIMA–SIPRI Workshop on An ASEAN Arms Register: Developing Transparency, Kuala Lumpur, Malaysia, 2–3 October 1995.

Nguen Buy Quy (ed.) (1992) *Unity in Diversity: Cooperation Between Vietnam and Other South-east Asian Countries* (Hanoi: Social Science Publishing House).

Niksch, Larry A. (1995) *The South China Sea Dispute* (CRS Report no. 95–934F) (Washington, DC: Congressional Research Service, The Library of Congress).

Nor, Commodore Ahmad Ramli. 'ASEAN Maritime Cooperation', Presented at the Defence Asia '89 Conference on Towards Greater ASEAN Military and Security Cooperation: Issues and Prospects, Singapore, 22–25 March 1989.

Nor, Vice Admiral Dato' Ahmad Ramli Hj. Mohd. 'The Royal Malaysian Navy's Roles: Adapting to Security Challenges?', Presented at the Conference on Changing Conceptions of Security in a Changing Pacific Asia, Kuala Lumpur, Malaysia, 25–26 April 1996.

Paribatra, Sukhumbhand. 'ASEAN Ten and Its Role in the Asia Pacific', Presented to the Conference on Asia in the XXI Century, organised by the Institute for International Relations, Hanoi, Vietnam, 28–29 April 1997.

Phanit, Thakur (1980) 'Regional Integration Attempts in Southeast Asia: A Study of ASEAN's Problems and Progress' (Ph.D. dissertation, Pennsylvania State University).

Pitsuwan, Surin (2011) ASEAN's Challenge: Some Reflections and Recommendations on Strengthening the ASEAN Secretariat, Submitted to H.E. Marty Natalegawa, Chair, ASEAN Coordinating Council, (Jakarta: 12 December).

Plummer, Michael and Chia Siow Yue (ed.) (2009). *Realizing the ASEAN Economic Community: A Comprehensive Assessment* (Singapore: Institute of Southeast Asian Studies, 2009)

Pye, Lucian (1985) *Asian Power and Politics: The Cultural Dimensions of Authority* (Cambridge, MA: The Belknap Press of Harvard University Press).

Roberts, Christopher (2012) *ASEAN Regionalism: Co-operation, Values and Institutionalisation* (New York: Routledge).

Scalapino, Robert, Seijabura Sato and Sung-Joo Han (eds) (1990) *Regional Dynamics: Security, Political and Economic Issues in the Asia Pacific Region* (Jakarta: Centre for Strategic and International Studies).

Severino, Rodolfo C. (2006) *Southeast Asia in Search of an ASEAN Community* (Singapore: Institute of Southeast Asian Studies).

—— (2009) *The ASEAN Regional Forum* (Singapore: Institute of Southeast Asian Studies).

Shafie, Mohammed Ghazalie bin (1982) *Malaysia: International Relations* (Kuala Lumpur: Creative Enterprises).

Shafie, Mohammed Ghazali bin. 'Reflections on ASEAN: 30 Years and Vision of the Future', Presented at the ASEAN Roundtable 1997, ASEAN in the New Millennium, jointly organised by the Institute of Southeast Asian Studies and the ASEAN Secretariat, Singapore, 4–5 August 1997.

Simon, Sheldon W. (1982) *The ASEAN States and Regional Security* (Stanford, CA: Hoover Institution Press).

—— (ed.) (1993) *East Asian Security in the Post-Cold War Era* (Armonk, NY: M.E. Sharpe).

Singh, Bilveer (1991) *ZOPFAN and the New Security Order in Asia-Pacific* (Petaling Jaya: Pelanduk Publications).

Snitwongse, Kusuma, and Sukhumbhand Paribatra (eds) (1987) *Durable Stability in South-east Asia* (Singapore: Institute of Southeast Asian Studies).

Soesastro, Hadi. 'Economic Integration and Interdependence in the Asia Pacific: Implications for Security', Presented at the Eighth Asia Pacific Roundtable, Kuala Lumpur, Malaysia, 5–8 June 1994.

Soesastro, Hadi (ed.) (1995) *ASEAN in a Changed Regional and International Political Economy* (Jakarta: Centre for Strategic and International Studies).

Soesastro, Hadi, and Anthony Bergin (eds) (1996) *The Role of Security and Economic Cooperation Structures in the Asia Pacific Region* (Jakarta: Centre for Strategic and International Studies).

Solidum, Estrella D. (1974) *Towards a Southeast Asian Community* (Quezon: University of the Philippines Press).

Sopiee, Noordin. 'ASEAN Towards 2020: Strategic Goals and Critical Pathways', Presented at the Second ASEAN Congress, Kuala Lumpur, Malaysia, 20–23 July 1997.

Sukma, Rizal (2003) 'ASEAN Cooperation: Challenges and Prospects in the Current International Situation', Presented at the Seminar on 'ASEAN Cooperation: Challenges and Prospects in the Current International Situation', Permanent Mission of the Republic of Indonesia to the United Nations, New York, 3 June 2003.

Sunardi, R.M. 'Maritime Security and Conflict Resolution: Indonesian Perspective', Presented at the Symposium on The Evolving Security Situation in the Asia Pacific Region: Indonesian and Canadian Perspectives, Jakarta, Indonesia, 26 June 1995.

Suriyamongkol, Marjorie L. (1988) *Politics of ASEAN Economic Co-operation: The Case of ASEAN Industrial Projects* (Singapore: Oxford University Press).

Tan, See Seng, and Amitav Acharya (eds) (2004) *Asia-Pacific Security Cooperation: Reconciling National Interest With Regional Order* (Armonk, NY: ME Sharpe).

Tang, James T.H. (ed.) (1995) *Human Rights and International Relations in the Asia-Pacific Region* (London: Frances Pinter).

Thambipillai, Pushpa, and Johan Saravanamuttu (1985) *ASEAN Negotiations: Two Insights* (Singapore: ASEAN Economic Research Unit, Institute of Southeast Asian Studies).

Thayer, Carlyle A. (1995) *Beyond Indochina* (Adelphi Paper no. 297) (London: International Institute for Strategic Studies).

Thayer, Carl. 'ASEAN's Expanding Membership', Presented at the Workshop on ASEAN in Transition: Implications for Australia, Brisbane, Australia, 9–10 December 1996.

Thongswasdi, Tarnthong (1979) 'ASEAN After the Vietnam War: Stability and Development Through Regional Cooperation' (Ph.D. dissertation, Claremont Graduate School).

Vanderbosch, Amy, and Richard Butwell (1966) *The Changing Face of Southeast Asia* (Lexington, KY: University of Kentucky Press).

Wanandi, Jusuf. 'Towards a New Regional Order for ASEAN', Presented to the Symposium on The Changing Role of the United Nations in Conflict Resolution and Peace-keeping, organised by the United Nations Department of Public Information and the Institute of Policy Studies, Singapore, 13–15 March 1991.

Weatherbee, Donald. 'Regional Economic Nodes: Transnational Growth Zones in East Asia', Presented at the Conference on National Strategies in the Asia-Pacific: The Effects of Interacting Trade, Industrial, and Defense Policies, organised by the National Bureau of Asian Research and the Center for Trade and Commercial Diplomacy, Monterey Institute of International Studies, Monterey, CA, 28–29 March 1996.

Young, Jeffrey D. (1992) *US Military Interaction with Southeast Asian Countries* (CRS Report no. 92–241F) (Washington, DC: Congressional Research Service, Library of Congress).

Index

9/11 attacks 175, 191, 212

Abdullah Fadzil Che Wan 126
Abdurrahman Wahid, President 125
Aceh refugees 120, 121, 230–1
ACMR (Air Combat Manoeuvring Range) 146
'action-reaction' dynamic 138
ACWC (ASEAN Commission on the Promotion and Protection of the Rights of Women and Children) 243, 245
ad hocism 62, 63, 64, 262
adjudication 124
Adler, E. 2, 14, 19, 20, 27, 29, 30, 31, 36
ADMM (ASEAN Defence Ministers Meeting) 61–2, 140, 148, 232
ADMM Plus 140, 148, 170, 259
AEC (ASEAN Economic Community) 144, 228, 235, 239, 240–3, 259
AFAS (ASEAN Framework Agreement on Services) 240
Afro-Asian unity 68
AFTA (ASEAN Free Trade Area) 113–14, 141, 235, 240, 241, 262
Agreement on Transboundary Haze Pollution, ASEAN 220
AHA (ASEAN Humanitarian Assistance Centre) 178
AHA (ASEAN Humanitatiran Assistance Centre) 219
AIA (ASEAN Investment Area) 141, 240
AICHR (ASEAN Intergovernmental Commission on Human Rights) 243–6
Air Combat Manoeuvring Range (ACMR) 146
air defence acquisitions 135–7, 138, 145
air space disputes 123, 127, 215
Alagappa, M. 94n.1
Alatas, A. 93, 97, 105, 108, 110, 114, 135, 151, 153, 169, 178, 247
Albar, Syed Hamid 222, 228
Ali, Hashim Mohammed 146
alliances 3, 17–18, 26, 87, 93, 148, 178, 254
Al-Qaeda 212, 213

ALTSEAN-Burma (Alternative ASEAN Network on Burma) 242
Ambalat dispute 127
AMM (ASEAN Ministerial Meetings) 131–2, 133, 176, 223, 237
AMMTC (ASEAN Ministerial Meeting on Transnational Crime) 214
anarchy 1, 3, 26, 264
Anderson, B. 24
Angkor Wat 125
Anoa-Singa army exercise 146
Anwar Ibrahim 110, 150, 152
APA (ASEAN People's Assembly) 242–3, 260
APCET (Asia-Pacific Coalition for East Timor) 242
APDMM (ASEAN Police and Defence Minister Meeting) 227
APEC (Asia-Pacific Economic Cooperation) 169, 171, 183, 186, 188, 189
APSC (ASEAN Political-Security Community) 233–4, 259, 266 see also ASC (ASEAN Security Community)
APT (ASEAN Plus Three) 184, 198, 217, 257, 262
Aquino, President 59, 128, 248n. 44
arbitration 124
'area denial' capability 130
ARF (ASEAN Regional Forum): ARF-SOM (ARF Senior Officials' Meeting) 173, 176; ASEAN as 'driver' into the future 262, 267; and ASEAN-ISIS 241; and the ASEAN Way 64, 102, 112, 171–8, 199, 257–8; cross-over with EAS (East Asia Summit) 186; and economic interdependence 140; evolution of 5, 165–71; and the Great Powers 198; limits and benefits of 178–83; and the Spratly Islands issue 128; and the testing of ASEAN norms 257–8
Armitage, R. 188
arms factory, proposed ASEAN 145
arms races/ arms build-up 15, 134–40, 145, 195, 257
arms registers 173, 229, 232

166, 179, 185, 188, 189; relationship with
Japan 166, 187; relationship with Thailand
148; relationship with the Phillipines 179,
191; relationship with Vietnam 112; removal
of forces 165, 168; sanctions on Burma 106;
as security community 26; and the South
China Seas dispute 133; threat to ASEAN's
survival 265; USA-Canada relations as
security community 17, 26; USA-Japan as
security community 26; US-ASEAN summit
(2010) 131; USA-Soviet Union relations as
security regime 17; US military presence 11n.
33
utility-maximisation 19, 20

values: common values essential for community
building 29; norms help create 21
Vasquez, J. 27
Vietnam: and the 1997 economic crisis 143;
admitted to ASEAN despite communist
system 58, 102; ASEAN and the Cambodia
conflict 79–94; ASEAN's relationship to 79,
255; bilateral defence cooperation 148; border
disputes 122; on Cambodian membership of
ASEAN 111; conflict in (general statistics)
120–1; entry to ASEAN easier than expected
256; and the expansion of ASEAN 98–102;
and the non-interference doctrine 58, 150–1,
152; relationship with China 113; Spratly
Islands issue 127–34; US withdrawal from 51
Vietnam War, relying on external powers 52
Visiting Forces Agreement 191
Voluntary Demonstration of Response (VDR)
177–8
voting mechanisms 235, 239
Vo Van Kiet 100
Vu Khoan 111

Wah, C.K. 76n. 94
Wanandi, J. 57, 261
war: absence of war or preparations for war as
key feature of security community 15;
ASEAN's record of war avoidance 261–2;
causes of 1; more likely in developing world
26; and multipolar systems 200; not yet
'unthinkable' in ASEAN 127, 264; war
avoidance and economic interdependence 28,
140; war avoidance and the commitment to
non-interference 227; war avoidance as key
norm 22; war not ruled out against *external*
threat 164
war on terror *see* terrorism
water disputes 123, 125, 127, 193
weak states: and the EAS (East Asia Summit)
186; and the principle of non-interference
57–9; and security communities 18
weapons *see* arms

'we feelings': and the ASC (ASEAN Security
Community) 227, 231; and the ASEAN
Socio-Cultural Community 240; challenge of
measurement 24–5; as crucial feature of
security community process 1, 3; and identity
23; and norms 22, 263; and security regimes
17; and the socialisation process 260
Wendt, A. 36
Western basis of security community concept 14,
26
Westphalian state system 22, 56, 211
Wezeman, S. 137
Wirayuda, H. 221
WMD (weapons of mass destruction) 229, 231
women and children, ASEAN Commission 243,
245
WTO (World Trade Organisation) 240

Yalem, R.J. 15, 27
Yang Jieche 130, 133
Yeo, G. 130, 196, 223, 234, 243
Yeo Ning Hong 135
Young, K.T. 4
Young, O. 38n. 21
Yudhoyono, President 192, 220
Yukioh Satoh 202n. 18

Zoellick, R. 104
ZOPFAN (Zone of Peace, Freedom and
Neutrality) 5, 52–6, 81, 101, 169, 200, 229,
257
ZoPFF/C (Zone of Peace, Freedom, Friendship
and Cooperation) 131